Mikhail
The Presentation of the Lamb

S ✠
O L

Ramez Mikhail

THE PRESENTATION OF THE LAMB

The Prothesis and Preparatory Rites of the Coptic Liturgy

Aschendorff
Verlag

Studies in Eastern Christian Liturgies (SECL)

On behalf of the
Society of Oriental Liturgy (SOL)

Edited by

Harald Buchinger, Tinatin Chronz, Mary Farag and Thomas Pott OSB

Volume 2

This series is peer reviewed.

Bibliografische Information der Deutschen Bibliothek
Die Deutsche Bibliothek verzeichnet diese Publikation in der
Deutschen Nationalbibliografie; detaillierte bibliografische Daten
sind im Internet über <http://dnb.ddb.de> abrufbar.

www.aschendorff-buchverlag.de

Printed in Germany
ISSN 2699-559X
ISBN 978-3-402-21766-5
ISBN 978-3-402-21767-2 (E-Book-PDF)

To my spiritual father
Abouna Bishoy Mikhail Brownfield

For his inspiring example of service, prayer, and integrity

CONTENTS

Preface and Acknowledgments 9
Editorial Notes 13
Tables and Figures 17
Abbreviations and Sigla 19
Introduction 23
1. The Current Rite 24
2. Previous Studies 27
3. Scope: Language, Time, and Place 30
4. Sources 37
5. Methodology 48

PART 1: HISTORICAL ORIGINS & PREPARATORY RITES
Chapter 1: Historical Origins 1: The Preparation of the Gifts 53
1. The Offering of the Gifts 55
2. The Location of the Preparation of the Gifts 68
3. Summary 88
Chapter 2: Historical Origins 2: The Transfer of the Gifts 91
1. The Transfer of the Gifts 91
2. The Transfer Chant 109
3. The Intermediate Ordo 117
4. The New Ordo 119
5. Conclusion 123
Excursus 1: The Vessels and Cloths of The Coptic Eucharist 125
1. Paten 126
2. Star 126
3. Chalice 127
4. Chalice Throne 127
5. Communion Spoon 128
6. Eucharistic Cloths 130
Chapter 3: Vesting and the Preparation of the Altar 133
1. The Vesting Rite 133
2. The Preparation of the Altar 141
3. The Prayers of Preparation 154
4. Conclusion 172
Excursus 2: The Prayers of the Hours and the Liturgy 175
1. The Daily Hours and the Liturgy: A Historical Overview 176

2. The Little Hours in East and West 197
3. The Little Hours in Current Practice 200
4. Issues in Current Practice 201

PART 2: THE PROTHESIS RITE

Introduction 207
Chapter 4: The Selection of the Offering and the Procession of the Lamb 209
1. The Selection of the Offering 212
2. The Hand Washing 220
3. The Commemorations 232
4. The Chant during the Selection of the Offering 237
5. The Procession of the Lamb 242
6. Glory and Honor 248
7. Processional Psalms 251
8. The Symbolism of Christ's Life 253
9. Conclusion 254
Chapter 5: The Blessing of the Offering and the Prayer of Thanksgiving 257
1. The Positions of the Celebrant and the Deacon 258
2. The Exchange of Blessing 262
3. The Blessing of the Offering 266
4. The Mixing of the Chalice 275
5. The Prayer of Thanksgiving 290
6. Conclusion 308
Chapter 6: The Prothesis Prayer and the Absolutions 311
1. The Prothesis Prayer 312
2. Chants Accompanying the Prothesis Prayer 333
3. Covering of the Gifts and the Absolutions 344
4. Conclusion 356
Excursus 3: Consecratory Language and its Implications 359
1. The Prothesis Prayer as an Epiclesis Prayer 360
2. The Prothesis Rite as an Ancient Anaphora 362
3. The Prothesis Prayer as a Moment of Consecration 371
Conclusions 377
1. Towards A Broad Historical View 378
2. Some Concluding Theological Remarks 383
Appendix 1: The Text of the Coptic Prothesis 397
Appendix 2: Chronological List of Liturgical Manuscripts 413
Appendix 3: Plans and Figures 427
Bibliography 435
Biblical Index 469
Manuscripts Index 471
General Index 477

PREFACE AND ACKNOWLEDGMENTS

This book presents to the readers the first study of the historical evolution of the prothesis rite, or the preparation of the eucharistic gifts, in the Coptic tradition. This stems from the following conviction: The spiritual ethos and beliefs of a community are best understood through a study of its worship practices. Within this framework, liturgical history is indispensable for the task of liturgical theology, pastoral practice, and ecumenical dialogue. While scholars have engaged with the sources of the Coptic Christian heritage for decades, even centuries, it will become immediately clear to the reader in the following pages that a comprehensive analysis of the history of the Coptic liturgy has simply never been written. Approaching the Coptic liturgy initially as an experienced practitioner and later as a scholar, I have sought to remedy this severe deficiency in this present work. Naturally, discretion had to be exercised in limiting the scope of the work, resulting in the decision to explore only the first stage in the Coptic liturgy of today; the prothesis rite.

The present work began as a doctoral dissertation at the Faculty of Catholic Theology of the University of Vienna in Austria. Subsequently, it was revised and enhanced in various ways during a one-year postdoctoral fellowship at the Yale Institute of Sacred Music in New Haven, Connecticut. During that year, I examined additional liturgical manuscripts at the Beinecke Rare Book & Manuscript Library (New Haven). I was also fortunate to examine a number of Euchologia–books containing the text of the eucharistic liturgy– located in the Monastery of the Virgin Mary known as al-Suryān (Egypt). Additionally, many errors were corrected, recent literature was added to the bibliography, and a few sections presented at academic conferences in Los Angeles, Vancouver, and Slovakia. Through it all, the language and presentation of the work have been considerably refined.

Unfortunately, I was unable to examine a large number of manuscripts belonging mainly to the collections of the Coptic Orthodox Patriarchate (Egypt), the Monastery of Saint Antony near the Red Sea (Egypt), and the Monasteries the Virgin Mary al-Baramūs in Wādī al-Naṭrūn (Egypt). Nonetheless, the large number of manuscripts that were examined have allowed me to reach what I believe are reliable results, even in the absence of information from a number of sources.

In the following pages, readers will find a thorough presentation and analysis of the Coptic ritual of the prothesis, in which the bread and wine for the Eucharist are chosen and ceremonially placed on the altar. The book assumes no prior knowledge of the Coptic liturgy, walking the reader systematically in explaining the current rite before proceeding to discuss each action and prayer through a detailed analysis of historical evidence. Each chapter concludes with a summary of its conclusions preparing the reader for the following stage in the ritual. The entire volume concludes with a broad view of the developmental phases of the Coptic prothesis rite, as well as a few theological reflections.

In addition, this volume was also conceived with the purpose of serving as a heretofore updated reference for manuscripts and bibliography on the Coptic liturgy. The reader will find at the end of this volume a complete list of liturgical manuscripts mentioned throughout the work, arranged chronologically, and supplied with dates of copying and relevant bibliography. In addition to manuscripts of the Coptic tradition, this list also includes Byzantine, Syriac, and Ethiopic manuscripts, underlining the cross-cultural nature of liturgical scholarship. Together with the extensive bibliography, it is my hope that readers interested in the historical evolution of the Coptic liturgy will find this a useful reference for further research.

A work of this magnitude and scope could not have been possible without the guidance and assistance of many, to whom I wish to express my deep gratitude. First, I wish to express my sincere thanks to my doctoral supervisor, Professor Hans-Jürgen Feulner (University of Vienna), who has given me the opportunity to study and complete this project at the prestigious Faculty of Catholic Theology of the University of Vienna. I also wish to express my sincere thanks to His Eminence Metropolitan Serapion of the Coptic Orthodox Diocese of Los Angeles, Southern California, and Hawaii, as well as His Grace Bishop Kyrillos, Dean of Saint Athanasius and Saint Cyril Theological School (ACTS) for their prayers, blessing, and constant support of my work.

I also wish to thank my two thesis readers, Ugo Zanetti (Monastère de Chevetogne) and Emmanuel Fritsch (Centre français des études éthiopiennes) for their expert comments and reading of the work; and Heinzgerd Brakmann for his frequent help in discussing a number of conceptual problems in this work. My heartfelt appreciation for the St. Shenouda the Archimandrite Coptic Society in Los Angeles, California and its president, Hany N. Takla, for awarding me the graduate student scholarship for two consecutive years, and for indispensable help in correcting and normalizing the Coptic texts in the following pages according to accepted scholarly norms. Daniel Galadza provided many important scholarly works on Byzantine liturgy that I consulted in this study, for which I am thankful.

The preparation of this work took place partially during a one-year fellowship at the Yale Institute of Sacred Music in New Haven, Connecticut. I wish to express my gratitude to the Institute and its director Prof. Martin Jean for the generous fellowship, scholarly experience, and the exceptional opportunities afforded to me during my stay. I also wish to thank my faculty mentor, Prof. Bryan D. Spinks for his continuous support and helpful suggestions and Vasileios Marinis for reading the first two chapters and providing valuable suggestions. My sincere thanks to Prof. Stephen J. Davis for inviting me to take part in the project to catalogue the manuscript library of the Monastery of the Syrians. Participating in this project has taught me a great deal about Coptic manuscript culture and codicology in the company of excellent experts in the field. All referenced manuscripts of the Monastery of the Syrians (al-Suryān) were inspected during my time on the project.

Preparation of this study continued during my stay as a postdoctoral researcher at the Chair of Liturgical Studies of the University of Regensburg (Germany) funded by the Alexander von Humboldt Foundation. My sincere thanks to Prof. Dr. Harald Buchinger for his generous hosting and untiring support of my work. I also thank Harald Buchinger, Tinatin Chronz, Thomas Pott, Mary K. Farag, dear colleagues of the Society of Oriental Liturgy (SOL) for their enthusiastic support for including my work in the new series Studies in Eastern Christian Liturgies published by the society. Magdy Said tirelessly provided the plans of churches in Appendix 3.

Access to the required manuscripts was a challenging aspect of making this work possible, and I wish to thank the many friends and colleagues who have contributed to providing access to rare materials. First, my sincere gratitude goes to the St. Shenouda the Archimandrite Coptic Society for providing digital access to the majority of Coptic manuscripts referenced in this work. Information about and/or images of other manuscripts were made available through the generosity of the following individuals: Archimandrite Justin Sinaites (Monastery of Saint Catherine, Mount Sinai), Fr. Amūn al-Suryānī (Monastery of the Virgin Mary, al-Suryān, Wādī al-Naṭrūn), Fr. Bertie al-Maqārī (Monastery of Saint Macarius, Wādī al-Naṭrūn), Fr. Gregorios al-Baramūsī (Monastery of the Virgin Mary, al-Baramūs, Wādī al-Naṭrūn), Fr. Zakka Labib (Coptic Orthodox Clerical College, Cairo), and Dr. Ibrahim Saweros (Sohag University).

My deep gratitude goes to Hegumen Fr. Bishoy Mikhail Brownfield, my parish priest, spiritual father, mentor, and at times even my personal trainer! His steadfast commitment to the Church, the priesthood, and the altar have shaped my relationship to the liturgy for most of my life. For this and for his unfailing love and support, I pray that we pray together many more liturgies at the altar of God.

My deepest gratitude to my family: My dear wife Marianne and our daughter Anastasia, whose continuous love and support have granted me the gift to enter into this rewarding journey of discovery; and my parents, Samira and Said, for nurturing in me love for the Church's liturgical life, as well as the discipline and industriousness necessary to study them. The following pages represent the coming together of these qualities, which they planted many years ago.

Regensburg
21 May 2020
13 Bašans 1736
Feast of Arsenius the Great

EDITORIAL NOTES

A work of this scope and objectives requires the close analysis of original texts in several languages. The majority of the sources utilized in this work are presented in the following chapters both in their original language and an English translation. To assist in referencing particular sections of a primary text, I have divided lengthy passages into smaller units, separated by English numerals in square brackets [...]. In many cases, these sources were never published and were thus examined directly in electronic copies of their respective manuscripts. This is the case with the majority of liturgical manuscripts, as well as other Coptic and Arabic documents that await independent publications. In these cases, the English translation is entirely mine. However, even when many sources were in fact published, it is often the case that the translation was made into a language other than English. This is the case for example with Ibn Sabbāʿ's *The Precious Jewel's* Latin translation, the Ps.-Sāwīrus *Order of the Priesthood's* German translation, and Gabriel V's *Ritual Order*'s Italian translation. In all such cases as well I present here my own English translation directly from the original language, while referring the reader in the footnotes to the page numbers for both the original text and its translation in the published editions.

On rare occasions, though an English translation of the source was already available, I have chosen to translate the text anew, finding what I consider a more accurate way to render the text. On the other hand, whenever the translation provided in the parallel English column has its own footnote reference, the reader can safely assume that the translation was copied faithfully from that source and is not my own translation work.

In many cases, it was necessary to adjust Coptic texts from the conventions followed in the original source. This was particularly the case with passages copied from the the Coptic Euchologion by Hegumen ʿAbd al-Masīḥ Ṣalīb (1902). In this work, the author has employed an obscure system of diacritics at variance from acceptable standards of editing and publishing Bohairic texts. This system employs three possible shapes for the Coptic *djinkim*. In the following pages, I have normalized the use of the *djinkim* to a single grave shape (ⲁ̀), and have otherwise followed the prevailing scholarly practices regarding the use of the *djinkim* as well as capitalization of Coptic words.

Medieval Arabic texts are often irregular in terms of spelling and orthography. This is particularly the case in Arabic texts written by Christian authors, so much so that scholars have come to recognize these consistent linguistic patterns as Christian Middle Arabic.[1] Care was taken to preserve the orthography of the original manuscript as much as possible, making only minor corrections when deemed necessary, and then without disturbing the "skeleton" of the word as written in the original. This often included making the following changes whenever applicable: *tā'* (ت) to *ṯā'* (ث), *dāl* (د) to *ḏāl* (ذ) and *hā' marbūṭa* (ه) to *tā' marbūṭa* (ة). Exceptions to this appear whenever the original manuscript was not examined. In these cases, the text presented corresponds exactly to the published edition cited in the footnotes.

Throughout the work, a consistent system of Arabic Romanization is applied, following the guidelines of the Deutsche Morgenländischen Gemeinschaft (DMG). The one exception to this general rule is the transcriptions of *hamza* (') and *'ayn* ('), rendered here with the indicated characters rather than (ʾ) and (ʿ), respectively. Names of authors and historical figures are usually given according to the Romanization system employed throughout the work. However, two exceptions to this general rule should be mentioned. First, when a commonly accepted English form of a personal name is available, this was preferred over a rigid transcription of the Arabic. Thus, I write Athanasius and not Aṯanāsiyūs, Gabriel and not Ġubriyāl, Christodoulus and not Ḫristūḏulūs. Second, when modern authors with Arabic names employ a preferred form in western scholarship, this was preferred over a strict Romanization of the name.

Titles of Greek, Coptic, and Arabic liturgical pieces and prayers appear throughout the texts in Coptic script. These have been presented in the edition and translation of the texts in their original Coptic script and spelling, while providing the standard Greek spelling whenever applicable. As deemed relevant, I also provide a translation and/or a transcription of such titles in parentheses.

1 For the definition of Christian Middle Arabic and a detailed analysis of its linguistic features, see Jacques Grand'Henry, "Christian Middle Arabic," in Kees Versteegh, et al, *Encyclopedia of Arabic Language and Linguistics*, vol. 1, A–Ed (Leiden: Brill, 2006), 383–387.

In most cases, Biblical quotations are from the Revised Standard Version (RSV) and using the Septuagint numbering. Exceptions to this general rule occur when the quoted verse occurs in the context of a Coptic hymnographic text, for example, when verses from the Psalter form proper chants in the Coptic liturgy. In such cases, I have chosen to present my own translation of the Coptic *textus receptus* of the hymn, which at times may stand at variance with common English Biblical translations.

TABLES AND FIGURES

Evolution of the Prayers of Preparation 172
The Hypothetical Shift of the Prothesis Prayer 333
Church of the Virgin in the Baramūs Monastery 431
Single-aisle Church in the temple in Taposiris Magna 431
The pastophoria doorways in various locations 432
Church number D (CHD87) in Narmuthis (Madīnat Māḍī) 432
Underground church in the Monastery of Abū Fānā 433
The Prepared Coptic Altar 433

ABBREVIATIONS AND SIGLA

Ambrosiana	Biblioteca Ambrosiana, Milan, Italy
Baramūs	Library of the Monastery of the Virgin Mary, al-Baramūs, Wādī al-Naṭrūn, Egypt
Barberini	The Barberini Collection of the Biblioteca Apostolica Vaticana, Vatican City, Italy
BAS	Liturgy of Saint Basil the Great
BAV	Biblioteca Apostolica Vaticana, Vatican City, Italy
BBGG	*Bollettino della Badia Greca di Grottaferrata*
BEL.S	Bibliotheca Ephemerides Liturgicae. Subsidia
BnF	Bibliothèque nationale de France, Paris, France
Bodleian	The Bodleian Libraries, Oxford, United Kingdom
Borgia	The Borgia Collection of the Biblioteca Apostolica Vaticana, Vatican City, Italy
British Library	The British Library, London, United Kingdom
BSAC	*Bulletin de la Société d'archéologie copte*
CE	*The Coptic Encyclopedia*, ed. Aziz S. Atiya. 8 volumes. New York: Macmillan, 1991.
CHR	The Liturgy of Saint John Chrysostom
CMR	*Christian-Muslim Relations: A Bibliographical History*, ed. David Thomas, et al. 8 volumes. Leiden: Brill, 2009–2016.
CPG	*Clavis Patrum Graecorum*, ed. Maurice Geerard. 5 volumes. Turnhout: Brepols, 1974–2003.
CSCO	Corpus Scriptorum Christianorum Orientalium
CYRIL	The Liturgy of Saint Cyril of Alexandria
EAE	*Encyclopaedia Aethiopica*, ed. Siegbert Uhlig and Alessandro Bausi. 5 volumes. Wiesbaden: Harrassowitz Verlag, 2003–2014.
GCAL	*Geschichte der christlichen arabischen Literatur*, ed. Georg Graf. 5 volumes. Studi e Testi 118, 133, 146, 147, 172. Vatican City: Biblioteca Apostolica Vaticana, 1944–1953.
GCS	Die griechischen christlichen Schriftsteller
GREG	The Liturgy of Saint Gregory the Theologian
Grottaferrata	Biblioteca Statale del Monumento nazionale di Grottaferrata, Grottaferrata, Italy

Hamburg	Staats- und Universitätsbibliothek, Hamburg, Germany
HP, 1.1	*History of the Patriarchs of the Coptic Church of Alexandria (S. Mark to Theonas 300)*, ed. B.T.A. Evetts. PO 1.2. Paris: Firmin-Didot, 1948.
HP, 1.3	*History of the Patriarchs of the Coptic Church of Alexandria: III Agathon to Michael I (766)*, ed. B.T.A. Evetts. PO 5.1 (21). Turnhout: Brepols, 2003.
HP, 1.4	*History of the Patriarchs of the Coptic Church of Alexandria: (Mennas I to Joseph, 767–849)*, ed. B.T.A. Evetts. PO 10.5 (50). Turnhout: Brepols, 1959.
HP, 2.1	*History of the Patriarchs of the Egyptian Church Known as the History of the Holy Church by Sawīrus ibn al-Mukaffa' Bishop of al-Ašmūnīn*, ed. Yassa 'Abd al-Masīḥ, and O.H.E. Burmester. Volume 2.1, *Khael II–Shenouti I (A.D. 849–880)*. Publications de la Société d'archéologie copte. Cairo: La Société d'archéologie copte, 1943.
HP, 2.2	*History of the Patriarchs of the Egyptian Church Known as the History of the Holy Church by Sawīrus ibn al-Muḳaffa' Bishop of al-Ašmūnīn*. Volume 2.2, *Khaël III–Šenouti II (A.D. 880–1066)*, ed. Atiya, Aziz Suryal, Yassā 'Abd al-Masiḥ, and O.H.E. khs-Burmester. Publications de la Société d'archéologie copte. Cairo: l'Institut français d'archéologie orientale, 1948.
HP, 2.3	*History of the Patriarchs of the Egyptian Church Known as the History of the Holy Church by Sawīrus ibn al-Muḳaffa' Bishop of al-Ašmūnīn*. Volume 2.3, *Christodoulus–Michael (A.D. 1046–1102)*, ed. Atiya, Aziz Suryal, Yassa 'Abd al-Masiḥ, and O.H.E. khs-Burmester. Publications de la Société d'archéologie copte. Cairo: La Société d'archéologie copte, 1959.
Hunt.	The Huntington Collection of the Bodleian Library, Oxford, United Kingdom
JAS	The Liturgy of Saint James Brother of the Lord
JThF	Jerusalemer Theologisches Forum
LEW	*Liturgies Eastern and Western Being the Texts Original or Translated of the Principal Liturgies of the Church*, ed. F.E. Brightman. Volume 1, Eastern Liturgies. Oxford, 1896.

MARK	The Liturgy of Saint Mark the Evangelist
Marsh	The Marsh Collection of the Bodleian Library, Oxford, United Kingdom
Messina	Biblioteca Regionale Universitaria, Messina, Italy
Missarum Sollemnia	*The Mass of the Roman Rite: Its Origins and Development (Missarum Sollemnia)*, Josef A. Jungmann, trans. Francis A. Brunner, 2nd edition, 2 volumes. Notre Dame, IN: Ave Maria, 2012.
MkPRES	The Presanctified Liturgy of Mark the Apostle
MLM	The Morgan Library and Museum, New York, USA
Modena	Biblioteca Estense, Modena, Italy
Muḥarraq	Library of the Monastery of the Virgin Mary, al-Muḥarraq, Asyūṭ, Egypt
NE	The *Sinai New Finds* Collection, Sinai, Egypt
NLR	The National Library of Russia, St. Petersburg, Russia
OC	*Oriens Christianus: Hefte für die Kunde des Christlichen Orients*
OCA	Orientalia Christiana Analecta
OCP	*Orientalia Christiana Periodica*
ÖNB	Österreichische Nationalbibliothek, Vienna, Austria
Ottoboni	The Ottoboni Collection of the Biblioteca Apostolica Vaticana, Vatican City, Italy
PETER	The Byzantine Liturgy of Saint Peter
PG	Patrologia Graeca
PL	Patrologia Latina
PO	Patrologia Orientalis
PRES	The Liturgy of the Presanctified Gifts
RMO	Rijksmuseum van Oudheden, Leiden, Netherlands
Rylands	The John Rylands Library, Manchester, United Kingdom
SC	Sources chrétiennes
Sinai	The Monastery of Saint Catherine, Mount Sinai, Egypt
SOC	Studia Orientalia Christiana
St. Antony	Library of the Monastery of Saint Antony by the Red Sea, Egypt
St. Macarius	Library of the Monastery of Saint Macarius, Wādī al-Naṭrūn, Egypt
St. Paul	Library of the Monastery of Saint Paul by the Red Sea, Egypt

Strasbourg	Bibliothèque nationale et universitaire de Strasbourg, France
Suryān	Library of the Monastery of the Virgin Mary, al-Suryān, Wādī al-Naṭrūn, Egypt
Uppsala	Uppsala University, Uppsala, Sweden
Vatican	The Vatican Collection of the Biblioteca Apostolica Vaticana, Vatican City, Italy

INTRODUCTION

The first major stage of the current order of the Coptic eucharistic liturgy is the bringing of the eucharistic gifts to the altar in the rite of *prothesis* or *Presentation of the Lamb* (تقديم الحمل, *taqdīm al-ḥamal*) as it is called in printed Euchologia. Unlike the Byzantine prothesis, in which the bread and wine for the Eucharist are prepared and placed upon a table of oblation in the northern end of the sanctuary,[1] the Coptic prothesis in its present form encapsulates the following actions at once: Selection of the gifts, their preparation, *and* their immediate placement on the altar. Thus, in its present state, the rite of prothesis is a very public part of the Coptic eucharistic liturgy that enjoys the same level of participation by the people as any other part of the liturgy. As such, the prothesis represents an integral element of the liturgical consciousness of the community, making it worthy of serious consideration in any discussion of Coptic eucharistic theology and ecclesiology. Although this is the rite today as it is practiced and experienced by Coptic Christians everywhere, there is clear evidence that the Coptic Rite[2] until the early fourteenth century separated the

1 An overview of the Byzantine prothesis rite including its historical development and an excellent analysis of the interplay between symbol and ritual appears in Thomas Pott, *Byzantine Liturgical Reform: A Study of Liturgical Change in the Byzantine Tradition*, Orthodox Liturgy Series 2 (Crestwood, NY: St Vladimir's Seminary Press, 2010), 197–228. This was in turn based on the classic study of the Byzantine prothesis by Georges Descoeudres. Cf. Georges Descoeudres, *Die Pastophorien im syro-byzantinischen Osten: Eine Untersuchung zu architektur- und liturgiegeschichtlichen Problemen*, Schriften zur Geistesgeschichte des östlichen Europa 16 (Wiesbaden: Otto Harrassowitz, 1983), 85–126. For a more recent treatment of the state of research concerning the Byzantine prothesis, cf. Steven Hawkes-Teeples, "The Prothesis of the Byzantine Divine Liturgy: What Has Been Done and What Remains," in *Rites and Rituals of the Christian East: Proceedings of the Fourth International Congress of the Society of Oriental Liturgy, Lebanon, 10–15 July 2012*, ed. Bert Groen, et al., Eastern Christian Studies 22 (Leuven: Peeters, 2014), 317-327.

2 Here and throughout this work, the term Rite, when capitalized, refers to the entire set of liturgical practices and customs of a given community, e.g. Coptic Rite, Byzantine Rite, or West-Syrian Rite. When not capitalized, rite simply refers to individual services and ceremonies, e.g. Prothesis rite, funeral rite, or marriage rite.

preparation of the gifts from their placement on the altar.[3] What follows is a brief overview of the Coptic prothesis rite in its current form and an outline of the scope, sources, and methodology that are used for a detailed study of the rite.

1. THE CURRENT RITE

Although the Coptic prothesis rite is similar to other traditions in the general sense of preparing the bread and wine for the anaphora, it is nonetheless unique in its details owing to its relatively late development to its present shape in the second millennium AD. Therefore, it would be beneficial to provide here a brief synopsis of the elements constituting this rite, as well as the preparatory rites that precede it.

The first preparatory act of the liturgy is the vesting of the clergy, which traditionally takes place after the conclusion of the *Matins Raising of Incense*. Having vested, the priest brings the eucharistic vessels and cloths to the altar, where he proceeds to arrange them in a specific arrangement in a process called the altar preparation. During and after this manual preparation of the altar, the priest recites two prayers of preparation, which are essentially prayers of access to the altar, in order for the celebrant to be made worthy to approach the divine service and to offer the sacrifice. The altar preparation and its prayers therefore constitute a second layer of preparatory rites before the commencement of the prothesis rite.

Following the altar preparation, the priest washes his hands and proceeds to select the appropriate bread offering. In doing so, the bread loaves are presented to him at the door of the sanctuary carried in a basket, and he is to choose a physically appropriate loaf from a total of three, five, seven, or more loaves (always an odd number). Having chosen the offering, the priest turns to the altar, where he wets his hand slightly and wipes the oblation. Afterwards, he makes the appropriate commemorations for those in need, the sick, the departed, and anyone else he wishes to commemorate, then wraps the oblation bread in a veil. Turning again towards the congregation, the priest elevates the oblation bread and proclaims aloud the prayer *Glory and Honor*, followed by the procession around the altar

[3] Evidence comes from two main sources: The manuscript *Paris BnF Ar. 100* (14th c.), fol. 9v. and *The Precious Jewel in Ecclesiastical Sciences* by Yūḥannā ibn Abī Zakariyyā ibn Sabbā' (14th c.) in *Paris BnF Ar. 207* (14th c.), fol. 121v. Cf. Vincentio Mistrīḥ, *Yūḥannā ibn Abī Zakarīā ibn Sibā', Pretiosa margarita de scientiis ecclesiasticis*, SOC, Aegyptiaca (Cairo: Centrum Franciscanum Studiorum Orientalium Christianorum, 1966), 179 (Arabic), 488 (Latin). The entire question is discussed in detail in chapters 1 and 2 of this work.

accompanied by the deacons and/or altar servants carrying the wine, water, and candles. This procession is accompanied by the congregational chanting of certain psalm selections according to season (Ps 117:24–26; 75:10, or 42:4 and 131:1).

At the conclusion of this procession, having returned to the front of the altar, the priest unwraps the offering. Making the sign of the cross over the bread, the wine, and the water, he pronounces the Trinitarian blessing, "In the name of the Father...Blessed be the Father...Blessed be his only-begotten Son...Blessed be the Holy Spirit..." This is in turn followed by a similarly Trinitarian proclamation by the deacon, "One is the Holy Father, one is the Holy Son, one is the Holy Spirit," followed by "Praise the Lord all nations" (Ps 116). Meanwhile, the priest places the bread on the paten, and takes the wine from the deacon to pour it into the chalice. After the deacon's proclamation, the people in turn chant *Glory to the Father.*

Now that the bread offering has been placed on the paten, the priest begins praying the *Prayer of Thanksgiving* as he pours the wine and water into the chalice. At the conclusion of this prayer, the chanters begin chanting ⲥⲱⲑⲏⲥ ⲁⲙⲏⲛ (*May you be saved, amen*). If a bishop is present, the chanters instead chant ⲛⲓⲥⲁⲃⲉⲩ ⲧⲏⲣⲟⲩ (*All the wise men of Israel*), a hymn that witnesses to the ancient custom of the bishop's vesting at this time, although in actual practice bishops vest at any time they arrive to the service. Irrespective of which hymn is chanted, the chanting takes place during the *Prothesis Prayer*, which the priest prays silently at the altar.[4] This prayer is certainly the oldest element of the entire rite and appears consistently in the oldest manuscripts of the Euchologion. At the conclusion of this prayer, the priest covers the eucharistic gifts on the altar with a large veil called *prospherin.* Afterwards, he goes around the altar counterclockwise, receiving prostrations from the deacons and servants. Everyone exits the sanctuary, while the priest stands at the entrance of the sanctuary facing the people and pronouncing the *Absolution of the Son*—or that of the Father if the anaphora of GREG is to be celebrated later—and the *Absolution of the Servants*, which concludes the entire rite. There are rules governing who is to pronounce this absolution in the case of

[4] In addition to Coptic sources, this prayer is also found in some Byzantine manuscripts, such as *BAV Barberini Gr. 336* (8th c.), and *BAV Vatican Gr. 2281* (AD 1207). Cf. Geoffrey J. Cuming, *The Liturgy of St Mark: Edited from the Manuscripts with a Commentary*, OCA 234 (Rome: Pontificium Institutum Studiorum Orientalium, 1990), 82; Gabriel Radle, "The Liturgical Ties between Egypt and Southern Italy: A Preliminary Investigation," in ⲥⲩⲛⲁⲝⲓⲥ ⲕⲁⲑⲟⲗⲓⲕⲏ: *Beiträge zu Gottesdienst und Geschichte der fünf altkirchlichen Patriarchate für Heinzgerd Brakmann zum 70. Geburtstag*, ed. Diliana Atanassova and Tinatin Chronz, Orientalia-Patristica-Oecumenica 6.2 (Vienna: Lit Verlag, 2014), 618–631.

multiple priests being present. In the case of a celebrating bishop, the right to pronounce the absolution is reserved for him alone.

As the research below demonstrates, both the *Prayer of Thanksgiving* and the *Absolution of the Servants* are not structurally or originally part of the prothesis rite. Rather, they have come to be associated with the preparation of the gifts only after the latter's relocation to the altar rather than being conducted in a separate adjacent room called the *pastophorion*. This shift in location of the preparation of the gifts is in fact the most profound change to have occurred in the historical development of the Coptic liturgy and forms the main subject of this present work. It suffices here to say that the *Prayer of Thanksgiving* and the absolutions belong originally to the *enarxis*, the public beginning of the liturgical ceremony, although they will be treated below precisely to make this point and because they are perceived today as important elements of the prothesis in its present form.

This is the rite in its current shape, which can thus be summarized as follows:

1. Preparation:
   a. Vesting of the clergy
   b. Prayer of Preparation, "O Lord who knows the hearts of everyone"
   c. Preparing the altar and placing of eucharistic vessels and cloths
   d. Prayer after the Preparation, "You O Lord have taught us this great mystery"
2. Prothesis:
   a. Selection of the eucharistic bread
   b. Commemorations
   c. Procession of the Lamb
   d. Trinitarian blessing over the gifts
   e. Mixing the chalice with wine and water
   f. Prayer of Thanksgiving
   g. *Prothesis Prayer*, "O Master Lord Jesus Christ, the co-eternal Logos"
   h. Covering of the paten and chalice
   i. Exiting the sanctuary
   j. Absolution of the Son or Absolution of the Father
   k. Absolution of the Servants[5]

5 For a standard description of the current Coptic liturgical tradition, see O.H.E. Burmester, *The Egyptian or Coptic Church: A Detailed Description of Her Liturgical Services and the Rites and Ceremonies Observed in the Administration of Her Sacraments*, Publications de la Société d'archéologie copte: Textes et

2. PREVIOUS STUDIES

It is hardly the fault of earlier works that they were written at a time when evidence from many centers of late-antique and medieval liturgy was yet to be published and analyzed. Such is the case for example in the classic work of Dom Gregory Dix, *The Shape of the Liturgy*. First published in 1945, it is one of the most well-known scholarly works to address the offering of the gifts and their transfer in East and West. Dix examines the difference in the manner of offering, categorizing it mainly to the western tradition of a people's offering of their gifts in person at the chancel barriers before the anaphora, and the eastern—i.e. Byzantine—tradition of the deacons receiving the offerings beforehand. Contrary to earlier scholarship, Dix argues that the western people's offertory was likely the more widespread custom in all of Christendom, while the eastern tradition, witnessed in the *Didascalia Apostolorum*, was likely only a Syrian peculiarity.[6] In support of his view that the people's offertory existed even in the East, he mentions the Coptic Rite, where the deacon commands before the anaphora to offer the gifts.[7] Unfortunately, Dix does not delve into the manuscript evidence used by Brightman. Nor does he account for the fact that the Coptic Rite as it stands today, and as it was published by Brightman, is attested only as far back as thirteenth-century manuscripts from the regions of Scetis and Cairo. This renders its inclusion in a discussion of the pre-Nicene origins of the offering quite unsatisfactory.

Another feature of earlier scholarship on the subject, and indeed earlier liturgical studies in general, is their frequent overlooking of non-Byzantine eastern traditions altogether. Such is the case for example in Josef A. Jungmann's *The Early Liturgy*. Jungmann indeed dedicates an entire chapter to discussing the various ecclesiastical and linguistic provinces, including such non-Byzantine eastern traditions as Jerusalem, Syria, and Egypt.[8] However, in the following chapter he succinctly presents what in his view are the major features distinguishing eastern liturgies from the Roman Rite. Among these features is the absence of the people's offertory, where, "The oriental

documents (Cairo: [La Société d'archéologie copte], 1967); Heinzgerd Brakmann, "Le déroulement de la Messe copte: Structure et histoire," in *L'Eucharistie: Célébrations, rites, piétés: Conférences Saint-Serge, XLIe semaine d'études liturgiques, Paris, 28 Juin–1 Juillet 1994*, ed. Achille M. Triacca and Alessandro Pistoia, BEL.S 79 (Rome: Edizioni Liturgiche, 1995), 107–132.

6 Gregory Dix, *The Shape of the Liturgy* (London: Bloomsbury, 2015), 123.

7 *LEW*, 164. For a discussion of this diaconal command, refer to chapter 1, section 1.2.

8 Josef A. Jungmann, *The Early Liturgy to the Time of Gregory the Great* (Notre Dame, IN: University of Notre Dame Press, 1959), 200–209.

liturgies have the Great Entry. The sacrificial gift is prepared before the beginning of the liturgy proper, on a special table and with a more or less complex rite."[9] After describing what is clearly the Byzantine prothesis strictly speaking, Jungmann continues, "After the Gospel, the offering is transferred in a solemn procession from this table to the altar."[10] As I demonstrate in this work, the current rite among non-Byzantine eastern traditions varies widely from the Byzantine rite described by Jungmann. Clearly, in this instance, speaking of eastern liturgies as synonymous with the Byzantine Rite is an unfortunate and gross generalization.

No overview of scholarship on the transfer of gifts would be adequate without mentioning the enduring work of Robert F. Taft, *The Great Entrance*. First published in 1975, it was republished in multiple editions, the latest of which is the Italian edition in 2014 with updates and revisions by Stefano Parenti. By far this is the most comprehensive work on the Great Entrance and transfer of gifts in the Byzantine East. Despite the Byzantine scope of the work, Taft offers valuable insights and conclusions of relevance to other non-Byzantine eastern rites as well. Throughout the present work, Taft's work is referenced as needed for a variety of points. Suffice it here to mention a few broad and relevant remarks.

First, contrary to earlier common theories, Taft begins his analysis by emphasizing that there is no evidence whatsoever that the people participated in a procession to bring the gifts to the altar before the anaphora.[11] At the same time, Taft is careful to emphasize that the people certainly offered gifts destined for the Eucharist, despite the lack of evidence for a people's offertory procession (i.e. a procession by the people bearing their gifts to the altar immediately before the anaphora).[12] As the present analysis shows, evidence from late antique and medieval Egypt is also ubiquitous that the people contributed their own offerings of bread and wine for the Eucharist. Finally, as mentioned above, Taft makes the useful general remarks that while a prothesis rite did not exist early on,[13] a pre-anaphoral transfer of gifts to the altar certainly did.[14]

Fortunately, quite a number of scholars have treated the preparation and transfer of gifts from a particularly Coptic

9 Ibid., 216.

10 Ibid., 217.

11 Robert F. Taft and Stefano Parenti, *Il Grande Ingresso: Edizione italiana rivista, ampliata e aggiornata*, Ἀνάλεκτα Κρυπτοφέρρης 10 (Grottaferrata: Monastero Esarchico, 2014), 102.

12 Ibid., 108.

13 Ibid., 125–126.

14 Ibid., 126.

perspective. In addition to specialized articles concerning specific points discussed in the course of this work, three general studies should be mentioned here. First, there is the useful description of the Coptic liturgy by Heinzgerd Brakmann, which contains a helpful section on the Coptic *avant-messe* or fore-mass.[15] Although Brakmann is concerned primarily with describing the current rite, he also provides helpful contextual information for earlier historical stages. For example, Brakmann explains that the modern day procession of the gifts around the altar during the prothesis is a remnant of an ancient true transfer of gifts from the prothesis table in the sanctuary, as seen in the fourteenth-century Ibn Sabbāʿ.[16] Brakmann regards it without doubt that, "the transfer and deposition of the gifts was once a pre-anaphoral rite among the Egyptians."[17] Besides Ibn Sabbāʿ, Brakmann also references the seventh-century story of Bishop Jacob of Wasīm, and later still, the tenth-century *Letter of Macarius Bishop of Manūf al-ʿuliyā*, both of which are key witnesses that are analyzed in detail in the second chapter of the present work.[18] However, as a brief article concerned mainly with providing a broad overview of the *déroulement* of the Coptic liturgy, Brakmann's article does not have the scope of a detailed analysis of the transfer of gifts.

Two years later in 1997, Roshdi W. B. Dous completed his doctoral dissertation at the Aristotle University of Thessaloniki, a critical edition of the Greek text of the Coptic liturgy of Basil. In a chapter dedicated to the transfer of gifts, Dous distinguishes between the prothesis, which he inexplicably describes as, "the offering (προσφορά) of bread and wine by the faithful," and "the preparation (προσκομιδή) of the lamb."[19] This distinction is confusing at best. First, there is no evidence of a ritual in which the faithful offered bread and wine. Second, the prothesis rite itself—whether in the Byzantine or Coptic traditions—is precisely the preparation of the lamb, which he considers to be a separate unit. Perhaps Dous used the term prothesis not to describe the ritual preparatory rite of that name, but the simple act of placing the gifts themselves on the altar, considering the literal meaning of the term. In his discussion of this first unit, the people's offering, he merely presents the text of the *Litany of the Oblations*, which is prayed both during matins and during the anaphoral

15 Brakmann, "Le déroulement," 111–115.

16 Ibid., 114.

17 Ibid.

18 Ibid., 114, 123.

19 Roshdi Wassef Behman Dous, "Η Αλεξανδρινή Θεία Λειτουργία του Αγίου Βασιλείου κατά την Κοπτική Παράδοση: Κριτική Έκδοση" [The Alexandrian Divine Liturgy of Saint Basil according to the Coptic tradition: A critical edition] (doctoral dissertation, Aristotle University of Thessaloniki, 1997), 52.

intercessions of Coptic MARK (CYRIL), and which calls for the acceptance of the various offerings of the people upon the heavenly altar in heaven. Dous postulates the introduction of this and other litanies into the anaphora of MARK as a result of the moving of the *proskomide*–the preparation of the gifts–from the pre-anaphora to the beginning of the liturgy.[20] Unfortunately, Dous makes no effort at exploring the matter further, nor does he seem aware of any supportive evidence for a people's offertory procession, or for a so-called rite of preparation or *proskomide* in the pre-anaphora, which never existed as such. In the subsequent section, Dous provides a description of the current prothesis rite, based on the *Ritual Order* of Gabriel V, discussed in detail below (see section 4.2).[21]

The most recent scholar to take up the topic of the transfer of gifts is Hegumen Athanasius al-Maqārī, author of a number of volumes in Arabic on diverse topics of Coptic liturgical history.[22] In the first volume of his two-volume work on the eucharistic liturgy, Fr. Athanasius succeeds in presenting two of the most important witnesses to the historical development of the transfer of gifts, *The Letter of Macarius* and *The Precious Jewel* of Ibn Sabbā'. I am in fact indebted to his work for bringing the existence of *The Letter of Macarius* to my attention, although as seen above, Heinzgerd Brakmann had already written about this important witness in 1995. Unfortunately, Fr. Athanasius' analysis makes a serious mistake in equating the rite described in *The Letter of Macarius* with that in *The Precious Jewel.* As I demonstrate here, these two sources described slightly variant rites, and strictly speaking should be grouped separately. Furthermore, Fr. Athanasius does not address other topics extensively, such as the people's bringing of their offerings, or the location where these offerings were stored until their transfer.

3. SCOPE: LANGUAGE, TIME, AND PLACE

Given the nature of such a study of the prothesis rite, certain chronological and geographic parameters should be defined. In terms of language, the Coptic Rite is here defined as the rite of the Coptic Church, regardless of whether it is transmitted in Coptic, Greek, or Arabic. Throughout their history, Copts have worshipped in three different languages, Greek, Coptic (in its Sahidic and later its Bohairic

20 Ibid., 53.

21 Ibid., 54–56.

22 Athanasius al-Maqārī, *Al-quddās al-ilāhī: Sirr malakūt allāh* [The Divine Liturgy: The mystery of the kingdom of God], 2nd ed., vol. 1, Ṭuqūs asrār wa-ṣalawāt al-kanīsa 3.5 (Cairo: Dār nūbār, 2011), 270–277.

dialects), and later Arabic. The question of when each language was phased out to give way to the next is a complex one, and at any rate, most surviving manuscripts of the Coptic liturgy in Greek are relatively late (16th–19th c.), while only a few date to the fourteenth century.[23] Suffice it to say that sources in all three languages will be utilized insofar as they are relevant to the subject.

Far from being a monolithic liturgical heritage, the liturgy of Egypt is a broad term encompassing a number of regional and historical subtypes. In his regular reports on the state of research on the liturgy of Egypt, Heinzgerd Brakmann has succeeded to establish a useful and accurate classification of the various stages and regional forms of the Egyptian liturgical family.[24] Throughout all of these writings, Brakmann speaks of a pre-Chalcedonian Alexandrian heritage,

[23] For an excellent analysis of the language shifts that occurred in Egypt, with reference to both liturgical and documentary evidence, see Maged S.A. Mikhail, *From Byzantine to Islamic Egypt: Religion, Identity and Politics after the Arab Conquest*, Library of Middle East History 45 (London: I.B. Tauris, 2014), 79–105.

[24] Heinzgerd Brakmann, "Neue Funde und Forschungen zur Liturgie der Kopten (1988–1992)," in *Acts of the Fifth International Congress of Coptic Studies, Washington, 12-15 August 1992*, ed. Tito Orlandi, vol. 1, *Reports on Recent Research* (Rome: CIM, 1993), 9-32. Cf. Heinzgerd Brakmann, "Neue Funde und Forschungen zur Liturgie der Kopten (1992-1996)," in *Ägypten und Nubien in spätantiker und christlicher Zeit: Akten des 6. Internationalen Koptologenkongresses Münster, 20.-26. Juli 1996*, ed. Stephen Emmel, et al., vol. 1, *Materielle Kultur, Kunst und religiöses Leben*, Sprachen und Kulturen des Christlichen Orients 6.1 (Wiesbaden: Ludwig Reichert Verlag, 1999), 451-464; Heinzgerd Brakmann, "Neue Funde und Forschungen zur Liturgie der Kopten, (1996-2000)," in *Coptic Studies on the Threshold of a New Millennium II: Proceedings of the Seventh International Congress of Coptic Studies, Leiden, 27 August–2 September 2000*, ed. Mat Immerzeel and Jacques van der Vliet, Orientalia Lovaniensia Analecta 133 (Leuven: Peeters, 2004), 575–606; Heinzgerd Brakmann, "Zwischen Pharos und Wüste: Die Erforschung alexandrinisch-ägyptischer Liturgie durch und nach Anton Baumstark (1872–1948)," in *Acts of the International Congress: Comparative Liturgy Fifty Years after Anton Baumstark (1872-1948), Rome, 25–29 September 1998*, ed. Robert F. Taft and Gabriele Winkler, OCA 265 (Rome: Pontificio Istituto Orientale, 2001), 323–376; Heinzgerd Brakmann, "Neue Funde und Forschungen zur Liturgie der Kopten (2000–2004)," in *Huitième congrès international d'études coptes (Paris 2004) I. Bilans et perspectives 2000–2004*, ed. Anne Boud'hors and Denyse Vaillancourt, Cahiers de la Bibliothèque copte 15 (Paris: De Boccard, 2006), 127–149; Heinzgerd Brakmann, "New Discoveries and Studies in the Liturgy of the Copts (2004–2012)," in *Coptic Society, Literature and Religion From Late Antiquity to Modern Times: Proceedings of the Tenth International Congress of Coptic Studies, Rome, September 17th -22nd, 2012 and Plenary Reports of the Ninth International Congress of Coptic Studies, Cairo, September 15th–19th, 2008*, ed. Paola Buzi, Alberto Camplani and Federico Contardi, vol. 1, Orientalia Lovaniensia Analecta 247 (Leuven: Peeters, 2016), 457–481. I wish to thank Prof. Heinzgerd Brakmann for his generous and patient explanation of his classification system through the numerous email messages we have exchanged.

followed by a slow diversification into the non-Chalcedonian and Chalcedonian communities as a result of the Chalcedonian controversy of the fifth century. Eventually, this natural process of divergence gave rise to the Melkite Alexandrian heritage on the one hand (more on this below) and to the non-Chalcedonian tradition of what later will be officially known as the Coptic Orthodox Church. This non-Chalcedonian system of liturgical practices is further divided regionally into the liturgies of Southern Egypt and Northern Egypt, respectively, the latter essentially synonymous with the Coptic liturgy practiced today. An intermediate stage in the liturgical development of the liturgy of the Coptic patriarchate is the so-called *neo-alexandrinische Liturgie*, known from a handful of sources and respresents what we know of the non-Chalcedonian liturgy in the city of Alexandria between the aftermath of Chalcedon and the relocation of the patriarchate to Cairo in the eleventh century.

The process of the formation of the Northern Egyptian Liturgy spanned centuries. Before the uniformity that today characterizes the Coptic Rite, local usages and traditions survived for a long time, particularly in Southern Egypt, as can be seen in the diversity of anaphoras preserved in the *Great Euchologion* of the White Monastery (nine in total), which dates to the end of the tenth century,[25] as well as the numerous Ethiopian anaphoras that were in use only locally within the Church of Ethiopia, of which twenty have been identified to this date. These local usages and most of what characterizes the liturgy of Southern Egypt were gradually abandoned in favor of the usages of Scetis and Cairo, particularly as the latter became the patriarchal center in the eleventh century, during the patriarchate of Christodoulus. In the twelfth century, the canons of Gabriel II ibn Turaik limited the anaphoras to be celebrated in the Coptic Church to the three currently in use (BAS, GREG, and CYRIL).[26] Finally, by the time of Gabriel V's *Ritual Order* the details of a rite more or less identical to the current one had become

25 Emmanuel Lanne, *Le grand euchologe du Monastère Blanc: Texte copte édité avec traduction française*, PO 28.2 (135) (Turnhout: Brepols, 2003). On the current state of knowledge of the liturgy of Southern Egypt, see Diliana Atanassova, "The Primary Sources of Southern Egyptian Liturgy: Retrospect and Prospect," in Groen, et al., *Rites and Rituals of the Christian East*, 47–96. For a recent discussion of the dating of this important codex from the perspective of paleography, cf. Alin Suciu, "À propos de la datation du manuscrit contenant le grand euchologe du Monastère Blanc," *Vigiliae Christianae* 65 (2011): 189–198.

26 Canon 26. See O.H.E. Burmester, "The Canons of Gabriel Ibn Turaik, LXX Patriarch of Alexandria," *OCP* 1 (1935): 5–45, here 40–41.

solidified, though certain local usages in distant Southern Egyptian towns surely lasted even longer.[27]

The Coptic Rite of today represents the victory of the Northern Egyptian liturgical tradition by the turn of the second millennium. More precisely, it is the product of juxtaposition of the liturgical traditions of the monasteries of Scetis–particularly that of the Monastery of Saint Macarius–with elements of the Alexandrian and the wider Northern Egyptian cathedral traditions. This process is thought to have taken place gradually between the seventh and tenth centuries influenced most by the central role of Scetis monasteries in that era, producing most of the Popes of the Coptic Church, among other examples of influence.[28] During the same period, certain liturgical influences of Syrian origin made their way into Coptic practice as well, a process partially related to the importance of Severus of Antioch, the two Coptic patriarchs of Syrian origin–Simon I (AD 689–701) and Abraham ibn Zur'a (AD 975–978)–as well as generally to the amicable relations between the two churches.[29]

This Northern Egyptian liturgy is known to us through the large number of liturgical Coptic-Arabic, and a few Greek-Arabic, manuscripts preserved in various libraries, museums, and monasteries in Egypt and elsewhere. The term Northern Egyptian liturgy is very accurate since it distinguishes very clearly between the liturgical heritage and texts of the North and South, which are–broadly defined–the two types of liturgical traditions within the one Coptic Orthodox patriarchate.

27 Alfonso 'Abdallah, *L'ordinamento liturgico di Gabriele V, 88° Patriarca Copto (1409–1427)*, SOC, Aegyptiaca (Cairo: Edizioni del Centro Francescano di Studi Orientali Cristiani, 1962).

28 In the period between the seventh and tenth centuries, eighteen out of twenty-eight patriarchs were monks from various Scetis monasteries. See Otto F.A. Meinardus, *Two Thousand Years of Coptic Christianity* (Cairo: American University in Cairo Press, 1999), 275–277.

29 On the strong Syrian influence in many aspects of the Coptic Church in the medieval period including liturgy, see Jean Maurice Fiey, "Coptes et syriaques: contacts et échanges," *SOC Collectanea* 15 (1972–1973): 295–365. This Syrian influence in terms of the shift from the anaphora of MARK to BAS in particular was discussed in Brakmann, "Neue Funde (1996–2000)," 582–583. More recently, the Syriac-Egyptian connection in terms of the "Syrian framework" of Coptic services was briefly mentioned in Heinzgerd Brakmann, "Le forme cultuali dell'antica Chiesa di Alessandria e la successive tradizione rituale della Chiesa copta," in *Popoli, Religioni e Chiese lungo il corso del Nilo: Dal Faraone Cristiano al Leone di Giuda*, ed. Cesare Alzati and Luciano Vaccaro, Storia Religiosa Euro-Mediterranea 4 (Vatican City: Liberia Editrice Vaticana, 2015), 247–264, here 262. Similar references to Syrian influence appear consistently in Brakmann's reports. Cf. Brakmann, "Neue Funde (2000–2004)," 132; Brakmann, "New Discoveries (2004–2012)," 462–463.

As for the post-Chalcedonian Melkite Alexandrian tradition as seen in medieval sources, it represents in many cases the blending of ancient Alexandrian traditions with Constantinopolitan influence. Examples of this latter branch of the Alexandrian liturgical tradition include the Melkite anaphora of MARK,[30] the *Blessing of the Waters of the Nile*,[31] the Alexandrian rite of matrimony,[32] and the Alexandrian Presanctified Liturgy of the Apostle Mark.[33]

The present study takes as its main preoccupation the current rite of the Coptic eucharistic liturgy, an essentially Northern Egyptian

[30] The Melkite Alexandrian liturgy of MARK was most recently published by Geoffrey J. Cuming from a number of medieval Greek manuscripts of Southern-Italian provenance. See Cuming, *The Liturgy of St Mark*, xxix–xxxi for a description of these manuscripts. These manuscripts are *BAV Vatican Gr. 2281* (AD 1207) with critical apparatus from *BAV Vatican Gr. 1970* (12th c.), the Messina Roll *Messina Gr. 177* (11th c.), *Sinai Gr. 2148* (13th c.), and *Greek Orthodox Patriarchate of Alexandria 173/36* (AD 1586), the so-called *Pegas Manuscript*. The dating of the first three manuscripts was recently adjusted from what it was thought to be at the time Cuming published his critical edition. Cf. Taft and Parenti, *Il Grande Ingresso*, 704–707. For other fragments of this anaphora, see Heinzgerd Brakmann, "Das alexandrinische Eucharistiegebet auf Wiener Papyrusfragmenten," *Jahrbuch für Antike und Christentum* 39 (1996): 149–164; Jürgen Hammerstaedt, *Griechische Anaphorenfragmente aus Ägypten und Nubien*, Papyrologica Coloniensa 28 (Opladen: Westdeutscher Verlag, 1999); as well as the Byzantine manuscripts of this anaphora found in the *Sinai New Finds*. See Michael Zheltov, "The Byzantine Manuscripts of the Liturgy of Mark in the Sinai New Finds," in Atanassova and Chronz, ⲥⲩⲛⲁⲝⲓⲥ ⲕⲁⲑⲟⲗⲓⲕⲏ, 801–808.

[31] Hieronymus Engberding, "Der Nil in der liturgischen Frömmigkeit des christlichen Ostens," *OC* 37 (1953): 56–88. Recently, Roshdi Dous studied this unique Alexandrian service and found not one, but two related Alexandrian Melkite services related to blessing the Nile in addition to a distinct Coptic tradition of a rite with the same purpose. See Roshdi Wassef Behman Dous, "Ο Αγιασμός των υδάτων του Νείλου Ποταμού στην Αλεξανδρινή Λειτουργική Παράδοση" [The sanctification of the waters of the Nile River in the Alexandrian liturgical tradition] (doctoral dissertation, Aristotle University of Thessaloniki, 2011). For a more synoptic treatment of the surviving witnesses of the Alexandrian Melkite liturgical tradition, cf. Brakmann, "Zwischen Pharos und Wüste," 350–352; Brakmann, "Neue Funde (1996–2000)," 584–588, and most recently, Brakmann, "Le forme cultuali," 254.

[32] The marriage rites of the Byzantine periphery were studied by Gabriel Radle in his doctoral dissertation at the Pontifical Oriental Institute. See Gabriel Radle, "The History of Nuptial Rites in the Byzantine Periphery" (doctoral dissertation, Pontificium Institutum Orientale, 2012). Regarding the Alexandrian rite of marriage in particular, see Gabriel Radle, "Uncovering the Alexandrian Greek Rite of Marriage: The Liturgical Evidence of *Sinai NF/MG 67* (9th/10th c.)," *Ecclesia Orans* 28 (2011): 49–73.

[33] Long thought to have been lost and known only from scattered references, it was recently found in Arabic translation in codex *Sinai Ar. 237* (13th c.) and displays an interesting blend of Melkite MARK with purely Constantinopolitan elements. See Ramez Mikhail, "The Presanctified Liturgy of the Apostle Mark in *Sinai Arabic 237*: Text and Commentary," *BBGG III* 12 (2015): 163–214.

ritual notwithstanding the myriad of textual and ritual variants over time and space that are the subject of this book. As such, local usages on the periphery of the Coptic sphere of influence are not of primary concern. The same can be said of the rich liturgical traditions of Nubia and the churches of Ethiopia and Eritrea, which are also genealogically Egyptian, although they are often instructive in the absence of Egyptian evidence. This book then is concerned specifically with analyzing the historical development of the prothesis rite within the Liturgy of Northern Egypt, the best witness of what Coptic Christians today everywhere recognize as their own liturgical heritage. Given the relative dearth of comparative historico-liturgical studies of the Coptic Rite, one is in fact compelled to begin with the center of the Coptic Rite, i.e. the liturgical traditions reflected in sources from Scetis, Cairo, and Northern Egypt generally. It is certainly hoped that future scholars and works can proceed to analyze those rites that are peripheral to the ecclesiastical center, much as the enormous body of work done in the twentieth century on Byzantine liturgical history moved from studying the rites of the Great Church of Constantinople first to the Byzantine liturgical periphery in more recent decades.

One implication of this chosen scope is that any rites not found in the Northern Egyptian liturgical tradition need not be analyzed in detail. This is the case for example regarding the ancient rites of entrance (*enarxis*). Once forming a grand procession of clergy and laity into the church at the commencement of the service, it has dropped from usage practically everywhere in Christendom, remaining only in vestigial form in the so-called *Prayers of Entrance* attested in various traditions. Since this deliberate ritual act of entrance into the church has not survived in the Northern Egyptian Liturgy attested in the sources, it will not be investigated in detail.

That being said, traditions beyond the dominant Scetis-Cairo axis will be referenced as the need arises for the sake of comparison and to fill lacunae in the evidence whenever sources from the area of primary concern cannot be located. Naturally, a comprehensive study of the Coptic liturgical heritage would have to include all such traditions. However, this selective geographical scope will be useful for a study, the ultimate goal of which is to investigate the historical development of the current rite of the Coptic Church.

Finally, the same purpose of the study naturally presents its own chronological scope. One can already declare most witnesses of the ancient Alexandrian Liturgy—Brakmann's *alt-alexandrinische Liturgie*—to be somewhat removed from the main scope. This should cause no great concern, since unfortunately the main liturgical sources between the fourth and tenth centuries (the *Prayers of*

Sarapion of Thmuis,[34] the *Barcelona Papyrus,*[35] and other such material) do not contain any prayers for the prothesis rite. Even later liturgical manuscripts predating the thirteenth century are rather scarce and consist mainly of fragments. This renders the bulk of the research into the historical development of the prothesis rite limited to Euchologia posterior to the thirteenth century, when one starts to see the earliest Copto-Arabic liturgical manuscripts. Nonetheless, one need not ignore the value of historical, hagiographical, and canonical literature for supplying precious liturgical information. As a terminal point for the development of the prothesis, the classic edition of the Euchologion by 'Abd al-Masīḥ Ṣalīb al-Mas'ūdī al-Baramūsī published in 1902 serves as a useful stopping point.[36] This landmark Euchologion was a great achievement in the history of Coptic liturgical books.[37] Textually comprehensive and meticulous in terms of rubrical details, this Euchologion became a standard for later editions, which tend to copy it verbatim, or differ only in the smallest details, thus rendering it a reliable witness to the current prothesis rite, and practically an *editio typica* for the Coptic liturgy. The status of this Euchologion as an *editio typica* was confirmed by the Holy Synod of the Coptic Orthodox Church in its session on 14 June, 1997, decreeing that Coptic Orthodox clergy in Egypt are to abide by the liturgical texts in the 'Abd al- Masīḥ edition unless otherwise corrected by the Synod itself.[38]

34 For the most updated study on the prayers of Sarapion with a review of previous studies, see Maxwell E. Johnson, *The Prayers of Sarapion of Thmuis: A Literary, Liturgical, and Theological Analysis,* OCA 249 (Rome: Pontificio Istituto Orientale, 1995).

35 The complete anaphoral prayers in the *Barcelona Papyrus* were first published in: Ramón Roca-Puig, *Anàfora de Barcelona i altres pregàries: Missa del segle IV,* 3rd ed. (Barcelona, 1999). It was subsequently published in English. Cf. Michael Zheltov, "The Anaphora and the Thanksgiving Prayer from the Barcelona Papyrus: An Underestimated Testimony to the Anaphoral History in the Fourth Century," *Vigiliae Christianae* 62 (2008): 467–504.

36 'Abd al-Masīḥ Ṣalīb, ⲡⲓϫⲱⲙ ⲛ̀ⲧⲉ ⲡⲓⲉⲩⲭⲟⲗⲟⲅⲓⲟⲛ ⲉⲑⲟⲩⲁⲃ ⲉ̀ⲧⲉ ⲫⲁⲓ ⲡⲉ ⲡⲓϫⲱⲙ ⲛ̀ⲧⲉ ϯϣⲟⲙϯ ⲛ̀ⲁⲛⲁⲫⲟⲣⲁ ⲛ̀ⲧⲉ ⲡⲓⲁⲅⲓⲟⲥ ⲃⲁⲥⲓⲗⲓⲟⲥ ⲛⲉⲙ ⲡⲓⲁⲅⲓⲟⲥ ⲅⲣⲏⲅⲟⲣⲓⲟⲥ ⲛⲉⲙ ⲡⲓⲁⲅⲓⲟⲥ ⲕⲩⲣⲓⲗⲗⲟⲥ ⲛⲉⲙ ϩⲁⲛⲕⲉⲉⲩⲭⲏ ⲉⲩⲟⲩⲁⲃ [The book of the Holy Euchologion, which is the book of the three Anaphoras of Saint Basil and Saint Gregory and Saint Cyril, and other holy prayers], (Cairo: 'Ayn šams, 1902).

37 On the history of liturgical books in the Coptic Rite, see Rafīq 'Ādil, "Al-kutub al-lītūrğiyya bayn al-maḫṭūṭ wa-l-maṭbū'. Taṭawurihā wa-marāḥil taqnīnuhā [Liturgical books between the manuscript and the printed, their evolution and stages of standardization]," *Madrasat al-iskandariyya* 16 (2014): 191–224.

38 Mattā'us, *Al-qarārāt al-mağma'iyya al-ḫāṣṣa bi-l-ṭuqūs al-kanasiyya* [The synodical decisions concerned with ecclesiastical rites], (Dayr al-Suryān, 2001), 24.

4. SOURCES

4.1. Liturgical Manuscripts

Before the Arabization of the Coptic Church, the text of the Coptic liturgy was transmitted in three languages, Greek, Bohairic Coptic, and Sahidic Coptic. Of these three, the Sahidic group is perhaps the oldest, surviving in manuscripts the oldest of which goes back to the seventh century.[39] Unfortunately, no Sahidic witness for the prayers of the prothesis has been found, and therefore the Sahidic recension itself is of little use for the present topic.

The Greek recension is perhaps the most interesting, yet likely also the more exceptional and not normative of Coptic practice. It survives in manuscripts of the fourteenth century and later, and has been judged by Budde as not directly descending from the original Greek ancestor of Egyptian BAS.[40] Budde further subdivided the Greek manuscripts into two families: the Scetiote family, with manuscripts written in the unique *majuscula Nitrensis* script, and the Antonian family, with later manuscripts possessing their own orthographical characteristics. Famous examples of the former group include the fourteenth-century *Paris BnF Gr. 325*[41] and *Coptic Museum Inv. 20*,[42]

39 The two oldest textual witnesses of BAS examined by Achim Budde are the so-called *Louvain Manuscript*, and *Bodleian Copt. f.1*, both from the seventh century. See Achim Budde, Die *ägyptische Basilios-Anaphora: Text, Kommentar, Geschichte*, JThF 7 (Münster: Aschendorff, 2004), 95–97.

40 Ibid., 88.

41 This manuscript was the basis for the Greek text of the Egyptian anaphoras of BAS and GREG published by Eusèbe Renaudot with a Latin translation. See Eusèbe Renaudot, *Liturgiarum Orientalium Collectio*, 2nd ed., vol. 1 (Frankfurt, 1847), 1–25. It was found in Cyprus and brought to Paris by the German scholar Johann Michael Wansleben in 1671. The texts of BAS and GREG in it exhibit clear signs of Byzantinization, which led Hieronymus Engberding initially to consider it an Alexandrian Melkite witness. Cf. Hieronymus Engberding, "Ein Problem in der Homologia vor der hl. Kommunion in der ägyptischen Liturgie," *OCP* 2 (1936): 145–154, here 147. However, Heinzgerd Brakmann demonstrated later that this manuscript in fact belongs to the Coptic community that lived in Cyprus since the twelfth century. Cf. Heinzgerd Brakmann, "Zur Stellung des Parisinus graecus 325 in der Geschichte der alexandrinisch-ägyptischen Liturgie," *Studi sull'Oriente Cristiano* 3 (1999): 97–110, here 99–105. For a full description of the manuscript and scholarship surrounding it, see Budde, *Die ägyptische Basilios-Anaphora*, 72–76. On Copts in Cyprus, see O.H.E. Burmester, "The Copts in Cyprus," *BSAC* 7 (1942): 9–13.

42 Hugh G. Evelyn-White, *The Monasteries of the Wadi 'N Natrûn Part I: New Coptic Texts from the Monastery of Saint Macarius*, Publications of the Metropolitan Museum of Art Egyptian Expedition 2 (New York: Metropolitan Museum of Art, 1926), 200–206. The contents of this manuscript were studied in detail by Heinzgerd

while the most famous example of the latter group is the so-called *Kacmarcik Codex*,[43] also from the fourteenth century.[44]

Recently, Roshdi Dous has added a group of nine additional manuscripts of later dating ranging from the sixteenth to the nineteenth centuries. These manuscripts are *Coptic Patriarchate Lit. 172* (AD 1599), *Coptic Patriarchate Lit. 184* (18th c.), *Coptic Patriarchate Lit. 175* (18th c.), *Abnūb St. Mīnā Lit. 1* (18th c.), *St. Mary al-Muḥarraq Lit. 13* (19th c.), *St. Paul Lit. 201* (AD 1818), *St. Antony Lit. 55* (AD 1824), *St. Macarius Lit. 156* (AD 1852), *St. Macarius Lit. 155* (AD 1894),[45] which, according to Budde, point to an attempt at the revival of the Greek liturgical heritage in monastic circles.[46] In some cases, the Greek text was likely a translation from Coptic.[47] Although it provides an interesting witness to the Greek translation of certain prayers of the prothesis, it cannot be considered an older or a more pristine recension compared to the more common Bohairic text. For this reason, euchological prayers examined in the course of this work are presented mainly in their Bohairic Coptic text. The Greek text will be referenced and included in the discussion only when it presents interesting information and clues for analysis.

The Bohairic Coptic text is by far the most commonly represented in the manuscript tradition, representing the dominant liturgical language of the Coptic Orthodox Church throughout Egypt since

Brakmann. See Heinzgerd Brakmann, "Zu den Fragmenten einer griechischen Basileios-Liturgie aus dem koptischen Makarios-Kloster," *OC* 66 (1982): 118–143. Cf. Budde, *Die ägyptische Basilios-Anaphora*, 76–77.

43 William F. Macomber, "The Kacmarcik Codex. A 14th Century Greek-Arabic Manuscript of the Coptic Mass," *Le Muséon* 88 (1975): 391–395. William F. Macomber, "The Anaphora of Saint Mark according to the Kacmarcik Codex," *OCP* 45 (1979): 75–98. William F. Macomber, "The Greek Text of the Coptic Mass and of the Anaphoras of Basil and Gregory according to the Kacmarcik Codex," *OCP* 43 (1977): 308–334. Cf. Budde, *Die ägyptische Basilios-Anaphora*, 77–82. For the place of this manuscript in the orthographical development of Greek liturgical texts from Egypt, see Achim Budde, "The Kacmarcik Codex as a Document of a Reformed Orthography in Greek Texts of the Coptic Church," *Journal of Coptic Studies* 7 (2005): 125–130.

44 The transfer of Coptic Christian manuscripts to European libraries as part of the western scholarly interest in Egypt between the fifteenth and nineteenth centuries is discussed in the famous study by Hamilton: Alistair Hamilton, *The Copts and the West, 1439–1822: The European Discovery of the Egyptian Church*, Oxford-Warburg Studies (Oxford: Oxford University Press, 2006), 250–258.

45 Dous, "Η Αλεξανδρινή Θεία Λειτουργία," 58–68.

46 Budde, *Die ägyptische Basilios-Anaphora*, 91.

47 For a philological demonstration of this process of translation in the case of the *Prayer of the Fraction* of GREG, see Ugo Zanetti, "Deux prières de la fraction de la liturgie Grégoire, en grec et en copte," *OCP* 78 (2012): 291–333.

approximately the tenth century.[48] The majority of the manuscripts examined for this work and including the priestly prayers of the prothesis come from the Bohairic recension of BAS. The prothesis is typically copied in the very beginning of any given manuscript, since its formulary is independent of which anaphora is celebrated. Throughout the work, references to manuscripts include the folio number whenever available. The folio numbering of Coptic manuscripts is highly irregular. Many times, European numbering systems were added to manuscripts after their acquisition by libraries, museums, or individuals. In fact, it is very common to encounter multiple conflicting numbering systems within a given manuscript. Throughout this work, whenever possible, the original Coptic numbering of a manuscript is followed.[49]

Finally, one may add a few remarks on the Arabic translation of the Coptic liturgies, found in most Euchologia in a parallel column.[50] These translations were studied independently by Wadī' al-Fransīskānī based on the oldest Euchologia from the thirteenth to the fourteenth centuries. He concluded the following: 1. The core or essence of the present-day Coptic liturgy does not differ from that in the manuscripts, 2. Some of the prayers used today are absent in all the older manuscripts, 3. There is no single Arabic translation used in all the manuscripts, but various independent attempts in each specimen, 4. The translations examined are noticeably literal renderings of the Coptic, at times even at the expense of Arabic grammatical rules, 5. Compared to current texts, the manuscripts studied show greater simplicity in avoiding repeating formulas and diaconal acclamations among other features of later prolixity, 6. Each liturgical manuscript, insofar as it represents a unique witness in a specific time and place,

48 An interesting ninth–eleventh century parchment sheet survives, which witnesses to the Bohairic Coptic liturgy in Scetis. See the most recent edition of this text in Tomasz Derda, ed., *Deir el-Naqlun: The Greek Papyri*, vol. 2 (P. Naqlun II), with contributions by Jakub Urbanik and Jaques van der Vliet, Supplements to the Journal of Juristic Papyrology 9 (Warsaw: Warsaw University, Faculty of Law and Administration, Institute of Archaeology, Department of Papyrology, 2008), 70–86. Achim Budde, "P. Naqlun 10/95 und seine Bedeutung für die Pflege des Griechischen in der Liturgie der koptischen Kirche," *OC* 86 (2002): 69–72.

49 For more information on Coptic codicology and manuscript culture, see Alessandro Bausi, et al., eds., *Comparative Oriental Manuscript Studies: An Introduction* (Hamburg: COMSt, 2015), 137–153.

50 The literature on the Arabization process in the Coptic Church is rich. For the classic treatment of the subject from the perspective of the written tradition, see Samuel Rubenson, "Translating the Tradition: Some Remarks on the Arabization of the Patristic Heritage in Egypt," *Medieval Encounters* 2, no. 1 (1996): 4–14.

should be studied and published separately.[51] Since the Arabic text was usually intended as a translation of the Coptic or Greek, it was decided not to include it as a separate text in this study when presenting the particular prayers of the prothesis rite.

4.2. Medieval Encyclopedias, Diataxeis and Commentaries

The thirteenth and fourteenth centuries alone produced three major liturgical sources of vital importance. The earliest of these is the work titled: دلاّل المبتدئين و تهذيب العلمانيين (*Dallāl al-mubtadi'īn wa-tahḏīb al-'almāniyyīn, The Guide to the Beginners and the Correction of the Laity*) traditionally—though likely falsely—attributed to Patriarch Cyril III ibn Laqlaq (AD 1235–1243). This short treatise contains short chapters on the proper behavior in church, the order of the sanctuary, a listing of the crosses signed by the celebrant throughout the service, the use of incense, and other ritual matters during the services.[52] It is preserved in a number of manuscripts, the oldest of which is *BAV Vatican Ar. 117* (AD 1323), fol. 197r–205v. A German translation of this treatise was published by Georg Graf.[53] For the present work, the manuscript was consulted directly in digital reproduction, while Graf's article is also cited.

Approximately a century later, two works of enduring significance for medieval Coptic liturgy were produced. The first of these is the ecclesiastical compendium: مصباح الظلمة و ايضاح الخدمة (*Miṣbāḥ al-ẓulma wa-īḍāḥ al-ḫidma, The Lamp of Darkness and the Elucidation of the Service*). This is the magnum opus of the fourteenth-century Šams al-Ri'āsa Abū l-Barakāt ibn Kabar (d. 1324).[54] Ibn Kabar was a member

51 Wadī' al-Fransīskānī, "Aqdam al-tarǧamāt al-'arabiyya (Qurūn 12–14) li-quddāsāt al-kanīsa al-qibṭiyya [The oldest Arabic translations (12th–14th centuries) of the liturgies of the Coptic Church]," *Madrasat al-iskandariyya* 7 (2011): 217–235, here 223–227. The author of this article dates the codex *British Library Or. 1239* to the twelfth century. Although traditionally dated as such, the more recent and cautious dating espoused by Heinzgerd Brakmann and Achim Budde assigns it to the thirteenth century. This explains the dating of this manuscript in the present work and the reference to Fr. Wadī''s work above as covering only the thirteenth to the fourteenth centuries, despite the explicit title of his article. Cf. Budde, *Die ägyptische Basilios-Anaphora*, 108–109. On the last conclusion by Fr. Wadī', which is more of a recommendation, see Ugo Zanetti, "Esquisse d'une typologie des euchologes coptes bohaïriques," *Le Muséon* 100 (1987): 407–418.

52 For more information, see *GCAL*, 2:364.

53 Georg Graf, "Liturgische Anweisungen des koptischen Patriarchen Kyrillos ibn Laklak," *Jahrbuch für Liturgiewissenschaft* 4 (1924): 119–134.

54 Samir Khalil Samir, "L'Encyclopédie liturgique d'Ibn Kabar († 1324) et son apologie d'usages coptes," in *Crossroad of Cultures: Studies in Liturgy and Patristics in Honor of Gabriele Winkler*, ed. Hans-Jürgen Feulner, Elena Velkovska, and Robert

of a wealthy Cairene family, and rose to the position of secretary to the Mamluk prince of Egypt Baybars Rukn al-Dīn al-Manṣūrī. After relinquishing his post, he was ordained a presbyter by the name of Barṣūma in the Patriarchal church al-Mu'allaqa (The Hanging Church), where he likely composed this work.[55] Covering many of the same topics as his near contemporary Ibn Sabbā', Ibn Kabar adds chapters on ecclesiastical canons and a bibliography of Copto-Arabic literature known to him. Fortunately, the chapter on the eucharistic liturgy in *The Lamp* has been translated from the two oldest manuscripts, *Paris BnF Ar. 203* (AD 1363–1369) and *Uppsala O. Vet. 12* (AD 1546) by Louis Villecourt.[56] For the present work, these two manuscripts were consulted directly in digital reproduction. Folio numbers in each manuscript are cited in addition to Villecourt's edition for convenience. Other manuscripts containing all or parts of this work remain to be analyzed and compared for what they may contribute to knowledge of this important work.[57]

The second of these fourteenth-century compositions is الجوهرة النفيسة في علوم الكنيسة (*Al-ğawhara al-nafīsa fī 'ulūm al-kanīsa, The Precious Jewel on the Church's Sciences*) by Yūḥannā ibn Abī Zakariyyā ibn Sabbā' (often also Romanized as Ibn Sibā', though the exact form of the name is unknown).[58] Little is known about the person of Ibn Sabbā' beyond that he lived in the fourteenth century.[59] In a recent work, Milad

F. Taft, OCA 260 (Rome: Pontificio Istituto Orientale, 2000), 619–655; Eugène Tisserant, Louis Villecourt, and Gaston Wiet, "Recherches sur la personnalité et la vie d'Abul Barakat Ibn Kubr," *Revue de l'Orient chrétien* 22 (1921–22): 373–394.

55 *GCAL*, 2:438–445. Cf. Wadī' Awaḍ, "Al-Shams ibn Kabar," *CMR*, 4:762–766.

56 Louis Villecourt, "Les observances liturgiques et la discipline du jeûne dans l'Eglise copte," *Le Muséon* 37 (1924): 201–280. This manuscript has the catalogue shelf number *Uppsala Or. 486*, and was copied from an earlier manuscript dated AD 1357. See Carl Johan Tornberg, *Codices Arabici, Persici et Turcici bibliothecae regiae Universitatis Upsaliensis* (Uppsala, 1849), 306–309; Louis Villecourt, "Les observances liturgiques et la discipline du jeûne dans l'Eglise copte (Ch. XVI–XIX de la Lampe des ténèbres)," *Le Muséon* 36 (1923): 249–292, here 250.

57 For a list of manuscripts containing the complete or partial contents of *The Lamp of Darkness*, see *GCAL*, 2:441–442. A more updated list appeared recently in Fādī Ra'fat Ramzī, "Tartīb al-quddās wa-l-qurbān (1): Naṣṣ al-bāb al-sābi' 'ašar min miṣbāḥ al-ẓulma fī īḍāḥ al-ḫidma ḥasab maḫṭūṭ bārīs [The order of the liturgy and the oblation (1): The text of the seventeenth chapter of the lamp of darkness in the elucidation of the service according to the Paris manuscript]," *Madrasat al-iskandariyya* 17 (2014): 193–214.

58 For more information, see *GCAL*, 2:448–449. Compare to the information provided by Mark N. Swanson with an up-to-date list of manuscripts in Mark N. Swanson, "Ibn Sabbā'," *CMR*, 4:918–923.

59 A remark in Chapter 26 of the work mentions that more than 1,300 years have passed since the time of the disciples, which, if true, would place Ibn Sabbā''s work around the middle of the fourteenth century, ca. AD 1350, perhaps about two or

Zakhary concludes that he was likely an archdeacon or cleric in the papal entourage, which would explain his intimate familiarity with Coptic rituals.[60] The work covers a variety of subjects, including theology, biblical exegesis, and ethics. The larger part of the work however is dedicated to ecclesiastical and liturgical topics, including a description of daily and seasonal services, and ordination rites. The *Precious Jewel* was published by the Fransciscan Victor Manṣūr Mistrīḥ from the manuscript *Egypt National Library Theology 221*.[61] Mistrīḥ took the date of this manuscript to be AM 1164 (= AD 1448). However, recent scholars agree that the date on fol. 115r should be understood as AH 1164 (= AD 1750), following the Hiğrī year calculation of the Muslim world, frequently employed in medieval Coptic manuscripts.[62] Taking this into account, the oldest manuscript of the *Precious Jewel* would in fact be *Paris BnF Ar. 207* (14th c.). Throughout this work, references to Ibn Sabbā' are provided from this manuscript in addition to referencing Mistrīḥ's edition and translation.

Much of the standardization of the Coptic liturgy that took place in the medieval period is thanks to the work: الترتيب الطقسي (*Al-tartīb al-ṭaqsī, The Ritual Order*) of Patriarch Gabriel V. This is perhaps the closest to an official *diataxis* of the Coptic liturgy, promoted by Patriarch Gabriel V (AD 1409–1427) in an attempt to standardize various Coptic liturgical practices in conformity with the rite of the patriarchal church in Cairo. The liturgy described in this work seems to have been written with a presbyteral liturgy in mind, since it omits any special rites in the presence of a celebrating bishop or patriarch. This work was published by Alfonso 'Abdallah from *Paris BnF Ar. 98*

three decades after the death of Ibn Kabar. The reference in question reads, "Those who believe it [the Gospel] have been for years, whose number now has reached more than [*yanīf*] one thousand three hundred years." See Mistrīḥ, *Pretiosa margarita*, 63 (Arabic), 424 (Latin). Taking the age of the Gospel to refer to the period after the life of Christ (i.e. more than AD 30) implies that Ibn Sabbā' must have written his work later than AD 1330 and likely even later. Curiously, a number of modern authors place Ibn Sabbā''s work in the middle or late thirteenth century instead. See e.g. Samir, "L'Encyclopédie liturgique d'Ibn Kabar," 620, and the study of Milad Zakhary cited in the following note as evidenced in its very title.

60 Milad Sidky Zakhary, *De la Trinité à la Trinité: La christologie liturgique d'Ibn Sabbā', auteur copte du XIIIe siècle*, BEL.S 140 (Rome: Edizioni Liturgiche, 2007), 98–130.

61 Mistrīḥ, *Pretiosa margarita*, b.

62 Kussaim Samir, "Contribution à l'étude du Moyen Arabe des Coptes," *Le Muséon* 80 (1967): 153–209, here 161–164. Cf. Zakhary's list in Zakhary, *De la Trinité à la Trinité*, 511–512.

(17th c.). The manuscript was consulted directly throughout this present work, while the edition by ʿAbdallah is also referenced.[63]

Less is known about the work titled ترتيب الكهنوت (*tartīb al-kahanūt*, *The Order of the Priesthood*), attributed to the tenth-century Coptic bishop of Ašmūnayn (Hermopolis) Sāwīrus ibn al-Muqaffaʿ, otherwise known as Sāwīrus of Ašmūnayn.[64] This work was certainly not the penmanship of Sāwīrus, as shown by Julius Assfalg through internal evidence. Nonetheless, also based on internal evidence analyzed by Assfalg, the work most likely dates to the thirteenth century, despite its pseudonymous authorship. This renders it a valuable resource in addition to the above-mentioned works.[65]

4.3. Sources for the Patriarchal Liturgy

Information regarding practice in the fifteenth and sixteenth centuries is sometimes supplemented by the rubrics for the patriarchal liturgy, or the liturgy when celebrated by a patriarch. Three particular sources are utilized throughout this work.[66]

The oldest of these sources is the description of the patriarchal liturgy in *Coptic Patriarchate Lit. 74* (AD 1444), a yet unpublished manuscript, and the oldest specimen belonging to the genre known as *tartīb al-bīʿa*. A type of hymnal, roughly equivalent to the Menaion in the Byzantine tradition, these manuscripts mostly offer the variable chants for each celebration arranged chronologically according to the liturgical year. This particular manuscript is the second volume of a two-codex collection covering the entire year, together with *Coptic Patriarchate Lit. 73* (AD 1444). This two-part collection is described in the catalogue of the manuscripts of the Coptic Orthodox Patriarchate by Marcus Simaika Pasha as follows: "The first [and second] part of the ordo of the Church (Rubrics in Arabic). Contains

63 For the section on the prothesis rite in this work, see *Paris BnF Ar. 98* (17th c.), fol. 45r–54v. Cf. ʿAbdallah, *L'ordinamento*, 171–181 (Arabic), 361–367 (Italian).

64 Julius Assfalg, *Die Ordnung des Priestertums: Ein altes liturgisches Handbuch der koptischen Kirche*, Publications du Centre d'etudes orientales de la Custodie Franciscaine de Terre-Sainte, Coptica 1 (Cairo: [Centre d'etudes orientales de la Custodie Franciscaine de Terre-Sainte], 1955). For more information on Sāwīrus, one of the most famous Copto-Arabic authors, see *GCAL*, 2:300–318; Mark N. Swanson, "Sāwīrus ibn al-Muqaffaʿ," *CMR*, 2:491–509.

65 Cf. Rafīq ʿĀdil, "Tartīb wa-šarḥ al-quddās al-ilāhī ʿind al-ābāʾ al-aqbāṭ [The order and explanation of the divine liturgy among the Coptic fathers]," *Madrasat al-iskandariyya* 18 (2015): 219–241.

66 For an edition, translation, and analysis of the patriarchal prothesis rite, see Ramez Mikhail, "The Liturgy *Coram Patriarcha* Revisited: The Prothesis of the Coptic Patriarchal Liturgy in Sources of the 15th–16th Centuries," *Le Muséon* 131, no. 3–4 (2018): 279–312.

the doxologies, canons, hymns and the responses of the Gospels."[67] The second volume consists of 98 folia of 14 lines each, and dimensions of 24 × 14 cm. Some folia are clearly restored, while the date on fol. 94v is AM 1161, which corresponds to AD 1444–45. The colophon is by the hand of Armīyā ibn al-Qummuṣ.

In addition to the hymnographical material, the manuscript provides instructions or a description of both vespers, matins, and the eucharistic liturgy in the presence of a patriarch. In each case, separate sections provide the rubrics for the event that the patriarch is celebrating the liturgy, or if he is simply in attendance without celebrating. This manuscript was inspected in a digital reproduction of the original, as well as in the publication of its text by Bishop Samuel of Šibīn al-Qanāṭir.[68]

Of slightly later date, a similar chapter on the patriarchal liturgy can be found in a later manuscript of the same genre, whose text was also published by Bishop Samuel, and given the title *Baramūs Codex*. This codex is shelved in the library of the Monastery of the Virgin Mary known as al-Baramūs under the shelfmark *Baramūs 6/278* (AD 1514). This slightly later description copied only seventy years after the one found in *Coptic Patriarchate Lit. 74* is mostly identical to it except in very minor details.

Finally, a description of the liturgy in the presence of the patriarch is found in the codex *Uppsala O. Vet. 12* (AD 1546).[69] The latter is a later copy of Ibn Kabar's *The Lamp of Darkness*, as remarked above. Absent from the oldest manuscript of this work, *Paris BnF Ar. 203* (AD 1363–1369), this section can be taken as reflective of practice in the mid-sixteenth century when *Uppsala O. Vet. 12* was copied. Thus, the Uppsala text is the youngest witness of the patriarchal liturgy in this general time period among the sources known so far. Overall, these three sources are much more valuable than Burmester's description of the patriarchal liturgy.[70] Unlike the sources presented

67 Marcus Simaika and Yassa ʿabd al-Masiḥ, *Catalogue of the Coptic and Arabic Manuscripts in the Coptic Museum, the Patriarchate, the Principal Churches of Cairo and Alexandria and the Monasteries of Egypt*, vol. 2 (Cairo: Government Press, 1942), 339.

68 Samuel, ed., *Tartīb al-bīʿa: ʿan maḫṭūṭāt al-baṭriyarkiyya bi-miṣr wa-l-iskandariyya wa-maḫṭūṭāt al-adyira wa-l-kanāʾis* [The church order: From the manuscripts of the Patriarchate in Cairo and Alexandria, and the manuscripts of the monasteries and churches], vol. 1, ([Cairo], 2000), 16–20. I would like to thank Dr. Ibrahim Saweros (Sohag University, Egypt) for making images of this important manuscript available to me.

69 *Uppsala O. Vet. 12* (AD 1546), fol. 188v–189v. Cf. Villecourt, "Les observances," 277–280.

70 O.H.E. Burmester, "The Liturgy Coram Patriarcha aut Episcopo in the Coptic Church," *Le Muséon* 49 (1936): 79–84.

here, Burmester's text only describes the liturgy when the patriarch is present but will not vest or participate in the liturgy.

4.4. Published Collections

One of the earliest attempts to publish the liturgies of the Alexandrian/Coptic Rite was Eusèbe Renaudot's *Liturgiarum Orientalium Collectio*, whose first edition in Paris (1716) was later republished in Frankfurt (1847).[71] This monumental work contained the text of the Coptic liturgies of BAS, GREG, and CYRIL in Latin translation, including the *Prayers of Preparation*, *Prayer of Thanksgiving*, and *Prothesis Prayer*. Although Renaudot does not state clearly the manuscript sources for his translation, Heinzgerd Brakmann identified Renaudot's translation as based on *Paris BnF Copt. 26* (15th c.).[72]

During the second half of the nineteenth century, English translations began appearing. One such example is the translation by John M. Rodwell of the three Coptic liturgies as well as the rest of the prothesis, the Liturgy of the Word, and the pre-anaphoral rites, based on *Rylands Copt. 426* (13th c.).[73] Another such example is that of Solomon Caesar Malan, vicar of Broadwindsor in 1875, "from an old Coptic manuscript,"[74] identified by Brakmann as *Bodleian Ind. Inst. Copt. 4* (13th/14th c.).[75] Malan also refers to comparisons being made to Ṭūḫī's Euchologion (1736), mentioned below,[76] as well as to Renaudot's Latin translation. Another classic English edition is that by John Marquess of Bute (1882), which explicitly sets itself apart from earlier works by focusing on current practice, "to provide English-speaking travelers in Egypt with a means of following intelligently the Sunday morning service of the native Christians," instead of relying on medieval manuscripts.[77]

71 Renaudot, *Liturgiarum Orientalium Collectio*, 1:1–25.

72 Brakmann, "Le déroulement," 107n4.

73 John M. Rodwell, *The Liturgies of S. Basil, S. Gregory, and S. Cyril, Translated from a Coptic Manuscript of the Thirteenth Century*, Occasional Paper of the Eastern Church Association 12 (London, 1870).

74 Solomon Caesar Malan, *The Divine ΕΥΧΟΛΟΓΙΟΝ, and the Divine Liturgy of S. Gregory the Theologian; Translated from an Old Coptic Manuscript*, Original Documents of the Coptic Church 6 (London, 1875).

75 Brakmann, "Le déroulement," 107n4.

76 Raphael al-Ṭūḫī, ⲡⲓϫⲱⲙ ⲛ̀ⲧⲉ ⲡⲓϣⲟⲙⲧ ⲛ̀ⲁⲛⲁⲫⲟⲣⲁ ⲉ̀ⲧⲉ ⲛⲁⲓ ⲛⲉ ⲙ̀ⲡⲓⲁⲅⲓⲟⲥ ⲃⲁⲥⲓⲗⲓⲟⲥ ⲛⲉⲙ ⲡⲓⲁⲅⲓⲟⲥ ⲅⲣⲏⲅⲟⲣⲓⲟⲥ ⲡⲓⲑⲉⲟⲗⲟⲅⲟⲥ ⲛⲉⲙ ⲡⲓⲁⲅⲓⲟⲥ ⲕⲩⲣⲓⲗⲗⲟⲥ ⲛⲉⲙ ⲛⲓⲕⲉⲉⲩⲭⲏ ⲉⲑⲟⲩⲁⲃ [The book of the three anaphoras, which are of Saint Basil and Saint Gregory the Theologian and Saint Cyril, and other holy prayers] (Rome, 1736).

77 John Marquess of Bute, *The Coptic Morning Service for the Lord's Day* (London, 1882).

However, a few years later in 1896 the first English translation of the Coptic liturgy based on a clearly referenced manuscript was published by Frank Edward Brightman.[78] This edition was based mainly on the thirteenth-century Euchologion *Bodleian Hunt. 360*, one of the earliest complete Copto-Arabic manuscripts of the liturgy available. Certain portions were also interpolated from the first printed *Deacon's Manual* (1887)[79] referenced below, as well as the codex *Bodleian Marsh 5* (14th c.).

4.5. Editions of Liturgical Books

The first printed Coptic Euchologion was published by Raphael al-Ṭūḫī in Rome (1736).[80] This Euchologion was part of an entire corpus of Coptic liturgical books published by Ṭūḫī for the future Coptic Catholic community. As expected from a liturgical book designed for liturgical use and not for academic work, it states no particular manuscript sources, although Brakmann identified the manuscript *BAV Vatican Copt. 17* (AD 1288) as the basis for this edition.[81] Although Ṭūḫī adjusted the text whenever appropriate to agree with certain teachings of the Roman Catholic Church,[82] this does not seem to affect the prothesis prayers particularly. For the earliest printed edition for the Coptic Orthodox community, there is the 1887 edition of Philotheos Ibrahīm,[83] who also published the *Deacon's Manual* used by Brightman and containing the diaconal responses for the entire liturgy. In addition, the landmark Euchologion by Hegumen ʿAbd al-Masīḥ Ṣalīb should be added.

78 *LEW*, 144–188.

79 [Philotheos Ibrāhīm], *Kitāb mā yağibu ʿala l-šamāmisa min al-qirāʾa fī l-ḫidma wa-l-tarātīl* [The book of what the deacons ought to read in the service and the chants] (Cairo, 1887). A *Deacon's Manual* or Diaconicon is a liturgical book containing mainly the portions of each service to be recited by the assisting deacon, as well as the hymns and chants sung by the chanters.

80 Ṭūḫī, ⲡⲓϫⲱⲙ ⲛ̀ⲧⲉ ⲡⲓϣⲟⲙⲧ ⲛ̀ⲁⲛⲁⲫⲟⲣⲁ.

81 Brakmann, "Le déroulement," 107n4. For an edition of the Arabic text of this manuscript, see Wadīʿ ʿAwaḍ, "Testo della Traduzione Araba della Messa Copta di San Basilio Secondo un Manoscritto del 1288," *SOC Collectanea* 41 (2008): 129–149. The text was also published in French translation in Mamdouh Chéhab, "Traduction de la version arabe de la messe copte de s. Basile. Vatican copte 17 (1288 AD)," *SOC Collectanea* 44 (2011): 49–68.

82 For example, inserting the Filioque into the Creed, and removing non-Chalcedonian saints, such as Dioscorus and Severus of Antioch.

83 [Philotheos Ibrāhīm], *Ḫulāgī al-qiddīs Basīliyūs* [The Euchologion of Saint Basil] (Cairo, 1887).

4.6 Other Sources

Finally, one must not ignore the important testimony of supplementary literature to knowledge of the liturgy in a given era. Included in this broad heading are three main types of evidence that certainly possess their own rich tradition of sources, publications, and methodologies. First, the canonical literature of the Coptic Church, particularly the canonical collections of some of the medieval patriarchs such as Christodoulus (AD 1047–1077), Cyril II (AD 1078–1092), Gabriel II ibn Turaik (AD 1131–1145), and Cyril III ibn Laqlaq (AD 1235–1243).[84] In many instances, these canonical collections provide unparalleled insights into church life in a particular era in a way that cannot be obtained from a reading of official commentaries and ideal representations of the liturgy.

In a similar vein is the vast and largely untapped field of Coptic hagiography.[85] Robert Taft has written repeatedly in recent years about the importance of hagiography and other popular literature to an accurate understanding of liturgy as it actually unfolded, and as it was experienced in the everyday lives of Christians of a given era.[86] Coptic hagiography is not merely stories of or about saints written in the Coptic language, but also includes those written in Greek with a

84 These collections have been published by Burmester. See O.H.E. Burmester, "The Canons of Christodulos, Patriarch of Alexandria (1047–1077)," *Le Muséon* 45 (1932): 71–84; O.H.E. Burmester, "The Canons of Gabriel Ibn Turaik, LXX Patriarch of Alexandria," *Le Muséon* 36 (1933): 43–54; O.H.E. Burmester, "The Canons of Gabriel Ibn Turaik, LXX Patriarch of Alexandria (First Series)," *OCP* 1 (1935): 5–45; O.H.E. Burmester, "The Canons of Cyril II, LXVII Patriarch of Alexandria," *Le Muséon* 49 (1936): 245–288; O.H.E. Burmester, "The Canons of Cyril III Ibn Laqlaq, 75th Patriarch of Alexandria," *BSAC* 12 (1946–1947): 81–136; O.H.E. Burmester, "The Canons of Cyril III Ibn Laklak, 75th Patriarch of Alexandria," *BSAC* 14 (1950): 113–150. For an introduction on Coptic canonical literature and its sources, see Hubert Kaufhold, "Sources of Canon Law in the Eastern Churches," in *The History of Byzantine and Eastern Canon Law to 1500*, ed. Wilfried Hartmann and Kenneth Pennington, History of Medieval Canon Law (Washington DC: Catholic University of America Press, 2012), 215–342.

85 For introductory surveys on hagiography, especially in Coptic, see Tito Orlandi, "Hagiography, Coptic," *CE*, 4:1191a–1197b; Theofried Baumeister, "Martyrology," *CE*, 5:1549b–1550b. Much has been written on the usefulness of hagiographical literature for historical research and how fact and fiction can be distinguished in this genre, which is not my concern here. See for example Hippolyte Delehaye, *Cinq leçons sur la méthode hagiographique*, Subsidia Hagiographica 21 (Brussels: Société des Bollandistes, 1934); Thomas Pratsch, "Exploring the Jungle: Hagiographical Literature between Fact and Fiction," in *Fifty Years of Prosopography: The Later Roman Empire, Byzantium and Beyond*, ed. Averil Cameron, Proceedings of the British Academy 118 (Oxford: Oxford University Press, 2003), 59–72.

86 See most recently, Robert F. Taft, *A History of the Liturgy of St. John Chrysostom*, vol. 6, *The Communion, Thanksgiving, and Concluding Rites*, OCA 281 (Rome, Pontificio Istituto Orientale, 2008), 74–76.

demonstrably Egyptian provenance, as well as later Arabic material.[87] Finally, church architecture is another area of potentially great opportunities for rediscovering the historical development of the Coptic liturgy. As is demonstrated in chapters 1 and 2, approaching the study of the Coptic prothesis from the perspective of church architecture complements existing knowledge of how the Coptic Rite, especially the prothesis, was carried out at various historical junctures.[88]

5. METHODOLOGY

This study was conceived as a history of the development and evolution of the Coptic rite of the prothesis. To write such a history will make it possible to answer some difficult liturgical and theological questions, based not on a priori assumptions of the purpose or meaning of this or that practice, but on how the individual elements of the Coptic prothesis developed historically, and what influences and factors shaped the rite to make it what it is today. Thus, first and foremost evidence from liturgical manuscripts as well as other sources introduced above is used to describe the development of the Coptic prothesis. In doing so, an attempt is made in the case of each ritual and textual element to identify its first appearance in the manuscript tradition, and then trace this element until the publication of the *editio typica* of 1902.

This attempt at locating the earliest forms for each ritual and liturgical element is not out of mere archaism, a romantic attempt to revive the past. Rather, it proceeds from Taft's observation that, to understand the purpose and function of a liturgical rite, "one seeks to go back to that point at which the unit under study emerges in its pristine integrity."[89] For frequently one finds that later additions to the rite tend to obscure its original integrity, especially if that original function is no longer well-understood, as Taft again has observed.

[87] For a discussion of the types of hagiographies in the Coptic language with an updated list of primary sources and scholarship, see Arietta Papaconstantinou, "Hagiography in Coptic," in *The Ashgate Research Companion to Byzantine Hagiography*, ed. Stephanos Efthymiadis, vol. 1, *Periods and Places* (Farnham, Surrey, England: Ashgate, 2011), 323–343.

[88] See Peter Grossmann, *Christliche Architektur in Ägypten*, Handbuch der Orientalistik, Section 1: The Near and Middle East 62 (Leiden: Brill, 2002), and the number of studies analyzing the intersection of architecture and liturgy in the Ethiopian context by Emmanuel Fritsch and referenced in chapters 1 and 2.

[89] Robert F. Taft, "The Structural Analysis of Liturgical Units: An Essay in Methodology," in *Beyond East and West: Problems in Liturgical Understanding*, 2nd ed., ed. Robert F. Taft (Rome: Edizioni Orientalia Christiana, Pontifical Oriental Institute, 2001), 187–202, here 200.

However, as the sources discussed above clearly show, there are entire centuries from which one may lack any liturgical manuscripts or other sources that could provide as complete a picture as possible of the development of the prothesis. In such cases, assistance is frequently sought in the comparative method to help formulate hypotheses. Much has been written about the utility of the comparative method of liturgical analysis, associated most famously with the name of Anton Baumstark (1872–1948).[90] In this method, primary sources of liturgical practice from various Christian communities are examined and compared contextually in order to elucidate their commonalities and differences. As a result of decades spent applying this method, Baumstark's name came to be traditionally associated with the so-called "laws" of liturgical evolution. Not quite laws in the traditional sense, these are general tendencies observed in the historical development of liturgical rites that can be of immense help in formulating working hypotheses in the absence of enough evidence. To these laws, one can add also a few more general tendencies observed by Taft, and listed in his writings on method.[91] Throughout this present work, the reader will find that evidence from Egyptian sources is frequently compared to analogous sources from the Christian East and West, namely, the Byzantine, Syrian, Ethiopian, and Roman traditions. For example, it was primarily thanks to primary sources from Syria and Ethiopia that it was possible to understand when and why the Coptic prothesis rite was moved from the adjacent pastophoria to the altar.

An extension of the comparative method is the structural analysis of liturgical units. This approach has gained great popularity as a useful method in liturgical analysis, particularly through Taft's work on the historical development of the Byzantine liturgy of St. John Chrysostom. According to this method, one must seek first to divide a certain rite under investigation into individual liturgical structures, then proceed to study each structure separately. Time and again this method has been shown to be useful in sifting through the liturgical data and formulating hypotheses as to the meaning of this data. That

90 Anton Baumstark, *Comparative Liturgy*, trans. F.L. Cross (Westminster, MD: A.R. Mowbray, 1958); Anton Baumstark, *Vom geschichtlichen Werden der Liturgie*, Ecclesia Orans 10 (Freiburg im Breisgau: Herder, 1923); Anton Baumstark, *On the Historical Development of the Liturgy*, trans. Fritz West (Collegeville, MN: Liturgical Press, 2011); Fritz West, *The Comparative Liturgy of Anton Baumstark*, Alcuin/GROW Liturgical Study 31 (Nottingham, England: Grove Books, 1995); to name a few of the studies by Baumstark available in English, as well as studies of Baumstark's own methodology and legacy.

91 Robert F. Taft, "Anton Baumstark's Comparative Liturgy Revisited," in Taft and Winkler, *Acts of the International Congress*, 191–232.

is because, as Taft observed in the Byzantine Rite, liturgical rites do not grow evenly–with additions to the rite added evenly to all of its elements–but tend to grow at certain so-called "soft points", namely the entrance rites, pre-anaphoral rites, and the communion and dismissal rites.[92]

Indeed, according to this method, the entire rite under study, the Coptic prothesis, may be considered a single liturgical unit, a "soft point" and thus the product of a rich developmental history. However, as Hans-Jürgen Feulner shows in his treatment of this method, one can certainly divide and sub-divide a single liturgical unit into smaller units.[93] These various sub-units within the larger single unit of the prothesis have grown unevenly, as some of these sub-units are certainly older than others.

The remainder of this book is an application of this well-established method–the comparative analysis of liturgical units–to uncover and analyze the historical development of the Coptic prothesis rite, the first part of the eucharistic liturgy as observed by Egypt's Coptic Christians.

92 Robert F. Taft, "How Liturgies Grow: The Evolution of the Byzantine Divine Liturgy," in Taft, *Beyond East and West*, 203–232, here 204.

93 Hans-Jürgen Feulner, "The Anglican Use within the Western Liturgical Tradition: Importance and Ecumenical Relevance from the Perspective of Comparative Liturgy," in *Anglicans and the Roman Catholic Church: Reflections on Recent Developments*, ed. Stephen E. Cavanaugh, (San Francisco, CA: Ignatius Press, 2011), 184–224, here 189.

PART 1

HISTORICAL ORIGINS AND PREPARATORY RITES

CHAPTER 1

HISTORICAL ORIGINS 1: THE PREPARATION OF THE GIFTS

If one were to follow the unfolding of the preparatory rites of the Coptic liturgy in their present form, the vesting of the celebrants would be immediately followed by the preparation of the altar, often performed today before or during the praying of the appropriate prayers of the liturgy of the hours from the Horologion.[1] However, before one can proceed to explaining the historical development of the preparation of the altar and its accompanying prayers, one must dedicate this chapter and the next to a topic far more crucial for the overall evolution of the Coptic prothesis rite, namely, the preparation and transfer of the eucharistic gifts. Although in the current rite the gifts are prepared and placed on the altar immediately at the beginning of the service, it will become clear through an examination of the sources that this was certainly not the case in earlier centuries.

It is necessary to make a few terminological distinctions clear from the outset. First, the preparation of the gifts in its earliest form consisted in no more than the reception of the offerings from the people by the deacons, and their keeping until the time of the transfer of gifts immediately before the anaphora. In such an early and practical form, the preparation of the gifts was yet to acquire the highly developed ritual, prayers, and symbols it would acquire later, and thus it will not be referenced here using the technical term prothesis. Instead, this term will be reserved solely for the solemn ritual that came to characterize the preparation of the gifts and included a number of formalized gestures and prayers in various traditions, most notably the *Prothesis Prayer* itself. The use of this terminological distinction is in agreement with the statement by Robert Taft, "There was no such thing as a prothesis rite at the

1 The *horologion,* known more popularly as the *ağbīyya* from the Coptic ⲁϫⲡ meaning hour, is the Coptic book of hours. See Georg Graf, *Verzeichnis arabischer kirchlicher Termini*, 2nd ed., CSCO 147, Subsidia 8 (Louvain: Secrétariat du Corpus, 1964), 4. For more information on the rubrics and history of praying select offices from the Horologion between the morning service and the prothesis, see Excursus 2.

beginning or anywhere else, nor any offertory prayer, in the early centuries."[2]

Second, it is also necessary to distinguish between the preparation of the gifts and their transfer to the altar. This distinction would be indeed unnecessary in rites that have preserved a sharp ritual distinction between the two acts until modern times, where the two are separated by the entire Liturgy of the Word. Such is the case in the Byzantine and Armenian Rites, where the prothesis is performed before the commencement of the public celebration, while the transfer of the gifts takes place as part of the pre-anaphoral rites. This is however not the case in the current rite of the Coptic liturgy, as well as that of the Ethiopian and Syrian rites, where the deposition of the gifts on the altar occurs at the very beginning of the liturgy, and any ritual formulas and prayers of prothesis take place afterwards, while the gifts are already on the altar. Thus, from the point of view of the current rite, the distinction between the prothesis and the transfer of gifts is merely theoretical, since the two actions happen in such close succession, and constitute one integral liturgical motion. This explains why the transfer of gifts, a pre-anaphoral rite in its original form, will be examined here in a work dedicated to the prothesis and other preparatory rites. Nonetheless, for the sake of analysis, and since this distinction was sharper in earlier stages of liturgical development, it will be employed here as needed.

Robert Taft stated in his analysis of the pre-anaphoral rites of the Byzantine liturgy, "That the transfer was done everywhere just before the anaphora is obvious."[3] As the evidence will demonstrate, this general statement holds true as well for the Alexandrian liturgical tradition and the Coptic Rite of the Northern Egyptian Liturgy. In fact, the main purpose of this chapter and the next is to demonstrate that the ancient and universal practice of placing the gifts on the altar immediately before the anaphora was indeed the case in Egypt as well. This ancient practice is referred to here as the *old ordo*, in contrast to the *new ordo*, where the deposition of the gifts occurs before the prothesis. This change in practice is indeed so drastic as to constitute a watershed event in the historical development of the Coptic liturgy of the Eucharist. Such large-scale ritual changes where an entire central action is moved so far away from its pristine location are incredibly rare. For this reason, as much evidence as possible will be marshalled from historical texts, liturgical sources, and church

2 Taft and Parenti, *Il Grande* Ingresso, 125. Cf. Robert F. Taft, *A History of the Liturgy of St. John Chrysostom*, vol. 2, *The Great Entrance: A History of the Transfer of Gifts and other Pre-anaphral [sic.] Rites*, 4th ed., OCA 200 (Rome: Pontificio Istituto Orientale, 2004), 32–33.

3 Taft and Parenti, *Il Grande Ingresso*, 126. Cf. Taft, *The Great Entrance*, 33.

architecture, in order not only to show that this shift did in fact occur, but to attempt as much as possible to understand its circumstances.

In order to arrive at a complete picture of the topic in question, the investigation over the course of this chapter and the next follows the eucharistic gifts from their initial bringing by the people, to their ultimate placement on the altar. Thus, the topic is here broken down to multiple phases: 1. The bringing of the offering by the people, 2. The location where the gifts were kept, and 3. The transfer of the gifts. In each phase, the historical development will be traced from its earliest discernible witnesses to its current form, paying close attention to the informative witness of the neighboring traditions of Byzantium, Syria, and Ethiopia.

1. THE OFFERING OF THE GIFTS

Unlike current practice, according to which the bread offering is baked in church in a special room commonly called Bethlehem, there is considerable evidence that people in fact brought their own offerings to church. However, the evidence does not permit the assumption that an offertory *procession* before the anaphora was ever the custom in Egypt.

1.1. The Bringing of the Offering by the People

One of the earliest witnesses that the faithful did indeed bring offerings to church for the Eucharist can be found in the writings of Shenoute of Atripe (ca. AD 347–465). In his homily *De lingua* found in *Paris BnF Copt. 130(3)*, he rebukes those who have recently left his monastic community and lists a number of virtuous acts that should be performed by all, namely, "bringing the offering (ϫⲓ ⲛⲧⲉⲡⲣⲟⲥⲫⲟⲣⲁ) to church, and giving one's bread to the hungry, and clothing the naked, and loving the stranger and the poor."[4]

In addition to literary witnesses to the people bringing their own offerings to church, further confirmation can also be found in the *Litany of Oblations*, a prayer for those who donated various offerings. Prayed today by the priest during the morning service, the prayer entreats God, "Remember the sacrifices, the offerings (ⲛⲓⲡⲣⲟⲥⲫⲟⲣⲁ), and the thanksgivings (ⲛⲓϣⲉⲡϩ̀ⲙⲟⲧ) of those who have offered."[5] The prayer continues, asking God to accept these offerings on his heavenly altar. In addition to its location in matins, the same prayer is repeated once later as part of the anaphoral litanies of Coptic MARK, as

4 Iohannes Leipoldt, ed., *Sinuthii archimandritae vita et opera omnia*, CSCO 42, Scriptores Coptici, Ser. 2, volume 4 (Paris: [E Typographeo reipublica], 1908), 114.

5 Ṣalīb, ⲡⲓϫⲱⲙ ⲛ̀ⲧⲉ ⲡⲓⲉⲩⲭⲟⲗⲟⲅⲓⲟⲛ, 68.

mentioned previously.[6] Not only is this prayer attested as early as the thirteenth-century *Bodleian Hunt. 360*,[7] it is also found with minor variants in all the Greek manuscripts of Melkite MARK, edited by Geoffrey Cuming,[8] and in the Ethiopian tradition both in the sixth-century Aksumite Collection as well as the Ethiopic *Statutes of the Apostles*.[9] This attests to its ancient presence in the liturgical tradition of the Church of Alexandria, and to the custom that this prayer represents, namely, that members of the faithful brought various offerings including those destined for the Eucharist frequently enough so as to merit a codified prayer on their behalf. A similar shorter prayer asks God, "Remember O Lord those who have brought unto you these gifts (ⲇⲱⲣⲟⲛ), and those on whose behalf they have been brought, and those by whom they have been brought, give them all the heavenly reward."[10] This latter however occurs mainly at the procession around the altar in the prothesis rite, and is frequently absent in manuscripts, as is shown below in chapter 4.

However, it seems that at least in some places the church stored such offerings for later use, after they were donated by the faithful. In the monastic *Canons of Shenoute* (5th c.), canon 13, the following injunction appears, "Cursed be whoever steals from the things of the sanctuary, whether it be bread or wine or any other articles that are from the sanctuary, whether inside the sanctuary or stored outside and not yet brought in."[11] A few centuries later, in *The Miracles of Apa Phoebammon* from *MLM M582* (AD 822/3–913/14), reference is made in the course of a miracle at the saint's shrine to a place "In the corner of the sanctuary," where one man found a *lakote* (ⲗⲁⲕⲟⲧⲉ)—a certain measurement—of wine.[12] This corner of the sanctuary may very well be a prothesis area, or a sacristy, where wine was kept along with other materials needed for the eucharistic rites. This would lead one to conclude that at least in some places—more affluent shrines of

6 Ibid., 609–610.

7 *Bodleian Hunt. 360* (13th c.), fol. 236r. Cf. *LEW*, 170.

8 Cuming, *The Liturgy of St Mark*, 31–32.

9 Information on the Aksumite Collection can be found in Bausi, *Comparative Oriental Manuscript Studies*, 367–372. Cf. George William Horner, *The Statutes of the Apostles or Canones Ecclesiastici: Edited with Translation and Collation from Ethiopic and Arabic MSS.; Also a Translation of the Saidic and Collation of the Bohairic Versions; and Saidic Fragments* (London: Williams & Norgate, 1904), 83 (Ethiopic), 227–228 (English). See also *LEW*, 203.

10 Ṣalīb, ⲡⲓϫⲱⲙ ⲛ̀ⲧⲉ ⲡⲓⲉⲩⲭⲟⲗⲟⲅⲓⲟⲛ, 214.

11 Bentley Layton, *The Canons of our Fathers: Monastic Rules of Shenoute*, Oxford Early Christian Studies (Oxford: Oxford University Press, 2014), 94–95.

12 Kerry E. Verrone, *Mighty Deeds and Miracles by Saint Apa Phoebammon: Edition and Translation of Coptic Manuscript M582 ff. 21r–30r in the Pierpont Morgan Library* (Providence, RI: Brown University, 2002), 28–29.

local saints and large monastic establishments—offerings for the Eucharist were provided in advance and stored on site.

If evidence from late antiquity as well as liturgical texts that may pre-date the Chalcedonian schism confirm that people brought eucharistic offerings, how late did this custom persist? As one begins to examine evidence from later centuries, the practice of preparing the offerings in church becomes more common, and eventually acquires canonical force. A reference to the people bringing their own offerings can still be found in the *Didascalia Arabica* (ca. 12th c.). The relevant passage appears in chapter 35, titled *Concerning the Order of the Building of the Holy Church*. Concerning the offerings, the *Didascalia Arabica* reads:

[1] وليكتب الشمامسة اسماء اصحاب القرابين الذين يأتون بها كل يوم، الأحياء منهم والاموات،[2] لكى إذا صلى الكاهن يذكرهم. [3] وهكذا يأتي الشماس بتذكارهم في ذلك الأسبوع. [4] ويكون مثال ما يكمل في السماوات.[13]

[1] And the deacons are to write the names for whom oblations are offered daily, the living among them and the dead, [2] so that when the priest prays he may remember them. [3] And thus the deacon brings their remembrance in that week, [4] and it becomes a likeness of what is fulfilled in heaven.

It may be difficult to date this passage precisely. According to Georg Graf, the *Didascalia Arabica* is transmitted in two recensions: An older vulgate version found in medieval Arabic nomocanons, and seems to be a translation from a Bohairic Coptic precursor, and a possibly younger version found only in *BAV Borgia Ar. 22* (AD 1295).[14] The passage in question appears only in the vulgate, and bears similarity to material in the *Testamentum Domini*, the pseudo-apostolic text of fifth-century West-Syrian provenance.[15] Taken by itself, the *Didascalia Arabica* cannot be considered a strong witness to the people's bringing their offering to church in the medieval period.

13 William Sulaymān Qilāda, *Ta'ālīm al-rusul al-disqūliyya*, 2nd ed. (Cairo: Dār al-ṯaqāfa, 1989), 842. Another edition of the *Didascalia Arabica* was published in Egypt by Ḥāfiẓ Dā'ūd (ordained later as Fr. Marqus Dā'ūd). Cf. Marqus Dā'ūd, *Al-disqūliyya aw ta'ālīm al-rusul*, 5th ed. (Cairo: Maktabat al-maḥabba, 1979), 176. For a Latin translation, cf. Franciscus Xaverius Funk, ed., *Didascalia et Constitutiones Apostolorum*, vol. 2, *Testimonia et Scripturae Propinquae* (Paderborn: In libraria Ferdinandi Schoeningh, 1906), 125. Translation of the canon above is mine.

14 *GCAL*, 1:564–569. Cf. Kaufhold, "Sources of Canon Law," 266–267.

15 *GCAL*, 1:565.

In fact, the witness of another canonical text of the Coptic tradition points to the contrary. In the Arabic *Canons of Ps.-Athanasius*,[16] canon 34 reads as follows:

[1] لا يجوز لكاهن ان يخرج بسبب خبيز القربان و لا يقف في الفرن [2] بل كما انه يخدم الشعب يخدمونه هو ايضاً الابودياقنيين. [3] لأن حزقيال النبي يقول من يعبد يتعبد له.[17]	[1] It is not permitted for the priest to leave on account of baking the oblation, nor to stand at the oven, [2] but just as he serves the people, likewise also the subdeacons serve him. [3] For Ezekiel the prophet says, he who worships is honored.

The Sahidic fragments of the *Canons of Ps.-Athanasius*, which date to the fifth–sixth century, do not contain this canon, while the Arabic text—presumably based on a Bohairic intermediary—was translated in the eleventh century by Bishop Mīḫā'īl of Tinnīs.[18] At least then, by the early medieval period when the Arabic version of these canons was composed, one can no longer speak of the people bringing their own offerings to church, but rather of an increased role of the deacons in preparing the gifts.

Another important witness is the canons of Patriarch Christodoulus (AD 1047–1077), in which the following canon has this to say regarding the eucharistic gifts:

16 Riedel edited the text based on three manuscripts, all from the fourteenth century. Multiple attempts have been made to date this collection of canons. Riedel advances the theory that the author of the lost Greek original may well have been Athanasius of Alexandria himself. See Wilhelm Riedel and W.E. Crum, *The Canons of Athanasius of Alexandria: The Arabic and Coptic Versions* (Oxford: Williams & Norgate, 1904), viii–xxvi. Coquin, noticing the absence of the feast of the Nativity from the collection, which was introduced in Egypt in the mid-fifth century, argued more cautiously that the canons must be earlier than that. Cf. René-Georges Coquin, "Canons of Pseudo-Athanasius," *CE*, 2:458b–459a. Finally, taking into account all the preceding scholarship on the subject, Athanasius al-Maqārī dismissed all the historical arguments dating the text to the time of Athanasius. Instead, he noted that the earliest witnesses of these canons do not refer to the author as Athanasius *the Apostolic*, his usual epithet in the Coptic tradition. He argues convincingly that the canons may in fact be the work of Patriarch Athanasius II (AD 488–494). Cf. Athanasius al-Maqārī, *Qawānīn al-bābā aṯanāsiyūs baṭriyark al-iskandariyya* [The canons of Pope Athanasius the patriarch of Alexandria], Maṣādir ṭuqūs al-kanīsa 1.10 (Cairo: Dār nūbār, 2006), 298. Wilhelm Riedel, *Die Kirchenrechtsquellen des Patriarchats Alexandrien* (Leipzig: A. Deichert'sche Verlagsbuchhandlung Nachf., 1900), 275.

17 Canon 34. *Paris BnF Ar. 251* (AD 1353), fol. 330r. Cf. Riedel and Crum, *The Canons of Athanasius of Alexandria*, 26 (Arabic), 32 (English). The translation was adjusted from Crum's for clarity and accuracy.

18 At least based on the information provided by Ibn Kabar in the *Lamp of Darkness*, chapter 5. See *GCAL*, 1:605–606; Kaufhold, "Sources of Canon Law," 275.

[1] وقد ابحنا للمؤمنين ان يعملوا القرابين في منازلهم ويحملوها الى البيعة على قدر طاقة كل واحد [2] فيكون له الاجر والثواب كقدر امانته [3] ويكون عمله على ما جرت به العادة [4] اولاً فان ذلك رفقاً بالبيعة [5] لئلا تكثر عليها المون.[19]

[1] We have allowed the faithful to make the oblations in their homes and to bear them to the church according to the ability of each. And to each there will be a reward according to his faithfulness. [3] They should be prepared according to custom; [4] foremost because this is a help to the church, so that there may not be an increase of expense upon it.

It may be tempting to view this canon in continuity with ancient practice. However, a closer analysis of the text demonstrates that the practice was likely already extinct by the eleventh century, the time of Patriarch Christodoulus. It is perhaps unlikely that this instruction would have been necessary if the practice of the people preparing the oblations themselves was considered normal. The language of the canon indicates that Christodoulus was allowing this practice himself, clearly indicating it was not practiced previously. The text of the canon also provides hints at the reason for this allowance, “[4] because this is an assistance to the church, [5] so that there may not be an increase of expense for it.” Finally, the canon also reveals that by the eleventh century, oblations had acquired a particular preparation method as seen in [3]. Although Christodoulus was allowing the people to prepare offerings in their own homes, he still sought to maintain the tradition of how the oblation bread was prepared, indicating that by his time, the oblations were baked in church following particular prescribed rubrics.[20]

A look at the historical circumstances of Christodoulus’ patriarchate explains the need for such an allowance. Mark Swanson, analyzing the biography of Christodoulus in *The History of the Patriarchs*, points to the severe persecutions suffered by the Coptic Church and the patriarch himself at that time. The local governor al-Yāzūrī closed churches, arrested the patriarch, tortured three bishops to death, and extorted funds. Later during the patriarchate of Christodoulus, during the so-called Great Tribulation of AD 1066–1073, armed conflict took place between military factions, disrupting agricultural life, and of course precipitating various episodes of

19 Burmester, “The Canons of Christodulos,” 77 (Arabic), 83 (English). Cf. *HP*, 2.3:168 (Arabic), 255 (English).

20 For a description of the Coptic oblation bread and the rubrics and canons observed in its baking, see Butler, *The Ancient Coptic Churches of Egypt*, vol. 2 (Oxford, 1884), 277–279.

burning and looting.[21] These events indeed explain the need for the patriarch to issue an exceptional decree allowing the people–whoever has the means to do so in such dire circumstances–to bake the oblation bread in their own homes and assist the churches. It can be concluded therefore that already by the eleventh century, Copts no longer typically brought their own offerings to church.

In contrast to the turbulent times of Christodoulus, the patriarchate of his successor Cyril II (AD 1078–1092) was relatively peaceful. This came about with the governorship of the Armenian general Badr al-Ǧamalī, who invaded Egypt to stabilize it at the request of the Fatimid Caliph al-Mustanṣir. Al-Ǧamalī's reign ushered in a period of peace for the Copts, as well as other Christian minorities, as Swanson relates.[22] It is no surprise then that soon after the exceptional permission by Christodoulus, one finds the following canon by Cyril II:

[1] يجب ان لا يُخبَز خبز القربان إلّا في فرن البيعة [2] ولا تعجنه امرأة.[23]	[1] The bread of the Eucharist must not be baked except in the oven of the church, [2] nor must a woman knead it.

It is certainly remarkable that two successive patriarchs would issue such diametrically opposed canons regarding the same issue. This seems to confirm that by the eleventh century, the tradition of the faithful providing the church with offerings of bread and wine for the Eucharist must have already become a thing of the past, allowed out of necessity by Christodoulus, and prohibited once again by Cyril II.[24]

21 Mark N. Swanson, *The Coptic Papacy in Islamic Egypt (641–1517)*, The Popes of Egypt 2 (Cairo: The American University in Cairo Press, 2010), 61–62.

22 Ibid., 63.

23 Burmester, "The Canons of Cyril II," 269 (Arabic), 282 (English). Cf. *HP*, 2.3:213. The canons of Cyril II appear also in the historical work by Yūsāb Bishop of Fuwwa. Cf. Samuel Al-Suryānī and Nabīh Kāmil, *Tārīḫ al-ābā' al-baṭārika li-l-anbā Yūsāb usquf Fuwwa* [The history of the fathers the patriarchs of Anba Yūsāb bishop of Fuwwa] (Cairo, 1987), 126.

24 It is important to note however that practice was far from uniform away from the center of Coptic ecclesiastical influence in Cairo and the North. A wall inscription in the Faras Cathedral in Nubia dated by its excavators between the tenth and eleventh centuries (given the numbers L.49a.3 = DBMNT 2927, and B.120a.3 = DBMNT 2928, respectively) preserved a list of people and donated goods, mostly consisting of bread and wine, which most likely represents a memorializing of certain key figures in the community–including also higher clergy–who have donated gifts for the Eucharist. See the transcription, translation, and analysis of these inscriptions: Adam Łajtar and Grzegorz Ochała, "Two Wall Inscriptions from the Faras Cathedral with Lists of People and Goods," in *Nubian Voices II: New Texts and Studies of Christian Nubian Culture*, ed. Adam Łajtar, Grzegorz Ochała, and Jacques van der Vliet, Supplements to the Journal of Juristic Papyrology 27 (Warsaw: Faculty of Law and Administration University of Warsaw / Institute of Archaeology / The Raphael Taubenschlag Foundation, 2015), 73–102.

The later witness of *The Order of the Priesthood* also confirms this. In chapter 3, *The Holy Sanctuary*, the author provides the following instructions regarding the bread and wine:

[1] واما الخبز المختوم والدم الزكي فلا يجوز ان يُقَرَّبوا الا من مال البيعة [2] او ما يُؤتَى به اليها من وجه حِل.[25]	[1] The sealed bread and precious wine must not be offered except from the money of the church, [2] or from what is brought to it as an allowance.

The text continues with a list of those who are not allowed to donate for such offerings, including those who lend with interest, wine merchants, fornicators, apostates, dishonest merchants, or anyone transgressing the Church's canons in any manner. Later in chapter 17, the duties of the sacristan are listed, including, "diligence in the baking of the oblation bread from the best and purest flour [...] and he ought to summon the priest to read near him the Davidic psalms while he kneads the bread."[26] This thirteenth-century treatise provides precious information on how the bread offering was prepared at the time. Taken together, the regulations on who can donate materials for the bread, who is to bake it, and the rubrics and rites observed during its baking all represent a far cry from the earlier witnesses of the faithful providing the church with their own baked oblations.

The rules surrounding the oblation bread are even taken as a type of confessional marker between Copts and Melkites (members of the Chalcedonian Church of Alexandria). In the final chapter of *The Order of the Priesthood*, a list of Melkite ritual practices considered abhorrent to the Coptic author include the following:

[1] عجين القربان عندهم من النساء والبنات وخبيزه في غير فرن البيعة فهو غير جائز بالشرع [2] اولاً انه غير مؤمن يلمسه بيده وهو غير متعمد [3] والثاني ان الكهنة عند القبط يقرأوا على العجين المزامير الداودية.[27]	[1] The kneading of the oblation among them by women and girls, and its baking elsewhere than the church's ovens, which is legaly forbidden. [2] First, that an unbeliever touches it with his hand, being unbaptized. [3] Second, because the priests among the Copts read the Davidic psalms over the dough.

By the thirteenth century, the manner by which the oblation bread was to be provided for the Eucharist had acquired such rigid regulations so as to be included among ten other cardinal issues

25 Assfalg, *Die Ordnung des Priestertums*, 16 (Arabic), 85–86 (German).

26 Ibid., 43 (Arabic), 120 (German).

27 Ibid., 55–56 (Arabic), 133 (German).

dividing the Copts and the Melkites ritually, a sure sign of the stabilization of the new order of things by that era.

1.2. Was there an Offertory Procession in Egypt?

As mentioned previously, scholarship before Robert Taft's monumental work on the eastern transfer of gifts tended to assume the existence of a people's offertory procession before the anaphora, where members of the faithful brought forward their oblations to be received by the deacons and placed on the altar. Such is the assumption made by Jungmann, who wrote that this offertory procession, "subsequently [after the third century] was to be found in all countries, and which flourished in the Occident for over a thousand years."[28] However, as Taft himself noted,[29] Jungmann was less confident about this statement in his earlier and more famous work, *Missarum Sollemnia*, where he acknowledges that, "There has been no comprehensive investigation of the offering of the gifts by the faithful in the Orient."[30]

Jungmann however was not alone in his certainty, which was shared by many previous liturgiologists. In addition to scholars mentioned by Taft who wrote primarily about the Byzantine liturgy,[31] one can also mention Gregory Dix, who strongly affirmed the existence of a people's procession everywhere except in Syria.[32] Likewise, Anton Baumstark in his work *Vom geschichtlichen Werden der Liturgie* declared, "In the East, the Great Entrance, symbolizing the entry of the Lord himself, took the place of the offertory procession performed by the community."[33] Taft however has convincingly argued that no evidence exists for an offertory procession by the people in the Byzantine Rite. It remains to be seen if this is true as well for Egypt, or, as has been claimed in passing,[34] a people's procession existed there as well as in Rome.

In his *Commentarius in Zachariam*, Cyril of Alexandria refers to the holy vessels of the altar, which are used instead of the people having their own vessels (ἴδιον σκεῦος).[35] Although the passage implies

28 Jungmann, *The Early Liturgy*, 117.
29 Taft and Parenti, *Il Grande Ingresso,* 103.
30 Jungmann, *Missarum Sollemnia*, 2:4n10.
31 Taft and Parenti, *Il Grande Ingresso,* 103–107.
32 Dix, *The Shape*, 123.
33 Baumstark, *On the Historical Development of the Liturgy*, 219. For Baumstark's original text, see Baumstark, *Vom geschichtlichen Werden der Liturgie*, 117.
34 Jungmann, *Missarum Sollemnia*, 2:4n10.
35 *In Zachariam* 6.14 (CPG 5204) (PG 72:273). For an English translation, see Robert C. Hill, *St. Cyril of Alexandria: Commentary on the Twelve Prophets,* vol. 1, The

that the people brought their own offerings—albeit not explicitly—this in no way implies that they presented them themselves in a ritual procession before the anaphora. In fact, the reference shows that for Cyril the vessels of the altar were preferred, which seems to point away from the people carrying their own oblations in the rite. This is especially so when he emphasizes that these holy vessels are to be used only by "the servants of the holy table,"[36] that is, the vessels containing such oblations were not to be touched by the people in the first place. The passage in Cyril's *In Zachariam* points to an already well-developed role for the deacons in preparing the offering, which also argues against the possibility of a people's procession.

Further evidence in this regard can be found in the *Historia monachorum* attributed to Paphnutius, though likely of later composition.[37] In one instance, Athanasius of Alexandria orders his deacon to "care for the offering (ϥι ⲡⲣⲟⲟⲩϣ ⲛ̄ⲧⲉⲡⲣⲟⲥⲫⲟⲣⲁ)."[38] Employing the same expression, Athanasius later returns to Alexandria, where he likewise, "ordered the offering to be cared for."[39] The same once again is said later on a visit, where Athanasius, "made them care for the offering and the altar."[40] Implicit in all these examples is that the servants were responsible for preparing the offering at the command of the bishop. If the people brought their own offerings and kept them until the pre-anaphora to be brought in a ritual procession, it would be difficult to explain what exactly this care for the offering entailed.

A later passage involving a certain Bishop John of Ephesus references the bishop in question preparing and depositing the gifts on the altar. The passage occurs in a later Coptic text, *A Discourse on the Compassion of God and on the Freedom of Speech of the Archangel Michael*, attributed to Severus of Antioch (AD 465–538), but confirmed at least as a tenth-century work given the date of

Fathers of the Church 124 (Washington, DC: Catholic University of America Press, 2007), 277. This reference seems to have been first used by Brightman to argue for a people's offertory procession in Egypt, cf. *LEW*, 508. It was later mentioned by Robert Taft, but ultimately discarded as irrelevant to a discussion of Byzantine practice. Cf. Taft and Parenti, *Il Grande Ingresso*, 107.

36 *In Zachariam* 6.14 (CPG 5204) (PG 72:273).

37 The text is published from the Sahidic manuscript *British Library Or. 7029* (AD 992) edited by Ernest Alfred Wallis Budge. See E. A. Wallis Budge, *Miscellaneous Coptic Texts in the Dialect of Upper Egypt* (London: British Museum, 1915), 432–502 (Coptic), 948–1011 (English). In this example and the following ones from Budge, translation is my own despite the availability of Budge's English translation.

38 Ibid., 463 (Coptic), 978 (English).

39 Ibid., 467 (Coptic), 982 (English).

40 Ibid., 468 (Coptic), 984 (English).

copying of its manuscript.[41] Dispatched by the emperor to baptize and establish Christianity in far-away Endikē, the bishop is said to have ordained a bishop and three presbyters, after which, "the archbishop took care of the offering, and elevated the offering upon the altar, and he presented it (ⲁϥⲡⲣⲟⲥⲫⲉⲣⲓ̈ ⲉϫⲱⲥ)."[42] It is unclear if this occurred before the anaphora or before the liturgy. However, considering he had just finished ordaining a bishop and some presbyters, one can presume that this elevation (i.e. transfer) and presentation on the altar was very likely in the pre-anaphora, since the ordination of presbyters takes place after the kiss of peace. In addition, since the elevation of the offering most likely refers to their deposition on the altar, one can only understand the term *presented* (ⲁϥⲡⲣⲟⲥⲫⲉⲣⲓ̈) as referring to the anaphora itself.

Naturally, this passage cannot be taken as evidence of a pre-anaphoral transfer of gifts in the time of Severus of Antioch in the sixth century. However, this reference can be assigned the *terminus ante quem* of the tenth century, the time of the copying of this discourse. At any rate, nothing here indicates that the people were directly involved with the preparation or bringing of these offerings to the altar at the time of the anaphora.

If all the available evidence presented here already shows that there was never an offertory procession of the gifts in Egypt by the people, how then can one explain the following diaconal command immediately before the anaphora?

ⲡⲣⲟⲥⲫⲉⲣⲓⲛ ⲕⲁⲧⲁ ⲧⲣⲟⲡⲟⲛ ⲥⲧⲁⲑⲏⲧⲉ ⲕⲁⲧⲁ ⲧⲣⲟⲙⲟⲩ ⲓⲥ ⲁⲛⲁⲧⲟⲗⲁⲥ ⲃⲗⲉⲯⲁⲧⲉ ⲡⲣⲟⲥⲭⲱⲙⲉⲛ.[43]	تَقَدَّموا على الرسم قِفُوا برعدة والى الشرق انظروا ننصت.	Come forward according to the pattern. Stand with trembling. Look to the east. Let us attend.

This diaconal command, presented here as it occurs in current text of Coptic BAS according to the 1902 Euchologion, appears also with slight variations in Coptic GREG,[44] and MARK.[45] It enjoys a long-standing tradition in the Coptic Rite, appearing in the oldest Coptic-Arabic Euchologia of Northern Egyptian provenance *BAV Vatican Copt. 17* (AD 1288), *Coptic Museum Lit. 463* (13th c.), *Rylands Copt.*

41 The text of this discourse was published by Budge from the Sahidic *British Library Or. 7597* (10th c.). See Ibid., 156–182 (Coptic), 735–760 (English).

42 Ibid., 176 (Coptic), 755 (English). Translation slightly modified.

43 Ṣalīb, ⲡⲓϫⲱⲙ ⲛ̀ⲧⲉ ⲡⲓⲉⲩⲭⲟⲗⲟⲅⲓⲟⲛ, 312. English translation is mine and is based on the Arabic for the purposes of the argument at hand.

44 Ibid., 470.

45 Ibid., 573.

426 (13th c.),[46] and *Bodleian Hunt. 360* (13th c.).[47] It is also attested in Greek manuscripts of Melkite MARK, appearing in its briefest form of προσφέρειν κατὰ τρόπον in *BAV Vatican Gr. 2281* (AD 1207).[48]

The Arabic text was presented above exactly as provided in the parallel column in the *editio typica* of 1902, which formed the basis for many future editions of the Euchologion. Judging from this translation, it would seem that the deacon is commanding the people to come forward at the commencement of the anaphora, which would in turn lend support to the theory that the people themselves may have brought forward their own offerings to the altar in an offertory procession. Fortunately, this mistranslation of the Greek verb προσφέρω as *approach* rather than the more accurate *offer* has been frequently corrected in more recent translations of the text, particularly those published in the Coptic communities outside Egypt.[49] Nonetheless, even an accurate translation of the command as "Offer in order, stand with trembling," can give the impression that the people are to stand in procession to offer at this juncture in the liturgy. If true, this would argue against all previous evidence showing that no such procession existed in Egypt.

However, this translation of the command as an infinitive can be analyzed further based on linguistic and comparative grounds. There is reason to believe that at least in the Egyptian tradition the command did not always contain the verb προσφέρω at all. Canon 97 of the Arabic *Canons of Ps.-Basil* only mentions the deacon at this point commanding the people to stand in their proper place.[50] Despite the late date of the manuscript transmitting these canons, the text in this case likely preserves an older tradition of this response, since by the fourteenth century Euchologia had already begun to include the infinitive προσφέρειν as part of the text. At least one other liturgical manuscript, the Sahidic diaconal parchment fragment *British Library Or. 3580A(11)*, has the response only as "Stand according to the pattern. Look towards the east in peace unto the Lord our God. Let us attend."[51] One notices here a certain syntactical balance, where the

46 Rodwell, *The Liturgies of S. Basil, S. Gregory, and S. Cyril*, 33.

47 *Bodleian Hunt. 360* (13th c.), fol. 68v; *LEW*, 164.

48 Cuming, *The Liturgy of St Mark*, 19.

49 The verb προσφέρω can be understood as, "approach, or enter upon," in the passive, i.e. προσφέρομαι, whose infinitive would be προσφέρεσθαι. See G.W.H. Lampe, *A Patristic Greek Lexicon* (Oxford: The Clarendon Press, 1961), 1183.

50 Canon 97. *Paris BnF Ar. 251* (AD 1353), fol. 187v: "يقول الشماس ليقف كل واحد في طقسه". Cf. Riedel, *Die Kirchenrechtsquellen*, 274.

51 ⲕⲁⲧⲁ ⲧⲣⲱⲡⲟⲛ ⲥⲧⲁⲑⲏⲧⲉ ⲉⲓⲥ ⲁⲛⲁⲧⲟⲗⲁⲥ ⲃⲗⲉϯⲁⲧⲉ ⲉⲛ ⲉⲓⲣⲏⲛⲏ ⲕ̅ⲱ̅ ⲧⲱ ⲑ̅ⲱ̅ ⲏⲙⲱⲛ ⲡⲣⲟⲥⲭⲱⲙⲉⲛ. See W. E. Crum, *Catalogue of the Coptic Manuscripts in the British Museum* (London: British Museum, 1906), 40. Although, one must add, the verb προσφέρω is attested

imperative in each command is placed in the final position. According to Budde, this is further support that the pristine text of this command likely possessed no initial infinitive.[52] In both of these witnesses, it would be difficult to argue that the text would omit what is supposed to be the main command/action of the diaconal bidding. That is, if one were to agree with the modern reading of this response as a command to offer. Naturally then, if the infinitive προσφέρειν is not original to this bidding, the entire argument for a pre-anaphoral people's offertory procession cannot be sustained, at least not on the grounds of this particular text.

Diaconal commands similar to this one in the pre-anaphora appear elsewhere in the East, such as the Byzantine liturgies of BAS and CHR as well as Hagiopolite JAS. In all cases, the command translates to, "Stand well, stand with fear. Let us attend to the holy anaphora *to offer* in peace."[53] This reading hearkens back to the Antiochene *Apostolic Constitutions* (ca. AD 380), where the similar command appears, "Arise unto the Lord with fear and trembling, let us be standing *to offer*."[54] In all cases, the sense of the response is clearly to stand well and look to the east, not for the people to advance or offer per se.

But if at any rate the response came to include this initial infinitive, how can it be translated? Unlike the examples from Byzantine and Hagiopolite sources, the text in the Coptic liturgy lacks a clear object of the verb such as, "to offer the anaphora." It is also certainly difficult to explain why a redactor would have appended an infinitive to the very beginning of the response rather than to the end, such as the case in Byzantine and Hagiopolite examples. The Greek infinitive could in theory function as an imperative, the so-called imperatival infinitive or *infinitivus pro imperativo*. However, this usage is extremely old and was particularly common only in Homer. In the New Testament, it appears only in two places in Paul's epistles (Rom 12:15, and Phil 3:16).[55] It is unlikely then that the infinitive in this response is intended

at least in the older Sahidic fragments *P. ÖNB K. 4854* (6th c.). See Jutta Henner, *Fragmenta Liturgica Coptica: Editionen und Kommentar liturgischer Texte der koptischen Kirche des ersten Jahrtausends*, Studien und Texte zu Antike und Christentum 5 (Tübingen: Mohr Siebeck, 2000), 40.

52 Budde, *Die ägyptische Basilios-Anaphora*, 222–226, here 225.

53 See the comparison of the texts in ibid., 224.

54 Ὀρθοὶ πρὸς Κύριον μετὰ φόβου καὶ τρόμου ἑστῶτες ὦμεν προσφέρειν. *Apostolic Constitutions* VIII, 12.2. See Marcel Metzger, *Les constitutions apostoliques*, vol. 3, *Livres 7–8: Introduction, texte critique, traduction et notes*, SC 336 (Paris: Cerf, 2008), 176–177.

55 F. Blass and A. Debrunner, *A Greek Grammar of the New Testament and Other Early Christian Literature*, tra. Robert W. Funk (Cambridge: Cambridge University Press, 1961), 197–198.

as a command, given how rare and unusual this use of the infinitive must have been by this late period. In fact, to admit this reading of the infinitive would mean this is the *only* instance in the entire repertoire of diaconal responses in the Coptic tradition where a command is given using an infinitive and not the usual imperative mood (προσεύξασθε, στάθητε, κλίνατε, βλέψατε), or a hortatory subjunctive (πρόσχωμεν, ἀκούσωμεν, κλίνωμεν).

It seems then that this Greek response was frequently misunderstood by later translators. In the ninth–eleventh century parchment sheet *P. Naqlun II 20*, the response is given in Greek with an accompanying Bohairic translation, which according to the most up to date reading by Jacques van der Vliet was likely [ⲉⲡ]ⲉⲣⲡⲣⲟⲥⲫⲉⲣⲓⲛ, certainly not an imperative.[56] Later Arabic translations would consistently read this infinitive as a command to approach or come forward, as shown above in the *textus receptus*, a reading I have argued cannot be the original sense of the Greek. A more accurate way to understand this command then would be the following: "Stand with trembling, look to the east, let us attend, *to offer* according to the established pattern." Similar interpretations of this command were proposed by Taft and Budde, in analyzing the Byzantine and the Coptic versions respectively.[57] Athanasius al-Maqārī has already noted this mistranslation, although he interpreted the corrected text to refer to the "rite of the presentation of the lamb," that presumably used to occur at that juncture.[58] It is unclear what Fr. Athanasius means by the rite of the presentation of the lamb. If he meant simply the transfer of gifts and their presentation on the altar, he would be certainly correct. If, however, he meant the fully developed prothesis rite of preparing the gifts, usually termed the presentation of the lamb in Arabic usage, he would be incorrect, since such a ritualized preparation never took place at this point.

Strictly speaking then, the deacon is not commanding the people to proceed physically and to present their offerings at this time, but rather to maintain good order and decorum so that the anaphora may proceed. An emphasis on maintaining good order is certainly necessary considering that even in the current rite the kiss of peace

56 Derda, *Deir el-Naqlun*, 2:74 (text), 78 (translation), 80 (discussion). There, the translators of the text struggle to render the infinitive as a command: "[in order to?] offer."

57 Robert F. Taft, "Textual Problems in the Diaconal Admonition before the Anaphora in the Byzantine Tradition," *OCP* 49 (1983): 340–365, here 363; Budde, *Die ägyptische Basilios-Anaphora*, 222.

58 Athanasius al-Maqārī, *Al-quddās al-ilāhī: Sirr malakūt allāh* [The Divine Liturgy: The mystery of the kingdom of God], 2nd ed., vol. 2, Ṭuqūs asrār wa-ṣalawāt al-kanīsa 3.6 (Cairo: Dār nūbār, 2011), 667.

takes place immediately before this admonition, exchanged among all members of the congregation. The text itself does not provide any evidence that the people offered anything at this point.

Thus, it can be concluded that while the people frequently provided bread and wine for the Eucharist in late antiquity and the early middle ages, they never did so as part of a ritual procession before the anaphora. Even by the eleventh century they seem to have no longer brought the actual offerings, but simply donated money or materials to provide for them.

2. THE LOCATION OF THE PREPARATION OF THE GIFTS

The next step in the journey is to examine where the gifts were placed until they were consecrated in the course of the anaphora. Either the gifts were always placed immediately on the altar—as in the current rite—or they were placed elsewhere and only later transferred to the altar for the anaphora. As evidence will soon demonstrate, both in Egypt and elsewhere in the East, the gifts were kept in a separate place until they were needed for the Eucharist, according to what is termed here the old ordo in the Coptic Rite. To be specific, the exact nature of the preparation of the gifts is not of concern here, nor whether this meant a simple collection and keeping of the gifts until the anaphora, or an elaborate rite similar to today's prothesis. Rather, the main point here is to establish this simple fact, namely, that unlike the current Coptic usage, the eucharistic gifts had another home besides the altar up until their transfer immediately before the anaphora.

To do so successfully, one will not find the answer in liturgical manuscripts. Unfortunately, the earliest such manuscripts witnessing to the liturgy of Northern Egypt are from the thirteenth century, when the old ordo had already become extinct. Instead, the main evidence comes from historical accounts and hagiography, supplemented by the comparative witness of liturgical celebration in nearby regions, namely Syria, Byzantium, Nubia, and Ethiopia. In addition, crucial information is supplied from an understanding of Coptic Church architecture and its development over time, as studied by Peter Grossmann and others. Although no single piece of evidence is in itself conclusive, the cumulative effect of all the following evidence makes a strong case for what can be called for the purpose of clarity the old ordo of the Coptic liturgy.

2.1. Early Canonical Collections (3rd–4th c.)

The earliest evidence from anywhere appears in the third-century Syrian *Didascalia Apostolorum,* which, according to Georg Graf and

Hubert Kaufhold, bears little relationship to the *Didascalia Arabica* more popular in the Copto-Arabic tradition.[59] In chapter 12 of the Syriac recension, the following directive appears: "As for the deacons, let one of them stand constantly over the gifts of thankfulness [i.e. of the Eucharist], and let another stand outside the door and look at those who come in."[60] Although it is not clear exactly where the deacon was to stand guarding the gifts, it may be safely assumed that it was not at the altar. As the visual focus of any church building, there would have been hardly any need for a dedicated deacon to stand guarding a place to which all eyes were directed in the first place! Incidentally, this passage was used by Taft as well from another angle, supporting the view that the people must have donated their offerings at the very beginning, rather than at the anaphora.[61]

A century later, one encounters the witness of the *Apostolic Constitutions*, a fourth-century canonical collection also of Syrian provenance. In Book 8, chapter 12, the following passage appears in the context of a hierarchical liturgy:

ὧν γενομένων οἱ διάκονοι προσαγέτωσαν τὰ δῶρα τῷ ἐπισκόπῳ πρὸς τὸ θυσιαστήριον.[62]	This having taken place, may the deacons present the gifts to the bishop at the altar.

Immediately after the dismissal of the catechumens, the deacons bring the eucharistic gifts to the bishop at the altar. This late-fourth century text is an important witness for the early history of the transfer of gifts both in the Syro-Byzantine East, as well as the universal Church, given the importance of the *Apostolic Constitutions* as a famous representative of the Church Order genre. For the present purpose, this passage shows clearly that in fourth-century Syria, the gifts were kept at a location other than the altar until the time of the anaphora. Additionally, the *Apostolic Constitutions* is frequently enlisted as one of the earliest witnesses to the transfer of gifts in the Byzantine tradition, reflecting a very primitive form of the Great Entrance.[63]

At the end of the same liturgy described here, the deacons do the following:

59 *GCAL*, 1:564. Kaufhold, "Sources of Canon Law," 266.

60 Book II, 57:6. Margaret Dunlop Gibson, *The Didascalia Apostolorum in English*, Horae Semiticae 2 (London: Cambridge University Press, 1903), 66. Cf. R.H. Connolly, *Didascalia Apostolorum: The Syriac Version Translated and Accompanied by the Verona Latin Fragments* (Oxford: The Clarendon Press, 1929), 120. For a Latin translation, cf. Franciscus Xaverius Funk, ed., *Didascalia et Constitutiones Apostolorum*, vol. 1 (Paderborn: In libraria Ferdinandi Schoeningh, 1906), 162.

61 Taft and Parenti, *Il Grande Ingresso*, 109.

62 Book VIII, 12.3. See Metzger, *Les constitutions apostoliques*, 3:178–179.

63 Taft and Parenti, *Il Grande Ingresso*, 134–135.

Καὶ ὅταν πάντες μεταλάβωσιν καὶ πᾶσαι, λαβόντες οἱ διάκονοι τὰ περισσεύσαντα εἰσφερέτωσαν εἰς τὰ παστοφόρια.[64]

And when all men and women have partaken, let the deacons taking the remains carry them to the pastophoria.

These so-called pastophoria are rooms on both sides of the apse. They were particularly prominent in Syro-Palestinian churches, where they served a variety of purposes including a sacristy, a diaconicon to store eucharistic vessels and books, and as a place to store, prepare, and store the eucharistic gifts.[65] Pastophoria were also part of church architecture in Ethiopia, Nubia, and Egypt. For the immediate purpose, it is crucial to recognize the *Apostolic Constitutions* as the first witness to this custom of using the adjacent pastophoria as a place to store the gifts before the anaphora as well as a location for certain post-communion rites, as Joseph Patrich has indicated in his study of the transfer of gifts in the Syro-Palestinian East.[66]

2.2. The Historia Ecclesiastica *of Theodoret (4th c.)*

Evidence is also clear that the gifts were kept elsewhere until the anaphora, or in other words, they were not immediately placed on the altar as in the current rite. Of particular relevance in this regard is a heated controversy surrounding Athanasius of Alexandria in the fourth century, and which was part of his ongoing struggle against the Arians in the aftermath of the ecumenical council of Nicaea in AD 325. The episode in question involves an accusation brought against Athanasius during the proceedings of the council of Sardica in AD 343. The accusation was that one of the presbyters of Athanasius, Macarius by name, had publicly broken a eucharistic chalice. Both the accusation and its rebuttal are reported multiple times, both in the *Historia Ecclesiastica* of Theodoret and in the *Apologia contra Arianos* of Athanasius. The passage is presented below from Theodoret, which references the testimony against Macarius by some catechumens:

[1] Ἐξ ὧν εἷς κατηχούμενος ἐρωτώμενος ἔφασκεν ἔνδον εἶναι ὅτε Μακάριος ἐπέστη τῷ τόπῳ, [2] καὶ ἕτερος ἐρωτώμενος ἔλεγε τὸν

[1] One of these catechumens, when asked, claimed that he was inside when Macarius entered the place. [2] And another, when asked, said that

64 Book VIII, 13.17. See Metzger, *Les constitutions apostoliques*, 3:210–211.

65 Peter Grossmann, "Pastophorium," *CE*, 1:216a–217a.

66 Joseph Patrich, "The Transfer of Gifts in the Early Christian Churches of Palestine: Archaeological and Literary Evidence for the Evolution of the "Great Entrance"," in *Pèlerinages et lieux saints dans l'Antiquité et le Moyen-Âge: Mélanges offerts à Pierre Maraval*, ed. Béatrice Caseau, Jean-Claude Cheynet, and Vincent Déroche, Monographies 3 (Paris: Association des amis du Centre d'histoire et civilisation de Byzance, 2006), 341–393, here 345.

θρυλούμενον παρ' αὐτῶν Ἰσχύραν νοσοῦντα κατακεῖσθαι ἐν κελλίῳ, [3] ὡς ἀπὸ τούτου φαίνεσθαι μηδ' ὅλως γεγενῆσθαί τι τῶν ὅλων μυστηρίων, [4] διὰ τὸ τοὺς κατηχουμένους ἔνδον εἶναι καὶ τὸν Ἰσχύραν μὴ παρεῖναι, ἀλλὰ νοσοῦντα κατακεῖσθαι.[67]

Ischyras, whom they had talked about so much, was then lying ill in his cell. [3] Hence it appears from this that the mysteries could not have been celebrated at that time, [4] as the catechumens were present, and as Ischyras was absent, but lay ill.

The passage appears verbatim in the *Apologia contra Arianos.*[68] Later still, Pope Julius of Rome, writing to the Eusebians at Antioch in defense of Athanasius, questions the very possibility of a catechumen having witnessed the alleged crime:

[1] Ἀπὸ δὴ τούτων ὧν ἔλεγε, καὶ ἡμεῖς ἀκολούθως στοχαζόμεθα, [2] ὅτι πῶς οἷόν τε τὸν ὄπισθεν τῆς θύρας νόσῳ κατακείμενον τότε ἑστηκέναι καὶ λειτουργεῖν καὶ προσφέρειν; [3] ἢ πῶς οἷόν τε ἦν προσφορὰν προκεῖσθαι ἔνδον ὄντων τῶν κατηχουμένων; [4] εἰ γὰρ ἔνδον ἦσαν οἱ κατηχούμενοι, οὔπω ἦν ὁ καιρὸς τῆς προσφορᾶς.[69]

[1] From these which he said, we too subsequently conjecture, [2] how was it possible that a man who was lying behind the door sick could get up, perform the liturgy, and offer? [3] Or how could it be that oblations were deposited when catechumens were within? [4] For if the catechumens were present inside, it was not yet the time of the offering.

The main defense brought by Athanasius and his supporters against the alleged crime–a crime he is not even accused of having perpetrated himself–was that it would be impossible for catechumens to witness such an act, since they were not present during the time of presenting the oblations. Now the fact that the catechumens were dismissed before the anaphora is well-known, albeit no longer represented in the Coptic liturgy. The point here is that the episode in question implies that the time of presenting the oblations occurred *later* in the course of the liturgy, at which point the catechumens were no longer allowed to remain. Clearly, the gifts were not already on the altar, but had to be presented at the commencement of the anaphora by carrying them from somewhere else. It may not be known based on these texts the exact location of the gifts until the anaphora. Nonetheless, it can be affirmed that in fourth-century Alexandria, the

67 *Historia Ecclesiastica* 2.6 (CPG 6222). Annick Martin and Pierre Canivet, *Théodoret de Cyr: Histoire ecclésiastique I (Livres I–II)*, SC 501 (Paris: Cerf, 2006), 358–359.

68 *Apologia contra Arianos* 46 (CPG 2123) (PG 25:329D–332A).

69 *Apologia contra Arianos* 28 (CPG 2123) (PG 25:296C). Cf. Dous, "Η Αλεξανδρινή Θεία Λειτουργία," 16. Dous cites only this passage from the *Apologia* as one among many Alexandrian patristic passages employing the term δωροφορία or transfer of gifts. Given the overall scope of his work, which was to publish a critical edition of the Greek recension of Coptic BAS, it is no surprise that he does not attempt to analyze or even quote the passage in question.

eucharistic gifts, likely at that early date brought by the faithful, were stored by the deacons until the time of the anaphora.

2.3. The Life of John of Scetis (ca. 7th c.)

Later Coptic witnesses may also shed light on the place where the eucharistic gifts may have been placed prior to the anaphora. One such witness is a subtle detail in the Arabic *Life of John of Scetis*, the famous seventh-century hegumen of Scetis.[70] This *Vita* was discovered and published by Ugo Zanetti from the manuscript *St. Macarius Hagiography 35* (AD 1549). Zanetti estimated that it was translated from a seventh-century Coptic precursor representing an expansion of a letter about the life of the saint written by Patriarch John III (AD 677–686).[71]

The relevant passage is in praise of the sanctity of the saint, who is said to have often witnessed miracles while celebrating the Eucharist:

[1] وبالأكثر اليوم الذي كان يريد ان يقدس فيه، كان يتحفظ لئلا يخرج كلمة بطالة من فيه [2] حتى انه، من قبل خوف الله الذى كان فيه و عظم تحفظه، استحق نعمة هكذا، [3] انه دفوعاً كثيرة، لما يقدم القربان المقدس ينظر من يرشم الخبز، [4]واذا صعد الى المذبح ليقدم القربان المقدس، ينزل نور وراحة عليه.[72]

[1] In particular, on the day in which he desired to celebrate [the liturgy], he used to watch lest an idle word come out of his mouth, [2] so that because of the fear of God that he possessed and the greatness of his discipline, he was worthy of such grace, [3] so that many times when he *offered* [*yuqaddim]* the holy oblation, he would see someone blessing the bread, [4] and when he would ascend to the altar to *offer* [*yuqaddim*] the holy offering, light and repose would descend upon him.

As can be seen, the passage contains two references to offering. First, the saint sees someone—presumably Christ—blessing the bread when he would offer the oblation. Later still, he ascends to the altar *to offer*, continuing to experience a certain Divine presence. The Arabic verb used in both cases is *yuqaddim* (يُقَدِّم), literally to present or place forward, most likely a translation of the Coptic ⲡⲣⲟⲥⲫⲉⲣⲓⲛ. Because the

70 Little is known with confidence about his life and monastic career. For a good summary, see Hugh G. Evelyn-White, *The Monasteries of the Wādi 'N Natrūn Part II: The History of the Monasteries of Nitria and of Scetis*, Publications of the Metropolitan Museum of Art Egyptian Expedition 4 (New York: Metropolitan Museum of Art, 1932), 275–277.

71 Ugo Zanetti, *Saint Jean, higoumène de Scété (VIIe siècle) Vie arabe et épitomé éthiopien*, Subsidia Hagiographica 94 (Brussels: Societé des Bollandistes, 2015), 48*.

72 Ibid., 342–345.

story implies a double offering–if one may say so–it could be interpreted to refer first to the prothesis and later to the anaphora. Further, because John is said to ascend to the altar the second time around to offer the holy oblation, one can indeed read this to mean that he was not at the altar earlier at the time of the first offering. This is how Emmanuel Fritsch understood the passage, which to him gave a strong indication of the rite of the prothesis conducted at a place other than the altar, that is, an adjacent pastophorion.[73] Interpreting this passage in light of the state of knowledge of how pastophoria were used in Egypt and Ethiopia, Ugo Zanetti also agreed with Emmanuel Fritsch that the passage refers to the preparation of the gifts away from the altar.[74]

In an effort to contextualize this isolated reference and provide some basis for evaluation, it is useful to examine church architecture in the relevant time and place. Since Zanetti has shown clearly that the Arabic *Vita* is based on a seventh-century Coptic *Vorlage*, written shortly after the departure of John of Scetis, this provides a rare opportunity, where one can more or less securely situate the eucharistic celebration described in seventh-century Scetis. Presumably, the seventh-century author of the life of a seventh-century saint would naturally describe events that presuppose the church architecture in his time and place.

Peter Grossmann, in discussing church architecture in monastic churches between the fourth and seventh centuries, provides the following information. Regarding the sanctuary area specifically, Grossmann indicates that all sanctuary rooms were initially "sharply divided from one another, and each accessible only from the nave."[75] The Church of the Virgin in the Baramūs Monastery (Appendix 3) represents one such example of a seventh-century Scetis church with pastophoria. In many cases, passageways between the central apse and the adjacent rooms were only constructed later. This description is consistent with some of the earliest examples of Ethiopian churches

73 Emmanuel Fritsch, "The Preparation of the Gifts and the Pre-Anaphora in the Ethiopian Eucharistic Liturgy in Around A.D. 1100," in *Rites and Rituals of the Christian East: Proceedings of the Fourth International Congress of the Society of Oriental Liturgy, Lebanon, 10–15 July 2012*, ed. Bert Groen et al., Eastern Christian Studies 22 (Leuven: Peeters, 2014), 97–152, here 111.

74 Zanetti, *Saint Jean*, 53–55. In an earlier publication of the *Life of John of Scetis*, Zanetti argued instead that the ascension to the altar refers to the praying of the *oratio veli* or *Prayer of the Veil* below the sanctuary, a prayer of *accessus ad altare* common in the Syrian and Coptic traditions. Cf. Ugo Zanetti, "La Vie de Saint Jean, higoumène de Scété au VIIe siècle," *Analecta Bollandiana* 114 (1996): 273–405, here 385.

75 Grossmann, *Christliche Architektur in Ägypten*, 54. For a full description of this church, see ibid., 499–501, with a floor plan in fig. 118.

with pastophoria, as shown below. Particularly remarkable is that these rooms adjacent to the central altar area were accessible only from the nave, which may even point to a procession to transfer the gifts that must exit into the nave before proceeding towards the altar.

Admittedly, neither the *Life of John of Scetis* nor the architectural evidence necessitate such an interpretation. The *Vita* does not explicitly mention that the gifts were placed elsewhere until the anaphora nor mentions any explicit transfer of gifts. The architectural evidence in itself does not indicate a particularly eucharistic function for the sharply divided side-rooms, as the ones in the church of Virgin Mary al-Baramūs. At the same time, such an interpretation of the two data types–textual and architectural–is certainly possible and can be admitted here in company with all the following textual, architectural, and comparative evidence.

2.4. The Coptic Life of Isaac *(8th c.)*

The expression in the *Life of John of Scetis* of ascending to the altar is by no means unique. In the eighth-century Coptic *Life of Isaac*, Patriarch of Alexandria (AD 686–689), one finds the following reference:

[1] ⲡⲁⲓⲁⲅⲓⲟⲥ ⲟⲩⲛ ⲛⲁⲙⲉⲛⲣⲁϯ ⲁ ⲫϯ ⲉⲣⲭⲁⲣⲓⲍⲉⲥⲑⲉ ⲛⲁϥ ⲛ̀ϩⲁⲛϩⲙⲟⲧ ⲛ̀ⲧⲁⲗϭⲟ ⲛ̀ⲟⲩⲙⲏϣ ⲛ̀ⲣⲏϯ. [2] ⲥⲟⲡ ⲛⲓⲃⲉⲛ ⲉ̀ⲧⲉϥⲛⲁϩⲱⲗ ⲉ̀ϫⲉⲛ ⲡⲓⲙⲁⲛⲉⲣϣⲱⲟⲩϣⲓ ⲉ̀ⲉⲣⲡⲣⲟⲥⲫⲉⲣⲓⲛ [3] ⲓⲥϫⲉⲛ ⲡⲓⲛⲁⲩ ⲉ̀ⲧⲉϥⲛⲁⲉⲣϩⲏⲧⲥ ⲉ̀ϯⲁⲛⲁⲫⲟⲣⲁ ⲉⲑⲟⲩⲁⲃ ϣⲁⲣⲉ ⲛⲉϥⲃⲁⲗ ⲓ̀ⲛⲓ ⲉ̀ⲡⲉⲥⲏⲧ ⲛ̀ϩⲁⲛⲉⲣⲙⲱⲟⲩⲓ [4] ϣⲁⲧⲉϥϫⲱⲕ ⲙ̀ⲡⲓϣⲉⲙϣⲓ ⲉ̀ⲃⲟⲗ.[76]

[1] Thus, my beloved, God granted this saint grace to heal many kinds [of diseases]. [2] Every time he would ascend upon the altar to offer, [3] from the moment when he would commence the holy anaphora his eyes would shed tears [4] until he had completed the service.

The Coptic *Life of Isaac* is certainly older and was written much closer to the Patriarch's life than the briefer Arabic biography in *The History of the Patriarchs*.[77] It survives in the manuscript *BAV Vatican Copt. 62* (9th–10th c.), fol. 211r–242v, and was written by Mina of Nikiu, a contemporary of Isaac.[78] Thus, the Coptic *Life of Isaac* provides a valuable testimony to the liturgical expressions–and perhaps even the liturgical setting–current in the seventh–eighth centuries, thanks to accurate knowledge of its authorship and date of composition.

Similar to the passage in the *Life of John of Scetis*, this passage mentions the offering twice: In [2], Isaac ascends to the altar *to offer*

76 Ernest Porcher, ed., *Vie d'Isaac, Patriarche d'Alexandrie de 686 a 689*, PO 11.3 (54) (Turnhout: Brepols, 2003), 356.

77 *HP*, 1.3:275–280.

78 Porcher, *Vie d'Isaac*, 301–302.

(ⲉ̀ⲣⲡⲣⲟⲥⲫⲉⲣⲓⲛ), and later in [3] he commences the anaphora (ϯⲁⲛⲁⲫⲟⲣⲁ). The passage can be interpreted in two ways: 1.The first offering refers to the prothesis rite, or at least to the preparation of the gifts, while the second, of course, refers to the anaphora, or 2.Both expressions refer to the anaphora, or to the liturgy as a whole, where the latter expression is used to define the former more technically. Understood as the preparation of the gifts, this would mean the gifts were prepared and placed on the altar at once according to the new ordo, a very early date given the rest of the evidence. If, however, the expression is understood as referring to the anaphora, this would render the passage very similar to that in the *Life of John of Scetis*, where again it could mean Isaac was not at the altar until the anaphora and the preparation was done elsewhere. Alternatively, it could mean that he simply ascended to the altar once again at the anaphora, and this is merely a reference to the pre-anaphoral *accessus ad altare*.

Once again when the textual evidence can be interpreted in a variety of ways, the witness of architectural development can be consulted for guidance. According to *The History of the Patriarchs*, Patriarch Isaac oversaw the completion of the restoration of the Cathedral of Saint Mark in Alexandria, begun earlier under Benjamin I (AD 622–661).[79] It is likely that the event above would have taken place at the usual patriarchal liturgies that Isaac celebrated in the cathedral that he himself had restored. Unfortunately, this cathedral itself has not survived, and it cannot be confirmed with accuracy whether the Cathedral of Saint Mark in Alexandria—particularly in its seventh-century renovated state—featured a prothesis pastophorion or not. Nonetheless, Grossmann writes that pastophoria were added to churches in the Mediterranean region of Egypt after the fourth century, after first appearing in Southern Egyptian churches.[80] An example of a Northern Egyptian church equipped with pastophoria is the small church in Taposiris Magna (modern day Abūṣīr), west of Lake Mareotis on the Mediterranean coast (Appendix 3).[81] Built in the 5th century, the church featured a central apse with two adjacent pastophoria on either side.[82]

79 For the concern Benjamin took for the renovation of the Cathedral of Saint Mark, see *HP*, 1.1:236. The renovation was continued and completed under Isaac. See *HP*, 1.3:278.

80 Grossmann, *Christliche Architektur in Ägypten*, 28.

81 Peter Grossmann, "Abuṣir," *CE*, 1:34b–36b.

82 Peter Grossmann, "Abusir," in *The Eerdmans Encyclopedia of Early Christian Art and Archaeology*, ed. Paul Corby Finney, vol. 1, A–J (Grand Rapids, MI: William B. Eerdmans Publishing Company, 2017), 7. For a full description of the church, see Grossmann, *Christliche Architektur in Ägypten*, 381–383, with a floor plan in fig. 3.

Given that pastophoria appear already in the fourth century in Northern Egypt, it would be perfectly logical to expect a newly-renovated cathedral in the seventh century to be equipped with a pastophorion as well. For a patriarch to obtain the opportunity and funds to rebuild such an important edifice for the entire Coptic Church and somehow adopt a more "minimalist" approach would simply be unthinkable. Thus, it is highly likely that the Coptic *Life of Isaac* witnesses to a practice whereby the patriarch ascended to the altar for the first time to celebrate the anaphora, after having prepared—or perhaps ordered the preparation of—the gifts elsewhere in an adjacent pastophorion.

2.5. The Order of the Priesthood *(13th c.)*

A slightly different disposition appears in the thirteenth-century *Order of the Priesthood.* In chapter 1, one finds the following description of the church building:

[1] ولها ثلاثة ابواب على ما نصت عليه الدسقولية [2] باب للرجال [3] و باب للنساء [4] و باب لبحري لدخول القربان منه.[83]	[1] And it [the church] has three doors as is written in the *disqūliyya*: [2] A door for men, [3] a door for women, [4] and a northern door, from which the oblations are to enter.

It is certainly true that this passage is *inspired* by the *Didascalia Arabica,* where one finds a similar reference to the doors of the church in chapter 35 of the Vulgate recension, mentioned previously. However, unlike the *Order of the Priesthood,* the passage in the *Didascalia Arabica* is slightly different:

[1] الكنيسة فليكن لها ثلاثة ابواب مثالاً للثالوث المقدس [2] احدهما يكون قبليها والاخر غربيها واخر بحريها. [3] ويكون بيت الخدمة عن يمين الباب القبلي [4] كي لا يبصر الشعب القرابين التي تأتيهم.[84]	[1] The church should have three doors in the likeness of the Holy Trinity. [2] One of them is to be to its south, and another to its west, and another to its north. [3] And the house of service should be to the right of the southern door, [4] so that the people may not see the oblations that come to them.

The *Didascalia Arabica* implies that the oblations came from a house of service, i.e. a diaconicon, to the right of the southern door. This could mean that this diaconicon was an external structure altogether that stood outside the floorplan of the church, which would explain

83 Assfalg, *Die Ordnung des Priestertums,* 4 (Arabic), 71 (German).

84 Qilāda, *Taʿālīm al-rusul al-disqūliyya,* 841. Cf. Funk, *Didascalia,* 2:124.

how the people thus would not be able to see the oblations until their entry. Similarly, the *Order of the Priesthood* describes a door through which the oblations entered at an unspecified time. Whether this entry took place in the pre-anaphora (old ordo) or in the very beginning (new ordo) is unclear and is not the point here.

The point in both texts—despite their minor disagreement on where the oblations came from—is that the oblations clearly were not placed in a pastophorion, which is not mentioned anywhere in the text. Thus, by the twelfth or thirteenth centuries, one sees that the older tradition of placing the gifts in an adjacent pastophorion was already disappearing. As the architectural evidence will soon demonstrate, this is perfectly in line with general developments in church building that started in Egypt a few centuries earlier.

2.6. The Preparation of the Gifts in the East

However, before the bulk of the architectural evidence from all around Egypt is presented more systematically, an overview of the situation elsewhere in the East should be provided. In particular, the practice in Syria, Ethiopia, and Nubia will prove to be very instructive in bolstering the case for the so-called old ordo, by which the gifts were not immediately placed on the altar at the very beginning of the service. For anyone strictly familiar with the current Coptic, Syrian, or Ethiopian rites, it will be surprising to find overwhelming evidence for this old ordo across diverse traditions.

2.6.1. The Syro-Byzantine East

Following the appearance of pastophoria in churches of Syria and Palestine in the fourth century, later witnesses as well as architectural monuments testify to the continued use of pastophoria as storage places for the gifts in the Syro-Antiochene liturgical tradition. The study by Joseph Patrich is perhaps the most detailed concerning the situation in Syria and Palestine from the fourth to the fifth centuries. Patrich seeks to make the case for the evolution of a Great Entrance procession in that region, not unlike that in the Byzantine capital. The textual evidence he provides is extensive, and includes the *Apostolic Constitutions*, the *Testamentum Domini* (5th c.), the *Scholia* of John Scholasticus (6th c.), and the *Mystagogia* of Maximus the Confessor (AD 580–662).[85] In addition, Patrich discusses evidence from ancient

[85] The *Mystagogia* of Maximus the Confessor is traditionally considered a witness to the Constantinopolitan liturgy, despite Patrich's argument for a Palestinian provenance. The evidence for the provenance of the liturgy described by Maximus

Palestinian churches that possessed either lockable pastophoria flanking the central apse, or apses flanked by open spaces with an attached prothesis chapel or chamber.[86]

The minutiae of Patrich's analysis need not be of concern. He concludes that by the mid-fifth century, the earlier pastophoria, which witnessed to a simple transfer of gifts, had given rise to the annexed prothesis chapel, which reflects a more solemnized Great Entrance procession.[87] Regardless of the degree of solemnity, the following can be gleaned from Patrich's study, namely, that a dedicated space in the church served the function of storing the eucharistic gifts of the people until the appointed time for their transfer to the altar. To establish this fact for Syria at such an early date (fourth-fifth century) is a crucial piece of information given the future influence the West-Syrian tradition will exert on the Northern Egyptian Coptic Rite. As I discuss below regarding the transfer of gifts, the West-Syrian rite–the non-Chalcedonian descendent of the ancient Antiochene tradition–also experienced its own shift from an old ordo of a pre-anaphoral transfer, to a new ordo of preparing the gifts directly on the altar.

The situation in Constantinople and other regions following the rite of the Byzantine capital was only slightly different. Although today the liturgical plan of Byzantine churches contains the adjacent prothesis chamber for the deposition of the gifts, earlier Constantinopolitan models did not have such an architectural feature, which appeared around the sixth century.[88] Instead, the eucharistic gifts in Constantinople were deposited in an adjacent building to the northeast called the *skeuophylakion*, which both Mathews and Taft have argued was the place where the gifts were stored and from which the transfer of the gifts before the anaphora began its route.[89] Thus, in both Syria-Palestine and the Byzantine capital–in many ways itself

has been most recently re-presented by Robert Taft. See Robert F. Taft, "Is the Liturgy Described in the Mystagogia of Maximus Confessor Byzantine, Palestinian or Neither?" *BBGG III* 8 (2011): 223–270.

86 For a useful table of churches and their respective types, see Patrich, "The Transfer of Gifts," 343. The most in-depth study of pastophoria in Syrian churches is that by Georges Descoeudres. For a discussion of the tripartite division of the early Syrian sanctuaries, cf. Descoeudres, *Die Pastophorien im syro-byzantinischen Osten*, 3–78.

87 Ibid., 358.

88 Taft and Parenti, *Il Grande Ingresso*, 343.

89 For the Byzantine skeuophylakion, its location, and its role in the liturgy, see ibid., 353–359, and Robert F. Taft, "*Quaestiones disputatae:* The Skeuophylakion of Hagia Sophia and the Entrances of the Liturgy Revisited," *OC* 81 (1997): 1–35. Taft's conclusions and information regarding the architecture of Constantinopolitan churches is based on Thomas F. Mathews, *The Early Churches of Constantinople: Architecture and Liturgy* (University Park, PA: Pennsylvania State University Press, 1971), 158–162.

inspired by Syro-Antiochene models–churches were equipped with special places for the deposition and keeping of the eucharistic gifts until a later transfer to the altar before the anaphora. The only difference between Syrian and Constantinopolitan churches in this regard was *where* exactly the gifts were placed, in an exterior structure as in the Constantinopolitan skeuophylakion or in an interior northeastern pastophorion as in Syria.

2.6.2 Ethiopia

Unlike the rich textual evidence for Syria and Constantinople, the situation in the Ethiopian tradition is much more challenging to establish. First, the earliest manuscripts of the Ethiopian *Qeddāsē* or eucharistic liturgy are from the fifteenth century, long after the new ordo, in conformity to Coptic usage, had become firmly established in Ethiopia as well.[90] Fortunately, monuments of ancient Ethiopian churches from various time periods have been preserved, providing valuable insight regarding the keeping and transfer of the eucharistic gifts in the Ethiopian tradition. Just as in Syria and Palestine, some of the earliest surviving Ethiopian monuments also had pastophoria adjacent to the central apse. These include the ruins of Adulis in Aksum and many other ruins of the Aksumite period, which possessed pastophoria open only westwards towards their respective aisles on either side.[91] Several such churches have pastophoria well preserved enough to provide a description. Usually, one pastophorion was used for the deposition of the gifts, judging from its usually more ornate furnishing with a table, compared to the simpler other pastophorion.[92] The entrance to the pastophoria varied over time. While the examples from Adulis and Aksum opened only to the west, elsewhere the pastophoria came to open to the sanctuary alone, or both to the aisles and the sanctuary (Appendix 3).[93]

This setup began to change in the second millennium, when churches began to be built with three parallel altars, thus taking over the place previously occupied by the prothesis pastophorion. Fritsch identifies the earliest Ethiopian church to be built with three sanctuaries as Mika'el Amba, consecrated by Metropolitan Mika'el in

90 Fritsch, "The Preparation of the Gifts," 102.

91 Ibid., 110, 137.

92 Ibid., 111. Sometimes, as in Dəgum, the table is no longer present. In its place, there can be seen four holes in the ground originally intended to hold the table in place.

93 Emmanuel Fritsch and Michael Gervers, "Pastophoria and Altars: Interaction in Ethiopian Liturgy and Church Architecture," *Aethiopica* 10 (2007): 7–51, here 12–14. For the complete chart of the various doorways of the pastophoria, see Fritsch, "The Preparation of the Gifts," 115.

AD 1150.[94] Older churches with pastophoria also began to be remodeled to reflect this new development in line with similar trends in Egypt. A few decades after the consecration of Mika'el Ambā (AD 1150), the churches in Lalibäla (12th–13th c.) were constructed with pastophoria. The church of Saint George at Zoz Amba is one example of such an arrangement. To reflect the new ordo however, this church contains three monoxyle portable altars.

This indicates that the new ordo had already developed in which the adjacent rooms can be used as additional sanctuaries. Although the architecture of the place still reflected the old ordo, the community adapted by using portable altars to be brought into the pastophoria when the need arises.[95] Thus, as in Syria-Palestine, Ethiopian churches also utilized these adjacent side-rooms or pastophoria for the deposition and keeping of the gifts until their transfer at the pre-anaphora, likely until some time in the eleventh or early twelfth centuries.

2.6.3 Nubia

Between Egypt and Ethiopia, there once thrived the civilization and Christianity of Nubia. Christianity in Nubia flourished between the fifth and fifteenth centuries among the three Nubian kingdoms of Nobatia, Makouria, and 'Alwā. Due to their proximity to Egypt, Nubian Christians were integrated into the Coptic Church ecclesiastical structure for most of their history, as textual and archaeological evidence suggests. Nubian bishops, often themselves Egyptian, were appointed directly by the Coptic Patriarch of Alexandria to various Nubian dioceses. Only one of the three kingdoms, Makouria, may have initially aligned itself with the Chalcedonian Alexandrian hierarchy, although it too began shifting its alliance to the Coptic Church by the seventh century.[96] In terms of liturgical tradition, as can be expected, the Nubians depended heavily on the liturgy of Egypt. Linguistically, they seem to have retained the use of Greek in ecclesiastical circles much longer than the Copts, although Coptic and Old Nubian are also attested.[97]

94 Ibid., 100. For brief information on Metropolitan Mika'el I, see Denis Nosnitsin, "Mika'el I," *EAE*, 3:953. For the rock-hewn church of Mika'el Amba, see Ewa Balicka-Witakowska, "Mika'el 'Amba," *EAE*, 3:959–961.

95 Fritsch and Gervers, "Pastophoria and Altars," 14.

96 William Y. Adams, "Nubian Church Organization," *CE*, 6:1813a–1814a. For more information on Nubian Christianity, see William Y. Adams, *Nubia: Corridor to Africa* (Princeton, NJ: Princeton University Press, 1977).

97 For a useful overview of the *status quaestionis* of the Nubian liturgical heritage, see Heinzgerd Brakmann, "Defunctus adhuc loquitur: Gottesdienst und Gebetsliteratur

The Nubian dossier is particularly useful in confirming the use of pastophoria for the keeping of the eucharistic gifts, or at the very least confirming a eucharistic function of some kind for these altar side-rooms. Prothesis pastophoria were discovered in churches in Banganarti, Faras,[98] and Sonqi Tino. In the room in Banganarti, there was found a chalice and paten, as well as what seems to be a relocated altar top.[99] This indicates that the northeastern pastophorion in Banganarti may have functioned as a prothesis room, or at least as a sacristy. More indicative of a eucharistic function is the northeastern pastophoria in Faras and Sonqi Tino, where inscriptions of liturgical prayers were found. The inscriptions in the cathedral in Faras included four prayers with clear eucharistic themes:

1. An incense prayer
2. The *Prothesis Prayer* of Alexandrian origin[100]
3. An epiclesis prayer over the chalice[101]
4. A prayer for blessing the chalice[102]

Similarly, Prayer 3—the epiclesis prayer of Nubian PRES—above was also discovered on the walls of the northeastern pastophorion of the church of Sonqi Tino, south of Wādī Ḥalfā.[103]

The two wall inscriptions that once appeared on the walls of the Faras Cathedral at key locations mentioned above (see note 22) provide yet another witness to the possible use of pastophoria in

der untergegangenen Kirche in Nubien," *Archiv für Liturgiewissenschaft* 48 (2006): 283–333.

98 Ibid., 289–290.

99 Ibid., 299–300.

100 This is the *Prothesis Prayer* of the Coptic prothesis rite, discussed below in chapter 6. It is also found in slightly variant recensions in the Ethiopian liturgy, and the Italo-Byzantine manuscript tradition. For the text of this prayer as it was found in the Faras Cathedral, see Jadwiga Kubińska, "Prothesis de la cathédrale de Faras. Documents et recherches," *Revue des Archéologues et Historiens d'Art de Louvain* 9 (1976): 7–37, here 20–21.

101 This is an epiclesis prayer to consecrate a new chalice from a presanctified particle of the body, constituting firm evidence for the existence of the presanctified liturgy in the Nubian Church. Cf. Stefanos Alexopoulos, *The Presanctified Liturgy in the Byzantine Rite: A Comparative Analysis of Its Origins, Evolution, and Structural Components*, Liturgia Condenda 21 (Leuven: Peeters, 2009), 115–116; Brakmann, "Defunctus adhuc loquitur," 320–324.

102 For an English translation of all four prayers, see Alexopoulos, *The Presanctified Liturgy*, 115–116; and more recently, Adam Łajtar and Dobrochna Zielińska, "The Northern Pastophorium of Nubian Churches: Ideology and Function (On the Basis of Inscriptions and Paintings)," in *Aegyptus et Nubia Christiana: The Włodzimierz Godlewski Jubilee Volume on the Occasion of his 70th Birthday*, ed. Adam Łajtar, Artur Obluski, and Iwona Zych, (Warsaw: Polish Centre of Mediterranean Archaeology, 2016), 435–457, here 439–441. For the Greek incipits of the prayers and their relevant bibliography, cf. Brakmann, "Defunctus adhuc loquitur," 321.

103 Ibid., 320.

Nubia for a eucharistic function. Both of these inscriptions record a list of people of various ranks–bishops, presbyters, laymen–and what appears to be donated foodstuffs, such as bread and wine. Not only is the type of material donated significant, the location of one of these inscriptions is of particular importance. This inscription, numbered L.491a.3, was located at the east end of the north wall in the northern vestibule of the cathedral, i.e., in an area of the church approximately in the northeast. The northeastern pastophorion of this very cathedral once stored several terracotta trays used as containers for food, which lends support to the use of this room to store the eucharistic gifts. Unfortunately, the inscriptions were both left in the cathedral, which was subsequently submerged under the waters of the artificial Lake Nubia (Lake Nasser), created as a result of the building of the Aswan Dam in the years 1958–1970.[104]

Interesting as the topic of the Nubian PRES may be, the information presented here is sufficient to show that Nubian northeastern pastophoria served some ritual function related to the Eucharist. From the nature of the prayers found, one can even venture a hypothesis that these rooms likely served as locations for the placement of the eucharistic gifts, and even for the prothesis rite, both in the context of the regular eucharistic liturgy and the presanctified liturgy.

2.7. Architectural Evidence

For a systematic treatment of the architectural evidence throughout Egypt, including the use of pastophoria, Grossmann's German monograph on the subject, as well as a series of English articles in the *Coptic Encyclopedia,* remain very useful. Grossmann approaches Egyptian church architecture systematically from its pre-fifth century beginnings until the Mamluk period (mid-thirteenth to mid-sixteenth centuries), while distinguishing in his treatment between urban and monastic churches. The discussion below follows the same organization of the evidence, focusing squarely on the topic of pastophoria.

104 See Łajtar and Ochała, "Two Wall Inscriptions from the Faras Cathedral," 73–102, especially the discussion in 97–102. The authors' argument that the hierarchical nature of the list of names indicates a solemn procession, which in turn seems to contradict Taft's long-proven assertion that no pre-anaphoral offertory procession existed in the Christian East fails to grasp Taft's point. The latter's main argument is that the deposition of the gifts in the east never took place in the *pre-anaphora,* which does not seem to be contradicted in the least by the Nubian wall inscriptions. That the list reflects a certain hierarchy of donors does not necessarily demonstrate a ritual procession that followed this order. Alternately, such a procession could have very well taken place as part of the entrance rites before the service began.

Although the term pastophorion itself is never attested in Egyptian texts, churches in the fourth century already feature triple-roomed sanctuary areas.[105] This is traditionally understood as a feature of Syrian churches, although Grossmann emphasizes that the earliest examples in Egypt antedate even those in Syria.[106] Sometimes, Egyptian churches even featured many apsidal rooms, not just two. Examples of this include the basilica of Hermopolis Magna and the White Monastery of Shenoute in Sūhāǧ.[107] Earlier examples ca. fifth century were also often irregular in proportion, that is, pastophoria on either side of the apse were not necessarily of equal size.[108] Although Grossmann does not make this point, this is very likely indicative of differing functions.

If such pastophoria antedate the earliest Syrian examples, this raises the question of their origin in the Egyptian context. Grossmann here offers no conclusive insight. It is unlikely in his view that the predecessor of such rooms is the multiple adjacent rooms usually found in Pharaonic temples, given the aversion of early Christians to most things pagan. Instead, he sees an even earlier prototype in the private homes of Christians, where the Eucharist was celebrated in the earliest centuries of Christianity, and which surely made use of multiple rooms.[109] As mentioned previously, Grossmann gives the general summary that pastophoria are more at home generally in Southern Egypt at such an early date, appearing only sporadically in Alexandria and near the coast, and often only added later.

In this regard, the small room in the northeastern corner of the sanctuary of the so-called Red Monastery near Sūhāǧ in Southern Egypt provides a particularly noteworthy example. This small room, an example of a Southern Egyptian pastophorion, features two phases of wall painting corresponding to the first and the third phases of

105 Grossmann, *Christliche Architektur in Ägypten*, 28; Peter Grossmann, "Architecture: Egypt (3rd–7th c. A.D.)," in Finney, *The Eerdmans Encyclopedia of Early Christian Art and Archaeology*, 1:108–110, here 108.

106 Grossmann, *Christliche Architektur in Ägypten*, 27. Cf. Peter Grossmann, "Pastophorium," *CE*, 1:216a–217a.

107 Ibid.

108 Grossmann, *Christliche Architektur in Ägypten*, 27.

109 Ibid. For the early Christian eucharistic gatherings in private homes, especially in connection with Greco-Roman symposium culture, see: Matthias Klinghardt, *Gemeinschaftsmahl und Mahlgemeinschaft: Soziologie und Liturgie frühchristlicher Mahlfeiern*, Texte und Arbeiten zum neutestamentlichen Zeitalter 13 (Tübingen: Francke Verlag, 1996); This approach is taken also in: Dennis E. Smith, *From Symposium to Eucharist: The Banquet in the Early Christian World* (Minneapolis, MN: Fortress Press, 2003); Valeriy A. Alikin, *The Earliest History of the Christian Gathering: Origin, Development and Content of the Christian Gathering in the First to Third Centuries*, Supplements to Vigiliae Christianae 102 (Leiden: Brill, 2010), 2–9.

work on the overall church, out of four total phases. The earliest of these phases dates to AD 533–566, while the later phase was likely finished ca. sixth–seventh centuries. Thus, according to Elizabeth Bolman, this room represents the earliest example of a northeastern pastophorion with an extant painting program.[110] The paintings themselves are diverse and are described in detail by Bolman. Overall, they include eagles, grapevines, wreaths, and crosses, which Bolman interprets in relation to themes of death, resurrection, and the Eucharist. Although the ubiquity of such representations in late antique Mediterranean paintings makes the task of ascertaining a particular liturgical function difficult, Bolman argues that at least a very likely function of this space was the preparation of the eucharistic gifts. This hypothesis is especially bolstered in view of the association between the prothesis rite and the sacrifice of Christ on the cross common in later commentaries, especially in Byzantium.[111] Even more certain, the later phase of wall painting depicts the archangels—most likely including Michael carrying a eucharistic oblation bread—as well as the four evangelists, Christ, the Virgin Mary, and Pshoi the founder of the monastery. Altogether, Bolman believes this later phase to be an even more certain sign that the room was used for the preparation of the gifts by the sixth or early seventh century.[112]

Between the fifth and seventh centuries, examples abound of small single-nave churches that lack any particular characteristics and are generally considered reductions in scale of large basilicas. This is where the small church in Taposiris Magna fits, which was mentioned above as an example of a Northern Egyptian church with adjacent pastophoria.[113] Built over a converted temple of Osiris as part of a larger fifth-century military camp, this small church testifies to the continued spread of pastophoria as a standard feature of Egyptian church buildings. Examples of similar small churches with apsidal side rooms include the church number D (CHD87) in Narmuthis (Madinat Māḍī) (App. 3),[114] and the underground church in the Monastery of

[110] Elizabeth S. Bolman, "Preparation of the Eucharist: Paintings in the Side Chambers," in *The Red Monastery Church: Beauty and Asceticism in Upper Egypt*, ed. Elizabeth S. Bolman (New Haven, CT: Yale University Press, 2016), 183–189. Cf. Bolman's earlier article on the same topic, Elizabeth S. Bolman, "The Iconography of the Eucharist? Early Byzantine Painting, the *Prothesis*, and the Red Monastery," in *ANAΘHMATA EOPTIKA: Studies in Honor of Thomas F. Mathews*, ed. Joseph D. Alchermes, Helen C. Evans, and Thelma K. Thomas (Mainz: Philipp von Zabern, 2009), 57–66.

[111] Bolman, "Preparation of the Eucharist," 185–186.

[112] Ibid., 188.

[113] Grossmann, *Christliche Architektur in Ägypten*, 41–42.

[114] Ibid., 42n91. For a full description of the church, see ibid., 421–422, and fig. 42.

Abū Fānā (Appendix 3).[115] Nothing more can be said by way of an overarching statement for urban churches in that era, given the irregular nature of such small churches, which defies attempts at a neat organization.

Meanwhile in seventh-century Scetis, as well as the White Monastery, the sanctuary area usually possessed sharply divided apsidal rooms, sometimes accessible only from the nave, as mentioned above in the example of the church of the Virgin in the Baramūs Monastery (Appendix 3), as well as other monastic churches of the region.[116] Other times, these adjacent rooms were accessible only from the apse, with one single entrance leading into the sanctuary. Examples of the latter type include the northern church of Quṣūr ʿĪsa South, the western church of Qaṣr al-Waḥā'ida, and the southern church of the Monastery of Apollo in Bawīṭ.[117] Later in the mid-seventh century, monastic churches particularly in Kellia, as well as the Baramūs Monastery church were modified to include passageways between apse and pastophoria, perhaps indicating a developing change in the liturgical usage of the space.

Thus far, no explanation has been given for the more common disposition of Coptic churches nowadays, which features a triple sanctuary room, with each room housing a consecrated altar. This characteristic began to appear in the last phase of Egyptian church architectural development, which took place some time during the Fatimid era (10th–12th c.). Grossmann identifies the oldest example of a triple-sanctuary room as that of Abū Qudāma, built during the patriarchate of Michael IV (AD 1092–1102).[118] However, Emmanuel Fritsch identified two earlier examples of such an arrangement: The new church of Saint Mercurius, consecrated by Patriarch Abraham ibn Zurʿa (AD 975–978),[119] and a church consecrated during the patriarchate of Christodoulus (AD 1047–1077) by George, bishop of Batū,[120] thus moving the phenomenon back to the tenth century at the earliest.[121] Another example found in *The Histories of the Monasteries and Churches* of Abū l-Makārim and not mentioned by either author belongs to the twelfth century. This church, dedicated to Saint Mennas and located in Fusṭāṭ Miṣr (Old Cairo) outside the fortress of Babylon,

115 Ibid. For a full description of the church, see ibid., 516, and fig. 134.

116 Ibid., 116. For a full description of this church, see ibid., 499–501, with a floor plan in fig. 118.

117 Ibid., 115n39.

118 *HP*, 2.3:397. Cf. Grossmann, *Christliche Architektur in Ägypten*, 96n323.

119 B.T.A. Evetts, *The Churches & Monasteries of Egypt and Some Neighbouring Countries Attributed to Abū Ṣāliḥ the Armenian* (Oxford, 1895), 119.

120 *HP*, 2.3:282.

121 Fritsch, "The Preparation of the Gifts," 99n3.

featured a northern altar and a door to the bake house, according to *The Histories*.[122] The account describes a fire that destroyed the church, which was later restored in the Caliphate of al-ʿĀḍiḍ (AD 1160–1171), dating the northern altar—and thus the reference to multiple altars—to at least the twelfth century when the church was restored, if not to the older building. Interestingly, accounts of Melkite churches in Egypt in the same work never mention the existence of multiple altars. This includes the church of Saint Arsenius in the Monastery of al-Quṣair, which, according to Grossmann, dates to after the destruction by al-Ḥākim (11th c.),[123] and the church of Saint Sabas in the same monastery.[124]

Grossmann, seemingly unaware of the earlier witnesses of this phenomenon, attributes the cause to renewed persecution under the Mamluk dynasty (12th–16th c.), as well as increased frequency of liturgical celebration.[125] Since under the Mamluks the building of new churches was heavily restricted—the theory goes—and since the Copts started celebrating the Eucharist more often, a solution was devised to re-purpose the existing pastophoria into sanctuary rooms with altars. Consequently, the place where the eucharistic gifts were previously placed and prepared was no longer available, and the gifts had to be placed directly on the altar from the start, as the next logical place, since they were destined there at any rate.

In his analysis of this phenomenon as it was adopted and implemented in Ethiopia, Emmanuel Fritsch touched upon the causes more than once. In an earlier study, he referenced both Grossmann's explanation—the need for extra altars for more celebrations—as well as possible Syrian influence.[126] In two later articles, Fritsch slightly rephrased the idea. In one instance, he referenced the need for more altars to honor more saints, rather than for an increased frequency of celebration per se. Later, he also added that a particular era in which Copts were under much pressure was the Ayyubid era (AD 1171–1254), although that was at least a century following the appearance of the earliest triple-sanctuary church.[127]

122 Evetts, *The Churches & Monasteries*, 105. Cf. Peter Grossmann, "Babylon," *CE*, 2:317a–323b.

123 Peter Grossmann, "Dayr al-Quṣayr," *CE*, 3:853a–855b.

124 Evetts, *The Churches & Monasteries*, 151.

125 Grossmann, *Christliche Architektur in Ägypten*, 95–96.

126 Fritsch and Gervers, "Pastophoria and Altars," 11.

127 Emmanuel Fritsch, "The Churches of Lalibäla (Ethiopia) Witnesses of Liturgical Changes," *BBGG III* 5 (2008): 69–112, here 71n10; Emmanuel Fritsch, "The Altar in the Ethiopian Church: History, Forms and Meanings," in *Inquiries into Eastern Christian Worship: Selected Papers of the Second International Congress of the Society of Oriental Liturgy, Rome, 17–21 September 2008*, ed. Bert Groen, Steven

However, the earliest known example of the triple-sanctuary church should adjust the understanding of the causes of this phenomenon. It is true that Copts experienced recurring pressures, particularly with respect to the building of new churches, both during the Ayyubid era and later under the Mamluks. However, this was generally not the case during the patriarchate of Abraham ibn Zur'a (AD 975–978), who was highly respected in the Fatimid court. Nor was this an exception made to a particular patriarch. As Swanson relates, the Fatimids were generally well disposed toward Christians out of pragmatic interest in a smoothly functioning society.[128] The Fatimids were also themselves a Shiite ruling minority among a majority Sunni population, which must have encouraged their tolerance of other minorities. Although there is no denying that the custom of equipping churches with three altars became very useful when the building of churches was severely restricted, it seems more in line with the evidence that the phenomenon *started* as an extension of the general trend in the seventh to the ninth centuries of adopting Syrian usage. This trend was surely accelerated by Patriarch Abraham, himself a Syrian merchant before his consecration.

In other places, the cause may have been simply a local adaptation to accommodate two communities within the same space. In 2002, a painting was discovered on an arched entrance of the northeastern pastophorion in the Church of the Virgin in the Monastery of the Syrians (Dayr al-Suryān), which was subsequently studied by Karel C. Innemée.[129] The church was initially constructed ca. AD 645. Later, the church was remodeled, changing this pastophorion to a sanctuary room with its own altar. Innemée posits that the painting in question was completed around the same time of the remodeling, after AD 700.[130] The painting itself represents a golden cross within a dark blue circle. Two figures flank the central shape. The one on the left is Saint James the Brother of the Lord, while the one on the right is unidentified, although there is a possibility it may be Peter the Apostle, based on a scene in the *Apocryphon of James*.[131] Based on the prominence of Saint James in the scene, and the suggested time of the remodeling and painting of this scene, Innemée postulated that the newly erected chapel was used by the fledgling community of Syrian monks, the first of whom arrived in Scetis in the early ninth

Hawkes-Teeples, and Stefanos Alexopoulos, Eastern Christian Studies 12 (Leuven: Peeters, 2012), 443–510, here 454; Fritsch, "The Preparation of the Gifts," 97–99.

128 Swanson, *The Coptic Papacy*, 48.

129 Karel C. Innemée, "A Newly Discovered Mural Painting in Deir al-Surian," *Eastern Chrisitan Art* 1 (2004): 61–66.

130 Ibid., 61.

131 Ibid., 62–64.

century. It would make sense for a chapel dedicated for Syrian monks to feature Saint James over its entrance, since he is the author of the main anaphora of the Syrian tradition (Syriac JAS). The witness of the new chapel in the Monastery of the Syrians is instructive and shows that in some cases the erection of multiple altars within the church—and thus the elimination of the pastophoria as places for the prothesis rite—may have had other reasons, unrelated to governmental oppression.

On the other hand, Grossmann's own opinion regarding the actual use of these apsidal adjacent rooms or pastophoria should be mentioned. Grossmann in fact questioned the validity of calling these rooms prothesis rooms, primarily because such a term presupposes the existence of an actual prothesis rite, that is, a ritualized preparation of the eucharistic gifts performed by the priest and involving a set of pre-appointed prayers and acts. Grossmann, citing Descoeudres and Taft,[132] declares categorically that such a rite did not exist until the seventh century, and that therefore these pastophoria cannot be called prothesis rooms before that time. However, Grossmann relies solely on scholarship from the Syro-Byzantine East, without showing that indeed the prothesis rite in Egypt is a post-seventh century development. As I argue below in chapter 6, the Coptic *Prothesis Prayer*, the central element in the whole prothesis rite, is quite ancient, and was already borrowed and found in the Italo-Byzantine manuscript tradition by the eighth century, suggesting that it may be older than the seventh century. Further evidence presented in the following chapter will also bolster the argument that the preparation of the gifts was already solemnized into a clerical ritual including the *Prothesis Prayer* perhaps around or shortly after the fifth century.

3. SUMMARY

Before proceeding in the next chapter to explore the historical development of the transfer of gifts, the following summary can be provided:

1. While no evidence exists that a pre-anaphoral offertory procession was ever the case in Egypt, people often brought offerings including bread and wine for the Eucharist. This practice was by no means without exceptions, as the *Canons of Shenoute*, and *Miracles of Apa Phoebammon* indicate. At any rate, by the eleventh century it is clear that the preparation of eucharistic bread

[132] Descoeudres, *Die Pastophorien im syro-byzantinischen Osten*, 91; Taft, "How Liturgies Grow," 207.

by the people had become nearly extinct, allowed only temporarily by Patriarch Christodoulus in the eleventh century.

2. That the gifts were placed elsewhere until the anaphora and not on the altar is clear from multiple sources. These include the *Didascalia Apostolorum* (3rd c.), and the *Apostolic Constitutions* (4th c.). This can also be implied from passages in the *Historia Ecclesiastica* of Theodoret (4th c.), the *Life of John of Scetis* (ca. 7th c.), the *Life of Isaac* (8th c.), and the *Order of the Priesthood* (13th c.). This is also consistent with the unequivocal witness of the neighboring eastern traditions of the Syro-Byzantine East, Nubia, and Ethiopia.
3. Architectural evidence in Egyptian churches indicates that churches with pastophoria already appear in the fourth century, often in Southern Egypt but also in the north.
4. Between the fifth and seventh centuries, the design seems to have spread further, appearing even in smaller churches near the coast, such as Taposiris Magna.
5. Pastophoria were also common in the large monasteries of Scetis and the White Monastery, where they were sharply divided from the apse. The method of entry into these pastophoria varied over time. Whereas older models were accessible only from the nave and completely blocked from the central apse, later renovations frequently added passageways between apse and pastophoria. This is highly significant for reasons that will become clear when the history of the transfer of gifts is analyzed.
6. Finally, pastophoria began to be converted to smaller adjacent sanctuaries with altars. This phenomenon can be documented at least since the tenth century, with more examples until the twelfth century. This was probably begun under Syrian influence, and later found further impetus in governmental restrictions on building of new churches. In one early example from Scetis, the conversion may have taken place to accommodate the new community of Syrian monks, who would have needed their own dedicated chapel. Today, the triple-sanctuary church is a standard feature of any building large enough to accommodate three altars.

The following chapter resumes the exploration of the historical origins of the preparation and transfer of gifts. The focus now shifts to the process of change from the old ordo, a pre-anaphoral transfer of gifts from the pastophorion to the altar, to the new ordo, in which the gifts are placed immediately on the altar at the commencement of the liturgy.

CHAPTER 2

HISTORICAL ORIGINS 2: THE TRANSFER OF THE GIFTS

Following the reception and preparation of the eucharistic gifts, they are to be transferred to the altar at some point during the unfolding of the liturgy. The central question here is whether there once existed a pre-anaphoral transfer of gifts in the Egyptian tradition, and if so, what evidence can be furnished to establish this fact in the clearest way possible. Naturally, much of the evidence presented in the previous chapter proving the use of adjacent pastophoria for the deposition of the gifts is relevant here as well. Clearly if the gifts were not immediately placed on the altar, they must have been transferred there at some point. Moreoever, ritual developments in Syria and Ethiopia continue to be useful to complete the understanding of the transition from the old ordo to the new ordo.

1. THE TRANSFER OF THE GIFTS

1.1. Early Witnesses (2nd–3rd c.)

It is clear from the very beginning that a pre-anaphoral transfer of gifts was the universal practice everywhere, even before the rise of particular regional Rites in the course of the fourth and fifth centuries. As early as the 2nd century, one finds the following brief description of a simple pre-anaphoral transfer of the gifts in the *First Apology* of Justin Martyr (AD 100–165):

[1] Ἀλλήλους φιλήματι ἀσπαζόμεθα παυσάμενοι τῶν εὐχῶν. [2] Ἔπειτα προσφέρεται τῷ προεστῶτι τῶν ἀδελφῶν ἄρτος καὶ ποτήριον ὕδατος καὶ κράματος, [3] καὶ οὗτος λαβὼν αἶνον καὶ δόξαν τῷ πατρὶ τῶν ὅλων διὰ τοῦ ὀνόματος τοῦ υἱοῦ καὶ τοῦ πνεύματος τοῦ ἁγίου ἀναπέμπει.[1]	[1] Having ceased the prayers, we greet one another with a kiss. [2] Then, bread and a cup of mixed wine are presented to the presider of the brothers. [3] And thus taking them, he gives praise and glory to the Father of all, through the name of the Son and the Holy Spirit.

1 *1 Apol.* 65 (CPG 1073). See Charles Munier, *Justin: Apologies pour les chrétiens*, SC 507 (Paris: Cerf, 2006), 302–304.

The same pre-anaphoral transfer of gifts is referenced in chapter 67 of the same text, where Justin describes the worship gathering on a regular Sunday.[2] From the point of view of the current Coptic rite, this already betrays a different arrangement. Unlike what one would expect to see today in a Coptic liturgy, in which the bread and wine are already found on the altar by the time of the kiss, here the bread and wine are brought to the presider after the kiss.

In the previous chapter, the *Apostolic Constitutions* was referenced as a witness to the bringing of the gifts to the bishop before the anaphora and for the return of the eucharist after communion to the pastophoria. In fact, analysis of the Coptic derivatives of the *Apostolic Constitutions* lends further support to the pre-anaphoral transfer of gifts. The Eighth Book of the *Apostolic Constitutions* was certainly influential beyond the Syro-Antiochene milieu in which it originated. In the Coptic canonical tradition, *Apostolic Constitutions VIII* appears in the Sahidic *Canons of the Apostles*, preserved in *British Library Or. 1320* (AD 1006).[3] The passage from the Greek recension cited above is presented here using Paul de Lagarde's Sahidic text and George Horner's English translation:

ⲛⲁⲓ ⲇⲉ ⲉⲩϣⲁⲛϣⲱⲡⲉ ⲙⲁⲣⲉ ⲛ̄ⲇⲓⲁⲕⲟⲛⲟⲥ ⲉⲓⲛⲉ ⲛ̄ⲛ̄ⲇⲱⲣⲟⲛ ⲉϩⲟⲩⲛ ⲙ̄ⲡⲉⲡⲓⲥⲕⲟⲡⲟⲥ ⲉⲡⲉⲑⲩⲥⲓⲁⲥⲧⲏⲣⲓⲟⲛ ⲉⲧⲟⲩⲁⲁⲃ.[4]	Further, when these things have been done, let the deacons bring the gifts to the bishop at the holy altar.[5]

The Sahidic text also inspired a later nineteenth-century Bohairic translation, which was edited and published by Henry Tattam.[6] Curiously, the reference to the pastophoria at the conclusion of the liturgy in the Greek recension is not found in either the Bohairic or Sahidic texts. Nonetheless, the earlier and more important passage for the immediate purpose is clearly well represented and shows beyond doubt that the gifts were kept by the deacons until the time of the anaphora.

This passage is also echoed in *Apostolic Tradition* 4, where the deacons bring in the oblations to the bishop after his ordination.[7] It

2 *1 Apol.* 67. See Munier, *Apologies pour les chrétiens*, 310–311.

3 Kaufhold, "Sources of Canon Law," 267. For a description and date of this important manuscript, see Crum, *Catalogue of the Coptic Manuscripts*, 52–53.

4 Paul de Lagarde, *Aegyptiaca* (Göttingen, 1883), 276.

5 Horner, *The Statutes of the Apostles*, 343.

6 Kaufhold, "Sources of Canon Law," 268. Henry Tattam, *The Apostolical Constitutions or Canons of the Apostles in Coptic with an English Translation* (London, 1848), 121–122.

7 *Traditio Apostolica* 4.2 (CPG 1737). For the Sahidic text, see Walter Till and Johannes Leipoldt, *Der koptische Text der Kirchenordnung Hippolyts*, Texte und

is also important to mention that the same chapter, and the pre-anaphoral transfer it mentions, is included in the *Canons of Hippolytus* (4th/5th c.), which shows almost a literal fidelity to it in this passage.[8] Later in Chapter 21 on Baptism, a similar transfer is recounted:

[1] ⲙⲁⲣⲉ ⲛⲓⲇⲓⲁⲕⲱⲛⲟⲥ ⲉⲛ ϯⲡⲣⲟⲥⲫⲟⲣⲁ ⲙ̀ⲡⲓⲉ̀ⲡⲓⲥⲕⲟⲡⲟⲥ [2] ⲟⲩⲟϩ ⲛ̀ⲑⲟϥ ⲉϥϣⲉⲡϩⲙⲟⲧ.[9]	[1] Let the deacons bring the offering to the bishop, [2] and he shall give thanks.[10]

This time, the passage is found in Bohairic rather than the older Sahidic version. Once again, one finds essentially the same idea in the Latin version–the oldest of all extant witnesses–as well as the Arabic and Ethiopic.[11] The *Apostolic Tradition* itself influenced the reference in the fifth-century *Testamentum Domini* to the same effect, which was mentioned in chapter 1 in the context of the Syro-Byzantine East.[12] Thus, early witnesses in the first centuries of the Church, as well as the local Syrian adaptation in the *Testamentum Domini*, attest to this pre-anaphoral transfer of gifts.

1.2. The Ethiopic Order of the Mystery *(ca. 5th c.)*

Also originating around the same period is a very important description of the liturgy contained in an Ethiopic Synaxarion reading for the 28th of the month of Ṭerr. The description comes in the form of a homily for the newly baptized on how to actively participate in the liturgical rites and can thus be said to be modeled after the

Untersuchungen zur Geschichte der altchristlichen Literatur 58 (Berlin: Akademie Verlag, 1954), 2–3. Cf. Paul F. Bradshaw, Maxwell E. Johnson, and L. Edward Phillips, *The Apostolic Tradition: A Commentary*, ed. Harold W. Attridge, Hermeneia–A Critical and Historical Commentary on the Bible (Minneapolis, MN: Fortress Press, 2002), 38. As seen in the textual comparison in the edition by Bradshaw et al, the reference to a pre-anaphoral transfer of gifts by the deacons is found also in the Latin version of the codex *Verona LV (53)* (5th c.), as well as in the Ethiopic and Arabic recensions of the *Traditio Apostolica*. The Ethiopian version may be especially instructive. It seems to have been made from an Arabic precursor older than the extant Arabic witnesses. Brakmann posits a probable date of ca. fifth century for the liturgy described in the Ethiopic version. See Brakmann, "Le déroulement," 109.

8 René-Georges Coquin, *Les canons d'Hippolyte: Édition critique de la version arabe, introduction et traduction française*, PO 31.2 (Paris: Firmin-Didot, 1966), 352–353. Although the Arabic recension published by Coquin is clearly not of fourth or fifth-century origin, it is posited that it relies on a Greek original of such antiquity.

9 Till and Leipoldt, *Der koptische Text der Kirchenordnung Hippolyts*, 22–23.

10 *Traditio Apostolica* 21.26 (CPG 1737). See Bradshaw, Johnson, and Phillips, *The Apostolic Tradition*, 120.

11 Bradshaw, Johnson, and Phillips, *The Apostolic Tradition*, 120.

12 Patrich, "The Transfer of Gifts," 360.

catechetical homily genre common in patristic writings of the fourth and fifth centuries. The Ethiopic text is found in *Paris BnF Ethiopic d'Abbadie 66–66bis* (15th c.) and was inserted into that particular Ethiopic Synaxarion in the course of its translation from Arabic in the early fifteenth century. During the course of the liturgy described in this text, the following is mentioned regarding the pre-anaphora:

> [1] And after the catechumens [*ne'usa krestiyān*] have been dismissed and the faithful [*ḥezba krestiyān*] remain and [the hymn] *The Hosts of Angels* [*sarāwita malā'ekt*] is read, [2] respond [*tasaṭawu*] to it with joy in order to join in the glorification with the hosts of angels [*sarāwita malā'ekt*] who stand and glorify and surround the mystery of Christ [*yekēlelewwo la-meśṭira Krestos*]. [3] Then the celebrants [*kāhnāt*] bring [*yāqarrebu*] the holy offering of Christ [*qwerbāno la-Krestos*], [4] the sacrifice [*maśwā'eta*] which is offered [*za-yetqērrab*] to God [*Egzi'abeḥēr*], [5] whereby he may forgive [*yesray*] the sins of all those who come near [*yeqarebu*] to him in righteousness [and] in faith, with good works.[13]

Despite its late appearance in the Ethiopic Synaxarion in the fifteenth century, Heinzgerd Brakmann suggested that the liturgy described in this homily may go back to fifth-century Alexandria, basing his conclusion on the absence of the Creed and the Lord's Prayer in the liturgy described.[14]

The passage is extremely valuable in attesting to a pre-anaphoral procession to transfer the gifts in the Ethiopian and the Egyptian contexts, two traditions which today do not possess such a procession. In addition, the degree of solemnity imparted to this procession already reveal that the liturgy in this text does not represent merely a practical preparation of the gifts, but more likely an already ritualized preparation, which perhaps included the *Prothesis Prayer*. Although the text provides no information on what takes place away from the view of the newly-baptized, one can at least sense that the transfer of gifts described here is no simple carrying of gifts to the altar, but a

13 Gérard Colin, ed., *Le Synaxaire éthiopien: Mois de Ṭerr*, PO 45.1 (Turnhout: Brepols, 1990), 220–221. See also the earlier edition of this text: Robert Beylot, "Sermon éthiopien anonyme sur l'eucharistie," *Abbay* 12 (1983): 79–116, 90 (Ge'ez), 109 (French). For an English translation and commentary on this important text, see Emmanuel Fritsch, "The Order of the Mystery: An Ancient Catechesis Preserved in BnF Ethiopic Ms d'Abbadie 66–66bis (Fifteenth Century) with a Liturgical Commentary," in *Studies in Oriental Liturgy: Proceedings of the Fifth International Congress of the Society of Oriental Liturgy, New York, 10–15 June 2014*, ed. Bert Groen, et al., Eastern Christian Studies 28 (Leuven: Peeters, 2019), 195–263, here 246 (English), 257 (Ge'ez).

14 Brakmann, "Le déroulement," 109. See also Brakmann's remark in: Brakmann, "Neue Funde (1988–1992)," 11–12.

formal ritual affair, not unlike the Byzantine Great Entrance in its significance.

1.3. Jacob of Wasīm (ca. 7th c.)

Another Ethiopian text is also instructive for the transfer of the gifts. This is the story of Bishop Jacob of Wasīm, assigned a seventh-century Northern Egyptian provenance by Heinzgerd Brakmann.[15] The story tells of the appearance of a mysterious saintly priest, and the subsequent celebration of the Eucharist the next morning. The relevant passage occurs during the description of that liturgy, and precisely at the pre-anaphora. Bishop Jacob reports, "And they dressed up the altar and brought the offering and he [the saintly mysterious priest] kept silent and we offered the offering."[16]

The context of this account is a liturgy in which the preparation of the altar, followed by the transfer of the gifts, takes place after the readings, that is, during the pre-anaphoral rites. It is not clear where the gifts were located until then, though based on the information presented earlier regarding the architectural arrangement of Scetis churches in the seventh century, one might expect the church in question to have sharply-divided apsidal side rooms that may have been used for such a function. Naturally, this involves a great amount of speculation that a story surviving today only in the Ethiopian tradition truly represents the reality in seventh-century Scetis architecturally speaking.[17] Thus, any attempt to conjecture the place of the gifts from this text would be stretching the evidence beyond its limits. Nonetheless, it is also unlikely that a later Ethiopian redactor altered the entire sequence of the liturgy described here from its seventh-century *Vorlage* posited by Brakmann. The witness of this story from the Ethiopian tradition can (only with extreme caution) be enlisted as evidence for a pre-anaphoral transfer of gifts in seventh-century Scetis. This suggestion is tentative *only* as long as Brakmann's dating and location are in fact accurate.

15 Brakmann, "Le déroulement," 118–119.

16 Victor Arras, ed., *Quadraginta historiae monachorum*, CSCO 505, Scriptores Aethiopici 85 (Leuven: Peeters, 1988), 235. For an English translation of the Ge'ez text of the relevant passage, see Fritsch, "The Preparation of the Gifts," 135.

17 Exceptional caution is warranted here in light of the manuscript history of this work, which survives in two fairly recent manuscripts: *British Library Or. 768* (18th c.) and *EMML 746* (20th c.). See Alessandro Bausi, "Monastic Literature," *EAE*, 3:993–999, here 995.

1.4. The Letter of Macarius of Manūf al-'uliyā *(10th c.)*

The witnesses presented so far belong overall either to the Ancient Church Order genre with its complex transmission history, or are Ethiopian witnesses presumed to betray an Egyptian ancestry. By far the most important and decisive witness to the old ordo in the Coptic Northern Egyptian Rite is found in a document of clearly and uniquely Coptic provenance, namely, the so-called *Letter of Macarius of Manūf al-'uliyā* from the tenth century.

First, some background information is in order. The letter appears as part of the contents of the codex *Paris BnF Ar. 100* (14th c.), fol. 9r–14r.[18] The codex itself is known as *The Book of the Chrism* and contains various writings concerning the making of the *myron* or chrism, including the text of the *Mystagogy* that is read during the liturgy of the chrism,[19] a description of the various substances used, and an account of the making of the chrism by various patriarchs.[20] The last account of these various consecrations took place in AD 1346 during the patriarchate of Peter V (AD 1340–1348),[21] indicating that the contents of the manuscript date to at least the mid-fourteenth century. The *Letter of Macarius* is written by a certain Macarius, bishop of *Manūf al-'uliyā* (Upper Manūf) in the northern Delta region.[22] The letter mentions that Macarius worked as scribe for

18 The codex displays multiple numbering attempts by folia and pages and using western and Coptic numbers. The folio numbers provided here are based on the Coptic cursive numbering located on the upper-left corner of each folio on the verso side.

19 The *Mystagogy* is a lengthy statement of faith read during the rite of the consecration of the chrism and based on *Testamentum Domini* I.28. See O.H.E. Burmester, "The Coptic and Arabic Versions of the Mystagogia," *Le Muséon* 46 (1933): 203–235; Heinzgerd Brakmann, "La 'Mystagogie' de la liturgie alexandrine et copte," in *Mystagogie: pensée liturgique d'aujourd'hui et liturgie ancienne, Conférences Saint-Serge, 39e semaine d'Études liturgiques, Paris, 30 juin–3 juillet 1992*, ed. Achille M. Triacca and Alessandro Pistoia, BEL.S 70 (Rome: Edizioni Liturgiche, 1992), 55–65.

20 For the complete contents of the manuscript, see Arnold van Lantschoot, "Le ms. Vatican copte 44 et le livre du Chrême (ms. Paris arabe 100)," *Le Muséon* 45 (1932): 181–234, here 185–186. Besides the manuscript, an Arabic edition of the text of the letter was recently published by Athanasius al-Maqārī, making it the first widely available edition in Arabic of *The Letter of Macarius*. See Athanasius al-Maqārī, *Sirr al-rūḥ al-qudus wa-l-mayrūn al-muqaddas* [The mystery of the Holy Spirit and the holy chrism], Ṭuqūs asrār wa-ṣalawāt al-kanīsa 3.2 (Cairo: Dār nūbār, 2007), 359–374.

21 *Paris BnF Ar. 100* (14th c.), fol. 93r–105r.

22 For more information on the various names and possible location of this city, as well as Bishop Macarius himself, see Stefan Timm, *Das christlich-koptische Ägypten in arabischer Zeit: Eine Sammlung christlicher Stätten in Ägypten in arabischer Zeit, unter Ausschluß von Alexandria, Kairo, des Apa-Mena-Klosters (Dēr Abū Mina), der Skētis (Wādi n-Naṭrūn) und der Sinai-Region*, vol. 4, (M–P), Beihefte zum Tübinger Atlas des Vorderen Orients, Reihe B (Geisteswissenschaften) 41.4 (Wiesbaden: Dr. Ludwig Reichert Verlag, 1988), 1575–1585.

Patriarch Cosmas III (AD 920–932), and that he also lived to see the patriarchate of Mīnā II (AD 956–974).[23] The letter is addressed to an anonymous group of archons, or rich laymen, concerning the chrism, its significance, history, making, and the various times in the year in which it was traditionally prepared. The letter is very significant in terms of the rich liturgical details it provides for a time period anterior to the earliest Copto-Arabic Euchologia of the thirteenth century and later. The letter begins with explaining the custom of the Copts in making the chrism in the context of the Lenten catechumenate period, at which point the following remark is made, quoted here in full:

[1] و في الجيل الاول ما كانوا يعمدوا اطفال بل من قد كَمَّلوا عمرهم يدعون كاتخومانس وهم الذين يعطوهم المعمودية [2] ويُعَلِّموهم دين النصرانية الى ثلث سنين ويُعَمَّدون. [3] ومن اجل هذا صار الرسم في الكنائس هذا الوقت في خروج قدس القديسين الى المذبح بعد قراءة الانجيل [4] وهو ان ينادي الشماس ويقول ينصرفوا الموعوظين ويغلقوا الابودياقُنيين الابواب.[24]

[1] In the first generation, they would not baptize infants, but those who had reached maturity were called catechumens,[25] and such ones are granted baptism. [2] And they teach them the Christian faith for three years and they are baptized. [3] Thus, the custom developed in the churches at that time, that the holy of the holies exits to the altar after the reading of the Gospel, [4] and that the deacon cries out and says "let the catechumens depart," and the subdeacons close the doors.

Immediately following this passage comes a gloss, likely added later at the time of copying the manuscript in the fourteenth century, which adds further explanation to the rites just described:

[1] كان يخرج القربان من الهيكل الذي هو هيكل التقدمة الى حيث يُقرأ الانجيل [2] يمضوا الكهنة مبدلين بالشمع والبخور ويقدم الى المذبح الذي للصعيدة. [3] عند ذلك يخرج الموعوظين [4] وهذا الرسم انقطع من ديار مصر عند القبط.[26]

[1] The offering used to exit from the sanctuary of offering to the place where the Gospel is read. [2] The clergy walk, vested, with candles and incense, and go to the altar of sacrifice. [3] At that time, the catechumens exit. [4] This arrangement has ceased in Egypt among the Copts.

[23] *Paris BnF Ar. 100* (14th c.), fol. 12r. See Louis Villecourt, "La lettre de Macaire, évêque de Memphis, sur la liturgie antique du chrême et du baptême à Alexandrie," *Le Muséon* 36 (1923): 33–46, here 39.

[24] *Paris BnF Ar. 100* (14th c.), fol. 9r–v. Cf. Villecourt, "La Lettre de Macaire," 34–35.

[25] The manuscript has كاتخومانس = Gr. Κατηχούμενος.

[26] *Paris BnF Ar. 100* (14th c.), fol. 9v. Cf. Villecourt, "La Lettre de Macaire," 34–35.

The description itself is clear enough so as to require no explanation. The author is explaining the level of participation of the catechumens, those for whom the chrism is made in the first place. Since, as he says, they are not allowed to see the mysteries, they are dismissed after the scriptural readings. At this point, the gifts are brought in procession by the clergy from the so-called sanctuary or altar of offering to the central altar. The procession itself seems to have been quite solemn, with vested clergy, carrying candles, and offering incense. The text of this comment alone at least witnesses to the existence of a Great Entrance-like procession of transferring the gifts in the Coptic Rite, at one point in history.

Commenting on this source, Athanasius al-Maqārī was quick to interpret the words of Macarius together with the explanatory note that the disappearance of the adult catechumenate was the natural reason for the disappearance of the old ordo of the pre-anaphoral transfer.[27] However, a closer reading of the text reveals this to be rather superficial. On the one hand, Macarius' own words simply say that the adult catechumens used to be dismissed from the liturgy before the solemn transfer of gifts, a fact that is well attested in East and West, and at least to be implied in Alexandria based on the witness of Theodoret's *Historia Ecclesiastica* cited previously. On the other hand, the later gloss is concerned only with explaining the logistics of this solemn transfer, since by then (mid-fourteenth century), this custom had already fallen into disuse. However, neither Macarius, nor the later author of the gloss, are linking the two phenomena as cause and effect. Simply put, the catechumens–as long as they existed as a distinct group of adults–were prevented from attending the eucharistic liturgy, while the transfer of gifts was originally part of the pre-anaphora irrespective of who was or was not allowed to witness it. That the pre-anaphoral transfer continued to be the custom even after the demise of the organized catechumenate can also be assumed, since it continued to be the custom in Byzantium, Rome, Armenia, and most likely Ethiopia long after.

Following the gloss, Macarius continues his description of the ancient custom in Alexandria. He writes, "But in recent times they have ceased the baptism of men and made it for infants, if they are born in the faith of Christ, the children of believers. But this is a current custom in the churches to this time."[28] Although it is not clear what custom Macarius is referring to, one can presume based on the overall topic of the letter that Macarius is referring to the consecration of the chrism by the patriarch and bishops, a rite–he recounts–that

27 Al-Maqārī, *Al-quddās al-ilāhī*, 1:276.

28 *Paris BnF Ar. 100* (14th c.), fol. 11v–12r. Cf. Villecourt, "La Lettre de Macaire," 35.

used to take place at some unspecified earlier period at the Angelion church in Alexandria.

Macarius in fact includes two lengthy explanations of the unfolding of this cathedral Alexandrian rite for the consecration of the chrism. In his second retelling, Macarius includes a further reference to the pre-anaphoral transfer, following a general baptism of the catechumens:

[1] ويعمد بيده ثلاثة نفر من الذكورة ويأمر القسوس ان يعمدوا من بقى [2] ثم يدهنهم البطريرك بالميرون وهو دهن البلسان بمفرده [3] ويخرج الى بيت الخدمة مع الاساقفة والشمامسة بين يديهم بالقراءة [4]فينزع عنه البدلة السَّليحية ويلبس بدلة القداس وتكون سواد. [5] ويخرج مع قدس القدس وهو الخبز والخمر الى المذبح والكهنة بين يديه بالقراءة والشمع والصلبان والبخور [6] فيقدس السرائر.[29]

[1] And he baptizes with his hand three males and commands the priests to baptize the remainder. [2] Then the patriarch alone anoints them with the chrism, which is the oil of the balm. [3] And he exits to the house of service with the bishops and the deacons, accompanied by readings. [4] And he takes off the apostolic vestment and puts on the vestment of the liturgy, and it is black. [5] And he exits with the holy of the holy [read: holies], which is the bread and the wine, to the altar, with the priests accompanying him with reading, as well as candles, crosses, and incense. [6] And he consecrates the mysteries.

Finally, Macarius writes that this solemn cathedral rite had already become down-scaled by his time as a result of its relocation to the Monastery of Saint Macarius:

[1] هذا طقس الكرسي السَّليحي الانجيلي بمدينة الاسكندرية [2] فلما لحقنا الاختلال والحيران حوَّلوا هذا الطقس الى دير القديس ابو مقار لكن ليس هو تام فيه [3] لا فيشيشين يوم الاربعاء ولا المعمودية يوم الجمعة إلّا تقديس الميرون.[30]

[1] This is the rite of the apostolic[31] evangelist throne in the city of Alexandria. [2] But when confusion and disturbance had reached us, they transferred this rite to the Monastery of Saint Macarius, but it is not perfect there. [3] There is no scrutiny[32] on Wednesday, nor baptism on Friday, except for the consecration of the chrism.

29 *Paris BnF Ar. 100* (14th c.), fol. 11v. Cf. Villecourt, "La Lettre de Macaire," 37–38.

30 *Paris BnF Ar. 100* (14th c.), fol. 11v–12r. Cf. Villecourt, "La Lettre de Macaire," 38.

31 The text reads *al-salīḥī* (السَّليحي) from the Syriac meaning apostolic. See Graf, *Verzeichnis*, 61.

32 The manuscript has *fīšīšīn* (فيشيشين), likely a derivative of the Greek ψηφίς: reckoning or calculation, understood here as the scrutiny of the candidates for baptism.

Macarius goes on to mention that he witnessed the rite performed in this vestige of its former splendor–i.e. without any actual catechumens to baptize–during the patriarchate of Cosmas III (AD 920–932), who is possibly the earliest documented patriarch to have consecrated the chrism in Scetis rather than in Alexandria.[33] This however does not mean that the transfer of the gifts described earlier was also excised out of the rite, although a more detailed discussion of the dating of this practice based on the witness of the *Letter of Macarius is* warranted.

That the explanatory gloss, presumably added at the time of copying after AD 1346, speaks of the pre-anaphoral transfer as an extinct custom among the Copts should come as no surprise. As was shown previously, both in Egypt and in Ethiopia, triple-altar churches began appearing in the tenth century and the twelfth century respectively. By the mid-fourteenth century, placing the gifts elsewhere and transferring them before the anaphora (the old ordo) was no longer feasible, a reality that is confirmed below through textual evidence when the new ordo is discussed. But what can one make of Macarius' own words, which mention the old ordo twice? The first passage speaks clearly of the way things were "in the first generation," and that the custom developed "at that time" to dismiss the catechumens before the transfer of the gifts. This strikes one not as a detailed account of the Coptic liturgy per se, but as a general impression of an idealized golden age, the olden days so to speak. Based on this reference alone, one cannot claim that the old ordo necessarily persisted until the tenth century, or even shortly before. However, the good news is that had there never been a pre-anaphoral transfer of gifts in Egypt, Macarius would not have mentioned this in the first place, a remark not even needed for his immediate topic.

The second reference, the detailed description of the rite as performed in Alexandria, provides more information. Twice, Macarius emphasizes that this rite was performed in the church of the Angelion, one of the ancient cathedrals of Alexandria. This church was built around the time of Patriarch Theodosius I (AD 535–567). It later fell into disrepair and was renovated by Patriarch Isaac I (AD 686–689).[34] However, the same account presupposes the existence of a large crowd of catechumens to be baptized and chrismated at the conclusion of the rites. If the entire account were to be understood as

33 Al-Maqārī, *Sirr al-rūḥ al-qudus,* 187. Roshdi W.B. Dous assumes the earliest consecration in Scetis to have been done by Macarius I (AD 932–952), the successor of Cosmas III. See Roshdi W.B. Dous, "History of Making the Holy Chrism in the Coptic Orthodox Church since Pope Athanasius (326–378) until Pope Shenouda the 3rd (1971–)," *Hallesche Beiträge zur Orientwissenschaft* 44 (2007): 27–63, here 39.

34 Aziz S. Atiya, "Alexandria, Historic Churches in," *CE,* 1:92b–95b.

having taken place after the seventh-century restoration of the church, it would be difficult to picture crowds of people joining the Coptic Church after centuries of the Chalcedonian conflict, and the Arab conquest of AD 642. In fact, even in Byzantium, which technically remained a Christian empire for much longer, there was already no organized adult catechumenate by the seventh century.[35] Thus, contrary to Athanasius al-Maqārī's hasty judgement,[36] it is again difficult to take the description by Macarius as an accurate historical account of Alexandrian cathedral rite given its historical inconsistency. In all likelihood, no large group of catechumens was ever baptized in the Angelion church post-seventh century.

Although the information in *The Letter of Macarius* cannot be dated confidently to the tenth century, one can still draw the following conclusions. Surely, such a transfer must have existed in medieval Egypt for Macarius to even suggest it, even if he may have had no first-hand experience of it. This is consistent with the evidence presented so far. Textual, comparative, and architectural evidence presented above all witnesses in the aggregate to placing the gifts elsewhere at first before eventually transferring them to the altar. Judging from the architectural developments in Egypt, one can even venture a hypothesis that the old ordo persisted until some time before Macarius, perhaps around the eighth century. This is because the firmest dating point is the introduction of triple-altar churches in the tenth century. It is likely that an abandonment of the pastophoria—such a traditional feature of church architecture—would not have been considered an option had they been still needed for such an important element in the liturgical rites, the preparation of the gifts. In other words, the evidence allows for the following development: 1. The old ordo likely lasted until ca. eighth century, 2. Between the eighth and tenth centuries the new ordo was slowly stabilizing, although at least learned clergymen such as Macarius knew of the older system, and finally, 3. By the tenth century, triple-altar churches emerge, reusing space that had already become more or less unused.

[35] Robert F. Taft, "Catechumenate," in *The Oxford Dictionary of Byzantium*, ed. Alexander P. Kazhdan, et al., vol. 1 (New York: Oxford University Press, 1991), 390. For more on the disappearance of the catechumenate in East and West, see Maxwell E. Johnson, *The Rites of Christian Initiation: Their Evolution and Interpretation*, rev. ed. (Collegeville, MN: Liturgical Press, 2007), 259–264. Although liturgical texts in the East, such as the ninth or tenth century Armenian rite of baptism and the fifth–eighth century *Georgian Lectionary* of Hagiopolite provenance still mention a lengthy adult catechumenate, it is likely that such references are merely vestiges of ancient practice. See Ibid., 277.

[36] Al-Maqārī, *Sirr al-rūḥ al-qudus*, 168.

1.5. The Transfer of the Gifts in East and West

Following the same methodology as the previous section, it would likewise be instructive to provide a general overview of the history of the transfer of the gifts in the neighboring traditions, namely, the Syro-Antiochene, Byzantine, and Ethiopian traditions. Among these, the Byzantine and Armenian Rites stand unique in having retained until today a pre-anaphoral transfer of gifts, greatly embellished by pomp and ritual into what is today called the Great Entrance. However, far from representing a Byzantine peculiarity, it will be shown soon that the Syrian and Ethiopian Rites as well used to observe the same custom of a pre-anaphoral transfer. That is, before ritual developments in each tradition–as in the Coptic Rite–spelled the demise of this once universal practice.

1.5.1. The Southern Egyptian Tradition

Unfortunately, extant sources of the Southern Egyptian liturgy do not provide very much in the question of the transfer of gifts. The so-called Great Euchologion of the White Monastery, the only Euchologion from this monastery collected and published so far, consists mainly of anaphoral prayers, providing no information on the preparation of the gifts or the pre-anaphoral rites. The manuscript collection of the Monastery of Archangel Michael in al-Ḥamūlī, preserved now in the Morgan Library and Museum in New York, contains no Euchologia at all, which unfortunately leaves a significant lacuna in our knowledge of Southern Egyptian rituals of the Eucharist.

Nonetheless, evidence from fragments of *typika* from the White Monastery may be the only subtle evidence known at this point for a pre-anaphoral transfer of gifts in that region. The term *typikon* in scholarship on Sahidic liturgy refers to manuscripts giving only the incipits of biblical readings and chants for each liturgical celebration.[37] One such typikon fragment, *RMO Copt. 85 (Insinger 40)*, is composed of four sheets of paper providing incipits for biblical readings and chants for various days of the year.[38] The chants are often taken from the psalms. Each chant incipit is assigned a title corresponding to the time in the service it is to be chanted. A common sequence of chant incipits is: 1. For the greeting (i.e. during the kiss), 2. For the bread, and 3. For the peace. These chants labeled "the bread" are of

37 Atanassova, "The Primary Sources of Southern Egyptian Liturgy," 76–78, 93–95.

38 W. Pleyte and P.A.A. Boeser, *Manuscrits coptes du Musée d'Antiquités des Pays-Bas à Leide* (Leiden: E.J. Brill, 1897), 217–228. I owe my knowledge of this type of chant in the White Monastery typika to my colleague Ágnes T. Mihálykó, both during the The Seventh International Congress of the Society of Oriental Liturgy, 9–14 July, 2018, Prešov, Slovakia and subsequently by providing the relevant literature.

particular interest. The heading is usually a variation of the Greek ἄρτος, with or without the Coptic definite article. Possibilities include, ⲁⲣⲧⲟⲥ, ⲡⲁⲣⲧⲟⲥ, ⲡⲁⲣⲧ, and even the highly irregular ⲁⲣⲧⲟⲡⲟ.[39]

Unfortunately, the date of this fragment is uncertain, though based on the use of paper and the script it is likely anywhere between the twelfth and thirteenth centuries.[40] No complete text of any of the chants indicated in this typikon fragment are known from other sources. The incipits are mostly in Greek, with some taken from the following psalms: Psalms 18:14, 117:15. Other incipits either refer to non-scriptural hymnography or are two vague to point clearly to a biblical psalm. At any rate, the most remarkable fact about these *artos* chants is precisely their consistent location in each sequence of chants for any given day. The incipits come after a chant for the kiss of peace—itself analogous to the *aspasmos* chants common in the Northern Egyptian liturgy and the received tradition for the same purpose—and is clearly related in some fashion to the eucharistic bread. Thus, it is highly likely that such artos chants witness to a transfer of the eucharistic gifts at this point in the pre-anaphora, shortly after the exchange of the kiss.[41] If the dating of this typikon fragment is correct, it would be a quite late testimony of the pre-anaphoral transfer of the gifts, a practice that the *Letter of Macarius* implies was already extinct in the tenth century. One possibility of course is that the Southern Egyptian liturgy may have been ritually conservative, holding on to a transfer and its associated chants long after it had become extinct in the North. Another possibility is that this particular manuscript may have been copied from an earlier source and thus transmits incipits for chants no longer executed. The last possibility may explain the absence of these artos chants in other Sahidic typikon fragments in the same collection.

39 Ibid., 218–219, 220, 223–226, 228.

40 Based on knowledge of the manuscript library of the White Monastery, it is thought that the use of paper for manuscript production generally began after the eleventh century. I am grateful for Alin Suciu and Diliana Atanassova for sharing their expert opinion on the possible date of this fragment.

41 For a brief discussion of the psalm selections in this and other typikon fragments, see Hans Quecke, "Psalmverse als »Hymnen« in der koptischen Liturgie?" in *Christianisme d'Egypte: Hommages à René-Georges Coquin*, ed. [Jean-Marc Rosenstiehl], Cahiers de la Bibliothèque copte 9 (Paris: Éditions Peeters, 1995), 101–114, esp. 108–110. See also the brief discussion with comprehensive references in Ugo Zanetti, "La liturgie dans les monastères de Shenoute," *BSAC* 53 (2014): 167–224, here 213. Zanetti also suggests a pre-anaphoral transfer as the likely context for these chants, though he also suggests the prayer of the fraction in the pre-communion rites as another possibility.

1.5.2. The Syro-Antiochene Tradition

The oldest evidence from the region of Syria-Antioch for a solemn pre-anaphoral transfer of gifts can be found in the *Mystagogical Catecheses* of Theodore of Mopsuestia, believed to have been delivered in Antioch before AD 392.[42] In Theodore's description, the simple and pristine transfer of gifts already seen in Justin Martyr and *The Apostolic Tradition* has given rise to a more solemn affair. It was still only performed by the deacons, but was understood with reference to the burial procession of Christ and the deposition of his body on the altar/tomb.[43] Similarly, the *Liturgical Homilies* of Ps.-Narsai (ca. 6th c.) speak of the deacons carrying the paten and the chalice to the altar with the same crucifixion motif.[44] From the same general time period, one may also add the witness of *The Apostolic Constitutions* and the *Testamentum Domini* mentioned earlier.[45]

This relative clarity in the sources of earlier centuries soon gives way to a multiplicity of conflicting information after the fifth century. At some point in its historical development, the West-Syrian tradition underwent the same shift encountered in the Coptic Rite from the old ordo to the new ordo. First, the sixth-century liturgy described in *Codex Syr. 303* (8th–9th c.) of *Bibliotheca Rahmani* still witnesses to a pre-anaphoral transfer of gifts.[46] However, Patriarch Mar Rahmani himself dated the ritual shift to the sixth century, based on certain canons attributed to John of Tella (6th c.), which describe a deposition of the gifts on the altar by the deacons at the very beginning of the liturgy.[47] Decades later, Gabriel Khouri-Sarkis argued initially that the shift occurred much later, and that the old ordo in fact persisted until the thirteenth century, deploring the shift in ritual and the new ordo of the Syrian Rite as "*une période vraiment sombre de leur histoire.*"[48] Ironically, Khouri-Sarkis completely changed his position later, arguing for a very early change in the rite.[49] The debate was nearly settled thanks to the work of Pierre-Edmond Gémayel, who in 1965

42 Taft and Parenti, *Il Grande Ingresso*, 129.

43 Ibid., 133.

44 Ibid., 134.

45 See Chapter 1, Section 2.1 and 2.6.1.

46 Taft and Parenti, *Il Grande Ingresso*, 138–140.

47 Ignatius Ephraem Rahmani, *Les liturgies orientales et occidentales, étudiées séparément et comparées entre elles* (Beirut: Patriarcale Syrienne, 1929), 149–150. Cf. Stéphane Verhelst, "La déposition des oblats sur l'autel en Syrie-Palestine. Contribution à l'histoire de la prothesis," *OC* 82 (1998): 184–203, here 184.

48 Gabriel Khouri-Sarkis, *La Liturgie syrienne. Anaphore des douze apôtres* (Paris: Mission Syrienne, 1950), 9. Cf. Verhelst, "La déposition des oblats," 185.

49 Gabriel Khouri-Sarkis, "L'anaphore syriaque de s. Jacques. Notes," *L'Orient Syrien* 7 (1962): 287–296, here 287. Cf. Verhelst, "La déposition des oblats," 185.

published his study of the Maronite foremass, in which he argued that the new ordo is possibly older than the tenth or eleventh centuries.[50] However, as Stéphane Verhelst later remarked, a more detailed analysis of the dating of the pertinent documents can nuance Gémayel's conclusions.

First, the authenticity of the six canons attributed to John of Tella (6th c.), which describe the new ordo, were contested by Verhelst, who concluded based on the canons' manuscript transmission and their absence in certain canonical collections that they are in fact from the ninth or tenth century at the earliest.[51] This should come as no surprise given other witnesses of the Syrian tradition. For example, the *De oblatione* of John of Dara (9th c.), while it does not explicitly mention when the gifts were placed on the altar, already speaks of the eucharistic vessels and veils at the very beginning of the text. This leads one to conclude that the gifts–and related paraphernalia–were likely already placed on the altar from the start.[52] The commentary by Moses bar Kepha (9th–10th c.) does mention a procession of the gifts from the altar to the nave and back to the altar. This is clearly a relic of the older procession of the gifts from the prothesis pastophorion to the altar, now instead beginning and ending at the same spot.[53]

Perhaps the most informative evidence regarding West-Syrian changes in the transfer of gifts comes from Severus of Antioch (6th c.). In a letter to Caesaria the Patrician during his period of exile in Egypt (AD 518–538), Severus wrote, "The veil therefore which, before the priest approaches, hides what is set forth and is removed after his entry, manifestly cries by the mouth of the facts themselves that the mystery [...] by means of this spiritual and rational priestly ministration reveals Christ."[54] Commenting on this passage, Verhelst convincingly argued that the gifts had been placed on the altar by deacons in the very beginning of the liturgy, according to what I have termed here the new ordo.[55] Surprisingly, Severus seems to have also known of the old ordo. In another letter addressed to Photius and Andrew, archimandrites of the monasteries in Caria, Severus provides ample details on the pre-anaphoral rites, especially regarding the

50 Pierre-Edmond Gémayel, *Avant-Messe maronite. Histoire et structure*, OCA 174 (Rome: Pontificium Institutum Orientalium Studiorum, 1965), 160–175.

51 Verhelst, "La déposition des oblats," 190.

52 Ibid., 196.

53 R. H. Connolly and H. W. Codrington, *Two Commentaries on the Jacobite Liturgy by George Bishop of the Arab Tribes and Moses Bār Kēpha: Together with the Syriac Anaphora of St. James and a Document Entitled the Book of Life* (Oxford: Williams & Norgate, 1913), 16–17 (English), 7 (Syriac).

54 Ernest Walter Brooks, ed., *A Collection of Letters of Severus of Antioch from Numerous Syriac Manuscripts*, vol. 2, PO 14 (67) (Turnhout: Brepols, 2003), 256.

55 Verhelst, "La déposition des oblats," 189.

dismissal of the catechumens. After the dismissal, he writes, "Further, when the holy symbols that are consecrated in the mysterious sacrifice are about to be brought out into the church, and to be placed on the holy altar, the first of the deacons, looking out of the door of the deacons' chamber, utters the fearful and awful words, 'No catechumen, no possessed person, no one that is incapable'."[56] The only possible explanation for such a discrepancy, according to Verhelst, is that Severus in fact knew of both ordos, indicating that the period of transition in the West-Syrian Rite took place some time during Severus' exile in Egypt between AD 518 and 538.[57] Writing in the same year, Baby Varghese also suggested the sixth century as a likely juncture for this shift.[58]

1.5.3. The Byzantine Tradition

In Constantinople, as mentioned previously, the eucharistic gifts were deposited in the exterior round structure called the skeuophylakion, which stood to the northeast of Hagia Sophia. In fact, as Robert Taft has clearly shown, the skeuophylakion is where everything began and ended: the deposition of the gifts, the storage of the vessels and vestments, the vesting of the clergy, and the ultimate return of the clergy carrying the mysteries after communion.[59]

Turning now to the procession itself, the earliest Constantinopolitan evidence for a Great Entrance procession appears in the *Sermo de paschate et de ss. eucharistia* attributed to Patriarch Eutychius (AD 552–565, 577–582), who speaks of a procession by deacons accompanied by a chant.[60] Explicit reference to the pre-anaphoral rites appears in the *Mystagogia* of Maximus the Confessor. Although mostly lacking rubrics, as most Euchologia tend to be, the oldest Byzantine Euchologion *BAV Barberini Gr. 336* (8th c.) is clear on the Great Entrance, mentioning also the accompanying chant and

[56] Ernest Walter Brooks, ed., *The Sixth Book of the Select Letters of Severus Patriarch of Antioch in the Syriac Version of Athanasius of Nisibis*, vol. 2 (Translation) pt. 1 (Oxford: Williams & Norgate, 1903), 187–188. The Syriac text can be consulted in Ernest Walter Brooks, ed., *The Sixth Book of the Select Letters of Severus Patriarch of Antioch in the Syriac Version of Athanasius of Nisibis*, vol. 1 (Text) pt. 1 (Oxford: Williams & Norgate, 1902), 209–210.

[57] Verhelst, "La déposition des oblats," 189.

[58] Baby Varghese, "Early History of the Preparation Rites in the Syrian Orthodox Anaphora," in *Symposium Syriacum VII: Uppsala University, Department of Asian and African Languages, 11–14 August 1996*, ed. René Lavenant, OCA 256 (Rome: Pontificio Istituto Orientale, 1998), 127–138, here 131.

[59] Taft and Parenti, *Il Grande Ingresso*, 356.

[60] *De paschate et ss. eucharistia* 8 (CPG 6939) (PG 86.2: 2400–2401). See Taft and Parenti, *Il Grande Ingresso*, 144.

the *Proskomide* prayer.[61] Unlike Syro-Antiochene sources that speak only of a carrying of the gifts or their deposition on the altar, Constantinopolitan sources are clear on calling this an entrance, which is accurate given that the skeuophylakion was an external structure, necessitating a procession from outside Hagia Sophia to bring in the gifts.[62]

In fact, aside from embellishments in the ritual and its interpretation, the most profound change to the Byzantine transfer of gifts was not *when* it was done, but *whence*. Eventually, the simpler idea of placing the gifts inside the church in a prothesis pastophorion won out over the skeuophylakion, which was surely more expensive to build. By the fourteenth century, *De officiis* of Ps.-Kodinos describes an imperial liturgy, which Taft understood to mean that the gifts were placed inside the church.[63]

1.5.4. The Ethiopian Tradition

An overview of Ethiopian church architectural history vis-à-vis the apsidal pastophoria was presented in the previous chapter, showing their evolution into altar rooms around the twelfth century. It was also briefly shown that the openings of these pastophoria fluctuated throughout their history, opening to the nave only, to the apse only, or to both as the case may be. It is based on this fluctuation in the architectural disposition of ancient Ethiopian churches that hypotheses can be made regarding the procession of the gifts itself; hypotheses, which here can also be extended to Coptic usage. This is especially helpful because textual evidence is lacking in the Ethiopian tradition anterior to the shift from the old ordo to the new ordo.

In churches where the earlier disposition is encountered, a procession of the gifts would have had to exit into the nave before approaching the central apse. This paints an image reminiscent of the pristine transfer procession encountered practically everywhere in the East at various points and is consistent with the fact that it is the oldest churches that display such an arrangement. Slightly later, Fritsch tells us, some innovations began to develop, shielding this procession from the view of the people. At Gāzēn (East-Təgray) in the early Middle Ages, a passage was made through the wall screening the area immediately in front of the northeastern pastophorion, allowing the procession to go directly to the apse without passing in full view of

[61] Stefano Parenti and Elena Velkovska, eds., *L'Eucologio Barberini gr. 336*, 2nd rev. ed., BEL.S 80 (Rome: Edizioni Liturgiche, 2000), 62–63 (Greek), 265–266 (Italian), section 12–13.

[62] Taft and Parenti, *Il Grande Ingresso*, 360–361.

[63] Ibid., 369.

the congregation.[64] In a similar vein, the church of the Trinity at Gundefru features a window connecting the pastophorion to the sanctuary directly.[65] Fluctuations in the direction of access to the pastophoria continue as explained before, but the final stage witnesses them opening both to the sanctuary and the aisle to the west, as in Giyorgis Zāramā and Wəqro Qirqos.

Based on all this evidence, difficult as it may be to sort out, Fritsch proposes that the changes in architecture may reflect changes in how the procession was performed. In the earliest period, corresponding to the oldest Aksumite churches, the procession may have been performed by deacons and/or presbyters in full view of the congregation, a true procession of the gifts reminiscent of the Byzantine Great Entrance, the West-Syrian procession seen in Moses bar Kepha (9th–10th c.), or in the *Letter of Macarius* (10th c.). The final stage however, with a passageway connecting the pastophorion to the sanctuary directly may have corresponded to a simple fetching of the gifts by the priest, the last vestige of an ancient solemn procession.[66] Fritsch's hypothesis is in fact very useful. Above, it was noted that Scetis monastic churches in the seventh century also had pastophoria that were sharply divided from the central apse, with passageways between the two added later.[67] This is precisely the same pattern found in Ethiopia, and it may indeed point to the same pattern of ritual development. As I demonstrate below from the *Precious Jewel* of Ibn Sabbā' (14th c.), it is precisely such a vestigial bringing of the gifts by the priest alone without any ceremony that is described in that text.

This general overview of the procession of the transfer of gifts in eastern rites was intended to demonstrate one central fact. Whether extant or extinct, every liturgical tradition observed in the East had at one point in its development a pre-anaphoral transfer of gifts, in conformity with ancient sources such as Justin Martyr. This point may seem superfluous and in need of no lengthy proof for anyone except those accustomed to the new ordo, whether they belong to the Syrian, Coptic, or Ethiopian Churches. Indeed, for communities following any of these traditions, a liturgy that starts with anything but the deposition of the gifts would seem strange, and lacking something of paramount importance. However, as the evidence–textual, comparative, and architectural–has demonstrated so far, a pre-

64 Fritsch, "The Preparation of the Gifts," 137.
65 Ibid., 138.
66 Ibid., 140–143.
67 Grossmann, *Christliche Architektur in Ägypten*, 54.

anaphoral deposition of the gifts is the most ancient, universal, and not to mention the most logical usage in the unfolding of the liturgy.

1.5.5. The Roman Tradition

In the previous chapter, the location of the deposition of the gifts was not discussed vis-à-vis the Roman Rite.[68] This is because, as Jungmann tells us, seventh-century Roman practice was for the clergy and their assistants to collect the offerings of the people after the reading of the gospel. First, the pope would approach the nobility accompanied by the archdeacon to receive their offerings of bread and wine. Next, they would proceed to the *confessio* to receive the offerings of high court officials, followed by the women's. Bread offerings were collected in a large cloth, while the wine was poured into a large chalice for the purpose.[69] This practice continued in Rome until approximately the twelfth century, according to the *Ordo ecclesiae Lateranensis*.[70] In the Frankish territories however, a people's offertory procession was the norm since at least the ninth century, according to the Synod of Mainz in AD 813. After the creed, the people assembled in line leading to the altar in order to bring their gifts.[71] Whether the gifts were collected by the clergy directly, or brought in procession by the people, it seems that the western tradition was for the people to withhold their gifts until the appropriate time to present them, in a marked difference from the eastern custom of depositing the gifts beforehand in a special location. Nonetheless, it remains the case that the gifts were indeed brought to the altar immediately before the eucharistic Mass proper, and not before the Scripture readings.

2. THE TRANSFER CHANT

The *Letter of Macarius* mentions that the clergy procession of the transfer of gifts was accompanied by incense and the carrying of candles. It would be logical to assume that a procession of such solemnity and ritual was likely accompanied by a chant of some sort, not unlike the Byzantine Great Entrance chants, and similar chants in other eastern Rites. What follows is an attempt to identify the exact nature of this chant.

68 Here and whenever the Roman Rite is discussed, the details are intended only for the Roman tradition as it was celebrated before the liturgical reforms of the Second Vatican Council (AD 1962–1965).

69 Jungmann, *Missarum Sollemnia*, 2:7.

70 Ibid., 7n30.

71 Ibid., 9.

2.1. The Hymn of the Hosts of Angels

In fact, the fifth-century Ethiopic catechesis *The Order of the Mystery* does mention a chant that accompanied the transfer procession. As seen above (section 1.2), a hymn identified as *The Host of Angels* is said after the dismissal of the catechumens and accompanying the transfer of the gifts.[72] Commenting on this, Emmanuel Fritsch saw in this reference to the "glorification of the hosts of angels" a possible witness to a hymn found today in the Ethiopian liturgy after Our Father:[73]

> [1] The hosts of the angels of the Savior of the world [2] stand before the Savior of the world and [3] encompass the Savior of the world [4] even the body and blood of the Savior of the world. [5] And let us come before the face of the Savior of the world. [6] In faith of him give we thanks to Christ.[74]

Without repeating here the interesting textual history of this post-Our Father hymn in the Ethiopian liturgy, suffice it to say that Fritsch concluded that this hymn is likely of Alexandrian, and even Hagiopolite, origin before appearing in this Ethiopian cathecetical homily. The Alexandrian provenance is simply in line with the overall Alexandrian origin of the liturgy described, in agreement with Brakmann. The Hagiopolite relationship is explained by the fact that the same hymn incipit is found in the Georgian translation of some Hagiopolite transfer chants found in the ancient Georgian *Octoechos*.[75]

This Jerusalem-Alexandria-Ethiopia hypothesis for a chant at the transfer of gifts is perfectly plausible as far as it goes. Further, the White Monastery typikon fragment *RMO Copt. 85* discussed previously seems to suggest an entire repertoire of transfer chants, though unfortunately only the incipits are given. But are these the *only* known candidates for an Egyptian chant at the transfer of gifts? The witness of certain processional chants in the current Coptic Rite would suggest another possibility.

72 Fritsch, "The Order of the Mystery," 246 (English), 257 (Geʿez). Cf. Colin, *Le Synaxaire éthiopien*, 220–221. See also Beylot, "Sermon éthiopien anonyme sur l'eucharistie," 90 (Geʿez), 109 (French).

73 Fritsch, "The Order of the Mystery," 218–219.

74 *LEW*, 235.

75 The connection was first noted by Brakmann and recently re-echoed by Fritsch. For the Georgian *Octoechos*, see Charles Renoux, "L'hymne des saints dons dans l'Octoéchos géorgien ancien," in *Θυσία αἰνέσεως. Mélanges liturgiques offerts à la mémoire de l'Archevêque Georges Wagner (1930–1993)*, ed. Job Getcha and André Lossky, Analecta Sergiana 2 (Paris: Presses Saint-Serge, Institut de théologie orthodoxe, 2005), 293–314, here 308.

2.2. Coptic Processional Psalms

In the current Coptic Rite, the clergy and assistants execute a procession around the altar carrying the gifts, which follows the selection of the bread by the celebrant and precedes its deposition on the altar. This procession is discussed in chapter 4 and is a relic of the ancient transfer procession from the northeastern pastophorion. In the current rubrics, the chanters are to execute one of a few psalm selections during this procession, depending on the season. The psalm verse indicated for all fasting days (except the weekdays of Lent) and Saturdays and Sundays of Lent is, "For the thought of man confesses you, and the remainder of the thought shall keep a feast to you," (Ps 75:11) followed by the following petition, "Accept unto you the sacrifices (ⲛⲓⲑⲩⲥⲓⲁ) and the offerings (ⲛⲓⲡⲣⲟⲥⲫⲟⲣⲁ)."[76]

Admittedly, there is no textual evidence that would allow dating this hymn prior to the fifteenth-century *Ritual Order* of Gabriel V,[77] thus it cannot be ascertained that it was in use in the old ordo. However, the idea expressed in the psalm verse emphasizes that the thought of man at this point confesses God, and the remainder—or all—the thought celebrates him. One cannot help but see a connection here with the Byzantine Cherubicon's theme: "Let us lay aside all earthly cares". This emphasis on leaving behind any other concern and focusing the attention solely on the Eucharist seems very appropriate immediately before the anaphora. To be fair however, this theme would be also appropriate as part of the entrance rites or the *accessus ad altare* within the new ordo, which, if in fact the case, would mean these psalm selections may have been adopted only after the shift to the new ordo and have always been chanted in their current location. Certainly, the argument from the theme of the psalm selections *alone* could not be decisive, though the theory that such selections may have functioned in the pre-anaphoral transfer of the old ordo cannot be ignored.

During the weekdays of Lent, the following psalm verse is prescribed: "I enter into the sanctuary of God, before the face of God my God, who gives joy to my youth. Remember O Lord David and all his meekness" (Ps 42:4; 131:1). Once again, the chant is mentioned in the *Ritual Order* and therefore cannot be attributed with certainty to the old ordo. However, the idea of entrance into the sanctuary would be perfectly appropriate for a transfer of gifts in the pre-anaphora. This idea would be somewhat weakened if the celebrant had already ascended to the altar to prepare it beforehand according to the new

[76] Ṣalīb, ⲡⲓϫⲱⲙ ⲛ̀ⲧⲉ ⲡⲓⲉⲩⲭⲟⲗⲟⲅⲓⲟⲛ, 216–217.

[77] *Paris BnF Ar. 98* (17th c.), fol. 47r. Cf. 'Abdallah, *L'ordinamento*, 173 (Arabic), 363 (Italian).

ordo, not to mention selecting the oblation bread from the holy doors, and commemorating those for whom the Eucharist is offered all while in the sanctuary already.

In addition, manuscripts preserve other processional psalm chants that maintain the same idea of entrance. For example, *Coptic Patriarchate Lit. 73* (AD 1444) includes the following chant for the weekdays of Lent instead:

[1] ⲁⲣⲓⲫⲙⲉⲩⲓ ⲡ̅ⲟ̅ⲥ̅ ⲛ̀ⲇⲁⲩⲓⲇ ⲛⲉⲙ ⲧⲉϥⲙⲉⲧⲣⲉⲙⲣⲁⲩϣ ⲧⲏⲣⲥ [2] ⲙ̀ⲫⲣⲏϯ ⲉⲧⲁϥⲱⲣⲕ ⲡ̅ⲟ̅ⲥ̅ ⲁϥⲧⲱⲃϩ ⲫϯ ⲛ̀ⲓⲁⲕⲱⲃ [3] ϫⲉ ⲁⲛ ⲉⲓⲉϣⲉ ⲛⲏⲓ ⲉ̀ϩⲣⲏⲓ ⲉ̀ϧⲟⲩⲛ ⲉ̀ⲫⲙⲁ ⲛ̀ϣⲱⲡⲓ ⲛ̀ⲧⲉ ⲡⲁⲏⲓ [4] ⲉⲛⲉϣⲉ ⲉ̀ϧⲟⲩⲛ ⲉ̀ⲡⲉϥⲙⲁⲛ̀ϣⲱⲡⲓ ⲛ̀ⲧⲉⲛⲟⲩⲱϣⲧ ⲉ̀ⲡⲓⲙⲁ ⲉ̀ⲧⲁⲛⲉⲕϭⲁⲗⲁⲩϫ ⲟ̀ϩⲓ ⲉ̀ⲣⲁⲧⲟⲩ ⲛ̀ϧⲏⲧϥ ⲁ̅ⲗ̅.[78]	[1] Remember O Lord David and all his meekness, [2] how he swore to the Lord and vowed to the God of Jacob, [3] will I enter into the dwelling of my house? [4] We will enter into his dwelling place, to worship at the place wherein your feet have stood. Alleluia [Ps 131:1–3, 7]

The chant is also attested in later manuscripts of the *tartīb al-bī'a*, such as *Baramūs 6/278* (AD 1514), the *St. Antony Codex* (AD 1661), the *Suryān Monastery Codex* (AD 1698),[79] as well as the *Alexandria Coptic Patriarchate Codex* (AD 1716), and *Coptic Patriarchate Lit. 117* (AD 1910), according to Athanasius al-Maqārī.[80] The chant is no longer used today, despite its similarity to the chant from Psalm 42:4 for the weekdays of Lent mentioned above.

Another alternate chant is found in the *Alexandria Coptic Patriarchate Codex* (AD 1716), and *Coptic Patriarchate Lit. 117* (AD 1910), according to Athanasius al-Maqārī,[81] as well as *Baramūs 6/278* (AD 1514), and the *St. Antony Codex* (AD 1661), according to Bishop Samuel.[82] Since none of these manuscripts were available to me, the text is presented here from Bishop Samuel's edition, which is based on the *Alexandria Coptic Patriarchate Codex* (AD 1716):

ⲁ̅ⲗ̅ ⲁ̀ⲛⲟⲕ ⲇⲉ ⲕⲁⲧⲁ ⲡ̀ⲁϣⲁⲓ ⲛ̀ⲧⲉ ⲡⲉⲕⲛⲁⲓ ⲉⲓⲉ̀ⲓ ⲉ̀ϧⲟⲩⲛ ⲉ̀ⲡⲉⲕⲏⲓ ⲟⲩⲟϩ ⲉⲓⲉ̀ⲟⲩⲱϣⲧ ⲛⲁϩⲣⲉⲛ ⲡⲉⲕⲉⲣⲫⲉⲓ ⲉ̅ⲑ̅ⲩ̅.[83]	But I, according to the abundance of your mercy, will enter into your house and worship before your holy sanctuary. [Ps 5:8]

78 *Coptic Patriarchate Lit. 73* (AD 1444), fol. 170r.

79 Samuel, *Tartīb al-bī'a*, 3:17, 20, 22.

80 Athanasius al-Maqārī, *Ṣawm nīnawa wa-l-ṣawm al-kabīr* [The fast of Nineveh and the great fast], Ṭuqūs aṣwām wa-a'yād al-kanīsa 4.4 (Cairo: Šarikat al-ṭibā'a al-miṣriyya, 2009), 152–153.

81 Ibid.

82 Samuel, *Tartīb al-bī'a*, 3:9, 20, 22.

83 Ibid., 9.

The attribution of any of these psalm chants to the old ordo is admittedly in need of further support, although it cannot be excluded outright. For further support of this hypothesis, the following arguments can be proposed. First, in the case of Psalm 42:4, there is nothing explicit about it that would make it appropriate for the weekdays of Lent. It is possible therefore that the association with Lent is simply an example of the retention of ancient usages in more solemn seasons.[84] If indeed the chanting of Psalm 42:4 or any of the other extinct examples featuring the idea of entrance at the procession around the altar is an ancient custom, it likely pre-dated Gabriel V by a few centuries, since he never mentions anything about it being the proper chant year-round either at his time or previously. This may very well place it at least around the time of the shift to the new ordo was completed by the thirteenth century if not before.

Second, another processional psalm chant prescribed for all non-fasting days, "This is the day the Lord has made, let us rejoice and be glad in it," (Ps 117:24–26) is associated today in current practice with the chanting of a long introductory Alleluia, the so-called *Alleluia al-Qurbān* or *Alleluia of the Offering*. The chant has been part of the rite as early as the *Precious Jewel* of Ibn Sabbāʻ (14th c.), who mentioned it as an introductory chant for the entire service, chanted once the celebrant begins his preparations to vest. In this regard, it is not unlike the analogous *Introit* or the *Offertory* chants of the Roman Mass.[85] Ibn Sabbāʻ adds the detail that the alleluia had various melodies either pensive during fasts, or joyous in feasts.[86] Since the alleluia essentially introduces the appropriate psalm verse for the season, it seems that its chanting lasted throughout the vesting, altar preparation, and the selection of the offering, or else it would have no real relation to the psalm verses chanted at the procession. Although today *Alleluia al-Qurbān* is associated only with the chanting of Psalm 117:24–26 on non-fasting days, there is no reason not to assume similar melodic alleluias likewise preceded the other psalm chants in other seasons, especially given Ibn Sabbāʻ's reference to its various seasonal melodies.

Is it possible that this introductory *Alleluia al-Qurbān* and its accompanying psalm verses one day formed the pristine processional chant accompanying the transfer of gifts in the old ordo? A conclusive

84 This liturgical "law" or phenomenon was popularized by Anton Baumstark. See Baumstark, *Comparative Liturgy*, 27–30. For a recent evaluation of this and others of Baumstark's "laws", together with illustrative examples from the Byzantine Rite, see Taft, "Anton Baumstark's Comparative Liturgy Revisited," 206–208.

85 Jungmann, *Missarum Sollemnia*, 1:324; 2: 27.

86 *Paris BnF Ar. 207* (14th c.), fol. 119r. Cf. Mistrīḥ, *Pretiosa margarita*, 174 (Arabic), 486 (Latin).

answer may be impossible to reach, but one can suggest this to be at least likely compared to the hymn of the hosts of angels found in the *Order of the Mystery.* First, there is the fact that the latter is a non-scriptural text, which tend to be of later adoption into the chant repertoire compared to biblical psalms.[87] In the Byzantine context, Robert Taft has argued that the pristine Great Entrance chant was also a psalm verse, Psalm 23:7–10, plus possibly Psalm 117:26, followed by alleluia as a refrain.[88] This was likely the case before the introduction of the Cherubic hymn in the time of Emperor Justinian I in the second half of the sixth century. The similarity is remarkable here with a psalm verse and alleluia, especially that the second psalm verse (Ps 117:26) is precisely the last verse in the Coptic processional psalm for non-fasting days, by far the most frequently chanted processional chant today, and known commonly as *Alleluia This is the Day* (ⲁⲗⲗⲏⲗⲟⲩⲓⲁ ⲫⲁⲓ ⲡⲉ ⲡⲓⲉϩⲟⲟⲩ). This similarity lends support to the hypothesis that an appropriate psalm verse(s) and alleluia likely formed the ancient chant at the transfer of gifts in the Coptic rite as well.

Furthermore, if one may push the boundaries of this hypothesis further, perhaps one of these psalms in its entirety—Psalm 75, 42, 131, or 117—was chanted, before later being abbreviated into the verses chanted today. The same could have also been the case with the psalm verse incipits in the White Monastery typikon *RMO Copt. 85.* A similar phenomenon occurred also to the Roman *Introit* and *Offertory* chants, which were gradually abbreviated from a full psalm to only a few verses some time between the ninth and eleventh centuries.[89] For the same reasons in the West, this may have also taken place in Egypt due to 1. The development of the lengthy *Alleluia al-Qurbān,* and 2. The eventual demise of the long transfer procession from the pastophorion to a more modest circuit around the altar. The *Alleluia al-Qurbān* itself, a complex and melodic piece with the majority of the musical notes on the initial A of alleluia is likely a later composition in comparison to the simplicity of a biblical psalm. One of course cannot dismiss the possibility that at some later stage the hymn of the hosts of angels may have functioned as a refrain for the psalm and its alleluia, much as the Cherubic hymn of the Byzantine liturgy also functioned as such, before supplanting the psalm altogether. Thus, the evolution of the processional chant at the transfer of gifts may have looked like this:

87 On the development and in many cases the replacement of biblical psalmody with ecclesiastical poetry, see Baumstark, *Comparative Liturgy,* 92–110.

88 Taft and Parenti, *Il Grande Ingresso,* 255.

89 Jungmann, *Missarum Sollemnia* 1:323–324.

1. An entire psalm was chanted. In Northern Egyptian sources, some of these psalms may have been Psalms 75, 42, 117 and/or 131.
2. This was later abridged to only a selection of verses from each.
3. Then, an introductory alleluia chant was added to compensate for the time lost in chanting the entire psalm.
4. Hymns such as the Ethiopic *Hosts of Angels* or the artos hymns of the White Monastery were added.
5. After the shift to the new ordo, the alleluia and accompanying psalm verses were retained, developing specific associations to different seasons.

Admittedly, this theory leaves some questions unanswered. For example, why is there no mention of an alleluia or psalm chant at the transfer of the gifts in the *Order of the Mystery*, a document said to be of fifth-century dating? Two possible reasons come to mind. Although the liturgy described in that source is *generally* of fifth-century dating based on the absence of the Nicene Creed and Our Father, this does not mean that all of its details represent fifth-century practice. It may be that some details were edited to reflect later usage, perhaps at a time when the old ordo was still practiced, yet with some of the accompanying chants having fallen out of use. Another possibility lies in the nature of the document itself. As a catechetical homily for the newly baptized, the *Order of the Mystery* is not an exact diataxis of the Ethiopian liturgy, expected to mention and comment on every liturgical detail. This is particularly the case considering a long-chanted alleluia–the length necessary to last the time it took to execute the transfer procession–which would not have been an element in which the newly baptized could participate or join. In short, arguing against the theory of an alleluia and psalm chant during the transfer based on the *Order of the Mystery* would be an argument from silence, and quite a shaky one at that.

2.3. The Theme of Angels in the Transfer Procession

The inverse may also be asked. If the brief mention to a certain hymn referencing the hosts of angels stands for the pristine Alexandrian transfer chant, can one find traces of this hymn in Coptic sources from the north? Unfortunately, not in the form it is found in the Ethiopian liturgy today after Our Father. In fact, in the Coptic prothesis rite, the theme of angels surrounding Christ is nowhere to be found, and there is no evidence that it ever existed. Nonetheless, Emmanuel Fritsch did point out the similarity between the Ethiopian version of the hymn and some ancient Hagiopolite chants in Georgian. Furthermore, similar references to the hosts of angels, and even the Trisagion of Isaiah 6:3 can be seen in other eastern rites, such as the Armenian

Hagiologies, the Syrian *Refrains of the Mysteries*, as well as other chants in the Chaldean Rite.[90] All of this leads one at least to expect a similar theme somewhere in the Coptic tradition, even if not found today in the prothesis of the new ordo, since elements of the old ordo with its separate preparation and transfer of gifts were combined to form today's new ordo prothesis rite.

In fact, it is not in today's prothesis at all that one can find similar references, but rather still in the original place of the transfer of gifts, in the pre-anaphora. The prayer before the kiss in Coptic BAS mentions that "the hosts of angels give you glory saying, glory to God in the heights, peace upon earth, and joy among men."[91] One can add to this an even more explicit reference found in the chant ⲡⲓⲭⲣⲓⲥⲧⲟⲥ ⲡⲉⲛⲥⲱⲧⲏⲣ (*Christ our Savior*), one of the so-called *aspasmos* chants that follow the prayer of the kiss and are meant to accompany the exchange of the kiss among the people. There are many such chants in the received Coptic repertoire, and this particular one is found prominently in two of the oldest Copto-Arabic Diaconicon manuscripts, *BAV Vatican Copt. 28* (AD 1306) and *BAV Vatican Copt. 27* (15th c.), as only the second of two options for such a chant. The text is identical to that in the *editio typica* provided here:

[1] ⲡⲓⲭⲣⲓⲥⲧⲟⲥ ⲡⲉⲛⲥⲱⲧⲏⲣ ⲁⲣⲓⲧⲉⲛ ⲛ̀ⲉⲙⲡϣⲁ ⲙ̀ⲡⲉⲕⲁⲥⲡⲁⲥⲙⲟⲥ ⲉⲑⲟⲩⲁⲃ ⲛ̀ϩⲣⲏⲓ ϧⲉⲛ ⲛⲓⲫⲏⲟⲩⲓ̀. [2] ϩⲓⲛⲁ ⲛ̀ⲧⲉⲛϩⲱⲥ ⲉ̀ⲣⲟⲕ ⲛⲉⲙ ⲛⲓⲭⲉⲣⲟⲩⲃⲓⲙ ⲛⲉⲙ ⲛⲓⲥⲉⲣⲁⲫⲓⲙ ⲉⲛⲱϣ ⲉ̀ⲃⲟⲗ ⲉⲛϫⲱ ⲙ̀ⲙⲟⲥ. [3] ϫⲉ ⲭⲟⲩⲁⲃ ⲭⲟⲩⲁⲃ ⲭⲟⲩⲁⲃ ⲡⲟ̅ⲥ̅ ⲡⲓⲡⲁⲛⲧⲟⲕⲣⲁⲧⲱⲣ ⲧⲫⲉ ⲛⲉⲙ ⲡⲕⲁϩⲓ ⲙⲉϩ ⲉ̀ⲃⲟⲗ ϧⲉⲛ ⲡⲉⲕⲱⲟⲩ ⲛⲉⲙ ⲡⲉⲕⲧⲁⲓⲟ.[92]	[1] Make us worthy, O Christ our Savior, of your holy greeting in the heavens, [2] so that we may praise you with the Cherubim and the Seraphim, crying out and saying: [3] Holy, Holy, Holy, Lord Pantocrator. Heaven and earth are full of your glory and your honor.

Judging from the thematic agreement with similar chants in other rites, especially the reference in the *Order of the Mystery*, it may indeed be true that a chant referencing the hosts of heaven or the Trisagion was at some point part of the transfer chants in Alexandria and the rest of Egypt. That no such chant can be found today near the procession around the altar in the prothesis may be explained in two ways. First, this procession takes place before any prayers or blessings—such as the *Prothesis Prayer*—have been prayed over the oblations, which may have played a role in diminishing the theme of heavenly liturgy and awe before the mysteries that would otherwise have been the case in the pre-anaphora. Second, this absence can be

90 Taft and Parenti, *Il Grande Ingresso*, 215–220.

91 Ṣalīb, ⲡⲓϫⲱⲙ ⲛ̀ⲧⲉ ⲡⲓⲉⲩⲭⲟⲗⲟⲅⲓⲟⲛ, 298.

92 Ibid., 306–307.

explained also in part by the diminishing length and solemnity of the whole affair. Having gone from a long procession from the northeastern pastophorion to the altar—the type described in the *Letter of Macarius* with such grandeur—to a mere single circuit around the altar in the current rite must have rendered any lengthy procession chants superfluous.

Thus, what may have been one—or even several—compositions referencing the hosts of angels were left in their old place in the pre-anaphora. That the chant presented above intertwines the themes of the kiss with the hosts of angels can be explained by the close proximity of the kiss and the transfer of gifts in their pristine forms, as well as the interdependence of the ideas of reconciliation and offering (Cf. Mt 5:23–24). Meanwhile, according to this hypothesis, the lengthy *Alleluia al-Qurbān* may have been re-purposed into an introductory chant for the entire liturgy, chanted during the altar preparation and selection of the offering, leaving behind only the short psalm verses to be chanted in haste while the priest and assistants circle around the altar. Today, the manner of executing the *Alleluia al-Qurbān* and its accompanying psalm verses is different from the way it is described in the sources. It is explained in more detail in chapter 4.

In the final analysis, one must keep in mind that both the initial rites of the liturgy as well as the pre-anaphoral rites in the old ordo have shared themes of offering, approaching the altar, and preparation for the subsequent rites of either the liturgy as a whole or the anaphora specifically. As such, it is ultimately difficult to sort out definitively what chants and hymns would have belonged originally to the pre-anaphoral rites of the old ordo, and what chants were only adopted after the new ordo, when the gifts came to be placed on the altar during the prothesis rite. In view of this difficulty, the hypothesis presented here regarding the history of the chant at the transfer of the gifts remains only one of various plausible scenarios. These hypotheses rest mainly on the appropriateness of the psalm verses in the Coptic repertoire—both extant and extinct—for the themes of *accessus* and bringing the gifts. Although such appropriateness is by no means conclusive, it nonetheless provides an interesting possibility that should be considered until such time when further evidence may help elucidate this complex issue.

3. THE INTERMEDIATE ORDO

The sources discussed so far have revealed only two ordos: An old ordo by which the gifts were placed in an adjacent room prior to the liturgy to be subsequently transferred in the pre-anaphora, and a new ordo—the current one—by which the gifts are placed on the altar immediately upon their selection in the beginning of the liturgy. There is however evidence of what can only be called an *intermediate ordo*. Such evidence can be seen mainly in the fourteenth-century *Precious Jewel* of Ibn Sabbāʿ. He describes the following, after the celebrant has prepared the altar, placing the eucharistic vessels and veils on it, and recited the appropriate prayers:

[1] ثم بعد ذلك يمضي الى هيكل التقدمة الصغير ويأخذ منه الحمل [2] وينظر فيه خشيةً من أن يكون مشقوق لأن الشق عيب والنص أن يكون حملاً لا عيب فيه [3] وذلك أن هذا القربان هو الخروف الحولي في العتيقة الذي لا عيب فيه.[93]

[1] Then afterwards he goes to the small sanctuary of offering and takes from it the lamb. [2] And he examines it, lest it be cracked, for a crack is a blemish, and the text is that it must be an unblemished lamb.[94] [3] And that is because this oblation is the lamb of one year of age in the Old Testament, in which there is no blemish.

And after explaining the rules regarding an acceptably prepared offering of bread and wine, the author continues:

[1] فاذا وُجِد ما يحتاج اليه من القربان والخمر والبخور والفحم وكل الة القداس إذا وجدها على ما ينبغي جيداً [2] يأخذ القربان ويمسحه كما مُسِح السيد له المجد بالماء قبل تسليمه لسمعان الكاهن [3] ثم يُدَوِره على يديه كدوران سمعان الكاهن به الهيكل [4] ثم يتسلمه الكاهن ويضعه في الصينية التي هي المذود ويلفه بالخرق كما فعلت العذرى عند الولادة [5] فالصينية اولاً بمثال المذود واخيراً بمثال القبر.[95]

[1] When the necessary bread, wine, incense, coal, and all the equipment for the liturgy have been found in good order, [2] he takes the bread, and anoints it as the Lord—to him be glory—was anointed with water before his presentation to Simeon the priest. [3] Then he turns it around in his hands, as Simeon the priest went around the sanctuary with him. [4] Then the priest receives it, places it in the paten, which is the manger, and wraps it with the cloths as the Virgin did at the birth. [5] For the paten is first in the likeness of the manger, and last in the likeness of the tomb.

Although Ibn Sabbāʿ's *Precious Jewel* was written in the mid-fourteenth century, contemporaneous with Ibn Kabar's *Lamp of Darkness* in the 1320s, it describes a ritual transfer of the gifts that is

93 *Paris BnF Ar. 207* (14th c.), fol. 121v. Cf. Mistrīḥ, *Pretiosa margarita*, 179 (Arabic), 488 (Latin).
94 Cf. Exodus 12:5.
95 Ibid., 180.

clearly intermediate from the point of view of ritual development.[96] Emmanuel Fritsch has already noted that Ibn Sabbā' mentioned the so-called sanctuary of the offering, where the priest went to retrieve the offering in the beginning of the liturgy.[97] However, it must be noted here that, though differing from the new ordo which knows no prothesis pastophorion, this description still maintains a transfer of gifts before the liturgy, which is not at all consistent with the old ordo of a pre-*anaphoral* transfer. Since the priest was described earlier as placing the eucharistic vessels and veils on the altar, and since now he is said to place the bread in the paten, it can be safely assumed that the priest retrieved the gifts and returned summarily to the altar, without much fanfare or procession of which to speak.

Thus, one can more accurately categorize Ibn Sabbā''s description as representing an intermediate ordo in terms of ritual evolution, lying somewhere between the old and the new systems. The fact that Ibn Sabbā' mentions this sanctuary of offering at all was noted as well by Alfonso 'Abdallah as a particularity of Ibn Sabbā', which must have fallen into disuse.[98] Although 'Abdallah's scope did not permit for a full treatment of the subject, his brief comment is correct as far as it goes, as will become clear through an examination of witnesses to later stages of the ritual. More recently, Athanasius al-Maqārī discussed this passage in the *Precious Jewel* in his analysis of the prothesis rite and its pristine location. Unfortunately, he makes no distinction between Ibn Sabbā''s description and that of Macarius of Manūf al-'uliyā, that is, between the intermediate ordo and the old ordo.[99]

4. THE NEW ORDO

As seen previously, the fourteenth century gloss in the *Letter of Macarius* already identified the pre-anaphoral transfer of gifts as an extinct custom among the Copts. In fact, a story found in the life of Pope Ḫā'īl III (AD 880–907) witnesses as well to a liturgy celebrated in the Northern Egyptian diocese of Saḫā, in which it would appear that the gifts were placed on the altar already prior to the scriptural

96 This is an important point to keep in mind throughout this work. While I hold that Ibn Sabbā' penned his work in the fourteenth and not the thirteenth century as frequently asserted, on the specific point of the transfer of the gifts he appears to represent an earlier stage of evolution (an intermediate ordo) than that represented by Ibn Kabar and later sources (the new ordo). For other ritual actions discussed throughout this work, the *Precious Jewel* is treated as basically contemporaneous with Ibn Kabar's *Lamp of Darkness* despite their often-different styles and approaches.

97 Fritsch, "The Preparation of the Gifts," 112.

98 'Abdallah, *L'ordinamento*, 83.

99 Al-Maqārī, *Al-quddās al-ilāhī*, 1:285.

readings. The account appears in the biography of Ḫā'īl III in the *History of the Patriarchs* as well as his biography in the Copto-Arabic Synaxarion.[100] During a visit by the pope and his entourage of bishops to consecrate a church in Saḫā, the local bishop delayed his arrival on account of preparing food for the high-profile guests. As the day was ending, the people asked the patriarch, "to bear the oblation (*al-qurbān,* القربان) upon the sanctuary (*al-haykal,* الهيكل), so that the priests might begin reading the books and their interpretation in a quiet and slow manner, until the bishop comes."[101] Upon the arrival of the bishop—described as evil by the narrative—he became angry and berated the patriarch for commencing the liturgy in his diocese without permission. Subsequently, he "went up to the sanctuary (*al-haykal,* الهيكل), and took the oblation (*al-dūrun,* الدورن, Gr = δῶρον)[102] which had been borne into it, and he broke it and threw it down and came out in anger."[103] This subtle detail indicating that the Scriptures were read *after* the bringing of the gifts to the sanctuary is thus another early witness to the new ordo besides the indirect tenth-century witness of the *Letter of Macarius* that the pre-anaphoral transfer was extinct by his time. Even more significant is that this story—if indeed goes back to the ninth/tenth century in the papacy of Ḫā'īl III—antedates the intermediate ordo of Ibn Sabbā' in the fourteenth century.[104] It would seem then that the shift from the old ordo to the new ordo was not uniform in all places, or that at least the so-called intermediate ordo was not followed everywhere.

We find the new ordo further confirmed by the time the *Lamp of Darkness* of Abū l-Barakāt ibn Kabar (14th c.), who provides the following description immediately following the preparation of the altar:

100 René Basset, *Le Synaxaire arabe jacobite (rédaction copte) (IV. Les mois de Barmahat, Barmoudah et Bachons)*, PO 16.2 (78) (Turnhout: Brepols, 1976), 241.

101 *HP*, 2.2:70–71 (Arabic), 103 (English).

102 Graf, *Verzeichnis*, 47.

103 *HP*, 2.2: 70–71 (Arabic), 103 (English).

104 This particular biography, and those of the following nine patriarchs until Šinūda II (AD 1032–1046), were written by Mīḫā'īl al-Damrāwī bishop of Tinnīs in AD 1051. Thus, both in view of the events described as well as the date of composition, the witness from the life of Pope Ḫā'īl III is significant. On the dating and composition of this set of biographies, see Swanson, *The Coptic Papacy*, 43. Swanson is citing the study by Johannes den Heijer. See Johannes den Heijer, *Mawhub ibn Mansur ibn Mufarrig et l'historiographie copto-arabe: Études sur la composition de l'Histoire des Patriarches d'Alexandrie*, CSCO 513, Subsidia 83 (Louvain: Peeters, 1989), 150–153.

[1] ويحضر الحمل ويغسل القس يديه بماء [2] ويمسح القربان بعد تصفحه واختيار ما يصلح منه.[105]

[1] Then he brings the lamb, and the priest washes his hands with water. [2] And he wipes the oblation after inspecting it and choosing what is appropriate from it.

The wording in the younger manuscript *Uppsala O. Vet. 12* (AD 1546) preserves essentially the same meaning: "And he brings the lamb and chooses from it what is suitable."[106] No reference is made here to any other location in which the oblations were kept, or in which this selection of the offering took place. One may argue that Ibn Kabar's silence or brevity do not convincingly point to the new ordo, but it would be difficult indeed to imagine Ibn Kabar, usually very detailed in his description, ignoring to mention such an important detail if there were some kind of procession to bring the offerings. This, and the gloss in the *Letter of Macarius* dating essentially to the same period, point unequivocally to the new ordo, in which the oblation was selected–most likely in the sanctuary area–and immediately placed on the altar from the very beginning of the liturgy.

This is also the same description found in the *Ritual Order* of Gabriel V (15th c.) despite the confusing repetition. First, the priest is said to do the following upon commencing the liturgy:

[1] وبعد ذلك يبتدئ الكاهن إذا اراد الخدمة الطاهرة فانه يتقدم اولاً ينظر القربان الذي يقدمه إن كان مختاراً والخمر ايضاً كما قيل فليكون زكياً لا عيب فيه. [2] و إذا اختاره الكاهن فليضعه على جناح الهيكل الايسر عندما يقف.[107]

[1] And after this the priest begins. If he desires the pure service, he proceeds first to examine the oblation that he is offering, whether it is of good quality, and the wine also as was said, is to be precious without blemish in it. [2] And when the priest has chosen it, he is to place it on the left side of the sanctuary where he stands.

It would seem here that the selection of the offering was executed. However, after the priest had placed the oblation on the altar and prepared the altar itself, the description continues:

105 *Paris BnF Ar. 203* (AD 1363–1369), fol. 203r. Cf. Villecourt, "Les observances," 249.

106 *Uppsala O. Vet. 12* (AD 1546), fol. 182v.

107 *Paris BnF Ar. 98* (17th c.), fol. 45v. Cf. 'Abdallah, *L'ordinamento*, 171–172 (Arabic), 361 (Italian).

[1] يُقَبّل الهيكل ويلتفت الى الغرب ليختار الحمل الذي هو خبز التقدمة. [2] ويستبرىء ذلك جيداً ليكون حملاً حولياً لا عيب فيه. [108]	[1] He kisses the altar and turns to the west to choose the lamb, which is the bread of the offering. [2] And he inspects this well to be a lamb of one year without blemish in it.

Surely, there would be no need for selecting the bread twice, and thus the matter stands in need of explanation. In his analysis of the rite of the prothesis in the fifteenth century, Athanasius al-Maqārī unfortunately did not mention or comment on this peculiarity whatsoever.[109] Roshdi Dous on the other hand mentions this detail in the course of his Modern Greek translation of the instructions of the *Ritual Order*. However, judging from his translation, he seems to understand the initial selection as a simple inspection (βλέπει) according to the literal meaning of the text, without it implying the actual selection of the offering, which is to be performed later.[110] The problem with this simple interpretation however is that it does not explain the placement of the offering on the altar at this point and how there can be a future selection of the offering, when it was already placed on the altar.

This discrepancy may in fact betray a layered nature of the *Ritual Order*. Perhaps in this particular point the text represents the compilation of disparate geographical and historical traditions, differing in the details of the prothesis. Another possible explanation is to consider the economic and political instability at the time of Gabriel V. As Samir Khalil notes, Gabriel V, "faced a difficult period for the Church. Politically Egypt was unstable, assassinations and revolts were frequent...More than any other group, with the possible exception of the Jews, the Copts suffered under these conditions."[111] It is probable then that, suffering from consistent shortages, poverty, and instability, Gabriel V sought to include such a precaution—perhaps common in his time—into his liturgical reforms. One thing is clear, and that is the latter selection following the preparation of the altar is more in line with current practice. It also seems to fit better the overall context of the rite, where the oblation would be placed on the altar after the latter was appropriately prepared by placing all the

108 *Paris BnF Ar. 98* (17th c.), fol. 47v. Cf. ʻAbdallah, *L'ordinamento*, 174 (Arabic), 364 (Italian).

109 Al-Maqārī, *Al-quddās al-ilāhī*, 1:286–287.

110 "ἀρχίζει ὁ ἱερέας ἐάν θέλει νά εἶναι ἁγνή ἡ διακονία, πηγαίνει καί βλέπει τό πρόσφορο τό ὁποῖο θά προσκομίσει, ἐάν εἶναι διαλεκτό καθώς ἐπίσης καί τό κρασί". See Dous, "Η Αλεξανδρινή Θεία Λειτουργία," 54.

111 Samir Khalil, "Gabriel V.," *CE*, 4:1130a–1133a, here 1130a.

appropriate vessels and veils upon it, a ritual process that occupies a considerable part of the next chapter.[112]

Suffice it here to say that by the fifteenth century, the new ordo had clearly gained the upper hand. As the evidence has demonstrated, this was already a reality even a century earlier per the gloss in the *Letter of Macarius*. By the time of Patriarch Gabriel V, sources no longer mention the old ordo or a sanctuary of offering ever having existed. If Gabriel V at least was aware of such an ancient practice, he clearly did not wish to even include it, thereby giving the new ordo a final and decisive victory as the official rite of the Coptic Orthodox Church in the celebration of the liturgy.

5. CONCLUSION

The first two chapters were occupied with exploring the historical origins of the preparation and transfer of gifts in the Coptic Rite. In particular, the focus was on the most profound shift in the order of the Coptic liturgy from a pre-anaphoral transfer of gifts, to a deposition of the gifts in the beginning of the liturgy, which I have given the terms the old ordo and the new ordo respectively. The overarching findings of this analysis show first that no evidence exists for a pre-anaphoral people's procession to bring the gifts to the altar in Egypt. More importantly, the current system of preparing and placing the gifts on the altar from the start is a product of the medieval period, some time between the eighth and thirteenth centuries. This may be judged either as late, from the perspective of general Christian history, or early considering the Coptic Northern Egyptian Rite, whose liturgical manuscripts are mostly younger than the thirteenth century.

This historical examination provides a strong footing from which to proceed to analyze the liturgical units of the prothesis rite according to the new ordo. Moving forward, these historical origins and the terms old ordo and new ordo are referenced continuously, in an effort to properly understand the origins and purpose of the various liturgical units that comprise the current rite of the prothesis in the Coptic eucharistic liturgy.

112 See chapter 3, sections 2–3.

EXCURSUS 1

THE VESSELS AND CLOTHS OF THE COPTIC EUCHARIST

As will be seen in Chapter 3, the rubrics of the altar preparation do not provide precise information on the number and placement of the veils. It would be appropriate at this time to present a list of all the vessels and veils that are involved in the preparation of the altar, before explaining their exact placement. As the eucharistic vessels used in the Coptic liturgy are listed, one will notice their overall adherence and similarity to those of neighboring liturgical traditions of the Christian East, the majority of which must have been in use since late antiquity. Exceptions to this general observation include the communion spoon, the subject of much speculation since it is closely connected to the manner of administering communion in various traditions.[1] Another exception is the so-called chalice throne, a hollow box that functions as a stand for the chalice throughout the celebration of the liturgy and is unique to the Coptic Rite.[2]

When appropriate, some brief historical remarks on the appearance of these vessels in the Coptic tradition will be presented. The following descriptions of eucharistic vessels is based on the list provided by Burmester in his monumental work on the Coptic Church and its rituals:[3]

1 For the history of the use of communion spoons for the administration of communion in the Byzantine Rite with references to other eastern traditions, see Robert F. Taft, "Byzantine Communion Spoons: A Review of the Evidence," *Dumbarton Oaks Papers* 50 (1996): 209–238. This was later updated in Taft, *Communion, Thanksgiving, and Concluding Rites*, 266–315.

2 Youhanna Nessim Youssef, "The Ark/Tabernacle/Throne/Chalice-Stand in the Coptic Church (Revisited)," *Ancient Near Eastern Studies* 48 (2011): 251–259.

3 Burmester, *The Egyptian Church*, 23–29. A lengthier, though not as clear, discussion chapter on Coptic eucharistic vessels appears also in Butler's work. See Butler, *The Ancient Coptic Churches*, 2:37–63. Finally, references are made occasionally to Braun's classic work on the subject of eucharistic vessels in East and West, Joseph Braun, *Das christliche Altargerät in seinem Sein und in seiner Entwicklung* (Munich, M. Hueber, 1932).

1. PATEN

Burmester gives the Greek name δίσκος to the ceremonial plate used for holding the eucharistic bread. Yet here as in all other instances he provides no literary source for this name. In fact, as James Drescher remarks, the use of δίσκος is very rare in Sahidic, and he provides compelling evidence from hagiographical texts that ⲧⲣⲁⲡⲉⲍⲁ was actually used for the paten.[4] That the Greek δίσκος was hardly—if ever—used in Egypt for the paten is further supported by papyri and ostraca. Examining lists of liturgical objects from churches and monasteries ranging from the fourth to the eighth century, Georg Schmelz could confirm that patens are not mentioned, whether by any special term or otherwise.[5]

In Arabic, it is simply referred to as *al-ṣīniyya* (الصينية), a general term that means tray or platter, usually china or porcelain.[6] Burmester also accurately describes it as a flat circular dish, about 23 cm in diameter, with a short edge, a depth of 3.5 cm, and no foot.[7] These dimensions however may vary in reality depending on the size of the congregation and the oblation bread needed. Butler gives a similar description, adding that the Coptic patens correspond closely to the earliest examples in the West.[8]

As can be expected of such an integral vessel to the celebration of the Eucharist, the paten is consecrated with holy chrism accompanied by the recitation of specific prayers. This has been the case at least since the thirteenth-century *Order of the Priesthood*, where the text mentions the paten as one of seven consecrated vessels, compared to another seven pieces of altar equipment that receive no consecration. The text also shows that by then the paten had already acquired particular significance as, "the likeness of the manger during [Christ's] childhood, and in the likeness of the wooden ark, wherein are the Scriptures."[9]

2. STAR

Not mentioned here in the rubrics, the *asteriskos* as it is called in Greek, meaning star, consists of two metal bands crossed at right

4 James Drescher, "Graeco-Coptica," *Le Muséon* 82 (1969): 85–100, here 98–100.

5 Georg Schmelz, *Kirchliche Amtsträger im spätantiken Ägypten nach den Aussagen der griechischen und koptischen Papyri und Ostraka*, Archiv für Papyrusforschung und verwandte Gebiete 13 (Munich: K. G. Saur, 2002), 102.

6 Hans Wehr, *A Dictionary of Modern Written Arabic (Arabic-English)*, ed. J. Milton Cowan, 4th ed. (Wiesbaden: Otto Harrassowitz, 1979), 533.

7 Burmester, *The Egyptian Church*, 24.

8 Butler, *The Ancient Coptic Churches*, 2: 39.

9 Assfalg, *Die Ordnung des Priestertums*, 15 (Arabic), 84 (German).

angles and riveted together.[10] Butler calls it a dome, a direct translation of its Arabic name *al-qubba* (القبة).[11] Its function is to fit on top of the paten and prevent the eucharistic veil covering the paten from touching the oblation bread.

3. CHALICE

Three papyri containing inventories of ecclesiastical objects clearly include silver chalices judged to be eucharistic by Georg Schmelz. Two of these papyri date to the fifth or sixth century, constituting one of the earliest witnesses to the chalice as a particular liturgical object.[12] Although Burmester gives the Coptic chalice a diameter of 10 cm,[13] this again varies in reality depending on the parish, the size of the congregation, and their financial means. It is called in Coptic ⲡⲓⲁⲫⲟⲧ or by the Greek loanword ⲡⲟⲧⲏⲣⲓⲟⲛ (Gr = ποτήριον), while in Arabic it is referred to as *al-kā's* (الكأس) a word used for any common stemmed glass.[14] Today, chalices are frequently made of silver or gold. However, Butler points out that glass chalices were used in the past, particularly at times of persecution when vessels were frequently stolen, such as during the great persecution ca. AD 700.[15] The author of *The Order of the Priesthood* regards the chalice as symbolic of the vessel of manna (Ex 16:33).[16]

4. CHALICE THRONE

Burmester gives this object two possible names in Coptic, the Greek loan word ⲕⲓⲃⲱⲧⲟⲥ (Gr = κιβωτός), and the natively Coptic word ⲑⲓⲟⲕⲉⲗⲓ, albeit without any source for the latter.[17] This altar object is a box of four or more sides, approximately the height of the chalice, with a round hole on the top. The sides are decorated with various iconographic scenes. During the preparation of the altar, the chalice is placed inside this box and remains there until communion.

Among all the other eucharistic vessels, the chalice throne is the most uniquely Coptic, having no exact parallel in other traditions. The

[10] Burmester, *The Egyptian Church*, 24. Burmester gives this object the Greek name *aster*, which, strictly speaking, is not used for this liturgical object in Byzantine sources. Cf. Lampe, *A Patristic Greek Lexicon*, 247.

[11] Butler, *The Ancient Coptic Churches*, 2: 39–40.

[12] Schmelz, *Kirchliche Amtsträger*, 102.

[13] Burmester, *The Egyptian Church*, 24.

[14] Wehr, *A Dictionary of Modern Written Arabic*, 808.

[15] Butler, *The Ancient Coptic Churches*, 2: 38.

[16] Assfalg, *Die Ordnung des Priestertums*, 15 (Arabic), 84 (German).

[17] Burmester, *The Egyptian Church*, 24. I have not been able to find any authority in Greek or Coptic lexica of this curious term.

origins of the chalice throne are also unclear. In his article on the chalice throne, Youhanna N. Youssef concluded that this object must be of very recent origin. This was based on the following arguments:[18] The chalice throne appears in *The Order of the Priesthood* as an object that receives no consecration by chrism, which presumably indicates its recent appearance, and its perception as a practical object to protect the chalice, rather than an object of a particular spiritual significance.[19] Additionally, the chalice throne does not appear in Ibn Kabar's *The Lamp of Darkness.* However, it appears in the rubric for a prayer of consecration in the oldest Coptic ordination/consecrations manuscript *Coptic Museum Lit. 253* (AD 1364), although the prayer itself makes no mention of the chalice throne.[20]

It is true that the chalice throne is an interesting object in terms of its unclear age and origin. A particular chalice throne from the church of Saint Mercurius in Old Cairo was dated by Alfred J. Butler to AD 1280,[21] although this dating was adjusted later by Georg Graf to AD 1564/5,[22] and finally corrected again by Linda Langen to AD 1765 based on a closer reading of the colophon on one of its icons.[23] However, iconograpical evidence may in fact demonstrate the existence of chalice thrones much earlier. An eighth-century wall painting in the Red Monastery near Sūhāğ depicts an angel carrying a communion spoon—discussed further below—and a chalice throne.[24]

5. COMMUNION SPOON

The spoon is used in the Coptic Rite to administer the blood to minor orders, the people, as well as for clergy to self-administer the chalice.

18 Youssef, "The Ark," 255.

19 Assfalg, *Die Ordnung des Priestertums,* 15 (Arabic), 84 (German).

20 *Coptic Museum Lit. 253* (AD 1364), fol. 149r.

21 Butler, *The Ancient Coptic Churches,* 1:109.

22 Georg Graf, "Ein alter Kelchthron in der Kirche Abū Sēfēn (mit einer Tafel)," *BSAC* 4 (1938): 29–36.

23 Linda Langen, "A Mysterious Altar-Casket in Abu Sefein Church in Old-Cairo," *BSAC* 28 (1986–1989): 75–79.

24 Dominique Bénazeth, "De l'autel au musée. Quelques objets liturgiques conserves au Musée Copte du Caire," in *Egypt 1350 BC-AD 1800: Art Historical and Archeological Studies for Gawdat Gabra,* ed. Marianne Eaton-Krauss, Căcilia Fluck, and Gertrud J.M. van Loon, Sprachen und Kulturen des Christlichen Orients 20 (Wiesbaden: Ludwig Reichert Verlag, 2011), 35–52, here 35, pl. 3. Cf. Elizabeth S. Bolman, "The Red Monastery Conservation Project, 2006 and 2007 Campaigns: Contributing to the Corpus of Late Antique Art," in *Christianity and Monasticism in Upper Egypt,* ed. Gawdat Gabra and Hany N. Takla, vol. 1, *Akhmim and Sohag* (Cairo: The American University in Cairo Press, 2008), 305–318, here 311, and fig. 25.4.

They are made of the same metal as the paten and chalice and are usually no more than 20 cm long. Burmester gives it two names in Coptic usage, from the Greek, κοχλιάριον and μυστήρ, though he provides no Coptic spelling. Both names are attested in late antique documentary sources, though currently, only the latter is used to refer to the spoon, even in Arabic (المستير, *al-mistīr*).[25] Graf took the latter name to be derived from the Greek μυστήριον, an opinion shared by many in the Coptic community.[26] However, the spoon is identified by the plural μίστρα in the church inventory in *P. Leiden Inst. 13* (7th/8th c.),[27] which points to the etymology of the Arabic *mistīr* rather to the Greek μύστρον, meaning spoon.[28] Contrary to Butler's assertion, the Coptic Church administers communion in both kinds separately, thus using the spoon only to administer the blood.[29] Unfortunately, Robert Taft repeated this same mistake later.[30]

Communion spoons are known to have been in use already during the course of the first millennium AD. In addition to the Red Monastery wall painting depicting a spoon and chalice throne, a graffito on the east wall of Chapel 36 of the Monastery of Apa Apollo in Bawīṭ depicts a priest administering communion from a chalice with a spoon and is dated some time between the sixth and eighth centuries.[31] In addition to the church inventory mentioned above, *P. Leiden Inst. 13* (7th/8th c.), an excavated church treasury in Ballana in Nubia from the fifth century confirms the use of liturgical spoons

25 Burmester, *The Egyptian Church*, 24.

26 Graf, *Verzeichnis*, 105.

27 Schmelz, *Kirchliche Amtsträger*, 103.

28 Henry George Liddell and Robert Scott, *A Greek-English Lexicon*, revised and augmented thoroughly by Sir Henry Stuart Jones with a revised supplement (Oxford: Clarendon Press, 1996), 1157.

29 Butler, *The Ancient Coptic Churches*, 2:40. An exception to this is in giving communion to the sick outside the context of the liturgy, where the body is administered already dipped in blood using the spoon.

30 In his earlier article on communion spoons, Robert Taft observed correctly that the Coptic Orthodox Church uses the spoon, not for intinction, but to administer the blood from the chalice. See Taft, "Byzantine Communion Spoons," 209. Unfortunately, he later reversed his observation intending to correct it, stating instead that the Coptic Orthodox Church uses the spoon to administer the unintincted particle of the body, then the chalice. Cf. Taft, *Communion, Thanksgiving, and Concluding Rites*, 268.

31 Gertrud J.M. van Loon, "The Meeting of Abraham and Melchizedek and the Communion of the Apostles," in *Coptic Studies on the Threshold of a New Millennium*, ed. Immerzeel and van der Vliet, 2:1373–1392, here 1388 (fig. 7). Cf. Bénazeth, "De l'autel au musée," 35n5. The graffito was originally published by Jean Clédat. See Jean Clédat, *Le monastère et la nécropole de Baouit*, vol. 2, Mémoires publiés par les membres de l'Institut français d'archéologie orientale du Caire 39 (Cairo: l'Institut français d'archéologie orientale, 1916), 37 (fig. 25).

at this early date.[32] The spoon also appears in *The Order of the Priesthood*, although it is given no symbolic meaning. The point is made there that the laity partake of the chalice via the spoon, unlike the priests who partake directly of the chalice.[33] In addition, as Braun observes, spoons appear in *The Lamp of Darkness* of Ibn Kabar (14th c.), and the *Ritual Order* of Gabriel V (15th c.) at communion.[34]

6. EUCHARISTIC CLOTHS

Various sizes and shapes of cloths and veils are employed in the Coptic tradition. Burmester divides this general category into four: A paten veil, a chalice veil, several smaller all-purpose veils, which he strangely calls mats, and finally a large cloth used to cover the entire altar called the *prospherin* veil. Both the paten and chalice veils are termed by Burmester ⲙⲁⲡⲡⲁ in Coptic,[35] a term that also occurs in the seventh-century *Life of Isaac*, Patriarch of Alexandria (AD 686–689), described as that "with which he [the priest] held the chalice,"[36] and is a Latin loanword, that likely entered Coptic via Greek.[37] The antiquity of this term in Egyptian usage is further attested in *P. Prag II 178* (5th/6th c.), another inventory of ecclesiastical objects containing the form μαππία.[38]

By the medieval period, the various veils had acquired symbolic significance. In the anonymous treatise titled *Kitāb al-īḍāḥ* (*The Book of Elucidation*), the author reflects on the sacrifice of Christ and its eucharistic content: "So that when we see him [Christ] wrapped on our behalf with cloths and placed in the paten, we may remember that likewise he was wrapped with graveclothes and placed in the tomb on our behalf."[39] This clear passion motif appears also in the treatise *The*

32 Schmelz, *Kirchliche Amtsträger*, 103.

33 Assfalg, *Die Ordnung des Priestertums*, 15 (Arabic), 84 (German).

34 Braun, *Das christliche Altargerät*, 277. See *Paris BnF Ar. 203* (AD 1363–1369), fol. 206r. Cf. Villecourt, "Les observances," 256; *Paris BnF Ar. 98* (17th c.), fol. 70v. Cf. ʿAbdallah, *L'ordinamento*, 197 (Arabic), 381 (Italian). To Braun's sources, one can also add *The Precious Jewel* of Ibn Sabbāʿ. *Paris BnF Ar. 207* (14th c.), fol. 171r. Cf. Mistrīḥ, *Pretiosa margarita*, 277 (Arabic), 538 (Latin).

35 Burmester, *The Egyptian Church*, 23.

36 Porcher, *Vie d'Isaac*, 344.

37 Lampe, *A Patristic Greek Lexicon*, 827.

38 Schmelz, *Kirchliche Amtsträger*, 105.

39 *Paris BnF Ar. 170* (13th c.), fol. 74v. This book is attributed to Sāwīrus ibn al-Muqaffaʿ. Although such attribution is doubtful, the text dates to the thirteenth-century at least, considering the date of its earliest manuscript. See *GCAL*, 2:309–311. Inexplicably, it was published in Cairo later for public readership under the title *Al-durr al-ṯamīn*, the title of another work attributed to Sāwīrus. See Marqus Ǧirǧis. *Al-durr al-ṯamīn fī īḍāḥ al-dīn* [The precious pearl in elucidating the faith], 2nd

Guide to the Beginners, where he writes, "Know that the holy sanctuary is a likeness of the tomb of Christ [...] The clothing of the altar is a likeness of the shroud, the cloths (*al-ḫiraq*, الخرق) are a likeness of the entombment cloths (*al-lafā'if*, اللفايف)."[40] To this passion symbolism is added another layer from the Nativity of Christ in *The Order of the Priesthood*, which explains the veils as, "equivalent to the cloths at [Christ's] death and entombment, and equivalent to the cloths, by which the body of our Lord–to him be glory–was wrapped in the manger."[41]

The development of passion symbolism surrounding the Eucharist, and particularly the altar was also central in Byzantine liturgical commentaries. In the *Historia Ecclesiastica* of Germanus, Patriarch of Constantinople from AD 715–730, one already finds ideas similar to those expressed above: "The altar corresponds to the holy tomb of Christ. On it Christ brought himself as a sacrifice to God the Father through the offering of his body as a sacrificial lamb."[42] Such emphasis on the passion of Christ, particularly in the ritual gestures of the Byzantine prothesis, developed in particular after the transfer of the lance, believed to have been used in Christ's crucifixion, from Jerusalem to Constantinople in AD 614.[43] The effects of these developments in the Byzantine liturgy were felt not only in the manual acts of the prothesis, but also in the interpration of the entire eucharistic liturgy by the famous Byzantine commentators, such as Germanus and others.[44] This marked a clear shift from the earlier

ed. (Cairo, [1992]), 95. On the authorship and dating of the *Book of Elucidation*, see Stephen J. Davis, *Coptic Christology in Practice: Incarnation and Divine Participation in Late Antique and Medieval Egypt*, Oxford Early Christian Studies (Oxford: Oxford University Press, 2008), 230–236; *GCAL*, 2:309–311; Mark N. Swanson, "*Kitāb al-īḍāḥ*," *CMR*, 3:265–269.

40 *BAV Vatican Ar. 117* (AD 1323), fol. 197v. Cf. Graf, "Liturgische Anweisungen," 121.

41 Assfalg, *Die Ordnung des Priestertums*, 15 (Arabic), 84 (German).

42 *Historia Ecclesiastica* 6 (CPG 8023) (PG 98:389). See Paul Meyendorff, St Germanus of Constantinople on the Divine Liturgy: The Greek Text with Translation, Introduction, and Commentary, Popular Patristics Series 8 (Crestwood, NY: St Vladimir's Seminary Press, 1984), 60–61. Meyendorff's text is based on an earlier work by Nilo Borgia, in turn based on BAV Vatican Gr. 790 (14th/15th c.), and Naples Gr. 63 (AD 1526). Meyendorff points out in the introduction that the text published by J.P. Migne in Patrologia Graecae is a corrupt medieval text. See ibid., 11–12.

43 Pott, *Byzantine Liturgical Reform*, 203.

44 The main classical Byzantine liturgical commentators include Maximus the Confessor (7th c.), Nicholas of Andida (11th c.), Nicholas Cabasilas (14th c.), and Symeon of Thessaloniki (15th c.). For the seminal study on the genre of Byzantine liturgical commentaries, see René Bornert, *Les commentaires byzantins de la Divine Liturgie du VIIe au XVe siècle*, Archives de l'Orient Chrétien 9 (Paris: Institut français d'études byzantines, 1966).

anagogical style of interpretation, such as that of Ps.-Dionysius and Maximus the Confessor–traditionally associated with the Alexandrian school of exegesis–to the more typological method associated with later authors, and which was traditionally associated with the Antiochene school.[45] Thus, to see later Coptic tradition likewise echoing the same passion symbolism shows just how such distinctions between the Alexandrian and Antiochene schools were abandoned over time.

Unfortunately, Butler's description of eucharistic veils leaves anyone intimately familiar with the Coptic Rite in confusion. First, he terms the veils mats or plates, although they clearly do not hold anything themselves to merit the term plate. He then writes, "Before the commencement of the mass, the sacred elements are covered with a veil or corporal called (*al-lifāfa*, اللفافة) in Arabic, and ⲡⲓⲡⲣⲟⲥⲫⲁⲣⲓⲛ in Coptic."[46] While it is true that at the end of the prothesis–and thus before the beginning of the Liturgy of the Word–the bread and wine are covered with a large veil called the *prospherin*, this is never referred to in Arabic as *al-lifāfa*, which is only used for small, hand-held cloths. Later, he also remarks that, "The Copts employ only these two eucharistic veils [paten veil and chalice veil]."[47] As remarked above and will be demonstrated further below, the fully prepared Coptic altar is in fact covered with many such veils, often twelve in number.

45 On the Alexandrian and Antiochene schools of exegesis as they are applied to liturgical commentaries, see Robert F. Taft, "The Liturgy of the Great Church: An Initial Synthesis of Structure and Interpretation on the Eve of Iconoclasm," *Dumbarton Oaks Papers* 34–35 (1980–1981): 45–75, here 61–65, reprinted in Robert F. Taft, *Liturgy in Byzantium and Beyond* (Hampshire, UK: Variorum, 1995), 45–75.

46 Butler, *The Ancient Coptic Churches*, 2:45.

47 Ibid., 46.

CHAPTER 3

VESTING AND THE PREPARATION OF THE ALTAR

The analysis now turns to the rite under investigation beginning with the vesting of the clergy and the preparation of the altar, two actions that are essentially components of the *accessus ad altare* of the Coptic liturgy in its present form. While the first two chapters focused on the larger issue of the shift from the old ordo to the new ordo, a process that can only be demonstrated from sources prior the tenth century, the rites examined starting with this chapter are never explicitly described before the sources of the Northern-Egyptian liturgy after the twelfth century. In this chapter, the vesting rite and its historical development is analyzed, while rescinding from analyzing the historical development of Coptic liturgical vestments themselves, a subject already treated elsewhere and not particularly relevant to the analysis of the rite.[1] Afterwards, the Coptic rite of the preparation of the altar is explained, situating it in relation to analogous rites in East and West. Finally, the prayers said during and after the preparation, themselves prayers of *accessus ad altare*, are presented and analyzed in terms of their origins.

1. THE VESTING RITE

In order to present a complete picture of all the ritual gestures associated with vesting, below are the instructions found in the

[1] The most comprehensive treatment of the history of liturgical vestments in the Coptic Church so far appears in Karel C. Innemée, *Ecclesiastical Dress in the Medieval Near East*, Studies in Textile and Costume History 1 (Leiden: Brill, 1992), 15–60. For more recent treatments of the historical evolution of Coptic liturgical vestments, cf. Ramez Mikhail, "Towards a History of Liturgical Vestments in the Coptic Rite: I-Minor Orders, Deacons, and Presbyters," *Coptica* 15 (2016): 55–70; Ramez Mikhail, "Towards a History of Liturgical Vestments in the Coptic Rite: II-Bishops and Patriarchs," *Coptica* 16 (2017): 55–66; Ramez Mikhail, "'And they Shall Stand Bareheaded': On the Historical Development of Liturgical Head-Covering in the Coptic Rite," forthcoming in Proceedings of the Eleventh International Congress of Coptic Studies, Claremont, California, July 25th–30th, 2016.

beginning of the *editio typica* of 1902 in addition to other clarifying notes:

[1] ثم يلبس الكاهن بدلة الكهنوت [2] وهو يقول المزمور التاسع والعشرين أعظمك يارب. [3] وبعده المزمور الثاني والتسعين الرب قد ملك والجمال لبس.[2]

[1] And the priest puts on the vestment of the priesthood, [2] while he says the twenty-ninth psalm, "I will exalt You O Lord," [3] and after it the ninety-second psalm, "The Lord reigns, he is clothed with majesty".

Here, the text adds the following footnote explaining precisely what is to be said before the priest puts on the vestments:

[1] وقبل لبس الكاهن التونية يرشمها ثلاثة رشوم وهو يقول ϧⲉⲛ ⲫ̀ⲣⲁⲛ و ϥ̀ⲥⲙⲁⲣⲱⲟⲩⲧ الخ. [2] ثم يلبسها. [3] وكذلك كل كاهن او شماس اراد التناول يرشم تونيته قبل لبسها. [4] فالكاهن يرشم بيده والشماس يقدمها الى أحد الكهنة فيرشمها له. [5] وان اشترك كاهنان في رشم تونية او جملة توانٍ. او ايضاً في رشم اشياء غير التواني فان أحدهما يرشم الرشمين الاول والثالث ويقول ما يخصهما والاخر يرشم فقط الرشم الثاني ويقول ما يخصه. [6] كما شُرح في رشم درج البخور قبل اوشية بخور عشية.[3]

[1] And before the priest wears the tunic, he signs it three times saying, "In the name," and "Blessed," etc., [2] then he puts it on. [3] And likewise every priest or deacon who wishes to receive communion has his tunic blessed before wearing it. [4] The priest signs it with his hand, and the deacon presents it to one of the priests and he signs it for him. [5] And if two priests participate in signing a tunic or a group of tunics, or also in signing other objects besides tunics, one of them performs the first and third signing saying what appertains to them, and the other performs only the second signing and says what appertains to it, [6] as was explained in the signing of the box of incense before the prayer[4] of the incense of vespers.

These rubrics for blessing the box of incense are provided in full earlier in the Euchologion:

[1] ثم يلتفت الى المذبح ويضع درج البخور مكانه ويضع اصبعه عليه ويقول ϧⲉⲛ ⲫ̀ⲣⲁⲛ ⲙ̀ⲫⲓⲱⲧ ⲛⲉⲙ ⲡϣⲏⲣⲓ ⲛⲉⲙ ⲡⲓⲡⲛⲁ ⲉⲑⲩ ⲟⲩⲛⲟⲩϯ ⲛ̀ⲟⲩⲱⲧ [2] ثم يرشم الدرج بمثال الصليب اولاً ويضع البخور في المجمرة يداً اولى كل ذلك وهو يقول ϥ̀ⲥⲙⲁⲣⲱⲟⲩⲧ ⲛ̀ϫⲉ ⲫϯ ⲫⲓⲱⲧ ⲡⲓⲡⲁⲛⲧⲟⲕⲣⲁⲧⲱⲣ ⲁⲙⲏⲛ. [3] ثم يرشم رشماً ثانياً ويضع البخور يداً ثانية وهو

[1] Then he turns to the altar and places the incense box in its place and puts his finger on it and says: "In the name of the Father and the Son and the Holy Spirit, one God." [2] Then he blesses the box with the sign of the cross first and places the incense in the censer the first time

2 Ṣalīb, ⲡⲓϫⲱⲙ ⲛ̀ⲧⲉ ⲡⲓⲉⲩⲭⲟⲗⲟⲅⲓⲟⲛ, 195–196.
3 Ibid.
4 The manuscript has "اوشية" = Gr εὐχή. Cf. Graf, *Verzeichnis*, 16.

يقول ⲁ̀ϥⲥⲙⲁⲣⲱⲟⲩⲧ ⲛ̀ϫⲉ ⲡⲉϥⲙⲟⲛⲟⲅⲉⲛⲏⲥ ⲛ̀ϣⲏⲣⲓ ⲓⲏ̅ⲥ̅ ⲡⲭ̅ⲥ̅ ⲡⲉⲛⲟ̅ⲥ̅ ⲁⲙⲏⲛ. [4] وان كان معه كاهن شريك او اكثر فلا يرشم الثاني ولا يضع اليد الثانية بل يصنع ذلك الكاهن الشريك. [5] وان كان معه شركاء قليلون او كثيرون فاليد الثانية لهم جميعاً واحداً بعد واحد. [6] وسواء كان معه شركاء ام لم يكن يرشم الكاهن الخديم رشماً ثالثاً ويضع البخور يداً ثالثةً وهو يقول ⲁ̀ϥⲥⲙⲁⲣⲱⲟⲩⲧ ⲛ̀ϫⲉ ⲡⲓⲡ̅ⲛ̅ⲁ̅ ⲉ̅ⲑ̅ⲩ̅ ⲙ̀ⲡⲁⲣⲁⲕⲗⲏⲧⲟⲛ ⲁⲙⲏⲛ. [7] ثم يضع يدين ايضاً بلا رشم لتتمة خمس ايادى بخور وهو يقول ⲟⲩⲱⲟⲩ ⲛⲉⲙ ⲟⲩⲧⲁⲓⲟ ⲟⲩⲧⲁⲓⲟ ⲛⲉⲙ ⲟⲩⲱⲟⲩ ⲛ̀ϯⲡⲁⲛⲁⲅⲓⲁ ⲧⲣⲓⲁⲥ: ⲫⲓⲱⲧ ⲛⲉⲙ ⲡϣⲏⲣⲓ ⲛⲉⲙ ⲡⲓⲡ̅ⲛ̅ⲁ̅ ⲉ̅ⲑ̅ⲩ̅. ϯⲛⲟⲩ ⲛⲉⲙ ⲛ̀ⲥⲏⲟⲩ ⲛⲓⲃⲉⲛ ⲛⲉⲙ ϣⲁ ⲉ̀ⲛⲉϩ ⲛ̀ⲧⲉ ⲡⲓⲉⲛⲉϩ ⲧⲏⲣⲟⲩ ⲁⲙⲏⲛ.[5]

saying, "Blessed be God the Father, the Pantocrator, amen." [3] Then he blesses a second time and places incense a second time saying, "Blessed is his only-begotten Son, Jesus Christ our Lord, amen." [4] And if there were an assisting priest with him or more, he does not perform the second signing and does not place the second spoon of incense, but the assisting priest does this. [5] And if there was with him assistant priests few or many, the second signing is for them all one after another. [6] And whether there were assisting priests with him or not, the celebrant priest makes a third signing and places a third spoon of incense saying, "Blessed be the Holy Spirit the paraclete, amen." [7] Then he places two spoons also without signing to make a total of five spoons of incense, saying, "Glory and honor, honor and glory, to the all-holy Trinity, the Father the Son and the Holy Spirit, now and at all times, and unto the ages of ages, amen."

The blessing of vestments is done in the same manner, using the same gestures and formulas. Following this rite of blessing the vestments and the details of how multiple participating priests can share in performing it, the rubrics on page 196 continue as follows:

[1] ثم يصافح اخوته الكهنة ويسألهم مساعدته في الطلب. [2] ثم يخضع للرب امام هيكله المقدس ويضرب مطانية لأخوته الكهنة وباقى الاكليرس.[6]

[1] Then he [the priest] greets his brothers the priests and asks them to assist him in entreating. [2] Then he bows to the Lord before his holy sanctuary and offers an obeisance[7] to his brothers the priests and the rest of the clergy.[8]

Today, the blessing of the vestments is still conducted in the manner described, with the addition that the priests and servants pray Our

5 Ṣalīb, ⲡⲓϫⲱⲙ ⲛ̀ⲧⲉ ⲡⲓⲉⲩⲭⲟⲗⲟⲅⲓⲟⲛ, 31–33.

6 Ibid., 196.

7 The manuscript has "مطانية", appearing also elsewhere as "مطانوة" = Gr μετάνοια. See Graf, *Verzeichnis,* 106.

8 The manuscript has "الاكليرس" = Gr κλῆρος. See Graf, *Verzeichnis,* 12.

Father before putting on their vestments and reciting Psalms 29 and 92.

1.1. Historical Development

As can be seen, the Coptic vesting rite is fairly simple in its outline. Even the moments of vesting in the ordination rites for various ranks do not contain any formulas or psalm verses particular to the vestments worn. This is the case even in the oldest manuscript of ordination rites, *Coptic Museum Lit. 253* (AD 1364), which was the source for later ordination texts with one exception. In a later manuscript containing the rite of consecration of the Patriarch of Alexandria, *Coptic Patriarchate Lit. 90* (19th c.), a more developed rite is recorded in which the patriarchal vestments are given one at a time accompanied by the recitation of appropriate psalm verses.[9] These psalm verses however correspond in almost every case to those accompanying the vesting of the bishop in the Byzantine Rite.[10] This developed ordination rite of vesting became—with minor modifications—the current practice at patriarchal consecrations, at least since the consecration of Pope Kīrillus VI (AD 1959–1971), as can be seen in the printed booklet used on the day of his consecration.[11] Appearing at such a late date, and manifesting such strong borrowing from the Byzantine Rite, the current rite of patriarchal vesting cannot be regarded as representative of Coptic vesting rites generally, especially that the Patriarch himself does not observe this vesting rite except on the day of his consecration.

In fact, the Coptic vesting rite with its simplicity bears no resemblance to other eastern vesting rites. This is the case not just when compared to the Byzantine tradition, but also the West-Syrian

9 O.H.E. Burmester, *The Rite of Consecration of the Patriarch of Alexandria: Text According to MS. 253 Lit., Coptic Museum* (Cairo: Société d'archéologie copte, 1960), 49–50 (Arabic), 85–88 (English). For a detailed analysis of the ordination rites of this manuscript in the context of the historical development of Coptic liturgical vestments, see Innemée, *Ecclesiastical Dress in the Medieval Near East*, 19–30.

10 Even in the Byzantine Rite, such vesting prayers do not appear before the twelfth or thirteenth centuries. See Vassa Larin, *The Byzantine Hierarchical Divine Liturgy in Arsenij Suxanov's Proskinitarij: Text, Translation, and Analysis of the Entrance Rites*, OCA 286 (Rome: Pontificio Istituto Orientale, 2010), 190.

11 *Barnāmaǧ ḥaflat risāmat ġibṭat al-ḥabr al-ǧalīl al-anbā Kīrillus al-sādis bābā al-iskandariyya wa-baṭrīyark al-kirāza al-marqusiyya* [The program of the ordination ceremony of His Beatitude the honored prelate Anba Kīrillus VI, Pope of Alexandria and Patriarch of the see of Mark] (Al-Faǧǧāla: Maṭba'at Samīr, 1959), 14–16. For a biography of Kīrillus VI, known both as a miracle-working modern saint and a reformer of ecclesiastical and monastic life, see most-recently Daniel Fanous, *A Silent Patriarch: Kyrillos VI (1902–1971) Life and Legacy* (Yonkers, NY: St. Vladimir's Seminary Press, 2019).

rite, which also includes psalm verses and prayers associated with each vestment item.[12] Perhaps the closest parallel can be found—quite expectedly—in the vesting rite of the Ethiopian tradition, in which the Lord's Prayer is recited as the main element of the rite.[13]

It is difficult to identify exactly when this ritual blessing and choice of Psalms 29 and 92 appeared. Liturgical manuscripts are quite unhelpful in describing the details of vesting, which leaves one more or less with works about the liturgy, such as ritual manuals and medieval guides. However, with the exception of the last segment about the priest bowing to the other clergy and asking them for their assistance, none of the other steps appear in the descriptions of the liturgy in *The Order of the Priesthood*,[14] *The Lamp of Darkness*,[15] *The Precious Jewel*,[16] or Gabriel V's *Ritual Order*.[17]

The Order of the Priesthood does not offer a description of the liturgy per se, but it presents information on vesting in the context of the rite of *Raising of Incense* for vespers and matins. In this context, what is described is a double process of preparation before the beginning of the service, which does not include a blessing of the vestments. Instead, it includes first a ritual washing of the feet in a designated basin in the back of the church, which is given a practical as well as spiritual significance.[18] Next, members of each rank take the head covering of those in the rank immediately superior to them and store them away for the duration of the service. That is, readers receive the hats of subdeacons, and subdeacons those of the deacons, and so on until the highest rank present whether priest or bishop. This clearly refers to the headgear worn as part of the clergy's street clothes and therefore has no significance for vesting per se, except as an initial act of humility exchanged among the servants. These two introductory rites are appropriate for vespers and matins, both of which are celebrated first thing upon entering the church in the evening and morning respectively. Since the liturgy—at least in theory—is always preceded by matins, it is understandable why current rubrics on vesting would not include such ritual ablutions or taking off street clothes.

12 *LEW*, 70.

13 Ibid., 197.

14 Assfalg, *Die Ordnung des Priestertums*, 39–40 (Arabic), 115–116 (German).

15 *Paris BnF Ar. 203* (AD 1363–1369), fol. 203r. Cf. Villecourt, "Les observances," 248.

16 *Paris BnF Ar. 207* (14th c.), fol. 120r–121v. Cf. Mistrīḥ, *Pretiosa margarita*, 176–178 (Arabic), 486–488 (Latin).

17 *Paris BnF Ar. 98* (17th c.), fol. 47r. Cf. 'Abdallah, *L'ordinamento*, 172–173 (Arabic), 361–363 (Italian).

18 Assfalg, *Die Ordnung des Priestertums*, 39–40 (Arabic), 115–116 (German).

This is not the case however in Ibn Sabbāʿ, who includes essentially the same rubrics in his description of the liturgy. This is because for unknown reasons Ibn Sabbāʿ does not provide a chapter on the rite of matins, giving the impression that the clergy begin the morning services directly with the liturgy without any morning prayers prior.

Finally, by the fifteenth century many elements of today's vesting rite make their first appearance. In the *Ritual Order* of Gabriel V, the priest is instructed in the beginning of vespers and matins to ask for the blessing of his brethren the clergy serving with him:

[1] اولاً يشارك اخوته الكهنة ويصافحهم فان بمصافحته لهم شهد قلوبهم انه طيب الخاطر من قبلهم وهم طيبين الخاطر من قبله. [2] ثم يتوجه الى امام هيكل الرب ويخضع للرب برأسه على الارض وهو يقول كاملة ⲧⲉⲛⲟⲩⲱϣⲧ ⲙ̀ⲙⲟⲕ ⲱ ⲡ̅ⲭ̅ⲥ̅ [3] ويقبل عتبة باب المذبح بفاه. [4] ثم يلتفت الى يمين المذبح ويضرب مطانوة لاخوته الكهنة وهو يقول ⲥⲙⲟⲩ ⲉⲣⲟⲓ ⲓⲥ ϯⲙⲉⲧⲁⲛⲟⲩⲃⲓ ⲭⲱ ⲛⲏⲓ ⲉⲃⲟⲗ ويضرب مطانوة الى الشمامسة ناحيتهم وهو يقول ⲥⲙⲟⲩ ⲉⲣⲟⲓ.[19]

[1] First, he [the priest] shares with his brothers the priests and greets them. For in his greeting them, he causes their hearts to witness that he is well disposed towards them and that they are well disposed towards him. [2] Then he goes in front of the sanctuary of the Lord and bows to the Lord with his head to the ground, saying fully: "We worship you O Christ,"[20] [3] and kisses the threshold of the door of the sanctuary with his mouth. [4] Then he turns to the right of the altar and makes a prostration to his brothers the priests saying, "Bless me, behold the prostration, forgive me." Then he makes a prostration to the deacons towards them saying, "Bless me."

In the chapter on the liturgy, the text provides similar rubrics after vesting, and after the ritual washing seen in previous sources. Thus, by the fifteenth century at the latest, the preparatory gestures surrounding the vesting had taken this shape:

1. Ritual washing in the church's basin.
2. Putting on the vestments.
3. Asking the other clergy and deacons for forgiveness and blessing.

Regarding the Trinitarian blessing seen in the *editio typica* cited above, none of these medieval sources mentions it with regards to vesting. However, the blessing itself is quite common. Since the

19 *Paris BnF Ar. 98* (17th c.), fol. 32bis r–v. Cf. ʿAbdallah, *L'ordinamento*, 157 (Arabic), 352 (Italian).

20 The full text of this formula is, ⲧⲉⲛⲟⲩⲱϣⲧ ⲙ̀ⲙⲟⲕ ⲱ ⲡⲓⲭⲣⲓⲥⲧⲟⲥ ⲛⲉⲙ ⲡⲉⲕⲓⲱⲧ ⲛ̀ⲁⲅⲁⲑⲟⲥ ⲛⲉⲙ ⲡⲓⲡⲛⲉⲩⲙⲁ ⲉ̀ⲑⲟⲩⲁⲃ ϫⲉ ⲁⲕⲓ̀ ⲁⲕⲥⲱϯ ⲙ̀ⲙⲟⲛ. (We worship you, O Christ, with your good Father, and the Holy Spirit, for you have come and saved us).

current rubrics refer this blessing to the one pronounced over the incense, it is noted that this blessing in fact appears as such in the context of placing incense in the censer in *The Order of the Priesthood*, albeit in rudimentary form: "And he places it [incense] in the censer and it is glory and honor to the Holy Trinity."[21] Similarly, a Trinitarian blessing is alluded to in Ibn Sabbāʿ: "And every time he carries the incense from the box to the censer he makes the sign of the cross. And after three times, he says glory and honor, honor and glory to the Holy Trinity, the Father, and the Son, and the Holy Spirit."[22] Finally, explicit description of this blessing over the incense appears in *The Ritual Order*.[23] However, it cannot be assumed that such a blessing was ever pronounced over the vestments in this early stage.

The earliest witness to the current vesting rite, complete with the Trinitarian blessing over the vestments and other ritual gestures, was published by Burmester from an eighteenth-century manuscript from the Monastery of Saint Paul by the Red Sea, although no shelfmark is given. The rite described in this text can be summarized as follows:

1. The priests ask each other for a mutual blessing.
2. Trinitarian blessing over the vestments by the celebrant priest
3. Reciting of Psalms 29 and 92
4. Bowing before the altar
5. Bowing before the other clergy, saying "Bless me, my fathers and brothers, forgive me."
6. Bowing before the deacons
7. Greeting the other clergy and asking them for assistance in prayer[24]

Thus, it can be concluded that the current vesting rite reached its fullest development some time between the sixteenth and eighteenth centuries. This final stage of development consisted in adding the Trinitarian blessing over the vestments, "In the name of the Father...Blessed be the Father...etc.," and the subsequent reciting of Psalms 29 and 92 by all vesting servants. As was seen, this Trinitarian blessing was borrowed from the blessing over the incense at any incense rite in vespers, matins, or the liturgy, in which context it is seen much earlier in the sources. In fact, this blessing is the standard priestly blessing for a number of purposes, including even the

21 Assfalg, *Die Ordnung des Priestertums*, 41 (Arabic), 117 (German).

22 *Paris BnF Ar. 207* (14th c.), fol. 127v. Cf. Mistrīḥ, *Pretiosa margarita*, 191 (Arabic), 493 (Latin).

23 *Paris BnF Ar. 98* (17th c.), fol. 33r–34r. Cf. ʿAbdallah, *L'ordinamento*, 158 (Arabic), 353 (Italian).

24 O.H.E. Burmester, "Vesting Prayers and Ceremonies of the Coptic Church," *OCP* 1 (1935): 305–314.

eucharistic bread and wine after their selection.[25] It was only natural then that this formula would be enlisted as a gesture to invoke and to bestow a blessing over the vestments, and by extension those who wear them, in order to perform their respective liturgical roles. Nonetheless, it is clear in the earliest sources available that the original content of the vesting process was not focused so much on blessing the vestments themselves, but on the personal cleansing of the clergy, and on the mutual exchange of forgiveness and blessing among those serving.

1.2. The Time of Vesting

Today, all clergy and servants vest before the prayers of the appointed hours of the Horologion. This includes any bishops, presbyters, deacons, and those in minor orders. However, this is not true in all the sources. There is strong evidence that bishops once vested after the prothesis rite completely and before the Liturgy of the Word.[26] There are also other variations regarding when the other ministers are to put on their vestments.

The current rite of vesting before the prothesis is encountered as early as the fourteenth-century Ibn Sabbāʿ's *The Precious Jewel*,[27] and Ibn Kabar's *The Lamp of Darkness*.[28] This natural flow of things was later included in the first printed Euchologion of Ṭūḫī.[29] Finally, it is the rite included in the *editio typica* of ʿAbd al-Masīḥ Ṣalīb, ensuring its permanence in current practice.[30]

However, a variant appears in which the priest first examines the offering of bread and wine, ensuring they are both properly prepared, and only then proceeds to put on the vestments. This rite is seen in the *Ritual Order* of Gabriel V from the fifteenth century, which has the following text:

[1] وبعد ذلك يبتدي الكاهن إذا اراد الخدمة الطاهرة فانه يتقدم اولاً ينظر القربان الذي يقدمه إن كان مختاراً والخمر ايضاً كما قيل فليكون زكياً لا عيب فيه. [2] وإذا اختاره الكاهن فليضعه

[1] Afterwards the priest begins. If he desires to serve purely, he proceeds first to examine the oblation that he is about to offer, whether it is of good quality. Likewise, the wine as was said, is to be precious without blemish. [2] And when the priest has

25 See chapter 5, section 3.

26 See chapter 6, section 2.2.

27 *Paris BnF Ar. 207* (14th c.), fol. 120r. Cf. Mistrīḥ, *Pretiosa margarita*, 176 (Arabic), 487 (Latin).

28 *Paris BnF Ar. 203* (AD 1363–1369), fol. 203r. Cf. Villecourt, "Les observances," 248–249.

29 Ṭūḫī, ⲡⲓϫⲱⲙ ⲛ̀ⲧⲉ ⲡⲓϣⲟⲙⲧ ⲛ̀ⲁⲛⲁⲫⲟⲣⲁ, 296.

30 Ṣalīb, ⲡⲓϫⲱⲙ ⲛ̀ⲧⲉ ⲡⲓⲉⲩⲭⲟⲗⲟⲅⲓⲟⲛ, 203.

على جناح الهيكل الايسر عندما يقف [3] ثم يتقدم يلبس آلة الكهنوت.[31]	chosen it, he is to place it on the left side of the altar where he stands, [3] then he proceeds to put on the garments of the priesthood.

In current usage, the selection of the eucharistic bread is a fully ritualized element of the prothesis rite, preceded by hand washing and accompanied by appropriate chants and the full participation of deacons and congregation. As such, it would be unthinkable for a priest to do this unvested. This minor practice then remains an obscure variation seen mainly in the *Ritual Order*.

The idea of inspecting the bread and wine even before vesting strikes one as exceptionally cautious and suggests that at least with some frequency the bread and/or wine were indeed found unacceptable or simply unavailable for the liturgy to proceed. Once again, one sees the marks of instability and insecurity that characterized the era of Gabriel V, where even the bread and wine for the Eucharist may have not been consistently available and appropriate. Nonetheless, given the special circumstances that made this precaution necessary at his time, the idea did not last. Certainly, it must have seemed foreign to later generations, for by the time of Ṭūḫī's edition, the vesting had been restored once again to its place before the prothesis, as mentioned above.

2. THE PREPARATION OF THE ALTAR

At this point in the unfolding of the rite, the eucharistic vessels make their first appearance, as the priest places them on the altar in preparation for the prothesis rite. For a detailed list of the altar vessels and cloths, the reader is referred to Excursus 1.

2.1. Current Rubrics

Since the rubrics instruct the priest to pray the first prayer of preparation during the manual acts of setting the vessels in their proper place, the *editio typica* of ʿAbd al-Masīḥ Ṣalīb interrupts the details of placing the vessels to provide the text of the prayer. However, for the sake of clarity, these manual acts are explained below in detail before advancing to the text of the prayers. After the priest and deacons had vested, the rubrics continue as follows:

[1] فيطلع الان كما شُرح. ويكون قنديل الشرق مُوقداً وكذلك شمعتان مُوقدتين على جانبي المذبح	[1] He [the priest] ascends now [to the altar] as was explained, and the

[31] *Paris BnF Ar. 98* (17th c.), fol. 45v. Cf. ʿAbdallah, *L'ordinamento*, 171–172 (Arabic), 361 (Italian).

على شمعدانين. والشماس يصعد ويقف امامه. [2] ثم ان الكاهن يكشف المائدة من الابروسفارين ويضع ألآنية أمامه ويحلّها من رباطها.[32]

eastern lamp should be lit, and likewise two candles lit on both sides of the altar on two candlestands. And the deacon ascends and stands opposite him. [2] Then the priest uncovers the table from the *prospherin*,[33] and he places the vessels before him and unties them.

First, before he is to do anything, an eastern lamp and two candles flanking the two sides of the altar are to be lit, likely inspired by Old Testament precedent (Ex 27:20–21). Historical evidence points both to the existence and particular importance of such lamps near the altar in the Coptic tradition. An oil lamp burning before the altar is mentioned in the *Encomium of Celestine of Rome on Victor the General*, where it is accorded miraculous healing power.[34] The Sahidic text of this encomium was published by Ernest Alfred Wallis Budge from the manuscript *British Library Or. 7022* (AD 951). An alleged daughter of Emperor Honorious, Kallieutropia, was possessed by a demon that caused her breasts to both swell up and shrivel at the same time. Upon hearing of the miracles that occurred at the shrine of Saint Victor, she travels there seeking her own healing. An angel appears to her at the shrine and instructs her, "When you rise up tomorrow morning, take a little of the oil which is in the lamp that is burning before the altar of sacrifice (пєѳүсιаст̄нрιон), and smear your breasts with it."[35] Although the miracle in question is said to have occurred in the martyrion of Saint Victor in Rome, the mention of a lamp before the altar is such a particular detail, and its familiarity appears to be taken for granted by this local Coptic text. Thus, one can safely assume hearers and readers of this encomium would have immediately recognized this altar lamp as a familiar feature of their own Coptic churches. A related witness to lamps or candles burning continuously around the altar occurs in *The Miracles of Apa Phoebammon*. During the annual feast of the saint, a thief attempts to rob his local shrine, and it is said, "He hurried, took the lampstand (птокарапτιон) down,

32 Ṣalīb, пιϫωм н̀тє пιєүхолоᴦιон, 196–197.

33 The manuscript has "الابروسفارين" = Gr προσφέρειν. See Graf, *Verzeichnis*, 2.

34 On Victor Stratelates in the Coptic tradition, including the encomium attributed to Celestine of Rome, see Michel van Esbroeck, "Victor Stratelates, Saint–Coptic Tradition," *CE* 7:2303a–2305a.

35 E. A. Wallis Budge, ed., *Coptic Martyrdoms etc. in the Dialect of Upper Egypt*, vol. 1 (Oxford, 1914), 57 (Coptic), 310 (English). Translation slightly modified.

which is a lamp burning on two sides (made of) fine bronze and took himself to the road to walk."[36]

Later in the medieval period, one encounters the earliest instance of the strict requirement for two lamps flanking the altar before the celebration of the liturgy. In the canons of Patriarch Gabriel II ibn Turaik (AD 1131–1145), the following injunction is included, "The liturgy shall not be celebrated without two candles around the altar."[37] Placing candles near or around the altar is of course common in many other traditions. Such is the case in the West-Syrian Rite, in which the priest begins to prepare the altar by lighting the two candles while reciting certain psalm verses.[38] Similarly, a multi-branch candlestand can be seen on the eastern side of altars in churches that follow the Byzantine tradition, while in the Roman Rite, candles—originally carried in the *introit* procession—are now placed on the altar from the very start, since at least the fourteenth century.[39]

That the deacon is to stand opposite the priest—facing west—may seem unnecessary today, since the deacon has no part in the preparation of the altar in the present day. It is very likely that this points to a larger role previously played by the deacon in the preparation of the altar. This is supported first by the story of Jacob bishop of Wasīm, where the deacon participated in the preparation of the altar: "And when the offering occurred [...] the presbyter put on the vestments and engaged in the hallowing, and the deacon too likewise, and they dressed up the altar."[40] Later in the thirteenth century, there is the similar witness of the treatise *The Guide to the Beginners and the Correction of the Laity*, which instructs that, "Every priest or deacon, who intends the service of the liturgy [...] prays the specific prayers for the clothing of the altar."[41] A century later, Ibn

[36] Verrone, *Mighty Deeds and Miracles by Saint Apa Phoebammon*, 38–39. The obscure word *tokaraption*, rendered as is in Verrone's edition, is likely a corruption of the Greek word κηριαπτάριον. The latter itself is a rare word, encountered only in Greek and Coptic documentary papyri from Egypt and in one Coptic translation of Homily 50 of John Chrysostom on the Gospel of Matthew, where it is used as a loan word to translate the Greek λαμπάς. It is most likely a Greek loanword attested only in Egypt and understood, as the text above indicates, as a lampstand. For a discussion of this word, its sources, and meanings, see Schmelz, *Kirchliche Amtsträger*, 122–123. See also Hans Förster, *Wörterbuch der griechischen Wörter in den koptischen dokumentarischen Texten*, Texte und Untersuchungen zur Geschichte der altchristlichen Literatur 148 (Berlin: Walter de Gruyter, 2002), 412.

[37] Burmester, "The Canons of Gabriel Ibn Turaik," (1933) 49 (Arabic), 54 (English).

[38] *LEW*, 70–71.

[39] Jungmann, *Missarum Sollemnia*, 1:271.

[40] Arras, *Quadraginta historia monachorum*, 155. Cf. Fritsch, "The Preparation of the Gifts," 134–135.

[41] *BAV Vatican Ar. 117* (AD 1323), fol. 197v. Cf. Graf, "Liturgische Anweisungen," 121.

Kabar echoed the same instructions in his chapter on the liturgy: "And the priest ascends to the sanctuary, accompanied by the deacon, and they clothe the altar together."[42]

Now, the celebrant is to uncover the altar from the so-called *prospherin*. This is a large white veil that covers the entire top of the altar, although contrary to these rubrics, it is today customarily stored away with the eucharistic vessels, and not left as an altar covering as the text might imply.[43] After the altar has been uncovered, the celebrant is to untie the vessels and place them in front of him on the altar. This untying of the vessels refers to the fact that the vessels and the various eucharistic cloths are usually stored away together in a large square white cloth that is then tied diagonally from its four corners to form a sort of large sack enclosing the vessels and altar cloths. This is done after every celebration of the liturgy, after which the entire bundle is stored somewhere in the sanctuary. It is unclear when this practice may have developed. However, it seems clear that this practice evolved with portability in mind. One cannot help but wonder if perhaps such a custom is a product of a time when raids on churches—whether in monasteries or the cities and villages—were frequent, necessitating that the precious eucharistic vessels be easily and quickly removed if needed.[44]

At this point Hegumen ʿAbd al-Masīḥ Ṣalīb presents the following footnote regarding the time at which the preparation of the altar is usually executed:

[1] العادة الجارية الآن انه اولاً يصلي الشعب صلاة مزامير الساعات [2] و يكون استعداد المذبح قبلها او في اثنائها.[45]	[1] The custom current now is that the people first pray the prayer of the psalms of the hours, [2] and that the preparation of the altar be done before or during it.

By the prayer of the psalms of the hours the text is referring to certain hours from the Horologion that are currently prayed between the service of *Matins Raising of Incense*, and the prothesis rite.

42 *Paris BnF Ar. 203* (AD 1363–1369), fol. 203r. Cf. Villecourt, "Les observances," 248.

43 The altar of course has its own permanent coverings, usually of dark burgundy or crimson color and extend to the ground on all sides of the altar. These coverings however are not called *prospherin* properly speaking. For a description of the coverings of the altar including the *prospherin*, see Burmester, *The Egyptian Church*, 23; Butler, *The Ancient Coptic Churches of* Egypt, 2:44–46; and Excursus 1.

44 The monasteries of Scetis in particular suffered from periodic raids and destruction by nearby tribes. For example, the monasteries were plundered in AD 817 by Arabs, and later in the mid-ninth century by local tribes. See Evelyn-White, *The Monasteries of Wadi 'N Natrun*, 2:249–251, 325–327.

45 Ṣalīb, ⲡⲓϫⲱⲙ ⲛ̀ⲧⲉ ⲡⲓⲉⲩⲭⲟⲗⲟⲅⲓⲟⲛ, 197n1.

Afterwards, the Euchologion presents the text of the first prayer of preparation, to be said during the placing of the vessels on the altar. Then, the rubrics for the placement of the vessels continue. They are presented here in full to preserve the flow of actions:

[1] ههنا يبتدئ الكاهن يمسح الصينية ويضعها مكانها. [2] ثم يمسح الكاس ويفتش داخل الكرسي ويمسحه من فوق ويضع الكاس فيه. [3] وكذلك يمسح الملعقة ويضعها على الكرسي قبليِّ الكاس [4] ويضع اللفائف فى اماكنها. ويكون قد وضع منها لفافة تحت الصينية وغطاها بلفافة اخرى وغطىَّ الكاس ايضاً بلفافة.[5] كل ذلك وهو يتلو بقية اوشية الاستعداد لكسوة المذبح و تهيئة الاوانى.[46]

[1] Here the priest begins to wipe the paten and to put it in its place. [2] Then he wipes the chalice, looks inside the throne, wipes it from the top, and places the chalice in it. [3] Likewise, he wipes the spoon and places it on the throne south of the chalice. [4] And he puts the veils in their places. And he is to have placed from them a veil under the paten and covered it [the paten] with another veil and covered the chalice also with a veil. [5] All this is while he recites the remainder of the *Prayer of Preparation* for the covering of the altar and the preparation of the vessels.

After the priest has finished the first prayer, the rubrics continue:

وإذا انتهى الكاهن من وضع الآنية كل شئٌ فى مكانه يقول هذه الصلاة سراً من بعد استعداد المذبح.[47]

And when the priest has finished placing the vessels everything in its place, he says this prayer secretly after the preparation of the altar.

The rubrics here do not provide precise information on the number and placement of the veils [4]. For a detailed list of Coptic eucharistic vessels and cloths with some brief remarks on historical origins, the reader is directed to the Excursus 1.

2.2. The Preparation in Current Usage

It is true that the *editio typica* of ʿAbd al-Masīḥ Ṣalīb is usually very detailed in its rubrics and explanations, and for this reason has become such an influential edition in the Coptic Orthodox Church. However, there still remains some aspects of the celebration of the liturgy, particularly manual acts by the priest, that are never explained in full in any printed book, or in which actual practice may be at variance with the literal meaning of the rubrics. The altar preparation is one of these aspects.

46 Ṣalīb, ⲡⲓϫⲱⲙ ⲛ̀ⲧⲉ ⲡⲓⲉⲩⲭⲟⲗⲟⲅⲓⲟⲛ, 199.

47 Ibid., 201.

Besides the paten veil and chalice veil mentioned in the rubrics, there is a large number of other cloths that are usually placed on the altar in a particular configuration. Since written sources do not provide a complete picture, the following description is by necessity anecdotal. Before the paten is placed on the altar, three square cloths are placed on the western edge–the priest's side–lying diagonally so that their triangular bottom half hangs off the edge of the altar. Then, two more veils of equal shape and size are placed on top of the altar, covering the gaps left between the veils placed diagonally. In the middle, in front of the priest, there is frequently placed an extra square cloth of red color. The difference in color is a practical choice, to facilitate seeing any small crumbs of the offering that may fall from the paten. Only then is the paten placed on top of the red cloth. Inside the paten itself is a circular cloth. On top of the star two square veils are placed, folded so as to form two triangles facing each other. Finally, the chalice is placed inside the chalice throne. Here also, there is frequently a square cloth with a circular hole in its center, designed to rest on top of the square shaped chalice throne, while leaving the round top of the chalice itself exposed. Another square veil is placed on the chalice covering it completely. The last veil, the large *prospherin*, covers both the chalice throne and the paten in front of it, although this is postponed until the end of the prothesis.[48] The resulting fully prepared Coptic altar can be seen in the appended image (Appendix 3).

Although the *editio typica* of 1902 explains the preparation of the altar in the beginning of the chapter on the liturgy, that is, after the chapter on the *Morning Raising of Incense*, this is not always when the preparation is executed in actual practice. Based on first-hand experience, the author has seen priests prepare the altar before beginning the matins service entirely, or during the chanting of the doxologies for the saints–roughly halfway through the morning service–or during the prayers of the Horologion that follow matins.

2.3. The Preparation in the Sources

As will be seen below, Bohairic Euchologia consistently refer to the preparation of the altar in the title of the accompanying prayers, making them the earliest witness to such an act. That aside however,

48 This anecdotal description is based on the practice of various clergy in the Coptic Orthodox Diocese of Los Angeles, Southern California, and Hawaii. I thank Fr. Bishoy Mikhail Brownfield (St. Cyril of Alexandria Coptic Orthodox Church, Irwindale, CA), and Fr. Daniel Habib (St. John Chrysostom American Coptic Orthodox Church, Laguna Niguel, CA) for their assistance in explaining the intricate details of the current practice.

the earliest source in the medieval period to describe the altar preparation and its accompanying prayers in detail is the *Precious Jewel* of Yūḥannā ibn Sabbā‘ in the fourteenth century. In chapter 63, he writes:

[1] ثم يضع الكاهن امامه كسوة الهيكل عليه [2] ويبسط يديه ويقول صلاة الكسوة الاولى من غير ان يكسي وعقله مجموع ويديه مبسوطتان الى نهاية الصلاة الأولى.[3] وبعد فراغها يكسي الهيكل بعقل مجموع. [4] وإذا فرغ من كسوة الهيكل ووضع الانية كل شيء في مكانه ومحله يقول الصلاة الثانية.[49]

[1] Then the priest places before him the covering of the altar upon it, [2] and raises his hands and says the first prayer of covering [the altar], without covering [it], with his mind collected and hands raised to the end of the first prayer. [3] And after it is finished, he covers the altar with an attentive mind. [4] When he has finished covering the altar, and has placed the vessels with everything in its place, he says the second prayer.

This text then refers to the two elements that make up this part of the liturgy, namely the physical setting of the eucharistic vessels and cloths in their appropriate place on the altar, and the near simultaneous recitation of two prayers that accompany these acts. Interestingly, Ibn Sabbā‘'s near contemporary, Ibn Kabar, did not mention the accompanying prayers, but focused his attention instead on the participation of the deacon in the process, as mentioned previously. However, it would be mistaken to conclude that the prayers did not exist in Ibn Kabar's liturgical practice, since they are mentioned here in Ibn Sabbā‘, and they are also a fixed element in the euchological manuscripts, at least since some of the oldest complete Copto-Arabic Euchologia of the thirteenth century, *British Library Or. 1239*, *Bodleian Hunt. 360*, and *BAV Vatican Copt. 17* (AD 1288). Although lacking in precise details, such as the exact placement of the vessels or the incipits of the prayers, Ibn Sabbā‘ can be considered reliably the earliest evidence for the rite of preparation of the altar besides the euchological manuscripts themselves.

By contrast, the *Ritual Order* of Gabriel V provides a much more explicit description of the preparation of the altar and accompanying prayers, although it too stops short of the level of detail seen in current practice. In the chapter on the liturgy, and after the description of vesting discussed in the previous section, the text continues:

[1] ثم إذا طلع فوق المذبح يقبله بفاه. [2] ويكون قنديل الشرق موقوداً وتكون الشمعتان

[1] And when he ascends to the altar, he kisses it with his mouth. [2] And

49 *Paris BnF Ar. 207* (14th c.), fol. 121v. Cf. Mistrīḥ, *Pretiosa margarita*, 178–179 (Arabic), 488 (Latin).

موقودان.[50] [3] ثم يكشف المائدة من الابرسفارين ويضع الانية امامه محلولة من رباطها. [4] والشماس يصعد ويقف امامه. [5] ويبتدي بصلاة الاستعداد وهي ⲡ̅ⲟ̅ⲥ̅ ⲫⲏⲉⲧⲥⲱⲟⲩⲛ ⲛ̀ⲛⲓϩⲏⲧ.[51]

the eastern lamp should be lit, and the two candles are to be lit. [3] Then he uncovers the table from the *prospherin*,[52] and places the vessels in front of him, untied from their bonds. [4] And the deacon ascends and stands in front of him. [5] And he [the priest] begins with the prayer of the preparation, and it is "O Lord who knows the hearts."

This is clearly, almost word for word, the description found today in the *editio typica* of 'Abd al-Masīḥ Ṣalīb. What follows is a description of what is to be chanted during the preparation of the altar by the choir. Namely, this is the alleluia and psalm selections discussed previously.[53] This particular detail was only included by 'Abd al-Masīḥ Ṣalīb as a footnote, since by his time the chanting of the alleluia with appropriate psalms—the so-called *Alleluia al-Qurbān*—was postponed until after the selection of the bread offering.[54] At any rate, the description continues:

[1] وإذا انتهى الكاهن في قراءة اوشية الاستعداد وهيⲡ̅ⲟ̅ⲥ̅ ⲫⲏⲉⲧⲥⲱⲟⲩⲛ ⲛ̀ⲛⲓϩⲏⲧ يقول الى عند ⲉⲑⲣⲓⲉⲣϩⲏⲧⲥ. [2] ومن هاهنا يبتدي الكاهن يمسح الانية الموضوعة امامه ويضع الصينية مكانها[3] والكاس مكانه بعد تفتيش كرسي الكاس [4] ويضع الملعقة فوق كرسي الكاس [5] واللفايف يضعهم مكانهم. [6] كل ذلك وهو يتلوا فى تتمة اوشية الاستعداد. [7] و إذا انتهى ذلك جميعه يقول الاوشية الذي بعد الاستعداد وهي ⲛ̀ⲑⲟⲕ ⲡ̅ⲟ̅ⲥ̅ ⲁⲕⲧ̀ⲥⲁⲃⲟⲛ ⲙ̀ الى اخرها.[55]

[1] And when he reads the prayer of preparation, "O Lord who knows the hearts," he reads until, "so that I begin," [2] and here the priest begins to wipe the vessels placed before him, and he puts the paten in its place. [3] And he puts the chalice in its place, after examining the chalice throne. [4] And he places the spoon on top of the chalice throne, [5] and places the veils in their places. [6] All this is while he reads the remainder of the *Prayer*[56] *of Preparation.* [7] And when he has finished all of this, he reads the prayer that is after the preparation, and it is, "You O Lord have taught us,"to its end.

50 More correctly, موقدتان.

51 *Paris BnF Ar. 98* (17th c.), fol. 47r. Cf, 'Abdallah, *L'ordinamento*, 173 (Arabic), 363 (Italian).

52 The manuscript has "الابروسفارين" = Gr προσφέρειν. Cf. Graf, *Verzeichnis*, 2.

53 See Chapter 2, Section 2.

54 For the selection of the oblations, see below Chapter 4, Section 1.

55 *Paris BnF Ar. 98* (17th c.), fol. 47v. Cf, 'Abdallah, *L'ordinamento*, 174 (Arabic), 363 (Italian).

56 The manuscript has "اوشية" = Gr εὐχή. Cf. Graf, *Verzeichnis*, 16.

Again, here is a description almost identical to the one in ʿAbd al-Masīḥ Ṣalīb's edition. Although Ibn Sabbāʿ previously did not provide as much detail, nothing there necessarily contradicts the later witness of the *Ritual Order* or ʿAbd al-Masīḥ Ṣalīb. The near identity in rubrics between the *Ritual Order* and Ṣalīb's edition probably occurred via the *editio princeps* of Ṭūḫī (1736). Heinzgerd Brakmann pointed out that the edition of Ṭūḫī is based on the codex *BAV Vatican Copt. 17* (AD 1288).[57] However, this manuscript is a classic Euchologion with very few rubrics, which means the rubrics in Ṭūḫī's edition must have come from elsewhere. At least in this point, this source seems to have been the *Ritual Order* itself, for the rubrics in Ṭūḫī read thus:

[1] ثم إذا طلع فوق المذبح يُقَبِّلَهُ بفاه [2] ويكون قنديل الشرق موقوداً. [3] ثم يكشف المائدة من الابرسفارين ويضع الانية محلولة من رباطها [4] وتكون شمعتان موقودتان على جانبي المذبح [5] والشماس يصعد ويقف امامه [6] ويبتدي بصلاة الاستعداد.[58]

[1] And when he ascends to the altar, he kisses it with his mouth. [2] And the eastern lamp is to be lit. [3] Then he uncovers the table from the *prospherin*, and places the vessels untied from their knots. [4] And on the two sides of the altar, there are to be two candles lit. [5] And the deacon ascends and stands in front of him. [6] And he [the priest] begins with the *Prayer of the Preparation*.

Later, the preparation of the altar continues, interrupted by the text of the prayers as in other sources:

[1] وهاهنا يحل العدة ويمسح الاواني ويضع الصينية مكانها [2] والكاس مكانه بعد تفتيش كرسي الكاس [3] ويضع الملعقة فوق الكرسي [4] واللفايف يضعهم مكانهم [5] هذا كله وهو يقول في بقية الاستعداد.[59]

[1] And at this point he unties the equipment and wipes the vessels and places the paten in its place, [2] and the chalice in its place after examining the chalice throne. [3] And he places the spoon on top of the chalice throne, [4] and the veils in their places. [5] All this is while he says the remainder of the [*Prayer*] *of Preparation*.

This is now followed by the second half of the first prayer, and by the full text of the second prayer, which is exactly the way this is presented in the *editio typica* of Ṣalīb and described in the *Ritual Order*. The fact that actual practice today is more complex than the details in any printed edition or source—mainly in the number of altar cloths and their placement—points to another aspect. Namely, that while the

57 Brakmann, "Le déroulement," 107n4.
58 Ṭūḫī, ⲡⲓϫⲱⲙ ⲛ̀ⲧⲉ ⲡⲓϣⲟⲙⲧ ⲛ̀ⲁⲛⲁⲫⲟⲣⲁ, 299–300.
59 Ibid., 305–306.

Northern Egyptian liturgy, had largely reached its current form by the thirteenth century–notwithstanding minor local variations in practice–many intricate details were never explicitly recorded and codified, making the task of charting their historical development or first appearance quite challenging.

As can be seen, post-thirteenth century medieval sources show that by then the manual acts of preparing the altar had become mostly fixed, showing no significant development or evolution. If one were to only consider the liturgy of Northern Egypt, it would be impossible to examine this topic any further. Fortunately, additional hypotheses can be formulated about the pre-history of the altar preparation, albeit using the comparative method rather than direct Egyptian sources.

2.4. A Hypothesis from the Comparative Method

It must be stated from the outset that this section is concerned only with the hypothetical origins of the manual acts of preparing the altar. A full discussion of the accompanying prayers of preparation can be found further below, after the texts of these prayers has been presented and analyzed. That the manual acts appearing in medieval sources do not show any particular development can be expected, since the Coptic tradition by the thirteenth century had already largely acquired its current shape.[60]

In reality, the physical placement of the eucharistic vessels and cloths on the altar must be intricately intertwined with the question of the location of the prothesis and the transfer of gifts, both architecturally in the church building, as well as chronologically in terms of the unfolding of the ritual. This topic was analyzed in the previous chapter to answer the questions of how, when, and why the Coptic prothesis rite shifted in location and time in the course of its historical development. In this section, a brief review of the evidence is presented with a view towards the results of this shift on the physical preparation of the altar, a process that was postulated to have begun around the the eighth century and was already firmly established by the tenth century.

The current hypothesis vis-à-vis the change in the location of the prothesis rite is based on the foregoing. In a situation in which the preparation of the gifts took place in a separate pastophorion away from the altar, naturally all the necessary eucharistic vessels and cloths would have been located there as well and transferred together with the gifts at the appropriate time. This would mean that no elaborate altar preparation of the kind seen in post-thirteenth century sources

60 Brakmann, "Zwischen Pharos und Wüste," 366.

would have taken place. Even if such a placement of cloths according to a specific arrangement on the altar took place after the transfer of the gifts (i.e. in the pre-anaphora), this would at least mean that the altar preparation as it is known today was not part of the prothesis or the preparation of the gifts that precedes the service. If true, this would place the development of the altar preparation somewhere between the change that occurred in the physical location of the prothesis rite and the earliest sources mentioning such a preparation, the earliest thirteenth-century Bohairic Euchologia, that is, between the eighth and thirteenth centuries.

This hypothesis can be tested by taking a second look at the transfer of gifts in East and West. As was presented previously, the Byzantine and Roman Rites still preserve a transfer of gifts before the eucharistic prayer. In the Byzantine East, during the Great Entrance procession, the gifts of bread and wine, as well as all the equipment and veils associated with the altar are carried along. Naturally, no preparation of the altar before the liturgy akin to the Coptic manner takes place, although the eucharistic veils are placed in their appropriate places covering the *diskos* and the chalice.[61] Likewise in the Roman Rite, the offertory takes place after the readings from Scripture. Before the offertory, the corporal is spread on the altar by a deacon, followed by the bringing in of the gifts.[62] Thus far, it is clear that in rites that preserve a pre-anaphoral transfer of gifts, no elaborate preparation of the altar takes place.

In the Syro-Antiochene tradition, a procession of the gifts similar to the Great Entrance was also practiced. Relying on the work of Joseph Patrich, it was established that this procession of the gifts existed by the late-fourth century, as seen in the *Apostolic Constitutions* (late 4th c.), *Testamentum Domini* (mid-5th c.), and the *Scholia* of John Scholasticus (mid-6th c.), as well as extensive architectural analysis of surviving churches in Palestine and Syria.[63] However, by the sixth century evidence for both ordos was encountered in the writings of Severus of Antioch (6th c.), and by the tenth-century commentary by Moses bar Kepha the ancient transfer procession had become a circular one, beginning and ending at the altar.

Today, the preparation of the altar indeed takes place before the prothesis, immediately following the vesting of the clergy. It is similar to the current Coptic Rite in the elaborate nature of placing the vessels

61 *LEW*, 356–361.

62 Jungmann, *Missarum Sollemnia* 2:52–53.

63 Patrich, "The Transfer of Gifts," 358. In agreement with Robert Taft, the witness of the *Mystagogy* of Maximus the Confessor (7th c.) is excluded here from the Palestinian sources advanced by Patrich.

and veils in a specific arrangement. The paten is placed on the left side of the priest with the sponge and spoon, the chalice on the right with the star and the cushion.[64] Finally, the paten veil is placed on the right (opposite from the paten), and the chalice veil on the left (opposite from the chalice).[65]

The Ethiopian tradition is perhaps the closest overall to the Coptic, although it is one of the hardest to analyze because of the scarcity of sources. Prior to the shift in the prothesis that occurred in Ethiopia by the twelfth century at the latest, the priest vested, then placed the altar-tablet on the altar covered with a cloth. This concluded the preparation of the altar at this early pre-twelfth century stage, according to Fritsch, after which the priest went to the prothesis chamber to begin the preparation of the gifts.[66]

Like the present-day Coptic practice, the Ethiopian preparation of the altar is not explicitly described in the written sources. One useful explanation of current practice–with some historical remarks–is that of Samuel A.B. Mercer. The preparation of the altar is more developed than its Coptic counterpart, with more prayers and gestures. The preparation of the vessels begins with a general prayer over all the vessels of the church, followed by a prayer over the *māḥfadāt*, or the eucharistic coverings.[67] What are not mentioned by Mercer or Brightman's rubrics, are the elaborate manual acts that constitute the preparation of the altar in current practice. A large white cloth covers the altar, and the paten is placed on top of it. A smaller veil is placed inside the paten. The chalice is then placed further towards the east, covered with a veil as well. The spoon is then placed at the eastern foot of the altar tablet. Two other veils are placed on the right of the priest, used later to wrap the bread and cover the

64 *LEW*, 70. Brightman's text is mainly from Guy Lefèvre de la Boderie, *D. Severi Alexandrini quondam patriarchae de ritibus baptismi, et sacrae synaxis apud Syros christianos receptis* (Antwerp, 1572), supplemented by a manuscript from Malabar belonging to Rev. G.B. Howard and manuscript *Bodleian Syr. E5*. See *LEW*, 2. The cushion, or cloud as Brightman calls it, is used to protect against spilling the blood during Communion. See Isḥaq Sākā, *Tafsīr ṭaqs al-kanīsa al-siryāniyya al-urṯuḏuksiyya al-anṭakiyya* [Explanation of the rite of the Syrian Antiochian Orthodox Church], 3rd rev. ed., (Lebanon: Manšūrāt dayr Mār Ya'qūb al-Barād'ī lil-rāhibāt al-suryānīyāt al-urṯuḏuksiyāt, 2003), 77.

65 *LEW*, 73. Cf. Sākā, *Tafsīr ṭaqs al-kanīsa al-siryāniyya*, 110. Unlike Brightman's description, Sākā describes the paten placed to the west (i.e. closer to the priest), and the chalice to the east (i.e. after the paten).

66 Fritsch, "The Preparation of the Gifts," 119–121.

67 Samuel A.B. Mercer, *The Ethiopic Liturgy: Its Sources, Development, and Present Form*, The Hale Lectures 1914–5 (London: A.R. Mowbray, 1915), 154. For the texts of these prayers, see *LEW*, 196.

chalice.[68] The prothesis itself includes specific prayers to bless each of the eucharistic vessels, for the paten, chalice, spoon, and the coverings, a feature not found in Coptic practice.[69] Although there is a lack of explicit sources on the Ethiopian prothesis before the switch of location, all the sources used by Mercer and Brightman are much more recent, and show a well-developed preparation of the altar in a situation where the prothesis is performed there from the start.[70]

This short survey of various liturgical traditions shows a strong connection between the presence or absence of a pre-anaphoral transfer of gifts and the presence or absence of rites of altar preparation before the prothesis. In the Byzantine and Roman Rites, no such altar preparation takes place, since all the eucharisic vessels and veils are brought to the altar with the gifts during the procession. However, in rites that have undergone a shift in the manner of preparing the gifts from an adjacent pastophorion to the altar, such as the West-Syrian, Coptic, and Ethiopian Rites, an elaborate rite of altar preparation developed, perhaps at a slightly later stage.

This change occurred in Syria around the sixth century, followed by Egypt between the eighth and tenth centuries, and finally Ethiopia by the beginning of the twelfth century. Despite the lack of sources earlier than the thirteenth century for the Northern Egyptian Coptic Rite, one can propose that the manual acts of preparing the altar before the prothesis developed in Egypt along with the shift from the old ordo, most likely under Syrian influence since the latter remains simpler in its details. The Coptic Rite—under no obligation to preserve the exact Syrian practice—seems to have developed these acts further, adding veils and their exact manner of placement at a later period. Finally, the practice of altar preparation seems to have been passed on to the Ethiopian Rite, following shortly after the change in the

68 I am grateful for Emmanuel Fritsch for sharing this practical information on the Ethiopian preparation of the altar and prothesis, which are not included in printed editions.

69 *LEW*, 199–200; Mercer, *The Ethiopic Liturgy*, 162–164. See also Ernst Hammerschmidt, *Studies in the Ethiopic Anaphoras*, 2nd rev. ed., Berliner Byzantinische Arbeiten 25 (Berlin: Akademie Verlag, 1988), 50–51.

70 The manuscripts listed by Samuel Mercer before his explanation of the unfolding of the Ethiopian liturgy are eleven in number, the earliest being *British Library Or. 545* (AD 1670–1675), and the latest a twentieth-century personal manuscript, *Mercer Ms. Eth. 3*, which he uses to explain the current rite. See Mercer, *The Ethiopic Liturgy*, 144. Brightman also relied on the same seventeenth-century manuscript used by Mercer as his earliest witness, while adding corrections and variants from four later manuscripts, of which only three contain the pre-anaphoral material, and were also used by Mercer: *British Library Or. 546* (AD 1730–1737), *British Library Or. 547* (AD 1784–1800), and *British Library Or. 548* (AD 1855–1868). See *LEW*, 112.

location of the prothesis, albeit before the Coptic Rite itself had acquired its fullest form seen today.

3. THE PRAYERS OF PREPARATION

As was mentioned previously, the celebrant is instructed in the rubrics to pray the first prayer of preparation while he is placing the vessels and eucharistic cloths in their proper places. After the preparation of the altar is completed, the second prayer is to be recited. The text of these prayers is presented here, accompanied by an English translation.

For this, the main text is provided in its Bohairic Coptic recension from the *editio typica* of ʿAbd al-Masīḥ Ṣalīb, while the Greek text comes from William Macomber's edition of the *Kacmarcik Codex* (14th c.). The choice of the *editio typica* for the Coptic text is obvious, while for the Greek text, the *Kacmarcik Codex* was chosen since it is the earliest extant witness of the Greek recension to contain the two prayers of preparation. The text of the prayers also agrees with later manuscripts of the Greek recension edited by Roshi W.B. Dous.[71]

3.1. The Prayer of Preparation of the Altar

[1] ⲡⲟ̅ⲥ̅ ⲫⲏⲉⲧⲥⲱⲟⲩⲛ ⲛ̀ⲛⲓϩⲏⲧ ⲛ̀ⲧⲉ ⲟⲩⲟⲛ ⲛⲓⲃⲉⲛ ⲫⲏⲉⲑⲟⲩⲁⲃ ⲟⲩⲟϩ ⲉⲑⲙⲟⲧⲉⲛ ⲙ̀ⲙⲟϥ ϧⲉⲛ ⲛⲏⲉⲑⲟⲩⲁⲃ ⲛ̀ⲧⲁϥ. [2] ⲫⲏⲉⲧⲟⲓ ⲛ̀ⲁⲑⲛⲟⲃⲓ ⲙ̀ⲙⲁⲩⲁⲧϥ ⲟⲩⲟϩ ⲉ̀ⲧⲉ ⲟⲩⲟⲛ ϣ̀ϫⲟⲙ ⲙ̀ⲙⲟϥ ⲉ̀ⲭⲁⲛⲟⲃⲓ ⲉ̀ⲃⲟⲗ. [3] ⲛ̀ⲑⲟⲕ ⲫⲛⲏⲃ ⲉⲧⲥⲱⲟⲩⲛ ⲛ̀ⲧⲁⲙⲉⲧⲁⲧⲉⲙⲡϣⲁ ⲛⲉⲙ ⲧⲁⲙⲉⲧⲁⲧⲥⲟⲃϯ ⲛⲉⲙ ⲧⲁⲙⲉⲧⲁⲧϩⲓⲕⲁⲛⲟⲥ ⲉ̀ϧⲟⲩⲛ ⲉ̀ⲡⲁⲓϣⲉⲙϣⲓ ⲉⲑⲟⲩⲁⲃ ⲛ̀ⲧⲁⲕ ⲫⲁⲓ. ⲟⲩⲟϩ ⲙ̀ⲙⲟⲛ ϩⲟ ⲙ̀ⲙⲟⲓ ⲉ̀ϧⲱⲛⲧ ⲉ̀ϧⲟⲩⲛ ⲟⲩⲟϩ ⲉ̀ⲁⲟⲩⲱⲛ ⲛ̀ⲣⲱⲓ ⲙ̀ⲡⲉⲙ̀ⲑⲟ ⲙ̀ⲡⲉⲕⲱ̀ⲟⲩ ⲉ̀ⲑⲩⲟⲁⲃ. [4] ⲁⲗⲗⲁ ⲕⲁⲧⲁ ⲡⲁ̀ϣⲁⲓ ⲛ̀ⲧⲉ ⲛⲉⲕⲙⲉⲧϣⲉⲛϩⲏⲧ ⲭⲱ ⲛⲏⲓ ⲉ̀ⲃⲟⲗ ⲁⲛⲟⲕ ϧⲁ ⲡⲓⲣⲉϥⲉⲣⲛⲟⲃⲓ. [5] ⲟⲩⲟϩ ⲙⲏⲓⲥ ⲛⲏⲓ ⲉⲑⲣⲓϫⲓⲙⲓ ⲛ̀ⲟⲩϩⲙⲟⲧ ⲛⲉⲙ ⲟⲩⲛⲁⲓ ϧⲉⲛ ⲧⲁⲓ ⲟⲩⲛⲟⲩ ⲑⲁⲓ. [6] ⲟⲩⲟϩ ⲟⲩⲱⲣⲡ ⲛⲏⲓ ⲉ̀ϧⲣⲏⲓ ⲛ̀ⲟⲩϫⲟⲙ ⲉ̀ⲃⲟⲗ ϧⲉⲛ ⲡϭⲓⲥⲓ ⲉⲑⲣⲓⲉⲣϩⲏⲧⲥ ⲟⲩⲟϩ ⲛ̀ⲧⲁⲥⲟⲃϯ ⲟⲩⲟϩ ⲛ̀ⲧⲁϫⲱⲕ ⲉ̀ⲃⲟⲗ ⲕⲁⲧⲁ ⲡⲉⲑⲣⲁⲛⲁⲕ ⲙ̀ⲡⲉⲕϣⲉⲙϣⲓ ⲉⲑⲟⲩⲁⲃ ⲕⲁⲧⲁ ⲡϯⲙⲁϯ ⲙ̀ⲡⲉⲕⲟⲩⲱϣ ⲉ̀ⲟⲩⲥⲑⲟⲓ ⲛ̀ⲥⲑⲟⲓⲛⲟⲩϥⲓ. [7] ⲥⲉ ⲡⲉⲛⲛⲏⲃ ϣⲱⲡⲓ ⲛⲉⲙⲁⲛ ⲁⲣⲓϣⲫⲏⲣ

[1] O Lord who knows the hearts of everyone [Acts 1:24; Lk 16:15], the holy one and who rests in his saints, [2] who alone is without sin, and is able to forgive sins [Mt 9:6]. [3] You, O Master, know my unworthiness, my unpreparedness, and my insufficiency unto this your holy service. And I do not have the face to draw near and to open my mouth before your holy glory. [4] But according to the multitude of your compassion, forgive me the sinner [Lk 18:13]. [5] And grant me to find grace and mercy at this hour. [6] And send unto me power from on high, that I may begin and prepare and fulfill your holy service as is pleasing to you, according to the pleasure of your will, unto a sweet-smelling savor [Eph 5:2]. [7] Yes, our Master, dwell with us, cooperate with us, bless us.

71 Dous, "Η Αλεξανδρινή Θεία Λειτουργία," 58–68.

ⲛ̀ⲛⲉⲣϩⲱⲃ ⲛⲉⲙⲁⲛ ⲥⲙⲟⲩ ⲉ̀ⲣⲟⲛ. [8] ⲛ̀ⲑⲟⲕ ⲅⲁⲣ ⲡⲉ ⲡⲭⲱ ⲉ̀ⲃⲟⲗ ⲛ̀ⲧⲉ ⲛⲉⲛⲛⲟⲃⲓ ⲫⲟⲩⲱⲓⲛⲓ ⲛ̀ⲧⲉ ⲛⲉⲛⲯⲩⲭⲏ ⲡⲉⲛⲱⲛϧ ⲛⲉⲙ ⲧⲉⲛϫⲟⲙ ⲛⲉⲙ ⲧⲉⲛⲡⲁⲣⲣⲏⲥⲓⲁ. [9] ⲟⲩⲟϩ ⲛ̀ⲑⲟⲕ ⲡⲉⲧⲉⲛⲟⲩⲱⲣⲡ ⲛⲁⲕ ⲉ̀ⲡϣⲱⲓ ⲙ̀ⲡⲓⲱⲟⲩ ⲛⲉⲙ ⲡⲓⲧⲁⲓⲟ ⲛⲉⲙ ϯⲡⲣⲟⲥⲕⲩⲛⲏⲥⲓⲥ ⲫⲓⲱⲧ ⲛⲉⲙ ⲡϣⲏⲣⲓ ⲛⲉⲙ ⲡⲓⲡⲛⲉⲩⲙⲁ ⲉⲑⲟⲩⲁⲃ. ϯⲛⲟⲩ ⲛⲉⲙ ⲛ̀ⲥⲏⲟⲩ ⲛⲓⲃⲉⲛ ⲛⲉⲙ ϣⲁ ⲉⲛⲉϩ ⲛ̀ⲧⲉ ⲛⲓⲉⲛⲉϩ ⲧⲏⲣⲟⲩ ⲁⲙⲏⲛ.[72]

[8] For you are the forgiveness of our sins, the light of our souls, our life, our strength, and our boldness. [9] And to you we send up the glory, the honor, and the worship, to the Father, and the Son, and the Holy Spirit, now and at all times, and unto ages of all the ages, amen.

[1] Δέσποτα Κύριε, καρδιόγνωστα πάντων, ὁ ἅγιος καὶ ἐν ἁγίοις ἀναπαυόμενος, [2] ὁ μόνος ἀναμάρτητος καὶ δυνάμενος ἀφιέναι ἁμαρτίας, [3] σὺ γινώσκεις, Δέσποτα, τὸ ἀνάξιόν μου καὶ ἀνέτοιμον καὶ ἀνίκανον πρὸς τὴν σὴν ἁγίαν λειτουργίαν ταύτην, καὶ ὅτι πρόσωπον οὐκ ἔχω προσεγγῦσαι καὶ ἀνοῖξαι τὸ στόμα μου ἐνώπιον τῆς ἁγίας σου δόξης. [4] Ἀλλά κατὰ τὸ πλῆθος τῶν οἰκτιρμῶν σου, ὁ Θεός, ἱλασθητί μοι τῷ ἁμαρτωλῷ, [5] καὶ δός μοι χάριν εὑρεῖν καὶ ἔλεος ἐν ταύτῃ τῇ ὥρᾳ. [6] Καὶ κατάπεμψόν μοι δύναμιν ἐξ ὕψους, τοῦ ἄρξασθαι καὶ ἑτοιμάσαι καὶ ἐν εὐθύτητι ἐπιτελέσαι τὴν ἁγίαν λατρείαν ταύτην, εἰς ὀσμὴν εὐωδίας κατὰ τὴν εὐδοκίαν τοῦ θελήματός σου. [7] Ναὶ Δέσποτα, συμπάρεσο ἡμῖν, συνέργησον, καὶ ἡμᾶς εὐλόγησον. [8] σὺ γάρ εἶ ἱλασμὸς τῶν ἁμαρτιῶν ἡμῶν, φωτισμὸς καὶ δύναμις τῶν ψυχῶν, [9] καὶ σοι τὴν δόξαν, τιμήν, καὶ προσκύνησιν ἀναπέμπομεν, τῷ Πατρὶ καὶ τῷ Υἱῷ καὶ τῷ Ἁγίῳ Πνεύματι, νῦν καὶ ἀεί, καὶ εἰς τοὺς αἰῶνας τῶν αἰώνων. Ἀμήν.[73]

[1] O Master Lord, the knower of the hearts of all [Acts 1:24; Lk 16:15], the holy one and who rests among saints, [2] who alone is sinless and able to forgive sins [Mt 9:6]. [3] You know, Master, my unworthiness, unpreparedness, and insufficiency unto this your holy service, and that I have no face to approach and open my mouth before your holy glory. [4] But according to the multitude of your compassion, O God, pardon me the sinner [Lk 18:13], [5] and grant me to find grace and mercy at this hour. [6] And send unto me power from on high, in order to begin, prepare, and uprightly fulfill this holy service, for a sweet-smelling savor [Eph 5:2], according to the good pleasure of your will. [7] Yes, O Master, be with us, cooperate, and bless us. [8] For you are the forgiveness of our sins and enlightenment and power of souls, [9] and to you we send up the glory, the honor, and the worship, to the Father and the Son, and the Holy Spirit, now and ever, and unto the ages of ages, amen.

72 Ṣalīb, ⲡⲓϫⲱⲙ ⲛ̀ⲧⲉ ⲡⲓⲉⲩⲭⲟⲗⲟⲅⲓⲟⲛ, 198–201.

73 Macomber, "The Greek Text of the Coptic Mass," 314; Dous, "Η Αλεξανδρινή Θεία Λειτουργία," 74.

3.2. The Prayer After the Preparation of the Altar

[1] ⲛ̀ⲑⲟⲕ ⲡ̅ⲟ̅ⲥ̅ ⲁⲕϯ̀ⲥⲁⲃⲟⲛ ⲉ̀ⲡⲁⲓⲛⲓϣϯ ⲙ̀ⲙⲩⲥⲧⲏⲣⲓⲟⲛ ⲛ̀ⲧⲉ ⲡⲓⲟⲩϫⲁⲓ. [2] ⲛ̀ⲑⲟⲕ ⲁⲕⲑⲁϩⲙⲉⲛ ϧⲁ ⲛⲏⲉⲧⲑⲉⲃⲓⲏⲟⲩⲧ ⲟⲩⲟϩ ⲛ̀ⲁⲧⲉⲙⲡϣⲁ ⲛ̀ⲉⲃⲓⲁⲓⲕ ⲛ̀ⲧⲁⲕ ⲉ̀ⲑⲣⲉⲛϣⲱⲡⲓ ⲛ̀ⲣⲉϥϣⲉⲙϣⲓ ⲙ̀ⲡⲉⲕⲑⲩⲥⲓⲁⲥⲧⲏⲣⲓⲟⲛ ⲉⲑⲩⲟⲁⲃ. [3] ⲛ̀ⲑⲟⲕ ⲡⲉⲛⲛⲏⲃ ⲁ̀ⲣⲓⲧⲉⲛ ⲛ̀ϩⲓⲕⲁⲛⲟⲥ ϧⲉⲛ ϯϫⲟⲙ ⲛ̀ⲧⲉ ⲡⲉⲕⲡ̅ⲛ̅ⲁ̅ ⲉ̅ⲑ̅ⲩ̅ ⲉ̀ϫⲱⲕ ⲉ̀ⲃⲟⲗ ⲛ̀ⲧⲁⲓⲇⲓⲁⲕⲟⲛⲓⲁ ⲑⲁⲓ. [4] ϩⲓⲛⲁ ϧⲉⲛ ⲟⲩⲙⲉⲧⲁⲧϩⲓⲧⲧⲉⲛ ⲉ̀ⲡϩⲁⲡ ⲙ̀ⲡⲉⲙⲑⲟ ⲙ̀ⲡⲉⲕⲛⲓϣϯ ⲛ̀ⲱⲟⲩ ⲛ̀ⲧⲉⲛⲓ̀ⲛⲓ ⲛⲁⲕ ⲉ̀ϧⲟⲩⲛ ⲛ̀ⲟⲩⲑⲩⲥⲓⲁ ⲛ̀ⲥⲙⲟⲩ. ⲟⲩⲱⲟⲩ ⲛⲉⲙ ⲟⲩⲛⲓϣϯ ⲙ̀ⲙⲉⲧⲥⲁⲓⲉ ϧⲉⲛ ⲡⲉⲑⲟⲩⲁⲃ ⲛ̀ⲧⲁⲕ. [5] ⲫϯ ⲫⲏ ⲉⲧϯ ⲛ̀ⲟⲩϩⲙⲟⲧ ⲫⲏ ⲉⲑⲟⲩⲱⲣⲡ ⲛ̀ⲟⲩⲥⲱϯ ⲫⲏ ⲉⲧⲉⲣⲛ̀ⲉⲣⲅⲓⲛ ⲛ̀ϩⲱⲃ ⲛⲓⲃⲉⲛ ϧⲉⲛ ⲟⲩⲟⲛ ⲛⲓⲃⲉⲛ. [6] ⲙⲏⲓⲥ ⲡ̅ⲟ̅ⲥ̅ ⲉⲑⲣⲉⲥϣⲱⲡⲓ ⲉⲥϣⲏⲡ ⲙ̀ⲡⲉⲕⲙⲑⲟ ⲛ̀ϫⲉ ⲧⲉⲛⲑⲩⲥⲓⲁ ⲉ̀ϩⲣⲏⲓ ⲉ̀ϫⲉⲛ ⲛⲏ ⲉ̀ⲧⲉ ⲛⲟⲩⲓ̀ ⲛ̀ⲛⲟⲃⲓ ⲛⲉⲙ ⲛⲓⲙⲉⲧⲁⲧⲉⲙⲓ ⲛ̀ⲧⲉ ⲡⲉⲕⲗⲁⲟⲥ. ⲟⲩⲟϩ ϫⲉ ⲥⲧⲟⲩⲃⲏⲟⲩⲧ ⲕⲁⲧⲁ ϯⲇⲱⲣⲉⲁ̀ ⲛ̀ⲧⲉ ⲡⲉⲕⲡⲛⲉⲩⲙⲁ ⲉⲑⲟⲩⲁⲃ ϧⲉⲛ ⲡⲓⲭⲣⲓⲥⲧⲟⲥ ⲓⲏⲥⲟⲩⲥ ⲡⲉⲛⲟ̅ⲥ̅. [7] ⲫⲁⲓ ⲉⲧⲉ ⲉ̀ⲃⲟⲗ ϩⲓⲧⲟⲧϥ ⲉⲣⲉ ⲡⲓⲱⲟⲩ ⲛⲉⲙ ⲡⲓⲧⲁⲓⲟ ⲛⲉⲙ ⲡⲓⲁⲙⲁϩⲓ ⲛⲉⲙ ϯⲡⲣⲟⲥⲕⲩⲛⲏⲥⲓⲥ ⲉⲣⲡⲣⲉⲡⲓ ⲛⲁⲕ ⲛⲉⲙⲁϥ ⲛⲉⲙ ⲡⲓⲡ̅ⲛ̅ⲁ̅ ⲉ̅ⲑ̅ⲩ̅ ⲛ̀ⲣⲉϥⲧⲁⲛϧⲟ ⲟⲩⲟϩ ⲛ̀ⲟⲙⲟⲟⲩⲥⲓⲟⲥ ⲛⲉⲙⲁⲕ. ϯⲛⲟⲩ ⲛⲉⲙ ⲛ̀ⲥⲏⲟⲩ ⲛⲓⲃⲉⲛ ⲛⲉⲙ ϣⲁ ⲉⲛⲉϩ ⲛ̀ⲧⲉ ⲛⲓⲉⲛⲉϩ ⲧⲏⲣⲟⲩ ⲁⲙⲏⲛ.[74]

[1] You, O Lord, have taught us this great mystery of salvation. [2] You called us, your lowly and unworthy servants, to become ministers of your holy altar. [3] O our Master, make us worthy by the power of your Holy Spirit to fulfill this ministry. [4] So that without falling into condemnation before your holy glory, we may offer unto you a sacrifice of praise [Heb 13:15], glory, and great beauty in your holy place. [5] O God who grants grace, who sends salvation, who works everything in everyone [1 Cor 12:16]. [6] Grant, O Lord, that our sacrifice may be acceptable before you [Phil 4:18], for my own sins and for the ignorances of your people [Heb 9:7], and that it may be pure according to the gift of your Holy Spirit [Rom 15:16], in Christ Jesus our Lord. [7] This is he through whom the glory, the honor, the dominion, and the worship are due unto you, with him and the Holy Spirit, the giver of life, who is of one essence with you, now and at all times, and unto the ages of all ages, amen.

[1] Σὺ Κύριε, κατέδειξας ἡμῖν τὸ μέγα τοῦτο τῆς σωτηρίας μυστήριον. [2] σὺ κατηξίωσας ἡμᾶς, τοὺς ταπεινούς καὶ ἁμαρτωλοὺς καὶ ἀναξίους δούλους σου, γενέσθαι λειτουργοὺς τοῦ ἁγίου θυσιαστηρίου σου. [3] σὺ ἱκάνωσον ἡμᾶς ἐν τῇ δυνάμει τοῦ Πνεύματός σου τοῦ Ἁγίου, εἰς τὴν διακονίαν ταύτην, [4] ἵνα ἀκατακρίτως στάντες ἐνώπιον τῆς ἁγίας δόξης σου, προσάγωμέν σοι θυσίαν αἰνέσεως καὶ δόξης καὶ

[1] You O Lord have revealed to us this great mystery of salvation. [2] You have made us worthy, we your lowly, sinful, and unworthy servants, to become ministers of your holy altar. [3] Make us fit by the power of your Holy Spirit unto this ministry, [4] so that standing uncondemned before your holy glory, we may present to you a sacrifice of praise [Heb 13:15], glory, and magnificence in your holy place. [5] O God, having

74 Ṣalīb, ⲡⲓϫⲱⲙ ⲛ̀ⲧⲉ ⲡⲓⲉⲩⲭⲟⲗⲟⲅⲓⲟⲛ, 201–203.

μεγαλοπρεπείας ἐν τῷ ἁγιαστηρίῳ σου. [5] Θεέ, δοὺς τὴν χάριν, πέμψας τὴν σωτηρίαν, σὺ γὰρ εἶ ὁ ἐνεργῶν τὰ πάντα ἐν πᾶσι, [6] δός, Κύριε, καὶ ὑπὲρ τῶν ἡμετέρων ἁμαρτημάτων καὶ τῶν τοῦ λαοῦ σου ἀγνοημάτων, δεκτὴν γενέσθαι τὴν θυσίαν ἡμῶν καὶ εὐπρόσδεκτον ἐνώπιόν σου, κατὰ τὴν δωρεὰν τοῦ Ἁγίου σου Πνεύματος, ἐν Χριστῷ Ἰησοῦ τῷ Κυρίῳ ἡμῶν, [7] δι' οὗ καὶ μεθ' οὗ σοι ἡ δόξα, τιμή, καὶ τὸ κράτος, σὺν τῷ παναγίῳ καὶ ἀγαθῷ καὶ ζωοποιῷ καὶ ὁμοουσίῳ σου Πνεύματι, νῦν καὶ ἀεί, καὶ εἰς τοὺς αἰῶνας τῶν αἰώνων. Ἀμήν.[75]

granted the grace, and having sent salvation, for you are he who works all in all [1 Cor 12:16], [6] grant also, O Lord, on behalf of our sins and the ignorances of your people [Heb 9:7], that our sacrifice be acceptable and well-pleasing before you [Phil 4:18], according to the gift of your Holy Spirit [Rom 15:16], in Christ Jesus our Lord, [7] through whom and with whom to you is the glory, the honor, and the dominion, with your all-Holy, good, life-giving, and consubstantial Spirit, now and ever, and unto the ages of ages, amen.

3.3. The Title of the Prayers

The title for these prayers in the *editio typica* is "The prayer of the preparation of the altar (صلاة الاستعداد الذي للمذبح)," and "Prayer secretly after the preparation (صلاة سراً من بعد الاستعداد)."[76] With the exception of the description of the second prayer as secret, this is rendered literally in Coptic in the *editio princeps* of Ṭūḫī as "A prayer of preparation of the altar (ⲟⲩⲉⲩⲭⲏ ⲛ̀ⲧⲉ ⲡⲓⲥⲟⲃϯ ⲙ̀ⲡⲓⲙⲁⲛ̀ⲉⲣϣⲱⲟⲩϣⲓ)," and, "A prayer after the preparation of the altar (ⲟⲩⲉⲩⲭⲏ ⲙⲉⲛⲉⲛⲥⲁ ⲡ̀ⲧⲓⲥⲟⲃϯ ⲙ̀ⲡⲓⲙⲁⲛ̀ⲉⲣϣⲱⲟⲩϣⲓ)," respectively.[77] With little variance, these two titles are matched as well in the majority of manuscripts.[78] Minor variatons include, "A prayer for the covering of the sanctuary (صلاة لكسوة الهيكل),"[79] and, "A prayer on behalf of the service of the altar (صلاة من اجل خدمة المذبح)."[80] Likewise, the title of the second prayer in all of these manuscripts tends to alternate

[75] Macomber, "The Greek Text of the Coptic Mass," 314–315; Dous, "Η Αλεξανδρινή Θεία Λειτουργία," 75.

[76] Ṣalīb, ⲡⲓϫⲱⲙ ⲛ̀ⲧⲉ ⲡⲓⲉⲩⲭⲟⲗⲟⲅⲓⲟⲛ, 198, 201.

[77] Ṭūḫī, ⲡⲓϫⲱⲙ ⲛ̀ⲧⲉ ⲡⲓϣⲟⲙⲧ ⲛ̀ⲁⲛⲁⲫⲟⲣⲁ, 304, 307.

[78] *BAV Vatican Copt. 17* (AD 1288), fol. 2r, *Bodleian Hunt. 572* (13th/14th c.), fol. 1r, *Bodleian Ind. Inst. Copt. 4* (13th/14th c.), fol. 1r, *Paris BnF Copt. 82* (AD 1307), fol. 1r, *BAV Borgia Copt. 7* (AD 1379), fol. 4r, *Kacmarcik Codex* (14th c.), fol. 1v, *Paris BnF Copt. 24* (15th c.), fol. 5r, *Paris BnF Copt. 73* (AD 1528), fol. 4r, *BAV Vatican Copt. 26* (AD 1616), fol. 1r, *Suryān Lit. 474* (AD 1666), fol. 3r, *Suryān Lit. 481* (AD 1752), fol. 3r, *Suryān Lit. 457* (AD 1758), fol. 3r, and *Suryān Lit. 482* (AD 1787), fol. 4r.

[79] *Suryān Lit. 466* (AD 1573), fol. 3r, and *Suryān Lit. 469* (before AD 1623), fol. 4r. A single manuscript, *Coptic Patriarchate Lit. 331* (AD 1678), fol. 3r combines the two titles into: صلاة الاستعداد لكسوة المذبح.

[80] *Suryān Lit. 468* (AD 1601), fol. 3r, *Suryān Lit. 472* (AD 1659), fol. 3r, *Suryān Lit. 473* (AD 1659), fol. 3r, and *Suryān Lit. 484* (AD 1841), fol. 99r.

between "A prayer after the preparation [of the altar]" and "A prayer after the covering [of the altar]." These manuscripts are representative of a wide geographical distribution including Scetis, the Eastern Desert, and even the Coptic communities in Jerusalem and in Cyprus.[81]

However, the titles of the prayers in other manuscripts are more diverse. Two of the earliest thirteenth-century Euchologia attribute the first prayer to Severus of Antioch.[82] Not all manuscripts attribute this prayer to the preparation of the altar per se. For example, *Bodleian Marsh 5* (14th c.) gives no title to the first prayer.[83] In *BAV Vatican Copt. 25* (17th c.), also from Scetis, the prayer is titled, "The prayer of the mystery of preparation (صلاة سر الاستعداد)," leaving it unclear for what or whom this preparation is intended.[84] In a similar fashion, *BAV Vatican Copt. 18* (AD 1531), *Suryān Lit. 465* (AD 1645) and *Suryān Lit. 477* (AD 1792) title the first prayer, "The prayer of preparation (صلاة الاستعداد)," [85] while *Beinecke Copt. 21* (AD 1877) calls both prayers collectively, "The prayers of preparation (صلوات الاستعداد)."[86] Some manuscripts are even more at variance from the standard titles. *Paris BnF Copt. 29* (AD 1639) has the Arabic title, "A mystery of preparation (سر استعداد)," while the Coptic reads, "*epiclesis* (ⲉⲡⲓⲕⲗⲏⲥⲓⲥ)," often used in Coptic rubrics to refer to the manner of reading the prayer secretly, making it equivalent to the Greek (μυστικῶς).[87] Similarly, *Suryān Lit. 461* (AD 1795) has, "The mystery of the preparation of the altar (سر استعداد المذبح)."[88] *Coptic Patriarchate Lit. 331* (AD 1678) calls the second prayer, "The mystery after the preparation (السر من بعد الاستعداد)."

Even more instructive—as will be demonstrated shortly—is the title in *Paris BnF Copt. 30* (AD 1642). Here, the introductory rubrics about the preparation of the altar begin abruptly with the title, "*Prayer of the Veil* (صلاة الحجاب)," which seems to confuse the prayer of altar

81 For the geographical provenance of these manuscripts and many others, see Budde, *Die ägyptische Basilios-Anaphora*, 139.

82 This is the case in *British Library Or. 1239* (13th c.), fol. 5r, and *Bodleian Hunt. 360* (13th c.), fol. 4r, both from the general area of the Scetis monasteries.

83 *Bodleian Marsh 5* (14th c.), fol. 1r.

84 *BAV Vatican Copt. 25* (17th c.), fol. 1r.

85 *BAV Vatican Copt. 18* (AD 1531), fol. 111v, *Suryān Lit. 465* (AD 1645), fol. 5r, *Suryān Lit. 477* (AD 1792), fol. 1r.

86 *Beinecke Copt. 21* (AD 1877), fol. 63r.

87 *Paris BnF Copt. 29* (AD 1639), fol. 2r. Regarding the term *epiclesis* as found in the heading of cetain Coptic euchological prayers, see O.H.E. Burmester, "Fragments of a Late 12th to Early 13th Century Bohairic Euchologion from the Monastery of St. Macarius in Scetis," *BSAC* 19 (1967–1968): 17–47, here 39n1; Brakmann, "Zu den Fragmenten," 127n53.

88 *Suryān Lit. 461* (AD 1795), fol. 12v.

preparation with the *oratio veli* or the *Prayer of the Veil*, which the priest recites before the anaphora.[89] However, by the end of the paragraph, the same manuscript refers to the same prayer again as, "A prayer for the preparation of the altar and the remainder of the vessels (صلاة الاستعداد لكسوة المذبح وبقية الاواني)," a title encountered also in *Coptic Museum Lit. 338* (18th c.).[90] Finally, *British Library Or. 1239* (13th c.) calls the second prayer, "A prayer of covering the altar by the prospherin (اوشية لتغطية الهيكل بالابرسفارين)," although this is clearly a confusion on the part of the copyist with the *Prothesis Prayer*, which follows soon after.[91]

3.4. The Text of the Prayers

Very little can be said about the text of the prayers. Analysis has shown that the text has been very stable in the manuscript tradition since the earliest thirteenth-century Euchologia *British Library Or. 1239*, *Bodleian Hunt. 360*, and *BAV Vatican Copt. 17*. The manuscripts examined displayed only those variants related to nonstandard spelling of Coptic, or occasional insignificant omissions. While the Arabic text for the entire liturgy displays less stability than the Coptic text in its choice of words, word order, and fidelity to a literal translation of the Coptic at the expense of proper style, none of these variants were found to be instructive in terms of the liturgico-theological analysis of the prayers.

The same is not true when comparing the Coptic recension to the Greek. As can be seen, although the two texts agree in the aggregate, they nonetheless differ in some key passages. In the first prayer, the Greek has "O Master Lord (Δέσποτα Κύριε)" as an introductory invocation, compared to the Coptic's "Lord (ⲡⲟ̅ⲥ̅)" in [1]. In the prayer's petition [6], the Greek adds a desire to *uprightly* fulfill the holy service (ἐν εὐθύτητι ἐπιτελέσαι τὴν ἁγίαν λατρείαν ταύτην), an expression absent in the Coptic. The Coptic itself however has an additional clause in the same petition [6] that the service be fulfilled "as is pleasing to you, according to the pleasure of your will (ⲕⲁⲧⲁ ⲡⲉⲑⲣⲁⲛⲁⲕ ⲙ̀ⲡⲉⲕϣⲉⲙϣⲓ ⲉⲑⲟⲩⲁⲃ ⲕⲁⲧⲁ ⲡϯⲙⲁϯ ⲙ̀ⲡⲉⲕⲟⲩⲱϣ)." The biggest difference between the two texts lies in [8]. While the Coptic has "For you are the forgiveness of our sins, the light of our souls, our life, our strength, and our boldness (ⲛ̀ⲑⲟⲕ ⲅⲁⲣ ⲡⲉ ⲡⲭⲱ ⲉ̀ⲃⲟⲗ ⲛ̀ⲧⲉ ⲛⲉⲛⲛⲟⲃⲓ ⲫⲟⲩⲱⲓⲛⲓ ⲛ̀ⲧⲉ ⲛⲉⲛⲯⲩⲭⲏ ⲡⲉⲛⲱⲛϧ ⲛⲉⲙ ⲧⲉⲛϫⲟⲙ ⲛⲉⲙ ⲧⲉⲛⲡⲁⲣⲣⲏⲥⲓⲁ)," the Greek has

89 *Paris BnF Copt. 30* (AD 1642), fol. 2r.
90 *Coptic Museum Lit. 338* (18th c.), fol. 2r.
91 *British Library Or. 1239* (13th c.), fol. 7v. Another possibility is that the *prospherin* is understood here as all the altar cloths and not just the large veil that covers the gifts at the conclusion of the prothesis rite.

"For you are the forgiveness of our sins and enlightenment and power of souls (σὺ γάρ εἶ ἱλασμὸς τῶν ἁμαρτιῶν ἡμῶν, φωτισμὸς καὶ δύναμις τῶν ψυχῶν)." Thus, the Greek text delays "soul" to govern both "enlightenment" and "power", while eliminating the two nouns, life and boldness, although the latter is a Greek loan word even in the Coptic text (ⲡⲁⲣⲣⲏⲥⲓⲁ).

The second prayer exhibits some key differences as well. Whereas the Lord in [2] is said to have "called us (ⲁⲕⲑⲁϩⲙⲉⲛ)" to become ministers in the Coptic text, this is rendered as "have made us worthy (κατηξίωσας ἡμᾶς)" in the Greek. The Coptic has the curious petition [6], "that it [our sacrifice] may be pure according to the gift of your Holy Spirit (ⲟⲩⲟϩ ϫⲉ ⲥⲧⲟⲩⲃⲏⲟⲩⲧ ⲕⲁⲧⲁ ϯⲇⲱⲣⲉⲁ̀ ⲛ̀ⲧⲉ ⲡⲉⲕⲡⲛⲉⲩⲙⲁ ⲉⲑⲟⲩⲁⲃ)," while the Greek simply has "that our sacrifice be acceptable and well-pleasing before you, according to the gift of your Holy Spirit (δεκτὴν γενέσθαι τὴν θυσίαν ἡμῶν καὶ εὐπροσδεκτὸν ἐνώπιόν σου, κατὰ τὴν δωρεὰν τοῦ Ἁγίου σου Πνεύματος)," without any reference to the purifying activity of the Holy Spirit. This brief analysis is sufficient to show the relative freedom of the Greek text of the Coptic liturgy from its more dominant Bohairic counterpart.

3.5. The History of the Prayers of Preparation

Although both prayers are linked in the formulary to the physical preparation of the altar, it is clear from a cursory glance at their texts that they are unrelated in any direct way to the eucharistic vessels and their preparation for the prothesis. This is also confirmed by the few manuscripts, such as *BAV Vatican Copt. 25* (17th c.), and *Paris BnF Copt. 29* (AD 1639), which do not claim the preparation to be of the altar, but simply "The Mystery of Preparation," as presented above. But, for whom is this preparation intended?

In both its Greek and Coptic texts, the first prayer has this following petition as its central core request in [6]: "send unto me power from on high, that I may begin and prepare and fulfill your holy service as is pleasing to you, according to the pleasure of your will, unto a sweet-smelling savor." Similarly, the second prayer asks the following in [3]: "O our Master, make us fit by the power of your Holy Spirit to fulfill this ministry," and adds to it later [6], "Grant, O Lord, that our sacrifice may be acceptable before you, for my own sins and for the ignorances of your people." Thus, they are prayers confessing the celebrant's unworthiness to offer the sacrifice and requesting divine assistance in order for the offering to be well pleasing for the forgiveness of the celebrant's and people's sins. This immediately places attempts at interpreting the function and origin of these two prayers within the larger context of the prayers of *accessus ad altare* in East and West. It will be instructive therefore to provide a tour through the prayers of *accessus* in different traditions. This will allow afterwards the proposing of some hypotheses regarding the history and function of the two prayers of preparation of the altar.

3.5.1. The Prayers of *Accessus ad Altare* in East and West

Prayers and rites preparing the clergy and asking for worthiness to approach and to serve the holy altar are common in East and West and are often titled by the Latin term, *accessus ad altare*. In addition to *apologiae* acknowledging the unworthiness of the clergy and asking for divine assistance, other elements of the *accessus* rites may include prayers for the acceptance of the future offering, as well as ancient rites such as the hand washing, and the kiss. The following is a sampling of these prayers in the various liturgical rites, though it is not intended as an exhaustive analysis, which would require its own study.

In the Roman Rite, such so-called *accessus* prayers in the pre-Vatican II, as well as the extraordinary form of the Roman Mass, developed in the ninth century as attested in the *Sacrementary of Saint Thierry*, and consisted of fourteen penitential prayers designated as *orationes ante missam*. These later developed into a selection of preparatory psalms that varied over time, only later to re-acquire the nature of an *apologia* through the addition of the *oratio Sancti Ambrosii, summe sacerdos* in the course of the eleventh century.[92]

In the Byzantine Rite, the Coptic prayer of preparation is matched most closely by the prayer *Nemo dignus* (οὐδεὶς ἄξιος), otherwise known as *The Prayer of the Cherubic Hymn* (εὐχὴ τοῦ Χερουβικοῦ ὕμνου), and is common today in both Byzantine CHR and BAS, as well as in the Armenian liturgy.[93] Here also the prayer entreats God: "With the power of your Holy Spirit, make me, who am clothed with the grace of the priesthood, to stand at this your holy table, and to offer your holy body and your honored blood."[94] In terms of the unfolding of the Byzantine liturgy, this prayer comes after the *synapte*, the silent recitation of *The Second Prayer of the Faithful*, and during the chanting of the Cherubic hymn.[95] That is, during the pre-anaphoral

[92] For the rites of *praeparatio ad Missam* in the Roman Rite, see Jungmann, *Missarum Sollemnia*, 1:271–276.

[93] *LEW*, 318, 401. For the text of the prayer in the oldest Byzantine Euchologion, *BAV Barberini Gr. 336* (8th c.), see Parenti and Velkovska, *L'Eucologio Barberini*, 62 (Greek), 265 (Italian), section 12. For the *Nemo dignus* prayer in the Armenian liturgy, see *LEW*, 430.

[94] Taft and Parenti, *Il Grande Ingresso*, 299. Translation is mine.

[95] *LEW*, 377–378.

rites, which separate the Liturgy of the Word from the eucharistic liturgy proper. In studying this prayer and its place in the history of the Byzantine liturgy, Robert Taft has shown that it is a late addition to the rites of the Church of Constantinople. He based his conclusion on multiple arguments, which included internal evidence from the text, the absence of the prayer in some early sources, and confusion in many manuscripts on the place of this prayer in the unfolding of the liturgy. Although the prayer is of Constantinopolitan origin, it remains part of a group of later elements that were added to the *accessus* rites of Constantinople.[96]

The Byzantine liturgies also express aspects of the *accessus* motif in other prayers. For example, in Byzantine BAS, the *Second Prayer of the Faithful*, Ὁ Θεός ὁ ἐπισκεψάμενος ἐν ἐλέει καὶ οἰκτιρμοῖς, asks God, "Strengthen us by the power of your Holy Spirit unto this ministry."[97] Other prayers such as the so-called *Proskomide* prayer in both CHR and BAS and other prayers of the faithful in CHR are also part of the *accessus* rites.[98]

Of particular importance for understanding the origin of the Coptic prayers of preparation is the *First Prayer of the Faithful* in Byzantine BAS, Σὺ Κύριε κατέδειξας ἡμῖν. This prayer is exactly the Coptic prayer after the preparation of the altar presented above. It is found in the Byzantine tradition without any variants from the Greek recension as early as the eighth century *BAV Barberini Gr. 336*.[99] It is also found in the *Pyromalus Codex*, an early archieratikon of BAS

96 The internal evidence for the late development of this prayer included: 1. Its addressing of Christ, not the Father, an unusual feature in most Byzantine prayers, 2. Its speaking of the priest in the first person, 3. The large amount of direct scriptural quotations, 4. The prayer's highly sacerdotal theology, and 5. The large number of variants in the manuscript tradition. For the entire analysis of the *Nemo dignus* prayer, see Taft and Parenti, *Il Grande Ingresso*, 257–296. On the other hand, the fact that the prayer addresses Christ makes it seem more at home in the anaphora of GREG, where it appears as an *oratio veli* in the codex *Paris BnF Gr. 325* (14th c.), fol. 66v–68v containing the Alexandrian liturgies of BAS and GREG. See Renaudot, *Liturgiarum Orientalium Collectio*, 1:88–89. This has led the late liturgiologist Ioannes Phountoules to see the origin of this prayer in Alexandria rather than Constantinople. Cf. Ioannes Phountoules, *Απαντήσεις εις Λειτουργικάς Απορίας* [Answers to liturgical questions], 6th ed., vol. 1 (1–150) (Athens: Ἀποστολική Διακονία τῆς Ἐκκλησίας τῆς Ἑλλάδος, 2006), 56.

97 *LEW*, 317, 401. Cf. Parenti and Velkovska, *L'Eucologio Barberini gr. 336*, 61 (Greek), 265 (Italian), section 11.

98 The rites and prayers of *accessus ad altare* in the Byzantine Rite were analyzed in the second part of Robert Taft's *The Great Entrance*, updated recently by Stefano Parenti. For the *Proskomide* prayers of CHR and BAS, see Taft and Parenti, *Il Grande Ingresso*, 568–603.

99 Parenti and Velkovska, *L'Eucologio Barberini gr. 336*, 61 (Greek), 265 (Italian), section 10.

from the tenth/eleventh century.[100] Robert Taft noted that both prayers of the faithful in Byzantine BAS are quite different from their counterparts in CHR and constitute prayers of *accessus*. He suggested that both prayers may have been originally one, and that the Urtext may have been the pristine *oratio accessus ad altare* of Byzantine BAS.[101] At any rate, the first prayer itself has been stable in the Byzantine traditions of Southern Italy and Constantinople at least since the period from the eighth to the tenth centuries, much earlier than the earliest Northern Egyptian Coptic Euchologia. Further analysis of the possible relationship between the two texts is presented further below.

The Hagiopolite tradition also preserves a large number of similar prayers. In JAS, there is the prayer Δέσποτα ζωοποιὲ before the Great Entrance, which asks to be made worthy, "to perform unto you this divine service."[102] A similar sentiment is expressed in the *Proskomide* prayer of JAS, Ὁ ἐπισκεψάμενος ἡμᾶς ἐν ἐλέει καὶ οἰκτιρμοῖς, which petitions, "Make me fit by the power of your all-Holy Spirit for this service."[103] This is immediately followed by the prayer, Ὁ Θεὸς ὁ διὰ πολλὴν καὶ ἄφατον φιλανθρωπίαν, which calls upon God, "do not turn us sinners backwards, having placed our hands on this fearful and bloodless sacrifice."[104] This is followed in some manuscripts of JAS

100 Jacques Goar, *ΕΥΧΟΛΟΓΙΟΝ sive Rituale Graecorum complectens ritus et ordines Divinae Liturgiae, officiorum, sacramentorum, consecrationum, benedictionum, funerum, orationum, &c. cuilibet personae, statui vel tempori congruos, juxta usum Orientalis Ecclesiae*, 2nd ed., (Graz: Akademische Druck- und Verlagsanstalt, 1960), 138. On the background and dating of this important testimony of liturgy in 10th-century Constantinople, see Taft, *Communion, Thanksgiving, and Concluding Rites*, 544–548.

101 Taft and Parenti, *Il Grande Ingresso*, 595.

102 *LEW*, 40. See also B. Charles Mercier, *La Liturgie de Saint Jacques: Édition critique du texte grec avec traduction latine*, PO 26.2 (126) (Turnhout: Brepols, 1997), 62–63. The prayer is also found in some Sinaitic witnesses of JAS among the *Sinai New Finds*, including *Sinai Gr. NE/MΓ 118* (8th/9th c.), and *Sinai Gr. NE/E 80* (11th/12th c.). For the Sinai witnesses, see Alkiviades Kazamias, *Η Θεία Λειτουργία του Αγίου Ιακώβου του Αδελφοθέου και τα Νέα Σιναϊτικά Χειρόγραφα* (Thessaloniki: Ἵδρυμα Ὄρους Σινᾶ, 2006), 168. It is also found in the Old Georgian version of JAS, attested in two tenth-century manuscripts. See Lili Khevsuriani, et al., *Liturgia Ibero-Graeca Sancti Iacobi: Editio, translatio, retroversio, commentarii*, JThF 17 (Münster: Aschendorff, 2011), 54–55. This prayer appears also in one Southern Italian formulary of CHR, *Grottaferrata Γβ IV* (10th c.), and in the Italo-Greek anaphora of PETER. See Taft and Parenti, *Il Grande Ingresso*, 294.

103 *LEW*, 45; Mercier, *La Liturgie de Saint Jacques*, 76–77; Kazamias, *Η Θεία Λειτουργία του Αγίου Ιακώβου*, 182–183; Khevsuriani, et al., *Liturgia Ibero-Graeca Sancti Iacobi*, 64–67.

104 *LEW*, 46; Mercier, *La Liturgie de Saint Jacques*, 78–79; Kazamias, *Η Θεία Λειτουργία του Αγίου Ιακώβου*, 184; Khevsuriani, et al., *Liturgia Ibero-Graeca Sancti Iacobi*, 70–73.

with another prayer, Εὐχαριστοῦμέν σοι Κύριε, and titled *Another Prayer of the Veil* (ἑτέρα εὐχὴ τοῦ καταπετάσματος), in which the grace of the Holy Spirit is requested, as the priest is "about to stand at the holy altar and offer this fearful and bloodless sacrifice."[105] Another prayer immediately before the anaphora in JAS with the incipit Ἀγαθὲ καὶ φιλάνθρωπε, asks to be made worthy, "with a pure conscience to serve you all the days of my life."[106] Although this prayer is missing from some manuscripts of JAS, *BAV Vatican Gr. 2282* (9th c.) and *Sinai Gr. 1040* (AD 1156–1169), it appears at least by the eleventh century in *Sinai Gr. NE/E 24* (11th c.), one of the manuscripts in the *Sinai New Finds.*[107] It also appears in some of the oldest manuscripts of Georgian JAS, *Sinai Geo. N. 26* (AD 965–973), *Sinai Geo. O. 53* (9th/10th c.), *Sinai Geo. N. 63* (10th c.), and *Graz Universitätsbibliothek 2058/4* (AD 985).[108]

On the other hand, the East-Syrian tradition is perhaps the briefest in its treatment of this theme. In the East-Syrian *Anaphora of Addai and Mari*, and before the recitation of the Creed, the priest says as he approaches the altar, "Having our hearts sprinkled and clean from an evil conscience, may we be accounted worthy to enter into the holy of holies."[109] This stands in marked contrast to the rich West-Syrian tradition, which places the most importance of all other Rites on the idea of *accessus ad altare.*[110] In the Second Service of the *qurbōno*, one can find the same prayer found in the East-Syrian liturgy. In addition, many of the large number of West-Syrian anaphoras contain prayers of *accessus* after the kiss, that it would be impractical to list them all here or to present their pertinent petitions. Suffice it to mention that at least two of these, *The Anaphora of Jacob Baradaeus*[111] and *The Anaphora of John of Bostra,*[112] have prayers of *accessus* titled explicitly *Prayers of the Veil.* This prayer in the latter anaphora in particular, as will be presented shortly, occurs verbatim in the Coptic anaphora of MARK, commonly ascribed to Cyril of Alexandria.

The Alexandrian tradition itself presents many examples of such prayers in its various anaphoras and recensions. The earliest manuscripts of the Melkite Alexandrian recension of MARK, *BAV*

105 *LEW,* 48; Mercier, *La Liturgie de Saint Jacques,* 80–83; Kazamias, *Η Θεία Λειτουργία του Αγίου Ιακώβου,* 186–187.

106 Mercier, *La Liturgie de Saint Jacques,* 82–85; Kazamias, *Η Θεία Λειτουργία του Αγίου Ιακώβου,* 187–188; Khevsuriani, et al., *Liturgia Ibero-Graeca Sancti Iacobi,* 72–73.

107 Kazamias, *Η Θεία Λειτουργία του Αγίου Ιακώβου,* 39.

108 Khevsuriani, et al., *Liturgia Ibero-Graeca Sancti Iacobi,* 37.

109 *LEW,* 270.

110 Taft and Parenti, *Il Grande Ingresso,* 471.

111 Eusèbe Renaudot, *Liturgiarum Orientalium Collectio,* 2nd ed., vol. 2 (Frankfurt: Ad Moenum, 1847), 371.

112 Ibid., 459.

Vatican Gr. 2281 (AD 1207) and *BAV Vatican Gr. 1970* (12th c.), have the prayer of the Cherubic hymn, Ὁ θεὸς ὁ παντοκράτωρ, which also asks God, "Send upon us the grace of your all-Holy Spirit [...] so that with a pure heart we may offer to you gifts."[113] This is in fact a shorter redaction of the *oratio veli* of JAS mentioned above. The same two manuscripts of Melkite MARK have the prayer Ἅγιε ὕψιστε φοβερέ, where in *BAV Vatican Gr. 2281* (AD 1207) it appears as a prayer of entrance before the Liturgy of the Word, while in *BAV Vatican Gr. 1970* (12th c.) it is a prayer after the deposition of the gifts. This prayer shows similarities to the prayer of preparation currently under investigation. It too starts with "O Holy one, exalted, and fearful, Lord who rests in the saints."[114] The central petition asks God, "Make us worthy of this holy sacrifice, and lead us closer to your holy altar."[115] The prayer was incorporated as well in one late manuscript of JAS, *BAV Borgia Gr. 24* (AD 1880).[116]

The formulary of BAS in the Byzantinized Egyptian-Cypriot Euchologion *Paris BnF Gr. 325* (14th c.) has two *Prayers of the Veil.* The first, δοξάζομέν σε δημιουργέ καὶ βασιλεῦ τῶν ὅλων, is quite unlike any other in its content and provides no basis for comparison.[117] The other, attributed to Syriac JAS, is the same prayer Ὁ Θεὸς ὁ διὰ πολλὴν καὶ ἄφατον φιλανθρωπίαν mentioned in JAS above.[118] As for the formulary of GREG in this manuscript, it starts with the prayer Ὁ ἐπισκεψάμενος ἡμᾶς ἐν ἐλέει καὶ οἰκτιρμοῖς,[119] which was already mentioned previously as the *Proskomide* prayer of JAS–its original location–and the *Second Prayer of the Faithful* in Byzantine BAS, and appears as well in various reworkings throughout the Byzantine tradition, including some Slavonic manuscripts of BAS.[120] This is followed by a *Prayer after the Preparation of the Altar*, Δέσποτα κύριε Ἰησοῦ Χριστέ, which is a longer redaction of Ἀγαθὲ καὶ φιλάνθρωπε from

[113] Cuming, *The Liturgy of St Mark*, 16.

[114] Ibid., 10; *LEW*, 122–123.

[115] Ibid.

[116] Mercier, *La Liturgie de Saint Jacques*, 84–85.

[117] *Paris BnF Gr. 325* (14th c.), fol. 1r–1v; Renaudot, *Liturgiarum Orientalium Collectio*, 1:57.

[118] *Paris BnF Gr. 325* (14th c.), fol. 1v–2v; Renaudot, *Liturgiarum Orientalium Collectio*, 1:58.

[119] *Paris BnF Gr. 325* (14th c.), fol. 60r–63r; Renaudot, *Liturgiarum Orientalium Collectio*, 1:85–86.

[120] Taft and Parenti, *Il Grande Ingresso*, 294–295. See also the comparison between the text of this prayer in *Paris BnF Gr. 325* (14th c.) and in JAS in Hammerschmidt, *Die koptische Gregoriosanaphora*, 80–82.

JAS.[121] Finally, for the *oratio veli* of this recension of GREG, there is the Constantinopolitan Οὐδεὶς ἄξιος, and another prayer with the incipit Κύριε ὁ θεὸς ἡμῶν ὁ παντοκράτωρ, which has the heading, "Another prayer of the veil among the Egyptians (Εὐχὴ ἄλλη καταπετάσματος παρ' Αἰγυπτίοις." This latter is also similar to the Coptic prayer of preparation in that it begins with "O Lord our God Pantocrator, who knows the thoughts of men, and examines the hearts and reins."[122] Following an admission of being called into the service despite his unworthiness, the priest asks, "Send to me the grace of your Holy Spirit, and make me worthy to stand at your holy altar."[123] The incipit in particular makes this prayer quite similar to the Coptic prayer of preparation.

The Coptic anaphoras themselves have a large number of similar prayers of *accessus*. In Bohairic BAS, one encounters again the same *Prayer of the Veil* of Greek Egyptian BAS and JAS Ὁ Θεὸς ὁ διὰ πολλὴν καὶ ἄφατον φιλανθρωπίαν, this time in Coptic, ⲫϯ ⲫⲏ ⲉⲧⲉ ⲉⲑⲃⲉ ⲧⲉⲕⲙⲉⲧⲙⲁⲓⲣⲱⲙⲓ.[124] An alternate prayer in Bohairic BAS, ⲡⲟ̅ⲥ̅ ⲡⲉⲛⲛⲟⲩϯ ⲫⲏⲉⲧⲁϥⲥⲟⲧⲧⲉⲛ,[125] is similar in some respects to the prayer of *Proskomide* of Byzantine BAS and to an alternate prayer before the anaphora in all manuscripts of JAS, Κύριε ὁ Θεὸς ὁ κτίσας ἡμᾶς.[126] In Bohairic GREG, a Coptic version of the same prayer found above in Greek GREG, Κύριε ὁ θεὸς ἡμῶν ὁ παντοκράτωρ, is preserved in Coptic: ⲡⲟ̅ⲥ̅ ⲫϯ ⲡⲓⲡⲁⲛⲧⲟⲕⲣⲁⲧⲱⲣ, [127] as well as an alternate prayer titled ⲉⲧⲓ ⲟⲛ ⲧⲉⲛⲧⲁⲥⲑⲟ, asking God for purification from all defilement, and to "Send to us the gift of your Holy Spirit, so that we may come to your holy altar and fulfill this ministry as is pleasing before you."[128] Nonetheless, it is the first prayer that is the more stable in the manuscript tradition, compared to the second prayer, which in the

[121] *Paris BnF Gr. 325* (14th c.), fol. 63r–64v; Renaudot, *Liturgiarum Orientalium Collectio*, 1:86–87. See the brief comparison in Hammerschmidt, *Die koptische Gregoriosanaphora*, 82–83.

[122] *Paris BnF Gr. 325* (14th c.), fol. 68v–70v; Renaudot, *Liturgiarum Orientalium Collectio*, 1:89–90.

[123] *Paris BnF Gr. 325* (14th c.), fol. 69v; Renaudot, *Liturgiarum Orientalium Collectio*, 1:90.

[124] Ṣalīb, ⲡⲓϫⲱⲙ ⸱ⲛⲧⲉ ⲡⲓⲉⲩⲭⲟⲗⲟⲅⲓⲟⲛ, 270.

[125] Ibid., 272–274.

[126] LEW, 47; Mercier, *La Liturgie de Saint Jacques*, 78-81; Kazamias, *Η Θεία Λειτουργία του Αγίου Ιακώβου*, 185–186; Khevsuriani, et al., *Liturgia Ibero-Graeca Sancti Iacobi*, 68–69.

[127] Ṣalīb, ⲡⲓϫⲱⲙ ⲛ̀ⲧⲉ ⲡⲓⲉⲩⲭⲟⲗⲟⲅⲓⲟⲛ, 453. See also Ernst Hammerschmidt, *Die koptische Gregoriosanaphora: Syrische und griechische Einflüsse auf eine ägyptische Liturgie*, Berliner byzantinistische Arbeiten 8 (Berlin: Akademie Verlag, 1957), 11–13.

[128] Ṣalīb, ⲡⲓϫⲱⲙ ⲛ̀ⲧⲉ ⲡⲓⲉⲩⲭⲟⲗⲟⲅⲓⲟⲛ, 456.

words of ʻAbd al-Masīḥ Ṣalīb was found in only two copies.[129] In the same way, two alternate prayers are printed in Coptic MARK/CYRIL. The first, ⲡⲓⲣⲉϥⲑⲁⲙⲓⲟ ⲛ̀ⲧⲉ ϯⲕⲧⲏⲥⲓⲥ ⲧⲏⲣⲥ, attributed to John of Bostra asks to be granted the Holy Spirit, "the immaterial and ineffable fire, which consumes all weaknesses and burns all wicked inventions [...] So that I make perfect this gift placed here, which is the mystery of all mysteries."[130] This prayer appears in exactly the same text in the Syriac anaphora of John of Bostra, as mentioned previously. The second prayer, ⲡⲟ̅ⲥ̅ ⲫϯ ⲛ̀ⲧⲉ ⲛⲓϫⲟⲙ, petitions God to "look upon our entreaties and grant us strength for this fearful ministry that is of the great and heavenly mystery."[131] Finally, it should be mentioned that the Ethiopian liturgy has the same two prayers of preparation of the Coptic liturgy, although it does not have the same tradition of the *Prayers of the Veil* before the anaphora.[132]

3.5.2. The Origins of the Coptic Prayers of Preparation

With such a large number of prayers of *accessus* in countless anaphoras and traditions, it would be futile to attempt to present all their texts in search for a taxonomy of *accessus* prayers that can shed light on the provenance of the Coptic prayers of preparation. It is indeed unfortunate that there are no Euchologia anterior to the thirteenth century that would provide a glimpse into the development of this part of the rite. It is precisely however when evidence is lacking that hypotheses can be advanced based on a comparison of texts and expected patterns of liturgical evolution, as will be demonstrated at this point. Of all the prayers examined in preparation for this analysis, the first point of comparison can be made between the Coptic *Prayer After the Preparation of the Altar* and the *First Prayer of the Faithful* in Byzantine BAS, which shows clearly that they share the same origin. Moreoever, the Byzantine version is likely older since it appears already in *BAV Barberini Gr. 336* (8th c.):[133]

129 Ibid., 455. According to the excellent research of Fr. Mīṣāʼīl al-Baramūsī on the manuscript sources oft he Euchologion of ʻAbd al-Masīḥ Ṣalīb, the two sources of this prayer are 1. the *editio typica* of Ṭūḫī, and 2. Manuscript *Coptic Patriarchate Lit. 160* (AD 1851), an Euchologion of the three liturgies from Mīr, a village near Assiyūṭ. The Euchologion is now allegedly lost. See Mīṣāʼīl al-Baramūsī, "Ḫūlāǧī al-qummuṣ ʻAbd al-Masīḥ Ṣālīb al-Baramūsī al-Masʻūdī al-maṭbūʻ sanat 1902 [The Euchologion of Hegumen ʻAbd al-Masīḥ Ṣālīb al-Baramūsī al-Masʻūdī printed in 1902]," *Madrasat al-iskandariyya* 22 (2017): 165–196, here 178.

130 Ibid., 557–558; *LEW*, 158.

131 Ṣalīb, ⲡⲓϫⲱⲙ ⲛ̀ⲧⲉ ⲡⲓⲉⲩⲭⲟⲗⲟⲅⲓⲟⲛ, 559.

132 *LEW*, 197.

133 The identity between these two prayes was already noted in Cuming, *The Liturgy of St Mark*, 81, and independently in Dous, "Η Αλεξανδρινή Θεία Λειτουργία," 17.

Prayer After the Preparation of the Altar	*First Prayer of the Faithful Byzantine BAS*
[1] You O Lord have revealed to us this great mystery of salvation.	[1] You O Lord have revealed to us this great mystery of salvation.
[2] You have made us worthy, we your lowly, sinful, and unworthy servants, to become ministers of your holy altar.	[2] You have judged us worthy, we your lowly, and unworthy servants, to be ministers of your holy altar.
[3] Make us fit by the power of your Holy Spirit unto this ministry,	[3] Authorize us for this ministry by the power of your Holy Spirit,
[4] So that standing uncondemned before your holy glory, we may present to you a sacrifice of praise, glory, and magnificence in your holy place.	[4] So that standing in the presence of your sacred majesty uncondemned, we may offer you a sacrifice of praise.
[5] O God, having granted the grace, and having sent salvation, for you are he who works all in all,	[5] For it is you alone who accomplish all things in all men.
[6] grant also, O Lord, on behalf of our sins and the ignorances of your people, that our sacrifice be acceptable and well-pleasing before you, according to the gift of your Holy Spirit, in Christ Jesus our Lord,	[6] Grant, Lord, that our sacrifice may be acceptable and welcome in your presence, for our sins and the faults of the people,
[7] through whom and with whom to you is the glory, the honor, and the dominion, with your all-Holy, good, life-giving, and consubstantial Spirit, now and ever, and unto the ages of ages, amen.[134]	[7] For to you belongs all glory, honor, and worship, to the Father, the Son, and the Holy Spirit. Now and ever, and unto the ages of ages, amen.[135]

A second point of comparison can be made between the two prayers of preparation combined and the *oratio veli* of Coptic GREG, ⲡ̅ⲟ̅ⲥ̅ ⲫϯ ⲡⲓⲡⲁⲛⲧⲟⲕⲣⲁⲧⲱⲣ. Below is a comparison, using my own translation of both prayers:

[134] Macomber, "The Greek Text of the Coptic Mass," 314–315; Dous, "Η Αλεξανδρινή Θεία Λειτουργία," 75.

[135] *LEW*, 316, 400. Translation is mine.

Prayers of Preparation of the Altar	*oratio veli* of GREG
[1] O Lord who knows the hearts of everyone, the holy one and who rests in his saints, who alone is without sin, and is able to forgive sins.	[1] O Lord God the Pantocrator, who knows the thoughts of men, and examines the hearts and reins.
[2] You, O Master, know my unworthiness, my unpreparedness, and my insufficiency unto this your holy service.	[2] While I am unworthy, you have called me to this your holy service.
[3] And I do not have the face to draw near and to open my mouth before your holy glory. But according to the multitude of your compassion, forgive me the sinner.	[3] Do not despise me, nor turn your face away from me, but wipe away all my transgressions, wash the blemish of my body and the defilement of my soul, and purify me completely. Lest while I ask of your goodness to grant forgiveness to others, I myself may not stand the test. Yes, O Lord, do not turn me away humiliated and ashamed.
[4] And grant me to find grace and mercy at this hour. And send unto me power from on high, that I may begin and prepare and fulfill your holy service as is pleasing to you, according to the pleasure of your will, unto a sweet-smelling savor. Yes, our Master, dwell with us, cooperate with us, bless us. For you are the forgiveness of our sins, the light of our souls, our life, our strength, and our boldness. You O Lord have taught us this great mystery of salvation. You called us, your lowly and unworthy servants, to become ministers of your holy altar. O our Master, make us worthy by the power of your Holy Spirit to fulfill this ministry.	[4] But send down to me the grace of your Holy Spirit,
[5] So that without falling into condemnation before your holy glory, we may offer unto you a sacrifice of praise, glory, and great beauty in your holy place. O God, who grants the grace, who sends	[5] And make me worthy to stand at your holy altar without falling into condemnation, and I will offer unto you this rational and bloodless sacrifice with a pure conscience,

salvation, who works everything in everyone.	
[6] Grant also, O Lord, that our sacrifice may be acceptable before you, for my own sins and for the ignorances of your people and that it may be pure	[6] for the pardoning of my sins and transgressions, and the forgiveness of the ignorances of your people; for the repose and rest of our fathers and brothers who have departed first in the Orthodox faith, and for the edification of all your people.
[7] according to the gift of your Holy Spirit, in Christ Jesus our Lord. This is he through whom the glory, the honor, the dominion, and the worship are due unto you, with him and the Holy Spirit, the giver of life, who is of one essence with you, now and at all times, and unto the ages of all ages, amen.	[7] For glory to you and your Only-begotten Son and the Holy Spirit the life-giver and co-essential with you. Now and at all times and unto the ages of all ages, amen.[136]

From this table, one can see that the two prayers share remarkable similarities in outline and in exact expressions. Looked at in this combined fashion, the question arises as to which came first: The *oratio veli* of GREG as it is today, the two prayers of preparation separated as they are today, or a combined Urtext of the two prayers as was presented now? By examining each possibility, a relative dating of these prayers can be surmised.

The *oratio veli* of GREG is written entirely in the first person, a usual sign of late composition, while at least the second prayer of preparation is written in the plural. It is also unnecessary to divide a perfectly flowing prayer in half, insert additional clauses and a concluding doxology to the first half, only to have them recited in succession anyway in their actual execution. Thus, it is unlikely that the *oratio veli* of GREG would be the origin of the two preparation prayers. A combined *Urtext* as presented above is also unlikely as the origin. The text changes from the first-person singular to the plural, making it unlikely that it ever existed in such a combined state. In addition, the second prayer—as was shown above—is found in the Byzantine tradition, and it is unlikely that a Byzantine redactor would take a prayer and copy only its second half, or for a Coptic redactor to combine two prayers—especially one foreign and the other native—to form one hybrid prayer. Therefore, this leaves the third possibility as the only plausible option, namely, that the *oratio veli* of GREG represents a later reworking of the two prayers of preparation into

136 Ṣalīb, ⲡⲓϫⲱⲙ ⲛ̀ⲧⲉ ⲡⲓⲉⲩⲭⲟⲗⲟⲅⲓⲟⲛ, 452–453 Translation from the Coptic text is mine.

one coherent prayer of *accessus ad altare.* That this prayer was not an original prayer of *accessus* in GREG can be shown as well from the fact that it addresses the Father, while the entire anaphora of Gregory is known for addressing the Son.

This leads to the next stage in the investigation, which is to compare the two prayers of preparation themselves. Already by suggesting that the two prayers were combined to form one *accessus* prayer, it becomes clear that the two prayers of preparation are somewhat redundant, repeating similar ideas of approach to the altar and offering an acceptable sacrifice. Thus, they cannot have been both original in this location. Between the two prayers, it is the second that seems a likely candidate for being more ancient overall. First, it is written in the plural, and takes into account all the servants and ministers of the altar rather than the one celebrant priest. Second, as was shown, it has a long tradition in the Byzantine periphery as well as Constantinople and was taken by Robert Taft to be the pristine prayer of *accessus ad altare* of Byzantine BAS. It is thus more likely that this prayer is originally Byzantine in provenance, since it is so integral to the more ancient anaphora of Constantinople, that of Basil the Great. This in turn leaves the *First Prayer of Preparation* as the original *accessus,* to which the prayer from Byzantine BAS was added later as an example of the common pattern of emphasis by duplication.[137]

The question therefore arises, why is there a prayer of *accessus ad altare* so early in the unfolding of the liturgy, when such classical rites of *accessus* generally appear immediately before the anaphora? The answer to this question again has to be attributed to the major shift that occurred to the time of the deposition of the eucharistic gifts on the altar in the course of the eighth century. Just as earlier it was suggested that elaborate rites of preparing the altar could not have existed before this radical shift took place, now also it can be added that this shift caused–even necessitated–the addition of *accessus* elements early on in the rite. This is because according to the new ordo, the priest is already standing at the altar and will soon place the bread and wine upon it for the anaphora, actions he would not have done until the pre-anaphora according to ancient usage. This new arrangement then resulted in a duplication of *accessus* rites before the prothesis and before the anaphora.

To summarize then, the following timeline of the historical evolution of the prayers of preparation can be proposed:

137 Taft, "Anton Baumstark's Comparative Liturgy Revisited," 214.

1. Before the eighth-century shift in the prothesis, the first *Prayer of Preparation* was likely a prayer of *accessus ad altare* found in the pre-anaphora.
2. After the shift to the new ordo, this prayer moved as well to the new location to satisfy the new need for prayers of *accessus* before the liturgy.
3. Shortly after, the *First Prayer of the Faithful* from Byzantine BAS was added to the preparatory rites before the prothesis as an example of emphasis through duplication. Likely itself a prayer of *accessus ad altare* for Byzantine BAS in origin, its borrowing as a prayer of preparation in the Coptic tradition is perfectly suitable.
4. Finally, before the earliest thirteenth-century Euchologia the two prayers had already been reworked into a single prayer to make a newly created *oratio veli* for GREG.

This proposed historical evolution can be depicted visually as follows:

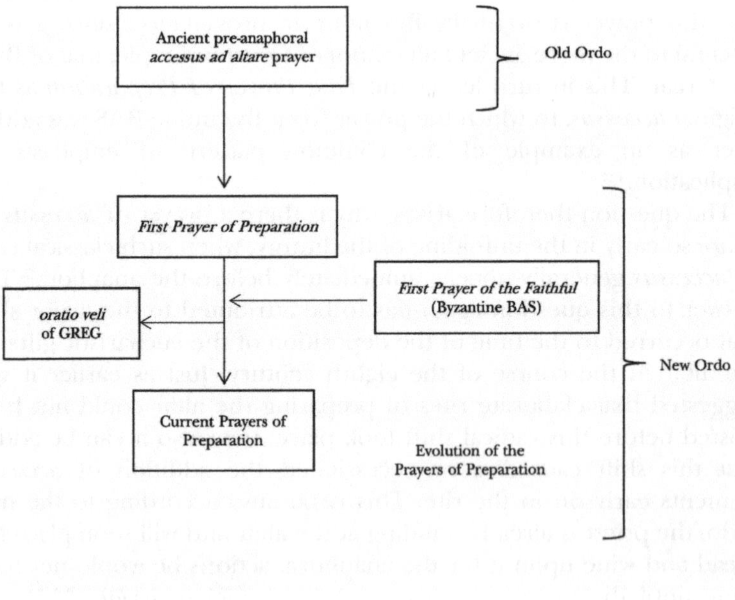

4. CONCLUSION

This chapter aimed to unpack and analyze two concurrent layers of action and words in the preparatory rites of the Coptic liturgy, which precede the prothesis rite. The action in this case was the physical preparation of the altar by placing upon it the eucharistic vessels and cloths in a specific arrangement, an arrangement found more or less stable in sources since the thirteenth century. The words accompanying this physical act are the so-called *Prayers of Preparation*, which the priest is to recite during and after the preparation of the altar.

Despite their titles however, these prayers are nothing but prayers of *accessus ad altare*, deliberately placed at this juncture after the major shift in the deposition of the eucharistic gifts that occurred between the eighth and tenth century AD, and through which the approach to the altar was moved to the very beginning of the liturgy. As such, they are not related in the least to the practical act of preparing the altar, except in the sense that the altar preparation constitutes the first act of a priestly character performed in the liturgy, excluding the morning raising of incense that usually precedes it. The first of these prayers was likely an ancient prayer of *accessus* in the pre-anaphora before the shift, while the second prayer, echoing similar ideas, is the pristine *accessus* prayer of Byzantine BAS, now titled the *First Prayer of the Faithful*, and was borrowed at a later stage for emphasis. Similarly, the physical acts of preparation are likely a product of the shift in the prothesis, which necessitated preparing the altar in advance for the placement of the eucharistic gifts that is about to occur shortly.

EXCURSUS 2

THE PRAYERS OF THE HOURS AND THE LITURGY

In the previous chapter, the following footnote in the Euchologion of 1902 was presented during the course of the discussion of the preparation of the altar:

[1] العادة الجارية الآن انه اولاً يصلي الشعب صلاة مزامير الساعات [2] و يكون استعداد المذبح قبلها او في اثنائها.[1]	[1] The custom current now is that the people first pray the prayer of the psalms of the hours, [2] and that the preparation of the altar be done before it or during it.

As remarked previously, this note refers to certain hours from the Horologion that are currently prayed between the service of *Matins Raising of Incense*, and the prothesis rite. These hours include at least the third and sixth hours, but may also include the ninth, vesper [= eleventh hour], and compline [= twelfth hour], according to specific seasonal rubrics explained below under current practice. The note implies that this practice is a recent development, although it gives no explanation or additional information to support this claim. This in itself makes the task of exploring this practice necessary and justifies dedicating this digression from the preparatory rites and the prothesis to accomplishing this goal. In addition, the manner in which the horologion hours are executed in current usage has an important impact on the unfolding of the prothesis rite, particularly regarding the chant that accompanies the selection of the eucharistic gifts.

In this excursus, I analyze the evidence that can be gathered regarding the intersection of the horologion hours—particularly the so-called little hours—and the liturgy. The purpose here is not to write a history of the development of the daily office per se, something that was done by others much more comprehensively and successfully.[2]

1 Ṣalīb, ⲡⲓϫⲱⲙ ⲛ̀ⲧⲉ ⲡⲓⲉⲩⲭⲟⲗⲟⲅⲓⲟⲛ, 197n1.

2 See Robert F. Taft, *The Liturgy of the Hours in East and West: The Origins of the Divine Office and its Meaning for Today*, 2nd rev. ed. (Collegeville, MN: Liturgical

Rather, the purpose is to explore the subset of this topic that has to do with praying the daily hours in the context of the eucharistic liturgy, particularly in the Coptic sources of the medieval period, the formative era of the Northern Egyptian or Coptic Rite. It will be found that while the daily hours have a long-standing tradition in the liturgical life of the Church, the practice of praying the hours as a precursor to the liturgy in particular seems to have emerged initially in the monastic tradition, and only later became standard elsewhere in the urban setting.

1. THE DAILY HOURS AND THE LITURGY: A HISTORICAL OVERVIEW

1.1. The Early Church (3rd–Early 4th c.)

Before one can proceed to the Coptic evidence relating to the intersection between the daily hours and the liturgy specifically, a brief history of the hours of daily prayer is warranted, which would provide perspective on the practice of praying at specific hours of the day (especially at the third, sixth, and ninth hours). From the earliest centuries from which evidence of daily prayers is available, it is clear that Christians prayed not just in the morning and the evening, but also during set times throughout the day. This is of course found as early as the New Testament accounts of Peter praying at the sixth hour (Acts 10:9), and of Peter and John going to the temple to pray at the third hour (Acts 3:1).

Later reference to prayers at specific times in the day is found in the *Stromateis* of Clement of Alexandria (ca. AD 150–215), where he writes, "But if some assign fixed hours for prayer, such as the third, sixth, and ninth, the gnostic, on the other hand, prays throughout his whole life."[3] Clement here is not referring to the Gnostic movement, but to the true Christian, who according to him should ideally pray always (1 Thes 5:17). Although Clement seems aware of these specific times of prayer, he himself is not claiming this to be the practice in Alexandria, but that of an unknown group of others. Later in the third century, Origen of Alexandria (ca. AD 185–254) refers to praying at least three times a day in his treatise *De oratione*. Although he

Press, 1993), for a detailed analysis of the history of the Liturgy of the Hours. In particular, see the firsthand account of the daily cycle of the monks of the Monastery of Saint Macarius in Scetis on pages 249–259; Paul F. Bradshaw, *Daily Prayer in the Early Church: A Study of the Origin and Early Development of the Divine Office* (Eugene, OR: Wipf & Stock, 1981).

3 *Stromateis* 7.7 (CPG 1377). See Alain le Boulluec, *Clément d'Alexandrie: Les Stromates VII*, SC 428 (Paris: Cerf, 1997), 128–129.

references the traditional times of the third hour in the example of Peter (Acts 10:9), he does not do so to call for praying at this specific time per se, but to simply provide biblical examples, in which particular times were set aside for prayer. He does so in support of his statement that prayer, "ought not to be performed less than three times each day."[4] In his analysis of this point, Paul Bradshaw points to the extensive previous literature that has interpreted Clement and Origen as indicative of prayers at the third, sixth, and ninth hours in third-century Alexandria. However, he instead takes the position that at this early stage, the Alexandrian system of daily prayer was in fact morning, noon, evening, and night.[5] Robert Taft agrees with this conclusion regarding the absence of explicit references to the third, sixth, and ninth hours, and suggests rather that the expression "morning, noon, and night" found in the sources may simply be interpreted as another way of saying, "Pray constantly" (1 Thes 5:17).[6]

In the West, further reasoning for prayer at these specific times is found in the treatise *De jejuniis* by Tertullian (AD 155–240). Besides precedence in Scripture, Tertullian points how "these three hours, as being more marked in human affairs, which divide the day, which distinguish businesses, which resound publicly, have likewise ever been of special solemnity in divine prayers."[7] Although it is not certain that these hours were indeed announced publicly in antiquity, they were certainly common points of reference in a world without modern, accessible time-keeping devices. Robert Taft accepts that these specific hours of the day became customary prayer times precisely because of their familiarity in the daily rhythm of life in late antiquity, in agreement with the same opinion expressed earlier by Clifford William Dugmore.[8]

Another third-century document important for the early development of daily prayers is the so-called *Apostolic Tradition*. The passage in question is found in the earliest version of the text, the Latin palimpsest folio of codex *Verona LV (53)* (5th c.), with lacunae supplied from the Sahidic Coptic version in *British Library Or. 1320* (AD 1006).[9] Taken together, the full daily cycle of prayers that emerges can be summarized as follows: Private prayer upon rising, a

4 *De oratione* 12.2 (CPG 1477). See Paul Koetschau, *Origenes Werke*, vol. 2, *Buch V–VII gegen Celsus, die Schrift vom Gebet*, GCS 3 (Leipzig, 1899), 325.

5 Bradshaw, *Daily Prayer*, 47–50.

6 Taft, *The Liturgy of the Hours*, 17.

7 *De jejuniis* 10 (PL 2:1017).

8 Taft, *The Liturgy of the Hours*, 19; C. W. Dugmore, *The Influence of the Synagogue upon the Divine Office*, Alcuin Club Collections 65 ([London]: The Faith Press, 1964), 66–67.

9 Taft, *The Liturgy of the Hours*, 22.

morning catechetical assembly, private prayers at the third, sixth, and ninth hours, a common evening agape meal, followed by more private prayers at home upon retiring, at midnight, and at cockcrow.[10] It is noteworthy that prayers at the third, sixth, and ninth hours, if they existed–and most likely not in Egypt–were practiced as a private devotion, and not as part of the organized worship life of third-century Christians.

The only exception to this last observation is found in the most important fourth-century source of cathedral worship in Jerusalem, the diaries of Egeria the nun, who visited the Holy Land between AD 381–384. During her visit, she reported what she witnessed of the public liturgical celebrations of Jerusalem. Famous for a liturgical life centered around the holy sites of Christ's life, public processions, and a tapestery of monastic and urban devotional practices, Jerusalem's liturgy left such an indelible impression on visitors of the time. Thus, the influence of Hagiopolite liturgy was felt throughout the Christian urban setting of the fourth century as far away as Alexandria, Rome, and further west.[11] In her description of the daily services in Jerusalem, Egeria describes services at midday and at three in the afternoon.[12] According to Taft, it is interesting to see the public celebration of the day hours at such an early date, which he attributes to the large number of monastics who lived and/or flocked to the Holy Land after the peace of Constantine to participate in its magnificent services.[13]

Thus, this brief overview of early Christian daily prayer can be concluded by observing that the day hours (third, sixth, and ninth) are not to be found in the earliest Egyptian evidence, which had a slightly different daily cursus of morning, noon, evening, and night. Traditions varied elsewhere, with Jerusalem being the only exception where the third and sixth hours were celebrated publicly.

1.2. Egyptian Monasticism (4th–5th c.)

In fact, much of the information regarding the development of daily prayers comes from the monastic tradition. In the fourth century, this

10 *Traditio Apostolica* 41 (CPG 1737). See Bradshaw, Johnson, and Phillips, *The Apostolic Tradition*, 194.

11 For the best and most recent summary of the liturgical life in early-Christian and Byzantine Jerusalem, see Daniel Galadza, *Liturgy and Byzantinization in Jerusalem*, Oxford Early Christian Studies (Oxford: Oxford University Press, 2018), 29–72, especially 43–46 on the diary of Egeria.

12 *Itinerarium* 24.3. See Pierre Maraval, *Égérie, Journal de voyage (Itinéraire): Introduction, texte critique, traduction, notes et cartes*, SC 296 (Paris: Cerf, 2017), 236–238.

13 Taft, *The Liturgy of the Hours*, 51.

includes the Scetis eremitic tradition in Northern Egypt, and the Pachomian coenobitic tradition in Southern Egypt, which together constitute what has been called the pure monastic office.[14] Thanks to the eyewitness account of John Cassian, who lived in Scetis between AD 380 and 399, scholars are able to reconstruct the daily prayer life of monks in that system of monasticism to a remarkably accurate degree. However, the purpose here is not the exact contents of the prayer assemblies in Scetis, but rather the times of prayer. In this regard, John Cassian has the following to say in his *Institutes*: "Except vespers and nocturns, there are no public services among them during the day except on Saturday and Sunday, when they meet together at the third hour for holy communion."[15] From this, it is clear that the only daytime assemblies took place on Saturdays and Sundays. Although these assemblies were held at the third hour for the Eucharist, there is no indication whatsoever that the liturgy was preceded by an office of the third hour from the Horologion, particularly that found today in the Coptic Horologion. More likely, the celebration of the Eucharist in the monasteries at that time followed more or less what was done in the nearby towns and cities, and there is no evidence from there either that it included the hours. During the week, the monks prayed the morning and evening prayers alone in their cells, or with any visitors.[16] Although the *Lausiac History*

14 The scholarly literature on the distinction between cathedral and monastic liturgy in the context of the daily office is very extensive and includes both staunch supporters and a few critics. This distinction seems to have been first formulated by Anton Baumstark in his work *Vom geschichtlichen Werden der Liturgie*. See Baumstark, *Vom geschichtlichen Werden der Liturgie*, 64–70; Baumstark, *On the Historical Development of the Liturgy*, 140–148. It was later mentioned as well in his *Liturgie comparée*. See Baumstark, *Comparative Liturgy*, 111–119. Among its most notable supporters, it suffices to mention the latest article, Robert F. Taft, "Cathedral vs. Monastic Liturgy in the Christian East: Vindicating a Distinction," *BBGG III* 2 (2005): 173–219. Taft maintained that the distinction did in fact correspond to actual concrete rites, and not to ideal types constructed by liturgists as an interpretative system. On the other hand, the distinction has been criticized for example in Peter Knowles, "A Renaissance in the Study of Byzantine Liturgy?" *Worship* 68 (1994): 232–41. Knowles cautioned against readily accepting this distinction. Paul Bradshaw preferred to see the distinction not in the outward tangible aspects of two traditions, but as two ways of prayer, differing in understanding of the role of prayer. See Paul F. Bradshaw, "Cathedral and Monastic: What's in a Name?" *Worship* 77 (2003): 341–353. Finally, the very existence of a pure monastic office was also questioned. See Stig Simeon Frøyshov, "The Cathedral-Monastic Distinction Revisited. Part I: Was Egyptian Desert Liturgy a Pure Monastic Office?" *Studia Liturgica* 37 (2007): 198–216.

15 *De coenobiorum Instit.* 3.2 (PL 49:115). See Jean-Claude Guy, *Jean Cassien, Institutions cénobitiques: Texte latin revu, introduction, traduction et notes*, SC 109 (Paris: Cerf, 1965), 93–95.

16 Taft, *The Liturgy of the Hours*, 61.

of Palladius refers to psalmody rising from each monastic habitation at the ninth hour, this is clearly not the later little hour of that name, but the evening time of prayer or vespers, one of the only two prayer times mentioned by Cassian above.[17]

The situation in the Pachomian communities of Tabennesi was largely similar. According to Armand Veilleux, the term "The canons of the *synaxis*," used frequently in Pachomian documents, did not imply the daily assembly of monks, but rather the actual daily and nightly prayers prescribed for those who joined the community.[18] In fact, the Pachomian corpus in many cases witnesses to the *synaxis* of daily prayer to be held in the morning and evening in common. The liturgical day likely started in the evening as the usual Egyptian custom current to the present day. An evening *synaxis* is attested in the *Precepts of Pachomius* 121,[19] the *Precepts and Laws* 10,[20] and the *Precepts and Institutes* 14.[21] The morning assembly is not as explicitly stated, although Veilleux surmises it was probably in the morning, based on *Precepts* 123, where, following this morning assembly, the monks are to reflect on what was taught until ordered by the housemaster to begin their manual labor.[22] Thus, Pachomian monks in the fourth century knew only two daily assemblies for prayer, with no mention whatsoever of any day hours.[23]

A century later, reference to multiple hours appears in the writings of Shenoute of Atripe (5th c.). Shenoute was the founder and leader of a federation of monasteries in Southern Egypt, the precursor of the so-called White Monastery, from which comes much of the information about Southern Egyptian liturgy in later centuries. In his *Discourses 1–3*, Shenoute speaks of those who are "first in church, morning and evening, at the hour of midday, and at the required hour

17 *Historia Lausiaca* 7.5 (CPG 6036). See Cuthbert Butler, *The Lausiac History of Palladius II: The Greek Text Edited with Introduction and Notes*, Texts and Studies Contributions to Biblical and Patristic Literature 6 (Cambridge: Cambridge University Press, 1904), 26.

18 Armand Veilleux, *La liturgie dans le cénobitisme pachômien au quatrième siècle*, Studia Anselmiana 57 (Rome: I.B.C. Liberia Herder, 1968), 294.

19 Armand Veilleux, *Pachomian Koinonia*, vol. 2, *Pachomian Chronicles and Rules*, Cistercian Studies 46 (Kalamazoo, MI: Cistercian Publications, 1981), 164.

20 Ibid., 182.

21 Ibid., 171.

22 Ibid., 164; Veilleux, *La liturgie*, 272.

23 Ibid., 297; Taft, *The Liturgy of the Hours*, 63; Hans Quecke, *Untersuchungen zum koptischen Stundengebet*, Publications de l'Institut orientaliste de Louvain 3 (Louvain: Université catholique de Louvain, Institut orientaliste, 1970), 150.

every day."[24] It is clear enough from this that by Shenoute's time certain midday hours had been added to the daily system of prayers. Although Taft is hesitant to accept this conclusion without further analysis,[25] Ugo Zanetti on the other hand accepted that the so-called little hours (prime, third, sixth, and ninth) were in fact prescribed by Shenoute.[26] This is certainly clear when one examines the monastic *Canons of Shenoute* (5th c.), where prayer offices are prescribed at dawn after the pre-dawn great gathering, the fifth or sixth hour, and the ninth or tenth hour, respectively.[27] Nonetheless, as with other evidence presented so far, there is no indication whatsoever that such hours accompanied the eucharistic celebration.

1.3. The Canons of Ps.-Basil *(6th–7th c.)*

Perhaps the earliest evidence of the association between the horologion hours and the eucharistic celebration appears in the *Canons of Ps.-Basil* in its extended Coptic recension. Canon 97 of this collection states:

[1] السَّابع والتسعون لاجل السراير. [2] إذا ابتدوا ان يَصنعَوا السرايَر لا يَصنعوا بقلق [3] بل يبتدوا الى ان يجتمع كل الشعب ويتلوا في المزامير الى ان يدخلوا.[28]

[1] The ninty-seventh [canon], for the mysteries: [2] When they commence to perform the mysteries, let them not perform with disturbance, [3] but let them begin until all the people has assembled, and recite from the psalms until they enter.

The Coptic version of this text contains 106 canons and is found mainly in Arabic medieval collections, but also in brief Coptic

24 Émile Amélineau, ed., *Oeuvres de Schenoudi: Texte copte et traduction française*, vol. 2 (Paris: Ernest Leroux, 1914), 233. For an English translation, see David Brakke and Andrew Crislip, *Selected Discourses of Shenoute the Great: Community, Theology, and Social Conflict in Late Antique Egypt* (Cambridge: Cambridge University Press, 2015), 140.

25 Taft, *The Liturgy of the Hours*, 252.

26 Ugo Zanetti, "La liturgie dans les monastères de Shenoute," *BSAC* 53 (2014): 167–224, here 186.

27 Canons 166–168 and 490. See Layton, *The Canons of our Fathers*, 156–157, 302–303. The basic unit of the office hours mentioned in this canonical collection is given the term "ⲥⲟⲟⲩ ⲛⲥⲟⲡ, The Six Rounds". For Layton's discussion of this term, see ibid., 70–72. For a detailed discussion of the daily office in Shenoutean monasticism, see Ugo Zanetti, "Questions liturgiques dans les 'Canons de Shenoute'," *OCP* 82 (2016): 67–99, here 69–78.

28 Canon 97. *Paris BnF Ar. 251* (AD 1353), fol. 187r. Cf. Riedel, *Die Rechtsquellen*, 273.

fragments dating from the sixth or seventh century.[29] This canon does not provide the much-desired information on the nature of these psalms that are to be prayed before the liturgy. Biblical psalms–strictly speaking–are used in various ways and can refer to many types of prayers, from the daily hours, to chants composed from the psalms, or even to the biblical canticles, some of which are psalms themselves. Nonetheless, it is a frequent custom to use the term psalms as *pars pro toto* for the prayers of the hours as a whole. Given the context of this reference, it is very plausible that this is indeed the case here as well, providing a relatively early witness to the praying of the hours before the liturgy. On the other hand, since this canon in particular is attested only in the later Arabic tradition without an early Coptic witness, there remains the possibility that this reference is a later insertion.

An earlier section of the same canonical collection, canon 28, also refers to the third, sixth, and ninth hours, albeit unrelated to the Eucharist:

[1] لنصَلي في السَّاعة الثالثة لأن في تلك الساعة صُلِب مخلصَنا. [2] لنصَلي في الساعة السَّادسة لأن في تلك السَّاعة كانت الظلمة. [3] لنصَلي في الساعة التاسعة لأن في تلك السَّاعة اسلم الكلمة روحَه في يد ابيه الله.[30]	[1] Let us pray at the third hour, for at that hour our Savior was crucified. [2] Let us pray at the sixth hour, for at that hour there was darkness. [3] Let us pray at the ninth hour, for at that hour the Word gave up his soul in the hands of God his Father.

Here, all the so-called little hours are mentioned and given justification from biblical events. Once again, this passage in particular is lacking in the Coptic fragments published by Crum, so the dating of this reference must be taken with caution, particularly when trying to hypothesize about the history of the little hours in Coptic practice and until such a time when the newly-discovered copy of these canons are published by Camplani and Contardi.

Nonetheless, even if this reference is dated much later in the medieval period, this already contradicts the assertion made by De

29 Crum, "Canons of Basil," 57–62. Unfortunately, the Coptic fragments published by Crum only reach to Canon 94. Crum's publication was based on the fragments identified as papyrus *Codex XIII* in the Egyptian Museum in Turin. More recently, a complete Coptic witness to the *Canons of Ps.-Basil* was discovered by the Polish Archaeological Mission in Šayḫ ʻabd al-Qurna near Luxor and currently preserved as *Coptic Ms. 1* in the National Museum of Alexandria. A complete edition of the text from this important witness is still awaited. See Alberto Camplani and Federico Contardi, "The Canons Attributed to Basil of Caesarea: A New Coptic Codex," in Buzi, Camplani, and Contardi, *Coptic Society, Literature and Religion*, 2:979–992.

30 Canon 28. *Paris BnF Ar. 251* (AD 1353), fol. 178v. Cf. Riedel, *Die Rechtsquellen*, 246.

Lacy O'Leary that, "the Divine Office had never passed outside the monasteries."[31] As a canonical collection that frequently appeared in Copto-Arabic *nomocanons*, the *Canons of Ps.-Basil* cannot be said to be of a particularly monastic provenance. This observation is strengthened by references found within the text. For example, the same canon 28, after listing all the canonical hours, adds, "Let us teach our children to pray these with all chastity,"[32] while a number of canons is addressed to married persons, clearly speaking to a non-monastic audience. That these canons were likely directed to non-monastics is very significant, for it shows that by their time one can already speak of an adoption of the monastic horologion into the urban or cathedral worship tradition. Although one cannot quite identify the current horologion cursus with the pure monastic office of the 4th century, particularly since the latter lacked the little hours as a common assembly, the overall monastic *character* of the present-day Coptic horologion–as distinguished from the cathedral-type matins and vespers services–is itself beyond doubt.[33]

At any rate, for a more unequivocal testimony to the praying of the hours in conjunction with the Eucharist, a later–and more accurately dateable–source for the Coptic liturgy of the hours is needed.

1.4. Codex MLM M574 *(AD 897-898)*

The earliest such source is the Sahidic manuscript *MLM M574* (AD 897-898), which contains the oldest known Horologion of Egyptian provenance. According to the catalogue of the Morgan Library and Museum, this is a parchment codex of 90 folia measuring 28 × 21 cm. The title of the codex in the colophon is ⲡⲓϫⲱⲱⲙⲉ ⲛϩⲉⲣⲙⲏⲛⲓⲁ (*The Book of Hermenia*).[34] This technical term, *hermenia*, refers to selections of psalm verses, sometimes arranged around a particular theme, and sometimes not, which were in frequent use in Southern Egyptian liturgy.[35] The codex is part of the large collection of manuscripts from the Monastery of Archangel Michael in al-Ḥāmūlī in the Fayyūm governorate of Middle Egypt. The colophon on folio

31 De Lacy Evans O'Leary, *The Daily Office and Theotokia of the Coptic Church* (London: Simpkin, Marshall, Hamilton, Kent, 1911), 70.

32 *Paris BnF Ar. 251* (AD 1353), fol. 178v. Cf. Riedel, *Die Rechtsquellen*, 246.

33 Quecke, *Untersuchungen*, 3.

34 Leo Depuydt, *Catalogue of Coptic Manuscripts in the Pierpont Morgan Library*, vol. 1, Oriental Series 1, Corpus of Illuminated Manuscripts 4 (Leuven: Peeters, 1993), 113.

35 For a discussion of the term *hermenia* in Southern Egyptian sources, see Quecke, *Untersuchungen*, 97–101. For a briefer treatment, cf. Ugo Zanetti, "Liturgy in the White Monastery," in Gabra and Takla, *Christianity and Monasticism*, 1:201–210, here 206; Zanetti, "La liturgie dans les monastères de Shenoute," 192–194.

91r indicates that the codex was donated to the library of the monastery by a certain Iōannēs, archimandrite and economos of the monastery, thereby establishing its monastic provenance.

The codex also contains certain prayers and texts that lend themselves to what would be identified today as the Horologion. However, in modern Coptic usage, the contents correspond more specifically to two separate but related books: The *ağbiyya* or book of hours, and the *abṣalmūdiyya* or the Book of the Psalmody, containing chants and canticles used in the offices of the *Morning Psalmody,* the *Evening Psalmody,* and the *Midnight Psalmody.* The prayers in the horologion part of *MLM M574* include the biblical canticles found in present usage (The Song of Moses in Exodus 15:1–21, Ps 135, The Song of the three youth in the furnace in LXX Dn 3:52–90, Ps 148–150), the *Gloria in excelsis,* the Trisagion, and other such prayers common to the Horologion.[36] Hans Quecke has analyzed the horologion part of this manuscript in great detail, which provides the bulk of the conclusions based on this important ninth-century witness.[37]

The first point of interest in this manuscript is that it contains the full hourly cursus of prayers found in the modern-day Coptic Rite. Beginning on folio 72r, a new section of the manuscript begins with the following heading:

[1] ⲥⲩⲛ ⲑ̅ⲱ̅. [2] ⲛⲁⲓ ⲛⲉ ⲛ̅ⲱϣ ⲉⲃⲟⲗ ⲙ̅ⲡⲛⲁⲩ ⲛ̅ⲣⲟⲩϩⲉ ⲙⲛ̅ ⲛⲁ ⲧⲉⲩϣⲏ. ⲙⲛ̅ ⲡⲛⲁⲩ ⲛ̅ⲥⲩⲛⲁⲅⲉ. [3] ⲙⲛ̅ ⲛⲉⲩⲛⲟⲟⲩ ⲙ̅ⲡⲉϩⲟⲟⲩ ⲉⲧϣ̅ϣⲉ ⲉϣⲗⲏⲗ ⲛ̅ϩⲏⲧⲟⲩ.[38]

[1] With God.[39] [2] These are the acclamations of the time of evening, and those of the nighttime, and those of the time of assembly, [3] and the hours of the day, in which one should pray.

What follows is a series of short prayers, mostly consisting of psalm verses in Greek with Coptic translation, prescribed for each of the following hours of prayer: Prime, third hour, sixth hour, ninth hour, the *lychnikon* at evening, and the night office. These are very brief psalm verses related in theme to each hour, unlike the full system of

36 For a full outline of the contents of this manuscript, see Depuydt, *Catalogue of Coptic Manuscripts,* 113–121.

37 The text of the horologion part of the manuscript with a German translation can be found in Quecke, *Untersuchungen,* 394–445. Photographs of the codex were published as part of the collection of photographs of the entire Pierpont Morgan collection in fifty six volumes by Henri Hyvernat. See Henri Hyvernat, *Bybliothecae Pierpont Morgan Codices Coptici photographice expressi,* vol. 13 (Rome, 1922).

38 *MLM M574* (AD 897–898), fol. 72r. Cf. Quecke, *Untersuchungen,* 422–423.

39 The phrase ⲥⲩⲛ ⲑ̅ⲱ̅ (with God) is a common introductory greeting in Coptic manuscript culture, which can perhaps be translated loosely as "in the name of God" or "by the help of God."

twelve psalms, troparia, and additional prayers that characterize the present-day Coptic Horologion of Northern Egyptian provenance. Nonetheless, this represents the earliest source to provide the content of these daytime or little hours.

In addition to merely mentioning the little hours, this passage is also significant for shedding light for the first time on the intersection between the daily hours and the Eucharist. As Hans Quecke has shown, the term ⲡ̄ⲛⲁⲩ ⲛ̄ⲥⲩⲛⲁⲅⲉ, which can be translated as "the time for assembly," occurs frequently in liturgical *typika* from Southern Egypt, usually referring to the eucharistic celebration.[40] Given the consistency of the meaning of this term in other sources, Quecke finds it difficult to imagine that the term here means something else, and thus concludes that in *MLM M574* (AD 897–898), the term should be understood as the time or hour of the Eucharist.[41]

This conclusion itself raises a few questions. First, the list of prayers in the heading does not correspond exactly to the titles of the prayers included afterwards in the text. While the general heading mentions evening, night, the Eucharist, and the hours of the day, the subsequent text includes prime, third hour, sixth hour, ninth hour, evening, and night. Quecke reasons that, since evening and night are accounted for in both places, and the little hours most probably correspond to the hours of the day (ⲛⲉⲩⲛⲟⲟⲩⲉ ⲙ̄ⲡⲉϩⲟⲟⲩ), this leaves "the time of the *synaxis*" to be somehow equivalent to prime.[42] If correct, this would mean that the Eucharist in this ninth-century monastic context was celebrated very early, before the third hour of the day (9 a.m.). This surely corresponds to actual practice today, in which the liturgy is usually celebrated in monasteries around dawn.[43] However, while in this manuscript the liturgy was listed in its proper spot within the chronological unfolding of the day between the nighttime prayer and the third hour, nowadays the liturgy is *preceded* by the third hour office regardless of how early or late it is celebrated. Perhaps this difference witnesses to the earliest stage in which the hours and the Eucharist were integrated in this fashion. At any rate for the present purpose, the Coptic horologion in *MLM M574* (AD 897–898) can be considered the earliest testimony of the eucharistic celebration and the daily hours forming one integrated cursus. However, it must be stressed, this source does not indicate that the hours were prayed *in the context of* the eucharistic liturgy, an entirely different matter.

40 Quecke, *Untersuchungen*, 118.
41 Quecke, *Untersuchungen*, 122.
42 Ibid., 122–123.
43 Taft, *The Liturgy of the Hours*, 258.

1.5. The Lamp of Darkness *of Ibn Kabar (14th c.)*

In the fourteenth century, Abū l-Barakāt ibn Kabar acknowledged the necessity of going to church both in the morning, "before any work," and in the evening, "to thank God—to him be glory—and to conduct the prayers and praises,"[44] even attributing this custom to apostolic command. For the rest of the hours "by day and by night," Ibn Kabar mentions them as encouraged for those who are free of occupation,[45] and obligatory for ascetics, clergy, and monks.[46] He later reinforces the same idea of daily matins and vespers, which are to be celebrated, "in church, particularly on Sunday and Saturday."[47]

After this general treatment of prayer, Ibn Kabar proceeds to describe the rites of vespers, the midnight vigil, and matins. Beginning with matins, Ibn Kabar writes:

[1] أمّا باكر وعشية فقد رُسِم فيها رفع البخور وبالخاصة باكراً فان ينبغي رفعه في كنايس الله سواء عقب الصلاة قداس او لم يعقبها [2] وقوم يرون برفع البخور اول الصلاة وقوم يرونه بعد قراءة المزامير وما يتلوها.[48]	[1] As for matins and vespers, it was appointed in them the raising of incense, especially matins, for it should be offered in the churches of God, whether the prayer is followed by a liturgy or not. [2] And there are those who think that incense is to be offered in the beginning of the prayer, and those who think it is to be after the reading of the psalms and what follows them.

Again, later for vespers, he writes:

[1] وأما صلاة عشية فالاعتماد فيها كالاعتماد باكراً في رفع البخور. [2] ومن الكهنة من يقرأ بعد الاجبية الهوس الرابع المشتمل على المزامير الثلثة مزمور ١٤٨ مزمور ١٤٩ مزمور ١٥٠ وايضا تاوضوكية ذلك اليوم كاملة في ليالي الاحاد والاعياد.[49]	[1] As for the prayer of vespers, it is done in the same manner as matins in the offering of incense. [2] And some priests, after the book of the hours, read the fourth ode, which includes the three psalms: Psalm 148, Psalm 149, and Psalm 150, and likewise the *theotokia* of that day in full on the eves of Sundays and feasts.

44 *Paris BnF Ar. 203* (AD 1363–1369), fol. 193v. Cf. Villecourt, "Les observances," 210.
45 *Paris BnF Ar. 203* (AD 1363–1369), fol. 194r. Cf. Villecourt, "Les observances," 210.
46 *Paris BnF Ar. 203* (AD 1363–1369), fol. 194r. Cf. Villecourt, "Les observances," 211.
47 *Paris BnF Ar. 203* (AD 1363–1369), fol. 195v–196r. Cf. Villecourt, "Les observances," 216.
48 *Paris BnF Ar. 203* (AD 1363–1369), fol. 196v. Cf. Villecourt, "Les observances," 218.
49 *Paris BnF Ar. 203* (AD 1363–1369), fol. 198r–v. Cf. Villecourt, "Les observances," 223.

The reference in [2] to praying the hours, since it is clearly an interjection, is not meant as the practice on the eves of Sundays and feasts. Rather, it is more likely that the fourth ode and the *theotokia* are what is meant as the special custom of feasts. What is useful here is that Ibn Kabar seems to espouse the practice of praying the hours as a matter of fact. In other words, those who did not do so, as referenced above, did not include Ibn Kabar and the practice in his church in Cairo.

An interesting variant occurs in the later manuscript of the same work, *Uppsala O. Vet. 12* (AD 1546). In the same chapter, a clarifying note added to the text states the following:

[1] لا يقال فى صلاة ليالي الاحاد الاجبية [2]
بل الخمس مزامير وهم ⲧⲁⲯⲩⲭⲏ ⲥⲙⲟⲩ ⲡ̅ⲟ̅ⲥ̅.
ⲡ̅ⲟ̅ⲥ̅ ⲁⲓⲱϣ ⲟⲩⲃⲏⲕ. ⲁⲓⲱϣ ⲛ̀ⲧⲁⲥⲙⲏ ⲡ̅ⲟ̅ⲥ̅.
ⲉ̀ⲃⲟⲗ ϧⲉⲛ ⲛⲏⲉⲧϣⲏⲕ. ϩⲏⲡⲡⲉ ⲇⲉ ⲥ̀ⲙⲟⲩ
ⲡ̅ⲟ̅ⲥ̅ ⲛⲏⲉⲑⲛⲟⲥ ⲧⲏⲣⲟⲩ.[50]

[1] The hours (*al-ağbiyya*) are not recited n the prayers on the eves of Sundays, [2] but the five psalms, and these are: Praise the Lord O my soul [Ps 103], Lord I have cried unto Thee [Ps 140], with my voice I cried unto the Lord [Ps 141], from the depths [Ps 129], Behold bless the Lord all you nations [Ps 116].

Ibn Kabar—or the copyist who added this note—is describing a Sunday vesper service that is different from that of the rest of the week. The difference lies in replacing the regular prayer of the hours with the five psalms (Pss 103, 140, 141, 129, and 116), familiar elsewhere in the Byantine Rite as the lamp-lighting psalms of the Byzantine Sabaitic cathedral vespers, as well as the present-day Byzantine Rite. This is certainly not an isolated Byzantinism. As Ugo Zanetti has shown, this system is found in some liturgical manuscripts, such as *St. Macarius Lit. 438* (14th c.), and *St. Macarius Lit. 440* (17th c.), and titled *The Prayer of the eleventh hour According to the Cairene Usage*, betraying its cathedral provenance.[51] Finally, regarding the liturgy, the following passage appears in *Paris BnF Ar. 203* (AD 1363–1369):

[1] والذي تداولته البيعة القبطية ان لا يكون
القداس الّا تلو صلاة. [2] والاحسن ان تكون
الصلاة التي تتقدمه برفع بخور هذا إذا كان
فصحاً. [3] واما اذا كان ايام الاربعين والاربعاء
والجمعة والاصوام الأخَر فيكون عقبي صلاة

[1] And the custom in the Coptic Church is that there be no liturgy except following a prayer. [2] And it is best if this prayer is the *Offering ot Incense*, that is, if it were a feast. [3]

50 *Uppsala O. Vet. 12* (AD 1546), fol. 179v. Cf. Villecourt, "Les observances," 240.

51 Ugo Zanetti, "Horologion copte et vêpres byzantines," *Le Muséon* 102 (1989): 237–254. For a further discussion of this and other ancient witnesses of evening prayer as they relate to current practice, cf. Ramez Mikhail, "On Evening Worship in Egypt: A Theological Evaluation of Contemporary Practice in Light of Patristic and Medieval Sources," *Coptica* 12 (2013): 77–94.

الساعة التي تتقدمه اعني التاسعة بالاجبية والقطع. [4] والرهبان في ايام الاربعين المقدسة يُصَلّون قبله صلاتي الغروب والنوم.[52]	But if it be the Forty Days, Wednesdays, Fridays, and the other fasts, it follows the prayer of the hour that precedes it, I mean, the ninth hour in the *ağbiyya* and the chants. [4] And the monks during the holy forty days pray the two prayers of evening and compline.

Once again, the distinction between monastic and non-monastic practice is very clear. In this case, Ibn Kabar prescribes the prayer of the hours appropriate to whatever time the liturgy is celebrated on fasting days, since liturgies during fasts are ideally celebrated later in the day. This is especially so, he continues, in the monastic environment, where they always pray vespers (again, this is the prayer of the eleventh hour in the Horologion, not the ritual evening raising of incense), and compline, presumably because the monks delay liturgies during the forty-day fast until after sunset. The exception to all this, it seems, is regular nonfasting days, in which the liturgy is preceded immediately by the morning incense service, which implies that no little hours are prayed.

The information in the *Lamp of Darkness* regarding monastic usage can be further corroborated by reference to the witness of the so-called *Book of the Holy Chrism* in the codex *Paris BnF Ar. 100* (14th c.). Besides containing the important *Letter of Macarius* discussed previously, the manuscript contains eyewitness accounts of the consecration of the chrism, which was performed by a number of patriarchs between the late thirteenth and mid-fourteenth centuries. Of particular interest is the account of the consecration of the chrism by Patriarch Benjamin II (AD 1327–1339) at the Monastery of Saint Macarius on the fourth Sunday of the Lenten fast in AD 1330. Upon arriving at the monastery on a Friday with his entourage of bishops, the patriarch took the blessing of the ancient sites of the monastery, then "began praying the ninth hour."[53] Afterwards, they began preparing the materials necessary for the consecration of the chrism until the appropriate time for the liturgy, when one of the hierarchs present, Metropolitan Gregorius of Damietta, "went out to the church and began the prayers of the evening and compline, and prayed the liturgy."[54] This agrees fully with the description by Ibn Kabar, in which the monks during Lent pray all the hours at their appropriate time, delaying the liturgy until after compline.

52 *Paris BnF Ar. 203* (AD 1363–1369), fol. 203r. Cf. Villecourt, "Les observances," 248.

53 *Paris BnF Ar. 100* (14th c.), fol. 53r.

54 *Paris BnF Ar. 100* (14th c.), fol. 53r.

Another narrative from the same source provides information on the practice on major feasts. The consecration of the chrism during the time of Patriarch Peter V (AD 1340–1348) took place during Holy Week of AD 1340. The patriarch, arriving to the Monastery of Saint Macarius on Lazarus Saturday, prayed the services of that day and Palm Sunday with the monks and his accompanying bishops. On Sunday, he is said to have prayed matins, followed by the procession of the cross.[55] At the conclusion of the procession, they re-entered the church, and they "continued the prayer [matins] according to the custom. Then they began praying the two hours the third and the sixth and they began the liturgy."[56] Since it was a Sunday, and especially a major feast, it is expected that the prayers of the hours would only include the third and sixth hours and not compline as is done on fasting days. The two examples from the *Book of the Holy Chrism* demonstrate that indeed in the fourteenth century, the praying of the little hours was an accepted custom in the monastic setting, observed even by visiting patriarchs and their accompanying hierarchs.

Thus, taking into account all the information from the two manuscripts of the *Lamp of Darkness* about the intersection of the prayers of the hours and the services of vespers, matins, and the liturgy, it can be summarized in the following way:

1. On regular days, practice varied in matins and vespers, with some praying the hours before the incense service (at least Cairo) and some who did not.
2. Shortly after Ibn Kabar's time, the custom of praying the introductory psalms of Byzantine vespers (Pss 103, 140, 141, 129, and 116) is witnessed for the eves of Sundays.
3. During fasts, when liturgies are customarily later in the day, the appropriate hour of the Horologion was prayed first. The particular hour varied depending on the time of day, with the ninth hour being frequently the case.
4. Monks did not stop at the ninth hour but added also the eleventh hour and compline.

Therefore, by the fourteenth century one sees the continued incorporation of the daily hours of the Horologion into the liturgical cycle of cathedral *Vespers*, and *Matins Raising of Incense*, and—most importantly—the eucharistic liturgy. Whereas Ibn Sabbāʿ as I discuss below mentions this phenomenon only in the context of particularly solemn occasions, in Ibn Kabar this usage extends also to praying the

55 Gérard Viaud, "La procession des deux fêtes de la Croix et du Dimanche des Rameaux dans l'Église copte d'après un manuscrit du monastère Al-Baramûs et du monastère Al-Muḥarraq," *BSAC* 19 (1970): 211–226. See also Burmester, *The Egyptian Church*, 264–268.

56 *Paris BnF Ar. 100* (14th c.), fol. 67r.

hours before the evening and morning *Raising of Incense* in some places, and certainly to praying the little hours between matins and the liturgy during fasts. This last detail is only because liturgies were celebrated later compared to nonfasting days. In other words, the practice of praying the little hours before the prothesis had not yet acquired a solid footing in the Coptic Rite outside the monastic setting, although at other times of the day (before morning and evening *Raising of Incense* for example), this had gradually become the custom in some places.

1.6. The Precious Jewel *of Ibn Sabbāʿ (14th c.)*

Around the same time as Ibn Kabar, one finds Ibn Sabbāʿ speaking generally about "the times of prayer obligatory for man,"[57] where he lists a full system of seven prayers, together with biblical justification, albeit not quite identical to that found elsewhere: 1. Dawn, 2. third hour, 3. sixth hour, 4. ninth hour, 5. sunset, 6. at the time of sleeping (compline), and 7. midnight.[58]

Ibn Sabbāʿ makes no distinction here between prayers obligatory for monks or laymen. Everyone, at least ideally, should pray the seven hours. In the chapter, *Concerning the Abbreviation of the Prayers of Laymen and the Lengthening of the Prayer of Monks* (في ذكر اختصار صلوات العلمانيين و تطويل صلاة الرهبان), he lays out more explicitly how laymen may be distinguished from monks in their system of prayer:

[1] أما صلاة العلمانيين فيجب ان تكون مختصرة لأجل اشتغالهم بالمعايش الدنيوية. [2] يجب عليهم ان يصلوا باكراً في الكنيسة بسجود وركوع وخلو بال وكذلك عشية بالشرح. [3] وأما الثالثة والسادسة والتاسعة فيجب عليهم الصلاة فيهم من غير تعطيل وهم جلوس في اشغالهم او مسافرين في البر والبحر او اي حالة كانوا فيها.[59]	[1] As for the prayer of the laity, it must be abbreviated on account of their occupation with worldly livelihood. [2] They ought to arrive to church early in the morning with prostration, kneeling, and a mind free of thoughts. Likewise, also in the evening as explained. [3] As for the prayers of the third, the sixth, and the ninth hours, they ought to pray them without delay while they are engaged in their occupations or traveling by land or sea, in any condition they may be in.

57 *Paris BnF Ar. 207* (14th c.), fol. 97r. Cf. Mistrīḥ, *Pretiosa margarita*, 135 (Arabic), 465 (Latin).

58 *Paris BnF Ar. 207* (14th c.), fol. 97r–v. Cf. Mistrīḥ, *Pretiosa margarita*, 135–136 (Arabic), 465 (Latin).

59 *Paris BnF Ar. 207* (14th c.), fol. 117r. Cf. Mistrīḥ, *Pretiosa margarita*, 170 (Arabic), 484 (Latin).

Although it may seem rather excessive to demand laymen to pray the entire daily cursus whether at work or travelling, Ibn Sabbāʿ goes on to outline the ideal monastic prayer in this way:

[1] فلَمّا تفرغوا لطلب الاخرة بعد ترك طلب الدنيا واسبابها [2] وادخلوا نفوسهم في شكل الملائكة العلوية [3] لزمهم اقتناء مايجب من التشكل بشكل الملائكة العلوية [4] وهو مداومة التسبيح والتقديس للباري تعالى على الدوام. [5] ولم يكن هذا النظام موقوفاً على اوقات محدودة بل يجب مداومة التسبيح والتقديس مع طلوع النفس ونزوله [6] لا يفرق بينهم وبينه غير النوم لراحة الطبيعة لانهم قد صاروا ملائكة ارضيين وبشر سمائيين.[60]

[1] Since [monks] have become free to seek after eternity after they have ceased from seeking after the world and its means of subsistence [2] and have put on themselves the likeness of the heavenly angels, [3] they have become obliged to obtain what befits the likeness of the heavenly angels. [4] That is, they ought to persevere in praising and hallowing the Creator (may he be exalted) at all times. [5] Nor was this order restricted to particular times, but they should continue praising and hallowing while breathing in and breathing out. [6] Nothing is to separate them from praying except sleep for bodily rest. For they have become angels on earth and heavenly men.

Of course, this is not to say that the specific seven hours of prayer mentioned earlier are only for laymen, but that monks are ideally to pray always (1 Thes 5:17), whether assembled together or praying in their heart, with every breath as it were. All this shows how important the daily hours were for Ibn Sabbāʿ. Although the idealistic tone of these passages cannot be overlooked, the very existence of such ideals means that daily prayer was highly regarded by the author, and not seen merely as the specialty of monks, but as part of the daily life of all Christians.

In light of the foregoing, it is quite telling that there is no mention of praying the little hours before the liturgy in Ibn Sabbāʿ's description in chapters 60-64 of the *Precious Jewel*. After presenting the different parts of the priest's vestments in chapter 61, followed by the preparation of the altar in chapter 63, the description moves directly to the prothesis, when the priest—according to the intermediate ordo—goes to the altar of offering to retrieve the oblations, and proceed with

[60] *Paris BnF Ar. 207* (14th c.), fol. 118r. Cf. Mistrīḥ, *Pretiosa margarita*, 171-172 (Arabic), 485 (Latin).

the rest of the prothesis.[61] If praying the hours were indeed the practice in Ibn Sabbā‘'s time in the celebration of every regular liturgy, one would have expected him to make even a brief mention of the practice, particularly given his emphasis on the place of the daily hours discussed above. Therefore, and despite this being an argument *ex silentio*, it may be concluded with sufficient confidence that the little hours did not form part of the unfolding of the liturgy known and described by Ibn Sabbā‘.

The same however is not true when one takes a closer look at special seasons and feasts. In a brief description of the Feast of the Annunciation in chapter 99, Ibn Sabbā‘ writes, "And the prayer on the eve of the feast shall be after the conclusion of the liturgy of the fast.[62] And they begin with the psalms (المزامير) and the *theotokia* according to the custom of feasts of the Lord (الاعياد السيدية)."[63] While this is not in reference to the little hours before the liturgy, it refers to another point in the daily cursus where the daily hours are prayed, namely, the eleventh hour and compline, which precede the evening service of vespers.

This remark is interesting because it may indicate that the practice of praying the monastic-style hours was becoming the custom, at least on solemn occasions. This is seen elsewhere in Ibn Sabbā‘, when he describes the unfolding of the rites of Holy Week, particularly Bright Saturday. In chapter 105, *Concerning the Order of the Saturday of Light and the Day of the Holy Resurrection*, Ibn Sabbā‘ writes the following: "And they assemble at the sixth hour and pray the hours (السواعي) in church." Later, he writes, "And when the reading of the Apocalypse is finished,[64] they pray the ninth hour with the psalms according to the custom of the year (الصلاة السنوية), and the liturgy is prayed."[65] This last remark to praying the ninth hour according to the regular custom can be interpreted to mean the ninth hour was regularly prayed before liturgies. However, given that in his regular description of the liturgy, Ibn Sabbā‘ makes no such reference, I take

61 *Paris BnF Ar. 207* (14th c.), fol. 121r–122v. Cf. Mistrīḥ, *Pretiosa margarita*, 179–180 (Arabic), 488 (Latin).

62 The Feast of the Annunciation is celebrated on 29 Baramhāt (= 25 March Julian), which falls during the Lenten fast.

63 *Paris BnF Ar. 207* (14th c.), fol. 185v–186r. Cf. Mistrīḥ, *Pretiosa margarita*, 310 (Arabic), 554 (Latin).

64 During the rites of Bright Saturday, the entire book of Revelation is read. See Burmester, *The Egyptian Church*, 270. For a detailed study of the rituals of Bright Saturday, see Athanasius al-Maqārī, *Sabt al-faraḥ wa-l-nūr: Al-tārīḫ al-ṭaqsī/ ṭuqūs al-ṣalawāt* [The Saturday of joy and light: The ritual history/the rites of the prayers], Ṭuqūs aṣwām wa-a‘yād al-kanīsa 4.7 (Cairo: Maṭābi‘ al-nūbār, 2012).

65 *Paris BnF Ar. 207* (14th c.), fol. 200v. Cf. Mistrīḥ, *Pretiosa margarita*, 346–347 (Arabic), 573 (Latin).

this instead to mean that the normal hours of the Horologion were prayed. That is, in distinction from the current ordo of Holy Week, in which Horologion hours are suspended from usage, and replaced instead by the special hourly cursus of Holy Week services.[66]

In summary, Ibn Sabbāʿ placed the daily hours in very high regard, even for non-monastics. Despite this, he makes no mention of the prayers of the hours as part of the normal everyday liturgy, while he clearly makes room for them on special solemn occasions such as the Feast of the Annunciation and Holy Week. It may be tempting to view this as an example of a frequently observed phenomenon or "law" of liturgical evolution, in which older practices are often retained in the more solemn celebrations.[67] However, since there is absolutely no evidence that the sixth or ninth hour were ever prayed in the context of the liturgy before this point, the evidence from the *Precious Jewel* of Ibn Sabbāʿ is another example of the gradual adoption of the Scetis liturgical tradition. This was likely the case particularly in solemn seasons such as Holy Week and feasts, which would have called for a

66 According to Maria Cramer, the current lectionary system for Holy Week in the Coptic tradition is attributed to Patriarch Gabriel II ibn Turaik (AD 1131–1145). See Maria Cramer, "Studien zu koptischen Pascha-Büchern: Der Ritus der Karwoche in der koptischen Kirche," *OC* 47 (1963): 118–130, here 121. This tradition is mentioned in a Coptic poem of AD 1626. See O.H.E. Burmester, "A Coptic Lectionary Poem (from MS. 408, Coptic Museum, Cairo)," *Le Muséon* 45 (1932): 21–70. This reform was undertaken by the assistance of the monks of Saint Macarius, in an effort to relax the strictness of the rite for parishes compared to their own monastic ordo, which consisted of reading the entire Old and New Testaments divided over the days of Holy Week. For general surveys of Coptic Holy Week, see Emmanuel Lanne, "Textes et rites de la liturgie pascale dans l'ancienne église copte," *L'Orient Syrien* 6 (1961): 279–300; Rafīq ʿĀdil, "Ṭaqs al-baṣẖa al-muqaddassa fī l-kanīsa al-qibṭiyya: Simātuhu al-aṣliyya wa-taṭawwuruhu ʿabr al-ʿuṣūr [The rite of Holy Pascha in the Coptic Church: Its original characteristics and its evolution throughout the ages]," *Madrasat al-Iskandariyya* 6 (2010): 189–215, here 196; Rafīq ʿĀdil, "Al-iṭār al-ʿām li-šakl wa-tartīb ṭaqs al-baṣẖa al-muqaddassa fī l-qarn al-rābiʿ ʿašar [The general framework for the structure and order of the rite of the Holy Pascha in the 14th century]," *Madrasat al-Iskandariyya* 13 (2013): 179–207. Later in the course of the twelfth or thirteenth century, according to Burmester, Bishop Peter of Bahnasā assisted in further reforms of the lectionary, adding Old Testament readings to every hour of prayer, and thus harmonizing all the hours of prayer throughout the week into more or less equal length. See O.H.E. Burmester, "Two Services of the Coptic Church Attributed to Peter, Bishop of Behnesā," *Le Muséon* 45 (1932): 235–254, here 236. On the relationship between the Coptic Holy Week lectionary and the Ethiopian *Gebra Ḥemāmāt*, see Ugo Zanetti, "Is the Ethiopian Holy Week Service Translated from Sahidic? Towards a Study of the *Gebra Ḥemāmāt*," in *Proceedings of the Eleventh International Conference of Ethiopian Studies, Addis Ababa, April 1–6 1991*, ed. Bahru Zewde, Richard Pankhurst, and Taddese Beyene, vol. 1 (Adis Ababa: Institute of Ethiopian Studies, 1994), 765–783.

67 Baumstark, *Comparative Liturgy*, 27–30; Taft, "Anton Baumstark's Comparative Liturgy Revisited," 206–208.

much more maximalistic ordo, with extra elements taken from the practice of monks, praised by Ibn Sabbāʿ as earthly angels and heavenly men.

1.7. The Ritual Order *of Gabriel V (15th c.)*

Although the gradual adoption of the daily hours generally into the daily rhythm was seen even in urban worship, the sources have yet to touch upon the particular point under investigation, the praying of the little hours before the prothesis in regular year-round liturgies. This was in fact still the case even by the time of Patriarch Gabriel V. In a chapter on the rites of evening and morning *Raising of Incense*, the text explains:

[1] يقول في صلاة باكر اوشية المرضى وهي ⲛⲓⲉⲧϣⲱⲛⲓ وبعدها اوشية المسافرين وهي ⲉⲧⲁⲩϣⲉ ⲡϣⲉⲙⲙⲱⲟⲩ. [2] وان كان عقيب صلاة باكر خدمة القداس فلا يقول اوشية المسافرين لكن يصعد الى المذبح بعد قراءة اوشية المرضى عندما يقول ϧⲉⲛ ⲡⲓϩⲙⲟⲧ يقول اوشية القرابين وهي ⲛⲓⲑⲩⲥⲓⲁ.[68]

[1] He [the priest] says in the prayer of the morning the litany of the sick, and after it the litany of the travellers. [2] And if the prayer of the morning is followed by the service of the liturgy, he does not say the prayer of the travellers, but ascends to the altar after the litany of the sick, when he says, "by the grace,"[69] and says the prayer of the oblations.

Although today the morning *Raising of Incense* always comes immediately before the liturgy, the *Ritual Order* is describing a rite in which this service was done every morning, irrespective of whether it is followed immediately by the liturgy, or if a liturgy is prayed at all on that day. This is not directly answering the particular question, but it demonstrates how in the rites of the patriarchal cathedral in the fifteenth century–at least ideally–the daily cycle of prayers was as of yet not thought of as a necessary element before the prothesis but could instead be prayed without a liturgy whatsoever. At any rate, in his next chapter on the rite of the liturgy of Saint Basil, Gabriel V

68 *Paris BnF Ar. 98* (17th c.), fol. 43v. Cf. ʿAbdallah, *L'ordinamento*, 169 (Arabic), 359 (Italian).

69 The reference here is to the concluding doxology of the prayer for the sick: "By the grace and compassion and love of man of your only-begotten Son, our Lord and our God and our Savior Jesus Christ. This is he through whom the glory and the honor and the majesty and the worship befit you with him, and the Holy Spirit the life-giver and consubstantial with you, now and at all times and unto the ages of all ages, amen," (ϧⲉⲛ ⲡⲓϩ̀ⲙⲟⲧ ⲛⲉⲙ ⲛⲓⲙⲉⲧϣⲉⲛϩⲏⲧ ⲛⲉⲙ ϯⲙⲉⲧⲙⲁⲓⲣⲱⲙⲓ ⲛ̀ⲧⲉ ⲡⲉⲕⲙⲟⲛⲟⲅⲉⲛⲏⲥ ⲛ̀ϣⲏⲣⲓ ⲡⲉⲛϭⲟⲓⲥ ⲟⲩⲟϩ ⲡⲉⲛⲛⲟⲩϯ ⲟⲩⲟϩ ⲡⲉⲛⲥⲱⲧⲏⲣ ⲓⲏⲥⲟⲩⲥ ⲡⲓⲭⲣⲓⲥⲧⲟⲥ. ⲫⲁⲓ ⲉⲧⲉ ⲉⲃⲟⲗ ϩⲓⲧⲟⲧϥ ⲉⲣⲉ ⲡⲓⲱ̀ⲟⲩ ⲛⲉⲙ ⲡⲓⲧⲁⲓⲟ ⲛⲉⲙ ⲡⲓⲁ̀ⲙⲁϩⲓ ⲛⲉⲙ ϯⲡⲣⲟⲥⲕⲩⲛⲏⲥⲓⲥ ⲉⲣ̀ⲡⲣⲉⲡⲓ ⲛⲁⲕ ⲛⲉⲙⲁϥ ⲛⲉⲙ ⲡⲓⲡⲛⲉⲩⲙⲁ ⲉⲑⲟⲩⲁⲃ ⲛ̀ⲣⲉϥⲧⲁⲛϧⲟ ⲟⲩⲟϩ ⲛ̀ⲟⲙⲟⲟⲩⲥⲓⲟⲥ ⲛⲉⲙⲁⲕ ϯⲛⲟⲩ ⲛⲉⲙ ⲛ̀ⲥⲏⲟⲩ ⲛⲓⲃⲉⲛ ⲛⲉⲙ ϣⲁ ⲉⲛⲉϩ ⲛ̀ⲧⲉ ⲛⲓⲉⲛⲉϩ ⲧⲏⲣⲟⲩ ⲁⲙⲏⲛ). See Ṣalīb, ⲡⲓϫⲱⲙ ⲛ̀ⲧⲉ ⲡⲓⲉⲩⲭⲟⲗⲟⲅⲓⲟⲛ, 55–56.

begins immediately with the vesting and altar preparation discussed previously, without even the slightest mention of the prayers of the hours.

In agreement with the *Ritual Order*, the patriarchal liturgy of *Coptic Patriarchate Lit. 74* (AD 1444) likewise makes no reference to the praying of the little hours. At the end of the morning *Raising of Incense*, the text continues:

[1] ثم يقرأ البطريرك البركة [2] ويبتدوا بعدها بقرآة الليلويا. [3] إن كان إفطار ⲁ̅ⲗ̅ ⲫⲁⲓ ⲡⲉ وان كان صوم ⲫⲙⲉⲩⲓ ⲭⲉ ⲁ̅ⲗ̅.[70]	[1] And the Patriarch reads the blessing.[71] [2] And after this they begin chanting Alleluia. [3] If it were nonfasting, Alleluia this is the day [Ps 117:24–26], and if it were a fast, Alleluia the thought of man [Ps 75:11].

The same is true in the later description of the patriarchal liturgy in *Baramūs 6/278* (AD 1514).[72] As can be seen, fifteenth-century sources of cathedral practice are unanimous in omitting the little hours from their description of the rite of the liturgy. This omission was also taken up a few centuries later by Ṭūẖī in his *editio princeps* of the Coptic Euchologion. This is expected, since he is likely to have supplied the rubrics for his edition from the *Ritual Order* itself, in addition to the texts of the prayers from *BAV Vatican Copt. 17* (AD 1288).[73]

Therefore, one can conclude based on the foregoing that the practice of praying the third, sixth, and ninth hours between the morning raising of incense and the prothesis by the fifteenth century was certainly the accepted practice in monasteries, and likewise adopted into the parishes and cathedrals on certain seasons (feasts, Holy Week, etc.). Nonetheless, it had not yet become the unassailable order of the liturgy any day there is a celebration, as the case is today. However, it is clear that by the early twentieth century, and likely for some time already before that, the practice had become the ritual norm. Unfortunately, the sources do not allow for a more precise dating for the solidification of this practice, though one would suspect it could not have been much later than the fifteenth century. This is because already a century earlier the canonical hours had made their

70 *Coptic Patriarchate Lit. 74* (AD 1444), fol. 74v. Cf. Samuel, *Tartīb al-bīʿa*, 1:17; Mikhail, "The Liturgy *Coram Patriarcha* Revisited," 307 (Arabic), 308 (English).

71 This is in reference to the dismissal blessing at the end of the morning and evening raising of incense services. See Burmester, *The Egyptian Church*, 45; Ṣalīb, ⲡⲓϫⲱⲙ ⲛ̀ⲧⲉ ⲡⲓⲉⲩⲭⲟⲗⲟⲅⲓⲟⲛ, 140–174.

72 Samuel, *Tartīb al-bīʿa*, 1:21; Mikhail, "The Liturgy *Coram Patriarcha* Revisited," 309 (Arabic), 310 (English).

73 Ṭūẖī, ⲡⲓϫⲱⲙ ⲛ̀ⲧⲉ ⲡⲓϣⲟⲙⲧ ⲛ̀ⲁⲛⲁⲫⲟⲣⲁ, 308–309.

way into the liturgical daily cycle at other times of the day such as vespers, as seen in Ibn Kabar.

Thus, returning to the note quoted in the beginning of this chapter from the Euchologion of 1902 by 'Abd al-Masīḥ Ṣalīb, which describes the praying of the little hours as a contemporary custom, it becomes clear that this practice cannot be as recent as an initial reading may suggest. One possibility is that Hegumen 'Abd al-Masīḥ may have judged this to be a recent practice simply because it does not appear in any of the Euchologia manuscripts he consulted in preparation for his edition of the Euchologion. Such a conclusion of course would be incorrect, since Euchologia by their very nature do not provide all the rubrics necessary for the service, but only the texts of the prayers of the celebrant. Another possibility, and perhaps more likely, is that Hegumen 'Abd al-Masīḥ did not mean that the practice of praying the hours itself was a recent innovation, but rather that the preparation of the altar during the prayers of the hours is the recent phenomenon in his judgement. It would surely be more logical to prepare the altar separately from the prayers of the hours, two elements that are essentially independent from one another.

At any rate, this one isolated note has unfortunately given rise to the common misconception that the practice is a recent innovation that has only gained acceptance only in the early twentieth century! Such is the position taken by Athanasius al-Maqārī, who in his work on the history of the Coptic liturgy started from this very note and set out to explore the same question. However, he mistakenly concluded within a few pages, "Even the Euchologion printed in 1902, and which was reviewed by Hegumen 'Abd al-Masīḥ Ṣalīb al-Baramūsī, when it speaks of the psalms of the hours *as a custom that has become current in his days*, does not mention the same order known to us today."[74] The evidence presented here has demonstrated that the practice in question has certainly developed over time. However, to conclude that it is as recent as the early twentieth century simply cannot be accepted without doing injustice to the historical record.

74 Al-Maqārī, *Al-quddās al-ilāhī*, 1:244. Translation and emphasis are mine. Fr. Athanasius seems to believe that the only order current today is to prepare the altar before the prayers of the hours, thus interpreting the two possibilities given in the Euchologion of 1902 as indicating that the practice must not have been stable by that time, if the altar preparation could still be done during the praying of the little hours. However, from personal observation the author has seen many priests prepare the altar at various points in the service.

2. THE LITTLE HOURS IN EAST AND WEST

It has been remarked that of all eastern traditions, the Coptic Rite has retained the purest monastic form.[75] While this is certainly true, it may be tempting for the untrained to regard the practice of praying the little hours before the prothesis as an example of this affinity toward monastic prayer. Similarly, this practice may appear as a recent innovation, perhaps unique to the Coptic Church with its fondness of its own monastic tradition. However, it is also the case that by the end of the fourth century the pure monastic and cathedral offices in many places blended to produce what is known as the urban monastic office. This was a result of the fact that monks often lived near cities in Palestine, Mesopotamia, Syria, and Cappadocia.[76] Although the distinction between the monastic and cathedral traditions is certainly useful for studying the daily hours in the fourth century, these two traditions hybridize in various ways in almost all traditions shortly afterwards. The exception to this is the Coptic and Ethiopian Rites, and even there, one finds parallel monastic and cathedral elements forming parts of a single liturgical tradition observed in both monasteries and parishes.

With this in mind, a cursory look at some other liturgical traditions will reveal that the praying of the third, sixth, and sometimes the ninth hours before the eucharistic liturgy is widespread. The Ethiopian tradition, in many ways an heir to Coptic usage, possesses a still extant set of cathedral services comprising vespers, nocturns, and matins. During Lent, one also finds the so-called little hours.[77] Unfortunately, knowledge of the historical development of the Ethiopian daily office is incomplete, which does not allow for a discussion of the historical development of this cathedral tradition. At this point, one can see that this system of cathedral services is native in character and not Coptic, since the Ethiopian Rite also possesses a translation of the Coptic horologion as a separate tradition titled the *sa'ātāt za-gebs* (Horologion of the Egyptians). As can be seen then, even the indigenous cathedral tradition of the Ethiopian Church has incorporated the little hours—albeit in Lent—into the daily liturgical cycle of hours at some unknown point in its historical development. The West-Syrian tradition of the Syrian Orthodox Church is even closer to current Coptic usage in that third and sixth hours are supposed to be prayed between matins (*ṣafro*) and the liturgy at any

[75] For example, see Taft, *The Liturgy of the Hours*, 249.
[76] The urban monastic synthesis is discussed in detail in ibid., 75–91.
[77] Ibid., 262.

time, and not just in Lent. This much at least was observed by Aelred Cody during his time in Jerusalem in 1962–1964.[78]

The Byzantine Rite of today is not purely of Constantinopolitan origin. In fact, the cathedral rite of the capital became largely extinct either around the time of the Fourth Crusade in AD 1204,[79] or certainly by the fifteenth century at the latest, as seen in the descriptions of it by Symeon of Thessaloniki (AD 1381–1429) in his treatise *On Sacred Prayer*.[80] At any rate, the cathedral office was eventually replaced by the monastic office. First, the Stoudios Monastery of Constantinople adopted the Palestinian monastic office of Saint Sabas after the first era of iconoclasm (AD 726–775). Later, a second wave of Sabaitic influence around the twelfth or thirteenth centuries resulted in the so-called neo-Sabaitic synthesis with the existing Stoudite tradition, which in turn was adopted even by the cathedrals and parishes in the capital. Thus, the Byzantine Rite of today is in fact the synthesis of monastic offices from Constantinople and Palestine.[81]

Although the older Stoudite office did not prescribe the little hours on Sundays and feasts, the Sabaitic office did exactly that.[82] This then is the ideal Byzantine practice today, despite what different jurisdictions and local parishes may do in actuality.[83] In the words of the Greek liturgiologist Ioannes Phountoules, "In essence, there are no two typika, but one [...] the only apparent difference of the monastic typikon from the typikon of the parishes consists today in the observance with strictness or *economia*—to use these two canonical terms analogously—of the instructions of the typikon that is common both to monks and to laymen."[84] Thus, according to this neo-Sabaitic

78 Aelred Cody, "L'eucharistie et les heures canoniales ches les Syriens jacobites. Une description des cérémonies," *L'Orient Syrien* 12 (1967): 55–81, here 70. See also Taft, *The Liturgy of the Hours*, 243.

79 For this and all subsequent information on the history of the Byzantine Divine Office, see Taft, *The Liturgy of the Hours*, 273–277. A more systematic treatment of the historical phases of evolution of the Byzantine Rite can be consulted in Robert F. Taft, *The Byzantine Rite: A Short History*, American Essays in Liturgy (Collegeville, MN: Liturgical Press, 1992).

80 Job Getcha, *The Typikon Decoded: An Explanation of Byzantine Liturgical Practice*, Orthodox Liturgy Series 3 (Yonkers, NY: St Vladimir's Seminary Press, 2012), 41.

81 Taft, *The Liturgy of the Hours*, 276–277; Getcha, *The Typikon Decoded*, 42–44.

82 Getcha, *The Typikon Decoded*, 45.

83 One readily available example of actual practice is quoted in Taft, *The Liturgy of the Hours*, 284. According to the testimony of a Greek Orthodox layman, orthros is followed immediately by the liturgy.

84 Ioannes Phountoules, *Τελετουργικά Θέματα* [Teleturgic topics], 2nd ed., vol. 1, Λογική Λατρεία 12 (Athens: Ἀποστολική Διακονία τής Ἐκκλησίας τής Ἑλλάδος, 2009), 12. Translation mine. This lecture, titled "The Monastic and Cathedral Typikon," was

typikon not only the little hours before the liturgy, but also the ninth hour is to be prayed before vespers, *mesonyktikon* (midnight) before orthros, and prime after orthros, to name only some of the elements that are frequently dropped in parish practice.[85] As is often the case, parish practice varies "according to the conservatism or progressivism of the minister, if not the chanters, who often form their preferences based not on liturgical grounds, but on musical criteria."[86]

In the Roman Rite, the Mass was preceded by *terce* and *sext* at least since the middle ages, specifically the time of John of Avranches, bishop of Avranches and later Rouen in France in the mid-eleventh century according to his treatise *Tractatus de officiis ecclesiasticis*.[87] This was the case not only in monasteries, but also in the parishes on Sundays and feast days. In fasts and particularly Lent by the Carolignian era, Mass was celebrated at the ninth hour, after *none*. However, already by the fourteenth century, the tendency arose to offer the Mass after *none*, but to pray the little hours much earlier, before noon.[88] As a form of regulation in response, the *Ordo Missae* of Johann Burchard (AD 1450–1506) laid down the exact hours to be prayed before Mass at any given season. This stipulated that *terce* would be prayed on Sundays and feasts, *sext* on simple feasts and ferial days, and *none* on days of penance,[89] which is quite similar to current Coptic practice, and stemming ultimately from the tradition of offering the Eucharist at a later hour on fasting days.

As one can see, it is clear from this overview that—at least in theory—the little hours are a standard component of the unfolding of the liturgy in many traditions, despite the ways in which this feature of the daily cycle has been modified or outright abandoned in actual practice.

delivered at the Panhellenic Monastic Congress held in Kalambaka, Greece in 1990. The entire lecture is very useful as a discussion of the current liturgical practice in the Church of Greece vis-à-vis the monastic typikon. For a full bibliography of the late Ioannes Phountoules, see Stefanos Alexopoulos, "Modern Greek Liturgical Scholarship: A Selective Bibliography (2000–2009)," in *ΤΟΞΟΤΗΣ: Studies for Stefano Parenti*, ed. Daniel Galadza, Nina Glibetic, and Gabriel Radle, Ἀνάλεκτα Κρυπτοφέρρης 9 (Grottaferrata: Monastero Esarchico, 2010), 19–47.

85 Ioannes Phountoules, *Απαντήσεις εις Λειτουργικάς Απορίας* [Answers to liturgical questions], 4th ed., vol. 3, (301–400) (Athens: Ἀποστολική Διακονία τῆς Ἐκκλησίας τῆς Ἑλλάδος, 2006), 249.

86 Ibid., 252.

87 Jungmann, *Missarum Sollemnia*, 1:248.

88 Ibid., 248–249.

89 Ibid.

3. THE LITTLE HOURS IN CURRENT PRACTICE

Today, the prayers of the hours of the Coptic Horologion are prayed between matins and the prothesis according to very specific rules. On Sundays, non-fasting days, and feasts, the third and sixth hours are prayed. The exception to this first rule is the three major feasts of the Nativity, Theophany, and Resurrection, prayed as evening liturgies, in which no hours at all are prayed between matins and the prothesis. This may very well be a relic of the earlier cathedral practice witnessed even until the fifteenth century (The *Ritual Order* and *Coptic Patriarchate 74 Lit.*). As such, this would be an example of the liturgical "law" of retention of older practices in particularly solemn celebrations.[90] On fasting days (i.e. days in which a total fast is prescribed until the ninth hour) the office of the ninth hour is added. Finally, during the three-day fast of Jonah and the Great Lenten fast, the horologion hour of vesper (the eleventh hour), and compline (the twelfth hour) are added. During Holy Week, the entire Horologion is suspended from use, and is replaced by the special services of Holy Week, which are themselves structured as a daily cursus of hours (first hour to eleventh hour).[91]

The way in which the hours are prayed is also not quite straightforward. Unlike the morning incense service, which is a self-contained service with its own dismissal blessing, the hours when prayed in this context are altered in some measure from the structure in the Horologion. Some elements of each hour are even dropped altogether. Below is the structure of the little hours (third, sixth, and ninth) as it is in the Horologion:

1. Introductory prayers
2. Prayer of Thanksgiving[92]
3. Psalm 50
4. The psalms of the hour (twelve in number)
5. Gospel passage
6. Troparia
7. *Kyrie eleison* 41 times
8. The prayer "Holy, Holy, Holy"
9. Our Father
10. Collect

[90] Baumstark, *Comparative Liturgy*, 27–30; Taft, "Anton Baumstark's Comparative Liturgy Revisited," 206–208.

[91] For a brief description of how the horologion is integrated into the daily liturgical cycle, see Burmester, *The Egyptian Church*, 98–99.

[92] This prayer is the introductory prayer for most Coptic liturgical services and today falls within the prothesis rite as well. As such, it is discussed later in chapter 5, section 5.

11. Final prayer
12. Our Father[93]

However, in the context of the liturgy, the third and sixth hours are usually blended together into one continuous unit according to the following scheme:

1. third hour psalms
2. sixth hour psalms
3. third hour Gospel
4. third hour Troparia
5. Trisagion
6. Our Father
7. The Prayer "Hail to you"
8. sixth hour Gospel
9. sixth hour Troparia
10. Introduction to the creed "We exalt you"
11. The creed
12. *Kyrie eleison* 41 times
13. The prayer "Holy, Holy, Holy"
14. Our Father

As can be seen, the two hours are blended together to produce one continuous unit, which departs quite noticeably from the structure of the hours in the Horologion itself. This composite structure also drops key elements such as the collect and the concluding prayer. In actual execution, the psalms are typically distributed among the chanters and congregation, and each person reads their assigned psalm silently.[94] This is surely a departure from the original intent of praying the psalms in common, a departure meant to shorten the duration of the prayers.

4. ISSUES IN CURRENT PRACTICE

Although it has been shown that the practice of praying the little hours before the prothesis itself is a long-standing tradition, there remain certain issues with the manner of praying the hours, their actual unfolding in the rite and the impact this has on other elements of preparatory rites of the Coptic liturgy. First, as already explained, the exact hours to be prayed are dictated by specific regulations tied to the liturgical cycles of fasting and non-fasting. This has certainly developed in connection with the traditional time of celebrating the

93 A synopsis of the structure of the hours can be found also in Burmester, *The Egyptian Church*, 101–103, and also in Taft, *The Liturgy of the Hours*, 252–253.

94 The same practice was observed by Robert Taft during a stay at the Monastery of Saint Macarius in the Scetis desert. See Taft, *The Liturgy of the Hours*, 257–258.

liturgy, which was later in the day during fasts and particularly Lent, and earlier on Sundays and non-fasting days. However, while current practice has shifted and varied in different places and in response to pastoral needs, the regulations regarding which hours to pray have not. Thus, in many parishes today a liturgy during Lent may be celebrated at 9 a.m. or even earlier, while still praying all the hours from third to compline! Thus, the various hours of the horologion have lost their connection to any real time that they are meant to sanctify. Similarly, under the current practice the hours also lose their connection to the time in which particular saving events have occurred, such as the descent of the Holy Spirit at the third hour, or the Lord's crucifixion at the sixth hour.

Another issue arises from a quick look at the two outlines presented above, in which the structure of the little hours in the Horologion is compared to the manner in which more than one hour are combined in the context of the liturgy. One is immediately struck, not so much by the practice of merging two offices together, but by the addition of prayers that are not part of either office, at least according to the received text of the Horologion. The prayers in question are the Trisagion, Our Father, and "Hail to you" [5, 6, 7], forming a sort of break separating the third hour troparia from the sixth hour Gospel passage and the prayer "We exalt you", and the creed [10, 11], which follow immediately after the sixth hour troparia. In the traditional text of the Horologion, these prayers appear only as part of the first hour (prime), and the twelfth hour (compline).[95] It is true that many manuscripts attest to the Trisagion and Our Father in the little hours between the third and fourth troparia. These manuscripts include *Coptic Museum Lit. 361* (AD 1234),[96] *Sinai Ar. 184* (13th c.), *Sinai Ar.*

95 Burmester, *The Egyptian Church*, 101, 104. The creed unit [Hail thee, we magnify thee, and the creed] are also found in the third nocturn of the Midnight Prayer. See ibid., 106–107.

96 O.H.E. Burmester, *The Horologion of the Egyptian Church: Coptic and Arabic Text from a Mediaeval Manuscript*, SOC Aegyptiaca (Cairo: Edizioni del Centro Francescano di Studi Orientali Cristiani, 1973), 43 (Coptic), 59 (Coptic), 73 (Coptic), 164 (English), 175 (English), 185 (English). Burmester proposed a dating of AD 1033–1034 for this manuscript. However, Maged (Basilios) Hanna in his dissertation on the Coptic horologion disagrees with the dating of this manuscript by Burmester, proposing instead a date of AD 1234. He based this opinion on paleographical analysis of the handwriting in the manuscript's colophon (fol. 170r), as well as generally that an eleventh-century dating for an Arabic translation of the Book of the Hours would be quite early. Cf. Maged Soubhy Rezk Hanna, "Το Ωρολόγιον της Κοπτικής Ορθόδοξης Εκκλησίας κατά τον Codex Parisinus 107 Arabe" [The horologion of the Coptic Orthodox Church according to the codex *Parisinius 107 Arabe*] (doctoral dissertation, National and Kapodistrian University of Athens, 2005), 20.

389 (13th c.), *BAV Vatican Copt. 40* (AD 1334),[97] and *BAV Barberini Or. 17* (AD 1396), to name a few.[98] It is never the case however that the Trisagion, Our Father, not to mention "Hail to you", would come after all six troparia, nor is it ever seen that the creed and its introductory prayer [10, 11] would appear in any of the little hours.

However, the most serious issue with the manner of praying the little hours today is that some of its elements actually overlap with the prothesis rite. Today, after the reading of the six troparia of the sixth hour (or whatever hour is prayed last), the priest begins to prepare for the prothesis by first washing his hands. This hand washing is a duplication of the more ancient hand washing in the pre-anaphora.[99] Simultaneously, the deacons or altar servants begin to prepare for the prothesis by carrying the wine and water in the sanctuary, while another servant stands at the entrance of the sanctuary carrying the basket of oblation bread. All this is done while the chanters and congregation are reciting the introduction to the creed and the creed. Since these prayers are not found as part of the third or sixth hours, and since they are recited while the prothesis rite is already underway, it may even seem that the prothesis rite itself begins with the recitation of the creed. What takes place then is an overlap of the end of the hours with the beginning of the prothesis rite, rather than their preservation as distinct liturgical units. Another possibility that may explain the addition of the creed in the first place is an attempt to harmonize this beginning stage of the prothesis with an analogous part in the pre-anaphora. There too, the priest washes his hands while the congregation recites the creed. Perhaps then with the doubling of some of these elements of the *accessus ad altare* such as the hand washing, the creed was added as well to level things out, a phenomenon observed frequently in liturgical evolution and termed *Angleichung* or harmonization.[100]

97 This manuscript was used by Raphael al-Ṭūḫī in publishing his editon of the Coptic *ağbiyya* in Rome 1750. See Raphael al-Ṭūḫī, ⲟⲩϫⲱⲙ ⲛ̀ⲧⲉ ⲛⲓⲉⲩⲭⲏ ⲙ̀ⲡⲓⲉϩⲟⲟⲩ ⲛⲉⲙ ⲡⲓⲉϫⲱⲣϩ ⲛ̀ⲍ̅ [The book of the seven prayers of the day and night] (Rome, 1750).

98 Hans Quecke, "Ein koptisch-arabisches horologion in der Bibliothek des Katharinenklosters auf dem Sinai (Cod. Sin. ar. 389)," *Le Muséon* 78 (1965): 99–117, here 112n50.

99 See Chapter 4, Section 2.

100 Described briefly, this is an observed phenomenon with many examples, where different liturgical services, or elements of such services, gradually become harmonized over time so that their celebration becomes more or less analogous and thus easier to perform. For example, ritual actions belonging to a frequently celebrated anaphora are generalized to all anaphoras. In this case, elements belonging to the pre-anaphora, the original *accessus ad altare*, are acquired as well by the preparatory rites before the prothesis. For examples of this phenomenon in

In fact, prayers from the horologion continue well into the prothesis. Today, the selection of the offering itself is accompanied by the chanting of *kyrie eleison* 41 times. This too is a horologion unit and has no business in the prothesis but is in fact found in all the little hours immediately following the troparia. Since this is not the place to discuss the chant accompanying the selection, suffice it to say here that none of the medieval sources or even the Euchologion of 1902 mention the chanting of *kyrie eleison* during the selection of the lamb.[101] Finally, after the conclusion of the *kyrie eleison*, whether the selection of the offering is finished or not, the congregation continues with "Holy, Holy, Holy" and Our Father [13, 14 in the outline above]. Therefore, given the silence of all the sources concerning this, and since at least in other hours of the Horologion (prime and compline) the creed, *kyrie eleison*, "Holy, Holy, Holy" and Our Father are all bound together as a single unit, it is certainly the case here that the chanting of *kyrie eleison* in particular cannot be the pristine chant accompanying the selection. Rather, it is a rogue element from the previous liturgical unit—the daily hours—that made its way into the rite of the prothesis.

It is therefore not the praying of the hours per se that is in any way problematic or untraditional as has been portrayed, but the exact *manner* in which they are prayed. This manner as it has developed into the modern era causes unnecessary confusion and overlapping of two ancient and highly traditional elements of Christian worship, the Liturgy of the Hours, and the selection of the oblation, the offering of the Church.

the Byzantine Rite, see Taft, "Anton Baumstark's Comparative Liturgy Revisited," 211–212.

101 Ṣalīb, ⲡⲓϫⲱⲙ ⲛ̀ⲧⲉ ⲡⲓⲉⲩⲭⲟⲗⲟⲅⲓⲟⲛ, 203.

PART 2

THE PROTHESIS RITE

INTRODUCTION

During the course of the preceding chapters, comprising the first part of this study, two particular goals were accomplished. First, the historical origins of the preparation and transfer of the eucharistic gifts in Alexandrian and Egyptian sources were explored. This process involved analyzing textual evidence spanning approximately ten centuries (ca. 4th–14th c.), as well as archaeological and comparative liturgical evidence. The result of this analysis was to definitively establish the details of the most impacting shift in the *deroulément* of the Coptic liturgy, in which the deposition of the gifts on the altar moved from its pristine pre-anaphoral location to the very beginning of the liturgy. The attempt to elucidate this process through a close reading of the evidence has allowed for distinguishing between a pre-anaphoral transfer (the old ordo) and the current rite (the new ordo). Moreover, an intermediate stage was seen in the fourteenth-century Ibn Sabbāʿ, in which the gifts were selected in the prothesis pastophorion before being brought in procession to the altar for the remainder of the prothesis rite.

Second, following this fascinating and necessary foundation, the stage was set to treat the preparatory rites of the Coptic liturgy, namely, the vesting of the clergy, the preparation of the altar, as well as the prayers of the hours that are prayed between matins and the liturgy. All of this has brought the discourse now to the threshold of the new ordo, the focus of the remainder of this study. For this remainder, the entire attention is directed at analyzing the liturgical units that comprise the new ordo, tracing their historical development from their earliest witnesses until the current rite as it stands today.

To put it more precisely, this new ordo is the result of the juxtaposition of the two elements of the preparation and transfer of gifts, which were far separated from one another by the Liturgy of the Word according to the old ordo. With this in mind, the first chapter in this analysis of the new ordo (Chapter 4) focuses on liturgical units that roughly equate to the preparation of the gifts and their journey to the altar. This includes the hand washing, the selection of the eucharistic bread, the commemorations pronounced by the celebrant over the chosen oblation, and the procession of the oblation around the altar. In a subsequent chapter (Chapter 5), the analysis continues with those elements of the rite conducted after the deposition of the gifts. This includes the blessing of the chosen offering, the pouring of the wine and water in the chalice, and the *Prayer of Thanksgiving*. A final chapter (Chapter 6) explores the central prayer of the entire rite, the *Prothesis Prayer*, as well as the absolution prayers that conclude the rite.

Throughout the investigation of the old ordo, evidence from liturgical manuscripts and Euchologia was hardly utilized, despite the large number of these manuscripts. This was due to the fact explained more than once, that the earliest surviving liturgical manuscripts witnessing to the Coptic or Northern Egyptian liturgy date from the thirteenth century and later, when the old ordo was already a matter of history. Fortunately, during the analysis of the new ordo and the development of the current rite, evidence from the large number of Copto-Arabic Euchologia scattered throughout the world's libraries and museums will play a more pronounced role in the overall arsenal of evidence. This is in addition to the already utilized classical sources of Ibn Kabar, Ibn Sabbā', Gabriel V, and other supportive textual and comparative evidence as the case may be.

Finally, from a theological standpoint, one can confidently say that the analysis of the current rite that follows is the key to understanding the theological significance and value of the Coptic prothesis, or the presentation of the lamb, as it is commonly called in the Coptic community. It is true that the foundational historical origins explored earlier provide a clear understanding of how the Coptic liturgy unfolded before accidents of history so to speak altered its course, which can in turn contribute to a more lucid understanding of its theology. However, despite the temptation to focus solely on the pristine old ordo–or any ordo considered ancient–it is a fact that rites, in addition to being conservative repositories of tradition, are also living expressions of piety. With this acknowledgement of the value of the contemporary ritual of any era to an understanding of its theology, the journey proceeds through the new ordo of the Coptic prothesis as it is celebrated and experienced today in the Coptic Church.

CHAPTER 4

THE SELECTION OF THE OFFERING AND THE PROCESSION OF THE LAMB

After the celebrant has prepared the altar and prayed the preparation prayers–during which, the appropriate hours of the Horologion have been prayed–the Euchologion of ʿAbd al-Masīḥ Ṣalīb continues with the prothesis rite as follows. The priest kisses the altar and turns to the west in order to begin the selection of the eucharistic bread offering, which is presented to him.[1] To the right of the celebrant stands an altar servant–or deacon if available–carrying a vessel of wine in his right hand on a veil and a lighted candle in the left.[2]

Before beginning the process of selecting the bread, the celebrant blesses the entire basket in the name of the Trinity: "In the name of the Father, and the Son, and the Holy Spirit, one God, amen. Blessed be the Father...Blessed be his only-begotten Son...Blessed be the Holy Spirit."[3] He then proceeds to examine each loaf, selecting the best one considering the quality of its baking, the presence of any cracks, and the clarity of its seal.[4] After selecting the best loaf, he wipes it with one of the altar cloths and places it on the right side of the altar.[5]

1 Although not described explicitly by ʿAbd al-Masīḥ Ṣalīb, while standing in this location, the priest faces an altar servant–or an assisting priest if available–holding a basket containing the oblation bread. The loaves are always presented in an odd number, commonly five, seven, or nine. They are to be arranged in the form of a cross in the circular basket. See Burmester, *The Egyptian Church*, 51.

2 Today, to the left of the celebrant stands another servant holding a vessel of water in his right hand and a lighted candle in his left in the same manner. This is the water that will be soon mixed with the wine in the chalice.

3 The same blessing was discussed earlier in chapter 3, section 1 in the course of the vesting prayers.

4 When the priest begins the selection, he crosses his arms the one over the other, picking up a loaf in each hand in this manner. For a detailed description of how the selection takes place, see Burmester, *The Egyptian Church*, 51.

5 Ṣalīb seems to have committed a mistake here, since he calls the right side of the altar the northern side, while in reality it would be the southern side of the altar. Considering actual practice today, this point is moot, since priests tend to hold the loaf in their hands standing at the center of the altar as usual.

Afterwards, he examines the wine by smelling it.[6] He is then to proceed to wash his hands, while reciting selections from the psalms (Pss 50:9–10, 25:6–7, or Ps 50:11–12).[7]

The instructions then specify that the priest is to dry his hands in a white towel only a little. This is because he is now to take the bread in his left hand and wipe it with his slightly wet hands both above and below. During this, he repeats the last section of the *Prayer After the Preparation of the Altar* discussed previously, "Grant, O Lord, that our sacrifice may be acceptable before you, for my own sins and for the ignorances of your people, for it is purified as the gift of your Holy Spirit, in Christ Jesus our Lord."[8] A footnote here points out that the current custom adds the three prayers for the peace of the Church, the hierarchs, and the assemblies recited silently as well over the bread.[9] Afterwards, the celebrant begins the silent commemorations, in which he prays for anyone in need, the sick, the travelers, the departed, or those who have provided the eucharistic gifts for this liturgy.[10] The commemorations are concluded with a general prayer on his own behalf, his physical relatives, and spiritual fathers.

Following the commemorations, the celebrant is to wrap the eucharistic bread in preparation for the procession of the lamb. He lifts the wrapped loaf above his head, while the deacon lifts the vessel of wine above his head as well behind the priest, followed by other altar servants carrying lighted candles. While circling around the altar once in procession, the celebrant recites the following prayer:[11]

> *The Priest*: Glory and honor, honor and glory to the all-holy Trinity, the Father, the Son, and the Holy Spirit. Peace and building up for the one and only, holy, catholic, and apostolic Church of God, amen. Remember O Lord those who have offered to you these gifts, those on whose behalf they have been offered, and those through whom they have been offered. Give them all the recompense from the heavens.

6 Burmester adds that after selecting the eucharistic loaf, the celebrant is to dip his thumb in the wine and make the sign of the cross with his wet thumb on both the chosen loaf, and all the rest. See Burmester, *The Egyptian Church*, 51–52.

7 Although the *editio typica* of Ṣalīb is considered the official edition of the Euchologion in the Coptic Orthodox Church by a Synodal decision of 1997, current practice differs on this point, where the priest washes his hands immediately after the preparation of the altar, and before the selection of the offering. Cf. Burmester, *The Egyptian Church*, 51.

8 Ṣalīb, ⲡⲓϫⲱⲙ ⲛ̀ⲧⲉ ⲡⲓⲉⲩⲭⲟⲗⲟⲅⲓⲟⲛ, 202–203.

9 Ibid., 206.

10 Ṣalīb provides specific formulas in Coptic and Arabic for each of these cases, in imitation of some late Euchologion manuscripts.

11 In actual practice, the celebrant pauses by the entrance to the sanctuary facing west while reciting this prayer.

The Deacon: Pray for these holy precious gifts, our sacrifices, and for the offerers.

The Priest continues: Remember O Lord everyone who has asked us to remember them in our entreaties and prayers. May the Lord remember them in his heavenly kingdom.[12]

The procession continues while the congregation chants the appropriate psalm selection for the procession, as seen in chapter 2. Currently, three such selections are available. On Saturdays, Sundays, feasts, and any non-fasting day, they chant "Alleluia. This is the day the Lord has made," (Ps 117:24–26). On Wednesdays, Fridays, and fasting days except weekdays of Lent, they chant, "Alleluia. The thought of man confesses you," (Ps 75:11). On the weekdays of Lent, they chant, "Alleluia. I enter into the sanctuary of God." (Ps 42:4; 131:1). At the conclusion of the procession, the celebrant returns to his position before the altar, escorted closely by the servants carrying the wine and the water. What follows is the remainder of the prothesis rite with its blessing of the offerings and their deposition in the chalice and paten.

This is the basic description of the rite as it is practiced today, relying mostly on the details found in the Euchologion of 1902, while supplying any missing information from Burmester's work, as well as personal observation, a reminder that one cannot fully equate actual practice even with authoritative liurgical books.

Returning once more to the earlier analysis of the old ordo and the new ordo, it can be said that the liturgical units described here, and which occupy our attention for this chapter, correspond roughly to the preparation of the gifts that preceded the liturgy in the old ordo. This rough correspondence is meant only in a general sense, and certainly not in the details, which are known from the early sources only vaguely and often by conjecture. Before the ritual evolution of the prothesis rite to its present form, the preparation of the gifts before the liturgy likely consisted in receiving the gifts in the prothesis pastophorion, the selection of the best bread and wine, and their placement in the paten and chalice respectively. Once this practical preparation had acquired a more ritualized clerical character, it came to be accompanied by the blessing of the oblations and the *Prothesis Prayer*, discussed in more detail in chapter 6. It is only with this in mind that one can speak of this chapter as corresponding roughly to the preparation of the gifts of the old ordo.

12 Ṣalīb, ⲡⲓϫⲱⲙ ⲛ̀ⲧⲉ ⲡⲓⲉⲩⲭⲟⲗⲟⲅⲓⲟⲛ, 213–215. In current practice, this final entreaty after the deacon's command is never said aloud.

What follows is a detailed analysis of this current rite of the prothesis witnessed since the earliest thirteenth-century Euchologia and other sources of the Northern Egyptian liturgy.

1. THE SELECTION OF THE OFFERING

Despite the relative complexity of the selection ritual in terms of the disposition of the priest and servants, and the large number of blessings and gestures made over the oblations, the basic purpose of this unit remains quite simple. Essentially, the priest is to select the most appropriate eucharistic loaf from a certain number presented to him, and to verify that the wine is suitable. It is therefore quite a practical matter, despite the evolved ceremonial surrounding it in the current rite.

Unfortunately, many Euchologion manuscripts lack all rubrics to describe this ritual selection. Manuscripts silent on this issue are many and span the chronological and geographical spectrum, although the tendency appears more in older ones that pre-date the fifteenth century. Examples include the thirteenth-century manuscripts *BAV Vatican Copt. 17* (AD 1288) from the Eastern Desert, the two oldest Scetis Euchologia *British Library Or. 1239* and *Bodleian Hunt. 360, Rylands Copt. 426*,[13] and the thirteenth/fourteenth-century *Bodleian Hunt. 572* and *Bodleian Ind. Inst. Copt. 4*. Examples of this silence continue into the fourteenth century with *Bodleian Marsh 5, Paris BnF Copt. 82* (AD 1307), *BAV Borgia Copt. 7* (AD 1379) and the *Kacmarcik Codex*, from the Eastern Desert, and *BAV Vatican Copt. 24* and *BAV Vatican Copt. 25*, both from Scetis.[14] Finally, from the fifteenth century, there are two further examples from the Coptic community in Cyprus, *Paris BnF Copt. 24* and *Paris BnF Copt. 31*. All of these examples, antedating and/or contemporaneous with the *Ritual Order* of Gabriel V, share the common feature of including only the euchological discursive prayers of the priest, and omitting any short formulas, rubrics, and all diaconal and congregational responses. Typical as this may be for a true classical Euchologion, this means that these manuscripts do not provide any information between the prayers of the preparation of the altar until the *Prayer of Thanksgiving* much later in the prothesis rite.

Nor is this tendency restricted only to those manuscripts older than the *Ritual Order*. Examples continue post-fifteenth century, even after

[13] Rodwell, *The Liturgies of S. Basil, S. Gregory, and S. Cyril*, 25–26.

[14] Though most of the prothesis in this manuscript falls within the seventeenth-century work of a second hand, the lack of rubrics here is likely caused by the later scribe's fidelity to the text of the original section he was seeking to replace.

the composition and establishment of the *Ritual Order* as a standard diataxis for the liturgy of the Coptic Rite. In fact, some of the latest manuscripts one can identify that lack all rubrics for the selection are *St. Macarius Lit. 155* (AD 1894) containing the Greek recension of the Coptic liturgy,[15] and *Coptic Museum Lit. 462* (19th c.), both of which date to only a few years prior to the Euchologion of 1902. Such Euchologia with no rubrics abound in the manuscript corpus and likely represent simple copies made economically and with everyday use in mind rather than indicating the complexity of actual ritual practice. This leads one to conclude without a doubt that the silence of many early manuscripts on this issue cannot be taken as evidence for a simpler rite of selection. The reasons for omission must be attributed to the fact that priests were generally expected to know such manual acts without the need to refer to written instructions during the service, which at any rate would have been cumbersome when everyone involved in the rite likely had their hands too busy to hold a codex.

1.1. The Lamp of Darkness *of Ibn Kabar (14th c.)*

But before one examines the evolution of the rubrics as they appear in the manuscripts post-*Ritual Order*, one must not forget the testimony of Ibn Kabar, which stands as an earlier witness to the rite before the reforms of Pope Gabriel V. About the selection of the offering, Ibn Kabar has the following to say:

[1] ويحضر الحمل [2] ويغسل القس يديه بماءٍ ويمسح القربان بعد تصفُحِهِ واختيار ما يصلح منه كما قلنا انفاً. [3] ويخرج مهما فضل منه عما قد حُمِل من الهيكل خارجا. [4] يمسح كل قربانة من وجهها وظهرها.[16]

[1] Then he brings the lamb. [2] And the priest washes his hands with water, and he wipes the oblation after inspecting it and choosing what is appropriate as we have said earlier. [3] And he removes outside the sanctuary whatever is left of [the bread] that was brought [4] And he wipes every bread on its front and back.

Clearly, Ibn Kabar's sequence of events is not in the best or most logical order. One glaring inconsistency is that the priest is said to bless all the oblation breads *after* they have been removed outside. Not only is this clearly impossible, it is simply the current practice reversed, in which all the oblations are indeed blessed after choosing the best one, but before their removal away from the sanctuary area.

[15] Dous, "Η Αλεξανδρινή Θεία Λειτουργία," 75–76.

[16] *Paris BnF Ar. 203* (AD 1363–1369), fol. 203r. Cf. Villecourt, "Les observances," 249.

While the place of the hand washing is discussed more closely below, one can at least say that the general strokes of the rite of selection, which include the bringing of a number of oblations from which the priest is to choose an appropriate one, can be seen in the fourteenth-century *Lamp of Darkness* at the earliest.

1.2. The Selection in The Ritual Order *and Similar Manuscripts*

Nonetheless, quite a number of manuscripts do include rubrics on this point, allowing a reconstruction of its development. The oldest manuscript with such instructions is *BAV Vatican Copt. 18* (AD 1531) from Cairo, which gives the following instructions for the selection.

[1] ويُقَبّل الكاهن المذبح ويلتفت الى الغرب ليختار الحمل الذي هو خبز التقدمة. [2] ويستبرئ ذلك جيدا ليكون حملاً حولياً لا عيب فيه. [3] ويأخذ الحمل بعد استبراه جيدا يمسح ظهره بستر نظيف ويقبله ويضعه على يمين المذبح في لفافة حرير. [4] ويستبرئ حال الخمر جيدا بالشم او يدع احد المفطرين يذوق منه في كفه. [5] فإن الخمر إذا مال صار خلاً والقربان إذا لم يجد غيره عن ضرورة ما يخرج عن حال الخبز.[17]

[1] And the priest kisses the altar and turns to the west to choose the lamb, which is the bread of offering. [2] And he inspects this well, so that it may be [as the] one-year-old lamb without blemish. [3] And he takes the lamb after inspecting it well, and wipes its back with a clean veil, kisses it, and places it on the right side of the altar in a silk veil. [4] Then he inspects the condition of the wine thoroughly by smelling or lets one of those not fasting taste from it in his palm. [5] For the wine, if it changes, becomes vinegar, while the oblation bread does not change from the nature of bread if out of necessity he does not find other than it.

These are essentially the same rubrics found in the *Ritual Order* quite verbatim.[18] The influence of the *Ritual Order* on subsequent manuscripts that include rubrics is to be expected of such an official diataxis of the Coptic liturgy. In fact, many later manuscripts share this noticeable feature of copying the instructions of the *Ritual Order* literally. These include *BAV Vatican Copt. 99* (AD 1718–1726), *Rylands Copt. 427* (AD 1764), *Coptic Patriarchate Lit. 331* (AD 1678), *Coptic Museum Lit. 80* (AD 1796), *British Library Or. 430* (AD 1832), *Coptic Museum Lit. 412* (AD 1867), and *Coptic Museum Lit. 16* (AD 1928–1942).

17 *BAV Vatican Copt. 18* (AD 1531), fol. 117v–118r.

18 *Paris BnF Ar. 98* (17th c.), fol. 47v–48r. Cf. 'Abdallah, *L'ordinamento*, 174 (Arabic), 364 (Italian).

Curiously, only two manuscripts examined for this section deviated in minor ways from the rubrics in the *Ritual Order*. In *Paris BnF Copt. 30* (AD 1642) and *Coptic Patriarchate Lit. 331* (AD 1678) from Cairo, the wine is inspected *after* the post-selection hand washing. The second manuscript is *Coptic Museum Lit. 265* (18th c.), where the rubrics are provided both in Coptic and Arabic—a certain rarity in these mansucripts—and are clearly a rephrasing of the rubrics of the *Ritual Order*, albeit with the same overall instructions.

Thus, the earliest steps for choosing the appropriate offering as seen in the *Ritual Order* of Gabriel V, as well as subsequent manuscripts that copied its text, can be summarized as follows:

1. After the preparation of the altar, the priest turns to the west, where the plate containing the offerings is presented to him.
2. The priest chooses the appropriate loaf from those presented. He wipes it clean with a veil, kisses it, and places it in a veil on the right side of the altar.
3. Then he turns again to inspect the wine by smelling it, or allowing a non-fasting person to taste it.[19]

1.3. The Selection According to Mīḫā'īl of Samannūd

As expected, the current rite is much more elaborate in its minor formulas and gestures compared to the bare bones ritual of Gabriel V. A middle stage can be found in two manuscripts of the eighteenth and nineteenth centuries, which attribute the rite of choosing the offering to a certain Mīḫā'īl of Samannūd. A bishop of Samannūd by the same name is attested in the fourteenth century and was one of the bishops that participated in the consecration of the chrism in AD 1374 with Pope Gabriel IV (AD 1370–1378).[20] Unfortunately, it cannot be ascertained that the Bishop Mīḫā'īl mentioned in the following manuscripts is the same fourteenth-century hierarch, especially that it is common for bishops to take the names of their predecessors in the same diocese. Thus, at the least, one may presume that the bishop associated here with the prothesis must have lived some time between

19 It is noteworthy that the latter method is never employed today. Not only would this imply involving a non-fasting member of the congregation in the performance of the rite, an absolute oddity, but it also implies offering to God something that was already in some measure received and consumed by a human being.

20 Youhanna Nessim Youssef and Ugo Zanetti, *La consécration du Myron par Gabriel IV 86e Patriarche d'Alexandrie en 1374 A.D.*, JThF 20 (Münster: Aschendorff, 2014), 79 (French), 329 (Arabic). See also an index of all the appearances of this bishop's name in this source in ibid., 192. For more information on the fourteenth-century Bishop Mīḫā'īl and the diocese of Samannūd, see Timm, *Das christlich-koptische Ägypten in arabischer Zeit*, 5:2254–2262.

the time of Gabriel V (15th c.) and the earliest witness to this person in the mid-eighteenth century.

The manuscript *British Library Add. 17725* (AD 1811) provides the following rubric in fol. 7v:

[1] ترتيب الاب الاسقف انبا ميخاييل اسقف سمنود. [2] يحضر اليه الحمل ويستبريه ويمسكه بيده و يقول

[3] ⲟⲩϩⲓⲣⲏⲛⲏ ⲛⲉⲙ ⲟⲩⲕⲱⲧ ⲛⲉⲙ ⲟⲩⲧⲁϫⲣⲟ ⲛ̀ⲧⲉ ϯⲁⲅⲓⲁ ⲛ̀ⲉⲕⲕⲗⲏⲥⲓⲁ ⲛ̀ⲧⲉ ⲫϯ ⲁⲙⲏⲛ.[21]

[1] The order of the father the bishop Abba Mīḫā'īl the bishop of Samannūd. [2] The lamb is brought to him [the priest], and he inspects it and holds it in his hands and says: [3] Peace and building up and strengthening of the holy Church of God, amen.

The same short *peace and building up* formula appears in an earlier manuscript, *Coptic Museum Lit. 344* (AD 1752), albeit after the hand washing. In both of these manuscripts, there is an additional formula not found in any of the earlier sources. The current practice—often unwritten—is for the priest to recite silently the prayer "Glory and honor," which he is later to proclaim again loudly during the procession. Clearly, such duplication cannot be original, and is likely the result of harmonizing this short prayer attested in the manuscripts with the similarly worded "Glory and honor," which contains the same phrase, "Peace and building up...etc." Regarding which of the two instances of saying the *Glory and Honor* prayer is original, it will be discussed shortly below.

In the Ethiopian liturgy, the priest blesses the bread while saying, "*Eulogios Kyrios Iēsous Christos*, Son of the living God, *hagiasma tōn pneumatōn hagios* in truth, amen."[22] Interestingly, this is done not at the entrance to the sanctuary as in Coptic usage, but rather at the north side of the altar, perhaps echoing the old ordo, in which the selection took place in the northeastern pastophorion. This blessing, certainly at variance with the Coptic one, is found in all manuscripts studied by Samuel A.B. Mercer.[23] However, the exception is the *Ordo Communis* of Täsfa Ṣəyon, published in Rome in 1548, which contains this prayer instead, "May the strength and blessing and light and sanctification of the Holy Trinity be on the church of the city N."[24] This prayer bears a strong similarity in idea to the prayer for the building up and peace of the Church of God. Given the late

21 *British Library Add. 17725* (AD 1811), fol. 7v–8r.

22 *LEW*, 199.

23 Mercer, *The Ethiopic Liturgy*, 160.

24 Ibid. For more information on the Ethiopian monk Täsfa Ṣəyon, also known as Peter the Ethiopian, see Alessandro Bausi and Gianfranco Fiaccadori, "Täsfa Ṣəyon," *EAE*, 5:525–528.

publication of Täsfa Ṣəyon's edition, it is difficult to date with precision when this formula began to be used either in the Ethiopian or the Coptic Rites. However, one can at least see the rough contours of the slow addition of prayers, gestures, and formulas that must have led to the complexity of the selection rite as it is practiced today.

1.4. The Selection in the Patriarchal Liturgy

An interesting variation on this common rite can be found in the patriarchal liturgy described in the manuscript *Coptic Patriarchate Lit. 74* (AD 1444).[25] The interesting setting of this liturgy is that the patriarch does not vest or participate in the prothesis, but rather does so at the conclusion of the prothesis and immediately before the Liturgy of the Word. That bishops generally do not serve as the ministers of the prothesis is an attested tradition also in the Byzantine Rite, a topic discussed in chapter 6, though this particular source seems to imply that only the patriarch remained unvested during the prothesis. This traditional arrangement—certainly unknown today in the current rite, in which the bishop serves from the very beginning—results in the following rite.

[1] ويتقدم كبير الكهنة او الارشي ويسأل البطريرك فيمن يكسي المذبح [2] فيأمر له اما بأحد الاساقفة او احد القسوس. [3] ويصعد الكاهن للمذبح ويتلوا اواشي الاستعداد. [4] ويقدموا القربان للبطريرك ليختار خبز التقدمة وكذلك وعاء الابركة ايضاً. [5] ثم يقدم ذلك الامنوت الى الكاهن الشريك.[26]

[1] And the senior priest or the arch[deacon][27] comes and asks the patriarch who is to cover the altar. [2] And he commands for it one of the bishops or priests. [3] The priest ascends to the altar and recites the prayers of the preparation [4] and they present the oblation to the patriarch to choose the bread of offering, and the vessel of wine.[28] [5] Then the sacristan[29] gives this to the assistant priest.[30]

25 Mikhail, "The Liturgy Coram Patriarcha Revisited," 282–288.

26 *Coptic Patriarchate Lit. 74* (AD 1444), fol. 74v. Cf. Samuel, *Tartīb al-bīʿa*, 1:17; Mikhail, "The Liturgy Coram Patriarcha Revisited," 307 (Arabic), 308 (English).

27 The manuscript reads: "الارشي", a contraction of "ارشيدياكون" = Gr ἀρχιδιάκονος. See Graf, *Verzeichnis*, 6.

28 The manuscript reads: "الابركة", = Gr ἀπαρχή, the first fruits, referring to the eucharistic wine. See Graf, *Verzeichnis*, 1.

29 The manuscript reads: "الامنوت" = Bohairic ⲉⲙⲛⲟⲩⲧ, a church servant or sacristan, a term employed frequently in medieval Copto-Arabic writings, though it has fallen out of use in more recent times. See Graf, *Verzeichnis*, 13.

30 Coptic usage does not observe the practice of "concelebration" in the strict sense. In any given liturgy, a single clergyman—be it a presbyter or a hierarch if present—is

The description indicates that, although the patriarch was present in the liturgy from the beginning, he did not vest or serve the rite of the prothesis fully, delegating instead other lower clergy to do so until the appropriate time for his vesting. One sees this in the preparation of the altar, a rite of *accessus ad altare*, and thus logically more appropriate for one of the clergy who was in fact vested and ready for such an entry into the sanctuary. However, it is clear that the selection of the offering was deemed on some level too important to be done by someone else in the presence of the patriarch. This resulted in the peculiar situation in which the gifts were brought to the patriarch at his throne outside the sanctuary and then transferred to the assisting priest inside the sanctuary after the selection. The same arrangement is indicated in another manuscript describing the patriarchal liturgy, *Baramūs 6/278* (AD 1514),[31] while the description in Ibn Kabar's the *Lamp of Darkness* according to *Uppsala O. Vet. 12* (AD 1546) of the pariarch's liturgy is not explicit on the matter.[32]

It is interesting that Pope Gabriel V makes no mention of this rite in his *Ritual Order*, written only a few years prior. One can only surmise that perhaps the *Ritual Order* was meant as a general diataxis for presbyteral liturgies, and thus eschewed the complexities of explaining the rites in the presence of a patriarch. The pomp and ceremony that comes across in this description are clear, especially the multiplicity of offices involved, expected of a patriarchal liturgy. Besides simply providing an alternative rite in the presence of the patriarch, it is also quite telling what liturgical units were considered of the highest ritual significance, and therefore reserved for the patriarch, despite the fact that he stood outside the sanctuary unvested.

the only true celebrant. As such, key liturgical acts and prayers are his sole privilege, such as the prothesis rite, the institution narrative, the epiclesis, and finally the pre-communion rites. During communion, it is he who administers the body, while any assisting priests–or deacons if present–may administer the blood. See Youssef and Zanetti, *La consécration du Myron*, 32. There is evidence however that a different form of concelebration closer to Byzantine practice may have existed in the Middle Ages. Cf. René-Georges Coquin, "Vestiges de concélébration ches les Melkites, les Coptes et les Éthiopiens," *Le Muséon* 80 (1967): 37–46. On the concelebration in the Byzantine Rite today, see Robert F. Taft, "Eucharistic Concelebration in Greek Orthodoxy Yesterday and Today," in Hawkes-Teeples, et al., *Studies on the Liturgies of the Christian East*, 259–277. Concelebration in the Ethiopian tradition was treated in the same volume: Emmanuel Fritsch, "Concelebration of the Eucharistic Liturgy in the Ethiopian Tradition," in Hawkes-Teeples, et al., *Studies on the Liturgies of the Christian East*, 11–29.

31 Samuel, *Tartīb al-bīʿa*, 1:21; Mikhail, "The Liturgy Coram Patriarcha Revisited," 309 (Arabic), 310 (English).

32 *Uppsala O. Vet. 12* (AD 1546), fol. 188v. Cf. Villecourt, "Les observances," 277; Mikhail, "The Liturgy *Coram Patriarcha* Revisited," 310 (Arabic), 311 (English).

That the selection of the offering–an originally practical matter performed by deacons in the early Church–came to be regarded with such reverence, witnesses to the increasing solemnity assigned to the preparation of the gifts in the new ordo. This had the unfortunate consequence of taking roles originally given to deacons in the oldest sources and assigning them to the priest, or even the patriarch or bishop if they are present. This tendency is seen in many subsequent liturgical elements of the rite of the prothesis.

1.5. Additional Acts and Prayers

Compared to the rite as found in the sources, current practice at the selection of the oblation is replete with additional gestures, acts, and formulas, not to mention departing even from the Euchologion of 1902 on more than one occasion. It has been mentioned already that the priest begins selecting the oblation by pronouncing a threefold Trinitarian blessing over the bread and the wine, and that he commences the selection by crossing his arms one over the other before lifting one loaf with each hand. What neither the Euchologion nor Burmester mention, is that the priest also blesses each oblation bread with the vessel of wine before beginning the selection process. Unlike the instructions in the Euchologion that allow for a non-fasting person to taste the wine, today the wine is inspected by having each altar servant smell it and respond in affirmation by saying, "Good and honored," implying that the wine is indeed in acceptable condition.

It is also no longer current practice–despite the instructions of the Euchologion–that the priest places the oblation bread on the altar *before* inspecting the wine. Today, the wine is inspected also while facing west at the entrance of the sanctuary, in the same ritual point as selecting the oblation bread. After the bread has been chosen, the priest blesses each remaining loaf once again with the chosen loaf. He also wets his finger with wine and makes the sign of the cross with it on all remaining loaves, saying the formula, "A sacrifice of glory, a sacrifice of praise, a sacrifice of Abraham, a sacrifice of Isaac, a sacrifice of Jacob, a sacrifice of Melchisedek." With the exception of the latter formula, which makes an appearance in some manuscripts, albeit for a different purpose, none of these practices are encountered in any of the sources.[33] Since these elements are missing even from manuals and medieval diataxeis such as Ibn Kabar and Gabriel V, one is led to conclude that the present state of the selection rite is a

[33] In *Coptic Patriarchate Lit. 331* (AD 1678), fol. 8r, a marginal note in red reads, "And when he turns to the west, he signs once and says [Coptic:] 'Blessed is he who comes.' And says, [Coptic:] 'A sacrifice of glory, a sacrifice of praise, a sacrifice of peace, a sacrifice of forgiveness.'"

product of various disparate customs, completely unknown in the fifteenth century, and passed down by oral tradition alone.

2. THE HAND WASHING

Of all the elements examined in this chapter, the hand washing is certainly the most complex in terms of its origin, significance, and original place in the unfolding of the rite. These aspects of the hand washing are explored below, after presenting the euchological and textual evidence available. As the evidence clearly demonstrates, the uncertainty surrounding the hand washing in the prothesis stems from the fact that it is simply a duplication of the pre-anaphoral hand washing, added so early in the liturgy because of the shift from the old ordo to the new ordo.

2.1. The Hand Washing in the Sources

As shown previously, the fourteenth-century *Precious Jewel* of Ibn Sabbāʿ makes no explicit mention of the hand washing at the prothesis. However, that a hand washing indeed took place can be certainly implied from this passage:

[1] فاذا وجد ما يحتاج اليه من القربان والخمر والبخور والفحم وكل الة القداس اذا وجدها على ما ينبغي جيداً [2] يأخذ القربان ويمسحه كما مُسِح السيد له المجد بالمآء قبل تسليمه لسمعان الكاهن [3]ثم يدوره على يديه كدوران سمعان الكاهن به الهيكل.[34]

[1] When the necessary bread, wine, incense, coal, and all the equipment for the liturgy have been found in good order, [2] he takes the bread, and anoints it as the Lord–to him be glory–was anointed with water before his presentation to Simeon the priest. [3] Then he turns it around in his hands, as Simeon the priest went around the sanctuary with him.

The fact that the so-called wiping or signing of the oblation is likened to the signing of Christ before his presentation to Simeon the elder is proof enough that the priest at this moment must have used water and not simply his dry hands. At any rate, as soon as witnesses to the hand washing are encountered, one immediately finds this washing connected in some way with the wiping of the oblation after its selection. The washing is explicitly mentioned as well in Ibn Kabar's *The Lamp of Darkness* as mentioned previously,[35] though the passage in reality can tolerate two variant meanings regarding the exact time of the washing, a topic that is addressed further below.

34 *Paris BnF Ar. 207* (14th c.), fol. 122v. Cf. Mistrīḥ, *Pretiosa margarita*, 180 (Arabic), 489 (Latin).

35 See above, chapter 4, section 1.1.

A century later, the two acts are clearly connected in the *Ritual Order* of Gabriel V. The psalm verses appearing in the original text in both Arabic and Coptic are both given in the English translation:

[1] ثم يغسل الكاهن يديه الاثنان ثلثة دفوع [2] وهو يقول الدفعة الاولى انضح علي زوفك فاطهر ⲉⲕⲉ̀ⲛⲟⲩϫ ϧⲁϫⲱⲓ ⲙ̀ⲡⲉⲕϣⲉⲛϩⲓⲥⲟⲡⲟⲛ ⲉⲓⲉ̀ⲧⲟⲩⲃⲟ. المرة الاولى. اغسلني به فابيض مثل الثلج. ⲉⲕⲉ̀ⲣⲁϧⲧ ⲉⲓⲉ̀ⲟⲩⲃⲁϣ ⲉϩⲟⲧⲉ ⲟⲩⲭⲓⲱⲛ. [3] ⲉⲕⲉ̀ⲑⲣⲓ ⲥⲱⲧⲉⲙ ⲉ̀ⲟⲩⲑⲉⲗⲏⲗ ⲛⲉⲙ ⲟⲩⲟⲩⲛⲟϥ ⲉⲩⲉ̀ⲑⲉⲗⲏⲗ ⲙ̀ⲙⲱⲟⲩ ⲛ̀ϫⲉ ⲛⲓⲕⲁⲥ ⲉⲧⲑⲉⲃⲓⲏⲟⲩⲧ. المرة الثانية اسمعني سروراً وفرحاً لتبتهج عظامي المتواضعة. [4] المرة الثالثة يقول ϯⲛⲁⲓⲁ ⲧⲟⲧ ⲉ̀ⲃⲟⲗ ϧⲉⲛ ⲛⲓⲉ̅ⲑ̅ⲩ̅. ⲟⲩⲟϩ ⲛ̀ⲧⲁⲕⲱϯ ⲉ̀ⲡⲉⲕⲙⲁⲛ̀ⲉⲣϣⲱⲟⲩϣⲓ ⲡ̅ⲟ̅ⲥ̅ ⲉ̀ⲡϫⲓⲛⲧⲁⲥⲱⲧⲉⲙ ⲉ̀ⲡϧⲣⲱⲟⲩ ⲛ̀ⲧⲉ ⲡⲉⲕⲥⲙⲟⲩ. غسلت بالطهر يداي وطفت مذبح يارب لاسمع صوت تسبحتك. [5] وان كان يحسن تلاوة المزمور لاخره يقوله. [6] ثم ينشف يديه فى ستر ابيض كتان نظيف قليل. [7] ويأخذ خبز التقدمة ويمسحه بيديه فوق واسفل. ويقول ⲙⲏⲓⲥ ⲡ̅ⲟ̅ⲥ̅.[36]

[1] Then the priest washes his hands three times, [2] while he says the first time, [Arabic:] "sprinkle upon me your hyssop and I will become pure" [Coptic:] "sprinkle upon me your hyssop, I will become pure," the first time. [Arabic:] "Wash me with it and I shall be as white as snow." [Coptic:] "Wash me and I will be whiter than snow." [3] [Coptic:] "You shall make me to hear joy and gladness, the humble bones shall rejoice," the second time. [Arabic:] "Cause me to hear joy and gladness, so that my humble bones may rejoice." [4] The third time he says, [Coptic:] "I will wash my hands of the holies, and I will go about your altar, O Lord, to hear the voice of your praise". [Arabic:] "I have washed my hands in purity and have gone around [your] altar, O Lord, to hear the voice of your praise." [5] And if he has mastered the recitation of the psalm to its end, he shall say it. [6] Then he dries his hands in a white linen clean veil only a little. [7] Then he takes the bread of offering and wipes it with his hands above and below, while saying, "Grant O Lord."

It is clear here that the wiping of the oblation, mentioned without further details in other sources, is associated here explicitly with the hand washing that precedes it. These instructions were copied verbatim in later manuscripts beginning with *BAV Vatican Copt. 18* (AD 1531). The same idea of washing the hands followed by wiping the oblation is seen also in later manuscripts, such as *Paris BnF Copt. 30* (AD 1642), *British Library Or. 429* (17th/18th c.), *BAV Vatican Copt. 99* (AD 1718–1726), *Coptic Museum Lit. 344* (AD 1752), *Rylands Copt. 427* (AD 1764), *Coptic Museum Lit. 80* (AD 1796),

[36] *Paris BnF Ar. 98* (17th c.), fol. 48r–v. Cf. 'Abdallah, *L'ordinamento*, 174–175 (Arabic), 364 (Italian).

Coptic Museum Lit. 265 (18th c.), *St. Macarius Lit. 147* (18th c.),[37] *St. Macarius Lit. 134* (18th/19th c.),[38] *British Library Add. 17725* (AD 1811), *British Library Or. 430* (AD 1832), *Coptic Museum Lit. 412* (AD 1867), *St. Macarius Lit. 133* (19th c.),[39] *St. Macarius Lit. 136* (19th c.), and *Coptic Museum Lit. 16* (AD 1928–1942).[40]

In other words, all available manuscripts that include rubrics on this issue mention the hand washing after the selection of the lamb, and in connection with the wiping of the oblation, as recently remarked by Athanasius al-Maqārī.[41] Unfortunately, Fr. Athanasius also understood the non-ritual washing mentioned in the beginning of the *Ritual Order* as another earlier ritual hand washing, while in reality the former is merely mentioned as a practical matter, not given any ritual significance, and should not be considered a double hand washing in the prothesis.[42]

It is clear from the survey of the evidence that the hand washing in the prothesis is clearly attested at least since Ibn Kabar in the fourteenth century, and that by the fifteenth-century *Ritual Order* it already possessed a fixed form, occupying a specific location in the unfolding of the rite, and accompanied by particular psalm verses.

2.2. The Place of the Hand Washing

It is clear that sources are nearly unanimous that the hand washing takes place *after* the selection of the offering. This was already seen above in Ibn Sabbā‘, Gabriel V's *Ritual Order*, and all subsequent manuscripts under investigation. The only possible exception may be the remark by Ibn Kabar, "Then the lamb is brought. And the priest washes his hands with water, and he wipes the oblation after inspecting it and choosing what is appropriate."[43] Unfortunately, Ibn Kabar's wording leaves room for two interpretations. Either the lamb is brought first–i.e. for the priest to perform the selection–followed by hand washing as all the other sources have indicated, or the hand washing took place before the selection, while only the wiping of the oblation is to be naturally understood as taking place after the selection. In the face of such unanimous agreement from the

37 Al-Maqārī, *Al-quddās al-ilāhī*, 1:297.

38 Ibid., 298.

39 Ibid.

40 Ibid., 297.

41 Ibid., 295.

42 Ibid., 219. Taft remarks that early Christian churches frequently included a fountain in the esonarthex for all the faithful to wash before entering. These ablutions are still performed in Ethiopia by the clergy. Fritsch, "The Preparation of the Gifts," 118–119; Taft and Parenti, *Il Grande Ingresso*, 320.

43 *Paris BnF Ar. 203* (AD 1363–1369), fol. 203r. Cf. Villecourt, "Les observances," 249.

fourteenth century and later, Ibn Kabar's somewhat ambiguous remark must be interpreted in the same vein, where the hand washing follows the selection of the appropriate offering. To this unanimity of sources, one can also add the patriarchal diataxis in *Coptic Patriarchate Lit. 74* (AD 1444), which refers to the patriarch washing his hands after the selection, although he has not yet vested nor entered the sanctuary.[44]

Confusion arises only much later. Although the *editio princeps* of Raphael al-Ṭūḫī (1736) and the *editio typica* of 1902 place the hand washing after the selection, current practice differs in that the hand washing without exception always takes place *before* the selection, and immediately following the preparation of the altar and the prayers of the hours. In fact, this swapping of units is reflected in later printed editions of the Euchologion, even those that otherwise copy the Euchologion of 1902 verbatim, such as the Euchologion published by the Monastery of the Virgin Mary al-Muḥarraq and is currently in its fifth edition.[45]

Grappling with this clear inconsistency, Athanasius al-Maqārī made the claim that the washing of the hands before the prothesis must be an imported rite, foreign to the Coptic tradition altogether. In support of this view, he cites the *Canons of the Apostles*, inspired by the *Apostolic Constitutions* VIII, which mention the subdeacons bringing water to the priests before bringing the offerings.[46] However, the theory of Fr. Athanasius is clearly mistaken, since the texts he uses are speaking of the pre-anaphoral hand washing, and do not refer in any way to the preparatory rites or the prothesis. Thus, while Fr. Athanasius is certainly correct that Coptic sources are nearly unanimous on the pristine location of the hand washing after the selection, he is certainly mistaken in claiming the current rite to be foreign altogether.

In fact, the reason for this discrepancy can be found in the major shift that occurred from the old ordo to the new ordo. Before the hand washing was ever part of the prothesis or preparatory rites, it had a long-standing place in the pre-anaphora. As early as Cyril of

44 The later patriarchal liturgy described in *Baramūs 6/278* (AD 1514) does not indicate that the patriarch washed his hands at all, but only the priest performing the prothesis before the patriarch's vesting. Samuel, *Tartīb al-bīʿa*, 1:21. Mikhail, "The Liturgy Coram Patriarcha Revisited," 288.

45 The Monastery of the Virgin Mary al-Muḥarraq, *Kitāb al-ḫūlāǧī al-muqaddas: Al-ṯalāṯat al-quddāsāt lil-qiddīsīn bāsīlyūs wa-iġrīġūryūs wa-kīrillus wa-yalīhum tartīb taʿmīr al-kaʾs wa-ṣalawāt uḫra mutanawiʿa* [The book of the Holy euchologion: The three liturgies of Saints Basil, Gregory, and Cyril, followed by the rite of the filling of the chalice, and miscellaneous other prayers], 5th ed. ([Asyūṭ]: The Monastery of the Virgin Mary al-Muḥarraq, 2014), 217.

46 Al-Maqārī, *Al-quddās al-ilāhī*, 1:299–300.

Jerusalem, and Theodore of Mopsuestia in the fourth century, the so-called *lavabo* is found as a veritable pre-anaphoral rite. In later centuries, the hand washing is still encountered in the *Apostolic Constitutions,* and the writings of Ps.-Dionysius, regardless of the slightly variant position of this unit among other pre-anaphoral rites, which is discussed in detail by Robert Taft.[47] Taft also argues that the hand washing, from its earliest history, was a spiritual rather than a practical matter.[48] Despite previous attempts to see in the *lavabo* a practical necessity after a supposed selection of the offering in the pre-anaphora, Taft lays this theory to rest by observing that it was deacons and not priests or bishops who handled the gifts in the early Church.

Seen thus as a spiritual gesture meant to emphasize the purity required before serving the eucharistic mystery, the hand washing is quite appropriate in the pre-anaphora as a rite of *accessus ad altare,* albeit in continuity with ritual ablutions found in Jewish and even pagan customs. Given the ancient and more original place of the hand washing in the pre-anaphora, it can be said with certainty that the hand washing in the prothesis is but a duplication of this act. Taft has also concluded as such for the Byzantine Rite, with its observable tendencies to repeat units from the pre-anaphora in the preparatory rites.[49] That this is true for the Coptic Rite as well can be further confirmed by noting that the psalm verses recited are identical in both locations (Pss 50:9–10, 25:6–7, or Ps 50:11–12).

Considering then that the hand washing in the prothesis is a duplicate, a foreign element belonging originally elsewhere, it is no surprise that its location would fluctuate. In the Byzantine Rite, the celebrant probably washed his hands during the transfer procession, since the procession itself was performed by deacons alone, at least in its most ancient historical form. Later, this position changed with the addition of other prayers and formulas during the Great Entrance chant.[50] A similar process may have occurred in the Coptic Rite in the course of its evolution. Perhaps at some initial stage—absent from the manuscript evidence—the deacons did the selection of the offering, in continuity with their ancient role as recipients and preparers of the offering. In such a situation, the priest may have likely washed his hands any time before, during, or after the selection, in preparation for the subsequent presbyteral rites of the prothesis. Later, by the time of the manuscript witnesses, the priest had already firmly acquired the function of selecting the offering, making it impossible for him to

47 Taft and Parenti, *Il Grande Ingresso,* 319–321.
48 Ibid., 319–320.
49 Ibid., 337–338.
50 Ibid., 328.

wash his hands at the same time. Thus, at first, the washing takes place consistently after the selection, a feature seen invariably in the sources. Only later, owing ultimately to the unstable location of this personal spiritual gesture, the washing is moved once again before the selection, probably to avoid the awkwardness of interrupting the flow of the rite by leaving the oblation on the altar to wash the hands.

Another theory may also be posited. According to the old ordo and even the intermediate ordo of Ibn Sabbāʿ, the selection of the offering never took place near the altar, but rather in the adjacent room or pastophorion. As such, this act is unrelated to the *accessus ad altare*, but is a purely practical matter in preparation for the liturgy. It follows then quite logically that the hand washing–a rite of *accessus* as shown above–would be saved so to speak until immediately before the ceremonies of the prothesis that are to take place on the altar. In the old ordo, of which there are no Euchologion manuscripts, the hand washing would have taken place in the pre-anaphora only, since no preparatory rites would have taken place on the altar prior to that. In the intermediate ordo, as was shown previously, the hand washing is implied by Ibn Sabbāʿ after the selection, which took place in the adjacent pastophorion. Finally, in the new ordo, it is expected that the washing would take place after the selection as well and before the priest continues with the rites of the prothesis (commemorations, procession, etc.) that take place on the altar.

Naturally, neither of these theories excludes the other, and both remain highly theoretical in the absence of Euchologion manuscripts prior to the new ordo. Returning once again to the new ordo, one thing is certain. For most of its history, the hand washing was performed after the selection of the offering, followed immediately by wiping the oblation with the priest's slightly moist hands.

2.3. Psalms and Prayers during the Hand Washing

As seen above in the *Ritual Order*, the priest is to wash his hands three times. In the first time, he says, "Sprinkle upon me your hyssop, I will become pure," (Ps 50:7) and in the second time, "Wash me and I shall be whiter than snow. You shall make me to hear joy and gladness, the humble bones shall rejoice," (Ps 50:8) and in the third time, "I will wash my hands of the holies, and I will go about your altar, O Lord, to hear the voice of your praise." (Ps 25:6–7).[51]

[51] According to the RSV translation, this verse reads, "I wash my hands in innocence, and go about thy altar, O Lord, singing aloud a song of thanksgiving, and telling all thy wondrous deeds." (Ps 25:6–7). The translation above is more faithful to the Coptic text.

For the sake of comprehensiveness, mention must be made of two groups of manuscripts with variant psalm readings. The first group has the same psalm verses for the first and second washings, but continue with Psalm 50 for the third washing, "Create in me a pure heart, O God, and renew a right spirit in my inward parts." (Ps 50:10) Manuscripts of this group include *Rylands Copt. 427* (AD 1764), *Coptic Museum Lit. 80* (AD 1796), *Coptic Museum Lit. 16* (AD 1928–1942), and *St. Macarius Lit. 136* (19th c.).[52] Additionally, manuscript *BAV Vatican Copt. 99* (AD 1718–1726) lengthens the psalm verse for the third washing to "Turn away your face from my sins, and blot out my iniquities." (Ps 50:9) This group in general, and particularly the latter manuscript's peculiarity, were noted by 'Abdel Masīḥ Ṣalīb in his *editio typica* and provided as an alternate practice.[53]

A third group of manuscripts inserts a non-scriptural prayer. To this group, belongs *British Library Add. 17725* (AD 1811), which provides the following prayer at the washing:

[1] ⲡⲁⲟ̅ⲥ̅ ⲓ̅ⲏ̅ⲥ̅ ⲡⲭ̅ⲥ̅ ⲙⲁⲧⲟⲩⲃⲟ ⲛ̀ⲛⲉⲛⲯⲩⲭⲏ ⲛⲉⲙ ⲛⲉⲛⲥⲱⲙⲁ ⲛⲉⲙ ⲛⲉⲛⲡ̅ⲛ̅ⲁ̅ [2] ⲛ̀ⲧⲉⲛϫⲓⲙⲓ ⲛ̀ⲟⲩⲙⲉⲣⲟⲥ ⲛⲉⲙ ⲛⲓⲉ̅ⲑ̅ⲩ̅ ⲉⲧⲁⲩⲣⲁⲛⲁⲕ ⲓⲥϫⲉⲛ ⲡⲉⲛⲉϩ. [3] ⲉⲕⲉ̀ⲛⲟⲩϫ ϧⲁϫⲱⲓ.[54]

[1] My Lord Jesus Christ, purify our souls and our bodies and our spirits, [2] so that we may find a share with the saints, who have pleased you since eternity. [3] Sprinkle me with hyssop.

The same instructions appear in *St. Macarius Lit. 134* (18th/19th c.) and *St. Macarius Lit. 133* (19th c.),[55] where in the former it is attributed to Bishop Mīḫā'īl of Samannūd. Finally, one can mention the *hapax* of Ibn Kabar's manuscript *Uppsala O. Vet. 12* (AD 1546), which has the following verse from Psalm 18 in the first washing, "Cleanse me from secret faults. Keep back your servant also from presumptuous sins; let them not have dominion over me." (Ps 18:12–13)[56] However, since it is unknown elsewhere, one can hardly consider this a distinct group.

It remains true that the majority of manuscripts that include the prayers and formulas said at the washing are generally faithful to the *Ritual Order,* as expected given its patriarchal authority as has been demonstrated repeatedly in the course of this study. It is quite inaccurate therefore when Fr. Athanasius, after presenting the latter group of manuscripts with their non-scriptural formula, regards the more widespread custom as an example of ritual practices "according

52 Al-Maqārī, *Al-quddās al-ilāhī,* 1:297.
53 Ṣalīb, ⲡⲓϫⲱⲙ ⲛ̀ⲧⲉ ⲡⲓⲉⲩⲭⲟⲗⲟⲅⲓⲟⲛ, 206.
54 *British Library Add. 17725* (AD 1811), fol. 8r.
55 Al-Maqārī, *Al-quddās al-ilāhī,* 1:298.
56 *Uppsala O. Vet. 12* (AD 1546), fol. 184r.

to one of the Euchologion manuscripts, or a few of them,"[57] while the reality is exactly the opposite.

2.4. The So-Called Baptism of the Lamb

In current practice, the priest wipes the oblation on two separate occasions. The first such instance is immediately after its selection while still facing west, and is understood merely as a practical ritual to remove any flour that may still be found on the bread. The second instance is more symbolic in character, performed after his return to the altar, and can be found explicitly mentioned in the *Ritual Order*'s instructions, "Then he takes the bread of offering and wipes it with his hands above and below, while saying, 'Grant O Lord...'."[58] Since this practice follows immediately after the hand washing, at least in the majority of the sources which include the hand washing at this point, it has come to be understood as a ceremonial gesture symbolic of Christ's baptism. An analysis of the sources on this point is therefore warranted to trace the development of this understanding.

As mentioned previously, Ibn Sabbāʿ does not explicitly mention any hand washing, neither before nor after the selection. Nonetheless, he did interpret the wiping of the oblation on the top and bottom as symbolic of the signing of Christ with water before his presentation to Simeon the Elder, a gesture that is at least not explicitly stated in Scripture. In the fourteenth century, Ibn Kabar mentions both the hand washing and the wiping of the oblation, though it is unclear if the two acts are at all connected, or if the priest wipes the oblation with his moist hands as the current custom dictates. Thus, none of the textual sources and ritual manuals—Ibn Kabar, Ibn Sabbāʿ, and Gabriel V—mention this so-called baptism of the lamb with the priest's moist hand.

The matter would have been settled at this point, if it were not for the consistent witness of liturgical manuscripts. The majority of manuscripts analyzed in this chapter mention that the priest, after washing his hands and reciting the appropriate psalm verses, dries his hands only a little, just as the *Ritual Order* has previously stated. A typical rubric for this can be seen in the earliest such manuscript, *BAV Vatican Copt. 18* (AD 1531):

57 Ibid., 299.

58 *Paris BnF Ar. 98* (17th c.), fol. 48v. Cf. ʿAbdallah, *L'ordinamento*, 174–175 (Arabic), 364 (Italian).

[1] ثم ينشف يديه في ستر ابيض كتان نظيف قليل لا يمسحهم قوي. [2] ويأخذ الحمل على راحة كفه ويمسحه بيديه فوق واسفل.[59]	[1] Then he dries his hands in a white linen clean veil only a little. He does not wipe them thoroughly. [2] And he takes the lamb on the palm of his hand, and wipes it above and below.

The idea that the priest is to dry his hand only a little before handling the oblation, found also in the *Ritual Order*, is encountered in the majority of the manuscripts. These include *Paris BnF Copt. 30* (AD 1642), *BAV Vatican Copt. 99* (AD 1718–1726), *Rylands Copt. 427* (AD 1764), *Coptic Museum Lit. 80* (AD 1796), *Coptic Museum Lit. 265* (18th c.), *St. Macarius Lit. 147* (18th c.),[60] *British Library Or. 430* (AD 1830), *Coptic Museum Lit. 412* (AD 1867), *St. Macarius Lit. 136* (19th c.),[61] and *Coptic Museum Lit. 16* (AD 1928–1942). Exceptions to this general rule are represented in *Coptic Museum Lit. 344* (AD 1752), which only mentions the hand washing and the wiping of the oblation without reference to drying the hands, and *British Library Add. 17725* (AD 1811), which goes so far as to say the following:

[1] ثم بعد ذلك ينشف يديه [2] وياخذ على اصابعه قليل ماء ويمسح [خبز] التقدمة.[62]	[1] And after this, he dries his hands. [2] And takes on his fingers a small amount of water, and wipes the bread of offering.

This specificity of detail is found also in *St. Macarius Lit. 133* (19th c.) and *St. Macarius Lit. 134* (18th/19th c.).[63] Thus, the manuscript tradition is nearly unanimous that the priest is only to dry his hands a little before wiping the oblation bread. One can hardly think of any practical value for this gesture, and the frequency of its appearance in the sources is too overwhelming to ignore. Therefore, despite the fact that no source explicity interprets this gesture as symbolic of baptism, it must be concluded that such an understanding did in fact develop slowly, providing a firm grounding for this practice to endure to the present day. This is especially the case when the current rite is considered, in which the actual hand washing is performed much earlier, but where nonetheless the celebrant uses a little water ceremoniously after the selection in order to perform this ritual baptizing of the lamb.

In analyzing this practice, Athanasius al-Maqārī reached a very different conclusion. Regarding the ceremonial wetting of the fingers

59 *BAV Vatican Copt. 18* (AD 1531), fol. 119r–v.
60 Al-Maqārī, *Al-quddās al-ilāhī*, 1:297.
61 Ibid.
62 *British Library Add. 17725* (AD 1811), fol. 8r.
63 Al-Maqārī, *Al-quddās al-ilāhī*, 1:305.

performed today after the selection, Athanasius al-Maqārī saw in this a relic of the full hand washing in its ancient place, which is correct as far as this observation goes. However, he also saw the two instances of wiping the oblation–once facing west without any water and later at the altar with water–as one and the same gesture doubled for no apparent reason. He then concluded that the wiping of the oblation has nothing to do with the hand washing, which in turn casts doubt into the very idea of baptizing the lamb. Given all the available evidence, the following objections to this conclusion can be presented:

1. The first wiping of the oblation from excess flour is a practical matter that does not need to be stated verbatim in the ritual instructions. Therefore, its absence in texts does not mean it was not performed.
2. The insistence of most manuscripts that the priest dries his hands *only a little* demands an explanation. Since it lacks any practical value, this leaves symbol itself as a likely origin of the practice.
3. A symbolic meaning for this gesture is in fact present even in the fourteenth-century *Precious Jewel* of Ibn Sabbā', albeit related to Christ's presentation to Simeon the Elder and not his baptism.

In fact, the last point regarding the symbolic interpretation of ritual gestures in correspondence to events in Christ's life is perfectly in accordance with developments elsewhere in the East. In the Byzantine tradition, the entire prothesis rite has long been associated with Christ's earthly ministry, particularly his passion.[64] In the Coptic tradition, the paten was understood as symbolic of both the manger and the tomb, in the words of Ibn Sabbā'.[65] Such a widespread tendency to interpret the preparatory rites of the liturgy in this manner cannot be ignored. Although again no prayers or audible phrases are attested in Coptic sources signifying that the wetting of the oblation is symbolic of Christ's baptism, al-Maqārī overlooked the fact that today many priests do in fact recite the following verses while doing so, "Behold the lamb of God, who takes away the sin of the world. John bore witness of him and cried out, saying, this was he of whom I said, he who comes after me is preferred before me, for he was before me. And of his fullness we have all received, and grace for grace. For the law was given through Moses, but grace and truth came through Jesus Christ." (Jn 1:29, 15–17) That this gesture is understood as symbolic of the baptism of Christ is further confirmed through a reading of any recent commentary on the liturgy. In one such popular commentary, Bishop Mattā'us, writes, "After putting the veil on the

64 Hawkes-Teeples, "The prothesis of the Byzantine Divine Liturgy," 323.

65 *Paris BnF Ar. 207* (14th c.), fol. 122v. Cf. Mistrīḥ, *Pretiosa margarita*, 179 (Arabic), 488 (Latin).

altar, the priest then carries the lamb and wets his right index finger and makes the sign of the cross on the bread from the top of the bread to the bottom, then around the bread from the left side to the right. This action symbolizes the baptism of Christ by Saint John in the river Jordan."[66] This interpretation was completely dismissed by al-Maqārī, who wrote, "Commentators could not see in this practice except that the priest baptizes the lamb, which is incorrect,"[67] and later again, "Thus, recent attempts have appeared to interpret this practice as symbolic of the baptism of the lamb with water, which is contrary to a study of ritual history."[68] However, there is no other way to explain this very ritual history, except that the rite had already acquired this symbolic interpretation early on, despite the fact that it was never explicitly sanctioned in official writings and manuals.

2.5. Formulas Accompanying the So-Called Baptism of the Lamb

As the priest is wiping the oblation with his moist hands, the sources indicate that he is to say a number of possible formulas and prayers. It would be useful therefore to examine these various short prayers one by one:

2.5.1. Grant O Lord that this Sacrifice may be Acceptable

By far the most common formula found in the sources accompanying the baptism of the lamb is, "Grant, O Lord, that our sacrifice may be acceptable before you, for my own sins and for the ignorances of your people, and that it may be pure according to the gift of your Holy Spirit, in Christ Jesus our Lord." This is the accompanying formula as found in the *Ritual Order*,[69] and every single manuscript that contains any rubrics whatsoever for this point in the rite. This is the formula found in the *editio typica* of 1902, and subsequently in current practice.[70] Any additional formulas listed below occur only in addition, and not in substitution to the "Grant O Lord" formula.

66 Mattā'us, *The Spirituality of the Rites of the Holy Liturgy in the Coptic Orthodox Church* (Alexandria, n.d.), 101.

67 Al-Maqārī, *Al-quddās al-ilāhī*, 1:308.

68 Ibid., 310.

69 *Paris BnF Ar. 98* (17th c.), fol. 48v–49r. Cf. 'Abdallah, *L'ordinamento*, 175 (Arabic), 364 (Italian).

70 Ṣalīb, ⲡⲓϫⲱⲙ ⲛ̀ⲧⲉ ⲡⲓⲉⲩⲭⲟⲗⲟⲅⲓⲟⲛ, 206.

2.5.2. A Sacrifice of Praise

Some manuscripts add the following prayer, presented here from the oldest such witness, *Coptic Museum Lit. 344* (AD 1752):

[1] ⲟⲩⲑⲩⲥⲓⲁ ⲛ̀ⲥⲙⲟⲩ ⲟⲩⲑⲩⲥⲓⲁ ⲙ̀ⲡⲭⲱ ⲉ̀ⲃⲟⲗ ⲛ̀ⲧⲉ ⲛⲉⲛⲛⲟⲃⲓ [2] ⲫⲟⲩⲱⲓⲛⲓ ⲛ̀ⲧⲉ ⲛⲉⲛⲯⲩⲭⲏ ⲛⲉⲙ ⲛⲉⲛⲥⲱⲙⲁ ⲛⲉⲙ ⲛⲉⲛⲡ︦ⲛ︦ⲁ︦. [3] ⲟⲩⲟϩ ⲛ̀ⲑⲟⲕ ⲡⲉⲧⲉⲛⲟⲩⲱⲣⲡ ⲛⲁⲕ ⲙ̀ⲡⲓⲱⲟⲩ ⲛⲉⲙ ⲡⲓⲧⲁⲓⲟ.[71]

[1] A sacrifice of praise, a sacrifice for the forgiveness of our sins. [2] The light for our souls, our bodies, and our spirits. [3] And unto you we send up glory and honor.

Other witnesses to this prayer are *British Library Add. 17725* (AD 1811), *St. Macarius Lit. 134* (18th/19th c.),[72] and *St. Macarius Lit. 133* (19th c.).[73] It is perhaps noteworthy that this short prayer lacks any internal coherence, nor does it refer directly to the so-called baptism of the lamb despite its late appearance in manuscripts of the eighteenth century and later. Also, three of its four witnesses—*Coptic Museum Lit. 344* (AD 1752), *British Library Add. 17725* (AD 1811), and *St. Macarius Lit. 134* (18th/19th c.)—attribute the order of the prothesis to Bishop Mīḫā'īl of Samannūd as discussed previously, leading one to posit a limited local usage for this formula. At any rate, it never made its way into printed editions including the Euchologion of 1902.

2.5.3. The Peace Formula and the Three Litanies

Finally, only one manuscript, *Coptic Museum Lit. 344* (AD 1752), adds two other elements at this juncture. First, the prayer, "Peace and building up and strengthening of the holy Church of God, Amen," mentioned previously, and found also in *British Library Add. 17725* (AD 1811), albeit before the hand washing. The second, is the instruction to pray the three litanies of the peace of the Church, the hierarchs, and the assemblies.[74] The latter is found in no other manuscript under consideration, though it survives in printed editions and current practice.

Largely, the manuscript witnesses all agree that the pristine formula at the wiping of the oblation is "Grant O Lord," which in itself cannot have been original in this place in the rite, since it is clearly borrowed from the last clause of the second prayer of preparation of the altar.

71 *Coptic Museum Lit. 344* (AD 1752), fol. 35r–v.

72 Al-Maqārī, *Al-quddās al-ilāhī*, 1:306.

73 Ibid., 305.

74 The full text of these litanies is found in the *editio typica* during the rite of matins. See Ṣalīb, ⲡⲓϫⲱⲙ ⲛ̀ⲧⲉ ⲡⲓⲉⲩⲭⲟⲗⲟⲅⲓⲟⲛ, 41–45. These three litanies form an authentic part of the Alexandrian liturgical tradition and can be found also in Melkite MARK in its various medieval manuscripts. Cf. Cuming, *The Liturgy of St Mark*, 14–15.

This is to be expected, since none of these formulas antedates the ritual reforms of Gabriel V in the *Ritual Order*. Thus, one faces the interesting fact that the gesture's symbolic interpretation as related to the birth of Christ—appearing since the fourteenth-century *Precious Jewel*—most likely predates the formulas accompanying it in the oldest sources. Given the long-standing tradition of interpreting the preparatory rites as related to the sufferings and birth of Christ, compared with the fact that the most frequent formula, "Grant O Lord," is clearly not original in this location, it is more appropriate to give precedence in this case to the symbolic interpretation as representing the more ancient tradition.

3. THE COMMEMORATIONS

Offerings for the Eucharist on behalf of the departed, the sick, or for various other needs of the community, have a long history in Christianity. This aspect has been explored already from the perspective of the people bringing their own offerings for the Eucharist, a tradition attested unanimously in the early sources, such as Shenoute of Atripe's *De lingua* (5th c.), the *Canons of Shenoute* (5th c.), the *Testamentum Domini* (5th c.), and the *Canons of Ps.-Athanasius* (5th–6th c.).[75] Offerings for the departed specifically are attested in the monastic communities of Shenoute of Atripe (5th c.). In one of the canons attributed to him, it is instructed upon the departure of a monk or nun, "And the Eucharist (ⲡⲣⲟⲥⲫⲟⲣⲁ) shall be celebrated for them each month until a year has elapsed."[76]

Offerings for the departed are also attested in the seventh-century *Testament of Abraham Bishop of Hermonthis*. One of many texts belonging to the genre of monastic foundational documents, this letter was written for the monks of the Monastery of Saint Phoebammon near Thebes in Egypt. As one of the many parting commandments of Bishop Abraham, he writes, "Wherefore, since thus it is necessary to abide by everything written in this invulnerable testament, I wish and order that, after my exit from this life, the wrapping of my body and my holy [eucharistic] offerings (προσφοραί) and meals [in my memory] (ἀγάπαι) and the designated days of my death [period] be fulfilled by your care according to the custom of the

75 See the earlier discussion on this topic in chapter 1, section 1.1.

76 Canon 229. Layton, *The Canons of Our Fathers*, 182–183. For a commentary on this and other Shenoutean canons of a liturgical character, see Zanetti, "Questions liturgiques," 81–84.

country, and according to my intention and plan."[77] It is thus no surprise that the mentioning of specific persons for whom offerings were made appears as a fixed element in the rite of the prothesis in the majority of the sources.

3.1. Commemorations in the Ritual Manuals

Surprisingly, among all of the sources, both the *Precious Jewel* of Ibn Sabbāʿ and the *Lamp of Darkness* of Ibn Kabar are silent about the commemorations. It would be difficult to guess why these two important sources would omit such a detail. At least in the case of the *Precious Jewel*, the text is quite abrupt, ending chapter 63 on the preparatory rites with the wiping of the oblation, and beginning immediately with chapter 64 and the deacon's role at the mixing of the chalice, thus omitting much more than just the commemorations.

At any rate, such a long-standing tradition attested since late antique sources in Egypt, and elsewhere, cannot be doubted simply through the witness of two fourteenth-century texts, despite their importance. A century later, Gabriel V provides once again what is to become the standard rubrics for the matter:

[1] وان كان القربان عن حي او ميت او ضعيف او مسافر او في شدة فيذكر اسمه ايضاً بعد ذلك. [2] ان كان حي يقول

ⲁⲣⲓⲫⲙⲉⲩⲓ̀ ⲡ̅ⲟ̅ⲥ̅ ⲙ̀ⲡⲉⲕⲃⲱⲕ ⲛ̅ⲓ̅ⲙ̅ ⲁⲣⲉϩ ⲉ̀ⲣⲟϥ ϧⲉⲛ ⲟⲩⲁⲅⲅⲉⲗⲟⲥ ⲛ̀ⲧⲉ ϯϩⲏⲣⲏⲛⲏ ⲟⲩⲟϩ ⲭⲱ ⲛⲁϥ ⲛ̀ⲛⲉϥⲛⲟⲃⲓ ⲛⲁϥ ⲉ̀ⲃⲟⲗ

اذكر يارب عبدك فلان. واحفظه بملاك السلامة واغفر له جميع خطاياه. [3] ان كان متنيح يقول هذا القبطي الذي هو هذا

ⲟⲩⲁⲛⲁⲡⲁⲩⲥⲓⲥ ⲛ̀ⲟⲩⲭⲃⲟⲃ ⲛ̀ⲧⲯⲩⲭⲏ ⲙ̀ⲡⲉⲕⲃⲱⲕ ⲛ̅ⲓ̅ⲙ̅ ⲙⲁⲙⲧⲟⲛ ⲛⲁⲥ ϧⲉⲛ ⲕⲉⲛϥ.

نياحاً وبرود لنفس عبدك فلان نيحه في حضن ابراهيم واسحق ويعقوب ويكملها كالعادة. [4] ان كان ضعيف يقول

[1] And if the offering [is] on behalf of [someone] living, or dead, or weak, or travelling, or in tribulation, he is to remember his name also after this. [2] If it were a living [person], he says "Remember O Lord your servant N.N. Preserve him by the angel of peace and forgive him his sins." [Arabic:] "Remember O Lord your servant N.N. and preserve him by the angel of safety and forgive him all his sins." [3] And if it were a reposed [person], he says this Coptic [saying], which is this, "Repose of refreshment for the soul of your servant N.N. Repose him in the bosom." [Arabic:] "Repose and refreshment for the soul of your servant N.N. Repose him in the bosom of Abraham, Isaac, and

77 Leslie S.B. MacCoull, "1. *Apa Abraham*: *Testament* of Apa Abraham, Bishop of Hermonthis, for the Monastery of St. Phoibammon near Thebes, Egypt," in *Byzantine Monastic Foundation Documents: A Complete Translation of the Surviving Founders' Typika and Testaments*, ed. John Thomas and Angela Constantinides Hero, vol. 1, Dumbarton Oaks Studies 35 (Washington DC: Dumbarton Oaks Research Library and Collection, 2000), 51–58, here 56.

ⲁⲣⲓⲫⲙⲉⲩⲓ̀ ⲡ̅ⲟ̅ⲥ̅ ⲙ̀ⲡⲉⲕⲃⲱⲕ ⲛ̅ⲓ̅ⲙ̅. ⲁⲣⲉϩ ⲉ̀ⲣⲟϥ ϧⲉⲛ ⲟⲩⲁⲅⲅⲉⲗⲟⲥ ⲛ̀ⲧⲉ ϯϩⲏⲣⲏⲛⲏ ⲟⲩⲟϩ ⲙⲁⲧⲁⲗϭⲟϥ ⲉ̀ⲃⲟⲗ ϧⲉⲛ ⲛⲉϥϣⲱⲛⲓ ⲧⲏⲣⲟⲩ

اذكر يارب عبدك فلان واحفظه بملاك السلامة واشفيه من سائر اوجاعه. [5] ان كانوا جماعة يقول

ⲁⲣⲉϩ ⲉ̀ⲣⲱⲟⲩ ϧⲉⲛ ⲟⲩⲁⲅⲅⲉⲗⲟⲥ ⲛ̀ⲧⲉ ϯϩⲓⲣⲏⲛⲏ ⲟⲩⲟϩ ⲙⲁⲧⲁⲗϭⲱⲟⲩ ⲉ̀ⲃⲟⲗ ϧⲉⲛ ⲛⲟⲩϣⲱⲛⲓ ⲧⲏⲣⲟⲩ

احفظهم بملاك السلامة واشفيهم من سائر امراضهم. [6] وان كان مسافر في بر او بحر يقول

ⲁⲣⲓⲫⲙⲉⲩⲓ̀ ⲡ̅ⲟ̅ⲥ̅ ⲟⲩⲟϩ ⲙⲁⲧⲁⲥⲑⲟϥ ⲉⲛⲏⲉⲧⲉ ⲛⲟⲩϥ ⲙⲁⲛ̀ϣⲱⲡⲓ ϧⲉⲛ ⲟⲩϩⲓⲣⲓⲛⲏ ⲛⲉⲙ ⲟⲩⲟⲩϫⲁⲓ

اذكر يارب عبدك فلان ورده الى مسكنه معافى بسلامة [7] وان كانوا جماعة يقول

ⲁⲣⲓⲫⲙⲉⲩⲓ̀ ⲡ̅ⲟ̅ⲥ̅ ⲟⲩⲟϩ ⲙⲁⲧⲁⲥⲑⲟ ⲉⲛⲏ ⲉⲧⲉ ⲛⲱⲟⲩ ⲙ̀ⲙⲁⲛϣⲱⲡⲓ ϧⲉⲛ ⲟⲩϩⲓⲣⲏⲛⲏ ⲛⲉⲙ ⲟⲩⲟⲩϫⲁⲓ

اذكر يارب عبيدك وردهم الى مساكنهم بسلامة معافين. [8] وان كانوا جماعة في شدة او في سجن او في ضائقة يقول

ⲁⲣⲓⲫⲙⲉⲩⲓ̀ ⲡ̅ⲟ̅ⲥ̅ ⲟⲩⲟϩ ⲛⲁϩⲙⲟⲩ ⲉ̀ⲃⲟⲗ ϧⲉⲛ ⲛⲟⲩϩⲟϫϩⲉϫ ⲧⲏⲣⲟⲩ

اذكر يارب عبيدك وخلصهم من جميع شدائدهم. [9] وان كان احد في شدة او سجن او ضائقة يقول

ⲁⲣⲓⲫⲙⲉⲩⲓ̀ ⲡ̅ⲟ̅ⲥ̅ ⲟⲩⲟϩ ⲛⲁϩⲙⲉϥ ⲉ̀ⲃⲟⲗ ϧⲉⲛ ⲛⲉϥϩⲟϫϩⲉϫ ⲧⲏⲣⲟⲩ

اذكر يارب عبدك فلان وخلصه من جميع شدائده [10] ان كان مذكر يقول ⲡⲉⲕⲃⲱⲕ مؤنث ⲧⲉⲕⲃⲱⲕⲓ جماعة ⲛⲉⲕⲉⲃⲓⲁⲓⲕ.[78]

Jacob," and he completes it as usual. [4] And if it were a weak [person], he says, "Remember O Lord your servant N.N. Preserve him by the angel of peace and heal him of all his sicknesses." [Arabic:] "Remember O Lord your servant N.N. and preserve him by the angel of safety and heal him of all his sufferings." [5] If it were a group, he says, "Preserve them with the angel of peace and heal them of all their sicknesses." [Arabic:] "Preserve them by the angel of safety and heal them of all their sicknesses." [6] And if it were a traveler by land or sea, he says, "Remember O Lord and return him to his own dwelling in peace and safety." [Arabic:] "Remember O Lord your servant N.N. and return him to his home healthy in safety." [7] And if it were a group, he says, "Remember O Lord and return them to their own dwelling in peace and safety." [Arabic:] "Remember O Lord your servants and return them to their homes healthy in safety." [8] And if it were a group in tribulation, prison, or necessity, he says, "Remember O Lord and deliver them from all their tribulations." [Arabic:] "Remember O Lord your servants and deliver them from all their tribulations." [9] And if it were someone in tribulation, prison, or necessity, he says, "Remember O Lord and deliver him from all his tribulations." [Arabic:] "Remember O Lord your servant N.N. and deliver him from all his tribulations." [10] If it be male, he says your male servant, if it be female, your female servant, and if it be a group, your servants.

78 *Paris BnF Ar. 98* (17th c.), fol. 49r–50r. Cf. 'Abdallah, *L'ordinamento*, 175–176 (Arabic), 364–365 (Italian).

The meticulousness in providing exact formulas for each situation, even as far as providing alternate gender and number forms, is a function of the declining level of competence in Coptic, which by then in the early fifteenth century was certainly reserved as a liturgical language.[79] In the Euchologion of 1902, the idea is expanded to include formulas for all the following possibilities:

1. A living person (male, female, plural)
2. A departed person (male, female, plural)
3. A sick person (male, female, plural)
4. A traveling person (male, female, plural)
5. A person in distress (male, female, plural)
6. Finally, the text adds the following petition for the priest personally:

[1] ⲁⲣⲓⲫⲙⲉⲩ̀ⲓ ⲡ̅ⲟ̅ⲥ̅ ⲛ̀ⲛⲉⲕⲉ̀ⲃⲓⲁⲓⲕ ⲛ̀ⲭⲣⲓⲥⲧⲓⲁⲛⲟⲥ ⲛ̀ⲟⲣⲑⲟⲇⲟⲝⲟⲥ ⲡⲓⲟⲩⲁⲓ ⲡⲓⲟⲩⲁⲓ ⲕⲁⲧⲁ ⲡⲉϥⲣⲁⲛ ⲛⲉⲙ ϯⲟⲩ̀ⲓ ϯⲟⲩ̀ⲓ ⲕⲁⲧⲁ ⲡⲉⲥⲣⲁⲛ. [2] ⲁⲣⲓⲫⲙⲉⲩ̀ⲓ ⲡ̅ⲟ̅ⲥ̅ ⲙ̀ⲡⲁⲓⲱⲧ ⲛⲉⲙ ⲧⲁⲙⲁⲩ ⲛⲉⲙ ⲛⲁⲥⲛⲏⲟⲩ ⲛⲉⲙ ⲛⲏ ⲉⲧϧⲉⲛⲧ ⲉ̀ⲣⲟⲓ ⲛ̀ⲥⲁⲣⲕⲓⲕⲟⲛ ⲛⲉⲙ ⲛⲁⲓⲟϯ ⲙ̀ⲡⲛⲉⲩⲙⲁⲧⲓⲕⲟⲛ [3] ⲛⲏ ⲙⲉⲛ ⲉⲧⲟⲛϧ ⲁ̀ⲣⲉϩ ⲉ̀ⲣⲱⲟⲩ ϧⲉⲛ ⲡⲁⲅⲅⲉⲗⲟⲥ ⲛ̀ⲧⲉ ϯϩⲓⲣⲏⲛⲏ ⲛⲏ ⲇⲉ ⲉⲧⲁⲩⲉⲛⲕⲟⲧ ⲙⲁⲙ̀ⲧⲟⲛ ⲛⲱⲟⲩ. [4] ⲁⲣⲓⲫⲙⲉⲩ̀ⲓ ⲡ̅ⲟ̅ⲥ̅ ⲛ̀ⲧⲁⲙⲉⲧϫⲱⲃ ⲁⲛⲟⲕ ϧⲁ ⲡⲓϩⲏⲕⲓ ⲟⲩⲟϩ ⲭⲱ ⲛⲏⲓ ⲉ̀ⲃⲟⲗ ⲛ̀ⲛⲁⲛⲟⲃⲓ ⲉⲧⲟϣ.[80]	[1] Remember O Lord your Orthodox Christian servants, each man by his name, and each woman by her name. [2] Remember O Lord my father, my mother, my siblings, my relatives in the flesh, and my spiritual fathers. [3] Those who are living, protect them by the angel of peace, and those who are departed, repose them. [4] Remember O Lord my weakness, I the poor, and forgive me my many sins.

It remains to be seen how the commemorations are represented in the various manuscripts under consideration.

3.2. The Commemorations in the Euchologia Manuscripts

Once again, analysis must be limited only to those manuscripts that contain any rubrics on this matter, since all older manuscripts from the thirteenth and fourteenth centuries, and indeed many later, lack any prayers between the preparation of the altar and the *Prayer of Thanksgiving*. Among those manuscripts that do provide information at this juncture, three groups can be distinguished. First, there are those manuscripts that provide a very brief mention of the commemorations, without providing any actual formulas. This group includes *Coptic Museum Lit. 344* (AD 1752), and *British Library Or. 429* (17th/18th c.). Second, manuscripts that provide the same lengthy listing of all possible formulas as the *Ritual Order* include *Coptic Museum Lit. 265* (18th c.), *British Library Or. 430* (AD 1832), and

79 Mikhail, *From Byzantine to Islamic Egypt*, 79–105.

80 Ṣalib, ⲡⲓϫⲱⲙ ⲛ̀ⲧⲉ ⲡⲓⲉⲩⲭⲟⲗⲟⲅⲓⲟⲛ, 212–213.

Coptic Museum Lit. 412 (AD 1867). Finally, a unique group of manuscripts mentions that the priest at this point remembers those who offered the oblations, and the children of the parish, which certainly refers to the congregation generally, and not particularly to children. This latter group includes *BAV Vatican Copt. 18* (AD 1531), *BAV Vatican Copt. 99* (AD 1718–1726), *Rylands Copt. 427* (AD 1764), *Coptic Museum Lit. 80* (AD 1796), and *Coptic Museum Lit. 16* (AD 1928–1942). Only in one case, *Paris BnF Copt. 30* (AD 1642) from Cairo, while including rubrics on the selection, hand washing, and accompanying formulas, did not mention the commemorations at all.

3.3. Commemorations in East and West

Such a universally attested custom took many expressions in various liturgical rites. In the West, the prayers accompanying the deposition of the gifts on the altar grew extensively ca. AD 1000, influenced by commemorations in the Gallican liturgy. The offering came to be frequently offered for certain persons and purposes. It appears that individual offerings and petitions eventually came to be offered for each person and cause, something which Walafrid Strabo in the ninth century criticized.[81] Jungmann remarks that after AD 1100 in Carolingian territory, Spain, and Monte Cassino, there was an increasing trend of multiplying the number of hosts for symbolic representations on different feasts.[82]

This late western trend is reminiscent also of the Byzantine tradition to arrange particles of bread on the diskos in a specific arrangement, in representation not only of Christ, the Virgin Mary, and the saints, but also of the living and departed to be commemorated at any particular liturgy. This Byzantine practice also began in the second millennium, attested initially in monastic circles in commemoration of their founders, clearly an extension of the earlier custom attested even in seventh-century Egypt.[83]

Finally, the Ethiopian liturgy with its very close affinity to the Coptic Rite, preserves commemorations at roughly the same juncture. After the wiping of the oblation with the priest's wet hands exactly as done in the Coptic liturgy, the priest says a prayer while going around the altar that contains the following petition, "Accept likewise the oblation

81 Jungmann, *Missarum Sollemnia*, 2:43.

82 Ibid., 43–44.

83 Hawkes-Teeples, "The prothesis of the Byzantine Divine Liturgy," 324. For a more detailed discussion of the multiplication of particles and the commemorations associated with this practice in the Byzantine Rite, see Pott, *Byzantine Liturgical Reform*, 210–218; Descoeudres, *Die Pastophorien im syro-byzantinischen Osten*, 103–111.

and offering of thy servant John, which he has brought unto thine holy name and let it be the redemption of his sins. Recompense him with a goodly recompense in this world and in that which is to come."[84] Mercer remarks that this prayer is practically the same in all manuscripts, except that the name of the priest is inserted.[85] However, the context of the prayer and its wording argues against this interpretation, preferring instead to read it as a prayer of commemoration on behalf of others who have offered. Indeed, it would be difficult to understand this petition as somehow implying that the Eucharist is offered solely by the priest–and not by the entire community–or that it is offered for the forgiveness of his sins alone.

4. THE CHANT DURING THE SELECTION OF THE OFFERING

Today, the selection of the offering, as well as the subsequent rites of baptizing the lamb and the commemorations, are accompanied by the chanting of *kyrie eleison* 41 times. However, the accompanying chant is a topic of more complexity in light of the previous conclusions regarding the transfer chant of the old ordo and the practice of praying the hours between matins and the liturgy. The choice of this chant also plays a profound role in communicating the intended mood or character of the prothesis rite from the very beginning, and thus derserves special attention.

Previous investigation into the historical origins of the transfer of gifts has shown that the shift from the pre-anaphoral old ordo to the new ordo likely began some time ca. eighth century. In the same vein, it was hypothesized that the pristine transfer chant could have been an alleluia followed by selections from–or the entire–Psalms 75, 42, 117 and/or 131. This alleluia chant may have been the ancestor of the modern day *Alleluia al-Qurbān* or *Alleluia of the Offering*, which was subsequently repurposed into an introit chant for the entire liturgy as one of the many results of the seismic shift from the old ordo to the new ordo. It is now time to pick up this investigation into the nature of this chant, except now not as a pre-anaphoral transfer chant, but as an introductory chant for the prothesis and the liturgy generally.

4.1. Alleluia as an Introit Chant

Evidence for an alleluia as an *introit* chant appears as early as the *Canons of Ps.-Athanasius,* where canon 40 reads as follows:

[84] *LEW*, 199.
[85] Mercer, *The Ethiopic Liturgy*, 162. However, this detail is unique in Mercer and is not encountered in current Ethiopian practice, according to Fr. Emmanuel Fritsch.

لا يقلق أحد من الكهنة عند ما يريد يقدس قبل ان يجتمع الشعب ويسمعوا الليلويا.86	Let no priest be troubled when he wishes to celebrate before the people be assembled and the alleluia is heard.

The canon appears also in the Coptic recension published by Crum from various fifth–sixth century papyrus fragments, although with a lacuna where the alleluia would have been mentioned. Since the alleluia only appears with certainty in the Arabic recension of the canons, one can thus conclude that it only became known as an introductory chant after the sixth century at the earliest.

Later Arabic sources are unanimous that the liturgy began with an alleluia chant. The first such witness is the fourteenth-century *Precious Jewel* of Ibn Sabbā‘, where the following description appears:

[1] ثم ان الكاهن اذا ابتدأ يقدم القداس ياذن الارشي دياقن رأس الشمامسة احد المرتلين ان يرتل ويقول في ترتيله الليلويا بلحن ينبغي لذلك الوقت والحين [2] ان كان الصوم محزن وان كان الاعياد السيدية فيكون بلحن الفرح [3] ليشتغل عقل كل حاضري الكنيسة بسماعه ويلتذوا به ليغنيهم عن احاديث الشيطان الذي تتداولها الامم الخارجة عن بيعة الله تعالى.87	[1] Then when the priest begins to offer the liturgy, the archdeacon, head of the deacons, grants permission to one of the chanters to chant and say alleluia with an appropriate melody for this time and season. [2] If it is a fast, a sad [melody], and if it is the Lordly feasts, it should be with a joyous melody, [3] so that the minds of all attending the church may be occupied with its hearing, and take pleasure in it, to guard them from the conversations of the devil, which are exchanged by the nations outside the Church of God the exalted.

Already in the fourteenth century, within the context of Ibn Sabbā‘'s intermediate ordo, the liturgy commenced with the solemn chanting of an alleluia. The melody of this chant varied by season, either pensive or joyous. Finally, a chant meant to occupy the attention of the congregation must have been intended to cover the duration of other liturgical acts, during which very little took place in their view. In other words, there must have been some sort of break in the service from the usual visible movement and audible prayers to necessitate a type of distraction—for lack of a better word—to maintain reverence among the congregation. Naturally, this concerns the time it took the

86 Canon 40. Riedel and Crum, *The Canons of Athanasius of Alexandria*, 27 (Arabic), 33 (English).

87 *Paris BnF Ar. 207* (14th c.), fol. 119r. Cf. Mistrīḥ, *Pretiosa margarita*, 173–174 (Arabic), 485–486 (Latin).

priest to go to the pastophorion, inspect and select the offering, and return to the altar, as well as any other unknown prothesis rituals according to the intermediate ordo.

Since Ibn Kabar does not mention any introductory chants, the next clear testimony appears in the *Ritual Order* of Gabriel V at the time of the preparation of the altar:

[1] وهم يرتلوا الليلويا ⲫⲁⲓ ⲡⲉ او غيرها كل وقت بما يلائمه. [2] الافطار جميعه والحدود والخمسين ⲫⲁⲓ ⲡⲉ. [3] واما صوم الميلاد وحدود الصوم الكبير وصوم التلاميذ وصوم العذراء الليلويا ϫⲉ ⲫⲙⲉⲩⲓ̀ وكذلك الاربعاء و الجمعة بطول السنة. [4] واما ايام الصوم الاربعين المقدسة وثلثة ايام يونان يقولوا الليلويا ⲉⲓⲉ̀ⲓ̀ ⲉ̀ϧⲟⲩⲛ والليلويا ⲁⲣⲓⲫⲙⲉⲩⲓ̀.[88]

[1] And they chant Alleluia this is [the day] or another chant, what befits every season. [2] In all non-fasting [days], Sundays, and the fifty days: This is [the day]. [3] But during the nativity fast, Sundays of the great fast, the fast of the disciples, and the fast of the Virgin: Alleluia for the thought [of man], and likewise Wednesday and Friday throughout the year. [4] But during the days of the fast of the holy forty [days], and the three days of Jonah, they say Alelluia I will enter, and Alleluia Remember [O Lord David].

By the fifteenth century, the following can be observed. The alleluia itself had remained by that time the introductory chant for the entire liturgy, commenced in conjunction with the preparation of the altar. Additionally, the psalm selections that follow the alleluia have become assigned to specific seasons, the details of which are identical to current practice. Perhaps the earlier reference in the *Precious Jewel* to various melodies according to season implied also variant psalm selections to go with each, or perhaps one of these psalms was still the single psalm chant, with the alleluia itself changing in melody. At any rate, the alleluia found today in the Coptic hymnological repertoire has only one melody across all seasons. The custom of chanting alleluia in the beginning of the liturgy is confirmed as well by the patriarchal diataxis in *Coptic Patriarchate Lit. 74* (AD 1444), as seen previously in Excursus 2.[89]

The same instructions of the *Ritual Order* were copied identically in the *editio princeps* of Ṭūḫī (1736), although one always has to be careful not to read this as indicative of actual practice in the eighteenth century. At any rate, Ṭūḫī provides the additional

88 *Paris BnF Ar. 98* (17th c.), fol. 47r–v. Cf. ʿAbdallah, *L'ordinamento*, 173–174 (Arabic), 363 (Italian).

89 See the previous remark in Excursus 2, Section 1.7.

confirmation that, "all of this takes place while the priest is reciting the *Prayer of Preparation*."[90]

By way of a valuable eyewitness account of nineteenth-century practice, one may include here the notes of John Patrick Crichton-Stuart, Marquess of Bute, in his valuable English translation of the Coptic liturgy, *The Coptic Morning Service for the Lord's Day* (1882). This publication has the advantage of not simply translating any one or group of manuscripts, but being based specifically on actual usage in the late nineteenth century, as the author states in the preface.[91] After the service of matins, the author writes, "The priest recites, inaudibly, the *Prayer of Preparation of the Altar*, during which the choir begins the alleluia."[92] Explaining the nature of this alleluia in a footnote, the author continues, "This is really the beginning of the hymn sung as the bread and wine are carried round the altar [...] but it is usual to begin it here, and to protract the first word alleluia till the procession starts, when it is continued."[93]

This confirms the hypothesis that the introductory alleluia witnessed in many earlier sources and associated with the selected psalm verses for each season is in fact the modern day *Alleluia al-Qurbān*. Thus, evidence is unanimous that—within the new ordo—the liturgy began with the chanting of alleluia, which lasted the entire duration of the preparation of the altar, the selection of the offering, the hand washing, and the commemorations. This alleluia was later resumed during the procession by the chanting of the appropriate psalm verses. Encountering the same description in Ṭūḫī, Hegumen ʿAbd al-Masīḥ unfortunately misunderstood the meaning intended, thinking that it implied the chanting of the psalm verses themselves during the altar preparation, as he explicitly states in a footnote.[94] This indicates that by the early twentieth century, this ancient usage had already become foreign even to a scholar such as himself. Additionally, since he left behind no chant book per se, it is not clear what if any chant accompanied the preparation, selection, and

90 Ṭūḫī, ⲡⲓϫⲱⲙ ⲛ̀ⲧⲉ ⲡⲓϣⲟⲙⲧ ⲛ̀ⲁⲛⲁⲫⲟⲣⲁ, 288.

91 Bute, *The Coptic Morning Service*, i.

92 Ibid., 35.

93 Ibid., 35n2.

94 Ṣalib, ⲡⲓϫⲱⲙ ⲛ̀ⲧⲉ ⲡⲓⲉⲩⲭⲟⲗⲟⲅⲓⲟⲛ, 197n1: "Note: Some rare copies mentioned here that the people say *alleluia this is the day* and its two alternates [lit. sisters] at the time of the prepration of the altar, each one in its [appointed] days and did not mention it [i.e. the chant] at the procession of the lamb. However, most copies—and the prevailing [custom] in our churches now—is that it is said during the procession of the lamb and we have placed it in this book in this manner. But as for the Euchologion printed in Rome in the year 1452 of the martyrs, it has indicated it to be said twice, that is, here and there, as though taking the two sayings together and this is not suitable."

commemorations if not the alleluia encountered in all the sources. For this last mystery, the answer can be found by revisiting current practice and the earlier conclusions regarding the prayers of the hours.

4.2. Current Practice at the Selection of the Offering

To review, the current practice is to prepare the altar during the hours of the Horologion or before. At the conclusion of the hours, the selection of the offering commences, accompanied by the chanting of *kyrie eleison* 41 times. This is followed by the prayer "Holy, Holy, Holy," which follows the *kyrie* in the Horologion, and at which point the celebrant has usually finished the selection and returned to the altar for the commemorations. If any time is left during such commemorations and before the procession of the gifts, the chanters may begin the *Alleluia al-Qurbān*. Such a long chant, meant originally to accompany a lot more than just the commemorations, is almost never chanted in its entirety. Rather, once the celebrant has finished the commemorations and has become ready for the procession, the chant is interrupted, to be resumed during the procession with only the psalm verses according to season. As seen in all the sources, the current usage is unattested anywhere, not even in Bute's eyewitness account.

In an earlier discussion of the horologion hours and their place between matins and the liturgy, it was concluded that the practice of praying the hours is indeed quite old, and likely came to be solidified ca. fifteenth century or slightly after. Additionally, the current manner of praying the hours was discussed, in which there is clear overlap between the end of the hours and the beginning of the prothesis, not only in chanting *kyrie eleison*, but in the following prayers, "Holy, Holy, Holy," and Our Father. Now, adding to the argument the medieval sources of the *Precious Jewel* (14th c.), *Ritual Order* (15th c.), *Coptic Patriarchate Lit. 74* (AD 1444), and the liturgy described by Bute, the evolution of the chant at the selection of the offering can be reconstructed as follows:

1. Already by the fourteenth-century intermediate ordo of Ibn Sabbāʿ, an introductory alleluia chant was utilized as the introit chant for the entire liturgy, lasting from the vesting and altar prepration until the procession of the oblations around the altar.
2. This chant survived intact until at least the fifteenth century, chanted in its entirety from the end of matins until the procession of the gifts (covering the altar preparation, the selection of the offering, the hand washing, and the commemorations). This is the

chant known as *Alleluia al-Qurbān* and its accompanying psalm verses.
3. Around the same time (ca. 15th c.), the practice of praying the horologion hours became well established, acquiring strict regulations. Initially, the *Alleluia al-Qurbān* remained untouched, chanted between the prayers of the hours and the procession.
4. Finally, perhaps in the name of efficiency, or perhaps for a lack of well-trained chanters, the horologion elements of *kyrie eleison* 41 times, "Holy, Holy, Holy," and Our Father made one last encroachment into the space reserved for *Alleluia al-Qurbān* during the selection of the offering, postponing the latter to the short time during the commemorations, according to current usage.

5. THE PROCESSION OF THE LAMB

After the celebrant has concluded the various commemorations prayed silently over the oblation at the altar, he prepares for the next unit in the rite, which is the procession of the oblations around the altar. This procession around the altar in its present form is a relic of the ancient procession of the transfer of the gifts from the northeastern pastophorion to the altar. It was performed in the pre-anaphora according to the old ordo as seen in the *Letter of Macarius of Manūf al-'uliyā* (10th c.). By the time of Ibn Sabbā' in the fourteenth century it had already moved to its present location before the Liturgy of the Word, albeit remaining a true transfer procession according to the intermediate ordo, as observed by Brakmann.[95] With the establishment of the new ordo as the standard rite of the prothesis, what used to be a true transfer procession became a circular procession of the gifts around the altar, preserving the form without the function of the ancient transfer procession. It is precisely in this vestigial form that one encounters the description of the procession in all sources of the new ordo, the minor differences among them notwithstanding.

5.1. The Procession in The Lamp of Darkness *(14th c.)*

Since the *Lamp of Darkness* does not include the commemorations, it continues with the rite after the wiping of the oblation with water and blessing the other oblations as follows:

[1] ويقول اولاً باركوا ⲉⲩⲗⲟⲅⲏⲥⲟⲛ [2] ثم يقول برشم القربان مجداً واكراماً للثالوث الى اخرها ⲟⲩⲱⲟⲩ ⲛⲉⲙ ⲟⲩⲧⲁⲓⲟ [3] ويناول	[1] And he says first, "Bless," [2] then he says in the signing of the oblation, "Glory and honor to the Trinity," to

95 Brakmann, "Le déroulement," 114.

القربان للشماس الخادم معه فيتلقاه من يده على خرقة من خرق الهيكل الكرزة ويغطيه باطرافها [4] ويدور به حول المذبح [5] ثم يسلمه للقس تجاهه عن يساره فيضعه في الصينية.[96]

its end. [3] Then he gives the oblation to the deacon that is serving with him, who receives it from his hand on one of the consecrated cloths of the altar and wraps it with its edges. [4] And he processes with it around the altar, [5] and hands it back to the priest on his left, who places it in the paten.

As is frequently the case, the steps described by Ibn Kabar are not identical to the current rite, although it should still be classified generally as a witness to the new ordo. First, the request, "bless," is addressed to other concelebrating priests. Throughout the Coptic Rite in its various services, the priest must ask for this blessing from other priests before beginning any prayer or litany. Since this permission is usually asked at the very beginning of a given ritual unit, it indicates that for Ibn Kabar the procession constituted the beginning of a new element, and one that was important enough to merit asking for this blessing before commencing it. In the current rite, this blessing takes place after the procession, and thus it is discussed further in chapter 5.[97]

The blessing of the oblation by the prayer *Glory and Honor* survives today as well, and is said by the priest either before or during the procession as will be evident soon starting with the *Ritual Order* of Gabriel V. Next, what makes Ibn Kabar's description stand out among all the sources is that the deacon is said to execute the procession alone. A specific deacon—one that is identified as serving with the priest—is said to receive the oblation on one of the altar cloths, and proceed with it around the altar wrapped in that veil. One can perhaps presume that the wine was also carried in that procession, either by the same deacon or by another. The idea of wrapping the oblation in a eucharistic veil survives today, where the priest does the same before the procession. Although the deacon's role in the procession as mentioned by Ibn Kabar cannot be corroborated—since all surviving Euchologia with rubrics are posterior to the thirteenth century—it is clear that this practice was not limited to this one text since vestiges of it survive in the current rite. While the priest is certainly permitted to handle the eucharistic bread directly throughout the liturgy, he still wraps it in the same manner today before the procession. This act

96 *Paris BnF Ar. 203* (AD 1363–1369), fol. 203r–v. Cf. Villecourt, "Les observances," 249.

97 See Chapter 5, Section 2.

lacks any particular explanation or logic,[98] which leads one to see in it the survival of what the deacon used to do according to Ibn Kabar, albeit now transferred to the priest.

In the same vein, it is also meaningful that the role of the deacon in this regard had already diminished by the time of the copying of the second oldest manuscript of the *Lamp of Darkness*, *Uppsala O. Vet. 12* (AD 1546), where the following rubric is found instead:

[1] ويلف الكاهن القربانة بخرقة وكذلك الشماس يلف الدم [2] ويطوفوا بهما حول المذبح مرة واحدة.[99]	[1] And the priest wraps the oblation bread in a veil, and likewise the deacon wraps the blood. [2] And they proceed with them around the altar once.

This is essentially the same set up as found in the *Ritual Order* below, and indicates that *Uppsala O. Vet. 12* (AD 1546) was likely adjusted to reflect the contemporary rite of the fifteenth century. This is but the first example in the rite of the prothesis that testifies to a former larger role for the deacon. More examples of this once central role will be seen in subsequent units of the prothesis rite.

5.2. The Procession in The Ritual Order *of Gabriel V (15th c.)*

Proceeding to the fifteenth-century rite attested in the *Ritual Order*, the following description is encountered immediately after the commemorations:

[1] واذا تكامل ذلك يلف الحمل في لفافة حرير ويرفعه على راسه [2] ويكون امامه شماس حاملاً شمعة.[3] وكذلك الشماس يرفع وعاء الخمر على راسه ملفوفة في لفافة حرير [4] وامامه شماس حامل شمعة. [5] ويدورا المذبح دورة واحدة.[100]	[1] And when this has been accomplished[101] he wraps the lamb in a silk veil and lifts it above his head. [2] And there is to be standing in front of him a deacon carrying a candle. [3] Likewise, the deacon lifts the vessel of wine above his head, wrapped in a silk veil, [4] and in front of him a deacon carrying a candle. [5] And they go around the altar one time.

98 Notwithstanding, of course, the common symbolic view that the wrapping represents the shrouding of Christ's body for his burial.

99 *Uppsala O. Vet. 12* (AD 1546), fol. 184r.

100 *Paris BnF Ar. 98* (17th c.), fol. 50r–v. Cf. 'Abdallah, *L'ordinamento*, 177 (Arabic), 365 (Italian).

101 i.e. the commemorations of those for whom the offering has been made, whether departed, sick, travelling, or in distress.

Unlike the *Lamp of Darkness,* here the priest himself holds the wrapped oblation bread, while the deacon only carries the wine in a clear sign of the diminishing role of the deaconate. There are also references to other deacons holding candles before both the bread and the wine. However, it is not likely that these other servants are deacons in the true sense, but rather simple altar assistants, who are referred to as deacons even today in a general sense. This is supported by the fact that the text seems clear in distinguishing between unspecified deacons on the one hand, and *the* deacon, who carries the wine.

This latest development in the procession logistics with the priest leading the way marks the last phase in the evolution of this liturgical unit. After the *Ritual Order*, the same rubrics were copied in all subsequent mansucripts with varying level of details, as will be shown below.

5.3. The Procession in the Euchologia Manuscripts

The oldest manuscript to describe the procession in terms identical to those in the *Ritual Order* is *BAV Vatican Copt. 18* (AD 1531), in which the following description appears:

[1] فاذا تكامل ذلك يلف الحمل في لفافة حرير ويرفعه على راسه [2] ويكون امامه شماس حامل شمعة. [3] وكذلك الشماس يرفع وعاء الخمر على راسه ملفوفة في لفافة حرير [4] وامامه شماس حامل شمعة. [5] ويدورا المذبح دورة واحدة.[102]	[1] And when this has been accomplished he wraps the lamb in a silk veil and lifts it above his head. [2] And there is to be standing in front of him a deacon carrying a candle. [3] Likewise, the deacon lifts the vessel of wine above his head, wrapped in a silk veil, [4] and in front of him a deacon carrying a candle. [5] And they go around the altar one time.

It is evident that these rubrics intentionally copied the *Ritual Order* verbatim. Nor is this an exception among the manuscripts analyzed for this chapter. Identical rubrics appear also in *Paris BnF Copt. 30* (AD 1642), *British Library Or. 429* (17th/18th c.), *BAV Vatican Copt. 99* (AD 1718–1726), *Rylands Copt. 427* (AD 1749), *Coptic Museum Lit. 265* (18th c.), *St. Macarius Lit. 147* (18th c.),[103] *St. Macarius Lit. 134* (18th/19th c.),[104] *British Library Add. 17725* (AD 1811), *British Library Or. 430* (AD 1832), *Coptic Museum Lit. 412* (AD 1867), *St.*

[102] *BAV Vatican Copt. 18* (AD 1531), fol. 123v.

[103] Al-Maqārī, *Al-quddās al-ilāhī*, 1:319.

[104] Ibid.

Macarius Lit. 133 (19th c.),[105] *St. Macarius Lit. 136* (19th c.),[106] and *Coptic Museum Lit. 16* (AD 1928–1942).

Exceptions to this overwhelming trend appear in a few manuscripts. As expected, earlier Euchologia from the thirteenth and fourteenth centuries do not include any mention of the procession or its directions. The seventeenth-century prothesis text in *BAV Vatican Copt. 25* mentions the procession and the prayer that accompanies it, but without any detailed instructions:

[1] دورة الحمل و وعاء الابركة [2] يقول الكاهن مجداً واكراماً.[107]	[1] The procession of the lamb and the vessel of wine. [2] The priest says, "Glory and honor".

In a similarly brief fashion—despite its late date—*Coptic Museum Lit. 80* (AD 1796) only mentions the procession briefly *after* the prayer *Glory and Honor* by the priest:

فاذا [كمل] الدورة يقف مكانه.[108]	And when the procession has been completed, he stands in his place.

While the slightly older *Coptic Museum Lit. 344* (AD 1752), stands somewhere in between this extreme brevity and the detailed instructions of the *Ritual Order*:

[1] ويحمل الحمل باعلا رأسه [2] وكذلك الشماس يحمل وعاء الابركة [3] وقدامهم الشموع موقودة [4] ويدوروا دورة واحدة.[109]	[1] And he carries the lamb above his head, [2] and likewise the deacon carries the vessel of wine, [3] and in front of them candles are to be lit. [4] And they process one time.

Thus, it is clear that the instructions reflected in the *Ritual Order* regarding the manner of the procession and the role assigned to the priest and deacon were copied in later centuries in a broad sample of liturgical manuscripts. The same instructions appeared as well in the *editio princeps* of Ṭūḫī (1736)[110] and the Euchologion of 1902.[111] In the current rite, the procession is performed in essentially the same manner, despite the frequent lack of proper deacons. In such cases, the priest carries the oblation bread wrapped in a veil, while altar assistants walk behind him carrying the wine and the water with candles. Any additional assistants follow as well carrying candles only.

105 Ibid.
106 Ibid.
107 *BAV Vatican Copt. 25* (17th c.), fol. 5r.
108 *Coptic Museum Lit. 80* (AD 1796), fol. 6v.
109 *Coptic Museum Lit. 344* (AD 1752), fol. 36r.
110 Ṭūḫī, ⲡⲓϫⲱⲙ ⲛ̀ⲧⲉ ⲡⲓϣⲟⲙⲧ ⲛ̀ⲁⲛⲁⲫⲟⲣⲁ, 301.
111 Ṣalib, ⲡⲓϫⲱⲙ ⲛ̀ⲧⲉ ⲡⲓⲉⲩⲭⲟⲗⲟⲅⲓⲟⲛ, 213.

Compared to the other minor acts after the selection such as the hand washing and commemorations, the procession constitutes an integral element in the rite of the prothesis, standing as a relic of the old ordo. As such, one would expect parallels of this procession elsewhere in nearby traditions. The Ethiopian liturgy today preserves exactly such a procession. According to Marqus Dā'ūd, the celebrant hands the oblation to the assisting priest after selecting and baptizing it, who in turn receives it in a veil, wraps it, and circles around the altar to the northern side. At this point, the assisting priest hands the oblation back to the celebrant, who has also walked to the southern side across from him. The celebrant then finishes the circuit around the altar and places the oblation in the paten.[112] Emmanuel Fritsch agrees that in the aggregate this procession is certainly a relic of the ancient procession to transfer the gifts from the pastophorion, given what is known of the old ordo of the Ethiopian liturgy as demonstrated earlier in chapters 1 and 2.[113] It is certainly interesting that the Ethiopian rite on this point has the deacon receive the oblation from the priest—in a fashion similar to that in Ibn Kabar—but then hand it back to the priest to carry in the procession, in a manner more similar to the current rite. Given the late date of most surviving Ethiopian liturgical manuscripts, it would be difficult to include this detail into the overall development of the Coptic prothesis rite, although one can easily presume the Ethiopian manner to be a sort of middle ground between the *Lamp of Darkness* and later developments. Regarding the West-Syrian Rite, it is important to remember that a procession survives there as well. In this case, the procession is performed from the altar to the nave and back to the altar, as seen in the commentary by Moses bar Kepha (9th–10th c.).[114]

In essence, the Coptic prothesis rite developed in a pattern similar to that in other neighboring traditions that underwent a shift to the new ordo. The ancient procession to transfer the gifts came to be replaced with a circular procession of the gifts. This procession has for all intents and purposes lost its original functional quality of transfer from one place to another, and has remained only as a ceremonial circular route to honor the eucharistic offerings before their deposition on the altar.

[112] Marqus Dā'ūd, *The Liturgy of the Ethiopian Church* (Cairo: The Egyptian Book Press, 1959), 23.

[113] Fritsch, "The Preparation of the Gifts," 127.

[114] Codrington, *Two Commentaries on the Jacobite Liturgy*, 16–17 (English), 7 (Syriac).

5. GLORY AND HONOR

The procession of the lamb is closely linked with the prayer *Glory and Honor,* which the priest pronounces either before beginning the procession or during it. The text of this prayer is very stable in those manuscripts that contain the full text. Thus, the text is presented here from the Euchologion of 1902:

[1] ⲟⲩⲱⲟⲩ ⲛⲉⲙ ⲟⲩⲧⲁⲓⲟ ⲟⲩⲧⲁⲓⲟ ⲛⲉⲙ ⲟⲩⲱⲟⲩ ⲛ̀ϯⲡⲁⲛⲁⲅⲓⲁ ⲧⲣⲓⲁⲥ ⲫⲓⲱⲧ ⲛⲉⲙ ⲡϣⲏⲣⲓ ⲛⲉⲙ ⲡⲓⲡⲛⲉⲩⲙⲁ ⲉⲑⲟⲩⲁⲃ. [2] ⲟⲩϩⲓⲣⲏⲛⲏ ⲛⲉⲙ ⲟⲩⲕⲱⲧ ⲉ̀ϫⲉⲛ ϯⲟⲩⲓ̀ ⲙ̀ⲙⲁⲩⲁⲧⲥ ⲉⲑⲟⲩⲁⲃ ⲛ̀ⲕⲁⲑⲟⲗⲓⲕⲏ ⲛ̀ⲁⲡⲟⲥⲧⲟⲗⲓⲕⲏ ⲛ̀ⲉⲕⲕⲗⲏⲥⲓⲁ ⲛ̀ⲧⲉ ⲫϯ ⲁⲙⲏⲛ. [3] ⲁⲣⲓⲫⲙⲉⲩⲓ̀ ⲡⲟ̅ⲥ̅ ⲛ̀ⲛⲏ ⲉⲧⲁⲩⲓ̀ⲛⲓ ⲛⲁⲕ ⲉ̀ϧⲟⲩⲛ ⲛ̀ⲛⲁⲓⲇⲱⲣⲟⲛ ⲛⲉⲙ ⲛⲏ ⲉⲧⲁⲩⲉ̀ⲛⲟⲩ ⲉ̀ϫⲱⲟⲩ ⲛⲉⲙ ⲛⲏ ⲉⲧⲁⲩⲉ̀ⲛⲟⲩ ⲉ̀ⲃⲟⲗ ϩⲓⲧⲟⲧⲟⲩ [4] ⲙⲟⲓ ⲛⲱⲟⲩ ⲧⲏⲣⲟⲩ ⲙ̀ⲡⲓⲃⲉⲭⲉ ⲡⲓⲉ̀ⲃⲟⲗ ϧⲉⲛ ⲛⲓⲫⲏⲟⲩⲓ̀.[115]

[1] Glory and honor, honor and glory [Rv 4:9] to the all-holy Trinity, the Father, the Son, and the Holy Spirit. [2] Peace and building up [Acts 9:31] for the one and only, holy, catholic, and apostolic Church of God, amen. [3] Remember O Lord those who have offered to you these gifts, those on whose behalf they have been offered, and those through whom they have been offered. [4] Give them all the recompense from the heavens [Mt 5:12].

The prayer must have been known at least since the fourteenth-century *Lamp of Darkness,* since its incipit is found there, and described as a blessing over the oblation before the procession.[116] One however has to wait until the *Ritual Order* of Gabriel V for the earliest source containing the entire text of the prayer, without any variants from the *textus receptus* used today.[117] Additionally, the *Ritual Order*—perhaps attempting to harmonize disparate usages—prescribes the same prayer to be said once more silently after the blessings over the oblations, which follow the procession, as the priest deposits the bread in the paten. Expectedly, this double recitation of the same prayer became the standard practice, and can be seen in the Euchologion as well, another sure sign of a practice regarded as normative today and found only in the *Ritual Order* at the earliest.

The manuscript tradition of this prayer is quite straightforward, with the majority of the manuscripts containing the text do not display any variants. Two exceptions to this include *British Library Add. 17725* (AD 1811), in which the text of the prayer is given only up to [2] "Peace and building up," to be continued—per the rubrics of the manuscript—with the earlier prayer recited at the selection and

115 Ṣalib, ⲡⲓϫⲱⲙ ⲛ̀ⲧⲉ ⲡⲓⲉⲩⲭⲟⲗⲟⲅⲓⲟⲛ, 213–214.

116 *Paris BnF Ar. 203* (AD 1363–1369), fol. 203r. Cf. Villecourt, "Les observances," 249.

117 *Paris BnF Ar. 98* (17th c.), fol. 50v. Cf. 'Abdallah, *L'ordinamento,* 177 (Arabic), 365 (Italian).

beginning with the same incipit (See section 1.3 above). If taken literally, this would render the full text of the prayer as such:

[1] ⲟⲩⲱⲟⲩ ⲛⲉⲙ ⲟⲩⲧⲁⲓⲟ ⲟⲩⲧⲁⲓⲟ ⲛⲉⲙ ⲟⲩⲱⲟⲩ ⲛ̀ϯⲡⲁⲛⲁⲅⲓⲁ ⲧⲣⲓⲁⲥ ⲫⲓⲱⲧ ⲛⲉⲙ ⲡϣⲏⲣⲓ ⲛⲉⲙ ⲡⲓⲡⲛⲉⲩⲙⲁ ⲉⲑⲟⲩⲁⲃ. [2] ⲟⲩϩⲓⲣⲏⲛⲏ ⲛⲉⲙ ⲟⲩⲕⲱⲧ ⲛⲉⲙ ⲟⲩⲧⲁϫⲣⲟ ⲛ̀ⲧⲉ ϯⲁⲅⲓⲁ ⲛ̀ⲉⲕⲕⲗⲏⲥⲓⲁ ⲛ̀ⲧⲉ ⲫϯ ⲁⲙⲏⲛ.[118]	[1] Glory and honor, honor and glory to the all-holy Trinity, the Father, the Son, and the Holy Spirit. [2] Peace and building up and strengthening of the holy Church of God, amen.

Once again, this is one of the manuscripts attributing the rite to Bishop Mīḫā'īl of Samannūd. It is perhaps noteworthy that the resulting prayer would be significantly shorter and lacking the final entreaty for those who offered the oblations. Perhaps this text preserves an older more pristine reading of this prayer? The text as such is not attested in any of the older Euchologia before the *Ritual Order*, but the possibility cannot be ignored. Curiously, another manuscript of the Samannūd type, *Coptic Museum Lit. 344* (AD 1752), while containing the same prayer, "Peace and building up" at the selection of the offering, makes absolutely no mention of any prayer to be said at the procession. Nonetheless, clearly by that date in the mid-eighteenth century the prayer *Glory and Honor* must have become a stable element of the rite, as seen in the overwhelming number of other manuscripts from the fifteenth to the nineteenth centuries.[119]

Immediately following the prayer, the deacon today responds with the following petition, one of many in the Coptic Rite received in Greek in the *textus receptus*:

[1] ⲡⲣⲟⲥⲉⲩⲝⲁⲥⲑⲉ ⲩⲡⲉⲣ ⲧⲱⲛ ⲁⲅⲓⲱⲛ ⲧⲓⲙⲓⲱⲛ ⲇⲱⲣⲱⲛ ⲧⲟⲩⲧⲱⲛ [2] ⲕⲉ ⲑⲩⲥⲓⲱⲛ ⲏⲙⲱⲛ [3] ⲕⲉ ⲡⲣⲟⲥⲫⲉⲣⲟⲛⲧⲱⲛ.120	[1] Pray for these holy honorable gifts, [2] our sacrifices, [3] and those who offer them.

The diaconal command is not mentioned in Ibn Kabar nor in the *Ritual Order*. As expected, it also makes no appearance in any Euchologia in the prothesis, which lack all congregation and diaconal parts. Interestingly however, the command is repeated later in the anaphora of BAS, and was known quite early in that location, appearing for example in one of the oldest known Euchologia of

118 *British Library Add. 17725* (AD 1811), fol. 8v, 7v–8r.

119 *Coptic Museum Lit. 344* (AD 1752), fol. 36r.

120 Ṣalib, ⲡⲓϫⲱⲙ ⲛ̀ⲧⲉ ⲡⲓⲉⲩⲭⲟⲗⲟⲅⲓⲟⲛ, 215. For the large number of Greek diaconal and congregational responses and hymns in the Coptic received tradition, see O.H.E. Burmester, "The Greek Kīrugmata Versicles & Responses and Hymns in the Coptic Liturgy," *OCP* 2, no. 3/4 (1936): 363–394, here 370. Burmester provides the text of this response corrected orthographically as such, "Προσεύξασθε ὑπὲρ τῶν ἁγίων τιμίων δώρων τούτων καὶ θυσιῶν ἡμῶν καὶ προσφερόντων."

Northern Egyptian provenance *Bodleian Hunt. 360* (13th c.), and the two oldest diaconal manuscripts, *BAV Vatican Copt. 28* (AD 1306), and *BAV Vatican Copt. 27* (15th c.). In both of its locations, the command follows the same priestly entreaty, "Remember O Lord those who have offered to you these gifts." This leads one therefore to conclude that its pristine location must have been in the anaphora, and was only added later to the prothesis as another example of the familiar liturgical phenomenon of *Angleichung*, already encountered more than once.[121]

After the diaconal command, proclaimed today by the deacon as the procession is underway, the Euchologion adds the following prayer for the priest:

[1] ويصل الكاهن هذه بالقول السابق قائلاً [2] ⲁⲣⲓⲫⲙⲉⲩⲓ̀ ⲡⲟ̅ⲥ̅ ⲛ̀ⲟⲩⲟⲛ ⲛⲓⲃⲉⲛ ⲉⲧⲁⲩϩⲟⲛϩⲉⲛ ⲛⲁⲛ ⲉ̀ⲉⲣⲡⲟⲩⲙⲉⲩⲓ̀ ϧⲉⲛ ⲛⲉⲛϯϩⲟ ⲛⲉⲙ ⲛⲉⲛⲧⲱⲃϩ [3] ⲡⲟ̅ⲥ̅ ⲉϥⲉ̀ⲉⲣⲡⲟⲩⲙⲉⲩⲓ̀ ϧⲉⲛ ⲧⲉϥⲙⲉⲧⲟⲩⲣⲟ ⲉⲧϧⲉⲛ ⲛⲓⲫⲏⲟⲩⲓ̀.[122]	[1] And the priest links this with the previous prayer, saying: [2] "Remember O Lord everyone who has asked us to remember them in our entreaties and prayers. [3] May the Lord remember them in his kingdom that is in the heavens."

Although not identified as such, this last segment is prayed silently today, and is marked out as such in printed Euchologia. It is however never identified as a secret prayer in the sources, despite the fact that it appears quite frequently. Its first appearance is once again in the *Ritual Order*, where it is written fully following the *Glory and Honor* without any instructions regarding its place or manner of recitation.[123] Subsequently, it makes various appearances in manuscripts. In every manuscript where this additional entreaty is included, it forms one unit with *Glory and Honor* without any breaks, since no manuscript includes the diaconal command that interjects the prayer today. These manuscripts include *BAV Vatican Copt. 18* (AD 1531), *Coptic Museum Lit. 265* (18th c.), *British Library Or. 430* (AD 1832), and *Coptic Museum Lit. 412* (AD 1867). On the other hand, the prayer is absent from any other manuscript under investigation, leading one to have expected this prayer to be likewise included.

All of this leads one to conclude again that the *Ritual Order* must have played a major role in shaping this unit–*Glory and Honor* and everything associated with it–into what it is today. This is supported by the fact that the Ethiopian prothesis, which generally follows the same outline of its Coptic relative, has only one parallel prayer to

121 Taft, "Anton Baumstark's Comparative Liturgy Revisited," 211–212.

122 Ṣalib, ⲡⲓϫⲱⲙ ⲛ̀ⲧⲉ ⲡⲓⲉⲩⲭⲟⲗⲟⲅⲓⲟⲛ, 215.

123 *Paris BnF Ar. 98* (17th c.), fol. 50v–51r. Cf. 'Abdallah, *L'ordinamento*, 177 (Arabic), 365 (Italian).

Glory and Honor, pronounced after placing the bread in the paten. The prayer reads: "Glory and honor are due unto the Holy Trinity, the Father and the Son and the Holy Ghost, coequal Trinity both now and ever and world without end."[124] Noticeable here is the absence of any entreaties on behalf of those who offered, or for those who have asked the priest to remember them. This briefer version matches closely the one found in *British Library Add. 17725* (AD 1811), despite the latter's late date. It is very likely then that the prayer in [3], "Remember O Lord those who have offered to you these gifts," and what follows came to be attached to *Glory and Honor* at a later date, possibly also added from the anaphora. At a third stage of development, the additional prayer, "Remember O Lord everyone who has asked us to remember them," was also added. This must have occurred at least shortly before the time of Gabriel V, if not through his direct influence. Finally, the borrowed entreaty from the anaphora must have attracted the diaconal command that goes with it as well.

The reconstruction of the evolution of this prayer can be bolstered by looking at the thematic progression of the entire prayer, where the first section [1] and [2] form a cohesive unit, in no need of further additions, while the entreaties that follow are independent in thought and idea. While the former proclaims the oblation as glory and honor to the holy Trinity and building up of the Church, the entreaties are about various members of the congregation, who were involved in one way or another in the oblation. In addition, such commemorations for those who offered, for whom the oblation was offered, and generally for anyone who asked to be remembered have their logical place as part of the commemorations before the procession. Therefore, once again, the pristine shape of this prayer was likely the one preserved in the late manuscript *British Library Add. 17725* (AD 1811). Additionally, the manner of saying this prayer seems to have also evolved from a merely silent blessing over the oblation in Ibn Kabar to a more proclamatory call, said while elevating the oblation and facing the congregation.

6. PROCESSIONAL PSALMS

Historically, the chanting of *Alleluia al-Qurbān* took place throughout the altar preparation, selection, and commemorations, according to the historical witnesses. Alternatively, in the current rite, the chant is relegated only to be executed during the commemorations and after *kyrie eleison* 41 times. In either case, after the procession of the lamb and the diaconal command said during it, comes the time for the

[124] *LEW*, 201.

continuation of the alleluia with the appropriate psalm selections. The received tradition of these seasonal psalm selections is as follows:

[1] ⲁⲗⲗⲏⲗⲟⲩⲓⲁ ⲫⲁⲓ ⲡⲉ ⲡⲓⲉϩⲟⲟⲩ ⲉⲧⲁ ⲡ̅ⲟ̅ⲥ̅ ⲑⲁⲙⲓⲟϥ ⲙⲁⲣⲉⲛⲑⲉⲗⲏⲗ ⲛ̀ⲧⲉⲛⲟⲩⲛⲟϥ ⲙ̀ⲙⲟⲛ ⲛ̀ϧⲏⲧϥ. ⲱ ⲡ̅ⲟ̅ⲥ̅ ⲉⲕⲉ̀ⲛⲁϩⲙⲉⲛ ⲱ ⲡ̅ⲟ̅ⲥ̅ ⲉⲕⲉ̀ⲥⲟⲩⲧⲉⲛ ⲛⲉⲛⲙⲱⲓⲧ. ϥ̀ⲥⲙⲁⲣⲱⲟⲩⲧ ⲛ̀ϫⲉ ⲫⲏ ⲉⲑⲛⲏⲟⲩ ϧⲉⲛ ⲫⲣⲁⲛ ⲙ̀ⲡ̅ⲟ̅ⲥ̅ ⲁⲗⲗⲏⲗⲟⲩⲓⲁ.	[1] This is the day the Lord has made; let us rejoice and be glad in it. O Lord save us, O Lord straighten our ways. Blessed is he who comes in the name of the Lord, Alleluia [Ps 117:24–26].
[2] ⲁⲗⲗⲏⲗⲟⲩⲓⲁ ϫⲉ ⲫⲙⲉⲩⲓ̀ ⲛ̀ⲟⲩⲣⲱⲙⲓ ⲉϥⲉ̀ⲟⲩⲱⲛϩ ⲛⲁⲕ ⲉ̀ⲃⲟⲗ ⲡ̅ⲟ̅ⲥ̅ ⲟⲩⲟϩ ⲡⲥⲱϫⲡ ⲛ̀ⲧⲉ ⲟⲩⲙⲉⲩⲓ̀ ⲉϥⲉⲣϣⲁⲓ ⲛⲁⲕ. ⲛⲓⲑⲩⲥⲓⲁ ⲛⲓⲡⲣⲟⲥⲫⲟⲣⲁ ϣⲟⲡⲟⲩ ⲉ̀ⲣⲟⲕ ⲁⲗⲗⲏⲗⲟⲩⲓⲁ.	[2] The thought of man shall confess to you, O Lord, and the remainder of thought shall keep a feast to you. [Ps 75:11] Accept unto you the sacrifices and the offerings, Alleluia.
[3] ⲁⲗⲗⲏⲗⲟⲩⲓⲁ ⲉⲓⲉ̀ⲓ̀ ⲉ̀ϧⲟⲩⲛ ϣⲁ ⲡⲓⲙⲁⲛ̀ⲉⲣϣⲱⲟⲩϣⲓ ⲛ̀ⲧⲉ ⲫϯ ⲛⲁϩⲣⲉⲛ ⲡϩⲟ ⲙ̀ⲫϯ ⲫⲏ ⲉⲧⲁϥϯ ⲙ̀ⲡⲟⲩⲛⲟϥ ⲛ̀ⲧⲉ ⲧⲁⲙⲉⲧⲁⲗⲟⲩ ϯⲛⲁⲟⲩⲱⲛϩ ⲛⲁⲕ ⲉ̀ⲃⲟⲗ ⲫϯ ⲡⲁⲛⲟⲩϯ ϧⲉⲛ ⲟⲩⲕⲩⲑⲁⲣⲁ ⲁⲗⲗⲏⲗⲟⲩⲓⲁ.125 ⲁⲣⲓⲫⲙⲉⲩⲓ̀ ⲡ̅ⲟ̅ⲥ̅ ⲛ̀ⲆⲁⲩⲓⲆ ⲛⲉⲙ ⲧⲉϥⲙⲉⲧⲣⲉⲙⲣⲁⲩϣ ⲧⲏⲣⲥ ⲁⲗⲗⲏⲗⲟⲩⲓⲁ.[126]	[3] I will go in to the altar of God, before the face of God, who gave joy to my youth. I will confess you, O God my God, with a harp, alleluia. Remember O Lord David and all his meekness, Alleluia [Ps 42:4; 131:1].

Since at least the fifteenth century in the *Ritual Order*, these three psalm selections had been linked to particular times of liturgical celebration according to the following pattern: [1] is chanted on feasts, Sundays, and generally any non-fasting day; [2] is chanted on all fasting days except the weekdays of Lent; and [3] is chanted on the weekdays of Lent.

There remains only one point regarding these chants to be made. Why would an alleluia and its associated psalm verses be separated today by the *Glory and Honor*, and the procession? In the hypothetical origin in the old ordo, the alleluia and psalms formed one unit as a transfer chant. Even in the *Precious Jewel* of Ibn Sabbāʿ, where the transfer occurs in its present place in the beginning of the liturgy, the alleluia began with the altar preparation with no sign that it was interrupted at any point.

Clearly, the only possible explanation for this unseemly interruption is that the *Glory and Honor* itself was not originally proclaimed out loud in such a manner as to interrupt the chant. As seen in Ibn Kabar, *Glory and Honor* was a simple blessing over the oblations before the procession. Even in the *Ritual Order*, a doubling of the prayer occurs, where its second iteration takes place as a silent

125 This alleluia is omitted today in actual practice.
126 Ṣalib, ⲡⲓϫⲱⲙ ⲛ̀ⲧⲉ ⲡⲓⲉⲩⲭⲟⲗⲟⲅⲓⲟⲛ, 216–217.

blessing before depositing the oblation in the paten, and this is exactly how the Ethiopian parallel takes place. As such, there would have been no public prayer with elevating the oblation, as is the present custom, which necessarily causes an interruption in the chanting.

Thus, eliminating the *Glory and Honor* and all its associated elements from the pristine rite, the following order emerges. This is admittedly hypothetical, but is intended specifically as a rite that would have been the custom within the new ordo but some time before the reforms of Gabriel V:

1. Preparation of the altar 2. Selection of the oblation 3. Hand washing and baptizing of the oblation 4. Commemorations 5. Procession around the altar	*Alleluia al-Qurbān* + Psalm verses

8. THE SYMBOLISM OF CHRIST'S LIFE

The liturgical units discussed in this chapter reveal an interesting theme, where ritual gestures are understood as symbolic of various episodes in Christ's earthly life, particularly his nativity and passion. This mode of interpretation appears most explicitly in the fourteenth-century *Precious Jewel*, where Ibn Sabbāʿ first compared the paten to both the manger and the tomb.[127] Other examples of this symbolic interpretation appear in such gestures as "baptizing" the eucharistic bread after its selection, as well as seeing in the eucharistic veils a symbol of the gravecloths of Christ or the cloths by which he was wrapped in the manger, as seen previously.[128]

The same tendency can be seen in the Byzantine tradition as well, where the passion narrative came to be integrated into the ritual gestures and understanding of the prothesis ca. eighth century, particularly with the introduction of the lance as a eucharistic implement.[129] Particularly in the Byzantine tradition, thanks to the large number of commentaries available, one can more accurately

127 *Paris BnF Ar. 207* (14th c.), fol. 122v. Cf. Mistrīḥ, *Pretiosa margarita*, 179 (Arabic), 488 (Latin).

128 See Excursus 1, Section 6.

129 Teeples, "The prothesis of the Byzantine Divine Liturgy," 323. For more on this theme as it was reflected in various Byzantine liturgical commentaries, see Pott, *Byzantine Liturgical Reform*, 202–206. Pott ultimately draws on the most detailed study of the historical development of the Byzantine prothesis by Georges Descoeudres. Descoeudres, *Die Pastophorien im syro-byzantinischen Osten*, 116–118.

describe a process by which the rite and its interpretation developed together, with symbolic interpretation influencing the development of the rite itself.[130]

Unfortunately, it is not possible to advance this far in understanding the process that gave rise to the same symbolic themes in the Coptic rite in the absence of as large a number of liturgical commentaries.[131] What can be affirmed is that the symbolic interpretation itself developed markedly over time. Today, not only is the baptism of the lamb and the paten seen in this vein, but the procession of the lamb is also understood as such. In the same gesture, the priest elevates the eucharistic loaf that is wrapped in a veil with a cross placed at an angle over it, said to be symbolic of Christ carrying the cross on his way to Golgotha. Similarly, the procession is also interpreted as the movement of Simeon carrying the child Jesus around the sanctuary.[132] Further gestures and elements of the prothesis examined in later chapters contribute to a broader vision of the extent of this nativity-passion theme.

9. CONCLUSION

Thus, one comes to the end of the initial rites of the prothesis, namely, the selection of the offering, the hand washing, the commemorations, and the subsequent procession around the altar. If one were to sum it all up in one broad theological statement, it would be the following. Through God's mercy, man is purified in his whole being in order to enter into the eucharistic mystery, in which the earthly join the heavenly in the ever-present memorial of Christ's incarnation and life-saving death, calling to remembrance fellow members of the body of Christ in need, while at the same time joyfully offering a sacrifice of praise before the Lord.

From a ritual and theological perspective, these specific elements were chosen to constitute their own chapter since they correspond roughly to the rites executed before the readings of Scripture according to the old ordo, albeit not necessarily as fully developed. By now, the priest would have also concluded any rites that can be considered preparatory or in some way corresponding to the *accessus ad altare*, such as prayers of preparation of the altar and the hand washing. What remains ahead is to continue with the rites of the prothesis proper, which as the subsequent analysis will show, are of a

[130] Pott, *Byzantine Liturgical Reform*, 220.

[131] For liturgical commentaries in the Coptic tradition, see ʿĀdil, "Tartīb wa-šarḥ al-quddās," 219–241.

[132] Mattāʾus, *The Spirituality of the Rites of the Holy Liturgy*, 104.

much more priestly character, forming the bulk of the euchological material and priestly prayers. These include mainly the *Prayer of Thanksgiving*, the *Prothesis Prayer*, and the concluding absolutions.

Throughout this chapter, the results of the shift to the new ordo were often quite palpable. The earliest sources of this new ordo, and in fact quite consistently since then, show everything being done in a very public and visible way, from the selection of the offering, to the hand washing at the altar, to the procession around the altar while elevating the gifts. This has had a tremendous effect on the place of the prothesis in the consciousness of the Church as a truly ecclesial and communal ceremony, making for a very rich ground for theological reflection, and indeed reticence to call this rite of the preparation of the gifts truly *preparatory* in the proper sense. In other words, while the rite is indeed preparatory strictly speaking since its tangible purpose is to prepare the offerings for the subsequent anaphora, it certainly does not play a secondary or supportive role as the word *preparatory* may be sometimes understood.

On a final note, one also clearly sees the influence of the *Ritual Order* of Gabriel V (15th c.) as an official diataxis of the Coptic liturgy, and the Coptic Rite generally, on future sources. Repeatedly, manuscripts after the fifteenth century copied the text of the *Ritual Order* almost verbatim, or at least preserve the same practices indicated in it. This usually came in clear contrast to earlier sources such as *The Lamp of Darkness* and *The Precious Jewel*, which often showed considerable variance in intricate ritual details. Although the current analysis is not primarily concerned with studying the diataxis of Gabriel V itself in any detail, these observations are certainly useful for a detailed and nuanced understanding of the place of this major source in the story of the Coptic liturgy. This is especially true where manual acts and short formulas–as opposed to lengthy euchological prayers–are the primary focus, as was the case in this current chapter.

CHAPTER 5

THE BLESSING OF THE OFFERING AND THE PRAYER OF THANKSGIVING

After the conclusion of the procession analyzed in the previous chapter, the celebrant priest takes his place once again in front of the altar, while the deacon or assistants stand to his left carrying the wine, the water, and candles. The celebrant exchanges a blessing with any other clergy of equal rank who may be present, while holding the oblation bread in his left hand. He then blesses the bread together with the wine and the water with the sign of the cross three times. While blessing the eucharistic gifts in this manner, the priest pronounces the same formula discussed earlier with respect to the blessing of the vestments: "In the name of the Father, and the Son, and the Holy Spirit, one God amen. Blessed be God the Father the Pantocrator, amen. Blessed be his only begotten Son, Jesus Christ our Lord, amen. Blessed be the Holy Spirit the Paraclete, amen."[1] Afterwards, the celebrant places the bread in the paten, while silently reciting the prayer *Glory and honor*, which he has already proclaimed aloud during the procession.

Meanwhile, the deacon—or one of the assisting altar servants in the absence of a deacon—pronounces the Trinitarian response: "One is the Holy Father, one is the Holy Son, one is the Holy Spirit, amen. Blessed be the Lord God forever amen." This is followed immediately by Psalm 116: "Praise the Lord, all nations. Let all the peoples praise him. For his mercy has been firmly established upon us, and the truth of the Lord endures forever, amen alleluia."[2] This is followed by the congregation's own Trinitarian acclamation: "Glory to the Father and the Son, and the Holy Spirit, both now and always and unto the ages of ages, amen alleluia."[3]

Meanwhile, the celebrant takes the wine and pours it in the chalice, which had been placed earlier inside the chalice throne during the

1 Ṣalīb, ⲡⲓϫⲱⲙ ⲛ̀ⲧⲉ ⲡⲓⲉⲩⲭⲟⲗⲟⲅⲓⲟⲛ, 213–219. See Chapter 3, Section 1.

2 Ibid., 221. Discussed more in detail below, the translation presented here is of the Coptic rather than quoting directly from the RSV English translation.

3 Ibid.

preparation of the altar.[4] This is followed by the addition of a small amount of water, which the Euchologion of 1902 identifies as no more than a third of the amount of wine. Afterwards, a new ritual unit begins, namely, the *Prayer of Thanksgiving*, as it is known generally in Coptic sources. This is a general prayer thanking God for his protection, salvation, and support until the present time, as well as asking him for his continued help for the remainder of the day. Although this prayer is offered in the context of the prothesis, oftentimes while the priest is still mixing the chalice with wine and water, a closer analysis of the prayer's text, usage, and history demonstrates that this prayer does not belong to the prothesis rite at all. Rather, the *Prayer of Thanksgiving* constitutes the first prayer of the public liturgical celebration or enarxis, which has become associated with the prothesis only because of the shift from the old ordo to the new ordo.

Thus, the triple blessing over the gifts and the *Prayer of Thanksgiving* make up the next stage in the rite examined in this chapter. The previous chapter was occupied with rituals and prayers, many of which belonged to the preparation of the gifts that preceded the liturgy in the old ordo as well, such as the selection of the gifts, and the commemorations. That chapter was concluded with a discussion of the procession, which is a remnant of the ancient transfer of the gifts that took place after the dismissal of the catechumens. Seen from this same perspective, the current chapter is concerned with elements that belong to the preparation of the gifts as well (e.g. the blessing over the gifts, the deposition of the bread in the paten, and the mixing of the chalice). The exception is the lone element of the *Prayer of Thanksgiving*, which can be considered neither as part of the ancient preparation nor the transfer of gifts. As was done previously in Chapter 4, and given the nature of the sources, the analysis will rely mostly on the classical commentaries/guides of Ibn Kabar, Ibn Sabbā', and Gabriel V. This is in addition to the number of liturgical manuscripts, most of which are posterior to the *Ritual Order* of Gabriel V.

1. THE POSITIONS OF THE CELEBRANT AND THE DEACON

The rubrics at this point in the Euchologion of Hegumen 'Abd al-Masīḥ Ṣalīb mention that the priest is to stand in his place facing east at the altar upon the conclusion of the procession.[5] Although the

4 See Chapter 3, Section 2.1.

5 Ṣalīb, ⲡⲓϫⲱⲙ ⲛ̀ⲧⲉ ⲡⲓⲉⲩⲭⲟⲗⲟⲅⲓⲟⲛ, 217.

rubrics do not mention explicitly where the deacon is to stand, it can be assumed that he is to be in close proximity to the priest, since the latter is instructed to bring the oblation bread closer to the wine vessel, which is carried by the deacon. In current practice, the deacon(s) stand to the left of the altar and the priest.

However, medieval sources are unanimous that deacons in the Coptic Church are to stand across from the priest, facing west and the people. This is seen at least since the twelfth-century *The Histories of the Monasteries and Churches* of Abū l-Makārim, where the Fatimid ruler al-Āmir bi-aḥkāmil-lāh (AD 1101–1130) is said to have visited the Monastery of Nahyā, near Giza to the southwest of Cairo.[6] Upon inquiring, the Caliph was informed that the priest stands at the altar facing east, while the deacon stands opposite him facing west throughout the liturgy.[7] Although the veracity of this account cannot be verified, it would be difficult to argue that the idea itself of the deacon's position during the liturgy was entirely fabricated.

The same information is found a century later in the *The Guide to the Beginners and the Correction of the Laity*. Here, the custom is given the following reasons: 1. The standing of the priest and deacon on opposite ends of the altar is likened to the two angels at the head and feet of Christ's tomb, 2. The priest prays to God, while the deacon is to face the people to address them in his various commands and responses, and 3. This is a custom handed down since the time of Saint Mark to the Copts, the Nubians, and the Ethiopians. The latter reason–if one can call it such–is argued by stating that deacons among the Alexandrian Melkites stand in this same position only when celebrating the liturgy of Saint Mark, while in other liturgies, presumably CHR or Byzantine BAS, the deacon faces east.[8]

6 René-Georges Coquin and Maurice Martin, "Dayr Nahya," *CE*, 2:843b–844a.

7 Evetts, *The Churches & Monasteries*, 182.

8 *BAV Vatican Ar. 117* (AD 1323), fol. 197v. Cf. Graf, "Liturgische Anweisungen," 121. The author here touches here upon a very important topic in the liturgical history of the Chalcedonian Eastern patriarchates of Alexandria, Antioch and Jerusalem, sometimes known collectively as Melkites. Between the eighth and thirteenth centuries, the local liturgical traditions of these three patriarchates were slowly replaced by the liturgical traditions of Constantinople, as the latter increasingly came to be regarded as the capital of Chalcedonian Orthodoxy. This process, termed Byzantinization by scholars of eastern liturgy, led to the gradual abandonment of the local anaphoras of the Eastern patriarchates, such as Melkite MARK, JAS, and various local services, lectionaries, and calendars. One very specific episode in the process of Byzantinization took place in the late twelfth century, when the Byzantine canonist and for some time absentee Chalcedonian patriarch of Antioch Theodore IV Balsamon (ca. AD 1185–1190) was asked by Patriarch Mark III of Alexandria (AD 1180–1209) about the authenticity of JAS and MARK. Balsamon responded that neither of these are acceptable since they were not

The following century, Ibn Sabbā' repeated the same observation. According to him, Coptic deacons stand opposite the priest unlike in all other confessions. The reason he gives however is quite simple: Because of increased attacks from heretics (either Chalcedonians or Muslims?), the Copts changed the traditional and universal position of the deacon out of necessity in order for the deacon to warn the priest in case of an attack, and to assist in quickly hiding the eucharistic gifts and vessels under the altar.[9]

Later sources that included the same instructions provided no new reasons. The *Order of the Priesthood* of Ps.-Sāwīrus explained the custom as 1. protection from attacks, 2. because the deacon's role is to speak to the people, as well as 3. the earlier allegorical intepretation of the priest and deacon as images of the angels at the tomb.[10] Ibn Kabar in the fourteenth-century *Lamp of Darkness* mentioned only the reason that the deacon is to address the people, and that he and the priest are images of the angels at the tomb.[11] Finally, the *Ritual Order* of Gabriel V included only the allegorical interpretation of the priest and deacon as representing the angels at the tomb.[12]

received in Constantinople. See *Interrogationes canonicae* (PG 138:953); Venance Grumel, "Les Réponses canoniques à Marc d'Alexandrie, leur caractère officiel, leur double rédaction," *Échos d'Orient* 38 (1939): 321–333; Patrick Demetrios Viscuso, *A Guide for a Church under Islam: The Sixty-Six Canonical Questions Attributed to Theodōros Balsamōn* (Brookline, MA: Holy Cross Orthodox Press, 2014), 66–68. Balsamon's canonical response took considerable time to take effect, since manuscripts of MARK and JAS continued to be copied well into the thirteenth century at least. See Joseph Nasrallah, "La liturgie des Patriarcats melchites de 969 à 1300," *OC* 71 (1987): 156–181. The Byzantinization of the Alexandrian Melkite tradition was addressed recently by Heinzgerd Brakmann in Brakmann, "Neue Funde (1996–2000)," 585. For the most exhaustive and updated study of the Byzantinization of the Jerusalem Patriarchate, including a discussion of Balsamon's canonical responses, see Galadza, *Liturgy and Byzantinization in Jerusalem*, 136–137. The present passage from *The Guide to the Beginners* is further proof of the continuity of the Eastern anaphoras of JAS and MARK among the Melkites in the thirteenth century.

9 *Paris BnF Ar. 207* (14th c.), fol. 123v–124r. Cf. Mistrīḥ, *Pretiosa margarita*, 182 (Arabic), 490 (Latin).

10 Assfalg, *Die Ordnung des Priestertums*, 36 (Arabic), 111–112 (German). These reasons are repeated later in the final chapter of the same work, titled "Concerning the Differences between the Melkites and the Copts." The passage is similar to the one from *The Guide to the Beginners* above in that it asserts the adherence of the Copts to their pristine Alexandrian tradition even when the Alexandrian Melkites have become accustomed to having the deacon face east. Once again, one encounters reference to the Melkite anaphoras of JAS and MARK, as well as Byzantine BAS and CHR, which interestingly point to the gradual adoption of the two Constantinopolitan anaphoras. See Ibid., 56 (Arabic), 134 (German).

11 *Paris BnF Ar. 203* (AD 1363–1369), fol. 204v. Cf. villecourt, "Les observances," 252.

12 *Paris BnF Ar. 98* (17th c.), fol. 53r. Cf. 'Abdallah, *L'ordinamento*, 180 (Arabic), 366 (Italian).

It would be difficult to accept the testimony of even so many medieval sources as indicative of a pristine Alexandrian tradition. First, the allegorical argument likening the priest and deacon to the angels at the tomb of Christ must be dismissed. Such spiritual meditations are seldom the original practical reason for a given custom. Further, the idea that the deacon, whose duty is to address the people, ought to face them, poses a few problems. It is true that it is one of the deacon's duties to address the people with the various *diakonika*, but this is likewise true in all liturgical traditions, which do not place the deacon across from the priest, a custom admitted as a peculiarity of the Coptic Church by the sources themselves. In fact, given the eastern orientation of the totality of eastern liturgy, it is far more likely that the westward orientation of any member of the clergy is an abnormality rather than the norm. Finally, there remains the assertion of *The Guide to the Beginners* that this custom is unanimous amongst the Churches following the Alexandrian liturgical tradition, including the Copts, the Nubians, the Ethiopians, and even the Alexandrian Melkites when celebrating the Liturgy of Saint Mark. However, to re-echo the remark by Emmanuel Fritsch, certain ancient Ethiopian churches such as in Dəgum seem to have had the altar placed very close to the eastern wall, leaving no room for a deacon to stand.[13] Therefore, the generalization of *The Guide* must be taken with a grain of salt, as perhaps indicative of accepted practice in his time, but certainly not of the universal or all-time practice in the Alexandrian liturgical realm.

Unfortunately, the demise of this peculiar medieval custom cannot be dated with any precision. Euchologia indebted to the *Ritual Order* of Gabriel V continued to assign the deacon a place facing west until the nineteenth century.[14] This is in addition to the majority of manuscripts between the fifteenth and nineteenth centuries that include the rubrics of this point, with the sole exception of *Paris BnF Copt. 30* (AD 1642) from Cairo, which omits any mention of the deacon's position. Nonethetless, it can be concluded at this point based on universality and an analysis of the sources that the position of the deacon in the Coptic liturgy shifted some time around the twelfth century. This was likely for exigent circumstances to protect the assemblies and the mysteries, before eventually reverting to the universal norm in the East, where everyone faces eastward.

13 Fritsch, "The Preparation of the Gifts," 108–110.

14 Examples include *British Library Add. 17725* (AD 1811), *British Library Or. 430* (AD 1832), *Coptic Museum Lit. 412* (AD 1867), and *Coptic Museum Lit. 16* (AD 1928–1942).

2. THE EXCHANGE OF BLESSING

At the conclusion of the procession around the altar, the Euchologion of Hegumen ‘Abd al-Masīḥ Ṣalīb prescribes the following:

[1] واذا اكمل الكاهن الدورة السابق ذكرها يقف مكانه اولاً غربي المذبح ووجهه الى الشرق. [2] ويضع الحمل اي القربانة على يده اليسرى. [3] ويطامن رأسه لاخوته الكهنة ويقول ⲉⲩⲗⲟⲅⲓⲧⲉ اي باركوا. [4] وفي المفرد اي اذا كان الحاضر عنده كاهناً واحداً يقول ⲉⲩⲗⲟⲅⲏⲥⲟⲛ اي بارك. [5] فيطامنون هم ايضاً رؤوسهم ويجاوبونه قائلين ⲛ̀ⲑⲟⲕ ⲉⲩⲗⲟⲅⲏⲥⲟⲛ اي انتَ بارك. [6] ثم ان الكاهن يلتفت الى القربانة ويقرب اليها وعاء الخمر ويكون الشماس ممسكاً لها بيده اليمنى بلفافة حرير. [7] ويرشم الكاهن الاثنين معاً ثلاثة رشوم بمثال الصليب كالعادة.[15]

[1] And when the priest has completed the aforementioned circuit, he stands in his original place west of the altar and his face to the east. [2] And he places the lamb, that is, the oblation bread, on his left hand, [3] and bows his head to his brothers the priests, and says, “bless.”[16] [4] and in the singular, that is, if he who is present with him is one priest, he says, “bless.”[17] [5] So, they also bow their heads and answer him saying, “You bless.” [6] And the priest turns to the oblation bread and brings the vessel of wine close to it. And the deacon is to be holding it with his right hand with a silk cloth. [7] And the priest signs the two together three signings with the sign of the cross according to the custom.

Before commencing the triple blessing of the chosen offerings, the celebrant must do one more thing, namely, to ask for the blessing of his brethren the clergy that are in attendance with him. The idea of asking for a blessing before serving is very common in the Coptic tradition, and also appears in various expressions in other traditions in East and West.[18] A similar exchange takes place in the West-Syrian anaphora of JAS before the kiss, “My brethren and my masters, pray for me that my sacrifice be accepted.”[19] The East-Syrian tradition has an even more elaborate exchange, where the other clergy respond: “God the Lord of all strengthen you to fulfill his will and receive your offering and be well pleased with your sacrifice for us and for yourself and for the four corners of the world by the grace of his compassion forever, amen.”[20] Similarly, one can find close parallels in the Roman

15 Ṣalīb, ⲡⲓϫⲱⲙ ⲛ̀ⲧⲉ ⲡⲓⲉⲩⲭⲟⲗⲟⲅⲓⲟⲛ, 217–218.

16 “ⲉⲩⲗⲟⲅⲓⲧⲉ” = Gr εὐλογῆτε.

17 “ⲉⲩⲗⲟⲅⲏⲥⲟⲛ” = Gr εὐλόγησον.

18 For a useful survey of these dialogues in eastern and western traditions, see Taft and Parenti, *Il Grande Ingresso*, 476–478.

19 *LEW*, 83.

20 Ibid., 272.

Orate fratres dialogue,[21] and the dialogue in the Byzantine Rite before the anaphora.[22] As can be seen, such exchanges of blessings and permission typically take place in the pre-anaphora, as part of the series of rites of *accessus ad altare*. The appearance of this gesture in the Coptic prothesis, far removed from the pre-anaphora, is another symptom of the major shift from the old ordo to the new ordo, which caused the duplication of many pre-anaphoral elements.

Many examples in hagiography support the antiquity of this practice in the Coptic tradition. In the biography of Gregory Thaumaturgus from the Coptic Synaxarion reading on 21 Hatūr, a priest that has lusted after a woman in the congregation was advised by the wonder-working saint not to enter the sanctuary, "at the time of prayer, [when] he took the blessing from the bishop and wished to enter the sanctuary."[23] The Sahidic *Life of Paul of Tamma* has a similar exchange during the course of a miraculous liturgy in which the apostles Peter and John joined Paul of Tamma and his disciple Ezekiel in the celebration. At Peter's invitation, John approached the altar asking those present, "Pray for me, so that I may do what he commanded me."[24]

Such exchanges are certainly common at various points in the liturgy, but particularly so at the same juncture in the Ethiopian Rite. After the triple blessing in the Ethiopian prothesis, the priest turns to his assistant and joins hands with him saying, "Remember me, my father presbyter," to which the latter responds, "The Lord keep your priesthood and accept your oblation."[25] A closer look at Coptic sources would allow one to observe the relative ubiquity of this exchange at this particular juncture.

2.1. The Exchange of Blessing in Medieval Coptic Sources

As was remarked before, earlier Euchologia typically lack explicit rubrics of the kind that would likely feature such an exchange of blessings. This is true not only of manuscripts predating the *Ritual*

21 Jungmann, *Missarum Sollemnia* 2:82–90.

22 Taft and Parenti, *Il Grande Ingresso*, 476–478.

23 René Basset, *Le Synaxaire arabe jacobite (II. Mois de Hatour et de Kihak)*, PO 3.3 (13) (Turnhout: Brepols, 1982), 320.

24 Enzo Lucchesi, "Trois nouveaux fragments coptes de la vie de Paul de Tamma par Ezéchiel," in *Ægyptus Christiana: Mélanges d'hagiographie égyptienne et orientale dédiés à la mémoire du P. Paul Devos, Bollandiste*, ed. Ugo Zanetti and Enzo Lucchesi, Cahiers d'orientalisme 25 (Geneva: Patrick Cramer, 2004), 211–224, here 214 (Coptic), 220 (French).

25 *LEW*, 201. Translation is slightly modernized. Brightman's text is based mainly on *British Library Or. 545* (AD 1670–1675), fol. 24–54. See *LEW*, 112. For alternative versions of this exchange, cf. Fritsch, "The Preparation of the Gifts," 130–131.

Order of Gabriel V in the fifteenth century, but also of many posterior manuscripts, which usually feature only the priest's prayers without any shorter formulas and proclamations. In fact, the *Precious Jewel* of Ibn Sabbāʿ does not mention this exchange of blessings, nor does it mention the triple blessing of the offerings discussed below. Once again, this is because the *Precious Jewel* is unique in dividing the prothesis rite over two chapters, one ending with the procession of the oblations from the prothesis pastophorion and the next beginning with the deacon mixing the chalice.[26] The earliest source to mention the exchange of blessings is the fourteenth-century *Lamp of Darkness* of Ibn Kabar. Curiously, in the *Lamp of Darkness* this exchange takes place before the procession around the altar and immediately after the selection of the offering:

[1] ويقول اولاً باركوا ⲉⲩⲗⲟⲅⲓⲥⲟⲛ. [2] ثم يقول برشم القربان مجداً وكرامة للثالوث الى اخرها ⲟⲩⲱⲟⲩ ⲛⲉⲙ ⲟⲩⲧⲁⲓⲟ[27]

[1] And he says first "Bless," [2] then he says in signing the oblation, "Glory and honor to the Trinity" to its end.

As was seen in the previous chapter, Ibn Kabar's order of the ritual elements of this juncture is quite different even from Gabriel V a century later. This is clear here in that the exchange of blessings is situated between the selection of the offering and the procession, although the current rite—as well as the *Ritual Order*—places this exchange after the procession. Nonetheless, the common aspect in either case is that the exchange of blessing is attached to the blessing over the oblations. While in Ibn Kabar this blessing was performed immediately after the selection of the offerings, in later centuries it came to be placed after the procession. This is seen already in the *Ritual Order*, where the following description is given at the conclusion of the procession, a description essentially identical to the Euchologion of 1902:

[2] يضع الكاهن القربانة على يده اليسار ويرشمها وَيَّا وعاء الخمر جملة ثلاثة صلبان. والشماس ماسك وعاء الخمر بلفافة حرير كما شُرِح. [3] اول ذلك يقول الكاهن بعد خضوعه للكهنة اخوته وقوله لهم ⲉⲩⲗⲟⲅⲓⲥⲟⲛ يجاوبوه الكهنة ⲛ̀ⲑⲟⲕ ⲉⲩⲗⲟⲅⲓⲥⲟⲛ[28]

[1] The priest places the oblation on his left hand and signs it with the vessel of wine a total of three crosses, while the deacon carries the vessel of wine with a silk veil as was explained. [3] First, the priest says to his brethren the priests, "bless," after bowing to them, and they respond to him, "You bless."

26 *Paris BnF Ar. 207* (14th c.), fol. 122v–13r. Cf. Mistrīḥ, *Pretiosa margarita*, 180–181 (Arabic), 489 (Latin).

27 *Paris BnF Ar. 203* (AD 1363–1369), fol. 203r. Cf. Villecourt, "Les observances," 249.

28 *Paris BnF Ar. 98* (17th c.), fol. 51r–v. Cf. ʿAbdallah, *L'ordinamento*, 178 (Arabic), 365 (Italian).

As can be expected by now, a considerable degree of uniformity can be observed in manuscripts dating after the ritual regulations of Gabriel V in the fifteenth century. Judging only based on manuscripts that are detailed enough to provide information on this point, one can still observe this exchange of blessings performed after the procession consistently until the nineteenth-century manuscripts that immediately predated the Euchologion of 1902.[29] Besides this consistent witness of manuscripts from the sixteenth to the nineteenth centuries, a few manuscripts omitted this exchange altogether despite being quite detailed otherwise. These include *BAV Vatican Copt. 25* (17th c.), though this might reflect the same irregularity in the pre-*Ritual Order* era, but also some rather late ones such as *BAV Vatican Copt. 99* (AD 1718–1726), *Rylands Copt. 427* (AD 1749), and *Coptic Museum Lit. 80* (AD 1796). In one single example, the exchange of blessings is implied in the priest bowing to the other priests, although no exact text is recorded. This is found in *British Library Or. 430* (AD 1832).

That the exchange is missing from certain manuscripts can be attributed to two causes. First, such gestures, short formulas, and movements are often not included in liturgical manuscripts but are passed down through oral tradition. Second, and more specific to this case, this is a point in the ritual in which much is taking place. A procession has just concluded—or is about to begin as in the case of the *Lamp of Darkness*—deacons and assistants are holding the wine, water, and candles, while the celebrant is carrying the oblation bread. It would not be difficult to see that for practical reasons manuscript copyists may choose to eschew verbosity and rely even more on each rank knowing their respective roles through oral tradition. At any rate, in such busy situations, it is unlikely that a priest would necessarily need to glance at a manuscript before exchanging such a common blessing. After all, this is the same verbal exchange that takes place among the priests at various points in the service, and before commencing any new unit in the rite.

More importantly, the question to ask is what significance does this exchange of blessings carry at this particular point? Observing the rite unfold at this point, things certainly seem to move rather rapidly from the selection of the offering, the commemorations, the procession, and finally the exchange of blessings and the blessing of the offerings that follow. It may seem somewhat unusual to interrupt this quick flow of events in order to exchange a blessing with other priests, in what

[29] This is the case in *BAV Vatican Copt. 18* (AD 1531), *Paris BnF Copt. 30* (AD 1642), *Coptic Museum Lit. 265* (18th c.), *British Library Add. 17725* (AD 1811), *Coptic Museum Lit. 412* (AD 1867), and *British Library Or. 429* (17th/18th c.).

may appear as a distraction from the matter at hand, namely, the eucharistic offering. Finally, again to the casual observer, this point does not seem to be the beginning of a new prayer or major liturgical unit that would merit this exchange.

However, it is only from the perspective of the new ordo that this transition from procession to blessing the oblations falls within the same ritual juncture. Returning once again to the shift from the old ordo to the new ordo, it is important to recall that the procession around the altar is simply a relic of the ancient transfer of the gifts from the prothesis pastophorion, performed as a true transfer even in the fourteenth-century *Precious Jewel* of Ibn Sabbāʿ. Seen as such, it becomes clear that the point of blessing the oblations after the procession is in reality the juncture between two distinct liturgical units, the transfer of the gifts and the subsequent rites of the prothesis performed exclusively on the altar. This juncture is also the beginning of the priestly elements of the prothesis rite, those elements that are the exclusive privilege of the priests and bishops, unlike the procession itself or even the selection of the offerings, which were performed by deacons in the early Church. It is natural therefore to expect an initial request for blessing at this point before the celebrant is to begin an entirely new phase in the rite.

Finally, this may explain why in Ibn Kabar this exchange of blessings would be placed before and not after the procession. At this period, not long after the final switch from Ibn Sabbāʿ's intermediate ordo, this juncture between the transfer and the subsequent rites seems to have been quite fluid, a true "soft point" in action. Naturally, elements such as this exchange of blessings–and the blessing of the oblations that follows–may have not yet acquired their fixed place in the unfolding of the rite.

3. THE BLESSING OF THE OFFERING

That some sort of blessing would be performed before placing the eucharistic gifts on the altar should be expected. Although lacking the exact formula of this blessing, the seventh-century *Life of John of Scetis*, mentioned before in the first chapter on the location of the prothesis, describes that the saint, "Oftentimes, when he was offering the oblation, he would be seeing someone blessing the bread."[30] This remark in the *Life of John of Scetis*, brief though it is, provides more evidence than even Euchologia from the thirteenth to the fifteenth century, which as was seen repeatedly, lack any such short formulas

30 Zanetti, *Saint Jean, higoumène de Scété*, 48*.

and blessings altogether. The same is true for the *Precious Jewel* of Ibn Sabbāʿ, which glosses over the entire matter.[31]

3.1. Glory and Honor as the Sole Blessing of the Oblations

It is therefore again in Ibn Kabar's *Lamp of Darkness*, and precisely to the oldest manuscript of this work *Paris BnF Ar. 203* (AD 1363–1369), where one finds the earliest information in the medieval period for the blessing over the oblations.[32] One has to be careful not to hastily call it a *triple* blessing in this case. As was shown above in analyzing the exchange of blessings among the priests, Ibn Kabar has the following to say regarding blessing the oblations, "Then he says in signing the offering (*qurbān*), 'Glory and honor to the Trinity' to its end."[33] The same information is found in a later section of Ibn Kabar's work. In the same chapter 17 on the order of the liturgy, Ibn Kabar includes a listing of the number of crosses the priest is to sign over himself, the gifts, and the people, which also includes signing the oblations with the cross three times, while saying *Glory and Honor*.[34]

31 Despite Ibn Sabbāʿ's silence on this point, as well as on everything between the transfer of the gifts and the mixing of the chalice by the deacon, Athanasius al-Maqārī erroneously grouped together Ibn Kabar's *Lamp of Darkness* and Ibn Sabbāʿ's *Precious Jewel* as sources that include the blessing of the oblations *before* the procession. While this is true for the former, one is at a loss as to how the author reached this conclusion for the latter. See Maqārī, *Al-quddās al-ilāhī*, 1:328n54.

32 A potentially earlier source should be mentioned, although its dating is quite uncertain. The manuscript *Bodleian Hunt. 572* (13th/14th c.) was dated as such by Brightman. See *LEW*, lx. This codex contains the liturgies of Saints Basil, Gregory, Cyril, and a number of fraction prayers. In addition, fol. 238r–243v contains an Arabic chapter outlining the number of crosses that the priest is to trace over himself, the gifts, and the people throughout the liturgy, including the blessing of the gifts after their selection. However, as Achim Budde pointed out, the first section of this manuscript until fol. 55r was added later, likely to repair the older codex. See Budde, *Die ägyptische Basilios-Anaphora*, 114–115. While the alleged older portion of the manuscript has Coptic page numbers in the upper left corner of each page, both the initial part of the codex, and the chapter on the number of crosses lack such numbering, leading to the conclusion that the relevant section was also a later addition to the codex.

33 *Paris BnF Ar. 203* (AD 1363–1369), fol. 203r. Cf. Villecourt, "Les observances," 249.

34 *Paris BnF Ar. 203* (AD 1363–1369), fol. 207v. Descriptions of the number of crosses to be performed during the liturgy became a sort of common liturgical genre in medieval sources. Witnessed in the Coptic tradition at least since *The Guide to the Beginners*, the Euchologion *Bodleian Hunt. 572* (13th/14th c.), and Ibn Kabar's the *Lamp of Darkness* (14th c.), it was often copied in later Euchologia as an additional section. The same genre is attested much earlier in the Syriac tradition, where it appears in the *Synodicon* of Jacob of Edessa (AD 633–708), and the commentary on the liturgy by Moses bar Kepha (AD 813–903). See Arthur Vööbus, *The Synodicon in the West Syrian Tradition I*, CSCO 367, Scriptores Syri 161 (Louvain: Secrétariat

For Ibn Kabar, the blessing over the oblations was nothing more than the prayer *Glory and Honor*. This prayer was analyzed extensively in the previous chapter, since from the perspective of the present-day unfolding of the rite it accompanies the procession around the altar. In the previous discussion, it was noted that Ibn Kabar mentions this prayer as a blessing over the oblations before the procession, though one must be cautious not to assume that the text implied here is identical to the full-length formula pronounced today at the procession. As is demonstrated below, the *Ritual Order* of Gabriel V as well as many later manuscripts attempted to harmonize these two variant locations for the prayer *Glory and Honor* by prescribing it again after the triple blessings, albeit in an abbreviated (or older?) form. At any rate, while Ibn Kabar's Paris manuscript certainly mentions the blessing over the oblations, it is not a triple blessing as the *textus receptus*, but the more general—albeit *Trinitarian*—prayer *Glory and Honor*.

3.2. The Triple Blessing of the Oblations

However, the blessing of the oblations eventually took on a triple form, whose development is somewhat unclear. One potential early witness is *BAV Vatican Copt. 25* (17th c.) from the Scetis region. As explained previously, this Euchologion was originally produced in the fourteenth century, though the pertinent section below and the entire prothesis text is the product of a second hand from the seventeenth century. As such, it is unclear whether the text below was found as such in the original folia from the fourteenth century. This manuscript provides the full text of the blessing as follows:

[1] رشم الحمل ووعاء الابركة ثلاثة مرات.

[2] ϧⲉⲛ ⲫⲣⲁⲛ ⲙ̀ⲫⲓⲱⲧ ⲛⲉⲙ ⲡϣⲏⲣⲓ ⲛⲉⲙ ⲡⲓⲡ︦ⲛ︦ⲁ︦ ⲉⲑⲟⲩⲁⲃ ⲟⲩⲛⲟⲩϯ ⲛ̀ⲟⲩⲱⲧ. [3] ϥ̀ⲥⲙⲁⲣⲱⲟⲩⲧ ⲛ̀ϫⲉ ⲫϯ ⲫⲓⲱⲧ ⲡⲓⲡⲁⲛⲧⲟⲕⲣⲁⲧⲱⲣ ⲁⲙⲏⲛ. [4] ϥ̀ⲥⲙⲁⲣⲱⲟⲩⲧ ⲛ̀ϫⲉ ⲡⲉϥⲙⲟⲛⲟⲅⲉⲛⲏⲥ ⲛ̀ϣⲏⲣⲓ ⲓ︦ⲏ︦ⲥ︦ ⲡⲭ︦ⲥ︦ ⲡⲉⲛⲟ︦ⲥ︦ ⲁⲙⲏⲛ. [5] ϥ̀ⲥⲙⲁⲣⲱⲟⲩⲧ ⲛ̀ϫⲉ ⲡ︦ⲛ︦ⲁ︦ ⲉ︦ⲑ︦ⲩ︦ ⲙ̀ⲡⲁⲣⲁⲕⲗⲏⲧⲟⲛ ⲁⲙⲏⲛ.[35]

[1] The signing of the lamb and the vessel of wine three times: [2] In the name of the Father and the Son and the Holy Spirit, one God, [3] Blessed is God the Father the Pantocrator amen. [4] Blessed is his only-begotten Son, Jesus Christ our Lord amen. [5] Blessed is the Holy Spirit, the Paraclete amen.

du Corpus SCO, 1975), 225–226 (Syriac); Arthur Vööbus, *The Synodicon in the West Syrian Tradition I*, CSCO 368, Scriptores Syri 162 (Louvain: Secrétariat du Corpus SCO, 1975), 209–210 (English); Connolly and Codrington, *Two Commentaries on the Jacobite Liturgy*, 70 (English), 64 (Syriac). *The Guide to the Beginners* is the earliest known example of this genre in the Coptic tradition. See Graf, "Liturgische Anweisungen," 122–123, for the German translation.

35 *BAV Vatican Copt. 25* (17th c.), fol. 6r–7v.

The text of the blessing in this manuscript is identical to the *textus receptus* as well as the edition of Hegumen 'Abd al-Masīḥ in 1902.[36] As mentioned in Chapter 3 regarding the vesting rite, this Trinitarian formula of blessing–and the *Glory and Honor* prayer that follows it–is ubiquitous in the Coptic tradition.[37] In addition to its usage as the formula for blessing the vestments and the oblations, it is also used to bless the incense before placing it in the censer,[38] in the ordination rites of various ranks,[39] and for blessing the crowns in the marriage rite,[40] to name a few examples. In other words, this particular formula has been enlisted as an appropriate form of blessing for any material offering or person to be blessed as part of the rites and sacraments of the Coptic Church.

The same exact formula appears also in the *Ritual Order* of Gabriel V only a century later, according to the following rubrics following the exchange of blessings among the priests and provided in both Coptic and Arabic:

[1] ثم يقول كاملة ϧⲉⲛ ⲫⲣⲁⲛ ⲙ̀ⲫⲓⲱⲧ. [2]
ثم يرشم الرشم الأول وهو يقول ϥ̀ⲥⲙⲁⲣⲱⲟⲩⲧ
ⲛ̀ϫⲉ ⲫϯ ⲫⲓⲱⲧ ⲡⲓⲡⲁⲛⲧⲟⲕⲣⲁⲧⲱⲣ
ⲁⲙⲏⲛ، مبارك الله الاب ضابط الكل. [3] الرشم
الثاني يقول ϥ̀ⲥⲙⲁⲣⲱⲟⲩⲧ ⲛ̀ϫⲉ
ⲡⲉϥⲙⲟⲛⲟⲅⲉⲛⲏⲥ ⲛ̀ϣⲏⲣⲓ ⲓ̅ⲏ̅ⲥ̅ ⲡⲭ̅ⲥ̅ ⲡⲉⲛⲟ̅ⲥ̅
ⲁⲙⲏⲛ، مبارك الابن الوحيد يسوع المسيح ربنا
امين. [4] يرشم الرشم الثالث ويقول
ϥ̀ⲥⲙⲁⲣⲱⲟⲩⲧ ⲛ̀ϫⲉ ⲡⲓⲡ̅ⲛ̅ⲁ̅ ⲉ̅ⲑ̅ⲩ̅
ⲙ̀ⲡⲁⲣⲁⲕⲗⲏⲧⲟⲛ ⲁⲙⲏⲛ، مبارك الروح القدس
البارقليط امين.[41]

[1] Then he says fully, "In the name of the Father," [2] then signs the first signing as he says, "Blessed is God the Father the Pantocrator, amen." [3] The second signing, he says, "Blessed is his only-begotten Son, Jesus Christ our Lord, amen." [4] He signs the third signing and says, "Blessed is the Holy Spirit the Paraclete, amen."

Finally, even the later manuscript of Ibn Kabar's *Lamp of Darkness*, *Uppsala O. Vet. 12* (AD 1546), seems to have been corrected to reflect the prevalent practice of its time and place, when compared to the earlier *Paris BnF Ar. 203* (AD 1363–1369), since it contains the exact formula as seen in *BAV Vatican Copt. 25* (17th c.), and the *Ritual Order*.[42] Additionally, as one would expect as a result of the standardizations of Gabriel V, a large number of later manuscripts

36 Ṣalīb, ⲡⲓϫⲱⲙ ⲛ̀ⲧⲉ ⲡⲓⲉⲩⲭⲟⲗⲟⲅⲓⲟⲛ, 217–218.
37 See chapter 3, section 1.
38 Burmester, *The Egyptian Church*, 36.
39 Ibid., 164.
40 Ibid., 133.
41 *Paris BnF Ar. 98* (17th c.), fol. 51v. Cf. 'Abdallah, *L'ordinamento*, 178 (Arabic), 365 (Italian).
42 *Uppsala O. Vet. 12* (AD 1546), fol. 184r.

preserves the text of the formula of blessing exactly as it appears in this source.[43]

Nonetheless, the *Glory and Honor* formula remained in the rubrics, albeit assigned second place after the Trinitarian formula. This is seen for example in *BAV Vatican Copt. 25* (17th c.):

[1] ثم يضع الحمل في الصينية [2] ويقول ⲟⲩⲱⲟⲩ ⲛⲉⲙ ⲟⲩⲧⲁⲓⲟ ⲟⲩⲧⲁⲓⲟ ⲛⲉⲙ ⲟⲩⲱⲟⲩ ⲛ̀ϯⲡⲁⲛⲁⲅⲓⲁ ⲧⲣⲓⲁⲥ ⲫⲓⲱⲧ ⲛⲉⲙ ⲡϣⲏⲣⲓ ⲛⲉⲙ ⲡⲓⲡ̅ⲛ̅ⲁ̅ ⲉ̅ⲑ̅ⲩ̅ ϯⲛⲟⲩ ⲛⲉⲙ ⲛ̀ⲥⲏⲟⲩ ⲛⲓⲃⲉⲛ.[44]	[1] Then he places the lamb in the paten [2] and says: "Glory and honor, honor and glory, to the all-holy Trinity, the Father and the Son and the Holy Spirit, now and at all times."

The *Ritual Order* repeats the same prayer after the Trinitarian blessing.[45] The incipit of the prayer also appears in the *Lamp of Darkness*'s *Uppsala O. Vet. 12* (AD 1546) without any specific instructions.[46] Additionally, the recitation of *Glory and Honor* is mentioned in many later manuscripts.[47]

3.3. The Blessing in the Patriarchal Liturgy of the fifteenth century

Previously, it was seen that even the selection of the offering, a practical matter traditionally the duty of deacons had become an act of the highest solemnity by the medieval period, and certainly by the fifteenth-century patriarchal liturgy of codex *Coptic Patriarchate Lit. 74* (AD 1444).[48] In this description of the liturgy in the presence of a patriarch, it is he who chooses the offering although he does not vest until after the prothesis rite has been concluded. It is no surprise then that in the case of the blessing of the oblations as well this act is reserved for the unvested patriarch according to the following description:

43 Manuscripts that include the blessing stated explicitly include: *BAV Vatican Copt. 18* (AD 1531), *Paris BnF Copt. 30* (AD 1642), *British Library Or. 429* (17th/18th c.), *British Library Or. 431* (AD 1718), *BAV Vatican Copt. 99* (AD 1718–1726), *Rylands Copt. 427* (AD 1749), *Coptic Museum Lit. 80* (AD 1796), *Coptic Museum Lit. 265* (18th c.), *British Library Add. 17725* (AD 1811), *British Library Or. 430* (AD 1832), *Coptic Museum Lit. 412* (AD 1867), *British Library Or. 5282* (AD 1872), and *Coptic Museum Lit. 16* (AD 1928–1942).

44 *BAV Vatican Copt. 25* (17th c.), fol. 6v–7r.

45 *Paris BnF Ar. 98* (17th c.), fol. 52r. Cf. 'Abdallah, *L'ordinamento*, 178 (Arabic), 365 (Italian).

46 *Uppsala O. Vet. 12* (AD 1546), fol. 184r.

47 *Paris BnF Copt. 30* (AD 1642), *British Library Or. 429* (17th/18th c.), *BAV Vatican Copt. 99* (AD 1718–1726), *Rylands Copt. 427* (AD 1749), *Coptic Museum Lit. 80* (AD 1796), *Coptic Museum Lit. 265* (18th c.), *British Library Add. 17725* (AD 1811), *Coptic Museum Lit. 412* (AD 1867), and *Coptic Museum Lit. 16* (AD 1928–1942).

48 Mikhail, "The Liturgy *Coram Patriarcha* Revisited," 288–290.

[1] وعندما يطوف الكاهن بالقربان والخمر المذبح [2] ينزل من المذبح ويتقدم الى البطريرك ليمسح الحمل ويرشمه وكذلك الخمر [3] ثم يعود الى المذبح بالحمل.[49]

[1] And when the priest circles the altar with the bread offering and the wine, [2] he descends from the sanctuary and advances to the patriarch, in order that he may wipe the lamb and sign it and likewise the wine. [3] Then, he [the priest] returns with the lamb to the sanctuary.

A century later, the patriarchal liturgy of the codex *Baramūs 6/278* (AD 1514) published by Bishop Samuel provides similar instructions,[50] as well as the patriarchal liturgy in codex *Uppsala O. Vet. 12* (AD 1546), the later copy of Ibn Kabar's *Lamp of Darkness*,[51] though in both cases a deacon accompanies the priest in his descent and ascent back to the sanctuary. Once again then, the significance of the ritual act–and therefore the desire to reserve it for the patriarch in his presence–is met with the fact that the patriarch has not yet vested nor is he a full participant in the prothesis. The compromise that seems to be followed consistently is to bring the offerings to him at key moments, as was seen so far in the selection of the gifts and their subsequent blessing after the procession.

This again allows for an understanding of the blessing of the oblations, encountered in some form since at least the seventh-century *Life of John of Scetis*, as an important juncture in the rite of the prothesis, constituting the first truly priestly act of the rite after the selection and procession of the gifts. From this point forward, the prothesis rite is dominated by actions and prayers that have always been the exclusive duty of the priest or bishop, and thus points to the results of the clericalization of the preparation of the gifts. So critical was this perception of the prothesis as a priestly act of the highest order that it features as a theme in the popular miracle attributed to Severus of Antioch according to the Coptic Synaxarion. During his clandestine sojourn in Egypt in AD 536, he is said to have entered a church during the liturgy, dressed as a simple monk. Unaware of his presence, the priest, "raised the oblation and went around with the incense to the people," presumably in reference to the prothesis and the incense rites before the Liturgy of the Word, respectively. At the beginning of the anaphora, when the priest uncovered the gifts, he

49 *Coptic Patriarchate Lit. 74* (AD 1444), fol. 74v. Cf. Samuel, *Tartīb al-bī'a*, 1:17; Mikhail, "The Liturgy *Coram Patriarcha* Revisited," 307 (Arabic), 308 (English).

50 Samuel, *Tartīb al-bī'a*, 1:17; Mikhail, "The Liturgy *Coram Patriarcha* Revisited," 309 (Arabic), 310 (English).

51 *Uppsala O. Vet. 12* (AD 1546), fol. 188v. Cf. Villecourt, "Les observances," 277; Mikhail, "The Liturgy *Coram Patriarcha* Revisited," 310 (Arabic), 311 (English).

saw that the gifts had disappeared, at which point an angel appeared to him to inform him that this has happened, "because you dared to raise the oblations, while the patriarch is standing."[52] Clearly, by the time this story was written the prothesis rite had acquired such a solemn priestly character that its performance without some form of participation by the hierarch—celebrating or not—was deemed an unthinkable transgression. During the remainder of this work, it will become clear exactly how the sources at various times made ritual room for the present hierarch in these originally practical diaconal preparations.

3.4. The Blessing of the Offerings in East and West

Many traditions in East and West possess similar blessings to be pronounced over the eucharistic oblations, either during their preparation in the prothesis, or after their deposition on the altar in the pre-anaphora. As always however, exceptions exist, and in this case, the exception is the Syrian and Byzantine traditions.[53] It is true that the Byzantine prothesis rite commences with the the deacon saying, "Bless, master," to which the priest responds with the usual, "Blessed be our God, always, now and ever, and unto the ages of ages, amen," before he handles the *prosphora*.[54] However, this exchange is so ubiquitous as an introduction to many Byzantine-Rite services that it would be erroneous to interpret it here as a blessing meant for the oblations specifically. Later at the mixing of the chalice, the deacon says, "Bless, master the holy union," to which the priest responds, "Blessed is the union of your holy things, always, now, and ever, and unto the ages of ages, amen."[55] However, here too the blessing is—strictly speaking—over the action of mixing the wine and water, and not for the oblations as such.

Curiously, the Armenian prothesis has a formula of blessing, though it is quite different from that in the Coptic tradition. During

52 René Basset, *Le Synaxaire arabe jacobite (I. Mois de Tout et de Babeh)*, PO 1.3 (3) (Turnhout: Brepols, 1980), 314. The story is also found in the Ethiopic *Conflict of Severus* by Athanasius, cf. Edgar J. Goodspeed, *The Conflict of Severus Patriarch of Antioch by Athanasius: Ethiopic Text Edited and Translated*, PO 4.6 (20) (Turnhout: Brepols, 2003), 714. For this and other instances of this story, cf. Heinzgerd Brakmann, "Hagiographie im Dienst hierarchischer Ambitionen. Eine ägyptische Wundererzählung im Umfeld der Vita *BHO* 1062 des Severos von Antiochien," in Zanetti and Lucchesi, *Ægyptus Christiana*, 279–286.

53 For the West-Syrian *Prothesis*, see *LEW*, 71–74. Likewise, the East-Syrian prothesis, which bears many similarities to its West-Syrian counterpart, lacks any similar blessing. Cf. ibid., 249–252.

54 Ibid., 356.

55 Ibid., 357.

the prothesis, the priest prays a prayer of John Chrysostom privately, in which he petitions, "Bless now, O Lord, this presentation. Receive it on your heavenly table."[56] However, the blessing over the oblations in the Ethiopian tradition has a form nearly identical to the triple blessing in the Coptic Rite. After a series of prayers over the chalice and the spoon, the priest makes the sign of the cross over the bread, saying, "Blessed be the Lord almighty, and blessed be the only Son our Lord Jesus Christ, and blessed be the Holy Ghost the Paraclete," followed by the *Glory and Honor* formula.[57] The latter is prescribed over the chalice alone in *British Library Or. 545* (AD 1670–1675), though it is indicated for both the chalice and the bread in *British Library Or. 546* (AD 1730–1737), only a century later, perhaps indicating a certain degree of regional variety on this point. Although there are no earlier witnesses, the blessing over the oblations was likely in practice much earlier, since it clearly follows the Coptic model. Additionally, Emmanuel Fritsch included the blessings in his reconstruction of the Ethiopian preparation of the gifts before AD 1100.[58]

Likewise, the Roman Rite is rich in various blessings at the deposition of the gifts, though none is quite like the Coptic and Ethiopian blessings. At the presentation of the gifts during the offertory procession, the deacon receives the bread offering with the blessing *Acceptum sit omnipotenti Deo*, although strictly speaking, this is more of a prayer for acceptance of the offering rather than for blessing it.[59] The closest analogue comes not at the deposition of the gifts, but at the mixing of the chalice. Jungmann believed the original blessing said at this point to have been *In nomine Patris et Filii et Spiritus Sancti*, found in a missal from Saint Peter (12th c.), and another from Valencia (AD 1417). Another similar formula also invokes each person of the Trinity and is adapted from similar formulas said at the commixture before communion.[60] Nonetheless, the difference in location and purpose between this blessing and the one over the oblations in the Coptic and Ethiopian Rites renders it unlikely that anything more than mere coincidence exists with the Roman tradition. Therefore, in all likelihood, the blessing of the eucharistic oblations in the name of the Holy Trinity is a uniquely Egyptian practice, which cannot even be attributed to West-Syrian influence in the absence of further evidence.

56 Ibid., 419. Translation slightly modernized.
57 Ibid., 200–201.
58 Fritsch, "The Preparation of the Gifts," 126.
59 Jungmann, *Missarum Sollemnia*, 2:54–57.
60 Ibid., 65.

3.5. Towards the Origins of the Blessing over the Oblations

It was shown that in the seventh-century *Life of John of Scetis*, only the bread was blessed. Additionally, in the fourteenth-century *Lamp of Darkness*, the blessing is also pronounced over the oblations (*qurbān*), leaving room for interpretation as to whether this included the wine, or only the bread, an ambiguity tolerated by the Arabic term. However, the *Ritual Order* of Gabriel V is quite explicit on the matter, stating clearly that the priest is to bless both the bread and the wine with the Trinitarian blessing, followed by *Glory and Honor* as he places the bread in the paten. On the other hand, in the Ethiopian liturgy, the Trinitarian blessing is pronounced over the bread first, and then repeated again over the wine, followed finally by the *Glory and Honor* over both.[61]

First, regarding the object of the blessings, it is very likely that the pristine blessing was over the bread alone. The *Life of John of Scetis*, as well as Ibn Kabar's *Lamp of Darkness* (14th c.) already support this, in which the blessing is pronounced immediately after the selection and before the procession. Additionally, the fact that the earliest Ethiopian evidence witnesses to a blessing of the bread separately from the wine can be a further indication that the blessing over the bread may have been the original blessing, with that over the wine added later and therefore separately. One can adduce to these sources the logical argument that, since the wine and water are only mixed in the chalice, which has not yet taken place at this point in the ritual, a blessing over the wine alone would be in a sense premature and incomplete. If true, it would mean that the instructions in *BAV Vatican Copt. 25* (17th c.), represents a development in the rite that may have taken place in Scetis, to be appropriated and normalized later in the *Ritual Order*.[62]

Second, regarding the original formula of blessing, the evidence is harder to interpret. The only source that separates the Trinitarian formula from the *Glory and Honor* is the *Lamp of Darkness*, which only mentions the latter. However, it must be remembered that the two formulas–the Trinitarian blessing and the *Glory and Honor* that follows–are so closely linked in Coptic practice so as to render attempts at separating them fruitless. As remarked in Chapter 3 on the vesting rite, the two blessings appear together in the context of the *Raising of Incense* of vespers and matins both in the *Order of the Priesthood* and the *Precious Jewel*. Given this consistent link between

61 *LEW*, 200–201.

62 That is, of course, assuming the surviving text on fol. 6r–7r, copied by a later hand in the seventeenth century, is faithful to the original text from the fourteenth century copied in Scetis.

the two formulas, it is more likely that they were always utilized together for the blessing of the oblations as well. Ibn Kabar's failure to mention the Trinitarian portion of it could have been a mere shorthand for such a familiar liturgical blessing.

4. THE MIXING OF THE CHALICE

Following the blessing of the oblations and the deposition of the bread in the paten, the rubrics instruct the priest at this point to pour the wine into the chalice and add a small amount of water. This brief act is today the exclusive privelege of the celebrant priest or bishop. First, he is to take the wine from the assistant carrying it and pour it in the chalice, which has been placed previously inside the chalice throne during the altar preparation. Next, the celebrant, or one of the assistants, pours water into the empty wine vessel according to a specified ratio, and then the celebrant in turn pours this water into the chalice.[63] The rubrics of the Euchologion imply that this takes place immediately after the triple blessing of the oblations and during the deacon's proclamation "One is the holy Father."[64] In reality, the process of mixing the chalice with wine and water could take place during the *Prayer of Thanksgiving* that follows, depending on the time it takes to recite the preceding prayers or to perform the accompanying ritual acts. This practical act of mixing the chalice suggests a few questions: 1. What is the origin of the mixing of the chalice with wine and water? 2. What do the sources say about the ratio of water to wine? and 3. Who was to perform this act?

4.1. Wine in Late Antique and Islamic Egypt

Although Egypt in antiquity was known more for its beer than its winemaking, Pliny the Elder mentioned a certain type of Egyptian wine, said to be of the highest quality.[65] In fact, based on documentary evidence, beer almost disappeared from papyri and records by the fourth century. This absence may testify to the shifting nature of the documentary records, reflecting more frequently the lives of middle and upper-class Hellenized Egyptians in the metropolises. Nonetheless, the absence of beer even from Coptic documentary sources after the fourth century may in fact signal that the drinking preferences of Egyptians, irrespective of class, had by late antiquity

63 Burmester, *The Egyptian Church*, 53.

64 Ṣalīb, ⲡⲓϫⲱⲙ ⲛ̀ⲧⲉ ⲡⲓⲉⲩⲭⲟⲗⲟⲅⲓⲟⲛ, 220.

65 *Naturalis Historia* XIV.9. See Harris Rackham, *Pliny Natural History: With an English Translation in Ten Volumes*, vol. 4, books 12–16, The Loeb Classical Library 370 (Cambridge, MA: Harvard University Press, 1986), 236–237.

more or less conformed to the surrounding Mediterranean culture's preference for wine.[66] In fact, late antique Alexandria was a major conduit for wine produced in the Egyptian hinterland, which was requisitioned by the imperial government in vast quanitities. In particular, the Mareotis region near Alexandria was famous during this period for its vineyards and wine production facilities, so much so that Mareotic wine enjoyed a good reputation well after the Arab conquest.[67]

The situation in Islamic Egypt continued for some time unchanged. Paulina Lewicka has studied wine consumption in medieval Cairo in detail and has shown conclusively that the local population—including Muslims—did not easily abandon the Greco-Roman customs prevalent in late antique and Byzantine Egypt. This was so despite the impression one may gather from the episodes of prohibition described in Christian and secular histories. The first such documented prohibition on the production and consumption of wine occured during the reign of ʿAlī ibn Sulaymān al-ʿAbbāsī, the Abbasid governor of Egypt in AD 786–787 as documented in the history of Yaḥyā al-Anṭākī (11th c.),[68] as well as the slightly later prohibition during the papacy of Cosmas II (AD 851–858).[69] Later, the first ruler to attempt a similar prohibition with more determination was the Fatimid Caliph al-Ḥākim (AD 996–1021). However, even this prohibition episode was not very effective. Egyptians, soon after the disappearance of al-Ḥākim, happily returned to their centuries-long Mediterranean lifestyle.[70]

The next major episode of prohibition took place during the reign of Ṣalāḥu l-Dīn al-Ayyūbī (Saladin) (AD 1174–1193). This time, the ban was soon overturned by Saladin's own son and successor, in view of the potential revenue that could be collected in alcohol taxation.[71]

66 Roger S. Bagnall, *Egypt in Late Antiquity* (Princeton, NJ: Princeton University Press, 1993), 32. Nonetheless, according to more recent research, beer did not completely disappear from the Egyptian diet, but continued to be the more easily obtainable beverage of the working class even in the Islamic period. Cf. Paulina B. Lewicka, "Alcohol and its Consumption in Medieval Cairo. The Story of a Habit," *Studia Arabistyczne i Islamistyczne* 12 (2004): 55–98, here 56–63.

67 Christopher Haas, *Alexandria in Late Antiquity: Topography and Social Conflict*, Ancient Society and History (Baltimore, MD: Johns Hopkins University Press, 1997), 36–38.

68 Lewicka, "Alcohol and its Consumption in Medieval Cairo," 71n59. For Yaḥyā al-Anṭākī, see *GCAL*, 2:49–50.

69 *HP*, 2.1:7 (English), 5 (Arabic). This particular biography falls within the series of biographies from the mid-eighth century to the late ninth century written by John the Writer. See Swanson, *The Coptic Papacy*, xii, 27–42.

70 Lewicka, "Alcohol and its Consumption in Medieval Cairo," 71–72.

71 Ibid., 76.

Throughout these spasmodic episodes of attempted prohibition, it was clear that the actual social mores of the Egyptian in the street—be it Christian, Muslim, or Jew—were not easily influenced by governmental pressure. Largely, as Lewicka put it, "The Mediterranean-minded Egypt was not eager to adapt itself to the newly imposed Islamic circumstances, nor was it eager to sacrifice its traditional habits for the sake of the rigorous doctrinal currents."[72] The situation only changed markedly during a much later episode during the reign of Sultan al-Ašraf Barsbāy (AD 1422–1438), in which mobs participated in the ransacking of churches and the destruction of any wine containers that were found, signaling a shift in the general attitude towards alcohol.[73]

It is important to keep in mind that these attempts at prohibition were most effective in Cairo, and that very little can be said about the situation in the rest of Egypt. Studying the question of alcohol bans during the Islamic period from the perspective of the Coptic Church specifically, Mennat Allah el-Dorry found consistent archaeological evidence for the continued production of wine in areas away from the capital, and especially in monasteries.[74] Usually safer from regular government interference compared to the cities, monasteries likely continued unchallenged in their centuries-old tradition of winemaking, both for liturgical as well as commercial purposes. Even when these prohibitions were most severe, Copts found various ways to circumvent the law, including soaking raisins or even vine branches in water, or using unfermented grape juice instead of wine,[75] though, she remarks, raisin wine was not merely a coping measure, but a unique beverage in its own right.[76]

The overarching point of all the foregoing is that Egyptians by late antiquity at the latest had assimilated the prevailing customs of the surrounding Mediterranean Greco-Roman culture with respect to alcohol consumption. These customs persisted well into the Islamic period, even among the Muslim population. With this understanding of the broader social context in mind, the liturgical questions regarding the mixed chalice can be explored.

72 Ibid., 96.

73 Ibid., 89.

74 Mennat Allah El-Dorry, "Wine Production in Medieval Egypt: The Case of the Coptic Church," in *Studies in Coptic Culture: Transmission and Interaction*, ed. Mariam Ayad (Cairo: The American University in Cairo Press, 2016), 55–63, here 60.

75 Ibid.

76 Ibid., 58.

4.2. The Cup of Mixed Wine

As Robert Taft remarks, everyone in antiquity and late antiquity drank their wine mixed with water.[77] This included both pagans and Jews. Thus, when Christians of the Early Church offered up a cup of wine mixed with water, as was mentioned explicitly in the *First Apology* of Justin Martyr for example,[78] it was primarily in line with common practice at the time whenever wine was consumed. Since social customs in Egypt were consistent with those elsewhere in late antiquity, one can safely assume that the practice of adding water to the wine goes back to late antiquity there as well. However, one should be cautious not to easily assume that Egyptians preferred hot water in this context like their Mediterranean counterparts elsewhere.[79] There is simply no evidence for this, not to mention that the hot weather would make it less favorable. Only later did symbolic meanings become attached to the practice of mixing water in the chalice. Most famously, this was explained with reference to the water and blood gushing from the side of Christ on the cross, although there is at least one instance in which the commentator—Yūḥannā ibn Sabbā'—linked it to the Virgin Mary allegedly drinking only wine mixed with water during her pregnancy.[80]

Symbolic explanations aside, the exact ratio of water to wine is something that appears repeatedly in the sources, albeit without any consistency. The earliest reference to the ratio of water to wine appears in a letter of Bishop Abraham of Hermonthis (6th c.) to one of his priests. Abraham is specific that the wine is to be mixed, "Three

77 Robert F. Taft, *A History of the Liturgy of St. John Chrysostom,* vol. 5, *The Precommunion Rites,* OCA 261 (Rome: Pontificio Istituto Orientale, 2000), 441–442.

78 *1 Apol.* 65 (CPG 1073). See Munier, *Justin: Apologies pour les chrétiens,* 302–304.

79 Taft, *The Precommunion Rites,* 442.

80 *Paris BnF Ar. 207* (14th c.), fol. 123r. Cf. Mistrīḥ, *Pretiosa margarita,* 181 (Arabic), 489 (Latin). The tradition that the Virgin Mary drank wine and water during her pregnancy makes a number of appearances in the Copto-Arabic literary tradition and goes back at least to *Kitāb al-īḍāḥ* or the *Book of Elucidation* attributed to the tenth-century Sāwīrus of Ašmūnayn. The idea seems to be that Christ's own flesh and blood, which he took of the Virgin Mary, were formed by the mixture of bread, wine, and water, which she drank during her pregnancy, an idea that attempts to explain how sacramentally bread, wine, and water can change into Christ's own body and blood. For the relevant passage in the *Book of Elucidation,* see Ǧirǧis, *Al-durr al-ṯamīn fī īḍāḥ al-dīn,* 97–100. For an English translation, cf. Davis, *Coptic Christology in Practice,* 297–298.

parts wine to one part water."[81] Canon 99 of the Arabic *Canons of Ps.-Basil* is even more conservative:

[1] والذين يناولون الكاس فليعرفوا ان لا يتركوا ماء كثيراً جداً خارجاً عن الحد. [2] ولا يزيدوا على الثلث واذا كان هناك حوائج كثيرة في موضع الاستعداد فيكفي العشر.[82]

[1] And those who administer the chalice let them know not to allow very much water beyond the limit. [2] And let them not exceed a third, and if there were many vessels[83] in the place of preparation, then a tenth suffices.

While Ibn Sabbā' does not specify the ratio of wine to water, Ibn Kabar slightly indicates only a tenth of water.[84] Surprisingly, even the usually very detailed *Ritual Order* of Gabriel V only hinted at a "known proportion" in mixing the wine and water, without specifiying an exact ratio.[85] Finally, the instructions of the *editio typica* of Ṣalīb allow for a third, a quarter, or even less.[86]

Thus, it appears that despite the care taken in many sources to dictate a ratio—or range of ratios—of water to wine, there is a certain degree of diversity in the details. Certainly, the most common ratio seen in the sources is one part water to three parts wine as seen initially in the archives of Abraham of Hermonthis (6th c.), although in later centuries smaller amounts of water were allowed, even as low as one part water to ten parts wine. One may have indeed expected that the periodic and often violent episodes of governmental prohibition would have motivated a development in the opposite direction, allowing for larger amounts of water to compensate for the precious and forbidden wine. Rather, it seems that in a general sense the official rubrics and canons were not influenced by these periodic

81 Samuel Moawad, "Liturgische Hinweise in koptischen literarischen Werken," in *From Old Cairo to the New World: Coptic Studies Presented to Gawdat Gabra on the Occasion of his Sixty-Fifth Birthday*, ed. Youhanna Nessim Youssef and Samuel Moawad, Colloquia Antiqua 9 (Leuven: Peeters, 2013), 125–145, here 129. The text is found in the collection of ostraca cataloged by Walter Ewing Crum as part of the collections of the Egypt Exploration Fund as *Ostracon 14 (E.82)*. Cf. W.E. Crum, ed., *Coptic Ostraca from the Collections of the Egypt Exploration Fund, the Cairo Museum and Others* (London, 1902), 14.

82 Canon 99. *Paris BnF Ar. 251* (AD 1353), fol. 188v. Cf. Riedel, *Die Rechtsquellen*, 277.

83 This is how Wilhelm Riedel translated this word in his German translation of the canons. Cf. Riedel, *Die Rechtsquellen*, 277. While literally "حوائج" means necessities or needs, here it means required objects, i.e. utensils. See Wehr, *A Dictionary of Modern Written Arabic*, 246–247.

84 *Paris BnF Ar. 203* (AD 1363–1369), fol. 203v. Cf. Villecourt, "Les observances," 249.

85 *Paris BnF Ar. 98* (17th c.), fol. 52r. Cf. 'Abdallah, *L'ordinamento*, 178 (Arabic), 365 (Italian).

86 Ṣalīb, ⲡⲓϫⲱⲙ ⲛ̀ⲧⲉ ⲡⲓⲉⲩⲭⲟⲗⲟⲅⲓⲟⲛ, 220.

pressures. One can only surmise that if anything, this decrease in the proportion of water used may signal the gradual abandonment of the ancient social custom of mixing wine with water, and instead retaining the practice only out of loyalty to tradition, as well as for its symbolic connotations.

4.3. The Minister of the Chalice

In agreement with ancient practice, the Coptic Rite assigned the mixing of the chalice to the deacon for most of its history. This should come as no surprise, though understandably it would seem very foreign today, centuries after this duty had been transferred to the celebrant priest or bishop in a clear sign of the clericalization of the rite.[87] The previous investigation in the first two chapters of this work into the origins of the preparation of the gifts has shown clearly that the process in its earliest stages was overseen by deacons, who received the gifts of the faithful, selected what was needed, and prepared them in view of their later transfer in the pre-anaphora. Sources implying the central role of the deacons in the preparation of the gifts included the *Didascalia Apostolorum* (ca. 3rd c.), *The Apostolic Constitutions* (4th c.), The *Historia Monachorum*, the *Apostolic Tradition,* and the *Canons of Ps.-Basil*, all of which hint that the deacons prepared the gifts without any mention of the priest. Naturally, in an era before the development of the prothesis as a liturgical rite and before the adoption of the *Prothesis Prayer* as the central function of the priest, the deacons would have also mixed the chalice with wine and water as part of their duty to prepare the gifts.

In addition to the sources listed above, and which were discussed in detail in the first two chapters, one can also add Canon 99 of the Arabic *Canons of Ps.-Basil* just mentioned. The canon gives instructions on mixing the chalice, not to priests specifically, but to the more general "those who administer the chalice," which implies at least that both acts—mixing the chalice and administering it—may have been performed by more than one rank. This indeed points to the continuing role of the deacons in mixing the chalice well into the medieval period, but also indicates that the priests may have begun to perform this function as well. Nonetheless, later medieval sources of the Coptic Rite witness to the continuity of the ancient role of the deacon in this point, as is shown below.

[87] It is beyond the scope of this work to discuss all the available examples of the process of clericalization in the Coptic Rite. For the similar process that took place in the development of the Byzantine prothesis, cf. Descoeudres, *Die Pastophorien im syro-byzantinischen Osten*, 113–114.

4.3.1. The Minister of the Chalice in the Medieval Guides (14th–15th c.)

The most striking feature of Ibn Sabbāʿ's *The Precious Jewel* is that it places much emphasis on the role of the deacon in the prothesis rite. Following the selection of the oblations in the pastophorion—called the small sanctuary of oblation in the text—everything that follows in the prothesis is given its own chapter, titled, "*Concerning the Explanation of the Liturgy of the Deacon,* (في ذكر شرح قداس الشماس)."[88] One of the first acts described in this chapter is the mixing of the chalice:

[1] حينئذ يقول الشماس عن اذن الكاهن والشعب كله ناصطين [2] اسباتير اجيوس ايسيوس اجيوس ابنوما اجيون امين [3] الذى شرحها واحد هو الاب القدوس واحد هو الابن القدوس واحد هو الروح القدس القدوس [4] وهو يسكب الخمر في الكاس [5] وبعد الخمر يسيراً من الماء حتى يصير ممزوج كما كانت العذرى مريم تشربه حال حملها.[89]

[1] At that time, the deacon says by permission from the priest, while all the people are listening, [2] *īsbātīr ağiūs īsiyūs ağiūs abnūma ağiūn āmīn,* [3] whose translation is, "one is the holy Father, one is the holy Son, one is the Holy Spirit the holy," [4] as he pours the wine in the chalice, [5] and after the wine a little water, so that it becomes mixed, as the Virgin Mary used to drink it during her pregnancy.

Postponing for now a discussion of the diaconal response accompanying the mixing of the chalice, one sees here that the deacon according to Ibn Sabbāʿ poured both the wine and the subsequent water and was thus responsible completely for the mixing of the chalice. The same exact tradition is documented by Ibn Kabar in his *Lamp of Darkness* (14th c.):

[1] ويصب الشماس الخمر في الكاس بعد استنشاق رائحته والتحرز من تغيير يكون قد خالطه [2] صباً مرتباً بمثال رشم الصليب بتؤدة. [3] ويمزجه بالماء الحلو مقدار عُشره مزجاً لطيفاً [4] ويبتدي بتوحيد الثالوث.[90]

[1] And the deacon pours the wine in the chalice after inhaling its smell and watching lest a change that may have befallen it, [2] pouring ordered in the likeness of the cross without haste. [3] And he mixes it calmly with fresh water the ratio of a tenth of it, [4] and begins with unifying the Trinity.

Aside from the few additional details, such as smelling the wine before pouring it in the form of a cross, Ibn Kabar is in agreement with the

88 *Paris BnF Ar. 207* (14th c.), fol. 123r. Cf. Mistrīḥ, *Pretiosa margarita,* 181 (Arabic), 489 (Latin).

89 *Paris BnF Ar. 207* (14th c.), fol. 123r. Cf. Mistrīḥ, *Pretiosa margarita,* 181 (Arabic), 489 (Latin).

90 *Paris BnF Ar. 203* (AD 1363–1369), fol. 203v. Cf. Villecourt, "Les observances," 249.

Precious Jewel in this regard. The final remark on "unifying the Trinity" simply refers to the diaconal response that accompanies the act of pouring the wine. Likewise, the later manuscript of the *Lamp of Darkness*, *Uppsala O. Vet. 12* (AD 1546), which occasionally differs from the earlier *Paris BnF Ar. 203* (AD 1363–1369), presents identical rubrics in this case.[91]

The situation persisted even in the fifteenth century, where one finds the following in the *Ritual Order* of Gabriel V:

[1] ثم يصب الشماس الخمر في الكاس [2] وهو يقول ⲁⲅⲓⲟⲥ ⲡⲁⲧⲏⲣ ⲁⲙⲏⲛ ⲉⲓⲥ الى اخر ⲛⲓⲉⲑⲛⲟⲥ ⲧⲏⲣⲟⲩ.[92]	[1] And the deacon pours the wine in the chalice, [2] while he says, "Amen, one is the holy Father," until the end of "All nations" [Ps. 116].

This is also witnessed in the patriarchal liturgy described in the codex *Baramūs 6/278* (AD 1514), where the deacon still added the wine to the chalice, although the water was reserved for the patriarch.[93] However, clearly the role of the deacon began to diminish shortly after. Although the treatise *The Mystery of the Trinity in the Service of the Priesthood* (سر الثالوث في خدمة الكهنوت) is a work generally dependent on the *Ritual Order*, it has been adjusted on this point to reflect the increasing tendency of the clericalization of the rite:

[1] ثم يضع الخبز في الصينية والخمر في الكاس [2] والكاهن يمزجه بالماء بيده.[94]	[1] Then he [the priest] places the bread in the paten and the wine in the chalice, [2] and the priest mixes it with water with his hand.

This last remark, emphasizing that the priest is the one that mixes the water as well, already betrays a certain sensitivity, or a wish to stress a point that may not be immediately apparent to the readers. Besides this, Ǧirǧis Fīlūṯā'us 'Awaḍ, the editor of the treatise, remarks in the critical apparatus that most copies do not contain this last statement. It is clear therefore that the text was edited over time to reflect evolving practices. This must have taken place well after the seventeenth century, since even the text according to the manuscript *Paris BnF Ar. 6147* (17th c.) still lacks reference to the priest adding

91 *Uppsala O. Vet. 12* (AD 1546), fol. 184r.

92 *Paris BnF Ar. 98* (17th c.), fol. 52r. Cf. 'Abdallah, *L'ordinamento*, 178 (Arabic), 365 (Italian).

93 Samuel, *Tartīb al-bī'a*, 1:21; Mikhail, "The Liturgy *Coram Patriarcha* Revisited," 309 (Arabic), 310 (English).

94 Ǧirǧis Fīlūṯā'us 'Awaḍ, *Kitāb sirr al-ṯālūṯ fī ḫidmat al-kahanūt: Ta'līf aḥad 'ulamā' al-kanīsa al-qibṭiyya fī l-qurūn al-wūsṭā* [The book of the mystery of the Trinity in the service of the priesthood, composed by one of the scholars of the Coptic Church in the middle ages] (Cairo: Al-maṭba'a al-miṣriyya al-ahliyya al-ḥadīṯa, 1942), 9. On this obscure source and its relation to the *Ritual Order* of Gabriel V, cf. *GCAL*, 2:466.

the water.[95] What remains now is to present the remaining evidence found in the Euchologia mansucripts.

4.3.2. The Minister of the Chalice in the Euchologia

In addition to the classical medieval commentaries and guides, there exists also a large amount of evidence in the euchological manuscripts, which can help understand the historical development of this point in greater detail.

Although the treatise *The Mystery of the Trinity* may be one of the earliest witnesses to the complete clericalization of the mixing of the chalice, several other sources may witness to an intermediate stage in which the deacon poured the wine, but the priest added the water. This is the case in the following manuscripts: *BAV Vatican Copt. 18* (AD 1531), *Rylands Copt. 427* (AD 1749) from Cairo, *Suryān Lit. 485* (AD 1784), *Coptic Museum Lit. 80* (AD 1796), and *Coptic Museum Lit. 16* (AD 1928–1942) from Jerusalem. Although most of these manuscripts are posterior to the seventeenth-century manuscript of *The Mystery of the Trinity*, they more likely transmit an older and intermediate tradition that remained alive in certain locations, such as Cairo and Jerusalem.

At the same time, at least some manuscripts continued to assign the entire process to the deacon despite their late date of copying. Such is the case in *British Library Or. 429* (17th/18th c.), *BAV Vatican Copt. 99* (AD 1718–1726), and *Cairo Franciscan Center 248* (AD 1878). Two further witnesses may point to this as well, though this is only by way of conjecture. In *BAV Vatican Copt. 38* (14th c.),[96] as well as *British Library Or. 431* (AD 1718), a new section begins at the diaconal response *One is the Holy Father* titled, "*The beginning of the service of the deacon* (بدو خدمة الشماس)," perhaps echoing the similar heading in the *Precious Jewel* by Ibn Sabbāʿ. Although neither manuscript mentions anything about the pouring of the wine, the idea that at this point in the rite the deacon's particular service or liturgical role begins must point to more than simply proclaiming any particular response.

95 Unfortunately, it was not possible to examine the two earlier manuscripts of this work: *Coptic Patriarchate Lit. 367* (AD 1493) and *Coptic Patriarchate Theo. 110* (AD 1562).

96 This codex consists mostly of a Psalmodia containing the chants appropriate for the Midnight Praise office. Beginning with fol. 268r, the codex contains the *diakonika* or diaconal responses for the liturgy. According to Achim Budde, the codex is a fourteenth-century copy with a later hand from the seventeenth century responsible for a portion of it. Inspection of the diaconal part of the manuscript reveals that the list of popes in the diptychs ends with Gabriel IV (AD 1370–1378). See Budde, *Die ägyptische Basilios-Anaphora*, 117.

Finally, the majority of later manuscripts testify to the solidification of the practice whereby the priest is the sole party responsible for pouring the wine and adding the water. This is the case in the following manuscripts: *Coptic Museum Lit. 344* (AD 1752), *Coptic Museum Lit. 265* (18th c.), *British Library Or. 430* (AD 1832), and *Coptic Museum Lit. 412* (AD 1867). Thus, this overview of the mixing of the chalice in the sources allows for the conclusion that the ancient tradition of allowing the deacon to pour the wine and the water in the chalice persisted in the Coptic Rite until some time between the fifteenth and the sixteenth centuries as witnessed in medieval commentaries up to the *Ritual Order*. This likely changed gradually to where the deacon still poured the wine, while the priest has become responsible for mixing the water in the appropriate ratio, as can be seen already in the sixteenth-century *BAV Vatican Copt. 18* (AD 1531). Finally, some time after the seventeenth century at the earliest and certainly by the eighteenth century, the entire ritual became the sole privilege of the priest, which remains the practice currently.

4.3.3. The Minister of the Chalice in East and West

As in the Coptic Rite so also in other traditions in East and West, the mixing of the chalice–and originally the entire preparation of the gifts–used to be the sole responsibility of the deacons. Nowhere is this more apparent than in the Byzantine tradition. The earliest Constantinopolitan evidence for a Great Entrance procession in the *Sermo de paschate et de ss. eucharistia* attributed to Patriarch Eutychius (AD 552–565, 577–582) mentions "the recently mixed chalice (κερασθὲν ἀρτίως ποτήριον)."[97] The fact that the deacons are said to bring this recently mixed chalice naturally leads to the conclusion that it is the deacons who also did the mixing. This is confirmed by the majority of later Byzantine liturgical commentaries, such as the *Hisrtoria Ecclesiastica* of Patriarch Germanus I of Constantinople (AD 715–730) in its ninth-century interpolation by Anastasius the Librarian,[98] and the *Protheoria* of Nicholas of Andida (11th c.), among other sources. The sole exception is Symeon of Thessaloniki (14th c.), who forbids the deacons to do the prothesis.[99]

Gradually, the Byzantine prothesis became increasingly clericalized, with acts initially performed by deacons slowly assigned to the priest. This process, according to Pott and Descoeudres, originated in

97 *De paschate et ss. eucharistia* 8 (CPG 6939) (PG 86.2: 2400–2401).

98 *Historia Ecclesiastica* 22 (CPG 8023). Cf. Meyendorff, *On the Divine Liturgy,* 72–73.

99 Taft and Parenti, *Il Grande Ingresso*, 465.

monastic circles and was finalized by the fourteenth century.[100] However, even after these developments, the mixing of the chalice remained—and remains today—the duty of the deacon, and is in fact the sole role of the deacon in the current Byzantine prothesis rite.[101]

By contrast, many other eastern traditions no longer allow the deacon to prepare the chalice. The current rubrics for the West-Syrian prothesis only mention the priest as the sole preparer of the gifts, including the mixing of the chalice.[102] This is contrary to the consistent witness of history, not only ancient and universal custom, but specifically Syrian sources such as the liturgical homilies of Narsai (5th c.), which imply that the deacons alone prepared and transferred the gifts much like the *Sermo* of Eutychius.[103] More explicitly, a canon attributed to John of Tella (6th c.) has clear instructions for the deacons regarding the mixing of the chalice.[104] Curiously, the East-Syrian preparation of the gifts according to a manuscript from the district of Jilu and utilized by Brightman retains echoes of the diaconal role, where the priest "goes out of the altar to the place of the deacon to mix the chalice."[105] Finally, the Ethiopian preparation of the gifts, always the closest to the Coptic, allowed the deacon to pour the wine in the chalice at least until the late seventeenth century, as seen in the rubrics of *British Library Or. 545* (AD 1670–1675).[106] However, as Emmanuel Fritsch points out, the current rubrics instruct the deacon to hand the wine to the priest—much like the current Coptic custom—who is then to pour it in the chalice. The rubrics assigning this to the deacon also appear in another seventeenth-century manuscript, *Uppsala Or. Ethiop. 20–23* (17th c.).[107]

The Roman Rite provides a peculiar parallel to some of our Coptic sources. The pouring of the wine in the chalice to this day remains the function of a priest or deacon. Historically, it was the duty of the deacon to do so before handing the chalice to the priest at the offertory.[108] In fact, many sources attest to the deacon not only

[100] Descoeudres, *Die Pastophorien im syro-byzantinischen Osten*, 114; Pott, *Byzantine Liturgical Reform*, 210.

[101] Descoeudres, *Die Pastophorien im syro-byzantinischen Osten*, 81.

[102] *LEW*, 71.

[103] R.H. Connolly, *The Liturgical Homilies of Narsai: Translated into English with an Introduction*, Texts and Studies Contributions to Biblical and Patristic Literature 8.1 (Cambridge: Cambridge University Press, 1909), 3.

[104] Rahmani, *Les liturgies orientales et occidentales*, 28–29. Cf. Varghese, "Early History of the Preparation Rites," 130.

[105] *LEW*, 251.

[106] Ibid., 199.

[107] Fritsch, "The Preparation of the Gifts," 123n51.

[108] Jungmann, *Missarum Sollemnia*, 2:54n63.

pouring the wine, but also offering the chalice on the altar.[109] Other sources have the subdeacon pour the wine in the chalice, as mentioned in the ordo of the Lateran Basilica (ca. AD 1140), Durandus (14th c.), and the *Ordinarium of Laon* (ca. AD 1400).[110] What is interesting however is the practice of reserving the adding of the water to the priest, which likely has to do with the symbolism of the mixture vis-à-vis the crucifixion, which ensured the practice a high degree of solemnity and importance. Jungmann identifies this practice in a number of sources, including Bonizo of Sutri's *De vita christiana* (11th c.), the *Ordo ecclesiae Lateranensis* (mid-12th c.), and a sermon by Pope Innocent III (AD 1198–1216) among many other sources.[111] However, this distinction in who pours the wine and the water must not have been widespread. Although it is explicitly stated as late as a fifteenth-century Graz Missal, the Benedictine *Liber ordinarius of Liége* allows any server to pour the wine and water.[112] As far as can be established, this is the only other instance besides the few Coptic witnesses of the sixteenth to nineteenth centuries where the water is given particular significance and reserved for the priest. Although there are no explicit commentaries from the Coptic tradition to provide the reason for this practice, one can presume that it had to do with the same understanding of the mixture as symbolic of the water and blood that gushed from Christ's side on the cross.

In a general sense, it is clear that the mixing of the chalice has consistently been the responsibility and privilege of the deacons everywhere. Without a doubt, this stemmed from the ancient arrangement attested at least since Justin's second-century *Apology*, in which the entire process of preparation of the gifts was within the purview of the deacons.[113] What occurred later in all places was one of two possibilities: 1. The mixing of the chalice remained a diaconal act as in the Byzantine and Roman traditions, or 2. The act was taken up by the priest as part of the general movement towards clericalization, as seen in the Syrian, Coptic, and Ethiopian traditions.

4.3.4. The Response Accompanying the Mixing of the Chalice

Whether the deacon mixes the chalice—according to earlier sources—or the priest does so after the blessing of the oblations, the deacon responds with the following response:

109 Ibid., 57.
110 Ibid., 60.
111 Ibid., 64.
112 Ibid.
113 See Chapter 2, Section 1.1.

[1] ⲓⲥ ⲡⲁⲧⲏⲣ ⲁⲅⲓⲟⲥ ⲓⲥ ⲩⲓⲟⲥ ⲁⲅⲓⲟⲥ ⲉⲛ ⲡⲛⲉⲩⲙⲁ ⲁⲅⲓⲟⲛ ⲁⲙⲏⲛ. [2] ⲉⲩⲗⲟⲅⲏⲧⲟⲥ ⲕⲩⲣⲓⲟⲥ ⲟ ⲑⲉⲟⲥ ⲓⲥ ⲧⲟⲩⲥ ⲉⲱⲛⲁⲥ ⲁⲙⲏⲛ. [3] ⲛⲓⲉⲑⲛⲟⲥ ⲧⲏⲣⲟⲩ ⲥⲙⲟⲩ ⲡ̅ⲟ̅ⲥ̅ ⲙⲁⲣⲟⲩⲥⲙⲟⲩ ⲉ̀ⲣⲟϥ ⲛ̀ϫⲉ ⲛⲓⲗⲁⲟⲥ ⲧⲏⲣⲟⲩ [4] ϫⲉ ⲁ ⲡⲉϥⲛⲁⲓ ⲧⲁϫⲣⲟ ⲉ̀ϩⲣⲏⲓ ⲉ̀ϫⲱⲛ ⲟⲩⲟϩ ϯⲙⲉⲑⲙⲏⲓ ⲛ̀ⲧⲉ ⲡ̅ⲟ̅ⲥ̅ ϣⲟⲡ ϣⲁ ⲉⲛⲉϩ ⲁⲙⲏⲛ ⲁⲗⲗⲏⲗⲟⲩⲓⲁ.[114]	[1] One is the holy Father, one is the holy Son, one is the Holy Spirit, amen. [2] Blessed is the Lord God, unto the ages amen. [3] Praise the Lord, all nations. Let all the peoples praise him. [4] For his mercy has been firmly established upon us, and the truth of the Lord endures forever, amen alleluia [Ps. 116:1–2].

This is in turn followed by the congregation's chanting of the *doxa:* "Glory to the Father, and the Son and the Holy Spirit, both now and ever, and unto the ages of ages, amen," a response that appears so consistently in the sources so as to demand no particular discussion or analysis.

Unlike the mixing of the chalice itself, which has been shown to have shifted from the deacon to the priest, this response has been very stable in the sources, both in its assignment to the deacon, as well as its text, minor variants notwithstanding. As was shown above, the text was stated explicitly in Ibn Sabbāʿ's *Precious Jewel* (14th c.), albeit only up to the end of the first clause [1].[115] Ibn Kabar, while not including the text or any portion thereof, referred to it in the deacon "unifying the Trinity," as he pours the wine.[116] In the *Ritual Order* of Gabriel V (15th c.), the text includes the incipit of the first clause, "Amen, one is the holy Father," and the incipit of Psalm 116 that follows in Coptic, "[Praise the Lord] all nations (ⲛⲓⲉⲑⲛⲟⲥ ⲧⲏⲣⲟⲩ)."[117]

The earliest manuscript to include the full text of the response is *Rylands Copt. 426* (13th c.),[118] followed by the diaconal manuscript *BAV Vatican Copt. 28* (AD 1306), which begins with the text in parallel Coptic and Arabic columns under the heading, "The Service of the Deacon (ⲡⲓϣⲉⲙϣⲓ ⲛ̀ⲧⲉ ⲡⲓⲇⲓⲁⲕⲱⲛ)."[119] The same occurs in the fifteenth-century diaconal *BAV Vatican Copt. 27* (15th c.).[120] Although these two earliest diaconal sources present no peculiarities compared

114 Ṣalīb, ⲡⲓϫⲱⲙ ⲛ̀ⲧⲉ ⲡⲓⲉⲩⲭⲟⲗⲟⲅⲓⲟⲛ, 221. The Greek portion of this response [1] and [2] are provided by Burmester, corrected to proper Greek orthography as such: "Εἷς Πατὴρ ἅγιος, εἷς Υἱὸς ἅγιος, ἓν Πνεῦμα ἅγιον ἀμήν. Εὐλογητὸς Κύριος ὁ Θεὸς εἰς τοὺς αἰῶνας ἀμήν." See Burmester, "The Greek Kīrugmata," 370.

115 *Paris BnF Ar. 207* (14th c.), fol. 123r. Cf. Mistrīḥ, *Pretiosa margarita*, 181 (Arabic), 489 (Latin).

116 *Paris BnF Ar. 203* (AD 1363–1369), fol. 203v. Cf. Villecourt, "Les observances," 249.

117 *Paris BnF Ar. 98* (17th c.), fol. 52r. Cf. ʿAbdallah, *L'ordinamento*, 178 (Arabic), 365 (Italian).

118 Rodwell, *The Liturgies of S. Basil, S. Gregory, and S. Cyril*, 25–26.

119 *BAV Vatican Copt. 28* (AD 1306), fol. 1r.

120 *BAV Vatican Copt. 27* (15th c.), fol. 255r.

to the *textus receptus*, later witnesses display a few interesting features. One such feature is the omission of the adjective *one* in the Arabic translation attested in *British Library Add. 17725* (AD 1811), rendering the text, "Holy is the Father, Holy is the Son, Holy is the Holy Spirit Amen (قدوس الاب قدوس الابن قدوس الروح القدس امين)."[121] Another tendency is to omit the *Blessed* clause [2], as seen in *Rylands Copt. 426* (13th c.), *BAV Vatican Copt. 18* (AD 1531), *BAV Vatican Copt. 38* (14th c.), and *British Library Or. 431* (AD 1718). In one case, *Coptic Museum Lit. 265* (18th c.), the scribe wrote Psalm 116 initially before crossing it out to make room for the *Blessed* clause, while *Coptic Museum Lit. 462* (19th c.) includes only the first clause [1]. This omission may not be a simple scribal oversight after all, since the response in the Ethiopian prothesis lacks this *Blessed* clause as well.[122] In most manuscripts, the response is followed by the congregational *Glory to the Father*, which poses no interpretative issues.

Minor textual errors aside, certainly the most intriguing question surrounding the response is its very existence in the prothesis. Comparison with other traditions demonstrates that the response bears no resemblance to anything similar said at the mixing of the chalice. In the Byzantine tradition, the deacon says, "Bless, master the holy union," to which the priest responds, "Blessed is the union of your holy things, always, now, and ever, and unto the ages of ages, amen."[123] The West-Syrian tradition has the priest pronounce the following much more suitable prayer at the mixing: "Our Lord Jesus Christ was crucified between two robbers in Jerusalem and was pierced in his side with the spear and there flowed out therefrom blood and water and he that saw it bare record and we know that his record is true."[124] Although the East-Syrian formula mentions the Holy Trinity, this is likely given the prescription to pour the wine in the likeness of the cross, and at any rate this is preceded by a reference to the crucifixion similar to the West-Syrian one: "The precious blood of our savior is poured into this chalice."[125] The only exception occurs in the Ethiopian prothesis, the one most likely to follow the Coptic arrangement, although even there the response is not associated with the mixing of the chalice, but is placed in the form of a dialogue between the priest and the people immediately before the enarxis.

Therefore, one must question the origins of this response in the Coptic prothesis and its very association with the mixing of the chalice. To be sure, this has to do once more with the hypothetical pre-

[121] *British Library Add. 17725* (AD 1811), fol. 9v.
[122] *LEW*, 199.
[123] Ibid., 357.
[124] Ibid., 71.
[125] Ibid., 251.

thirteenth century origins of the practice, since most witnesses of the Northern Egyptian Coptic liturgy are consistent in its inclusion in the same location it is found today. One must also distinguish between the first two clauses [1] and [2] and the recitation of Psalm 116 that follows. Aside from the natural distinction in content and source between a Trinitarian blessing such as "One is the holy Father," and the Psalm that follows, at least one manuscript–*BAV Vatican Copt. 28* (AD 1306)–makes this distinction clear by separating the psalm from the remainder of the response by the heading, "Psalm 116 (ⲯⲁⲗⲙⲟⲥ ⲣⲓⲋ)."[126]

One possible theory could relate to the blending–or rather blurring–of the lines between the prothesis and the enarxis that took place after the shift from the old ordo to the new ordo. As a result, elements of the enarxis may have come to be performed during the prothesis and even before the *Prothesis Prayer*. It is likely then that Psalm 116 could be one such element that may have originally belonged to the enarxis. This may already be hinted at even in the later manuscript tradition. In *British Library Or. 431* (AD 1718) and *British Library Add. 17725* (AD 1811), this response is placed as the beginning of a new section of the formulary titled in Coptic and Arabic, "The Service of the Deacon (ⲡⲓϣⲉⲙϣⲓ ⲛ̀ⲇⲓⲁⲕⲟⲛ),"[127] and, "The beginning of the holy liturgy (بدوا القداس المقدس),"[128] respectively. The Ethiopian prothesis lends support to this idea as well, with its placing of the response immediately before the enarxis and away from the mixing of the chalice. Finally, the very idea of Psalm 116 as an enarxis or introit of some sort is not foreign to the current Coptic Rite, where this very psalm is chanted at the beginning of the cathedral office of *Vespers Praise* that precedes the *Vespers Raising of Incense* and practically ushers in the beginning of the liturgical day.[129]

As for the initial part of the response, "One is the holy Father," it is clearly identical to the congregation's response to the elevation and *sancta sanctis* in the pre-communion rites. In its later location in the pre-communion, the Trinitarian text of this response represents the later recension, in contrast to the earlier Christological recension, "One is holy, one Lord, Jesus Christ, to the glory of God the Father," which is still in use in the Byzantine liturgies.[130] This Trinitarian form is attested as early as Theodore of Mopsuestia (4th c.) and the *Homilies* of Narsai (5th c.), and was soon adopted throughout the

126 *BAV Vatican Copt. 28* (14th c.), fol. 2v.
127 *British Library Or. 431* (AD 1718), fol. 5v.
128 *British Library Add. 17725* (AD 1811), fol. 9v.
129 Mikhail, "On Evening Worship in Egypt," 89; Taft, *The Liturgy of the Hours*, 255.
130 On the history of this response in its two traditions–the Christological and Trinitarian–see Taft, *The Precommunion Rites*, 240–248.

Syrian and Egyptian liturgical regions. Naturally, with an acclamation attested so early in multiple traditions as a response to the even more ancient call to communion, the *sancta sanctis*, one has to conclude that its presence in the prothesis must be a duplicate and not its original location. If true, it would be more plausible that this duplication was intended for the prothesis and not the enarxis, given the association of both the prothesis and the pre-communion rites with the eucharistic gifts. Thus, what originally was a people's response to the call for communion may have been slowly adopted as an acclamation over the gifts that were just deposited on the altar and the chalice that was recently mixed. The theory that the response is unoriginal in the prothesis may also explain why its assignment varied from the deacon in the Coptic Rite to the priest in the Ethiopian Rite.

5. THE PRAYER OF THANKSGIVING

The people's chanting of the *doxa* is followed by the celebrant's praying of the *Prayer of Thanksgiving*, a prayer found with some degree of variation in its text both in the Coptic tradition and in the Alexandrian tradition of Melkite MARK. This prayer stands as the next element in the Euchologia. Even in those earlier manuscripts that lack rubrics and formulas for the selection of the offering, the procession, and the blessings—and which generally predate the fifteenth-century *Ritual Order* of Gabriel V—the *Prayer of Thanksgiving* is usually found immediately after the prayers accompanying the altar preparation, discussed previously in the third chapter. The *Prayer of Thanksgiving* is interesting in terms of its proper or pristine location in the Coptic liturgy. From the perspective of the casual observer—or even the experienced practitioner—of the Coptic Rite, the prayer is easily perceived as a proper and natural element of the prothesis. First, in actual practice, the celebrant can often be seen mixing the chalice while reciting this prayer, which gives the impression of some kind of connection between word and act. Second, the prayer precedes two ritual elements that are certainly part of the prothesis: the *Prothesis Prayer*, and the covering of the gifts, further strengthening the perception that everything preceding—the *Prayer of Thanksgiving* included—falls within the prothesis. This common perception is further confirmed by examining many recent works of commentary on the Coptic liturgy, which usually feature the prayer as one of the elements of the prothesis, or the presentation of the lamb as it is usually titled in Arabic.[131]

However, as the analysis below will demonstrate, the *Prayer of Thanksgiving* is another example of a ritual element that originally belonged to the enarxis or the beginning of the public prayers of the liturgy. As was seen above regarding Psalm 116, the *Prayer of Thanksgiving* has become awkwardly placed within the prothesis rite as a result of the profound shift from the old ordo to the new ordo in the unfolding of the Coptic liturgy.

5.1. The Title of the Prayer

In the Coptic tradition, the majority of the manuscripts give this prayer the Coptic title ⲟⲩⲉⲩⲭⲏ ⲛ̀ϣⲉⲡϩⲙⲟⲧ, or the Arabic صلاة الشكر, both meaning: *A Prayer of Thanksgiving*. This is true for the ubiquitous post-fifteenth century manuscripts that have been examined,[132] as well as most pre-fifteenth century ones that pre-date the *Ritual Order* of Gabriel V.[133] Nonetheless, some minor variants do occur in the

[131] Examples to demonstrate this are many. Some of the more famous Arabic commentaries on the Coptic liturgy include: Youhanna Salāma, *Al-la'āli' al-nafīsa fī šarḥ ṭuqūs wa-mu'taqadāt al-kanīsa* [The precious pearls in the explanation of the rites and beliefs of the Church], 3rd ed., vol. 1 (Cairo: Maktabat Mār Ǧirǧis bi-šīkūlānī, 1965), 337. Mattā'us, *The Spirituality of the Rites of the Holy Liturgy*, 105–106. In his major work on the Eucharist originally published in 1977, Hegumen Mattā al-Miskīn frequently interpreted the prayer as a form of consecration over the chalice in the tradition of Jewish and early Christian thanksgiving over the cup at meals. This idea, together with the broader topic of interpreting the prothesis as a self-contained anaphora is discussed at length in Excursus 3 of the present work. See Mattā al-Miskīn, *Al-ifḫāristiyyā 'ašā' al-rabb* [The Eucharist the supper of the Lord], 3rd ed. (Wādī al-Naṭrūn: Dayr al-qiddīs anbā Maqār, 2007), 309n9; 570, 572, 641. Following largely the same interpretation, Fr. Athanasius al-Maqārī included the prayer in his analysis of the prothesis as well, making no point that it may not originally belong to this rite. Cf. Al-Maqārī, *Al-quddās al-ilāhī*, 1:341–346.

[132] These include *Paris BnF Copt. 28* (13th/14th c.), fol. 5v, *Paris BnF Copt. 24* (15th c.), fol. 3v, *Paris BnF Copt. 31* (15th c.), fol. 5r, *Paris BnF Copt. 25* (15th/16th c.), fol. 6v, *Paris BnF Copt. 26* (before AD 1523), fol. 8v, *Paris BnF Copt. 73* (AD 1528), fol. 9r, *BAV Vatican Copt. 18* (AD 1531), fol. 5v, *Suryān Lit. 469* (before AD 1623), fol. 8r, *Paris BnF Copt. 29* (AD 1629), fol. 6r, *BAV Vatican Copt. 25* (14th c.), fol. 7r, *British Library Or. 429* (17th/18th c.), fol. 9v, *BAV Vatican Copt. 99* (AD 1718–1726), fol. 80r, *BAV Vatican Copt. 78* (AD 1722), fol. 7r, *British Library Or. 8778* (AD 1726), fol. 7v, *Rylands Copt. 427* (AD 1749), fol. 11v, *Coptic Museum Lit. 80* (AD 1796), fol. 7v, *British Library Add. 17725* (AD 1811), fol. 10r, *Beinecke Copt. 21* (AD 1877), fol. 70v, *Coptic Museum Lit. 462* (19th c.), fol. 61r, and *Coptic Museum Lit. 16* (AD 1928–1942), fol. 3v.

[133] *BAV Vatican Copt. 17* (AD 1288), fol. 5v, *Rylands Copt. 426* (13th c.). See Rodwell, *The Liturgies of S. Basil, S. Gregory, and S. Cyril*, 26, *Bodleian Ind. Inst. Copt. 4* (13th/14th c.), fol. 4v. See Malan, *The Divine ΕΥΧΟΛΟΓΙΟΝ*, 3, *Bodleian Hunt. 572*

manuscripts.[134] The near unanimity of this title is a function of its opening line in the Coptic tradition, a call to give thanks to God for his protection and salvation.

The only exception in the Coptic tradition occurs in the important manuscript *Bodleian Hunt. 360* (13th c.), where the title in fol. 9r reads, "The First Prayer of the Mornings (ϯϩⲟⲩⲓϯ ⲛ̀ⲉⲩⲭⲏ ⲛ̀ⲧⲉ ϩⲁⲛⲁⲧⲟⲟⲩⲓ, الصلاة الاولى للغدوات). This title has support as far back as the prayers of Sarapion of Thmuis, where Prayer 19 is titled, "The First Prayer of Sunday (Εὐχὴ πρώτη κυριακῆς)," though the similarity between the two prayers ends there.[135] Thus, it has become customary to refer to this prayer as the *First Prayer of the Morning* in scholarship on the Melkite tradition, though strictly speaking the title is not supported in any of the known manuscripts of Melkite MARK. These include the Messina Roll, *Messina Gr. 177* (11th c.), *BAV Vatican Gr. 1970* (12th c.), *BAV Vatican Gr. 2281* (AD 1207), and *Greek Orthodox Patriarchate of Alexandria 173/36* (AD 1586), otherwise known as the *Pegas Manuscript*.[136] Although by far the title most common in Coptic sources is the *Prayer of Thanksgiving*, and is retained here in fidelity to the sources, the title *First Prayer of the Morning* is much more indicative of the proper location and function of this important Alexandrian prayer.

5.2. The Text of the Prayer

To begin with, below is the *textus receptus* of the *Prayer of Thanksgiving*. Upon comparison of all the available Coptic Euchologia, it was found that the text has been very stable since its

(13th/14th c.), fol. 6v, *Paris BnF Copt. 82* (AD 1307), fol. 5r, *BAV Borgia Copt. 7* (AD 1379), fol. 8v, *Bodleian Marsh 5* (14th c.), fol. 4v, and *BAV Vatican Copt. 24* (14th c.), fol. 9v.

134 Examples include the following: الشبهموت *al-šibihmūt* from the initial verb in the Coptic text of the prayer ⲙⲁⲣⲉⲛϣⲉⲡϩⲙⲟⲧ. See *Coptic Patriarchate Lit. 74* (AD 1444), fol. 74v, *BAV Vatican Copt. 18* (AD 1531), fol. 127v, *Coptic Museum Lit. 344* (AD 1752), fol. 36r, *Coptic Museum Lit. 265* (18th c.), fol. 27r, *British Library Or. 430* (AD 1831), fol. 40v, *Coptic Museum Lit. 412* (AD 1867), fol. 69r. One manuscript has, "The Prayer of Thanksgiving to the Father (صلاة الشكر للاب)," found in *Paris BnF Copt. 39* (15th c.), fol. 9v. Both *Paris BnF Copt. 30* (AD 1642), fol. 12v, and *Coptic Patriarchate Lit. 331* (AD 1678), fol. 11r have, "The Prayer of Thanksgiving (اوشية الشكر)," using an Arabic derivation from the Coptic ⲉⲩⲭⲏ [Gr = εὐχή], rather than the native Arabic word for prayer [Ar = صلاة]. Cf. Graf, *Verzeichnis*, 16.

135 Johnson, *The Prayers of Sarapion of Thmuis*, 70–71.

136 Cuming, *The Liturgy of St Mark*, xxix–xxxi. For the most recent dating of these manuscripts, cf. Taft and Parenti, *Il Grande Ingresso*, 704–710. Of the six manuscripts of Melkite MARK found in the *Sinai New Finds* and published by Michael Zheltov, only one, parchment roll *Sinai Gr. NE/E66* (12th/13th c.) opens with the last line of the prayer, thus rendering it of little use for an analysis of the title and text. Cf. Zheltov, "The Byzantine Manuscripts of the Liturgy of Mark," 802.

earliest complete witnesses in the thirteenth-century manuscripts, though the Arabic translation across mansucripts is never uniform, and usually betrays the individual and local attempts behind each codex. Thus, the text is presented here using the Euchologion of 1902:

> [1] *Priest*: Let us give thanks to the beneficent and merciful God, the Father of our Lord, God, and Savior Jesus Christ. [2] For he has protected us, helped us, kept us, accepted us to himself, spared us, supported us, and has brought us to this hour. [3] Let us also ask the Pantocrator our God to keep us this holy day and all the days of our life in all peace.
>
> [4] *Deacon*: Pray. *People*: Lord have mercy
>
> [5] *Priest*: O Master, Lord, God the Pantocrator, the Father of our Lord, God, and Savior Jesus Christ, [6] we thank you for everything, concerning everything, and in everything, [7] for you have covered us, helped us, kept us, accepted us to yourself, spared us, supported us, and have brought us to this hour.
>
> [8] *Deacon*: Pray that God may have mercy on us, have compassion on us, hear us, help us, and receive the entreaties and prayers of his saints from them on our behalf for the good at all times, and to make us worthy to receive of the communion of his holy and blessed mysteries for the forgiveness of our sins. *People*: Lord have mercy.
>
> [9] *Priest*: Therefore, we ask and entreat your goodness, O lover of mankind, grant us also to complete this holy day and all the days of our life in all peace and your fear. [10] All envy, all temptation, all the work of Satan, the counsel of wicked men and the rising up of enemies, hidden and manifest, take them away from us, and from all your people, and from this table,[137] and from this, your holy place. [11] But those things which are good and profitable do provide for us, for it is you who have given us the authority to tread on serpents and scorpions, and upon all the power of the enemy [Lk 10:19] [12] And lead us not into temptation, but deliver us from the evil one [Mt 6:13], through the grace, compassion and love of mankind, of your only-begotten Son, our Lord, God, and Savior, Jesus Christ. [13] Through whom the glory, the honor, the dominion, and the worship are due unto you, with him and the Holy Spirit, the

137 Modern Euchologia include additional phrases here depending on the context in which the prayer is recited. For example, during a baptism, "and from this font," during the rite of matrimony, "and from this vestment," and in a funeral, "and from this soul." See Ṣalīb, ⲡⲓϫⲱⲙ ⲛ̀ⲧⲉ ⲡⲓⲉⲩⲭⲟⲗⲟⲅⲓⲟⲛ, 27–28.

giver of life, who is of one essence with you, now and at all times, and unto the age of all ages, amen.[138]

The *Prayer of Thanksgiving* is also known in the Alexandrian Melkite tradition, where it is found in some manuscripts of Melkite MARK. In his critical edition of MARK, Geoffrey Cuming compared the text of this prayer in the two main manuscripts of this liturgy, *BAV Vatican Gr. 2281* (AD 1207) and *BAV Vatican Gr. 1970* (12th c.).[139] His comparison shows clearly that, while the former is somewhat younger than the latter, it nonetheless transmits a more ancient version of MARK, particularly in this prayer. For example, *BAV Vatican Gr. 1970* (12th c.) thanks God for having made us worthy to stand before him seeking forgiveness of sins, which is entirely lacking from *BAV Vatican Gr. 2281* (AD 1207). Also lacking from the latter is the petition to complete this day with all joy, health, salvation and sanctification.[140]

This prayer is also found in Arabic translation in another Melkite Alexandrian source unknown to Cuming, the codex *Sinai Ar. 237* (13th c.), a sort of encyclopedic collection of liturgical texts. Among its many contents, the codex contains an Arabic translation of Melkite MARK, in which the prayer appears, albeit written out of place at the conclusion of the formulary. Below is a comparison of the Greek text of the prayer and the Arabic witness of *Sinai Ar. 237* (13th c.):

BAV Vatican Gr. 2281 (AD 1207)	*Sinai Ar. 237* (13th c.)
[1] Δέσποτα Κύριε ὁ Θεός ἡμῶν ὁ παντοκράτωρ, ὁ Πατὴρ τοῦ Κυρίου καὶ Θεοῦ καὶ Σωτῆρος ἡμῶν Ἰησοῦ Χριστοῦ, εὐχαριστοῦμέν σοι κατὰ πάντα καὶ διὰ πάντων καὶ ἐν πᾶσιν,	[1] ايها السيد الاله ربنا والاهنا ماسك الكل وضابطه ابو ربنا والاهنا ومخلصنا يسوع المسيح نشكرك في الكل ومع الكل وفي كل حال وعلى كل حال.
[2] ὅτι ἐσκέπασας, ἐβοήθησας, ἀντελάβου ἡμῶν μέχρι τῆς ἁγίας σου ὥρας ταύτης.	[2] لانك ظللتنا وسترتنا واعنتنا وعضدتنا والى هذه الساعة المقدسة.
[3] Καὶ δεόμεθα καὶ παρακαλοῦμέν σε, φιλάνθρωπε, ἀγαθέ, καὶ τὴν ἁγίαν σου ἡμέραν ταύτην καὶ πάσας τὰς ἡμέρας τῆς ζωῆς ἡμῶν ἐν εἰρήνῃ ἡμᾶς διαφύλαξον. [4] Πάντα δὲ φθόνον, πάντα πειρασμόν, πᾶσαν σατανικὴν ἐνέργειαν καὶ ἀνθρώπων πονηρῶν ἐπιβουλὴν	[3] فمنك نطلب واليك نرغب ايها الصالح محب البشر ان تقدس [هذا اليوم المقدس] وكل ايام حياتنا بالسلامة. [4] لكيما نكون محفوظين من كل حسد [ومن كل التجارب] وكل عمل شيطاني ومن مشاورة الناس الشريرين وعن هذا الموضع المقدس.

138 Ibid., 22–30.

139 Cuming, *The Liturgy of St Mark*, 90. The other medieval witnesses of MARK utilized by Cuming, *Messina Gr. 177* (11th c.), and *Greek Orthodox Patriarchate of Alexandria 173/36* (AD 1586), do not feature this prayer.

140 Ibid.

ἀποδίωξον ἀφ'ἡμῶν καὶ ἀπο τοῦ ἁγίου τόπου τούτου, ὁ Θεός. [5] Τὰ ἀγαθὰ καὶ τὰ συμφέροντα ἐπιχορήγησον ἡμῖν, καὶ τὴν ζωὴν ἡμῖν οἰκονόμησον. καὶ εἴ τι σοι ἡμάρτομεν εἴτε ἐν λόγῳ εἴτε ἐν ἔργῳ, εἴτε ἐν γνώσει εἴτε ἐν ἀγνοίᾳ, συ ὡς ἀγαθὸς καὶ φιλάνθρωπος Θεός παριδεῖν καταξίωσον, [6] καὶ μή εἰσενέγκῃς ἡμᾶς εἰς πειρασμόν, ὅν ὑπενεγκεῖν οὐ δυνάμεθα. Χάριτι καὶ οἰκτιρμοῖς καὶ φιλανθρωπίᾳ τοῦ μονογενοῦς σου Υἱοῦ, δι'οὗ καὶ μεθ'οὗ σοὶ ἡ δόξα καὶ τὸ κράτος, σὺν τῷ παναγίῳ καὶ ἀγαθῷ καὶ ζωοποιῷ σου Πνεύματι, νῦν καὶ ἀεὶ καὶ εἰς τοὺς αἰῶνας τῶν αἰώνων ἀμήν.[141]

[5] اللهم وهب لنا العطايا الصالحات الموافقات ودبر حياتنا وان نخطئ اليك اذ كنا اخطينا بكلمة او بعمل او بمعرفة او بغير معرفة كانت فانت ايها الصالح محب البشر اجعلنا اهلاً للمغفرة والمسامحة.

[6] لا تدخلنا فى التجارب فانا لا نقوا لها لكن نجينا من الشرير ومن كل اعماله التى لا نستطيع مقاومتها بنعمة ورافة ابنك الوحيد محب البشر الذي انت معه مبارك وروحك الكلي قدسه الان والى كل اوان امين.[142]

With very few differences in wording—and a missing initial address—the prayer appears in another formulary in the same codex, this time as part of the presanctified liturgy of Mark (MkPRES).[143] This particular version of the PRES is based on the complete anaphora of Melkite MARK. As such, it contains the *Prayer of Thanksgiving* as its enarxis prayer, immediately following the prothesis, in the same location it is found in MARK.

In either case, this comparison demonstrates that in the aggregate the text in *Sinai Ar. 237* (13th c.) is closer to that of *BAV Vatican Gr. 2281* (AD 1207) in its succinctness and lacks the same additional clauses that distinguish *BAV Vatican Gr. 1970* (12th c.). One should thus speak more appropriately of a more dominant recension of this prayer within the Melkite tradition, represented by at least two thirteenth-century witnesses, *BAV Vatican Gr. 2281* and *Sinai Ar. 237*. The remaining witness, *BAV Vatican Gr. 1970* (12th c.), represents a more elaborate recension.

Compared to this more developed recension of the prayer as found in *BAV Vatican Gr. 1970* (12th c.), the Coptic *textus receptus* clearly lacks most of the additional clauses that distinguish the former. Thus, comparing the Coptic text with the more pristine *BAV Vatican Gr. 2281* (AD 1207) presents the following:

141 Cuming, *The Liturgy of St Mark*, 90.

142 *Sinai Ar. 237* (13th c.), fol. 238r–v.

143 Mikhail, "The Presanctified Liturgy of the Apostle Mark in *Sinai Arabic 237*," 166 (Arabic), 170–171 (English).

BAV Vatican Gr. 2281 (AD 1207)	Coptic *textus receptus*
	[1] ⲙⲁⲣⲉⲛϣⲉⲡϩⲙⲟⲧ ⲛ̀ⲧⲟⲧϥ ⲙ̀ⲡⲓⲣⲉϥⲉⲣⲡⲉⲑⲛⲁⲛⲉϥ ⲟⲩⲟϩ ⲛ̀ⲛⲁⲏⲧ ⲫϯ ⲫⲓⲱⲧ ⲙ̀ⲡⲉⲛⲟ̅ⲥ̅ ⲟⲩⲟϩ ⲡⲉⲛⲛⲟⲩϯ ⲟⲩⲟϩ ⲡⲉⲛⲥ̅ⲱ̅ⲣ̅ ⲓ̅ⲏ̅ⲥ̅ ⲡⲭ̅ⲥ̅. [2] ϫⲉ ⲁϥⲉⲣⲥⲕⲉⲡⲁⲍⲓⲛ ⲉ̀ϫⲱⲛ ⲁϥⲉⲣⲃⲟⲏⲑⲓⲛ ⲉ̀ⲣⲟⲛ ⲁϥⲁⲣⲉϩ ⲉ̀ⲣⲟⲛ ⲁϥϣⲟⲡⲧⲉⲛ ⲉ̀ⲣⲟϥ ⲁϥϯⲁⲥⲟ ⲉ̀ⲣⲟⲛ ⲁϥϯⲧⲟⲧⲉⲛ ⲁϥⲉⲛⲧⲉⲛ ϣⲁ ⲉ̀ϩⲣⲏⲓ ⲉ̀ⲧⲁⲓⲟⲩⲛⲟⲩ ⲑⲁⲓ. [3] ⲛ̀ⲑⲟϥ ⲟⲛ ⲙⲁⲣⲉⲛϯϩⲟ ⲉ̀ⲣⲟϥ ϩⲟⲡⲱⲥ ⲛ̀ⲧⲉϥⲁⲣⲉϩ ⲉ̀ⲣⲟⲛ ϧⲉⲛ ⲡⲁⲓⲉϩⲟⲟⲩ ⲉ̅ⲑ̅ⲩ̅ ⲫⲁⲓ ⲛⲉⲙ ⲛⲓⲉϩⲟⲟⲩ ⲧⲏⲣⲟⲩ ⲛ̀ⲧⲉ ⲡⲉⲛⲱⲛϧ ϧⲉⲛ ϩⲓⲣⲏⲛⲏ ⲛⲓⲃⲉⲛ ⲛ̀ϫⲉ ⲡⲓⲡⲁⲛⲧⲟⲕⲣⲁⲧⲱⲣ ⲡⲟ̅ⲥ̅ ⲡⲉⲛⲛⲟⲩϯ.
[4] Δέσποτα Κύριε ὁ Θεός ἡμῶν ὁ παντοκράτωρ, ὁ Πατὴρ τοῦ Κυρίου καὶ Θεοῦ καὶ Σωτῆρος ἡμῶν Ἰησοῦ Χριστοῦ, [5] εὐχαριστοῦμέν σοι κατὰ πάντα καὶ διὰ πάντων καὶ ἐν πᾶσιν, [6] ὅτι ἐσκέπασας, ἐβοήθησας, ἀντελάβου ἡμῶν μέχρι τῆς ἁγίας σου ὥρας ταύτης.	[4] ⲫⲏⲏⲃ ⲡⲟ̅ⲥ̅ ⲫϯ ⲡⲓⲡⲁⲛⲧⲟⲕⲣⲁⲧⲱⲣ ⲫⲓⲱⲧ ⲙ̀ⲡⲉⲛⲟ̅ⲥ̅ ⲟⲩⲟϩ ⲡⲉⲛⲛⲟⲩϯ ⲟⲩⲟϩ ⲡⲉⲛⲥ̅ⲱ̅ⲣ̅ ⲓ̅ⲏ̅ⲥ̅ ⲡⲭ̅ⲥ̅. [5] ⲧⲉⲛϣⲉⲡϩⲙⲟⲧ ⲛ̀ⲧⲟⲧⲕ ⲕⲁⲧⲁ ϩⲱⲃ ⲛⲓⲃⲉⲛ ⲛⲉⲙ ⲉⲑⲃⲉ ϩⲱⲃ ⲛⲓⲃⲉⲛ ⲛⲉⲙ ϧⲉⲛ ϩⲱⲃ ⲛⲓⲃⲉⲛ. [6] ϫⲉ ⲁⲕⲉⲣⲥⲕⲉⲡⲁⲍⲓⲛ ⲉ̀ϫⲱⲛ ⲁⲕⲉⲣⲃⲟⲏⲑⲓⲛ ⲉ̀ⲣⲟⲛ ⲁⲕⲁⲣⲉϩ ⲉ̀ⲣⲟⲛ ⲁⲕϣⲟⲡⲧⲉⲛ ⲉ̀ⲣⲟⲕ ⲁⲕϯⲁⲥⲟ ⲉ̀ⲣⲟⲛ ⲁⲕϯⲧⲟⲧⲉⲛ ⲁⲕⲉⲛⲧⲉⲛ ϣⲁ ⲉ̀ϩⲣⲏⲓ ⲉⲧⲁⲓⲟⲩⲟⲛⲟⲩ ⲑⲁⲓ.
[7] Καὶ δεόμεθα καὶ παρακαλοῦμέν σε, φιλάνθρωπε, ἀγαθέ, καὶ τὴν ἁγίαν σου ἡμέραν ταύτην καὶ πάσας τὰς ἡμέρας τῆς ζωῆς ἡμῶν ἐν εἰρήνῃ ἡμᾶς διαφύλαξον.	[7] ⲉⲑⲃⲉ ⲫⲁⲓ ⲧⲉⲛϯϩⲟ ⲟⲩⲟϩ ⲧⲉⲛⲧⲱⲃϩ ⲛ̀ⲧⲉⲕⲙⲉⲧⲁⲅⲁⲑⲟⲥ ⲡⲓⲙⲁⲓⲣⲱⲙⲓ ⲙⲏⲓⲥ ⲛⲁⲛ ⲉ̀ⲑⲣⲉⲛϫⲱⲕ ⲉ̀ⲃⲟⲗ ⲙ̀ⲡⲁⲓⲕⲉⲉϩⲟⲟⲩ ⲉ̅ⲑ̅ⲩ̅ ⲫⲁⲓ ⲛⲉⲙ ⲛⲓⲉϩⲟⲟⲩ ⲧⲏⲣⲟⲩ ⲛ̀ⲧⲉ ⲡⲉⲛⲱⲛϧ ϧⲉⲛ ϩⲓⲣⲏⲛⲏ ⲛⲓⲃⲉⲛ ⲛⲉⲙ ⲧⲉⲕϩⲟϯ.
[8] Πάντα δὲ φθόνον, πάντα πειρασμόν, πᾶσαν σατανικὴν ἐνέργειαν καὶ ἀνθρώπων πονηρῶν ἐπιβουλὴν ἀποδίωξον ἀφ'ἡμῶν καὶ ἀπο τοῦ ἁγίου τόπου τούτου, ὁ Θεός.	[8] ⲫⲑⲟⲛⲟⲥ ⲛⲓⲃⲉⲛ ⲡⲓⲣⲁⲥⲙⲟⲥ ⲛⲓⲃⲉⲛ ⲉⲛⲉⲣⲅⲓⲁ ⲛⲓⲃⲉⲛ ⲛ̀ⲧⲉ ⲡⲥⲁⲧⲁⲛⲁⲥ ⲡⲥⲟϭⲛⲓ ⲛ̀ⲧⲉ ϩⲁⲛⲣⲱⲙⲓ ⲉⲩϩⲱⲟⲩ ⲛⲉⲙ ⲡⲧⲱⲛϥ ⲉ̀ⲡϣⲱⲓ ⲛ̀ⲧⲉ ϩⲁⲛϫⲁϫⲓ ⲛⲏ ⲉⲧϩⲏⲡ ⲛⲉⲙ ⲛⲏ ⲉⲑⲟⲩⲱⲛϩ ⲉ̀ⲃⲟⲗ ⲁⲗⲓⲧⲟⲩ ⲉ̀ⲃⲟⲗ ϩⲁⲣⲟⲛ ⲛⲉⲙ ⲉ̀ⲃⲟⲗ ϩⲁ ⲡⲉⲕⲗⲁⲟⲥ ⲧⲏⲣϥ ⲛⲉⲙ ⲉ̀ⲃⲟⲗ ϩⲁ ⲧⲁⲓⲧⲣⲁⲡⲉⲍⲁ ⲑⲁⲓ ⲛⲉⲙ ⲉ̀ⲃⲟⲗ ϩⲁ ⲡⲁⲓⲙⲁ ⲉⲑⲟⲩⲁⲃ ⲛ̀ⲧⲁⲕ ⲫⲁⲓ.
[9] Τὰ ἀγαθὰ καὶ τὰ συμφέροντα ἐπιχορήγησον ἡμῖν, καὶ τὴν ζωὴν ἡμῖν οἰκονόμησον. καὶ εἴ τι σοι ἡμάρτομεν εἴτε ἐν λόγῳ εἴτε ἐν ἔργῳ, εἴτε ἐν γνώσει εἴτε ἐν ἀγνοίᾳ, συ ὡς ἀγαθὸς καὶ φιλάνθρωπος Θεός παριδεῖν καταξίωσον, [10] καὶ μή εἰσενέγκῃς ἡμᾶς εἰς πειρασμόν, ὅν ὑπενεγκεῖν οὐ δυνάμεθα. [11] Χάριτι καὶ οἰκτιρμοῖς καὶ φιλανθρωπίᾳ τοῦ μονογενοῦς σου Υἱοῦ,	[9] ⲛⲏ ⲇⲉ ⲉⲑⲛⲁⲛⲉⲩ ⲛⲉⲙ ⲛⲏ ⲉⲧⲉⲣⲛⲟϥⲣⲓ ⲥⲁϩⲛⲓ ⲙ̀ⲙⲱⲟⲩ ⲛⲁⲛ ϫⲉ ⲛ̀ⲑⲟⲕ ⲡⲉ ⲉⲧⲁⲕϯ ⲙ̀ⲡⲓⲉⲣϣⲓϣⲓ ⲛⲁⲛ ⲉ̀ϩⲱⲙⲓ ⲉ̀ϫⲉⲛ ⲛⲓϩⲟϥ ⲛⲉⲙ ⲛⲓϭⲗⲏ ⲛⲉⲙ ⲉ̀ϫⲉⲛ ϯϫⲟⲙ ⲧⲏⲣⲥ ⲛ̀ⲧⲉ ⲡⲓϫⲁϫⲓ. [10] ⲟⲩⲟϩ ⲙ̀ⲡⲉ̀ⲣⲉⲛⲧⲉⲛ ⲉ̀ϧⲟⲩⲛ ⲉ̀ⲡⲓⲣⲁⲥⲙⲟⲥ ⲁⲗⲗⲁ ⲛⲁϩⲙⲉⲛ ⲉ̀ⲃⲟⲗ ϩⲁ ⲡⲓⲡⲉⲧϩⲱⲟⲩ [11] ϧⲉⲛ ⲡⲓϩⲙⲟⲧ ⲛⲉⲙ ⲛⲓⲙⲉⲧϣⲉⲛϩⲏⲧ ⲛⲉⲙ ϯⲙⲉⲧⲙⲁⲓⲣⲱⲙⲓ ⲛ̀ⲧⲉ ⲡⲉⲕⲙⲟⲛⲟⲅⲉⲛⲏⲥ ⲛ̀ϣⲏⲣⲓ ⲡⲉⲛⲟ̅ⲥ̅ ⲟⲩⲟϩ ⲡⲉⲛⲛⲟⲩϯ ⲟⲩⲟϩ ⲡⲉⲛⲥ̅ⲱ̅ⲣ̅ ⲓ̅ⲏ̅ⲥ̅ ⲡⲭ̅ⲥ̅.

[12] δι᾽οὗ καὶ μεθ᾽οὗ σοὶ ἡ δόξα καὶ τὸ κράτος, σὺν τῷ παναγίῳ καὶ ἀγαθῷ καὶ ζωοποιῷ σου Πνεύματι, νῦν καὶ ἀεὶ καὶ εἰς τοὺς αἰῶνας τῶν αἰώνων ἀμήν.[144]	[12] ⲫⲁⲓ ⲉⲧⲉ ⲉ̀ⲃⲟⲗ ϩⲓⲧⲟⲧϥ ⲉⲣⲉ ⲡⲓⲱⲟⲩ ⲛⲉⲙ ⲡⲓⲧⲁⲓⲟ ⲛⲉⲙ ⲡⲓⲁⲙⲁϩⲓ ⲛⲉⲙ ϯⲡⲣⲟⲥⲕⲩⲛⲏⲥⲓⲥ ⲉⲣⲡⲣⲉⲡⲓ ⲛⲁⲕ ⲛⲉⲙⲁϥ ⲛⲉⲙ ⲡⲓⲡ̅ⲛ̅ⲁ̅ ⲉ̅ⲑ̅ⲩ̅ ⲛ̀ⲣⲉϥⲧⲁⲛϧⲟ ⲟⲩⲟϩ ⲛ̀ⲟⲙⲟⲟⲩⲥⲓⲟⲥ ⲛⲉⲙⲁⲕ. ϯⲛⲟⲩ ⲛⲉⲙ ⲛ̀ⲥⲏⲟⲩ ⲛⲓⲃⲉⲛ ⲛⲉⲙ ϣⲁ ⲉⲛⲉϩ ⲛ̀ⲧⲉ ⲛⲓⲉⲛⲉϩ ⲧⲏⲣⲟⲩ ⲁⲙⲏⲛ.[145]

The most distinguishing characteristic of the Coptic text is its double opening address [1–3], which is surely not original. In addition, the Coptic text adds the mention of hidden and manifest enemies [8], and the scriptural reference to treading on serpents and scorpions in [9] (Cf. Lk 10:19) which is absent from all Melkite witnesses. On the other hand, the more pristine Melkite text in *BAV Vatican Gr. 2281* (AD 1207) has a lengthy petition for forgiveness of sins committed in word or deed, knowingly or unknowningly in [9], which is absent from the Coptic text. Overall, however, the Coptic *textus receptus* of the *Prayer of Thanksgiving* is textually closest to the ancient Melkite recension found in this early thirteenth-century witnesses.

One final comparison should be presented here, this time between the Melkite recension from *BAV Vatican Gr. 1970* (12th c.) and the Greek text of the Coptic recension, as found in the *Kacmarcik Codex* (14th c.).

BAV Vatican Gr. 1970 (12th c.)	*Kacmarcik Codex* (14th c.)
	[1] Εὐχαριστοῦμεν τῷ εὐεργέτῃ καὶ ἐλεήμονι Θεῷ τῷ Πατρὶ τοῦ Κυρίου δὲ καὶ Θεοῦ καὶ Σωτῆρος ἡμῶν Ἰησοῦ Χριστοῦ, [2] ὅτι ἐσκέπασεν, ἐβοήθησεν, ἐφύλαξεν, ἀντελάβετο, καὶ διήγαγεν ἡμᾶς μέχρι τῆς ὥρας ταύτης. [3] Αὐτὸν οὖν παρακαλέσωμεν ὅπως φυλάσσῃ ἡμᾶς ἐν τῇ ἁγίᾳ ἡμέρᾳ ταύτῃ καὶ ἐν πάσαις ταῖς ἡμέραις τῆς ζωῆς ἡμῶν, ἐν πάσῃ εἰρήνῃ ὁ παντοκράτωρ Κύριος ὁ Θεός ἡμῶν.
[4] Εὐχαριστοῦμεν καὶ ὑπερευχαριστοῦμεν σοι Δέσποτα Κύριε ὁ Θεός ἡμῶν, ὁ Πατὴρ τοῦ Κυρίου καὶ Θεοῦ καὶ Σωτῆρος ἡμῶν Ἰησοῦ Χριστοῦ, [5] κατὰ πάντα καὶ διὰ πάντων καὶ ἐν πᾶσιν,	[4] Δέσποτα Κύριε ὁ Θεός ὁ παντοκράτωρ, ὁ Πατὴρ τοῦ Κυρίου δὲ καὶ Θεοῦ καὶ Σωτῆρος ἡμῶν Ἰησοῦ Χριστοῦ, [5] εὐχαριστοῦμέν σοι Κύριε ὁ Θεός ἡμῶν κατὰ πάντα καὶ διὰ πάντα καὶ ἐν πᾶσιν,

144 Cuming, *The Liturgy of St Mark*, 90.

145 Ṣalīb, ⲡⲓϫⲱⲙ ⲛ̀ⲧⲉ ⲡⲓⲉⲩⲭⲟⲗⲟⲅⲓⲟⲛ, 22–30.

[6] ὅτι ἐσκέπασας, ἐβοήθησας, ἀντελάβου παρήγαγες ἡμᾶς τὸν παρελθόντα χρόνον τῆς ζωῆς ἡμῶν καὶ ἤγαγες ἡμᾶς ἕως τῆς ὥρας ταύτης, ἀξιώσας πάλιν παραστῆναι ἐνώπιόν σου ἐν τόπῳ ἁγίῳ σου ἄφεσιν αἰτοῦντες τῶν ἁμαρτιῶν ἡμῶν καὶ ἱλασμὸν παντὶ τῷ λαῷ σου.

[7] Καὶ δεόμεθα καὶ παρακαλοῦμέν σε, φιλάνθρωπε, ἀγαθέ, δὸς ἡμῖν τὴν ἁγίαν ἡμέραν ταύτην καὶ ἅπαντα τὸν χρόνον τῆς ζωῆς ἡμῶν ἐπιτελέσαι ἀναμαρτήτως μετὰ πάσης χαρᾶς, ὑγείας, σωτηρίας καὶ παντός ἁγιασμοῦ καὶ τοῦ σου φόβου.

[8] Πάντα δὲ φθόνον, πάντα φόβον πάντα πειρασμόν, πᾶσαν σατανικὴν ἐνέργειαν πᾶσαν πονηρῶν ἀνθρώπων ἐπιβουλὴν ἐκδίωξον ἀφ'ἡμῶν, ὁ Θεός, καὶ ἀπο τῆς ἁγίας σου καθολικῆς καὶ ἀποστολικῆς ἐκκλησίας.
[9] Τὰ ἀγαθὰ καὶ τὰ συμφέροντα ἡμῖν ἐπιχορήγησον. καὶ εἴ τι σοι ἡμάρτομεν ἐν λόγῳ ἢ ἔργῳ, ἢ κατὰ διάνοιαν, συ ὡς ἀγαθὸς καὶ φιλάνθρωπος Θεός παριδεῖν καταξίωσον,

[10] Καὶ μὴ ἐγκαταλίπῃς ἡμᾶς, ὁ Θεός, τοὺς ἐλπίζοντας ἐπὶ σοι, μηδὲ εἰσενέγκῃς ἡμᾶς εἰς πειρασμόν, ἀλλὰ ῥῦσαι ἡμᾶς ἀπὸ τοῦ πονηροῦ καὶ ἐκ τῶν ἔργων αὐτου.
[11] Χάριτι καὶ οἰκτιρμοῖς καὶ φιλανθρωπίᾳ τοῦ μονογενοῦς σου Υἱοῦ, δι'οὗ καὶ μεθ'οὗ σοὶ ἡ δόξα καὶ τὸ κράτος, σὺν τῷ παναγίῳ καὶ ἀγαθῷ καὶ ζωοποιῷ σου Πνεύματι, νῦν καὶ ἀεὶ καὶ εἰς τοὺς αἰῶνας τῶν αἰώνων ἀμήν.[146]

[6] ὅτι ἐσκέπασας, ἐβοήθησας, ἐφύλαξας, ἀντελάβου καλῶς καὶ εἰρηνικῶς διήγαγες ἡμᾶς μέχρι τῆς ὥρας ταύτης, παντοκράτωρ Κύριε ὁ θεός ἡμῶν.

[7] Καὶ δεόμεθα καὶ παρακαλοῦμέν σε, φιλάνθρωπε, ἀγαθέ, Κύριε ὅπως καὶ τὴν ἁγίαν σου ἡμέραν ταύτην καὶ πάσας τὰς ἡμέρας τῆς ζωῆς ἡμῶν, δὸς ἡμῖν Κύριε ὁ θεός ἀναμαρτήτως διελθεῖν μετὰ πάσης χαρᾶς, ὑγείας, εἰρήνης, σωτηρίας εὐεργεσίας, παντός ἁγιασμοῦ καὶ τοῦ σου φόβου ἐπιτελεῖν. [8] Πάντα δὲ φθόνον, πάντα φόβον πάντα πειρασμόν, πᾶσαν σατανικὴν ἐνέργειαν καὶ ἀνθρώπων πονηρῶν ἐπιβουλὴν αἰσθητῶν καὶ νοητῶν, παράγαγε ὁ θεός ἀφ'ἡμῶν καὶ ἀπὸ τοῦ λαοῦ σου καὶ ἀπὸ τοῦ ἁγίου τόπου τούτου. [9] ὁ θεός τὰ καλὰ καὶ τὰ συμφέροντα ἡμῖν ἐπιχορήγησον. τὰ ἔργα τῶν χειρῶν ἡμῶν εὐλόγησον, τὴν ζωὴν ἡμῶν οἰκονόμησον. Σὺ γὰρ ἔδωκας ἡμῖν τὴν ἐξουσίαν τοῦ πατεῖν ἐπάνω ὄφεων καὶ σκορπίων καὶ ἐπὶ πᾶσαν τὴν δύναμιν τοῦ ἐχθροῦ. [10] καὶ μή εἰσενέγκῃς ἡμᾶς εἰς πειρασμόν, ἀλλὰ ῥῦσαι ἡμᾶς ἀπὸ τοῦ πονηροῦ πάσας τὰς ἡμέρας τῆς ζωῆς ἡμῶν,

[11] ἐν Χριστῷ Ἰησοῦ τῷ Κυρίῳ ἡμῶν, δι'οὗ καὶ μεθ'οὗ σοι ἡ δόξα καὶ τὸ κράτος, σὺν τῷ παναγίῳ καὶ ἀγαθῷ καὶ ζωοποιῷ σου Πνεύματι, νῦν καὶ ἀεὶ καὶ εἰς τοὺς αἰῶνας τῶν αἰώνων ἀμήν.[147]

First, the *Kacmarcik* text shows the same duplication of the opening address seen in the Coptic text above and found here in the beginning

[146] Cuming, *The Liturgy of St Mark*, 90.
[147] Macomber, "The Greek Text," 315–316.

in [1–3], which shows the dependency of the Greek text on the Coptic original. Furthermore, usually the Greek witnesses of the Coptic liturgies are identical to the Coptic text. However, in this particular case the text of the prayer in the *Kacmarcik Codex* (14th c.) features particular additions not found in the Coptic text in any of its witnesses, and in fact found only in the more elaborate *BAV Vatican Gr. 1970* (12th c.). This is clearest in [7], where the prayer asks for God to complete this day with joy, health, peace, salvation, benefit, and all sanctification. This addition appears also in later witnesses of the Greek text of the Coptic liturgy, which were published by Roshdi Dous.[148] All other differences between the two texts presented in this table are additions found only in *BAV Vatican Gr. 1970* (12th c.). Thus, it appears that at least in the *Prayer of Thanksgiving* the Greek textual tradition, which likely arose in Scetis and the Monastery of Saint Antony by the Red Sea, was influenced by the Alexandrian tradition of Melkite MARK.

5.3. Origins of the Prayer

Naturally, a prayer that is shared between both branches of the Alexandrian tradition, the Coptic and Melkite, would be expectedly ancient in origin and should be attested in some manner much earlier than the thirteenth-century sources and Euchologia. One such attempt to locate the earliest references to the *Prayer of Thanksgiving* was made by Hegumen Mattā al-Miskīn in his seminal work on the Eucharist. Among other references to the Eucharist in patristic literature, Mattā al-Miskīn identified what he judged to be a reference to the *Prayer of Thanksgiving* in the *Stromateis* of Clement of Alexandria (2nd–3rd c.): "Thus, receiving lordly power, the soul meditates to be God; regarding nothing bad but ignorance and work contrary to right reason. And giving thanks always (εὐχαριστοῦσα ἐπὶ πᾶσι) for all things to God."[149] However, such a general exhortation to continuous thanksgiving cannot reasonably be connected specifically to the *Prayer of Thanksgiving*. Unfortunately, two other Coptic scholars, copied the reference later in their dissertations on the Coptic liturgy and Horologion respectively.[150]

148 Dous, "Η Αλεξανδρινή Θεία Λειτουργία," 77. The text of the *Prayer of Thanksgiving* in the work by Dous is presented from the following mansucripts: *Coptic Patriarchate Lit. 172* (AD 1599), *Coptic Patriarchate Lit. 184* (18th c.), *Abnūb St. Mīnā Lit. 1* (18th c.), and *St. Macarius Lit. 155* (AD 1894).

149 *Stromateis* 6.14 (CPG 1377). Cf. Al-Miskīn, *Al-ifḫāristiyya*, 435. Cf. Patrick Descourtieux, *Clément d'Alexandrie: Les Stromaties VI*, SC 446 (Paris: Cerf, 1999), 286–287.

150 Dous, "Η Αλεξανδρινή Θεία Λειτουργία," 15; Hanna, "Το Ωρολόγιον της Κοπτικής Ορθόδοξης Εκκλησίας," 31.

Yet, Coptic liturgy seems to have known prayers of this kind early on. A limestone ostracon from Thebes dated to the seventh or early-eighth century attests to a Sahidic prayer of thanksgiving based on a Greek original. Although the text can hardly be said to be similar to the Bohairic *Prayer of Thanksgiving*, references to thanking God, "who acquired us, who quickened us," and, "for the day, for the sun, and the light," hint at a similar function of thanksgiving at the beginning of a morning liturgical assembly.[151] The earliest unequivocal witness of the text of the *Prayer of Thanksgiving* survives in Sahidic (with Fayyumic tendencies) in a manuscript from the eleventh/twelfth century, *Prague Or. Inst. MS I p.1–3*, a five-folio fragment of a book of miscellaneous prayers. In this witness, the *Prayer of Thanksgiving* appears essentially identical to the received text at the head of a series of four prayers: Thanksgiving, for the sick, the travelers, and a prayer of incense.[152] The order of these prayers notwithstanding, this group of prayers is strongly suggestive of the *Morning Raising of Incense* service in the Bohairic Northern tradition.

Allusions to the *Prayer of Thanksgiving* appear also in the biography of Pope John III (AD 677–686) also known as John of Samannūd. In the *History of the Patriarchs* in the codex *Hamburg 304 (Or. 26)* (AD 1266), the pope enters the cathedral of Saint Mark in Alexandria near the end of his life, where the following takes place:

[1] ولما وصل الى بيعة القديس ماري مرقس الانجيلي التى بناها باحكام الله الغير مدروكة [2] فحُمِلَ ودخلوا به الى المذبح الكبير. [3] فوقف بقوة الروح وقال الشبهمات.[153]	[1] And when he arrived at the church of Saint Mark the Evangelist, which he built according to the incomprehensible judgements of God, [2] he was carried and they entered with him into the large altar. [3] So he stood by the power of the Spirit and said the *šibihmāt*.

The text refers to the *Prayer of Thanksgiving* using the term *šibihmāt*, a common designation based on the first word of the prayer in Coptic:

[151] Ágnes T. Mihálykó, "Two Coptic Prayers on Ostracon (P. Berol. 709 and 9444+4790)," *Archiv für Papyrusforschung* 65, no. 1 (2019): 133–155, here 145–155. According to Mihálykó, the fifth-century Aksumite Collection already contains a variant of the *Prayer of Thanksgiving*. Since this important corpus remains unpublished, I was unable to comment further on this witness. See Ágnes T. Mihálykó, *The Christian Liturgical Papyri: An Introduction*, Studien und Texte zu Antike und Christentum 114 (Tübingen: Mohr Siebeck, 2019), 142.

[152] Valerie Hažmuková, "Miscellaneous Coptic Prayers," *Archiv Orientální* 8 (1936): 318–333, here 325–327.

[153] Christian Friedrich Seybold, *Severus ibn al Muqaffa' alexandrinische Patriarchengeschichte von S. Marcus bis Michael I, 61–767 nach der ältesten 1266 geschriebenen Hamburger Handschrift*, Veröffentlichungen aus der Hamburger Stadtbibliothek 3 (Hamburg: Lucas Gräfe, 1912), 120.

ⲙⲁⲣⲉⲛϣⲉⲡϩⲙⲟⲧ (*Let us give thanks*), and one seen above among the variants in the title found in manuscripts. The reference appears as well in the *History of the Patriarchs*, based on *Paris BnF Ar. 301* (15th c.) and *Paris BnF Ar. 302* (15th c.). This time, the pope is said to have "said the whole of the *Prayer of Thanksgiving*."[154] In both cases, the language used is highly specific, leaving no doubt that this prayer was intended. Incidentally, even today the *Prayer of Thanksgiving* is precisely what any hierarch would likely pray upon arriving from a journey or upon visiting a church. The title of the prayer is likewise mentioned explicitly in the biography of Patriarch Mīnā I (AD 767-774). The *History of the Patriarchs* mentions that a certain would-be usurper of the patriarchal chair entered the cathedral one Sunday morning with the help of the governor's soldiers, and "ascended to the sanctuary to say the *Prayer of Thanksgiving* (صلاة الشكر) and [the prayer of] peace as the patriarch."[155] The fact that the biographies of two patriarchs from the seventh and eighth centuries respectively clearly point to the prayer may potentially indicate that the prayer was known within the Coptic Rite as early as the seventh century, or at least by the time of the copying of the oldest manuscripts of the *History of the Patriarchs* in the thirteenth century. One can however favor a somewhat earlier date within this broad range, considering the integral place of this prayer in manuscripts of Melkite MARK, as well as the general tendency towards growth and development of the Coptic Rite during the crucial period between the seventh to the ninth centuries, as previously explained. Hypotheses aside, only this much can be stated with certainty: Prayers of thanksgiving seem to have enjoyed currency in Egyptian liturgy at least since the seventh/eighth centuries (or even the fifth pending the publication of the Aksumite Collection), with our specific prayer text attested clearly since the eleventh or twelfth centuries in the region of Fayyum at some distance from the centers of Bohairic liturgy in the north.

On the other hand, the prayer is noticeably absent from the *Order of the Mystery*, the post-baptismal homily and description of the liturgy preserved in Ethiopic but describing an Alexandrian liturgy of the fifth century according to Heinzgerd Brakmann.[156] As a text directed at newly-baptized faithful to help them participate in the visible and public rites of the liturgy, it is surprising that it does not refer at all to what is known to be the enarxis prayer of the liturgy in the entire Church of Alexandria. Thus, the fifth century can be posited

[154] *HP*, 1.3:275.

[155] *HP*, 1.4:485.

[156] Brakmann, "Le déroulement," 109. See also Brakmann's remark in: Brakmann, "Neue Funde (1988–1992)," 11–12. See the full bibliography in Fritsch, "The Order of the Mystery," 196n5.

as a *terminus post quem* for the development of the *Prayer of Thanksgiving*, since it is absent from this fifth-century source. While a definitive dating of the appearance of this prayer may not be possible at this time, a hypothesis of ca. seventh century is at least permissible.

5.4. The Place of the Prayer in the Unfolding of the Liturgy

Within the unfolding of the prothesis rite, the *Prayer of Thanksgiving* may easily appear as an integral element of the rite, recited immediately following the deposition of the gifts on the altar, often while the celebrant is still mixing the chalice, and even preceding the *Prothesis Prayer*. However, a preponderance of evidence shows this to be a misunderstanding of the function or location of this prayer in the Coptic liturgy.

First, a striking feature of the *Prayer of Thanksgiving* is precisely that it does not once mention the eucharistic gifts, their transformation, or the partaking of them in communion that is expected. Liturgical formularies consistently feature prayers of thanksgiving *after* communion. One would have expected a prayer at the prothesis to feature some explicit offering of thanks for the gifts that are now presented or will be offered up in the anaphora to become Christ's body and blood, but nothing of this sort is expressed. Based on content alone then, one cannot automatically—or through force of popular perception—consider this prayer an element of the prothesis rite.

Second, the general character of the prayer is exactly why it has come to appear so frequently in practically every Coptic rite and service as an introductory prayer. It occupies this position in the *Vespers* and *Matins Raising of Incense*,[157] every hour of the Coptic Horologion,[158] the service of absolution for women after giving birth, the baptismal rite,[159] the marriage rite,[160] the anointing of the sick,[161] ordination to any rank of the deaconate or priesthood,[162] and funerals.[163] This is in addition to seasonal services such as the sanctification of water on Theophany and the Feast of the Apostles

157 Burmester, *The Egyptian Church*, 36.

158 O.H.E. Burmester, "The Canonical Hours of the Coptic Church," *OCP* 2, no. 1/2 (1936): 78–100, here 89.

159 Burmester, *The Egyptian Church*, 112, 114. O.H.E. Burmester, "The Baptismal Rite of the Coptic Church (A Critical Study)," *BSAC* 11 (1945): 27–86, here 47, 49.

160 Burmester, *The Egyptian Church*, 136.

161 Ibid., 145.

162 Ibid., 154–187.

163 Ibid., 202.

Peter and Paul,[164] and the Kneeling Service on Pentecost.[165] Certainly, broadening the view of the function of this prayer to include the totality of the Coptic Rite is enough by itself to show that the prayer is not an element of the prothesis, but is simply an enarxis prayer suited for any liturgical gathering or function.

Third, the function of the prayer as an enarxis prayer is confirmed in the Melkite tradition of MARK, where it functions precisely as such. Coming immediately *after* the prothesis rite and the introductory greeting, "Blessed is the kingdom," the prayer is clearly intended in Melkite MARK as the first prayer of the public part of the liturgy in the Alexandrian Melkite tradition, later Byzantinisms of the manuscripts notwithstanding. As was shown previously, the title "First Prayer of the Morning" is itself attested in one very important Coptic Euchologion, *Bodleian Hunt. 360* (13th c.). In addition, Prayer 19 in Sarapion, which has the similar title "First Prayer of Sunday," also functions as an *enarxis* prayer, even asking explicitly to properly learn and interpret the scriptural readings that are to follow.[166]

Fourth, the idea that the *Prayer of Thanksgiving* represents not the continuation of a liturgical rite, but the *beginning* of a new unit is certainly not absent in the Euchologia. In *Paris BnF Copt. 29* (AD 1639) and *Paris BnF Copt. 30* (AD 1642), the *Prayer of Thanksgiving* begins a new section in the manuscript. Instead of following immediately on the same folio as the preceding prayers of the preparation of the altar, the scribe of each manuscript chose to begin a new folio, adding a geometric headpiece to the top of the page followed by the title, "With God (ⲥⲩⲛ ⲑⲉⲱ)." This phrase is used frequently in Coptic manuscript culture to denote the beginning of a new work, chapter, or section. The visual appearance of these two late manuscripts certainly gives the strong impression that the prayer was intended as the beginning of a new liturgical unit. This, together with all the other arguments from content and usage in the Coptic and Melkite traditions leaves no room any longer to regard this prayer as an original element to the prothesis.

5.5. The Diaconal Responses during the Prayer

Any time the *Prayer of Thanksgiving* is recited today, it is preceded by the diaconal command, "Stand up for prayer (ⲉⲡⲓ ⲡⲣⲟⲥⲉⲩⲭⲏ

164 Ibid., 261. Burmester, "Two Services of the Coptic Church," 238.

165 Ibid., 304. O.H.E. Burmester, "The Office of Genuflection on Whitsunday," *Le Muséon* 47 (1934): 205–257.

166 Johnson, *The Prayers of Sarapion of Thmuis*, 70–71.

ⲥⲧⲁⲑⲏⲧⲉ)."[167] It is also interrupted by two other diaconal commands: "Pray (ⲡⲣⲟⲥⲉⲩⲝⲁⲥⲑⲉ),"[168] and the following lengthier response with an added clause during the prothesis:

[1] ⲧⲱⲃϩ ϩⲓⲛⲁ ⲛ̀ⲧⲉ ⲫϯ ⲛⲁⲓ ⲛⲁⲛ ⲛ̀ⲧⲉϥϣⲉⲛϩⲏⲧ ϧⲁⲣⲟⲛ ⲛ̀ⲧⲉϥⲥⲱⲧⲉⲙ ⲉ̀ⲣⲟⲛ ⲛ̀ⲧⲉϥⲉⲣⲃⲟⲏⲑⲓⲛ ⲉ̀ⲣⲟⲛ [2] ⲛ̀ⲧⲉϥϭⲓ ⲛ̀ⲛⲓϯϩⲟ ⲛⲉⲙ ⲛⲓⲧⲱⲃϩ ⲛ̀ⲧⲉ ⲛⲏ ⲉ̅ⲑ̅ⲩ̅ ⲛ̀ⲧⲁϥ ⲛ̀ⲧⲟⲧⲟⲩ ⲉ̀ϩⲣⲏⲓ ⲉ̀ϫⲱⲛ ⲉ̀ⲡⲓⲁⲅⲁⲑⲟⲛ ⲛ̀ⲥⲏⲟⲩ ⲛⲓⲃⲉⲛ [3] ⲛ̀ⲧⲉϥⲁⲓⲧⲉⲛ ⲛ̀ⲉⲙⲡϣⲁ ⲉ̀ⲑⲣⲉⲛϭⲓ ⲉ̀ⲃⲟⲗ ϧⲉⲛ ϯⲕⲟⲓⲛⲱⲛⲓⲁ ⲛ̀ⲧⲉ ⲛⲉϥⲙⲩⲥⲧⲏⲣⲓⲟⲛ ⲉⲑⲟⲩⲁⲃ ⲉⲧⲥⲙⲁⲣⲱⲟⲩⲧ ⲉ̀ⲡⲓⲭⲱ ⲉ̀ⲃⲟⲗ ⲛ̀ⲧⲉ ⲛⲉⲛⲛⲟⲃⲓ.[169]	[1] Pray that God may have mercy on us, have compassion on us, hear us, help us, [2] and receive the entreaties and prayers of his saints from them on our behalf for the good at all times, [3] to make us worthy to receive of the communion of his holy and blessed mysteries for the forgiveness of our sins.

Since these diaconal biddings are not integral to the prayer itself, their history in the sources should be explained.

The first two responses, "Stand up for prayer," and, "Pray," are in fact attested quite early in the manuscripts. The parchment sheet *P. Naqlun II 20* (9th–11th c.) contains the responses of the deacon during the liturgy in Greek and Coptic translation, and features these two responses in the very beginning.[170] Judging from the remainder of the text, it can be affirmed that the responses for the *Prayer of Thanksgiving* here are in the context of the liturgy and not another service where the prayer may be employed, such as vespers or matins. The papyrus serves to give the Coptic translation of the diaconal responses and congregational chants that are performed in Greek, clearly to a reader without knowledge of the latter. As such, it cannot be ascertained that the third diaconal response for the *Prayer of Thanksgiving*, "Pray that God may have mercy," was not in use at the time and place of the copying of this manuscript, since it is already in Coptic, which was presumably understood by the reader.

Regarding this third diaconal response, the earliest evidence for its usage is found in the Euchologion *Bodleian Hunt. 360* (13th c.) and the diaconal *BAV Vatican Copt. 28* (AD 1306). Nonetheless, in all likelihood the third response is a somewhat later addition. The response is missing from the following manuscripts: *BAV Vatican Copt. 17* (AD 1288), *Bodleian Ind. Inst. Copt. 4* (13th/14th c.), *Bodleian Hunt. 572* (13th/14th c.), *Paris BnF Copt. 82* (AD 1307), *BAV Borgia Copt. 7* (AD 1379), *Paris BnF Copt. 39* (15th c.), *BAV*

167 Corrected orthographically, the response would be "Ἐπὶ προσευχὴν στάθητε." Cf. Burmester, "The Greek Kīrugmata," 366.

168 Corrected orthographically, the response would be "Προσεύξασθε." Cf. Burmester, "The Greek Kīrugmata," 366.

169 Ṣalīb, ⲡⲓϫⲱⲙ ⲛ̀ⲧⲉ ⲡⲓⲉⲩⲭⲟⲗⲟⲅⲓⲟⲛ, 223–224.

170 Derda, *Deir el-Naqlun*, 2:71.

Vatican Copt. 25 (17th c.), *BAV Vatican Copt. 19* (AD 1715), *BAV Vatican Copt. 78* (AD 1722), *BAV Vatican Copt. 81* (AD 1722), and *British Library Or. 8778* (AD 1726). It is true that as Euchologia, they should not be expected necessarily to include all diaconal responses. However, in every manuscript where the third response, "Pray that God may have mercy," is missing, the second response, "Pray,"—and a number of other diaconal commands throughout the formulary–are included. At any rate, it is common in the Coptic manuscript tradition for the strict distinction between Euchologia and diaconals to be gradually abandoned over time, which weakens the argument that the Euchologia listed here *should* not include the third response. Thus, it can be concluded, based on the number of manuscripts, that the first and second response (Stand up for prayer, and Pray), are certainly older and more stable in the history of the *Prayer of Thanksgiving* than the third response, "Pray that God may have mercy."

The other observation to be made regarding these diaconal commands is their clear instability in terms of location within the prayer. In one case, *Bodleian Hunt. 360* (13th c.), the second command, "Pray," is grouped together with the first, rather than interrupting the prayer in its current position. In another case, *BAV Borgia Copt. 7* (AD 1379), the first command was moved to immediately precede the second. The general conclusion that can be advanced then is that the diaconal commands that today accompany the *Prayer of Thanksgiving* are later accretions that remained unstable in their usage and location within the prayer for a long time.

5.6. The Concluding Doxology

Today in actual practice, the celebrant proclaims the *Prayer of Thanksgiving* audibly only until [12] in the English text above: "and upon all the power of the enemy [Lk 10:19]," reciting the remainder of the prayer silently. While one cannot venture a hypothesis based on the available sources for the reason why the biblical reference from Matthew 6:13 would be said inaudibly, there is in fact clear evidence that the concluding doxology, "through the grace, compassion, and love of man, etc.," was never traditionally recited inaudibly. Rather, the concluding doxologies of all litanies and prayers functioned as a clear marker of hierarchical seniority and were reserved for the bishop or patriarch whenever they presided, which implies that they were proclaimed audibly.

First, the liturgical manuscripts themselves are entirely silent on the issue. Not a single Euchologion examined for this work, ranging from the thirteenth to the twentieth centuries, indicated that the concluding doxology or any part of the prayer is to be read inaudibly. This is quite indicative and not an argument *ex silentio* as it may seem. Coptic Euchologia as early as the thirteenth century have indicated some prayers as to be said secretly, as was seen in the fragments published by O.H.E. Burmester,[171] and also later in *BAV Vatican Copt. 25* (17th c.) with respect to the prayers of the altar preparation. It is then very significant that the concluding doxology is never indicated as such.

The concluding doxology was consistently mentioned in commentaries and guides as a phrase reserved for the presiding hierarch. This appears first in the *Precious Jewel* of Ibn Sabbāʿ (14th c.), where he writes:

[1] فيبتدي الكاهن بصلاة الشكر الى اخرها. [2] وعند نهايتها ان كان رئيس الكهنه حاضرا يقول باي اداوول هي ضدف. [3] وفي كل الاواشي تتمتها كذلك.[172]

[1] And the priest begins with the *Prayer of Thanksgiving* to its end. [2] And at its conclusion, if the high priest is present, he says, "This is He through whom." [3] And all prayers are concluded in this manner.

Ibn Sabbāʿ goes on to give this practice an anagogical interpretation that is quite elaborate. According to him, man was created in order to replace the fallen angels in offering praise and adoration to the Triune God. In Ibn Sabbāʿ's conception of the heavenly liturgy, Satan's duty was to transfer and elevate the praise of lower-ranking angels to God. However, by refusing to do so and being deluded that this praise was offered to him personally, he fell from grace. Thus, the author continues, the bishop is appointed, "head of the priests, the earthly priestly rank, who are earthly angels and heavenly men. And he seals the *Prayer of Thanksgiving*, which is offered by those whom he rules, and he completes it with his own mouth."[173]

Although lacking the anagogical interpretation of Ibn Sabbāʿ, the *Lamp of Darkness* of Ibn Kabar confirms the practice in its later manuscript *Uppsala O. Vet. 12* (AD 1546). In a chapter describing the patriarchal services following the description of regular presbyteral liturgies, Ibn Kabar indicates that the patriarch is to say the concluding doxology for the litany in the context of vespers or matins.[174] The same instructions can be found in the patriarchal liturgy in codex *Coptic Patriarchate Lit. 74* (AD 1444), where the patriarch is to say the concluding doxology of the litany of the departed, a standard

171 Burmester, "Fragments of a Late 12th to Early 13th Century Bohairic Euchologion," 39n1; Brakmann, "Zu den Fragmenten," 127n53.

172 *Paris BnF Ar. 207* (14th c.), fol. 124v. Cf. Mistrīḥ, *Pretiosa margarita*, 184 (Arabic), 490–491 (Latin).

173 Ibid., 185.

174 *Uppsala O. Vet. 12* (AD 1546), fol. 188r. Cf. Villecourt, "Les observances," 276.

element of the Coptic *Vespers Raising of Incense*.[175] Finally, nowhere is this custom more highlighted than in the later patriarchal liturgy found in the codex *Baramūs 6/278* (AD 1514), where the priests are instructed the following:

[1] وفي اخر كل سر يلتفت يخضع للبطريرك وهو يقول اخر القول [2] والبطريرك يكمل ان كان ⲫⲁⲓ ⲉⲧⲉ او ⲟⲩⲟϩ ⲛ̀ⲑⲟⲕ [3] لا يبديهم الكاهن لكن يقول اخر كلامه والبطريرك هو الذي يكمل.[176]

[1] At the end of each prayer,[177] he is to turn to the patriarch as he is saying the last clause, [2] while the patriarch completes, whether it is "To whom..." or "And to You...," [3] and no priest is to begin [this], but he is to say the last of his words and the patriarch is the one to complete.

It is important to note that—unlike the *Precious Jewel* of Ibn Sabbāʿ—in later fifteenth and sixteenth century patriarchal liturgies, it was the patriarch himself that recited the entire prayer, which marked his ascent to the altar and the first prayer he was to pronounce even while unvested.[178] Thus, these sources do not directly speak of the silent doxology in the context of the *Prayer of Thanksgiving* in the prothesis rite.

Nonetheless, it is clear that the concluding doxology was regarded as a solemn seal of the entire prayer, whether concerning the *Prayer of Thanksgiving* specifically or all other prayers. As such, it was consistently reserved for the patriarch or hierarch in his presence as a sign of respect, something highly emphasized in one source above, where the priest is also instructed to turn to the patriarch in a clear sign of reverence. It would be quite unthinkable for such great emphasis to be placed on a phrase that was at any rate recited silently, rendering all such instructions for the priest not to say the doxology irrelevant. The evidence then strongly indicates that at least between the thirteenth and sixteenth centuries the concluding doxologies of all prayers—the *Prayer of Thanksgiving* included—were recited aloud by the celebrant in presbyteral liturgies.

175 *Coptic Patriarchate Lit. 74* (AD 1444), fol. 70v. Cf. Samuel, *Tartīb al-bīʿa*, 1:9.

176 Samuel, *Tartīb al-bīʿa*, 1:21; Mikhail, "The Liturgy *Coram Patriarcha* Revisited," 309 (Arabic), 310 (English).

177 Literally, "mystery (سر)," typically used for inaudible prayers, though here seemingly applied in a general sense to any priestly prayer.

178 *Coptic Patriarchate Lit. 74* (AD 1444), fol. 74v; Cf. Samuel, *Tartīb al-bīʿa*, 1:17, 21; *Uppsala O. Vet. 12* (AD 1514), fol. 188v; Villecourt, "Les observances," 278; Mikhail, "The Liturgy *Coram Patriarcha* Revisited," 307–312.

6. CONCLUSION

During the course of this chapter, three liturgical units were analyzed in detail. These are the blessing over the oblations, the mixing of the chalice, and the *Prayer of Thanksgiving*. Repeatedly, the shift from the old ordo to the new ordo has made it possible to properly contextualize the elements under discussion and to understand their pristine function and location. It is now time to give a broad summary of what has been accomplished in this chapter.

Although the previous chapter ended with the procession around the altar, which is surely the descendant of the pre-anaphoral procession of the gifts from the pastophorion, the subsequent rites analyzed in this chapter—with the exception of the *Prayer of* Thanksgiving—still largely concern the preparation of the gifts. These rites would have been performed—albeit embryonically—in the prothesis pastophorion until the intermediate ordo of Ibn Sabbāʻ at the latest. However, unlike the earliest stages of the preparation of the gifts, which involved deacons alone and contained no ritual elements strictly speaking, one sees here a clear stamp of the ritualization of the prothesis, where the practical matters of selecting and setting the eucharistic gifts transition into the ritual preparation of the gifts in the form of blessings and prayers.

This move towards the ritual phase of the rite is marked clearly by the initial exchange of blessings among the clergy. This is followed by the blessing over the gifts, which was likely only over the bread before evolving to be pronounced over the wine as well. So important is this blessing, that it was reserved for the hierarch in the patriarchal liturgy of *Coptic Patriarchate Lit. 74* (AD 1444) and all later patriarchal liturgies in *Baramūs 6/278* (AD 1514) and the *Lamp of Darkness* of *Uppsala O. Vet. 12* (AD 1546), despite the fact that he would not vest or enter the sanctuary until later. Next, the mixing of the chalice was done, a function that was retained as a duty of the deacon in most of the sources. Beginning ca. seventeenth century, this function came to be assigned to the priest instead, as seen in the treatise *The Mystery of the Trinity*. Although the mixing of the chalice today is accompanied by the deacon's proclamation *One is the Holy Father* followed by Psalm 116, neither of these were likely original or formed part of the preparation of the gifts in the old ordo. While the former is clearly a duplication of the pre-communion response to the *sancta sanctis*, the latter has no parallel elsewhere and is more suitable as the beginning of the enarxis, or the liturgy proper.

Finally, the *Prayer of Thanksgiving* is firmly within the domain of the enarxis and can no longer be regarded—as has been the custom—as part of the prothesis rite. The prayer functions as an enarxis prayer elsewhere, not just in other Coptic services, but also in the Melkite Alexandrian tradition as seen in Melkite MARK. Representing a unique Alexandrian liturgical feature, the prayer likely appeared after the fifth century, but well before the turn of the second millennium. Compared to other witnesses of this prayer in the Melkite tradition, the Coptic *textus receptus* is closer to the older recension found in *BAV Vatican Gr. 2281* (AD 1207), except for a major duplication of a few initial clauses. As the enarxis prayer par excellence in the Patriarchate of Alexandria, it is no surprise that its concluding doxology was reserved for the patriarch at least in the *Precious Jewel*, despite the fact that, once again, he was not to vest until afterwards according to the patriarchal rubrics of *Coptic Patriarchate Lit. 74* (AD 1444). Although the prayer is clearly unrelated to the prothesis in its original purpose, it was nonetheless necessary to treat it here at length given the popular perception that it is in fact an integral element of the rite.

This will make it possible below in Excursus 3 to address a particularly fascinating theory, which attempted to see in the prothesis a truly self-sufficient ancient eucharistic prayer with its own anaphoral/thanksgiving prayer over the cup in continuity with Jewish meal traditions and early Christian eucharistic gatherings. Conclusions in this chapter regarding the *Prayer of Thanksgiving* already set the stage for a rigorous evaluation of this theory. In addition, authentic and ancient elements of the prothesis continue after the *Prayer of Thanksgiving* in the unfolding of the Coptic liturgy. This includes the *Prothesis Prayer* itself, which constitutes the most ancient priestly element of the entire preparation of the gifts in the old ordo. The incongruity of this crucial prayer today following and not preceding the enarxis is analyzed in the following chapter.

CHAPTER 6

THE PROTHESIS PRAYER AND THE ABSOLUTIONS

After the celebrant has concluded the *Prayer of Thanksgiving*, he begins praying the *Prothesis Prayer* secretly. During this time, the congregation or chanters intone the first syllable of the melodic acclamation ⲥⲱⲑⲏⲥ ⲁⲙⲏⲛ, usually translated as "Saved, amen," although its exact meaning is analyzed below. Alternatively, if a bishop is in attendance, the hymn *All the wise men of Israel* (ⲛⲓⲥⲁⲃⲉⲩ ⲧⲏⲣⲟⲩ), is chanted instead, which corresponds to the ancient place of the hierarchical vesting, though the vesting itself is no longer postponed to this point. At the conclusion of the *Prothesis Prayer*, the celebrant covers the altar with the *prospherin* veil, which extends from the western end of the altar covering the paten and reaches to the eastern end, thus covering the chalice throne with the mixed chalice in it. This act of covering is done with the help of a deacon or altar servant standing across from the celebrant. Finally, according to current practice, the priest folds a small altar cloth into a triangle and places it on top of the *prospherin*, precisely at the place where it covers the top of the chalice.

Afterwards, the celebrant is to venerate the altar and walk around to its southern side. There, he is to prostrate to the east and venerate the altar once more. Continuing his tour around the altar, the celebrant goes to the eastern side, where he receives a prostration from the deacon and other assistants. Everyone then exits the sanctuary. The deacons and assistants bow before the sanctuary entrance, while reads the absolution over them. This privilege is appointed to a bishop if celebrating. If two or more priests are celebrating, the absolution is to be pronounced by a non-celebrating priest, that is, a priest who is not the celebrant. While the rubrics appoint two absolutions at this point–the *Absolution of the Son* or *Absolution of the Father*, depending on which of the three anaphoras will be prayed, followed by the *Absolution of the Servants*–only the last of these is pronounced aloud in actual practice. After the conclusion of the absolution, the bowing servants now rise and re-enter the sanctuary with the celebrant to commence the incense rites before the Liturgy of the Word. Meanwhile, the chanters and congregation continue the chanting of either *May you be saved* or *All the wise men of Israel,* which are interrupted for the absolutions.[1]

Thus, in just such a smooth and almost imperceptible way, the new ordo of the Coptic liturgy transitions from the prothesis rite through the enarxis and to the Liturgy of the Word. This chapter then is the final stage in the liturgical and historical analysis of the prothesis rite, taking the absolutions as a terminal point. This choice is based on the perception that the absolutions represent the *conclusion* of the prothesis, though the discussion below argues that this is a misunderstanding of their original function.

The fact of the matter is that the *Prothesis Prayer*, as in the Syro-Byzantine East, is the most ancient element of the entire rite. Although the preparation of the gifts as such goes back much earlier, it is precisely the *Prothesis Prayer* which first imparted the quality of a liturgical rite to what was originally a simple and practical preparation. Among all the prayers and formulas comprising the prothesis rite, this prayer is also the one with the most theological content and significance. The central petition of the prayer calls upon the Logos to shine his face upon the bread and wine and to bless, sanctify, purify, and change them into his body and blood, using language typically reserved for the epiclesis prayer in the anaphora. In a sense, this prayer communicates the entire theological content of the prothesis rite, and as such, it occupies the major part of this final chapter. In addition to the consecratory language of the prayer and the questions it raises regarding the theology of consecration in the Coptic liturgy, the prayer is also interesting in terms of its textual history, as well as its location in the unfolding of the Coptic liturgy. While the latter is explored in this chapter, a separate excursus discusses the consecratory language of this prayer and its implications for the understanding of eucharistic consecration in the Coptic Orthodox Church.

1. THE PROTHESIS PRAYER

The prayer appears with interesting variants first in the Southern Italian Byzantine tradition, as well as in practically all the local rites comprising the Alexandrian liturgical realm, such as Melkite MARK, the Nubian, and Ethiopian liturgies. After the relationship among these various versions has been elucidated, the issue of the location of this prayer in the unfolding of the Coptic liturgy is addressed. As it stands today, the prayer comes *after* the *Prayer of Thanksgiving*, a

1 Ṣalīb, ⲡⲓϫⲱⲙ ⲛ̀ⲧⲉ ⲡⲓⲉⲩⲭⲟⲗⲟⲅⲓⲟⲛ, 225–234. Cf. Burmester, *The Egyptian Church*, 54–55.

prayer that was judged in the previous chapter to be an enarxis prayer, with no relation to the prothesis rite whatsoever. This fact raises the question as to why the *Prothesis Prayer*, the oldest and most central to the rite, would appear after and not before the enarxis prayer as one would expect it.

1.1. The Title of the Prayer

Remaining withing the Coptic tradition, it should be noted that the title of the prayer varies considerably among manuscripts, printed editions, and commentaries. First, the title of the prayer in the *editio typica* of 1902 is, "The prayer of the prothesis of the bread and the chalice to the Son."[2] The use of the terms ⲡⲣⲟⲑⲉⲥⲓⲥ or التقدمة, rendered here as *prothesis* is attested in the manuscript tradition with minor variations. The two oldest examples are *Bodleian Hunt. 360* (13th c.), in which the title is, "A prayer over the prothesis of the holy oblation when you elevate it upon the altar, for the Son,"[3] as well as *BAV Vatican Copt. 17* (AD 1288), in which the title is, "A prayer for the prothesis of the bread and the chalice."[4]

By far, the most common title in the manuscripts is, "The Prayer of/upon the prothesis,"[5] also attested in *The Guide to the Beginners*

2 (صلاة تقدمة الخبز والكاس للابن): Ṣalīb, ⲡⲓϫⲱⲙ ⲛ̀ⲧⲉ ⲡⲓⲉⲩⲭⲟⲗⲟⲅⲓⲟⲛ, 225. The Arabic word,تقدمة (*taqdima*) could be translated as: presentation, offering, placing forward, all meanings that can be captured nicely with the technical term, *prothesis*. Cf. Wehr, *A Dictionary of Modern Written Arabic*, 878.

3 (ⲟⲩⲉⲩⲭⲏ ⲛ̀ϯⲡⲣⲟⲑⲉⲥⲓⲥ ⲛ̀ⲧⲉ ϯⲡⲣⲟⲥⲫⲟⲣⲁ ⲉ̅ⲑ̅ⲩ̅ ⲁⲕϣⲁⲛⲧⲁⲗⲟⲥ ⲉ̀ϫⲉⲛ ⲡⲓⲙⲁⲛ̀ⲉⲣϣⲱⲟⲩϣⲓ, صلاة على تقدمة القربان المقدس اذا ما رفعته على المذبح مختصة بالابن): *Bodleian Hunt. 360* (13th c.), fol. 14r. The Arabic title above adds the reference to the Son.

4 (صلاة على تقدمة الخبز والكاس): *BAV Vatican Copt. 17* (AD 1288), fol. 8r. Cf. Wadi, "Testo della Traduzione Araba," 133; also seen in *Paris BnF Copt. 26* (before AD 1523), fol. 12v, *Suryān Lit. 466* (AD 1573), fol. 11r, *Suryān Lit. 468* (AD 1601), fol. 11r, *Suryān Lit. 469* (before AD 1623), fol. 12v, *Suryān Lit. 472* (AD 1659), fol. 11v, *Suryān Lit. 473* (AD 1659), fol. 12r, *Suryān Lit. 474* (AD 1666), fol. 11v, *Suryān Lit. 457* (AD 1758), fol. 5r, *Suryān Lit. 482* (AD 1787), fol. 13v, *Coptic Museum Lit. 80* (AD 1796), fol. 13v, *Suryān Lit. 484* (AD 1841), fol. 94r, and *British Library Or. 5282* (AD 1872), fol. 38v.

5 (ⲟⲩⲉⲩⲭⲏ ⲛ̀ⲧⲉ ϯⲡⲣⲟⲑⲉⲥⲓⲥ, اوشية التقدمة, صلاة التقدمة, or ⲟⲩⲉⲩⲭⲏ ⲉ̀ϫⲉⲛ ϯⲡⲣⲟⲑⲉⲥⲓⲥ, صلاة على التقدمة): *Paris BnF Copt. 82* (AD 1307), fol. 5r, *BAV Borgia Copt. 7* (AD 1379), fol. 12r, *Kacmarcik Codex* (14th c.), fol. 7r, *BAV Vatican Copt. 25* (14th c.), fol. 10v, *Coptic Patriarchate Lit. 74* (AD 1444), fol. 74v, *Baramūs 6/278* (AD 1514), *Paris BnF Copt. 73* (AD 1528), fol. 13r, *BAV Vatican Copt. 18* (AD 1531), fol. 123v, *BAV Vatican Copt.* 26 (AD 1616), fol. 16v, *Paris BnF Copt. 29* (AD 1639), fol. 10r, *Paris BnF Copt. 30* (AD 1642), fol. 17r, *Coptic Patriarchate Lit. 331* (AD 1678), fol. 15r, *British Library Or. 429* (17th/18th c.), fol. 14r, *British Library Or. 431* (AD 1718), fol. 9v, *Suryān Lit. 481* (AD 1752), fol. 10r, and *Hamburg Bishoy Euchol. 6* (18th/19th c.), fol. 2r.

and the Correction of the Laity attributed to Cyril III ibn Laqlaq,[6] and the *Ritual Order* of Gabriel V.[7] Other similar examples include, "Prayer for the prothesis of the oblation and the chalice,"[8] "Prayer of the prothesis of the bread and chalice,"[9] "The prayer of the prothesis secretly over the bread and the chalice,"[10] "The prayer of the prothesis to the Son, secretly,"[11] "A prayer for the bread of the prothesis and the chalice,"[12] "A prayer over the bread of the prothesis,"[13] "A prayer over the bread of the prothesis, to the Son,"[14] "A prayer on the prothesis of the oblation,"[15] or the slightly wordier, "Prayer on the prothesis of the Holy oblation to the Son."[16]

In other instances, the title is more general and does not include the term prothesis at all. This is the case in the title: "A prayer [said over] the bread and the chalice,"[17] or only on the bread.[18] Other examples include "A prayer of the table,"[19] a title attested also in Ibn Kabar's the *Lamp of Darkness*,[20] and the most fascinating, "A prayer to consecrate the bread and the chalice."[21]

Finally, some manuscripts seem to have been based on the assumption that the *Prothesis Prayer* itself is in fact an enarxis prayer,

6 *BAV Vatican Ar. 117* (AD 1323), fol. 198r. Cf. Graf, "Liturgische Anweisungen," 122.

7 *Paris BnF Ar. 98* (17th c.), fol. 52v. Cf. ʻAbdallah, *L'ordinamento*, 179 (Arabic), 366 (Italian).

8 (صلاة لتقدمة القربان والكاس): *Coptic Museum Lit. 462* (19th c.), fol. 63r.

9 (ⲟⲩⲉⲩⲭⲏ ⲛ̀ϯⲡⲣⲟⲑⲉⲥⲓⲥ ⲛ̀ⲧⲉ ⲡⲓⲱⲓⲕ ⲛⲉⲙ ⲡⲓⲁⲫⲟⲧ, اوشية تقدمة الخبز والكاس): Paris *BnF Copt. 31* (15th c.), fol. 8r, and the similar title in *Hamburg Macarius Euchol. 30* (17th/18th c.), fol. 1v replacing the ⲛ̀ (of) with ⲉ̀ϫⲉⲛ (upon).

10 (صلاة التقدمة سراً على الخبز و الكاس): *Beinecke Copt. 21* (AD 1877), fol. 70v.

11 (اوشية التقدمة للابن سراً): *Suryān Lit. 465* (AD 1645), fol. 20v.

12 (صلاة على خبز التقدمة والكاس): *Coptic Museum Lit. 344* (AD 1752), fol. 36r.

13 (صلاة على خبز التقدمة): *Rylands Copt. 427* (AD 1749), fol. 16v; *Suryān Lit. 459* (AD 1788), fol. 15v.

14 (صلاة على خبز التقدمة للابن): *Suryān Lit. 477* (AD 1792), fol. 16v.

15 (ⲟⲩⲉⲩⲭⲏ ⲛ̀ϯⲡⲣⲟⲑⲉⲥⲓⲥ ⲛ̀ⲧⲉ ⲡⲓⲱⲓⲕ, صلاة على تقدمة القربان): *Paris BnF Copt. 39* (15th c.), fol. 14r.

16 (صلاة على تقدمة القربان المقدس للابن): *Paris BnF Copt. 25* (15th/16th c.), fol. 11v.

17 (ⲟⲩⲉⲩⲭⲏ ⲉ̀ϫⲉⲛ ⲡⲓⲱⲓⲕ ⲛⲉⲙ ⲡⲓⲁⲫⲟⲧ, صلاة تقال على الخبز والكاس): *BAV Vatican Copt. 19* (18th c.), fol. 12r, *British Library Add. 17725* (AD 1811), fol. 13r, *BAV Vatican Copt. 78* (AD 1722), fol. 12v, *BAV Vatican Copt. 81* (AD 1722), fol. 12v. In all cases, the Arabic adds the phrase [said over], absent in the Coptic.

18 (صلاة على الخبز): *Coptic Museum Lit. 16* (AD 1928–1942), fol. 5v.

19 (ⲟⲩⲉⲩⲭⲏ ⲛ̀ⲧⲉ ϯⲧⲣⲁⲡⲉⲍⲁ, صلاة [لتقدمة] المائدة): *British Library Or. 8778* (AD 1726), fol. 11r. The Arabic adds to the Coptic title, rendering it "A Prayer *for the offering* of the table". Also, *Paris BnF Copt. 28* (13th/14th c.), fol. 13r, and *Beinecke Copt. 20* (19th c.), with no remaining folio number.

20 *Paris BnF Ar. 203* (AD 1363–1369), fol. 203v. Cf. Villecourt, "Les observances," 249.

21 (صلاة لتقديس الخبز والكاس): *British Library Or. 430* (AD 1832), fol. 41r.

giving it the title "A prayer of the beginning."[22] This is the case with minor variations combining ideas of offering or prothesis of the bread and/or chalice in the following manuscripts: *Paris BnF Copt. 26* (before AD 1523), fol. 12r,[23] *Suryān Lit. 485* (AD 1784), fol. 65r, *Coptic Museum Lit. 265* (18th c.), fol. 34r, *Coptic Museum Lit. 412* (AD 1867), fol. 72r, and *Coptic Museum Lit. 462* (19th c.), fol. 63r. At any rate, as can be seen here, the most ubiquitous title in the manuscripts, and the one appearing in some of the oldest sources contains the word *taqdima* or prothesis in some variation.

1.2. The Text of the Prayer

Once again, limiting the discussion at first to the text in the Coptic tradition, the *textus receptus* appears to be quite stable with no significant variants. It is presented below translated from the Euchologion of 1902:

> [1] O Master Lord Jesus Christ, the co-eternal Logos of the immaculate Father, who is co-essential with him and the Holy Spirit, [2] for you are the living bread, which came down from heaven [Jn 6:51], and has made yourself a spotless lamb for the life of the world [Jn 1:29]. [3] We ask and entreat your goodness, O lover of mankind, shine your face upon this bread and upon this cup, these which have been placed upon this your priestly table: [4] bless them, sanctify them, purify, and change them. [5] So that this bread may become your holy body, and the mixture in this cup your honored blood. [6] And may they become unto all of us communion, healing, and salvation of our souls, our bodies, and our spirits. [7] For you are our God, and to you belongs glory with your good Father and the Holy Spirit the life-giver and co-essential with you. [8] Now and at all times and unto ages of all ages, amen.[24]

In order to aid the analysis of the text, the ideas of the prayer in its Coptic *textus receptus* can be summarized as follows: 1. Opening address, 2. identification of Christ as the bread coming down from heaven and the spotless lamb, 3. entreaty for Christ to shine his face upon the bread and wine placed on the altar, 4. in order to bless, sanctify, purify, and change them, 5. to the body and blood, 6. for communion, healing, and salvation, 7. followed by the concluding doxology.

22 (ⲟⲩⲉⲩⲭⲏ ⲙ̀ⲡⲣⲱⲙⲓⲟⲛ صلاة بداية). ⲡⲣⲱⲙⲓⲟⲛ = Gr προοίμιον, a beginning or introduction.

23 This is the case in the Coptic title of the prayer in this manuscript, which differs from the Arabic translation, "A prayer of the prothesis of the bread and chalice," as stated above.

24 Ṣalīb, ⲡⲓϫⲱⲙ ⲛ̀ⲧⲉ ⲡⲓⲉⲩⲭⲟⲗⲟⲅⲓⲟⲛ, 225–228.

Among all the prayers analyzed in this work and found in the Coptic prothesis rite, this prayer is by far the most widespread, appearing in five liturgical traditions, and represented broadly in three main recensions or types, which can be called ancient, intermediate, and modern, respectively. The following analysis attempts to sort out these various versions and identify their interrelationship as well as the textual evolution of this prayer.

1.2.1. The Ancient Recension

Although, as will be explained below, scholars generally agree that this prayer is Egyptian in origin, the ancient recension of this prayer is preserved in Byzantine manuscripts of Southern Italy. The earliest witness to this version is the codex *BAV Barberini Gr. 336* (8th c.), in which the prayer is found as the *Prothesis Prayer* of CHR and as the first prayer in the entire formulary:

[1] Κύριε ὁ θεὸς ἡμῶν, [2] ὁ προθεὶς ἑαυτὸν ἀμνὸν ἄμωμον ὑπὲρ τῆς τοῦ κόσμου ζωῆς, [3] ἔφιδε ἐφ'ἡμᾶς καὶ ἐπὶ τὸν ἄρτον τοῦτον καὶ ἐπὶ τὸ ποτήριον τοῦτο, [4] καὶ ποίησον ἀυτὸ ἄχραντόν σου σῶμα καὶ τίμιόν σου αἷμα [5] εἰς μετάληψιν ψυχῶν καὶ σωμάτων. [6] Ὅτι ἡγίασται καὶ δεδόξασται τὸ πάντιμον καὶ μεγαλοπρεπές [ὄνομά σου].[25]	[1] O Lord our God, [2] who offered himself a blameless lamb for the life of the world, [3] Look upon us, and upon this bread and upon this cup, [4] and make it your pure body and honorable blood, [5] for the communion of souls and bodies. [6] For hallowed and glorified is your all-honored and majestic name.

The prayer appears frequently in later manuscripts of the Southern Italian region, especially as a *Prothesis Prayer* of CHR. Jacob and Parenti provide the most comprehensive list, with Parenti adding a helpful indication of the variants whenever applicable.[26] Examples include *Grottaferrata Γβ IV* (10th c.), *St. Petersburg NLR 226* (10th c.),[27] the Sinai Slavic leaflets *Sinai Glagol. 37* or the so-called *Euchologium Sinaiticum* (11th c.),[28] *Messina Gr. 160* (11th c.),

25 Parenti and Velkovska, *L'Eucologio Barberini gr. 336*, 71 (Greek), 272 (Italian). As is common in most liturgical manuscripts, the final doxology is frequently omitted in the process of copying. Above, ὄνομά σου is added for clarity.

26 André Jacob, "Histoire du formulaire grec de la liturgie de saint Jean Chrysostome" (doctoral dissertation, Université de Louvain, 1968), 197–202; Stefano Parenti, "Influssi italo-greci nei testi eucaristici bizantini dei 'Fogli Slavi' del Sinai (XI sec.)," *OCP* 57 (1991): 145–177, here 158–167.

27 André Jacob, "L'euchologe de Porphyre Uspenski Cod. Leningr. Gr. 226 (Xe siècle)," *Le Muséon* 68 (1965): 173–214, here 183.

28 For the Glagolitic text with a French translation and a Greek retroversion, see Jean Frček, *Euchologium Sinaiticum: Texte Slave avec sources grecques et traduction*

Grottaferrata Γβ VIII (12th c.), *BAV Vatican Gr. 2005* (AD 1194–1195), *Grottaferrata Γβ XIII* (13th c.), *BAV Vatican Gr. 2012* (16th c.), *Strasbourg Gr. 1899* (AD 1523), and *Modena Gr. 16* (16th c.).

In addition to CHR, the prayer is also indicated in certain manuscripts of the Southern-Italian liturgy of PETER. This includes the manuscripts *Grottaferrata Γβ VII* (10th c.),[29] where it is only an incipit implying that perhaps the prayer was included earlier in CHR as well. Other examples include *BAV Vatican Gr. 1970* (12th c.),[30] *BAV Vatican Borghes. Ser. I 506* (AD 1581), *BAV Ottoboni Gr. 189* (16th c.), and *Paris BnF Gr. 322* (16th c.).[31] It can also be found–though with expected modification–in some formularies of Byzantine PRES, such as *Ambrosiana Gr. 276* (13th c.), and *Munich Bayerische Staatsbibliothek Gr. 540* (AD 1416). Finally, the ancient recension is found in Arabic translation in the version published by Constantin Bacha, which is considered to represent eleventh-century practice.[32]

Although some of the later Byzantine manuscripts in this group add certain common phrases to the pristine text of *BAV Barberini Gr. 336* (8th c.), the additions are considered minor and do not substantially add to the basic six points comprising the ancient recension in its briefest witnesses.[33] The notable differences between this ancient recension and the Coptic *textus receptus* lie in the latter's 1. expanded greeting, 2. the reference to Christ, the bread that came down from heaven, 3. the petition is for Christ to shine his face, rather than to look down, 4. explicit verbs of consecration, and 5. expanded benefits of communion.

française, vol. 2, PO 25.3 (123) (Turnhout: Brepols, 1989), 489–617, here 606–607. These leaflets are discussed in detail in Parenti, "Influssi italo-greci".

29 Gaetano Passarelli, *L'Eucologio Cryptense Γ.β. VII (sec. X)*, Ἀνάλεκτα Βλατάδων 36 (Thessaloniki: Πατριαρχηκόν Ἵδρυμα Πατερικῶν Μελετῶν, 1982), 167; H.W. Codrington, *The Liturgy of Saint Peter*, Liturgiegeschichtliche Quellen und Forschungen 30 (Münster: Aschendorff, 1936), 130.

30 Ibid., 137.

31 The prayer also appears in a late manuscript of PETER, *BAV Ottoboni Gr. 384* (AD 1581), though in this case it varies significantly from all available texts to merit excluding it from this general scheme. Cf. Ibid., 168–169.

32 Constantin Bacha, "*Notions générales sur les versions arabes de la liturgie de S. Jean Chrysostome suivies d'une ancienne version inédite*," in *ΧΡΥΣΟΣΤΟΜΙΚΑ*: *Studi e ricerche intorno a S. Giovanni Crisostomo a cura del comitato per il XVo centenario della sua morte* (Rome: Libreria Pustet, 1908), 405–471, here 411 (Arabic), 442 (French).

33 For details concerning these minor additions, see Parenti, "Influssi italo-greci," 145–177.

1.2.2. The Intermediate Recension

Interestingly, all witnesses of this intermediate recension are found in sources that are directly Alexandrian, rather than in Byzantine texts, such as CHR, PETER, or PRES. In fact, most of the witnesses of this intermediate recension appear in Melkite MARK, with the exception of one source whose exact textual context is unclear. This latter witness also happens to be the shortest and makes for a logical bridge from the ancient recension of *BAV Barberini Gr. 336* (8th c.). The witness in question is Prayer 2 in the Nubian liturgical texts, attested specifically in 1. the *Qaṣr Ibrīm Codex*,[34] 2. the northern pastophorion in the Faras Cathedral,[35] 3. the northern pastophorion of Building 5, a Church of Archangel Raphael, in the citadel of Dongola, 4. Room 27 of the northwestern annex of a monastery on Kom H in Dongola, and 5. Room 7 of the commemorative complex of the northwestern annex in the same monastery.[36] Of all the witnesses of the prayer in the Nubian evidence, the text as found in Room 7 of the commemorative complex in the monastery on Kom H in Dongola was published most recently and provides a good example of the text as follows:

[1] Κύριε Ἰησοῦ Χριστέ, ἀκατάληπτε λόγε καὶ συνάναρχε τοῦ ἀχράντου σου Πατρὸς καὶ Πνεῦματος ἁγίου, [2] σὺ εἶ ὁ ἄρτος ὁ ἐκ τοῦ οὐρανοῦ καταβάς, [3] σὺ εἰσπροσέθησας σεαυτὸν ἀμνὸν ἄμωμον ὑπὲρ τῆς τοῦ κόσμου ζωῆς. [4] ἐπίφανον τὸ πρόσωπόν σου ἐπὶ τὸν ἄρτον τοῦτον καὶ ἐπὶ τὸ ποτήριον τοῦτο [5] εἰς μεταποίησιν τοῦ ἀχράντου σου σώματος καὶ τοῦ τιμίου αἵματος [6] ἐν οἷς σε ὑποδέχεται τράπεζα ἀποστολικῇ λειτουργίᾳ καὶ ἱερατικῇ ὑμνῳδίᾳ [7] εἰς περιποίησιν καὶ ἀντίλημψιν ψυχῶν καὶ τῶν σωμάτων, ὅτι εὐλογεῖται.[37]	[1] O Lord Jesus Christ, the Logos incomprehensible and without beginning with your immaculate Father and the Holy Spirit, [2] you are the bread that came down from heaven. [3] You offered yourself a spotless lamb for the life of the world. [4] Shine your face upon this bread and upon this cup, [5] unto changing [them] to your immaculate body and honored blood, [6] in which [form] [this] table receives you with apostolic service and priestly chant, [7] unto preservation and refreshment of souls and bodies, for blessed.

34 W.H.C. Frend and I.A. Muirhead, "The Greek Manuscripts from the Cathedral of Q'asr Ibrim," *Le Muséon* 89 (1976): 43–49

35 Kubińska, "Prothesis de la cathédrale de Faras," 20–21.

36 The prayers found in these locations, including the Prothesis Prayer, mostly remain unpublished, with the exception of 1, 2, and 5 above.

37 Adam Łajtar and Jacques van der Vliet, *Empowering the Dead in Christian Nubia: The Texts from a Medieval Funerary Complex in Dongola*, Supplements to the

This version of the prayer is somewhat closer to the Coptic *textus receptus*, albeit with significant differences. The opening address has been expanded from the ancient recension to include the Father and the Holy Spirit, although they are not directly addressed. Christ is now identified as the bread of life. The prayer changes the Byzantine "look upon us," to the distinctly Egyptian "shine your face," characteristic of all non-Byzantine versions. However, the clear difference is that the text still lacks any specific verbs of consecration, asking simply for the bread and wine to be changed.

Also falling within the intermediate recension is the version in Melkite MARK in *BAV Vatican Gr. 2281* (AD 1207):

[1] Δέσποτα Κύριε Ἰησοῦ Χριστέ, ὁ συνάναρχος Υἱὸς τοῦ ἀχράντου Πατρὸς καὶ Πνεύματος ἁγίου, [2] ὁ μέγας ἀρχιερεύς, ὁ προσθεὶς ἑαυτὸν ἀμνὸν ἄμωμον ὑπέρ τῆς τοῦ κόσμου ζωῆς, [3] δεόμεθα καὶ παρακαλοῦμέν σε, φιλάνθρωπε ἀγαθέ, ἐπίφανον, Κύριε, τὸ πρόσωπόν σου ἐπὶ τὸν ἄρτον τοῦτον καὶ ἐπὶ τὸ ποτήριον τοῦτο, [4] εἰς μεταποίησιν τοῦ ἀχράντου σώματος καὶ τοῦ τιμίου σου αἵματος, [5] ἐν οἷς σε ὑποδέχεται τράπεζα παναγία, ἱερατικῇ ὑμνῳδίᾳ, ἀγγελικῇ χοροστασίᾳ, [6] εἰς μετάληψιν ψυχῶν καὶ σωμάτων. [7] Χάριτι καὶ οἰκτιρμοῖς καὶ φιλανθρωπίᾳ τοῦ μονογενοῦς σου Υἱοῦ, δι' οὗ καὶ

[1] O Master Lord Jesus Christ, the coeternal Son of the immaculate Father and the Holy Spirit, [2] the great high priest, who offered himself a blameless lamb for the life of the world. [3] We ask and entreat you, O good lover of mankind, shine your face, O Lord, upon this bread and upon this cup, [4] unto changing [them] to [your] immaculate body and your precious blood, [5] in which [form] the all-holy table receives you with priestly chant and angelic choir, [6] unto communion of souls and bodies. [7] By the grace and compassion and love of mankind of your only-begotten Son, through whom and with whom to you is the

Journal of Juristic Papyrology 32 (Warsaw: Faculty of Law and Administration University of Warsaw / Institute of Archaeology / The Raphael Taubenschlag Foundation, 2017), 54–55. This latest edition of the text from Dongola provides clear images of the actual wall inscriptions, a diplomatic text, as well as an orthographically corrected text of the prayer. This Prayer 2 was connected and attributed to the Nubian PRES by Prof. Adam Łajtar first in a 1996 article about the *Qaṣr Ibrīm codex*, which also contains a prayer of accepting the offerings before and an epiclesis prayer over the bread alone through the presanctified blood after. See Adam Łajtar, "Varia Nubica III: Ein liturgisches Gebet aus Qasr Ibrim," *Zeitschrift für Papyrologie und Epigraphik* 112 (1996): 140–142. The assertion was repeated most recently for the same sequence of prayers as found in the funerary vault in Dongola. See Łajtar and van der Vliet, *Empowering the Dead in Christian Nubia*, 58–59. However, the sequence of prayers need not be necessarily connected to a single service. The text in the *Qaṣr Ibrīm codex* asks Christ to shine his face on the bread and the chalice, but only to change the bread to the body, which indeed suggests the PRES, though imperfectly. However, this assertion for Prayer 2 cannot be accepted for the text in the Dongola funerary vault, which explicitly calls for the change of both bread and wine to body and blood.

μεθ' οὗ σοὶ ἡ δόξα καὶ τὸ κράτος, σὺν τῷ παναγίῳ καὶ ἀγαθῷ καὶ ζωοποιῷ σου Πνεύματι, νῦν καὶ ἀεὶ καὶ εἰς τοὺς αἰῶνας τῶν αἰώνων. Ἀμήν.[38]

glory and the power, with your all-holy, good, and life-giving Spirit, now and ever and unto the ages of ages, amen.

Finally, the same prayer appears in *BAV Vatican Gr. 1970* (12th c.) as such:

[1] Δέσποτα Ἰησοῦ Χριστέ, Κύριε, ὁ συνάναρχος Λόγος τοῦ ἀνάρχου Πατρὸς καὶ τοῦ ἁγίου Πνεύματος, [2] ὁ μέγας ἀρχιερεύς, ὁ ἄρτος ὁ ἐκ τοῦ οὐρανοῦ καταβὰς καὶ ἀναγαγὼν ἐκ φθορᾶς τὴν ζωὴν ἡμῶν, ὁ δοὺς ἑαυτὸν ἀμνὸν ἄμωμον ὑπὲρ τῆς τοῦ κόσμου ζωῆς, [3] δεόμεθα καὶ παρακαλοῦμέν σε, Κύριε φιλάνθρωπε, ἐπίφανον τὸ πρόσωπόν σου ἐπὶ τὸν ἄρτον τοῦτον καὶ ἐπὶ τὰ ποτήρια ταῦτα, ἅ ἡ παναγία τράπεζα ὑποδέχεται, δι'ἀγγελικῆς λειτουργίας καὶ ἀρχαγγελικῆς χοροστασίας καὶ ἱερατικῆς ἱερουργίας, [4] εἰς σὴν δόξαν καὶ ἀνακαινισμὸν τῶν ἡμετερῶν ψυχῶν, [5] χάριτι καὶ οἰκτιρμοῖς καὶ φιλανθρωπίᾳ τοῦ μονογενοῦς σου Υἱοῦ, δι' οὗ καὶ μεθ' οὗ σοὶ ἡ δόξα καὶ τὸ κράτος σὺν τῷ παναγίῳ καὶ ἀγαθῷ καὶ ζωοποιῷ σου Πνεύματι, νῦν καὶ ἀεὶ καὶ εἰς τοὺς αἰῶνας τῶν αἰώνων. Ἀμήν.[39]

[1] O Master Jesus Christ, Lord, the coeternal Word of the Father without beginning, and the Holy Spirit, [2] the great high priest, the bread that came down from heaven, and lifts our life from corruption, who has given himself a blameless lamb for the life of the world, [3] we ask and entreat you, O Lord the lover of mankind, shine your face upon this bread and upon these cups, which the all-holy table receives, through the angelic liturgy and the archangelic choir and the priestly service, [4] unto glory to you and renewal of our souls, [5] by the grace, compassion, and love of mankind of your only-begotten Son, through whom and with whom to you is the glory and the power with your all-holy, good, and life-giving Spirit, now and ever and unto the ages of ages, amen.

Notwithstanding some minor differences in the opening address, *BAV Vatican Gr. 1970* (12th c.) adds the reference to Christ the bread that came down from heaven in [2] and adds also, "and lifts our life from corruption." The petition in [3] entreats for a plurality of cups. The table accepts the bread and the cups through the "angelic liturgy, archangelic choir, and priestly service." Finally, the benefits of communion are changed to "glory to you and renewal of our souls."[40] Besides these minor expansions, the two witnesses of Melkite MARK are noticeably expanded from the Nubian text, especially in

38 Cuming, *The Liturgy of St Mark*, 4.

39 Ibid., 4–5. Cf. Charles Anthony Swainson, *The Greek Liturgies Chiefly from Original Authorities* (Cambridge, 1884), 26–28.

40 Ibid., 5.

describing Christ as both the high priest and the bread. Nonetheless, all three witnesses avoid explicit or specific consecratory verbs besides the general "to change," seen consistently so far in both the ancient and the intermediate recensions. The same is also true for the Arabic version of Melkite MARK found in *Sinai Ar. 237* (13th c.), despite the fragmentary nature of the text. Sections of the prayer represented by an ellipsis in square brackets [...] correspond to parts of the text that were not legible:

[1] ايها السيد الرب يسوع المسيح الذي في البدئ وفي البدئ [اتباركى] دائماً مع الاب وروح القدس. [2] الكاهن العظيم قدمت كخروف الذي لا عيب فيه من اجل حياة كل العالم. [3] نطلب منك ونسأل لك انت الصالح محب البشر ليضىء وجهك على هذا الخبز القربان النقي جسدك الذكي وكذلك في هذا الكاس دم لك طاهر ذكي [4] ولينتقلان الى طباع جسدك [x الذكى وكذلك فى هذا الكاس x][41] و دمك الزكيين وعلى هذه المائدة المقدسة المملوءة قدس [5] اقتبله [...] مجده لا تنقطع بمجامع ملايكته [6] والذى يقتبله يكون خلاص للنفوس والاجساد بموهبة ومحبتك للبشر.[42]

[1] O Master Lord Jesus Christ, who is from the beginning, and in the beginning [blessed?] always with the Father and the Holy Spirit, [2] the high priest, you have been offered as a lamb without blemish for the life of the world. [3] We ask of you and entreat you, O you the good lover of man, let your face shine upon this bread, the pure oblation, your precious body, and likewise [what] is in this cup, your pure and precious blood, [4] to be transformed into the nature of your precious body and blood, which you have received upon this holy table, full of holiness [5] Accept it [...] his ceaseless glory by the choir of his angels. [6] And whoever receives it, may it be salvation of souls and bodies, by the gift and your love of mankind.

The particularly elaborate language in [4] perhaps betrays a free reworking or explanation of the Greek text, rather than a rigid or literal translation. Overall, one can identify the intermediate recension particularly with its verbosity in the opening greeting [1], the addition of high priest to Christ's attributes [2], the petition for Christ to shine his face [3], and in the adjective-noun pairs in [4], such as angelic choirs and priestly chant.

41 The manuscript here has: [xالذكى وكذلك فى هذا الكاسx] = [x the precious and likewise [what is] in this cup x], indicating the scribe wished to cross out this clause after writing it. For clarity, this clause was likewise ignored in the translation.

42 *Sinai Ar. 237* (13th c.), fol. 227r–v.

1.2.3. The Modern Recension

Finally, the most expanded version of the prayer is found in the Coptic and Ethiopian traditions. Within this broad category, the Greek text of the Coptic liturgies is in itself slightly more conservative, as seen particularly in the Greek fragments discovered by Hugh Gerard Evelyn-White and collected as *Coptic Museum Inv. 20* (14th c.):

[1] Δέσποτα Κύριε Ἰησοῦ Χριστέ ὁ συναΐδιος λόγος τοῦ ἀχράντου σου Πατρὸς καὶ Πνεύματος ἁγίου, [2] ὁ ἄρτος ὁ ἐκ τοῦ οὐρανοῦ καταβάς καὶ προθεὶς σεαυτὸν ἀμνὸν ἄμωμον ὑπὲρ τῆς τοῦ κόσμου ζωῆς. [3] Δεόμεθα καὶ παρακαλοῦμέν σε φιλάνθρωπε ἀγαθέ Κύριε, ἐπίφανον τὸ πρόσωπόν σου ἐπὶ τὸν ἄρτον τοῦτον καὶ ἐπὶ τὸ ποτήριον τοῦτο [ἅ] προεθήκαμεν ἐν ταύτῃ τῇ ἱερατικῇ σου τραπέζῃ [4] καὶ ἁγίασον αὐτὰ καὶ μεταποίησον [5] ἵνα ὅ μεν ἄρτος οὗτος γένηται εἰς τὸ ἅγιόν σου σῶμα τὸ δὲ ποτήριον σου αἷμα [6] εἰς ἄφεσιν ἁμαρτιῶν. [7] Χάριτι καὶ οἰκτιρμοῖς καὶ φιλανθρωπίᾳ τοῦ μονογενοῦς σου Υἱοῦ, δι' οὗ καὶ μεθ' οὗ σοὶ ἡ δόξα καὶ τὸ κράτος σὺν τῷ παναγίῳ καὶ ἀγαθῷ καὶ ζωοποιῷ σου Πνεύματι, νῦν καὶ ἀεὶ καὶ εἰς τοὺς αἰῶνας τῶν αἰώνων. Ἀμήν.[43]

[1] O Master Lord Jesus Christ, the coeternal Logos of your immaculate Father and the Holy Spirit, [2] the bread which came down from heaven, who have offered yourself a blameless lamb for the life of the world. [3] We ask and entreat you, O Lord the good lover of mankind, shine your face upon this bread and upon this cup, which we have placed on this your priestly table. [4] And sanctify them and change [them], [5] so that this bread may become your holy body, and the cup your blood, [6] unto the forgiveness of sins, [7] by the grace and compassion and love of mankind of your only-begotten Son, through whom and with whom to you is the glory and the power with your all-holy, good, and life-giving Spirit, now and ever and unto the ages of ages, amen.

Compared to this text, the likely contemporaneous *Kacmarcik Codex* (14th c.) differs only in one respect, adding bless (εὐλόγησον) to the beginning of the consecratory verbs in [4].[44] This is only one step away from the Coptic *textus receptus*, as shown below:

[1] ⲫⲛⲏⲃ ⲡⲟ̅ⲥ̅ ⲓ̅ⲏ̅ⲥ̅ ⲡⲭ̅ⲥ̅ ⲡⲓϣ̀ⲫⲏⲣ ⲛ̀ⲁⲓⲇⲓⲟⲥ ⲟⲩⲟϩ ⲡⲗⲟⲅⲟⲥ ⲛ̀ⲧⲉ ⲡⲓⲁⲧⲑⲱⲗⲉⲃ ⲫⲓⲱⲧ ⲛ̀ⲟⲙⲟⲟⲩⲥⲓⲟⲥ ⲛⲉⲙⲁϥ ⲛⲉⲙ ⲡⲓⲡⲛⲉⲩⲙⲁ ⲉⲑⲟⲩⲁⲃ. [2] ⲛ̀ⲑⲟⲕ ⲅⲁⲣ ⲡⲉ ⲡⲓⲱⲓⲕ ⲉⲧⲟⲛϧ ⲉⲧⲁϥⲓ̀ ⲉ̀ⲡⲉⲥⲏⲧ ⲉ̀ⲃⲟⲗ ϧⲉⲛ ⲧⲫⲉ ⲟⲩⲟϩ ⲁⲕⲉⲣϣⲟⲣⲡ ⲛ̀ⲭⲁⲕ ⲛ̀ⲟⲩϩⲓⲏⲃ ⲛ̀ⲁⲧⲁϭⲛⲓ ⲉ̀ϩⲣⲏⲓ ⲉ̀ϫⲉⲛ ⲡⲱⲛϧ ⲙ̀ⲡⲓⲕⲟⲥⲙⲟⲥ. [3] ⲧⲉⲛϯϩⲟ ⲟⲩⲟϩ ⲧⲉⲛⲧⲱⲃϩ ⲛ̀ⲧⲉⲕⲙⲉⲧⲁⲅⲁⲑⲟⲥ

[1] O Master Lord Jesus Christ, the co-eternal and the Logos of the immaculate Father, who is co-essential with him and the Holy Spirit, [2] for you are the living bread, which came down from heaven, and has made yourself a spotless lamb for the life of the world. [3] We ask and entreat your

[43] Evelyn-White, *The Monasteries of the Wadi 'N Natrun*, 1:202.

[44] *Kacmarcik Codex* (14th c.), fol. 8r. Cf. Macomber, "The Greek Text," 316.

ⲡⲓⲙⲁⲓⲣⲱⲙⲓ ⲟⲩⲱⲛϩ ⲙ̀ⲡⲉⲕϩⲟ ⲉ̀ϩⲣⲏⲓ ⲉ̀ϫⲉⲛ ⲡⲁⲓⲱⲓⲕ ⲫⲁⲓ ⲛⲉⲙ ⲉ̀ϫⲉⲛ ⲡⲁⲓⲁⲫⲟⲧ ⲫⲁⲓ ⲛⲁⲓ ⲉⲧⲁⲛⲭⲁⲩ ⲉ̀ϧⲣⲏⲓ ⲉ̀ϫⲉⲛ ⲧⲁⲓⲧⲣⲁⲡⲉⲍⲁ ⲛ̀ⲓⲉⲣⲁⲧⲓⲕⲏ ⲛ̀ⲧⲁⲕ ⲑⲁⲓ. [4] ⲥⲙⲟⲩ ⲉ̀ⲣⲱⲟⲩ ⲁⲣⲓⲁⲅⲓⲁⲍⲓⲛ ⲙ̀ⲙⲱⲟⲩ ⲙⲁⲧⲟⲩⲃⲱⲟⲩ ⲟⲩⲟϩ ⲟⲩⲟⲑⲃⲟⲩ. [5] ϩⲓⲛⲁ ⲡⲁⲓⲱⲓⲕ ⲙⲉⲛ ⲛ̀ⲧⲉϥϣⲱⲡⲓ ⲛ̀ⲑⲟϥ ⲡⲉ ⲡⲉⲕⲥⲱⲙⲁ ⲉⲑⲟⲩⲁⲃ. ⲡⲓⲑⲱⲧ ⲇⲉ ⲉⲧϧⲉⲛ ⲡⲁⲓⲁⲫⲟⲧ ⲛ̀ⲑⲟϥ ⲡⲉ ⲡⲉⲕⲥⲛⲟϥ ⲉⲧⲧⲁⲓⲏⲟⲩⲧ. [6] ⲟⲩⲟϩ ⲙⲁⲣⲟⲩϣⲱⲡⲓ ⲛⲁⲛ ⲧⲏⲣⲟⲩ ⲉⲩⲙⲉⲧⲁⲗⲩⲙⲯⲓⲥ ⲛⲉⲙ ⲟⲩⲧⲁⲗϭⲟ ⲛⲉⲙ ⲟⲩⲥⲱⲧⲏⲣⲓⲁ ⲛ̀ⲧⲉ ⲛⲉⲛⲯⲩⲭⲏ ⲛⲉⲙ ⲛⲉⲛⲥⲱⲙⲁ ⲛⲉⲙ ⲛⲉⲛⲡⲛⲉⲩⲙⲁ. [7] ϫⲉ ⲛ̀ⲑⲟⲕ ⲅⲁⲣ ⲡⲉ ⲡⲉⲛⲛⲟⲩϯ ⲉⲣⲉ ⲡⲓⲱⲟⲩ ⲉⲣⲡⲣⲉⲡⲓ ⲛⲁⲕ ⲛⲉⲙ ⲡⲉⲕⲓⲱⲧ ⲛ̀ⲁⲅⲁⲑⲟⲥ ⲛⲉⲙ ⲡⲓⲡⲛⲉⲩⲙⲁ ⲉⲑⲟⲩⲁⲃ ⲛ̀ⲣⲉϥⲧⲁⲛϧⲟ ⲟⲩⲟϩ ⲛ̀ⲟⲙⲟⲟⲩⲥⲓⲟⲥ ⲛⲉⲙⲁⲕ ϯⲛⲟⲩ ⲛⲉⲙ ⲛ̀ⲥⲏⲟⲩ ⲛⲓⲃⲉⲛ ⲛⲉⲙ ϣⲁ ⲉⲛⲉϩ ⲛ̀ⲧⲉ ⲛⲓⲉⲛⲉϩ ⲧⲏⲣⲟⲩ ⲁⲙⲏⲛ.[45]

goodness, O lover of mankind, shine your face upon this bread and upon this cup, these which we have placed upon this, your priestly table: [4] bless them, sanctify them, purify them and change them. [5] So that this bread may become your holy body, and the mixture in this cup your honored blood. [6] And may they become unto all of us communion, healing, and salvation of our souls, our bodies, and our spirits, [7] for you are our God; to you belongs the glory with your good Father and the Holy Spirit, the life-giver, and coessential with you, now and at all times and unto ages of all ages, amen.

The Coptic text adds the adjective co-essential (ⲟⲙⲟⲟⲩⲥⲓⲟⲥ), in the opening address in [1],[46] and adds a fourth consecratory verb: purify (ⲙⲁⲧⲟⲩⲃⲱⲟⲩ). Finally, instead of forgiveness of sins, the Coptic version elaborates the gifts of communion into healing and salvation for our souls and bodies. With minor adjectival additions, this is also the text as it appears in the Ethiopian liturgy published by Brightman, especially where the verbs of consecration—bless, hallow, cleanse, and change—are concerned.[47]

In broad terms, the intermediate recension expands the ancient with a longer opening address, and describes Christ as the bread that came down from heaven and/or the great high priest. This is followed by the modern recension, which continues the expansion by adding specific consecratory verbs up to four in the Coptic and Ethiopian texts.

1.3. Origins of the Prayer

It would be certainly logical to conclude that the *Prothesis Prayer* of the Coptic Rite originated in the Byzantine tradition, since it is within that tradition that the prayer is found both in its briefest recension

45 Ṣalīb, ⲡⲓϫⲱⲙ ⲛ̀ⲧⲉ ⲡⲓⲉⲩⲭⲟⲗⲟⲅⲓⲟⲛ, 225–228.

46 This is absent from the majority of manuscripts, appearing only as late as the eighteenth-century *Coptic Museum 265 Lit*, fol. 34v, and *BAV Vatican Copt. 19* (AD 1715), fol. 12r.

47 *LEW*, 204.

and in the oldest manuscript witness, *BAV Barberini Gr. 336* (8th c.). Despite this appearance however, scholars for decades have concluded that the prayer is not native to the Byzantine tradition, but is more likely oriental, i.e. originating somewhere in the non-Byzantine eastern liturgical traditions. This was the opinion, first of all, of Hieronymus Engberding,[48] followed by André Jacob,[49] Robert Taft,[50] Heinzgerd Brakmann,[51] Geoffrey Cuming,[52] and Stefano Parenti.[53] Nonetheless, it would be worthwhile to clearly state the evidence against the prayer's Byzantine origin, and—more importantly—the evidence demonstrating its Egyptian provenance. This is particularly important since more than one scholar have followed the opinion of Engberding that the prayer originated as the epiclesis prayer of MARK.

1.3.1. Arguments against a Byzantine Provenance

It is certainly true that the prayer in its ancient recension and its oldest witnesses appears predominantly in manuscripts of CHR, an ultimately Constantinopolitan liturgy, and one that has become the main liturgy of Constantinople by the end of the first millennium.[54] However, it is not in any Constantinopolitan manuscripts that one encounters the *Prothesis Prayer* within the Byzantine tradition. In fact,

48 Hieronymus Engberding, "Neues Licht über die Geschichte des Textes der ägyptischen Markusliturgie," *OC* 40 (1956): 51–68, here 56–57.

49 Jacob, "Histoire du formulaire," 85. See also André Jacob, "La tradition manuscrite de la liturgie de Saint Jean Chrysostome (VIIIe–XIIe siècles)," in *Eucharisties d'Orient et d'Occident. Semaine liturgique de l'Institut Saint-Serge 2*, ed. Bernard Botte, et al., Lex Orandi 47 (Paris: Cerf, 1970), 109–138, here 117.

50 Taft and Parenti, *Il Grande Ingresso*, 464.

51 Brakmann, "Zu den Fragmenten," 129.

52 Cuming, *The Liturgy of St Mark*, 85.

53 Parenti, "Influssi italo-greci," 170. See also, Stefano Parenti, "Vino e olio nelle liturgie bizantine," in *Olio e vino nell'alto Medioevo. Spoleto, 20–26 aprile 2006*, Settimane di studio della Fondazione Centro italiano di studi sull'alto Medioevo 54 (Spoleto: Fondazione Centro italiano di studi sull'alto Medioevo, 2007), 1251–1289, here 1258.

54 On the process of the replacement of Byzantine BAS with CHR as the principal liturgy of the Church of Constantinople, see Stefano Parenti, "La 'vittoria' nella chiesa di Constantinopoli della Liturgia di Crisostomo sulla Liturgia di Basilio," in *A Oriente e Occidente di Constantinopoli. Temi e problemi liturgici di ieri e di oggi*, ed. Stefano Parenti, Monumenta, Studia, Instrumenta Liturgica 54 (Vatican City: Libreria editrice vaticana, 2010), 27–73. For an attempt to link the shift to the crisis of Iconoclasm, cf. Stefanos Alexopoulos, "The Influence of Iconoclasm on Liturgy: A Case Study," in *Worship Traditions in Armenia and the Neighboring Christian East: An International Symposium in Honor of the 40th Anniversary of St Nerses Armenian Seminary*, ed. Roberta R. Ervine, AVANT Series 3 (Crestwood, NY: St Vladimir's Seminary Press, 2006), 127–137.

all Byzantine manuscripts featuring this prayer are from the region of Southern Italy, a liturgical area possessing its own peculiar recension of Byzantine BAS and CHR, the product of fusion of Constantinopolitan, oriental, and even some western elements.[55] In the oldest such witness, *BAV Barberini Gr. 336* (8th c.), the *Prothesis Prayer* under investigation appears only in the CHR formulary, while the formulary for Byzantine BAS—preceding that of CHR—has the *Prothesis Prayer* in use today in the Byzantine Rite, Ὁ Θεός ὁ Θεός ἡμῶν, ὁ τὸν οὐράνιον ἄρτον.[56] It is indeed significant that the prayer never appears in the context of Byzantine BAS, even in Southern Italian manuscripts, a strong indication that the prayer is not original to the principal Constantinopolitan liturgy, and therefore not of Constantinopolitan origin itself. This conclusion is further bolstered by the absence of this prayer even from the ancient Constantinopolitan recension of CHR, pointing its origin definitively away from the Byzantine capital.

Another argument against the Constantinopolitan origin of the prayer is the fact that it includes the chalice in its consecratory petition, even in its ancient recension. As Taft has shown, the custom at Constantinople was to prepare the chalice immediately before the Great Entrance and not during the prothesis, as betrayed in the *Sermo de paschate et de ss. eucharistia* of Eutychius (6th c.).[57]

The usage of non-Constantinopolitan prayers within the formulary of CHR in Southern Italian mansucripts is a well-documented phenomenon. This can be seen consistently in manuscripts of the ancient Italo-Greek recension of CHR, where precisely the *Prothesis Prayer*, together with the *Trisagion Prayer*, and the *Entrance Prayer* were imported from external sources. In most cases, non-Constantinopolitan elements in Southern Italian manuscripts tend to be of Middle Eastern origin, a fact that has been attributed to the influx of Chalcedonian Christian migrants from the Middle East to Sicily and Southern Italy after the Persian and Arab invasions of the sixth and seventh centuries.[58] The ubiquity of this prayer therefore in Byzantine manuscripts of CHR much earlier than Egyptian sources is not an indication that the prayer is Byzantine in origin.

55 On the Southern Italian ancient recension of CHR, see Jacob, "Histoire du formulaire," 62–206.

56 Parenti and Velkovska, *L'Eucologio Barberini gr. 336*, 57 (Greek), 263 (Italian).

57 *De paschate et ss. eucharistia* 8 (CPG 6939) (PG 86.2: 2400–2401). Cf. Taft and Parenti, *Il Grande Ingresso*, 463.

58 Radle, "The Liturgical Ties," 618.

1.3.2. Arguments for an Egyptian Provenance

First, the number of manuscripts notwithstanding, the prayer appears in far more distinct *traditions* within the Egyptian realm. Compared to witnesses of the prayer in the single non-Egyptian tradition–the Italo-Byzantine–the prayer otherwise appears in the Alexandrian Melkite MARK, the Coptic, Nubian, and Ethiopian liturgies. This in itself is enough to point clearly to the Egyptian tradition as the origin of the prayer, since it is far more likely that the Italo-Byzantine tradition–eclectic as it is by nature–would borrow from Egypt than vice versa, especially given Greek migration patterns in the sixth and seventh centuries.[59] Since the Middle Eastern provenance of the prayer is highly likely, one should also remark that the prayer is not attested anywhere in the Syro-Palestinian realm, such as in Greek JAS or the West-Syrian tradition, leaving naturally the Patriarchate of Alexandria as the likely conclusion. It is true that the prayer appears in the Arabic version of CHR of the eleventh century from the Patriarchate of Antioch, but this cannot be considered a native Antiochene tradition, since by then the Byzantinization of the eastern patriarchates was well underway.[60]

The witness of the prayer in the Egyptian sphere with the most certain date is Melkite MARK, and precisely *BAV Vatican Gr. 1970* (12th c.). Since the text in that witness was shown to be of the intermediate recension and slightly more developed than the version in the *Qaṣr Ibrīm Codex* and *BAV Vatican Gr. 2281* (AD 1207), one can even push the origin of the prayer in Egyptian sources slightly backwards to pre-twelfth century. This is still much later than the eighth-century Byzantine source, *BAV Barberini Gr. 336.* Unfortunately, the Coptic sources do not help, since the prayer is only seen there as early as the thirteenth century in sources such as *BAV Vatican Copt. 17* (AD 1288), *Bodleian Hunt. 360* (13th c.), and *The Guide to the Beginners and the Correction of the Laity.*[61]

It was noted by Descoeudres that the Constantinopolitan *Prothesis Prayer* was introduced to the rite of the Byzantine capital before the time of the *Mystagogia* of Maximus the Confessor (7th c.), since he speaks clearly of the entrance of the holy and venerable mysteries. This solemn language regarding what Patriarch Eutychius a century

59 A similar argument was made by Gabriel Radle with respect to the Alexandrian crowning prayer. Cf. Gabriel Radle, "The Byzantine Marriage Tradition in Calabria: *Vatican Reginensis Gr. 75* (a. 982/3)," *BBGG III* 9 (2012): 221–245, here 233.

60 On the Byzantinization of the Middle Eastern Chalcedonian patriarchates, see above Chapter 5, Section 1.

61 *BAV Vatican Ar. 117* (AD 1323), fol. 198r. Cf. Graf, "Liturgische Anweisungen," 122.

earlier emphasized was merely bread and wine signals a marked shift in understanding the nature of the eucharistic gifts at the Great Entrance. This shift was attributed by Descoeudres to the introduction of the *Prothesis Prayer* with its consecratory language.[62]

Taking inspiration from this line of thought, the *Prothesis Prayer* of the Coptic liturgy can be likewise detected implicitly in sources much earlier than the twelfth century. Already in the Ethiopic sermon *Order of the Mystery*, one encounters a transfer procession imbued with solemnity that rivals that described by Maximus the Confessor. The eucharistic gifts are described in the text as "the mystery of Christ (*la-meśṭira Krestos*)," surrounded by hosts of angels, and even as "the holy offering of Christ (*qwerbāno la-Krestos*), the sacrifice (*maśwā'eta*)," before the gifts have been offered on the altar.[63] The language used here by the author of the sermon is strongly suggestive of the gifts having been already consecrated, offered, or otherwise blessed in some fashion, which in turn points to the *Prothesis Prayer*. Although the text does not reveal the text of the prayer that likely fulfilled this function, the Egyptian *Prothesis Prayer* with its most explicit consecratory language is the most likely candidate. At any rate, the *Order of the Mystery* may be the earliest evidence there is for a *Prothesis Prayer* in Egypt and indeed anywhere, given the fifth-century date assigned to this source by Heinzgerd Brakmann.[64]

Furthermore, the text of the prayer itself betrays an Egyptian connection. Not only is the prayer explicit in calling for the consecration of the gifts, it does so using language of the ancient Logos-epiclesis prayers, and not the more familiar Spirit-epiclesis found today in most anaphoras.[65] Such Logos-epicleses were quite common before the Council of Constantinople (AD 381) and the development of the orthodox formulation of the work and person of

62 Descoeudres, *Die Pastophorien im Syro-byzantinischen Osten*, 93. On the other hand, Taft argued that the prayer was introduced after Maximus and before *BAV Barberini Gr. 336*, in other words, between the seventh and eighth centuries, since Maximus does not explicitly mention the prothesis rite at all. Cf. Taft and Parenti, *Il Grande Ingresso*, 462. On the difference in locating the point at which the prayer was introduced in Constantinople between Taft and Descoeudres, cf. Pott, *Byzantine Liturgical Reform*, 201–202.

63 Colin, *Le Synaxaire éthiopien*, 220–221. Cf. Beylot, "Sermon éthiopien," 90 (Ge'ez), 109 (French); Fritsch, "The Order of the Mystery," 246 (English), 257 (Ge'ez).

64 Brakmann, "Le déroulement," 109; Idem., "Neue Funde (1988–1992)," 11–12.

65 On the history of the epiclesis prayer and the shift from prayers addressing the Logos to those addressing the Holy Spirit, see Robert F. Taft, "From Logos to Spirit: On the Early History of the Epiclesis," in *Gratias Agamus: Studien zum eucharistischen Hochgebet: Für Balthasar Fischer*, ed. Andreas Heinz and Heinrich Rennings (Freiburg: Herder, 1992), 489–502; John H. McKenna, *The Eucharistic Epiclesis: A Detailed History from the Patristic to the Modern Era*, 2nd ed. (Chicago, IL: Hillenbrand Books, 2009).

the Holy Spirit. Leaving aside the thorny issue of whether the Logos-epiclesis is an Alexandrian innovation, one can at least remark safely that such Logos-epicleses are common in Egyptian liturgical texts even after the fourth-century rise of the Spirit-epiclesis.[66] Such an epiclesis prayer addressed to Christ appears in the Egyptian prayers of Sarapion of Thmuis in the anaphora,[67] and for the sanctification of water.[68] Later Coptic texts from Southern Egypt feature similar prayers as well, such as the eleventh-century fragment *British Library Or. 3580A(7)*.[69] This manuscript features a fragment of a Sahidic anaphoral text containing the end of the anamnesis and an invocation similar to the one in the *Prothesis Prayer*:

[1] ⲧⲛ̄ϩⲟⲙⲟⲗⲟⲅⲉⲓ ⲛ̄ⲧⲉⲕⲁⲛⲁⲥⲧⲁⲥⲓⲥ ⲙⲛ̄ ⲧⲉⲕⲁⲛⲁⲗⲩⲙⲯⲓⲥ [2] ⲁⲩⲱ ⲧⲛ̄ⲁⲓⲧⲉⲓ ⲉⲃⲟⲗ ϩⲓⲧⲟⲟⲧⲕ ϫⲉⲕⲁⲥ ⲉⲕⲉⲟⲩⲱⲛϩ ⲉⲃⲟⲗ ⲙ̄ⲡⲉⲕϩⲟ ⲉϩⲣⲁⲓ ⲉϫⲙ̄ ⲡⲓⲟⲉⲓⲕ ⲙⲛ̄ ⲡⲓⲡⲟⲧⲏⲣⲓⲟⲛ. ⲱⲥⲥⲁⲛⲁ. [3] ⲧⲉⲡⲓⲕⲁⲗⲩⲙⲯⲓⲥ ⲧⲛ̄ⲥⲟⲡ̄ⲥ̄ ⲁⲩⲱ ⲧⲛ̄ⲡⲁⲣⲁⲕⲁⲗⲉⲓ ⲙ̄ⲙⲟⲕ ⲡⲁⲅⲁⲑⲟⲥ ⲉⲧⲣⲉⲕⲧⲛ̄ⲛⲟⲟⲩ ⲙ̄ⲡⲉⲕⲡ̄ⲛ̄ⲁ̄ ⲉⲧⲟⲩⲁⲁⲃ ⲁⲩⲱ ⲙ̄ⲡⲁⲣⲁⲕⲗⲩⲧⲟⲛ ⲉⲃⲟⲗϩⲛ̄ ⲙⲡⲏⲩⲉ ⲉϩⲣⲁⲓ ⲉϫⲙ̄ ⲡⲓⲟⲉⲓⲕ ⲙⲛ̄ ⲡⲉⲧϩⲙ̄ ⲡⲓⲡⲟⲧⲏⲣⲓⲟⲛ[70]	[1] We confess your Resurrection and your ascension, [2] and we entreat you, shine your face upon the bread and the cup. Hosanna. [3] Epiclesis: We ask and entreat you, O good one, to send your Holy Spirit the Paraclete from the heavens upon the bread and that which is in the cup.

The exact anaphoral source of this text is unknown, but it shows clearly an anamnesis followed by a Logos-epiclesis, much like the *Prothesis Prayer* in language, especially in [2]: "show your face upon this bread and the cup." This is followed immediately by a Spirit-epiclesis.

Another possible example of such a Logos-epiclesis appearing fairly late in liturgical texts is the Sahidic *Paris BnF Copt. 129(20)* (10th–11th c.), fol. 157v. This Sahidic fragment from the White Monastery in Southern Egypt contains three consecutive prayers of offering, the third of which is titled, "Another Prayer of Offering, of the Son

66 For a full discussion of the arguments for and against this view, with a conclusion against such an opinion, see Johnson, *The Prayers of Sarapion of Thmuis*, 233–253.

67 Ibid., 48–49.

68 Ibid., 54–55.

69 Crum, *Catalogue of the Coptic Manuscripts*, 35. According to Geoffrey Cuming, the eleventh-century dating was suggested by Prof. Karl Heinz Kuhn in a private letter to Cuming. On this fragment, see Engberding, "Neues Licht," 51–57; Jacob, "Histoire du formulaire," 82–83. For a brief description of the fragment and its related literature, see Henner, *Fragmenta Liturgica Coptica*, 8.

70 Crum, *Catalogue of the Coptic Manuscripts*, 35–36.

(κεεγχη ⲛ̀ⲧⲁⲗⲟ ⲉϩⲣⲁⲓ ⲧⲁⲡⲱⲏⲣⲉ ⲧⲉ)."[71] Unfortunately, nothing remains of the prayer itself except the incipit, "O Master Lord Jesus Christ, the holy Logos." One is even tempted to identify this fragment with the *Prothesis Prayer*, since the title in the manuscript resembles the title of the *Prothesis Prayer* in *Suryān 465* (AD 1645), fol. 20v, and *Paris BnF Copt. 25* (15th/16th c.), fol. 11v. Nonetheless, it is certainly enough to point to this piece of evidence as an indication of the strength of the Logos-epiclesis tradition in Egypt long after the spread of the Spirit-epiclesis in all eastern traditions, including that of Egypt as well. The Coptic *Prothesis Prayer* with its clear relationship to other Logos-epicleses sits comfortably in this regard within the Egyptian tradition.

Finally, the Egyptian provenance of the prayer is at least somewhat hinted within the Glagolitic leaves of *Sinai Glagol. 37* (11th c.), otherwise known as the *Euchologium Sinaiticum*. These are three folia that formed part of a Glagolitic Euchologion discovered in Sinai in 1850 by Archimandrite Porphyry Uspensky. More recently, 28 more folia were added to this Euchologion as part of the *Sinai New Finds*.[72] The three original folia include the *Prothesis Prayer* in Slavonic translation, situated as an epiclesis within the anaphora of CHR. The title is given as "Prayer of Saint Basil for the Prothesis of the Bread."[73] Although such attributions are generally suspect, the fact that the prayer would be attributed to Basil within CHR betrays consciousness of its foreign, non-CHR origin. Since this prayer is also foreign to the Constantinopolitan recension of Byzantine BAS, and given the Sinai provenance of the folia, it is likely that the attribution to Basil is a hint of the prayer's Egyptian provenance and origin within the Egyptian BAS formulary, an opinion shared between Jacob and Parenti.[74]

Although previous scholarship has not been very clear on why this prayer is Egyptian in origin, the reasons can be summarized as follows: 1. The prevalence of the prayer in sources that fall within the Alexandrian liturgical region, 2. A *Prothesis Prayer* of some kind most likely existed in the Alexandrian tradition even earlier than the Byzantine, as betrayed by the language of the *Order of the Mystery*

71 The fragment is discussed, albeit only with regards to the second prayer of offering, in Ágnes T. Mihálykó, "Witnesses of A 'Prayer of Offering' in Sahidic from the White Monastery and the Thebaid," *Journal of Coptic Studies* 17 (2015): 127–139, here 129–131.

72 For a discussion of the newly found folia and their place within the original manuscript, as well as helpful previous scholarship on this important ancient source, see Ioannis C. Tarnanidis, *The Slavonic Manuscripts Discovered in 1975 at St Catherine's Monastery on Mount Sinai* (Thessaloniki: Saint Catherine's Monastery, 1988), 65–87.

73 Frček, *Euchologium Sinaiticum*, 606.

74 Jacob, "Histoire du formulaire," 81; Parenti, "Influssi italo-greci," 171.

(ca. 5th c.), 3. The classification of the prayer as a Logos-epiclesis places it comfortably in Egypt, and 4. At least one Byzantine source expressed awareness of the foreign and likely Egyptian provenance of the prayer.

1.4. The Place of the Prayer in the Unfolding of the Liturgy

As remarked above, the *Prothesis Prayer* has a peculiar location within the unfolding of the Coptic liturgy. The previous chapter has demonstrated clearly that the *Prayer of Thanksgiving* is an enarxis prayer and is unrelated to the prothesis rite. However, the *Prothesis Prayer*, the most important element of this rite, comes after and not before the *Prayer of Thanksgiving*. This is the case in all thirteenth-century sources, the oldest sources of the Northern Egyptian Coptic liturgy. Examples of this include the manuscripts *BAV Vatican Copt. 17* (AD 1288), *Bodleian Hunt. 360* (13th c.), *Rylands Copt. 426* (13th c.),[75] *Bodleian Ind. Inst. Copt. 4* (13th/14th c.), *Bodleian Hunt. 572* (13th/14th c.), *Paris BnF Copt. 28* (13th/14th c.), and *Hamburg Bishoy Euchol. 7* (13th/14th c.). Even *British Library Or. 1239* (13th c.), one of the oldest Euchologia, shows the *Prothesis Prayer* after the *Prayer of Thanksgiving*, though the order there is unique in placing the latter even before the altar preparation prayers.[76]

1.4.1. The Location of the Prayer in Melkite MARK

In its earliest sources, the prayer appears in the very beginning of the formulary as the only euchological element of the prothesis rite. This is the case in *BAV Barberini Gr. 336* (8th c.), as well as in Melkite MARK in *BAV Vatican Gr. 2281* (AD 1207). Nonetheless, the prayer is found at the Great Entrance in the other manuscript of Melkite MARK, *BAV Vatican Gr. 1970* (12th c.). This has led Engberding to conclude that the Great Entrance was the original location of the prayer, relying on the language used, "angelic liturgy and archangelic choir," as more suitable near the Great Entrance, and holding its position in the prothesis elsewhere as merely Byzantine influence.[77] On the other hand, Cuming's view was that the prayer's position in the prothesis rite is the original location. Not only is this the position in the earliest witnesses including those of Italo-Byzantine CHR, the text of Melkite MARK itself in *BAV Vatican Gr. 1970* (12th c.) begins

75 Rodwell, *The Liturgies of S. Basil, S. Gregory, and S. Cyril*, 26–27.
76 *British Library Or. 1239* (13th c.), fol. 8v.
77 Engberding, "Neues Licht," 54.

with the title of a prothesis prayer, although no such prayer is found in that location.[78]

The issue is easily settled by taking into account all witnesses of the prayer. In most cases, the prayer appears either within the prothesis rite or at least immediately following the enarxis as in the Coptic liturgy. The few exceptions are: 1. *BAV Vatican Gr. 1970* (12th c.), in which the prayer was likely moved, 2. the Nubian evidence, in which the prayer seems to come after the Trisagion prayer, and 3. The *Euchologium Sinaiticum*, in which the prayer is used as the anaphoral epiclesis. However, even the latter two cases are not complete formularies but a few isolated folia and/or wall inscriptions, from which it would be difficult to prove anything regarding the order of prayers. However, the fact remains that the *precise* location of the prayer in the Coptic Rite is unusual. Faced with this oddity of location as well as the unanimity of sources from the thirteenth century and later on this issue, a hypothesis could be proposed.

1.4.2. A Deliberate Adjustment?

Already, the evidence from Melkite MARK and Italo-Byzantine CHR being much older makes it far more likely that the place of the prayer in the Coptic liturgy was a later adjustment and not its original location, contrary to what Cuming briefly indicated.[79] Unfortunately, there is no available sources for the Coptic liturgy before the thirteenth century on this point that make it possible to prove definitively that the prayer was moved in the Coptic Rite, and if so, when or why. This is precisely the kind of problem that has been solved many times so far by examining the issue from the perspective of the shift from the old ordo to the new ordo, and this time is no exception.

Naturally, while the old ordo lasted, there was likely no conflict between the *Prothesis Prayer* and the *Prayer of Thanksgiving*, since the former was said in the pastophorion, while the latter before the sanctuary. The issue only arises from the lifting of the entire prothesis rite and placing it quite literally on the altar, where it would come up against such enarxis rites according to the new ordo and even the intermediate ordo of Ibn Sabbāʿ.[80] The impact of this shift on the sequence of prayers was that now, what was originally the actual

78 Cuming, *The Liturgy of St Mark*, 80–81.

79 Ibid.

80 Quite surprisingly, the *Precious Jewel* of Ibn Sabbāʿ, interesting and detailed as it is in other respects, makes no explicit mention of the *Prothesis Prayer* as such, a fact that has no satisfactory explanation. See *Paris BnF Ar. 207* (14th c.), fol. 125v. Cf. Mistrīḥ, *Pretiosa margarita*, 186–187 (Arabic), 491 (Latin).

beginning of the liturgy has come to be preceded by an entire rite of preparation of the gifts. This must have seemed discordant for anyone at the time familiar with both ordos. This is for two reasons: 1. A prayer familiar to everyone as the beginning of *every* liturgical service in the Coptic Church has now come to be found far into the liturgy, and 2. The *Prothesis Prayer*, previously prayed in the pastophorion as the *climax* of the rite of preparation is now prayed–hypothetically anyway–very near to the beginning of the service, preceded only by the newly adopted prayers of altar preparation, which in all likelihood were prayed secretly. It is certainly unusual for a liturgical rite to place its most central element, its heaviest load so to speak, near the very beginning. The *Prothesis Prayer* was indeed a heavy load theologically speaking with its clear consecratory language, and to begin nearly the entire affair with such a key and important prayer would have been an undesirable side effect of the shift. Fortunately, this was something that can easily be remedied by the addition of preliminaries and introductions so common in liturgical development along the "soft points" of the liturgy.

It would not be difficult then to imagine a scenario in which the *Prayer of Thanksgiving* was deliberately moved up to precede this important consecratory *Prothesis Prayer*, as a way to preface and introduce the latter. It is important to recall here that the acts and prayers comprising the remainder of the prothesis rite so far either are practical preparatory acts, or have arisen from the shift of the rite to the altar, such as the procession of the gifts. If the theory of a deliberate adjustment is correct, this means the *Prayer of Thanksgiving* was moved closer to the beginning of the liturgy and immediately following what was understood and accepted as practical preliminaries, and therefore seem to have caused no discomfort.

It has been shown previously that the blessing of the oblations was probably understood as the first properly ritual and clerical act in terms of the unfolding of the rite, alluded to the seventh century and preceded in many manuscripts by an exchange of blessings among the clergy, a sure sign of its importance. Why was the *Prayer of Thanksgiving* not moved prior to these blessings instead? Admittedly, this hypothesis does not allow for a satisfactory answer to this point. However, there is at least one very early witness in which the *Prayer of Thanksgiving* indeed comes at the very beginning of the entire formulary of BAS, and that is *British Library Or. 1239* (13th c.).

Finally, such a deliberate change to the order of the prayers could not have been possible, and could not have achieved such popularity, unless it had arisen from official circles. The two likely candidates in this regard would be the Scetis monasteries or the patriarchal cathedral in Alexandria, assuming this change took place before the relocation of the Patriarchate to Cairo in the eleventh century. If all this is true, it would be a very interesting episode of deliberate liturgical change, and not merely the random cumulative effects of minor changes over centuries, nor yet the type of liturgical change partially in response to external circumstances, such as the very shift to the new ordo. In the aftermath of the liturgical change of abandoning the prothesis pastophorion and transferring the rite to the altar, it seems the Coptic Church—or some of its members or hierarchs at some point—were not content with simply transposing the prothesis rite as an integrated whole onto the beginning of the liturgy. Instead, it was decided to make a deliberate attempt at re-shuffling some elements at the border between the prothesis and the enarxis to make for a smoother transition and for a more "palatable" *déroulement* of these initial rites, which by then had acquired a very solemn and consecratory character by virtue of the *Prothesis Prayer*. The table below is a representation of the hypothetical shift in the location of this prayer:

Old ordo	Intermediate/New ordo	
In pastophorion: 1. Vesting 2. Selection of the gifts 3. Hand washing 4. Commemorations 5. Blessing of the bread 6. Mixing of the chalice 7. *Prothesis Prayer* At the Altar: 1. Ps 116 2. *P. of Thanksgiving* 3. Liturgy of the Word	Hypothetical Intermediate Phase 1. Vesting 2. Altar preparation 3. Selection of gifts 4. Hand washing 5. Commemorations 6. Procession (to the altar in intermediate ordo) 7. Blessing of the bread 8. Mixing the chalice (+ *Eis Pater Agios* + Ps 116) 9. *Prothesis Prayer* 10. *P. of Thanksgiving* 11. Liturgy of the Word	Current Rite 1. Vesting 2. Altar preparation 3. Selection of gifts 4. Hand washing 5. Commemorations 6. Procession 7. Blessing of the bread 8. Mixing the chalice (+ *Eis Pater Agios* + Ps 116) 9. *P. of Thanksgiving* 10. *Prothesis Prayer* 11. Liturgy of the Word

The Hypothetical Shift of the Prothesis Prayer.

2. CHANTS ACCOMPANYING THE PROTHESIS PRAYER

Once the celebrant has finished the *Prayer of Thanksgiving* and began the silent praying of the *Prothesis Prayer*, the chanters begin one of two chants depending on whether it is a normal presbyteral liturgy or if a bishop is celebrating.[81] In either case, the chant lasts throughout the *Prothesis Prayer,* the subsequent covering of the gifts on the altar and the orderly exit of the clergy and deacons from the sanctuary. Both of these chants are analyzed below in terms of their texts and function in the rite.

2.1. The People's Acclamation: May You Be Saved

The first of these chants is *May you be saved* (ⲥⲱⲑⲏⲥ ⲁⲙⲏⲛ), whose full text reads as follows:

[1] ⲥⲱⲑⲏⲥ ⲁⲙⲏⲛ [2] ⲕⲉ ⲧⲱ ⲡⲛⲉⲩⲙⲁⲧⲓ ⲥⲟⲩ.[82]	[1] May you be saved, amen. [2] And with your spirit.

In actual execution, the first syllable of this acclamation, ⲥⲱ-, is given a lengthy melody that lasts throughout the *Prothesis Prayer,* the covering of the gifts, and the process of exiting the sanctuary by the clergy and assistants. The remainder of the acclamation is then resumed after the absolution, thus leading directly into the chants that accompany the censing and precede the reading of Scripture in a smooth transition. This is the way this acclamation is executed at any rate in ordinary liturgies when no bishop is celebrating, at least since the fourteenth century, as seen in the *Lamp of Darkness.*[83]

Besides the use of this acclamation as a congregational melodic chant at this point in the prothesis rite, the words of the acclamation itself occur elsewhere in the liturgy, albeit without such melodic setting. The earliest witness of the word ⲥⲱⲑⲏⲥ in a liturgical context may be *P. Berlin 12683,* a small ostracon (ca. 21 × 14 cm) with Greek acclamations from Elephantine near Aswan in Southern Egypt. According to Ágnes Mihálykó, this single item likely dates from AD 597–626.[84] Its entire content consists of the *Doxa patri,* followed by the shorter doxology, "δόξα σοι κύριε," and the two words, "ξωθης

81 The third possibility–which falls outside the scope of this work given its seasonal character–occurs only during the weekdays of Lent, i.e. all days except Saturdays and Sundays, in which neither chants are performed in the customary way. Instead, ⲥⲱⲑⲏⲥ ⲁⲙⲏⲛ, the first syllable of which usually lasts throughout the *Prothesis Prayer* and the covering of the gifts, is said without this long melodic introduction. This is followed by the chanting of Ps 87:1–3, 5, "His foundations are in the holy mountains." This is concluded by three full prostrations by all those present, clergy included, before exiting the sanctuary. See Ṣalīb, ⲡⲓϫⲱⲙ ⲛ̀ⲧⲉ ⲡⲉⲩⲭⲟⲗⲟⲅⲓⲟⲛ, 224–225.

82 Ibid.

83 *Paris BnF Ar. 203* (AD 1363–1369), fol. 203v. Cf. Villecourt, "Les observances," 250.

84 Mihálykó, *The Christian Liturgical Papyri,* 115.

εὐλόγησον."[85] The first word in this pair is likely our ⲥⲱⲑⲏⲥ, though unfortunately nothing more can be discerned regarding the liturgical context for which this small ostracon was intended. Today, the only other instance in the liturgy is limited to the point immediately following the *Absolution of the Father* after the Lord's Prayer in the pre-communion rites, where it is proclaimed by the deacon.[86] This particular usage is attested since the fourteenth century as seen in the diaconal portion of *BAV Vatican Copt. 38* (14th c.),[87] and was later standardized in the *Ritual Order* of Gabriel V.[88] Besides the eucharistic liturgy, it is also important to keep in mind that many other liturgical services tend to follow the same general structure of the liturgy, including adding this response after the same absolution prayers.

Other instances of this acclamation appear as well in three other usages, though these have disappeared from current practice. René-Georges Coquin noted two of these:[89] 1. By the people after the Gospel at the conclusion of the Liturgy of the Word,[90] and 2. By the deacon as part of the dismissal rites at the conclusion of the liturgy.[91] The latter is a *hapax* witnessed only in *Paris BnF Gr. 325* (14th c.), which is heavily Byzantinized.[92] Although this acclamation is unknown in the Byzantine Rite, it is also unusual in this place in the Coptic Rite, and is absent from other Greek manuscripts of the Coptic liturgy, such as the *Kacmarcik Codex* (14th c.). The former usage after the Gospel is no longer in practice, though it is attested in Ibn Kabar's the *Lamp of Darkness* (14th c.),[93] Gabriel V's *Ritual Order* (15th c.),[94] and in the contemporaneous diaconal *BAV Vatican Copt. 27* (15th c.).[95] The final noteworthy instance of this acclamation, which was unknown to Coquin, occurs in the rite of the consecration of the holy chrism or *myron* according to *Coptic Patriarchate Lit. 106* (AD 1377), where it is said during the rites of making the chrism, this time preceding the

85 Otto Stegmüller, "Christliche Texte aus der Berliner Papyrussammlung," *Aegyptus* 17 (1937): 452–462, here 459–462.

86 Ṣalīb, ⲡⲓϫⲱⲙ ⲛ̀ⲧⲉ ⲡⲓⲉⲩⲭⲟⲗⲟⲅⲓⲟⲛ, 402.

87 *BAV Vatican Copt. 38* (14th c.), fol. 291v.

88 *Paris BnF Ar. 98* (17th c.), fol. 67v. Cf. 'Abdallah, *L'ordinamento*, 194 (Arabic), 378 (Italian).

89 René-Georges Coquin, "Les formes de participation du peuple dans le rit copte," *Proche Orient chrétien* 18 (1968): 122–139, here 131.

90 Ṣalīb, ⲡⲓϫⲱⲙ ⲛ̀ⲧⲉ ⲡⲓⲉⲩⲭⲟⲗⲟⲅⲓⲟⲛ, 275.

91 Renaudot, *Liturgiarum Orientalium Collectio*, 1:84.

92 Paris BnF Gr. 325 (14th c.), fol. 76r.

93 *Paris BnF Ar. 203* (AD 1363–1369), fol. 204v. Cf. Villecourt, "Les observances," 252.

94 *Paris BnF Ar. 98* (17th c.), fol. 58v. Cf. 'Abdallah, *L'ordinamento*, 185 (Arabic), 371 (Italian).

95 *BAV Vatican Copt. 27* (15th c.), fol. 7r.

reading of the absolutions by the patriarch and is likewise followed by epistle readings and incense rites similar to the Liturgy of the Word.[96]

There are strong indications that the usage of the acclamation as a chant meant to cover the entirety of the *Prothesis Prayer* may have slowly developed at least in the late fourteenth century. In the fourteenth-century *Precious Jewel* of Ibn Sabbā‘, no mention is made of this acclamation at any of its attested points mentioned above. Moreover, the author mentions the diaconal command, "stand up for prayer," after the conclusion of the *Prayer of Thanksgiving*. Coming at the point when the *Prothesis Prayer* would be expected, it would be unusual if this command was followed immediately by a secret prayer or by a chant.[97] Of relatively the same period, *BAV Vatican Copt. 28* (AD 1306) includes a diaconal response: "Pray for the holy table (ⲡⲣⲟⲥⲉⲩⲝⲁⲥⲑⲉ ⲩⲡⲉⲣ ⲧⲏⲥ ⲁⲅⲓⲁ ⲟⲩⲧⲣⲁⲡⲉⲍⲁ).[98] Both the location of the response in the manuscript and its meaning indicates that it accompanied the *Prothesis Prayer*, which in turn means the latter was likely prayed audibly and not silenced by any chant.

The most intriguing aspect of this acclamation however is its exact meaning and grammatical form. Burmester expressed his bewilderment regarding this, when he wrote, "In its actual form this response is hard to understand."[99] The acclamation is clearly Greek in origin, and is usually translated to Arabic–and by extension other international languages used in the celebration of the Coptic liturgy–as "[You are] saved amen." In Arabic, this form, خَلَصت is in the second person singular past indicative, while in English for example this is even more ambiguous, leaving room either for a plural or singular reading.

However, the expression has nothing to do with salvation as such. Coquin in particular quoted a story of John of Thebes in the Greek *Apophthegmata Patrum*, in which the saint is described ministering to the sickly elder Abba Ammoes for twelve years, who, "never told him thank you (σωθείης)."[100] Other times, the expression carries the meaning of a simple greeting, equivalent to the Latin *salve* or the Greek χαίρε, such as is found in two sayings of Macarius the Great,

96 Youssef and Zanetti, *La consécration du Myron*, 136 (French), 250 (Arabic).

97 *Paris BnF Ar. 207* (14th c.), fol. 184v. Cf. Mistrīḥ, *Pretiosa margarita*, 186 (Arabic), 491 (Latin).

98 *BAV Vatican Copt. 28* (AD 1306), fol. 3r. The command appears to be corrupted from "Προσεύξασθε ὑπερ τῆς ἁγίας τραπέζης," though it remains unattested elsewhere.

99 Burmester, *The Egyptian Church*, 54.

100 John of Thebes 53 (CPG 5562). Cf. Jean-Claude Guy, *Les Apophtegmes des Pères. Collection systématique, chapitres X–XVI*, vol 2, SC 474 (Paris: Cerf, 2003), 394–395. Cf. Coquin, "Les formes de participation," 131; Lampe, *A Patristic Greek Lexicon*, 1361.

one of which was mentioned by Lampe.[101] To these, Andrea Nicolotti adds a few more examples from the epistles of Theodore the Stoudite illustrating this usage of the second person aorist optative (σωθείης) in the sense of a Christian greeting.[102]

Recently however, Youhanna N. Youssef and Ugo Zanetti preferred a subjunctive reading of this greeting based on the edition of the *Apophthegmata* by Jean-Claude Guy, rendering it instead σωθῇς.[103] Their preference was based on the following arguments: 1. The optative mood was no longer current in the Greek of the fourth century AD, and 2. The optative spelling would theoretically render the Coptic version ⲥⲱⲑⲉⲓⲏⲥ.[104] While the idea that the expression is intended as a greeting or an expression of thanks is clear enough from context, the arguments presented for the subjunctive reading are unconvincing. First, it is true that the optative mood had already sharply declined by the time of the New Testament authors, where it is very rare and appears mostly in the writings attributed to the apostles Luke and Paul. Nonetheless, languages have a way of preserving archaic grammatical structures in stereotyped formulaic expressions. Even Modern Greek, which took its final shape much later than the fourth century, has retained certain fixed expressions in the now-obsolete dative, such as εντάξει [lit. in order] to imply agreement, or τοις εκατό to denote percentage. The optative itself still survives—albeit in a very limited fashion—in the wish γένοιτο or μη γένοιτο to express a positive or negative wish respectively.

It is thus not entirely inconceivable that an archaic expression such as σωθείης in the optative mood would survive in this fixed form and usage long after the optative itself has ceased to be a living grammatical feature of spoken Byzantine Greek. This is especially likely among conservative monastic circles and given the Christian undertone of the greeting's literal sense. Finally, the argument based on the ideal Coptic spelling of the optative form can be easily challenged given the irregular and inconsistent nature of the Coptic rendering of Greek loan words. In this case, σωθείης itself has been

101 Macarius 3 (CPG 5562). Cf. Jean-Claude Guy, *Les Apophtegmes des Pères. Collection systématique, chapitres XVII–XXI*, vol. 3, SC 498 (Paris: Cerf, 2005), 54–55; Macarius 39 (CPG 5562) (PG 65: 280). Lampe, *A Patristic Greek Lexicon*, 1361. For accessible English translations of these *apophthegmata*, cf. Benedicta Ward, tra., *The Sayings of the Desert Fathers: The Alphabetical Listing*, rev. ed., Cistercian Studies 59 (Kalamazoo, MI: Cistercian Publications, 1984), 126, 137.

102 Andrea Nicolotti, "Forme di partecipazione alla liturgia eucaristica nel rito copto," in *Liturgia e partecipazione: Forme del coinvolgimento rituale*, ed. Luigi Girardi, Caro salutis cardo. Contributi 27 (Padua: Messaggero, 2013), 223–267, here 259.

103 Guy, *Les Apophtegmes des Pères*, 2:394–395.

104 Youssef and Zanetti, *La consécration du Myron*, 37n150.

rendered variously as ⲥⲱⲑⲓⲥ,[105] ⲥⲱⲑⲏⲥ,[106] and ⲥⲱⲑⲉⲓⲥ.[107] As for the rare form of the acclamation (ⲥⲱⲑⲏⲥⲟⲙⲉⲛ) or (ⲥⲱⲑⲏⲥⲱⲙⲉⲛ) found in a few sources,[108] such as *Hamburg Macarius Euchol. 46* (13th/14th c.), fol. 1v, Ibn Kabar, and *BAV Vatican Copt. 28* (AD 1306), fol. 3v, it seems to have been an isolated mistake, perhaps intending a first person plural future indicative, "we will be saved." However, as Athanasius al-Maqārī points out, the passive form of this future would be (σωθησόμεθα) and not (σωθῆσομεν), the latter being in fact in the active voice, distorting the meaning to "we will save!"[109]

At any rate, the sense of a general wish of good health and/or greeting provides good insight into the function of this acclamation in the Coptic liturgy. The expression was likely a common colloquial expression in Scetis during the formative period of the Northern Egyptian liturgy, and has entered into the liturgy there as a popular expression of gratitude and wish for good health directed solely to the celebrant.[110] Judging from the examples seen in the liturgical tradition, this always came as the response or conclusion of particular actions perceived as emblematic of the priestly office in some sense, most frequently after absolution prayers, but also after delivering a homily. In this regard then, σωθειης is not unlike the Greek εἰς πολλὰ ἔτη δέσποτα, ἄξιος, and other such expressions of popular approval so common in late antiquity both in the secular and the ecclesiastical realms.[111]

105 Ṣalīb, ⲡⲓϫⲱⲙ ⲛ̀ⲧⲉ ⲡⲓⲉⲩⲭⲟⲗⲟⲅⲓⲟⲛ, 224. Manuscripts include *BAV Vatican Copt. 38* (14th c.), fol. 283v, *Coptic Patriarchate Lit. 74* (AD 1444), fol. 74v, *BAV Vatican Copt. 27* (15th c.), fol. 7r, *BAV Vatican Copt. 18* (AD 1531), fol. 228r, *Paris BnF Copt. 29* (AD 1639), fol. 10r, *Paris BnF Copt. 30* (AD 1642), fol. 17r, and *Coptic Museum Lit. 462* (19th c.), fol. 63v.

106 Ṭūḫī, ⲡⲓϫⲱⲙ ⲛ̀ⲧⲉ ⲡⲓϣⲟⲙⲧ ⲛ̀ⲁⲛⲁⲫⲟⲣⲁ, 312. Manuscripts include *Bodleian Copt. f. 3* (15th/16th c.), fol. 66r, *British Library Or. 429* (17th/18th c.), fol. 14r, *British Library Or. 431* (AD 1718), fol. 9r, *Coptic Museum Lit. 265* (18th c.), fol. 33v, *British Library Or. 430* (AD 1832), fol. 41r.

107 Youssef and Zanetti, *La consécration du Myron*, 136 (French), 250 (Arabic).

108 *Hamburg Macarius Euchol. 46* (13th/14th c.), fol. 1v, *Hamburg Macarius Hymns 30* (14th/15th c.), fol. 13v, Ibn Kabar in *Paris BnF Ar. 203* (AD 1363–1369), fol. 3v (Cf. Villecourt, "Les observances," 252), and *BAV Vatican Copt. 28* (AD 1306), fol. 3v.

109 Al-Maqārī, *Al-quddās al-ilāhī*, 2:350.

110 Athanasius al-Maqārī went as far as seeing the people as reciprocating the act of being absolved of their sins, which the priest expressed through the reading of the absolution. This exaggerates the simple sense of the acclamation, and it is probably unlikely that the people offered any kind of absolution to the priest in return. See ibid., 351.

111 A great summary of the Jewish, pagan, and Christian uses of such acclamations can be found in Robert F. Taft, "The Dialogue before the Anaphora in the Byzantine Eucharistic Liturgy III: 'Let us Give Thanks to the Lord–It is Fitting and Right',"

As for the second part of this acclamation in its received text, [2] and with your spirit, it is the people's response to the presider's greeting of peace common throughout the East. As such, it stands to reason that it is not meant to be read together with [1] May you be saved. Thus, rather than attempting to understand this common greeting as somehow a wish that the celebrant be saved together with his spirit, it would be much easier to interpret this common response as originally connected to a peace greeting, "Peace be to all," that has disappeared from the formulary at some point. With this in mind, two candidates can be suggested. First, there is reason to believe that the *Prothesis Prayer* itself may have been preceded by a peace greeting, at least based on the testimony of the *Precious Jewel*, which mentions the diaconal command, "Stand up for prayer," itself usually part of the common sequence of initial greetings/commands before priestly prayers in Northern Egyptian liturgy. The second possibility would be the incense prayer that initiates the Liturgy of the Word, "O God the great the eternal." The latter in fact possesses precisely this initial peace greeting–at least theoretically though not in practice–even in the Euchologion of 'Abd al-Masīḥ Ṣalīb, surely a remnant of when this prayer was recited audibly.[112] Thus, what is today a single chant thought to consist of one continuous sentence is in fact two different acclamations/responses: A wish for good health common after absolution prayers and another, even more common, response to the celebrant's peace greeting.

2.2. All the Wise Men of Israel: *A Witness to the Hierarch's Vesting*

In liturgies in which a bishop is presiding, the following hymn is chanted instead at the conclusion of the *Prayer of Thanksgiving* and replacing the long melody of ⲥⲱⲑⲏⲥ ⲁⲙⲏⲛ:

[1] ⲛⲓⲥⲁⲃⲉⲩ ⲧⲏⲣⲟⲩ ⲛ̀ⲧⲉ ⲡⲓⲥⲣⲁⲏⲗ [2] ⲛⲏ ⲉⲧⲉⲣϩⲱⲃ ⲉ̀ⲛⲓⲕⲁⲡ ⲛ̀ⲛⲟⲩⲃ [3] ⲙⲁⲑⲁⲙⲓⲟ ⲛ̀ⲟⲩϣⲑⲏⲛ ⲛ̀ⲁⲁⲣⲱⲛ [4] ⲕⲁⲧⲁ ⲡⲧⲁⲓⲟ ⲛ̀ϯⲙⲉⲧⲟⲩⲏⲃ [5] ⲙ̀ⲡⲉⲛⲓⲱⲧ ⲉⲧⲧⲁⲓⲏⲟⲩⲧ ⲛ̀ⲁⲣⲭⲏⲉⲣⲉⲩⲥ ⲡⲁⲡⲁ ⲁⲃⲃⲁ [...] [6] ⲛⲉⲙ ⲡⲉⲛⲓⲱⲧ ⲛ̀ⲉⲡⲓⲥⲕⲟⲡⲟⲥ ⲁⲃⲃⲁ [...] ⲛⲓⲙⲉⲛⲣⲁϯ ⲛ̀ⲧⲉ ⲡⲓⲭⲣⲓⲥⲧⲟⲥ.[113]

[1] All the wise men of Israel, [2] who weave golden threads, [3] make an Aaronic garment [Ex 28:1–5] [4] according to the honor of the priesthood [5] of our honorable father, the high priest, Pope Abba N.N. [6] and our father the bishop Abba N.N. the beloved of Christ.

OCP 55 (1989): 63–74, here 69–72. See also the extensive bibliography in Robert F. Taft, *A History of the Liturgy of St. John Chrysostom,* vol. 4, *The Diptychs*, OCA 238 (Rome: Pontificium Institutum Studiorum Orientalium, 1991), 2–3.

112 Ṣalīb, ⲡⲓϫⲱⲙ ⲛ̀ⲧⲉ ⲡⲓⲉⲩⲭⲟⲗⲟⲅⲓⲟⲛ, 234.

113 [Ibrāhīm], *Kitāb ma yağibu 'ala al-šamāmisa*, 70.

Similar to the ⲥⲱⲑⲏⲥ ⲁⲙⲏⲛ chant, this hymn is also interrupted once the clergy and assistants exit the sanctuary and the absolution is pronounced. Regardless of how much of the hymn was chanted prior to that point, the chanters continue after the absolution starting with [5]: "Of our honorable father." This is followed still by ⲥⲱⲑⲏⲥ ⲁⲙⲏⲛ, which is performed without its customary long melody. The retention of the latter is perhaps due to cognizance of its place in the rite as an acclamation of approval following the absolution, an appropriate gesture whether the one giving this absolution is a bishop or presbyter.

The text of this chant indicates that it has to do with the patriarch or bishop's vesting for the liturgy. This is clear from its mention in [2] of "weaving golden threads," and the subsequent exhortation for those wise men of Israel in [3] to "make an Aaronic garment [Ex 28:1–5]," that is, a priestly garment befitting the honor of the hierarch(s) present. However, the fact of the matter is that bishops generally vest for the liturgy much earlier according to the current rite. Observing no special rite of their own, bishops usually arrive to the church at any point before, during, or after matins at the latest, at which point the service is interrupted to welcome them with appropriate chants. Once they enter the sanctuary, they vest in the same way described for other clergy, without any accompanying special chants. This hymn *All the Wise Men of Israel* then remains at this point in the unfolding of the hierarchical liturgy without any relation to the act it is meant to indicate.

The tradition of delaying the hierarch's vesting until after the prothesis rite and immediately before the absolutions is well documented in the sources. The fourteenth-century *Precious Jewel* of Ibn Sabbā' emphasizes this point, not once, but twice. In chapter 61 on the vestments of the clergy, he writes:

[1] ولباس البدلة يكون من قبل طلوع الهيكل للكاهن. [2] وان كان راس كهنة فيكون لباسه البدلة بعد تقدمة القربان قبل التحليل [3] ليتميز بذلك رؤساء الكهنة من الكهنة بوضع الرياسة.[114]	[1] The wearing of the vestment is to be before the ascent to the sanctuary for the priest. [2] And if there was a a hierarch, his wearing of the vestment is to be after the offering of the oblation before the absolution, [3] in order for the hierarchs to be distinguished thereby from the priests with [respect to] the position of leadership.

114 *Paris BnF Ar. 207* (14th c.), fol. 120r. Cf. Mistrīḥ, *Pretiosa margarita*, 176 (Arabic), 487 (Latin).

Later in chapter 64, one finds the following description at the conclusion of the *Prothesis Prayer*:

[1] ثم ان المُقَدس ان كان رئيس كهنة لبس البدلة ذلك الوقت كمثل هرون [2] والمرتلين يرتلوا بما يليق بلباس بدلة الكهنوت.[115]

[1] And if the celebrant were a head of priests [i.e. a hierarch], he is to wear the vestment at this time in the likeness of Aaron, [2] and the chanters chant what is appropriate to the putting on of the priestly vestment.

The latter passage clearly refers to an appropriate chant, which may even include the words "priestly vestment," and a possible reference to Aaron, both of which are very similar to the words of the chant under discussion, though the passage stops short of providing the incipit of the hymn. More details on how this unfolds precisely are given in the patriarchal liturgy in *Coptic Patriarchate Lit. 74* (AD 1444) as follows:

[1] فيصعد الاب البطرك الى المذبح ويقبله [2] ويتناول الحمل من الكاهن ويضعه فى الصينية [3] ويبتدي بالخدمة كالعادة الى اخر قراءة الشبهموت. [4] يبتدوا يقولوا ⲥⲱⲑⲓⲥ ⲁⲙⲏⲛ ⲕⲉ ⲧⲟ ⲡ̅ⲛ̅ⲁ̅ⲧ̅ⲓ ⲥⲟ. [5] وعندما تنتهي اوشية التقدمة يغطي بالابرسفارين [6] ويتوجه الى جانب المذبح ليبدل بدلة القداس. [7] يبتدوا يقولوا هكذا بلحنها المعروف هنا ⲚⲒⲤⲀⲂⲈⲨ.[116]

[1] And the father the patriarch ascends to the altar and venerates it. [2] And he takes the lamb from the priest and places it in the paten. [3] And he begins the service according to the custom until the end of the reading of the the *Prayer of Thanksgiving*. [4] They begin and say *May you be saved amen*, and with your spirit. [5] And when the *Prothesis Prayer* is concluded, he covers with the *prospherin*. [6] And he goes to the side of the altar to put on the vestment of the liturgy. [7] And they begin to chant thus in the melody known here: *[All] the Wise Men*.

The manuscript then provides the entire text of the chant, which is identical to the current version presented above. This is essentially the same rubrics in the slightly later *Baramūs 6/278* (AD 1514), besides mentioning that the patriarch at this point wears a white *burnus* (i.e.

115 *Paris BnF Ar. 207* (14th c.), fol. 125v–126r. Cf. Mistrīḥ, *Pretiosa margarita*, 187 (Arabic), 492 (Latin).

116 *Coptic Patriarchate Lit. 74* (AD 1444), fol. 74v. Cf. Samuel, *Tartīb al-bīʿa*, 1:17; Mikhail, "The Liturgy *Coram Patriarcha* Revisited," 307 (Arabic), 308 (English), and the discussion in 292–297.

a *phelonion* or cope).[117] It is also noteworthy that both manuscripts depart from current practice in the order of the chants, postponing *All the wise men of Israel* until after *May you be saved.*

A slightly different order still is implied in the patriarchal liturgy described in *Uppsala O. Vet. 12* (AD 1546):

[1] فيصعد البطريرك ويتناوله منه [2] فيضعه في الصينية ويبدأ بالسلام والشكر وصلاة المائدة. [3] ويغطي المذبح ويرتل الشعب ويقولون ⲥⲱⲑⲓⲥⲁ[ⲙⲏⲛ] [4] فيقلع البطريرك برنسه ويلبس البدلة [...][5] فاذا ابدل يقرأ التحليل على الخدام والشعب يرتلون ويقولون ⲛⲓⲥⲁⲃⲉⲩ ⲧⲏⲣⲟⲩ ⲛ̀ⲧⲉ.[118]

[1] And the patriarch ascends [to the altar] and takes it [the oblation] from him [the priest]. [2] And he places it in the paten and begins with the peace and the thanksgiving and the *Prothesis Prayer.* [3] And he covers the altar and the people chant and say *May you be saved,* [4] So the patriarch removes his *burnus* and puts on the vestment [...][119] [5] And when he has vested, he reads the absolution over the servants, while the people chant and say: *All the Wise Men of [Israel].*

Here it seems that the hymn in question, ⲛⲓⲥⲁⲃⲉⲩ ⲧⲏⲣⲟⲩ, is chanted *while* the patriarch is reading the absolution. This may indicate that the absolution was at some point read silently, since it was meant for a select group of persons–the servants–and not for the entire congregation.

Postponing a discussion of the full implications of this piece of information until the absolutions themselves are presented below, it is clear from these sources that the vesting of the bishop or patriarch took place consistently after the prothesis rite. This is not only supported by the Copto-Arabic sources presented here, but by the very ancient character of the preparation of the gifts as discussed previously. While originally this fell within the responsibilities of deacons alone, it only came to be the privilege of presbyters through the introduction of the *Prothesis Prayer*, which necessitated the presence and participation of a priest as well. It is only natural then to find the bishop in sources up to the sixteenth century practically waiting in the nave on his throne until the appropriate time to enter the sanctuary, to deposit the gifts in the paten and pray the subsequent prayers. These prayers are the *Prayer of Thanksgiving,* the presidential enarxis prayer that expectedly belongs to the presider, and the

117 Samuel, *Tartīb al-bī'a,* 1:21; Mikhail, "The Liturgy *Coram Patriarcha* Revisited," 309 (Arabic), 310 (English). For *burnus,* see Graf, *Verzeichnis,* 23.

118 *Uppsala O. Vet. 12* (AD 1546), fol. 188v–189r. Cf. Villecourt, "Les observances," 278; Mikhail, "The Liturgy *Coram Patriarcha* Revisited," 311.

119 Here the text provides a list of all the vestments of the patriarch.

Prothesis Prayer, the clerical and most ancient blessing over the oblations. This image of a hierarch awaiting his turn in the nave to enter the sanctuary at the appropriate time is reminiscent of the traditional Byzantine usage, in which the bishop typically takes no part in the prothesis and only enters the sanctuary at the Little Entrance.[120] In fact, certain Byzantine sources provide an even closer parallel, such as the tenth-century liturgy described in the Latin translation of Byzantine BAS in the Johannisberg manuscript,[121] in which the hierarch vests, places the oblations in the paten, and prays the *Prothesis Prayer*.[122]

The only apparent incongruity in this arrangement is that the hierarch is said to perform these important liturgical acts unvested, delaying his vesting until the conclusion of the *Prothesis Prayer*.[123] However, even this apparent oddity of a bishop praying at the altar unvested while all lower rank clergy have put on their vestments can be explained as a sort of transitional phase. According to the old ordo, the entire prothesis rite was performed away from the altar, and as such may not have been considered part of the liturgy proper. It is then conceivable that such preparatory rites, shielded away from the people's observation and participation, and thus hardly constituting a public liturgy at all, would be conducted at some point in its historical trajectory before the vesting took place. Seen thus, the sources

[120] The Little Entrance of the Byzantine Divine Liturgy is the ancient beginning of the liturgical assembly, at which point both the clergy and laity entered the nave. Already by the eighth century, the liturgy had come to begin with the chanting of the three antiphons, reducing this entrance procession to a clergy procession into the sanctuary with the Gospel book, as seen in the commentary attributed to Germanus of Constantinople. The earliest reference to the name Little Entrance–and not simply, the entrance–is found in the *diataxis* of Philotheos Kokkinos (14th c.). See Juan Mateos, *La célébration de la Parole dans la liturgie byzantine. Étude historique*, OCA 191 (Rome: Pontificium Institutum Studiorum Orientalium, 1971), 71–90.

[121] The Johannisberg manuscript is a Latin translation of Byzantine BAS, discovered in the Monastery of Johannisberg on the Rhine near Mainz by Georg Witzel. Together with the so-called *Pyromalus Codex*, they represent precious witnesses to the tenth-century hierarchical liturgy of Constantinople. On these two sources and their value as witnesses of the Byzantine hierarchical liturgy, see Taft, *Communion, Thanksgiving, and Concluding Rites*, 544–548.

[122] For an excellent presentation of the different ways the bishop was or was not involved in the prothesis in the Byzantine Rite, cf. Vassa Larin, "The Bishop as Minister of the Prothesis? Reconsidering the Evidence in Byzantine and Muscovite Sources," in Groen, Hawkes-Teeples, and Alexopoulos, *Inquiries into Eastern Christian Worship*, 319–330, here 322.

[123] In the patriarchal diataxis of Demetrius Gemistos (AD 1390), the bishop too vests after the prothesis. However, there, as in Byzantine usage generally, the bishop appears to take no part in the prothesis rite. Cf. ibid., 325n22; Alexander Rentel, "The 14th Century Patriarchal Liturgical Diataxis of Dimitrios Gemistos: Edition and Commentary," (doctoral dissertation, Pontifical Oriental Institute, 2003), 185–189.

between the thirteenth and sixteenth century presented here could be witnesses to a hold over of this practice in the hierarchical liturgy, long after the presbyters and deacons had adapted to the newer arrangement of the new ordo, in which the prothesis is practically the first part of the liturgy. As is well known, holdovers of this kind in the rites of hierarchs and solemn celebrations is a commonly encountered liturgical phenomenon.[124] This would also signal that the absolution that followed was not perceived as part of the prothesis as such, but as part of the enarxis, preceded only by the *Prayer of Thanksgiving*, whose present position is surely not original. A fuller discussion of the place of the absolutions is provided below.

Having said this, the hymn itself *All Wise Men of Israel* may not have been as consistent everywhere as an accompaniment to the hierarchical vesting. True, its absence from the oldest manuscript of the *Lamp of Darkness* by Ibn Kabar (14th c.) and the *Ritual Order* of Gabriel V can be excused by the nature of the works themselves, which generally omit any mention of rites at a patriarchal liturgy. However, the hymn is also lacking in all three oldest diaconal manuscripts: *BAV Vatican Copt. 38* (14th c.), *BAV Vatican Copt. 28* (AD 1306), and *BAV Vatican Copt. 27* (15th c.), despite the fact that all three include other chants for the bishop. Finally, the hymn seems to have been unknown to Ṭūḫī, who replaced it in his Rome *editio princeps* with another popular hierarchical chant, ⲏ ⲁⲅⲁⲡⲏ.[125] Although today this hymn is exclusively chanted in the presence of a hierarch after the reading of the Pauline epistle, Ṭūḫī's rubric adds to this, "and when they [i.e. the hierarchs] vest according to the custom."[126]

3. COVERING THE GIFTS AND THE ABSOLUTIONS

As mentioned briefly in the beginning of this chapter, the priest covers the gifts after the conclusion of the *Prothesis Prayer*. First, he covers the paten and chalice with a small veil each, and then the entire altar is covered with the *prospherin*, the large veil that spreads over the entire altar. On the one hand, Ibn Sabbāʿ saw in this the spiritual meaning of "veiling Christ who is present from the minds of the people until the creed."[127] On the other hand, both Ibn Kabar and Gabriel V after him explained the covering of the gifts as symbolic of

[124] Taft, "Anton Baumstark's Comparative Liturgy Revisited," 206–208.

[125] For the corrected Greek text of this chant, see Burmester, "The Greek Kīrugmata," 385.

[126] Ṭūḫī, ⲡⲓϫⲱⲙ ⲛ̀ⲧⲉ ⲡⲓϣⲟⲙⲧ ⲛ̀ⲁⲛⲁⲫⲟⲣⲁ, 173.

[127] *Paris BnF Ar. 207* (14th c.), fol. 126r. Cf. Mistrīḥ, *Pretiosa margarita*, 187 (Arabic), 492 (Latin).

the wrapping of Christ's body for his burial, and the *prospherin* in particular as a symbol of the stone on the tomb.[128]

Afterwards, the priest venerates the altar and walks to the southern side, where he prostrates, "thanking God who made him worthy of this pure service."[129] After rising and venerating the altar once more, he walks to the northern side, where he receives a prostration from the deacon and blesses him. This prostration was perceived in Ibn Sabbāʿ as particularly fitting given the deacon's position, "higher than the priest in his proximity to the east," in reference to the deacon's standing at the eastern end of the altar.[130] Both priest and deacon then venerate the altar and descend from the sanctuary, together with the other servants and clergy if any. Finally, everyone prostrates to the east, except for the one priest or bishop who is to read the absolution prayers. This is done either by a priest other than the main celebrant, or if present, a hierarch. If neither were available, that is, in a liturgy with a single priest, naturally he would also pronounce the absolutions. This particular arrangement of having a hierarch read the absolutions is likewise interpreted by Ibn Sabbāʿ as a form of reciprocal humility. While during the prothesis the hierarch stood for the most part outside the sanctuary, below the other clergy in a sense, it is now their turn to bow to him for the absolution in a gesture that is perhaps intended to restore proper hierarchical order as expressed liturgically.[131] These instructions are repeated verbatim from the *Ritual Order* of Gabriel V in a number of mansucripts.[132]

3.1. The Absolutions

Absolution prayers are utilized frequently in the Coptic Rite, particularly as concluding priestly blessings at the end of services. This is particularly the case at the end of vespers and matins, as well as in the pre-communion rites following the *Fraction Prayer*. There are two absolution prayers, one titled *Absolution of the Father* and the other

128 *Paris BnF Ar. 203* (AD 1363–1369), fol. 203v. Cf. Villecourt, "Les observances," 249–250. *Paris BnF Ar. 98* (17th c.), fol. 53r. Cf. ʿAbdallah, *L'ordinamento*, 179 (Arabic), 366 (Italian).

129 *Paris BnF Ar. 98* (17th c.), fol. 53v. Cf. ʿAbdallah, *L'ordinamento*, 180 (Arabic), 366 (Italian).

130 *Paris BnF Ar. 207* (14th c.), fol. 126r. Cf. Mistrīḥ, *Pretiosa margarita*, 187 (Arabic), 492 (Latin).

131 *Paris BnF Ar. 207* (14th c.), fol. 126v. Cf. Mistrīḥ, *Pretiosa margarita*, 188 (Arabic), 492 (Latin).

132 *Paris BnF Ar. 98* (17th c.), fol. 53r–v. Cf. ʿAbdallah, *L'ordinamento*, 179–180 (Arabic), 366 (Italian). These manuscripts are *BAV Vatican Copt. 18* (AD 1531), fol. 126v–127v, *British Library Or. 429* (17th/18th c.), fol. 16r–v, *Rylands Copt. 427* (AD 1749), fol. 19r, *Coptic Museum Lit. 265* (18th c.), fol. 37r–38r, *British Library Add. 17725* (AD 1811), fol. 14r, and *British Library Or. 430* (AD 1832), fol. 42r–v.

Absolution of the Son. While they are addressed to the Father and the Son respectively, both share in common their invoking of the apostolic authority to forgive sins, followed by a petition to forgive the sins of the people. As part of the pre-communion rites, the *Absolution of the Father* is included in the formularies of BAS and CYRIL, while the *Absolution of the Son* is included in the formulary of GREG, in agreement with the addressee of each of these anaphoras.

In the context of the prothesis, ritual instructions at least since the *Ritual Order* of Gabriel V (15th c.) have prescribed the following arrangement. The priest is to read the *Absolution of the Son* if the anaphora to be celebrated is BAS, while in the case of GREG, the *Absolution of the Father* is read instead. In other words, the absolution in the prothesis is to be the opposite of the one that will be read in the pre-communion rites.[133] Although these instructions are repeated faithfully in Ṣalīb's Euchologion,[134] in actual practice this absolution prayer is never recited audibly at this point in the rite. Instead, what *is* recited audibly is the so-called *Absolution of the Servants.* This is a unique absolution prayer not found anywhere else in the Coptic Rite invoking an absolution upon the servants of this particular liturgy from the mouths of the Holy Trinity, the Church, and a number of saints. The text of these absolution prayers follows:

3.1.1. *Absolution of the Son*

[1] ⲫⲛⲏⲃ ⲡⲟ̅ⲥ̅ ⲓⲏⲥⲟⲩⲥ ⲡⲭ̅ⲥ̅ ⲡⲓⲙⲟⲛⲟⲅⲉⲛⲏⲥ ⲛ̀ϣⲏⲣⲓ ⲟⲩⲟϩ ⲡⲗⲟⲅⲟⲥ ⲛ̀ⲧⲉ ⲫϯ ⲫⲓⲱⲧ ⲫⲏ ⲉⲧⲁϥⲥⲱⲗⲡ ⲛ̀ⲥⲛⲁⲩϩ ⲛⲓⲃⲉⲛ ⲛ̀ⲧⲉ ⲛⲉⲛⲛⲟⲃⲓ ϩⲓⲧⲉⲛ ⲛⲉϥⲙⲕⲁⲩϩ ⲛ̀ⲟⲩϫⲁⲓ ⲛ̀ⲣⲉϥⲧⲁⲛϧⲟ. [2] ⲫⲏ ⲉⲧⲁϥⲛⲓϥⲓ ⲉ̀ϧⲟⲩⲛ ϧⲉⲛ ⲡϩⲟ ⲛ̀ⲛⲉϥⲁⲅⲓⲟⲥ ⲙ̀ⲙⲁⲑⲏⲧⲏⲥ ⲟⲩⲟϩ ⲛ̀ⲁⲡⲟⲥⲧⲟⲗⲟⲥ ⲉⲑⲟⲩⲁⲃ ⲉ̀ⲁϥϫⲟⲥ ⲛⲱⲟⲩ. ϫⲉ ϭⲓ ⲛⲱⲧⲉⲛ ⲛ̀ⲟⲩⲡ̅ⲛ̅ⲁ̅ ⲉϥⲟⲩⲁⲃ ⲛⲏ ⲉⲧⲉⲧⲉⲛⲛⲁⲭⲁ ⲛⲟⲩⲛⲟⲃⲓ ⲛⲱⲟⲩ ⲉ̀ⲃⲟⲗ ⲥⲉⲭⲏ ⲛⲱⲟⲩ ⲉ̀ⲃⲟⲗ ⲟⲩⲟϩ ⲛⲏ ⲉⲧⲉⲧⲉⲛⲛⲁⲁⲙⲟⲛⲓ ⲙ̀ⲙⲙⲱⲟⲩ ⲥⲉⲛⲁⲁⲙⲟⲛⲓ ⲙ̀ⲙⲱⲟⲩ. [3] ⲛ̀ⲑⲟⲕ ⲟⲛ ϯⲛⲟⲩ ⲡⲉⲛⲛⲏⲃ ϩⲓⲧⲉⲛ ⲛⲉⲕⲁⲡⲟⲥⲧⲟⲗⲟⲥ

[1] O Master, Lord Jesus Christ, the only-begotten Son and Logos of God the Father, who has broken every bond of our sins through his saving, life-giving sufferings. [2] Who breathed into the face of his saints the disciples and holy apostles, saying to them, "Receive unto you the Holy Spirit. If you forgive the sins of any, they are forgiven. If you bind the sins of any, they are bound." [Jn 20:22–23] [3] You also now, O our Master, have given grace through your holy

[133] The manuscript of the *Ritual Order* adds CYRIL above the line after GREG, indicating it was added later to the text. This indicates that by then already the Coptic anaphora of MARK/CYRIL was seldom celebrated. It is also inconsistent with the intended arrangement of reciting the opposite absolution to the one in each respective anaphora, since the anaphora of CYRIL itself includes the *Absolution of the Father* in the pre-communion rites. *Paris BnF Ar. 98* (17th c.), fol. 53v. Cf. 'Abdallah, *L'ordinamento,* 180 (Arabic), 366 (Italian).

[134] Ṣalīb, ⲡⲓϫⲱⲙ ⲛ̀ⲧⲉ ⲡⲓⲉⲩⲭⲟⲗⲟⲅⲓⲟⲛ, 229.

ⲉ̅ⲑ̅ⲩ̅ ⲁⲕⲉⲣϩⲙⲟⲧ ⲛ̀ⲛⲏ ⲉⲧⲉⲣϩⲱⲃ ϧⲉⲛ ⲟⲩⲙⲉⲧⲟⲩⲏⲃ ⲕⲁⲧⲁ ⲥⲏⲟⲩ ϧⲉⲛ ⲧⲉⲕⲉⲕⲕⲗⲏⲥⲓⲁ ⲉ̅ⲑ̅ⲩ̅ ⲉ̀ⲭⲁ ⲛⲟⲃⲓ ⲉ̀ⲃⲟⲗ ϩⲓϫⲉⲛ ⲡⲓⲕⲁϩⲓ ⲟⲩⲟϩ ⲉ̀ⲥⲱⲛϩ ⲟⲩⲟϩ ⲉ̀ⲃⲱⲗ ⲉ̀ⲃⲟⲗ ⲛ̀ⲥⲛⲁⲩϩ ⲛⲓⲃⲉⲛ ⲛ̀ⲧⲉ ϯⲁⲇⲓⲕⲓⲁ. [4] ϯⲛⲟⲩ ⲟⲛ ⲧⲉⲛϯϩⲟ ⲟⲩⲟϩ ⲧⲉⲛⲧⲱⲃϩ ⲛ̀ⲧⲉⲕⲙⲉⲧⲁⲅⲁⲑⲟⲥ ⲡⲓⲙⲁⲓⲣⲱⲙⲓ ⲉ̀ϩⲣⲏⲓ ⲉ̀ϫⲉⲛ ⲛⲉⲕⲉⲃⲓⲁⲓⲕ ⲛⲁⲓⲟϯ ⲛⲉⲙ ⲛⲁⲥⲛⲏⲟⲩ ⲛⲉⲙ ⲧⲁⲙⲉⲧϫⲱⲃ ⲛⲁⲓ ⲉⲧⲕⲱⲗϫ ⲛ̀ⲛⲟⲩⲁⲫⲏⲟⲩⲓ̀ ⲙ̀ⲡⲉⲙⲑⲟ ⲙ̀ⲡⲉⲕⲱⲟⲩ ⲉ̅ⲑ̅ⲩ̅. [5] ⲥⲁϩⲛⲓ ⲛⲁⲛ ⲙ̀ⲡⲉⲕⲛⲁⲓ ⲟⲩⲟϩ ⲥⲱⲗⲡ ⲛ̀ⲥⲛⲁⲩϩ ⲛⲓⲃⲉⲛ ⲛ̀ⲧⲉ ⲛⲉⲛⲛⲟⲃⲓ. ⲓⲥϫⲉ ⲇⲉ ⲁⲛⲉⲣ ϩ̀ⲗⲓ ⲛ̀ⲛⲟⲃⲓ ⲉ̀ⲣⲟⲕ ϧⲉⲛ ⲟⲩⲉⲙⲓ ⲓⲉ ϧⲉⲛ ⲟⲩⲙⲉⲧⲁⲧⲉⲙⲓ ⲓⲉ ϧⲉⲛ ⲟⲩⲙⲉⲧϣⲗⲁϩ ⲛ̀ϩⲏⲧ ⲓⲧⲉ ϧⲉⲛ ⲡϩⲱⲃ ⲓⲧⲉ ϧⲉⲛ ⲡⲥⲁϫⲓ ⲓⲧⲉ ⲉ̀ⲃⲟⲗ ϧⲉⲛ ⲟⲩⲙⲉⲧⲕⲟⲩϫⲓ ⲛ̀ϩⲏⲧ. [6] ⲛ̀ⲑⲟⲕ ⲫⲏⲛⲏⲃ ⲫⲏ ⲉⲧⲥⲱⲟⲩⲛ ⲛ̀ⲑⲙⲉⲧⲁⲥⲑⲉⲛⲏⲥ ⲛ̀ⲧⲉ ⲛⲓⲣⲱⲙⲓ ϩⲱⲥ ⲁⲅⲁⲑⲟⲥ ⲟⲩⲟϩ ⲙ̀ⲙⲁⲓⲣⲱⲙⲓ ⲫϯ ⲁⲣⲓⲭⲁⲣⲓⲍⲉⲥⲑⲉ ⲛⲁⲛ ⲙ̀ⲡⲭⲱ ⲉ̀ⲃⲟⲗ ⲛ̀ⲧⲉ ⲛⲉⲛⲛⲟⲃⲓ. ⲥⲙⲟⲩ ⲉ̀ⲣⲟⲛ ⲙⲁⲧⲟⲩⲃⲟⲛ ⲁⲣⲓⲧⲉⲛ ⲛ̀ⲣⲉⲙϩⲉ [7] ⲙⲁϩⲧⲉⲛ ⲉ̀ⲃⲟⲗ ϧⲉⲛ ⲧⲉⲕϩⲟϯ ⲟⲩⲟϩ ⲥⲟⲩⲧⲱⲛ ⲉ̀ϧⲟⲩⲛ ⲉ̀ⲡⲉⲕⲟⲩⲱϣ ⲉ̅ⲑ̅ⲩ̅ ⲛ̀ⲁⲅⲁⲑⲟⲛ. [8] ϫⲉ ⲛ̀ⲑⲟⲕ ⲅⲁⲣ ⲡⲉ ⲡⲉⲛⲛⲟⲩϯ ⲉ̀ⲣⲉ ⲡⲓⲱⲟⲩ ⲛⲉⲙ ⲡⲓⲧⲁⲓⲟ ⲛⲉⲙ ⲡⲓⲁⲙⲁϩⲓ ⲛⲉⲙ ϯⲡⲣⲟⲥⲕⲩⲛⲏⲥⲓⲥ ⲉⲣⲡⲣⲉⲡⲓ ⲛⲁⲕ ⲛⲉⲙ ⲡⲉⲕⲓⲱⲧ ⲛ̀ⲁⲅⲁⲑⲟⲥ ⲛⲉⲙ ⲡⲓⲡ̅ⲛ̅ⲁ̅ ⲉ̅ⲑ̅ⲩ̅ ⲛ̀ⲣⲉϥⲧⲁⲛϧⲟ ⲟⲩⲟϩ ⲛ̀ⲟⲙⲟⲟⲩⲥⲓⲟⲥ ⲛⲉⲙⲁⲕ. ϯⲛⲟⲩ ⲛⲉⲙ ⲛ̀ⲥⲏⲟⲩ ⲛⲓⲃⲉⲛ ⲛⲉⲙ ϣⲁ ⲉⲛⲉϩ ⲛ̀ⲧⲉ ⲛⲓⲉⲛⲉϩ ⲧⲏⲣⲟⲩ ⲁⲙⲏⲛ.[135]

apostles to those who for a time work in the priesthood in your holy Church to forgive sin upon the earth and to bind and to loosen every bond of iniquity. [4] Now also we ask and entreat your goodness, O lover of mankind, for your servants, my fathers, my brothers, and my weakness, those who are bowing their heads before your holy glory. [5] Dispense to us your mercy and break every bond of our sins, and if we have committed any sin against you knowingly or unknowingly, or through cowardice, or in deed or word, or from pusillanimity, [6] O Master who knows the weakness of men, as a good one and lover of man, O God, grant us the forgiveness of our sins. Bless us, purify us, absolve us, and all your people. [7] Fill us with your fear and direct us towards your holy good will, [8] for you are our God, and the glory, the honor, the dominion, and the worship are due unto you, with your good Father and the Holy Spirit, the giver of life, who is of one essence with you, now and at all times and unto the age of all ages, amen.

3.1.2. *Absolution of the Father*

[1] ⲫⲏⲛⲏⲃ ⲡ̅ⲟ̅ⲥ̅ ⲫϯ ⲡⲓⲡⲁⲛⲧⲟⲕⲣⲁⲧⲱⲣ ⲡⲓⲣⲉϥⲧⲁⲗϭⲟ ⲛ̀ⲧⲉ ⲛⲉⲛⲯⲩⲭⲏ ⲛⲉⲙ ⲛⲉⲛⲥⲱⲙⲁ ⲛⲉⲙ ⲛⲉⲛⲡⲛⲉⲩⲙⲁ. [2] ⲛ̀ⲑⲟⲕ ⲡⲉ ⲉⲧⲁⲕϫⲟⲥ ⲙ̀ⲡⲉⲛⲓⲱⲧ ⲡⲉⲧⲣⲟⲥ ⲉ̀ⲃⲟⲗ ϧⲉⲛ ⲣⲱϥ ⲙ̀ⲡⲉⲕⲙⲟⲛⲟⲅⲉⲛⲏⲥ ⲛ̀ϣⲏⲣⲓ ⲡⲉⲛⲟ̅ⲥ̅ ⲟⲩⲟϩ ⲡⲉⲛⲛⲟⲩϯ ⲟⲩⲟϩ ⲡⲉⲛⲥⲱⲧⲏⲣ ⲓⲏⲥⲟⲩⲥ ⲡⲓⲭⲣⲓⲥⲧⲟⲥ. ϫⲉ ⲛ̀ⲑⲟⲕ ⲡⲉ ⲡⲉⲧⲣⲟⲥ ⲉⲓⲉ̀ⲕⲱⲧ ⲛ̀ⲧⲁⲉⲕⲕⲗⲏⲥⲓⲁ ⲉ̀ϩⲣⲏⲓ ⲉ̀ϫⲉⲛ ⲧⲁⲓⲡⲉⲧⲣⲁ ⲟⲩⲟϩ ⲛⲓⲡⲩⲗⲏ ⲛ̀ⲧⲉ ⲁⲙⲉⲛϯ ⲛ̀ⲛⲟⲩϣ̀ϫⲉⲙϫⲟⲙ ⲉ̀ⲣⲟⲥ. ⲉⲓⲉ̀ϯ ϫⲉ ⲛⲁⲕ

[1] O Master, Lord God the Pantocrator, healer of our souls, our bodies, and our spirits. [2] You are he who said to our father Peter, from the mouth of your only-begotten Son, our Lord, God, and Savior Jesus Christ, "You are Peter, and on this rock, I will build my Church, and the gates of hades shall not prevail against it. I will give you the keys of the kingdom of the heavens. That

[135] Ibid., 128–133.

ⲛ̀ⲛⲓϣⲟϣⲧ ⲛ̀ⲧⲉ ⲑⲙⲉⲧⲟⲩⲣⲟ ⲛ̀ⲧⲉ ⲛⲓⲫⲏⲟⲩⲓ̀. ⲛⲏ ⲉⲧⲉⲕⲛⲁⲥⲟⲛϩⲟⲩ ϩⲓϫⲉⲛ ⲡⲓⲕⲁϩⲓ ⲉⲩⲉ̀ϣⲱⲡⲓ ⲉⲩⲥⲱⲛϩ ϧⲉⲛ ⲛⲓⲫⲏⲟⲩⲓ̀ ⲟⲩⲟϩ ⲛⲏ ⲉⲧⲉⲕⲛⲁⲃⲟⲗⲟⲩ ⲉ̀ⲃⲟⲗ ϩⲓϫⲉⲛ ⲡⲓⲕⲁϩⲓ ⲉⲩⲉ̀ϣⲱⲡⲓ ⲉⲩⲃⲏⲗ ϧⲉⲛ ⲛⲓⲫⲏⲟⲩⲓ̀. [3] ⲙⲁⲣⲟⲩϣⲱⲡⲓ ⲟⲩⲛ ⲫⲏⲏⲃ ⲛ̀ϫⲉ ⲛⲉⲕⲉⲃⲓⲁⲓⲕ ⲛⲁⲓⲟϯ ⲛⲉⲙ ⲛⲁⲥⲛⲏⲟⲩ ⲛⲉⲙ ⲧⲁⲙⲉⲧϫⲱⲃ ⲉⲩⲃⲏⲗ ⲉ̀ⲃⲟⲗ ϧⲉⲛ ⲣⲱⲓ ϩⲓⲧⲉⲛ ⲡⲉⲕⲡⲛⲉⲩⲙⲁ ⲉⲑⲟⲩⲁⲃ ⲡⲓⲁⲅⲁⲑⲟⲥ ⲟⲩⲟϩ ⲙ̀ⲙⲁⲓⲣⲱⲙⲓ. [4] ⲫϯ ⲫⲏ ⲉⲧⲱⲗⲓ ⲙ̀ⲫⲛⲟⲃⲓ ⲛ̀ⲧⲉ ⲡⲓⲕⲟⲥⲙⲟⲥ ⲁⲣⲓϣⲟⲣⲡ ⲛ̀ϭⲓ ⲛ̀ⲑⲙⲉⲧⲁⲛⲟⲓⲁ ⲛ̀ⲧⲉ ⲛⲉⲕⲉⲃⲓⲁⲓⲕ ⲛ̀ⲧⲟⲧⲟⲩ ⲉ̀ⲟⲩⲟⲩⲱⲓⲛⲓ ⲛ̀ⲧⲉ ⲡⲉⲙⲓ ⲛⲉⲙ ⲟⲩⲭⲱ ⲉ̀ⲃⲟⲗ ⲛ̀ⲧⲉ ⲛⲓⲛⲟⲃⲓ. [5] ϫⲉ ⲛ̀ⲑⲟⲕ ⲟⲩⲛⲟⲩϯ ⲛ̀ⲣⲉϥϣⲉⲛϩⲏⲧ ⲟⲩⲟϩ ⲛ̀ⲛⲁⲏⲧ ⲛ̀ⲑⲟⲕ ⲟⲩⲣⲉϥⲱⲟⲩⲛϩⲏⲧ ⲛⲁϣⲉ ⲡⲉⲕⲛⲁⲓ ⲟⲩⲟϩ ⲛ̀ⲑⲙⲏⲓ. [6] ⲓⲥϫⲉ ⲇⲉ ⲁⲛⲉⲣⲛⲟⲃⲓ ⲉ̀ⲣⲟⲕ ⲓⲧⲉ ϧⲉⲛ ⲡⲥⲁϫⲓ ⲓⲧⲉ ϧⲉⲛ ⲛⲓϩⲃⲏⲟⲩⲓ ⲁⲣⲓⲥⲩⲛⲭⲱⲣⲓⲛ ⲭⲱ ⲛⲁⲛ ⲉ̀ⲃⲟⲗ ϩⲱⲥ ⲁⲅⲁⲑⲟⲥ ⲟⲩⲟϩ ⲙ̀ⲙⲁⲓⲣⲱⲙⲓ. [7] ⲫϯ ⲁⲣⲓⲧⲉⲛ ⲛ̀ⲣⲉⲙϩⲉ ⲛⲉⲙ ⲡⲉⲕⲗⲁⲟⲥ ⲧⲏⲣϥ ⲛ̀ⲣⲉⲙϩⲉ ⲉ̀ⲃⲟⲗ ϩⲁ ⲛⲟⲃⲓ ⲛⲓⲃⲉⲛ ⲛⲉⲙ ⲉ̀ⲃⲟⲗ ϩⲁ ⲥⲁϩⲟⲩⲓ ⲛⲓⲃⲉⲛ ⲛⲉⲙ ⲉ̀ⲃⲟⲗ ϩⲁ ϫⲱⲗ ⲉ̀ⲃⲟⲗ ⲛⲓⲃⲉⲛ ⲛⲉⲙ ⲉ̀ⲃⲟⲗ ϩⲁ ⲱⲣⲕ ⲛ̀ⲛⲟⲩϫ ⲛⲓⲃⲉⲛ ⲛⲉⲙ ⲉ̀ⲃⲟⲗ ϩⲁ ϫⲓⲛⲉⲣⲁⲡⲁⲛⲧⲁⲛ ⲛⲓⲃⲉⲛ ⲛ̀ⲧⲉ ⲛⲓϩⲉⲣⲉⲧⲓⲕⲟⲥ ⲛⲉⲙ ⲛⲓⲉⲑⲛⲓⲕⲟⲥ. [8] ⲁⲣⲓⲭⲁⲣⲓⲍⲉⲥⲑⲉ ⲛⲁⲛ ⲡⲉⲛⲛⲏⲃ ⲛ̀ⲟⲩⲛⲟⲩⲥ ⲛⲉⲙ ⲟⲩϫⲟⲙ ⲛⲉⲙ ⲟⲩⲕⲁϯ ⲉⲑⲣⲉⲛⲫⲱⲧ ϣⲁ ⲉ̀ⲃⲟⲗ ⲉ̀ⲃⲟⲗ ϩⲁ ϩⲱⲃ ⲛⲓⲃⲉⲛ ⲉ̀ⲧϩⲱⲟⲩ ⲛ̀ⲧⲉ ⲡⲓⲁⲛⲧⲓⲕⲓⲙⲉⲛⲟⲥ ⲟⲩⲟϩ ⲙⲏⲓⲥ ⲛⲁⲛ ⲉⲑⲉⲣⲛⲓ̀ⲣⲓ ⲙ̀ⲡⲉⲑⲣⲁⲛⲁⲕ ⲛ̀ⲥⲏⲟⲩ ⲛⲓⲃⲉⲛ. [9] ⲥ̀ϧⲉ ⲡⲉⲛⲣⲁⲛ ⲛⲉⲙ ⲡⲭⲟⲣⲟⲥ ⲧⲏⲣϥ ⲛ̀ⲧⲉ ⲛⲏ ⲉⲑⲟⲩⲁⲃ ⲛ̀ⲧⲁⲕ ⲛ̀ϩⲣⲏⲓ ϧⲉⲛ ⲑⲙⲉⲧⲟⲩⲣⲟ ⲛ̀ⲧⲉ ⲛⲓⲫⲏⲟⲩⲓ̀ ϧⲉⲛ ⲡⲓⲭⲣⲓⲥⲧⲟⲥ ⲓⲏⲥⲟⲩⲥ ⲡⲉⲛⲟ̅ⲥ̅ [10] ⲫⲁⲓ ⲉ̀ⲧⲉ ⲉ̀ⲃⲟⲗ ϩⲓⲧⲟⲧϥ ⲉⲣⲉ ⲡⲓⲱⲟⲩ ⲛⲉⲙ ⲡⲓⲧⲁⲓⲟ ⲛⲉⲙ ⲡⲓⲁⲙⲁϩⲓ ⲛⲉⲙ ϯⲡⲣⲟⲥⲕⲩⲛⲏⲥⲓⲥ ⲉⲣⲡⲣⲉⲡⲓ ⲛⲁⲕ ⲛⲉⲙⲁϥ ⲛⲉⲙ ⲡⲓⲡ̅ⲛ̅ⲁ̅ ⲉ̅ⲑ̅ⲩ̅ ⲛ̀ⲣⲉϥⲧⲁⲛϧⲟ ⲟⲩⲟϩ ⲛ̀ⲟⲙⲟⲟⲩⲥⲓⲟⲥ ⲛⲉⲙⲁⲕ. ϯⲛⲟⲩ ⲛⲉⲙ ⲛ̀ⲥⲏⲟⲩ ⲛⲓⲃⲉⲛ ⲛⲉⲙ ϣⲁ ⲉⲛⲉϩ ⲛ̀ⲧⲉ ⲛⲓⲉⲛⲉϩ ⲧⲏⲣⲟⲩ ⲁⲙⲏⲛ.[136]

which you bind on earth shall be bound in the heavens, and that which you loose on earth shall be loosed in the heavens." [Mt 16:18–19] [3] Therefore, Master, let your servants, my fathers, my brothers, and my weakness, be absolved by my mouth, through your Holy Spirit, O good one and lover of man. [4] O God, who takes away the sin of the world [Jn 1:29], hasten to accept the repentance of your servants, unto a light of understanding and forgiveness of sins. [5] For you are a compassionate and merciful God. You are longsuffering. Your mercy is great and true [Ps 85:15]. [6] If we have sinned against you, either by word or by deed, pardon and forgive us, as a good one and lover of mankind. [7] O God, absolve us, and absolve all your people from every sin, and from every curse, and from every denial, and from every false oath, and from every encounter with the heretics and the heathen. [8] O our Master, grant us a reason and strength and understanding to flee from every evil deed of the adversary, and grant us to do what is pleasing to you at all times. [9] Inscribe our names with all the choir of your saints in the kingdom of the heavens [Lk 10:20] in Christ Jesus our Lord. [10] Through whom the glory, the honor, the dominion, and the worship are due unto you, with him and the Holy Spirit, the giver of life, who is of one essence with you, now and at all times, and unto the age of all ages, amen.

136 Ibid., 396–400.

3.1.3. *Absolution of the Servants*

[1] ⲛⲉⲕⲉ̀ⲃⲓⲁⲓⲕ ⲛ̀ⲣⲉϥϣⲉⲙϣⲓ ⲛ̀ⲧⲉ ⲡⲁⲓⲉϩⲟⲟⲩ ⲫⲁⲓ ⲡⲓϩⲓⲅⲟⲩⲙⲉⲛⲟⲥ ⲡⲓⲡⲣⲉⲥⲃⲩⲧⲉⲣⲟⲥ ⲛⲉⲙ ⲡⲓⲇⲓⲁⲕⲱⲛ ⲛⲉⲙ ⲡⲓⲕⲗⲏⲣⲟⲥ ⲛⲉⲙ ⲡⲓⲗⲁⲟⲥ ⲧⲏⲣϥ ⲛⲉⲙ ⲧⲁⲙⲉⲧϫⲱⲃ. ⲉⲩⲉ̀ϣⲱⲡⲓ ⲉⲩⲟⲓ ⲛ̀ⲉⲣⲙϩⲉ ⲉ̀ⲃⲟⲗ ϧⲉⲛ ⲣⲱⲥ ⲛ̀ϯⲡⲁⲛⲁⲅⲓⲁ ⲧⲣⲓⲁⲥ ⲫⲓⲱⲧ ⲛⲉⲙ ⲡϣⲏⲣⲓ ⲛⲉⲙ ⲡⲓⲡⲛⲉⲩⲙⲁ ⲉⲑⲟⲩⲁⲃ. [2] ⲛⲉⲙ ⲉ̀ⲃⲟⲗ ϧⲉⲛ ⲣⲱⲥ ⲛ̀ϯⲟⲩⲓ̀ ⲙ̀ⲙⲁⲩⲁⲧⲥ ⲉⲑⲟⲩⲁⲃ ⲛ̀ⲕⲁⲑⲟⲗⲓⲕⲏ ⲛ̀ⲁⲡⲟⲥⲧⲟⲗⲓⲕⲏ ⲛ̀ⲉⲕⲕⲗⲏⲥⲓⲁ. [3] ⲛⲉⲙ ⲉ̀ⲃⲟⲗ ϧⲉⲛ ⲣⲱⲟⲩ ⲙ̀ⲡⲓⲓ̅ⲃ̅ ⲛ̀ⲁⲡⲟⲥⲧⲟⲗⲟⲥ. ⲛⲉⲙ ⲉ̀ⲃⲟⲗ ϧⲉⲛ ⲣⲱϥ ⲙ̀ⲡⲓⲑⲉⲱⲣⲓⲙⲟⲥ ⲛ̀ⲉⲩⲁⲅⲅⲉⲗⲓⲥⲧⲏⲥ ⲙⲁⲣⲕⲟⲥ ⲡⲓⲁⲡⲟⲥⲧⲟⲗⲟⲥ ⲉⲑⲟⲩⲁⲃ ⲟⲩⲟϩ ⲙ̀ⲙⲁⲣⲧⲩⲣⲟⲥ. [4] ⲛⲉⲙ ⲡⲓⲡⲁⲧⲣⲓⲁⲣⲭⲏⲥ ⲉ̀ⲑⲟⲩⲁⲃ ⲥⲉⲩⲏⲣⲟⲥ ⲛⲉⲙ ⲡⲉⲛⲥⲁϧ ⲇⲓⲟⲥⲕⲟⲣⲟⲥ ⲛⲉⲙ ⲡⲓⲁⲅⲓⲟⲥ ⲁⲑⲁⲛⲁⲥⲓⲟⲥ ⲡⲓⲁⲡⲟⲥⲧⲟⲗⲓⲕⲟⲥ ⲛⲉⲙ ⲡⲓⲁⲅⲓⲟⲥ ⲡⲉⲧⲣⲟⲥ ⲓⲉⲣⲟⲙⲁⲣⲧⲩⲣⲟⲥ ⲡⲓⲁⲣⲭⲏⲉ̀ⲣⲉⲩⲥ ⲛⲉⲙ ⲡⲓⲁⲅⲓⲟⲥ ⲓⲱⲁⲛⲛⲏⲥ ⲡⲓⲭⲣⲩⲥⲟⲥⲧⲟⲙⲟⲥ ⲛⲉⲙ ⲡⲓⲁⲅⲓⲟⲥ ⲕⲩⲣⲓⲗⲗⲟⲥ ⲛⲉⲙ ⲡⲓⲁⲅⲓⲟⲥ ⲃⲁⲥⲓⲗⲓⲟⲥ ⲛⲉⲙ ⲡⲓⲁⲅⲓⲟⲥ ⲅⲣⲏⲅⲟⲣⲓⲟⲥ. [5] ⲛⲉⲙ ⲉ̀ⲃⲟⲗ ϧⲉⲛ ⲣⲱⲟⲩ ⲙ̀ⲡⲓⲧ̅ⲓ̅ⲏ̅ ⲉⲧⲁⲩⲑⲱⲟⲩϯ ϧⲉⲛ ⲛⲓⲕⲉⲁ ⲛⲉⲙ ⲡⲓⲣ̅ⲛ̅ ⲛ̀ⲧⲉ ⲕⲱⲥⲧⲁⲛⲧⲓⲛⲟⲩⲡⲟⲗⲓⲥ ⲛⲉⲙ ⲡⲓⲥ̅ ⲛ̀ⲧⲉ ⲉⲫⲉⲥⲟⲥ. [6] ⲛⲉⲙ ⲉ̀ⲃⲟⲗ ϧⲉⲛ ⲣⲱϥ ⲙ̀ⲡⲉⲛⲓⲱⲧ ⲉⲧⲧⲁⲏⲟⲩⲧ ⲛ̀ⲁⲣⲭⲏⲉ̀ⲣⲉⲩⲥ ⲁⲃⲃⲁ ⲛ̅ⲓ̅ⲙ̅. ⲛⲉⲙ ⲉ̀ⲃⲟⲗ ϧⲉⲛ ⲣⲱⲥ ⲛ̀ⲧⲁⲙⲉⲧⲉⲗⲁⲭⲓⲥⲧⲟⲥ. [7] ϫⲉ ϥ̀ⲥⲙⲁⲣⲱⲟⲩⲧ ⲟⲩⲟϩ ϥ̀ⲙⲉϩ ⲛ̀ⲱⲟⲩ ⲛ̀ϫⲉ ⲡⲉⲕⲣⲁⲛ ⲉⲑⲟⲩⲁⲃ ⲫⲓⲱⲧ ⲛⲉⲙ ⲡϣⲏⲣⲓ ⲛⲉⲙ ⲡⲓⲡⲛⲉⲩⲙⲁ ⲉⲑⲟⲩⲁⲃ ϯⲛⲟⲩ ⲛⲉⲙ ⲛ̀ⲥⲏⲟⲩ ⲛⲓⲃⲉⲛ ⲛⲉⲙ ϣⲁ ⲉⲛⲉϩ ⲛ̀ⲧⲉ ⲛⲓⲉⲛⲉϩ ⲧⲏⲣⲟⲩ ⲁⲙⲏⲛ.[137]

[1] May your servants, the ministers of this day, the hegumen, the priest, the deacon, the clergy, all the people, and my weakness, be absolved from the mouth of the all-holy Trinity, the Father and the Son and the Holy Spirit; [2] and from the mouth of the one and only, Holy, catholic and apostolic Church. [3] And from the mouths of the twelve apostles; and from the mouth of the beholder of God the Evangelist Mark, the holy apostle and martyr; [4] the patriarch Saint Severus, our teacher Dioscorus, Saint Athanasius the apostolic, Saint Peter the hieromartyr the high priest, Saint John Chrysostom, Saint Cyril, Saint Basil, and Saint Gregory. [5] And from the mouths of the three hundred and eighteen assembled at Nicea, the one hundred and fifty at Constantinople, and the two hundred at Ephesus. [6] And from the mouth of our honorable father the high priest Abba N.N. and from the mouth of my lowliness. [7] For blessed and full of glory is your holy Name, O Father and Son and Holy Spirit, now and at all times and unto the age of all ages, amen.

Since it is common in the Coptic Rite to pronounce such absolutions at the conclusion of services or ritual units, it is tempting to see these absolutions as a conclusion to the prothesis rite. It is also tempting in view of current practice to see the *Absolution of the Servants* as the only original absolution in this place, and to see the other two absolutions as duplications from the end of other services. However, closer scrutiny and comparative analysis demonstrates that as a matter of fact, the *Absolution of the Son* is more likely the pristine prayer in

[137] Ibid., 230–234.

this location and makes far more sense as part of the enarxis rites of the liturgy. On the other hand, the *Absolution of the Servants* likely developed later as part of the final stages of the ritualization and clericalization of the prothesis rite before the shift to the new ordo moved both absolutions to be said in succession before the sanctuary.

3.2. The Origin of the Absolutions at the Prothesis

In 1979, Hans Quecke published what is so far considered the most ancient witness of the *Absolution of the Father*, from *British Library Or. 4718(1)*, a parchment manuscript in the Fayyumic dialect of Coptic, first cataloged by Crum, and dated by Quecke to the tenth century.[138] Compared to the *textus receptus*, this text is considerably shorter, particularly in its quotation of Matthew 16, which only includes the verse, "whatever you bind on earth shall be bound in heaven, and whatever you loose on earth shall be loosed in heaven" (Mt 16:19). However, while there are no witnesses of the other two absolutions as old as the tenth century, the *Absolution of the Father* can be disregarded as the pristine prayer in the Coptic prothesis rite. Very simply, the inclusion of this absolution in the rubrics is only found in Gabriel V in the fifteenth century, and even there only as an alternative when GREG is celebrated. This instruction is not found in Ibn Sabbāʿ and Ibn Kabar, nor even in any of the Euchologia examined for this study from the thirteenth nineteenth centuries, where neither the text nor even a brief reference to this possibility is mentioned. The Ethiopian liturgy also has the same absolution to the Son at the same point in the liturgy, lending credence to its antiquity.[139] The prescription to read the *Absolution of the Father* thus seems more as an artificial attempt in the time of Gabriel V to avoid repeating the same absolution twice in the prothesis and the pre-communion rites when GREG is celebrated.

Focusing on the two remaining absolutions, an *Entrance Prayer* in Melkite MARK proves very helpful for comparison:

[1] Δέσποτα Χριστέ ὁ Θεὸς ἡμῶν, [2] ὁ τὴν δωδεκάφωτον λαμπάδα τῶν δώδεκα ἀποστόλων ἐκλεξάμενος, καὶ ἐξαποστείλας αὐτοὺς ἐν ὅλῳ τῷ κόσμῳ κηρῦξαι καὶ διδάξαι τὸ εὐαγγέλιον τῆς

[1] O Master Christ our God, [2] who have chosen the twelve-lighted lamp of the twelve apostles, and have sent them to the whole world, to preach and teach the gospel of your kingdom, and to heal all sickness and

[138] Crum, *Catalogue of the Coptic Manuscripts*, 245–246. Cf. Hans Quecke, "Zum 'Gebet der Lossprechung des Vaters' in der ägyptischen Basilius-Liturgie. Ein bisher unbeachteter Textzeuge: Brit. Libr., Ms. Or. 4718(1) 3," *Orientalia* 48 (1979): 68–81.

[139] *LEW*, 205.

βασιλείας σου, καὶ θεραπεύειν πᾶσαν νόσον καὶ πᾶσαν μαλακίαν ἐν τῷ λαῷ. [3] καὶ ἐμφυσήσας εἰς τὰ πρόσωπα αὐτῶν, καὶ εἰπὼν αὐτοῖς, Λάβετε πνεῦμα ἅγιον, τὸν παράκλητον. ἄν τινων ἀφίετε τὰς ἁμαρτίας, ἀφέονται. ἄν τινων κρατεῖτε, κεκράτηνται. [4] οὕτως καὶ ἐφ'ἡμᾶς τοὺς παρεστηκότας δούλους σου, ἐν τῇ εἰσόδῳ τῆς ἱερουργίας ταύτης, ἐπισκόπους, πρεσβυτέρους, διακόνους, ὑποδιακόνους, ἀναγνώστας, ψάλτας τε καὶ λαϊκούς, σὺν παντὶ τῷ πληρώματι τῆς ἁγίας καθολικῆς καὶ ἀποστολικῆς ὀρθοδόξου τοῦ Θεοῦ ἐκκλησίας. [5] ῥῦσαι ἡμᾶς, Κύριε, ἀπὸ κατάρας καὶ δεσμοῦ καὶ ἀφορισμοῦ καὶ ἐκ τῆς μερίδος τοῦ ἀντικειμένου. [6] καὶ καθάρισον ἡμῶν τὰ χείλη καὶ τὴν καρδίαν ἀπὸ παντὸς μολυσμοῦ καὶ ἀπὸ πάσης ῥαδιουργίας. [7] ἵνα ἐν καθαρᾷ καρδίᾳ καὶ καθαρῷ συνειδότι προσφέρωμέν σοι τὸ θυμίαμα τοῦτο, εἰς ὀσμὴν εὐωδίας καὶ εἰς ἄφεσιν τῶν ἁμαρτιῶν ἡμῶν καὶ παντὸς τοῦ λαοῦ σου.[140]

every infirmity among the people [Mt 4:23], [3] and have breathed into their faces and said to them, "Receive the Holy Spirit the comforter. Whose sins you forgive, they are forgiven; whose sins you bind, they are bound." [Jn 20:22-23] [4] Likewise also upon us your servants who are standing here in the entrance of this holy service, the bishops, presbyters, deacons, subdeacons, readers, chanters, and the laity, with all the fullness of the holy, catholic and apostolic Orthodox Church of God, [5] deliver us, O Lord, from curses, bondage, excommunication, and from the share of the adversary. [6] And purify our lips and heart from all blemish and from all deceit. [7] So that with a pure heart and pure conscience we may offer to you this incense, unto a sweet-smelling fragrance and unto the forgiveness of our sins and of all your people.

This prayer is located in Melkite MARK at the Little Entrance, a position analogous to the conclusion of the prothesis in the Coptic Rite, since both come at the beginning of the Liturgy of the Word. Both the *Entrance Prayer* of Melkite MARK and the *Absolution of the Son* share this common structure: 1. An opening address to Christ, 2. followed by a reference to the apostolic authority to bind and loose from Matthew 16, 3. which leads to a petition to forgive the sins of the servants standing—or bowing their heads—at this place at the entrance of this service, or before God's glory.[141] Additionally, it is important to note that the *Absolution of the Son* in the *Kacmarcik Codex* (14th c.), does in fact replace the clause in the Coptic text, "bowing down their heads," with, "those who are standing before your

140 Cuming, *The Liturgy of St Mark*, 9–10.

141 The *Entrance Prayer* in Melkite MARK noticeably repeats a clause from the *Trisagion Prayer* of the same liturgy in [2] and concludes with a clause that is more suitable as an *Incense Prayer*, natural as part of the incense rites before the Liturgy of the Word in [7].

holy glory (τοῖς παρεστηκόσιν ἐνώπιον τῆς ἁγίας σου δόξης)," which is even more similar to [4] in Melkite MARK.[142] This, in addition to the clear similarity in the listing of ecclesiastical ranks in [4] with the *Absolution of the Servants*, shows clearly the general interrelationship between all three prayers to the exclusion of the *Absolution of the Father*. This clear similarity to such an ancient prayer of entrance in Melkite MARK–in addition to the consistency of the *Absolution of the Son* in all Coptic sources as well as the Ethiopian liturgy–makes a very strong case that this absolution prayer is in fact the more original in the formulary.[143]

As for the *Absolution of the Servants*, the one more prominent today by virtue of being recited audibly, it seems to have developed somewhat later than the *Absolution of the Son*. Besides being unique and not used elsewhere in the Coptic Rite, it is also unique in its structure in dedicating much of the prayer to listing saints from whose mouths the servants are to be absolved. This idea of absolving from the mouth finds its parallel in the *Absolution of the Father*, a surely older text, in which the petition in [3] "Therefore, O Lord, let your servants [...] be absolved by my mouth," figures prominently as the central petition of the prayer, as also observed by Engberding.[144] Compared to the *textus receptus*, the manuscripts vary widely on the inclusion of certain saints in the list, a sure sign of the prayer's late development even by the standards of the already late Euchologia from the thirteenth century and later.[145] At least one manuscript

142 Macomber, "The Greek Text," 317.

143 Engberding's argument that the *Absolution of the Father* is more original since it addresses the Father like the remainder of BAS is unconvincing. First, prayers in the prothesis, Liturgy of the Word, and much of the pre-anaphora are common to all three liturgies. Second, the *Prayer of the Gospel*, to name one example, is addressed to Christ. Cf. Hieronymus Engberding, "Untersuchungen zu den jüngst veröffentlichten Bruchstücken ṣa'idischer Liturgie," *OC* 43 (1959): 59–102, here 74. Even if this perceived mismatch between the addressee of the prayer and the rest of BAS is admitted, it could be interpreted as a perfect example of the "*lectio difficilior praeferenda*" principle, which argues that precisely because this prayer is seemingly out of place by virtue of its address to Christ it is more likely the original prayer in BAS at this point. On this principle, see Taft, "Anton Baumstark's Comparative Liturgy Revisited," 212–213.

144 Engberding, "Untersuchungen," 74

145 Sampling only the earliest Euchologia between the thirteenth and fourteenth centuries, one notes that most lack the names of Dioscorus, Athanasius, Peter of Alexandria, and John Chrysostom, such as *BAV Vatican Copt. 17* (AD 1288), *Bodleian Hunt. 360* (13th c.), *British Library Or. 1239* (13th c.), *Rylands Copt. 426* (13th c.), *Coptic Museum Lit. 463* (13th c.), *Paris BnF Copt. 82* (AD 1307), *BAV Borgia Copt. 7* (AD 1379), and *BAV Vatican Copt. 24* (14th c.). Other manuscripts of the same general period lack Athanasius, Peter of Alexandria, and John

includes the *Absolution of the Servants* directly following the *Absolution of the Son* without so much as a title or any form of separation.[146] While it cannot be said that the two absolutions once formed one continuous prayer, since the *Absolution of the Son* is found alone at the conclusion of many liturgical rites, this may still mean that the *Absolution of the Servants* developed as a later addition and never really stood alone in the formulary of BAS. This generally agrees with Engberding's observations on the similarity between the *Absolution of the Father* on the one hand and clauses in both the *Absolution of the Son* and the *Absolution of the Servants*. However, to qualify Engberding's view that the first absolution influenced the other two, it seems more likely that all three developed out of a common stock, a *Formelgut* of absolution phraseology common in Egypt, which also includes the *Entrance Prayer* of Melkite MARK.[147]

Besides this common stock, the *Absolution of the Servants* language of listing particular fathers may have shared distant common origins with the idea found in another prayer of entrance in Melkite MARK, in which it is petitioned: "Grant us to fulfill the worship of the holy fathers (δὸς ἡμῖν τὴν τῶν ἁγίων πατέρων ἐπιτελεῖν λατρείαν)."[148] The idea of bringing to mind that the service about to commence is part of a long tradition of fathers may have inspired the listing of such fathers by name in the *Absolution of the Servants*. This is particularly the case in seeing that among those fathers listed, many are central to Coptic Christianity in particular, such as Mark the Evangelist, Severus of Antioch, Dioscorus, Athanasius, Peter, and Cyril of Alexandria.[149]

Chrysostom, but do include Dioscorus, such as *Bodleian Hunt. 572* (13th/14th c.) and *Bodleian Marsh 5* (14th c.).

146 For example, *Bodleian Hunt. 572* (13th/14th c.), fol. 17r. The title of the *Absolution of the Servants* in *British Library Or. 431* (AD 1718), fol. 14v, and in *Paris BnF Copt. 25* (15th/16th c.), fol. 16v is simply, "The rest (البقية)." In *Paris BnF Copt. 29* (AD 1639), fol. 15v, it is, "The remainder of the absolution (بقية التحليل)."

147 Engberding, "Untersuchungen," 74. The idea of a common *Formelgut* for these prayers is strengthened when, strictly speaking, the *Absolution of the Father* calls for the absolution through the mouth of the priest in the first person, while that of the servants attributes this absolution first to the Trinity, then all the saints, and only finally to the priest pronouncing the absolution as an afterthought.

148 Cuming, *The Liturgy of St Mark*, 10.

149 On the polemics between the Chalcedonian and non-Chalcedonian factions in Egypt in the aftermath of the Council of Chalcedon (AD 451) and the central role of the eucharistic celebration in such polemics, see Leslie S.B. MacCoull, "'A Dwelling Place of Christ, a Healing Place of Knowledge': The Non-Chalcedonian Eucharist in Late Antique Egypt and its Setting," in *Varieties of Devotion in the Middle Ages and Renaissance*, ed. Susan C. Karant-Nunn, Arizona Studies in the Middle Ages and the Renaissance 7 (Turnhout: Brepols, 2003), 1–16, reprinted in: Leslie S.B. MacCoull, *Documenting Christianity in Egypt, Sixth to Fourteenth Centuries*, Variorum Collected Studies Series CS 981 (Burlington, VT: Ashgate Variorum, 2011), 1–16.

Even excluding those saints that seem to have been consistently missing from earlier Euchologia (i.e. Dioscorus, Athanasius, and Peter of Alexandria), the list retains the names of two key figures in non-Chalcedonian orthodoxy, namely Severus of Antioch and Cyril of Alexandria.

Having thus argued for the more ancient place of the *Absolution of the Son*, followed by the introduction of the *Absolution of the Servants* during the formative centuries of the Northern Egyptian liturgy before the ninth century, the picture can be completed in the fifteenth century at the latest. At that juncture, the introduction of the *Absolution of the Father* in the *Ritual Order* of Gabriel V likely took place as a way to balance things. Since the *Absolution of the Son* was already there and it did not match the addressing of BAS to the Father, the *Absolution of the Father* was introduced to render things tidier and more logical. Finally, in actual practice at any rate, the heavy weight of having two lengthy absolution prayers recited at this time gave way, resulting in the *Absolution of the Son* (or *the Father*)–either of which are recited elsewhere in the service aloud–to be recited silently this time. This development left room for the audible recitation of only one absolution prayer: The *Absolution of the Servants.*[150]

3.3. The Function of the Absolutions

Moving on from the historical development of these absolutions, what was likely the *function* of these absolutions at this ritual juncture? Once again, the easy answer may be that these are concluding absolutions in keeping with the tradition to end many a liturgical service with an absolution of some sort. However, it could be suggested that while the *Absolution of the Servants* likely functioned as such, the more ancient *Absolution of the Son* functioned more as an entrance prayer. This is so for the following reasons. A prayer at the beginning of the liturgy asking for forgiveness of sins is already found in the fourth-century *Sacramentary of Sarapion*, the prayer titled *The First Prayer of Sundays.*[151] Second, the very similar *Entrance Prayer* of Melkite MARK functions as such and there is no reason to suppose that it ever occupied a different place in Melkite MARK. Third, later Coptic sources for the patriarchal liturgy are consistent in

150 This case is a very clear example of Baumstark's second law, in which liturgical development proceeds from simplicity to increasing enrichment, followed by a retrograde development of abbreviation, usually at the expense of the older elements. See Taft, "Anton Baumstark's Comparative Liturgy Revisited," 198–200.

151 Johnson, *The Prayers of Sarapion of Thmuis*, 70–71; Brakmann, "Le déroulement," 112–113.

indicating that the patriarch–or any hierarch–is to vest immediately before this absolution. This signals that the absolutions were understood as belonging to what follows, namely the Liturgy of the Word, and not the preceding prothesis rite. All of this of course is in addition to the very language of the absolution, which asks for forgiveness for the servants who–according to the Greek text–are standing before God's holy glory. It would be very logical to assume here that the prayer has its intent set on what is to follow, the fulfillment of the divine service, rather than what has just ended, which is its practical preparation.

Since the *Absolution of the Servants* likely developed before the ninth century, this would have fallen well within the old ordo. If true, it would have made sense initially as a prayer recited in the prothesis pastophorion, as an additional prayer absolving the clergy and deacons specifically before commencing the liturgy. This would explain for example how the absolution seems to have been recited silently in *Uppsala O. Vet. 12* (AD 1546) as seen above.[152] This would also give it a particular parallelism with a *Prayer of Inclination after Communion* in BAS, pronounced also for the servants alone and likely read in the prothesis pastophorion after communion.[153]

Finally, this idea would explain why the rubrics unanimously emphasize that a priest other than the one celebrating is to read this absolution. Perhaps under the old ordo the priest whose duty it was to prepare the gifts, to read the *Prothesis Prayer* and the absolution would have been one of the assisting clergy other than the presider of the assembly. This is of course at a time before the transfer of the prothesis to the altar and its understandnig as a rite of the highest solemnity reserved for the celebrant and the patriarch himself, including this very absolution. This hypothetical development can be summarized as follows:

1. First, the *Absolution of the Son* or a related ancestor stood alone as the entrance prayer of the *enarxis*, likely following the *Prayer of Thanksgiving* directly.
2. Next, as part of the overall ritualization of the preparation of the gifts, the *Absolution of the Servants* developed to be said over the servants in the prothesis pastophorion before their entry into the service. This likely took place before the ninth century, or at any rate before the rise to prominence of the new ordo by the tenth century.
3. With the development of the intermediate and eventually the new ordo, the two prayers were brought together in close proximity.

152 *Uppsala O. Vet. 12* (AD 1546), fol. 189r. Cf. Villecourt, "Les observances," 278.
153 Ṣalīb, ⲡⲓϫⲱⲙ ⲛ̀ⲧⲉ ⲡⲓⲉⲩⲭⲟⲗⲟⲅⲓⲟⲛ, 425–426.

Many manuscripts, ultimately aware of the secondary nature of the *Absolution of the Servants*, include it without title or heading in one continuous text with the *Absolution of the Son*. As with the intermediate and new ordo generally, this must be dated to before the thirteenth century, since the absolutions are stable in all Bohairic Euchologia of Northern Egypt.
4. By the fifteenth century, in an attempt at a balanced variety, Gabriel V introduces the *Absolution of the Father* in this location, previously only read in the pre-communion of BAS and CYRIL.
5. Actual practice however eventually acknowledges the impracticality of having two absolution prayers in succession. Thus, a later development relegates the first–and more ancient–to be read silently.

4. CONCLUSION

Certainly, the *Prothesis Prayer* of the Coptic liturgy is the most significant element in the entire rite of the prothesis, both in its textual history as well as in its consecratory language. Although this prayer has received much attention within the Byzantine tradition as the more common prayer in Italo-Byzantine manuscripts of CHR, such studies seldom took into account all the witnesses of this prayer in the Coptic, Nubian, and Ethiopian liturgy as well. The present analysis of the textual history of this prayer given all its witnesses groups them into three main recensions, ancient, intermediate, and modern, in order of verbal complexity. Within this scheme, the Coptic *textus receptus* represents the modern recension, seen mainly in its addition of consecratory verbs similar to the epiclesis prayer of the anaphora. However, it was also shown that the prayer's ancient recension is clearly of Egyptian origin despite its earliest witnesses in the Italo-Byzantine manuscripts of CHR. This was also the opinion of Engberding and Jacob, though the discussion here confirms this conclusion more clearly and with more evidence. Finally, the position of the prayer in the unfolding of the Coptic prothesis was studied. The result was to propose a new hypothesis that the *Prayer of Thanksgiving* was deliberately placed before the *Prothesis Prayer* in order to preface the latter, to solemnize it in a sense, and to delay what was certainly perceived as the central priestly prayer of the entire rite.

The other major section of this chapter was occupied with the absolutions pronounced after the *Prothesis Prayer* and exiting the sanctuary. Although today only one absolution is said audibly, it was demonstrated that the *Absolution of the Son*, now said inaudibly, is the more ancient entrance prayer of the Coptic liturgy, while the

Absolution of the Servants was likely a later development pronounced only over the servants in the pastophorion. The historical development of these absolutions and their manner of recitation is a classic and perfect example of Baumstark's law of increasing complexity, followed by a retrograde simplification.

By way of a broad statement on the rites analyzed in this chapter, one can clearly see the complexity of trying to discern the proper place and pristine order of each prayer. This already began in the previous chapter, when the *Prayer of Thanksgiving* was discussed, a prayer that is clearly an enarxis prayer although it is placed and understood today as part of the prothesis rite. This chapter has continued in this same line of investigation in trying to explain the current place of the *Prothesis Prayer*, as well as the function and pristine location of the absolutions. Although the latter are easily perceived as concluding prayers of the prothesis, it was shown that they are more likely entrance prayers that introduce the Liturgy of the Word. This complexity is a direct result of the shift to the new ordo, which has given rise to very interesting developments in the order of the prayers.

These developments, to summarize, are the deliberate re-ordering of elements to adapt to this new arrangement, as well as a blurring of the lines separating the preparation of the gifts from the enarxis and Liturgy of the Word. While beforehand these two distinct elements of the eucharistic celebration were separated physically in terms of their location in the church, their newly-adopted physical proximity makes the duty of the liturgical historian analyzing them—to say nothing of the inquisitive faithful participating in them—more challenging. This interface between the prothesis rite and the Liturgy of the Word constitutes an authentic "soft point" of the Coptic eucharistic liturgy that has truly merited the attention and meticulous research that gave rise to this entire work.

EXCURSUS 3

CONSECRATORY LANGUAGE AND ITS IMPLICATIONS

That the *Prothesis Prayer* calls for the change of the gifts to the body and blood of the Lord in language identical to that of the epiclesis prayers in the various eucharistic anaphoras is beyond doubt. Not only is the text of the prayer explicit in this regard, but the prayer seems to have been understood as in fact effecting this change. This is seen explicitly in Ibn Sabbā' in his fourteenth-century work *The Precious Jewel*, where he writes, "Then the priest and the deacon cover *Christ who is present*, which is the offering, with the veil of the *prospherin*, in order to veil Christ from the minds of the people until the time of the creed."[1] The language is very explicit that already at the conclusion of the prothesis rite Christ is understood as present in the oblations. Although Ibn Sabbā' mysteriously does not mention the *Prothesis Prayer* itself, it is very likely that such clear language was motivated by precisely this prayer.

Such clear consecratory language may seem strange at first, and can raise a few questions. How is the presence of a prayer with such an epicletic character in a rite considered preparatory to be understood? What is the place of this prayer within the wider topic of eucharistic consecration in the eastern Churches generally, and the Coptic Church particularly? Since the anaphoral epiclesis is commonly understood as the one moment in which the eucharistic gifts change, can an analysis of the *Prothesis Prayer* on this level nuance or even alter this perception entirely? Finally, what are the implications of this prayer on the very nature of the Coptic prothesis rite, both in terms of its historical development and its function in the Coptic liturgy? The following analysis sheds light on these issues.

In fact, scholarship has grappled with the consecratory language of the *Prothesis Prayer* in multiple ways. First, there were attempts to identify the prayer as an actual ancient epiclesis prayer of either the Coptic version of MARK or BAS that was somehow moved into the prothesis rite at some point. Taking the discussion further, Mattā al-

1 *Paris BnF Ar. 207* (14th c.), fol. 126r. Cf. Mistrīḥ, *Pretiosa margarita*, 187 (Arabic), 492 (Latin). Emphasis mine.

Miskīn saw in the entire prothesis rite a complete and self-contained anaphora, given its structure of blessing over the bread, a thanksgiving prayer over the cup, followed by an epiclesis. The natural implication of this theory is that everything that follows—the anaphora itself included—would be viewed as a later addition, a verbal expression of a mystery already accomplished in the prothesis, and which Mattā al-Miskīn argued was an ancient Egyptian eucharistic prayer in its own right. Extreme as this view certainly is, the view that the prothesis rite at least mirrors in some way the shape of the anaphora is an idea in itself worth examining. This question was already examined with respect to the Byzantine Rite as presented below.

1. THE PROTHESIS PRAYER AS AN EPICLESIS PRAYER

Arguments that the *Prothesis Prayer* was originally the epiclesis of Coptic MARK are based generally on three pieces of evidence. However, all three are unconvincing upon closer scrutiny. The first of these is the heading of the prayer in the fourteenth-century Greek fragments of the Coptic liturgy published by Hugh Gerard Evelyn-White and preserved today as *Coptic Museum Inv. 20* (14th c.). The prayer in this text is given the title Epiclesis prayer (ⲉⲩⲭⲏ ⲉⲡⲓⲕⲗⲏⲥⲉⲱⲥ = Gr εὐχή ἐπικλῆσεως), which has led Engberding to argue that the ancient epiclesis character of the prayer was still alive in the fourteenth century.[2] In fact, the prayer is given this title also in *BAV Borgia Copt. 7* (AD 1379), *Paris BnF Copt. 24* (15th c.), *Paris BnF Copt. 39* (15th c.), *Paris BnF Copt. 26* (before AD 1523), *Paris BnF Copt. 73* (AD 1528), and *Coptic Museum Supp. Lit. 432* (19th/20th c.). However, as Burmester and Brakmann have noted, the designation ⲉⲡⲓⲕⲗⲏⲥⲓⲥ simply refers to the inaudible manner of reciting the prayer and not to an identification of it as an actual epiclesis prayer.[3]

Second, the Sahidic fragment *British Library Or. 3580A(7)* was utilized by Engberding as a source—albeit partial—of the *Prothesis Prayer* in its Sahidic version, which he presented in the form of a Greek retroversion. As presented in the previous chapter, the fragment contains the following clause, similar to the Coptic *Prothesis Prayer*, “We entreat you, shine your face upon the bread and the cup.” This is preceded by an anamnesis phrase and followed by a Spirit-epiclesis. Engberding considered this a “crown witness *in petto*,” to the original epiclesis function of this prayer in the anaphora of MARK.[4] On the other hand, Cuming cautioned against placing too

[2] Engberding, “Neues Licht,” 55.

[3] Burmester, “Fragments,” 39n1; Brakmann, “Zu den Fragmenten,” 127n53.

[4] Engberding, “Neues Licht,” 56.

much weight on this one fragment. He reasoned that what follows this short epicletic phrase is closer to the wording of Coptic BAS than MARK, since it appears that the intercessions followed the epiclesis. Additionally, the text refers to "*your* precious blood," an indication that the rest of the anaphora may have been directed to Christ, similar to GREG and not MARK or BAS. Cuming concludes that the entire fragment has the appearance of a local usage and not necessarily MARK at all.[5] Similarly, Hans Quecke cautioned against interpreting this fragment as a direct witness of MARK.[6] Unfortunately, Jacob also repeated Engberding's assertions regarding the ancient function of the prayer as an epiclesis in MARK, which is perhaps understandable given that Jacob was primarily investigating the Byzantine manuscript tradition, and not the Coptic.[7] Fortunately, even Jacob seems to have modified this judgement in a later article.[8]

At any rate, the witness of *British Library Or. 3580A(7)* can be entirely discounted, since the textual correspondence between it and the *Prothesis Prayer* is negligible. Indeed, the only reason why this fragment is considered in scholarship on the *Prothesis Prayer* at all lies in the single phrase, "we entreat you, shine your face upon the bread and the cup." One can hardly consider this enough to identify the fragment with the *Prothesis Prayer*, rendering its inclusion by Engberding in the table comparing the various recensions of the prayer somewhat misleading. At best, this fragment shows the common nature of the expression, "shine your face," in the Egyptian liturgical heritage, a point already made in the previous chapter, but it can in no way be taken as evidence that the *Prothesis Prayer* was ever used as an anaphoral epiclesis in MARK or elsewhere.

The final witness is the Sinai Slavonic leaflets *Sinai Glagol. 37* or the so-called *Euchologium Sinaiticum* (11th c.).[9] In this case, the text of the *Prothesis Prayer* does appear in full as an anaphoral epiclesis. This has led Burmester to conclude that this indeed was the ancient place of this prayer before it came to be used in the prothesis instead.[10] However, Jacob later examined the matter and cast doubt on Burmester's apparent certainty. As Jacob noted, the leaves are not

5 Cuming, *The Liturgy of St Mark*, 128–129.

6 Hans Quecke, "Ein saidischer Zeuge der Markusliturgie (Brit. Mus. Nr. 54 036)," *OCP* 37 (1971): 40–57, here 40n3.

7 Jacob, "Histoire du formulaire," 82–83; André Jacob, "La tradition," 117.

8 André Jacob, "L'evoluzione dei libri liturgici bizantini in Calabria e in Sicilia dall'VIII al XVI secolo, con particolare riguardo ai riti eucaristici," in *Calabria bizantina. Vita religiosa e strutture amministrative, Atti del primo e secondo Incontro di studi bizantini* (Reggio Calabria: Edizioni Parallelo 38, 1974), 47–69, here 52. Cf. Parenti, "Vino e olio," 1258n34.

9 Frček, *Euchologium Sinaiticum*, 606–607.

10 Burmester, "Fragments," 31–32.

necessarily consecutive, and the very end of the prayer is lost, making it difficult to argue that the *Prothesis Prayer* was indeed the epiclesis prayer, even in the original *Euchologium Sinaiticum*, of which only a few scattered folia remain.[11] In addition to Jacob's doubts, one should keep in mind that after all this is but a single source representing an anomaly even within its own Slav-Byzantine tradition. In the final analysis, there is not a single shred of evidence that this prayer was ever anywhere but the prothesis rite as far as the Coptic liturgy is concerned.

2. THE PROTHESIS RITE AS AN ANCIENT ANAPHORA

There is no denying that the act of accepting and blessing the eucharistic gifts, followed by their deposition on the altar accompanied by ritualized formulas, gestures, and prayers already renders the rite broadly similar to the anaphora itself, insofar as both contain and express ideas of offering and consecration of common food and drink as holy and dedicated to God. Even in rites where this preparation of the gifts takes place on a separate table of prothesis such as the Byzantine Rite, the increasing ritualization of this originally practical diaconal duty naturally imparted to the rite aspects of offering and consecration. In other words, the ritual preparation and/or placement of the gifts on the altar eventually came to be a sort of anaphora within an anaphora.

This is seen also in the Roman Rite. Although there is no Roman prothesis per se, the offertory that precedes the Roman Mass and involves placing the gifts on the altar accompanied by the praying of the *secreta* or *oratio super oblata* naturally constituted a duplication of the sorts of ideas contained within the Roman Canon of the Mass. This is precisely why in the middle ages the offertory acquired the title Little or Lesser Canon, seen in fifteenth-century Hungary, Missals from Regensburg between the fifteenth and sixteenth century, and even as early as the late fourteenth-century Missals from Augsburg.[12] As Jungmann points out however, the idea of the offertory as an anticipation or even a duplication of the Canon stood unexpressed long before the middle ages.

Similar ideas were observed regarding the Byzantine prothesis, despite the fact that it is performed away from the altar as a private clerical rite. Already in one of the earliest studies of the topic, Marco Mandalà described the structure of the Byzantine liturgy as a tripartite: "Messa della protesi, Messa dei catecumeni, Messa dei

11 Jacob, "Histoire du formulaire," 81.
12 Jungmann, *Missarum Sollemnia*, 2:97n2.

fedeli," in light of the structure of the prothesis rite which resembles the liturgy with its ideas of offering, commemorations, *Prothesis Prayer*, and even a dismissal.[13] Descoeudres in turn remarked that this development of the prothesis to parallel the liturgy has also caused a development in the symbolic understanding of the liturgy.[14]

Similarly focusing on meaning rather than the structure per se, Hans-Joachim Schulz saw in the prothesis—as in the Roman offertory—a reflection of the same basic ideas found in the anaphora, seeing all three as connected together by the theme of offering.[15] Of course, the Roman offertory is not the Byzantine prothesis, which was never located in the pre-anaphora, nor included a popular procession of the faithful. Nonetheless, Schulz's basic premise is that the offering of the eucharistic gifts renders both the Roman offertory and the Byzantine prothesis into rites of offering in their own way not unlike the anaphoral prayer. It is precisely in view of the structural and theological parallelism between the prothesis and the liturgy that Ioannes Phountoules described the latter as a miniature sketch (σμικρογραφία) of the Divine Liturgy,[16] an idea that has recently given inspiration to a detailed analysis of this parallelism by Stelyios Muksuris.[17]

So far, all is fine and well. It was only however in the work of Hegumen Mattā al-Miskīn on the Eucharist that this parallelism was taken to a completely different level. In his writings, the prothesis rite was argued to be, not a younger liturgical unit developed in parallel to the anaphora, but a more ancient and self-contained eucharistic celebration that goes back to the earliest decades of Christianity. Mattā al-Miskīn's radical theory on the origin of the prothesis rite is an extension of the clear consecratory language of the *Prothesis Prayer* and is an attempt to explain the entire place of the prothesis rite in the progression of ideas of eucharistic theology in the course of the Coptic liturgy. Given this theory's bold assertions and the prominence of Fr. Matta's legacy in the contemporary Coptic Orthodox Church as

13 Marco Mandalà, *La protesi della liturgia nel rito bizantino-greco* (Grottaferrata: Scuola Tipografica Italo-Orientale S. Nilo, 1935), 107. Cf. Descoeudres, *Die Pastophorien im syro-byzantinischen Osten*, 114.

14 Descoeudres, *Die Pastophorien im Syro-byzantinischen Osten*, 114.

15 Hans-Joachim Schulz, *The Byzantine Liturgy: Symbolic Structure and Faith Expression*, trans. Matthew J. O'Connell (New York: Pueblo Publishing, 1986), 184. Cf. Hans-Joachim Schulz, *Die byzantinische Liturgie: Glaubenszeugnis und Symbolgestalt*, 3rd rev. ed., Sophia: Quellen östlicher Theologie 5 (Trier: Paulinus, 2000), 153–154,

16 Phountoules, *Απαντήσεις εις Λειτουργικάς Απορίας*, 3:43.

17 Stelyios S. Muksuris, *Economia & Eschatology: Liturgical Mystagogy in the Byzantine Prothesis Rite* (Brookline, MA: Holy Cross Orthodox Press, 2013), 195–213.

an ascetic and a theologian,[18] it is necessary that his reasoning be examined in detail.[19]

2.1. The Theory of Mattā al-Miskīn

Appearing throughout his volume of nearly eight hundred pages on the Eucharist, the theory of Fr. Mattā can be summarized thus. Building on several observations made by earlier western scholars on the continuity of early Christian eucharistic prayers with Jewish meal blessings, Fr. Mattā noted that the structure of the prothesis in its current shape reflects many elements found in the Last Supper accounts and its Jewish antecedents. These include the taking of bread, blessing it by calling the name of God upon it, and giving thanks over the mixed cup, in addition to a final epiclesis prayer for consecrating the gifts.

Fr. Mattā thus reached the conclusion that the prothesis rite in the Coptic Church is the descendant of the most ancient form of celebrating the Eucharist originating in Jerusalem. The celebrant simply pronounced a blessing over the bread and a thanksgiving over the cup in imitation of Christ's actions at the Last Supper. This was done without any lengthy anaphoral prayers, mention of the Divine economy of salvation, or the addition of ideas of the atoning sacrifice of the cross as a foundational basis for the eucharistic mystery. According to him, only at a later historical period–ca. fourth century–were these latter elements added to the pristine simple form of this Ur-Eucharist thus forming the Liturgy of the Faithful. These elements–the anaphoral prayer and all that follows–were added simply to describe and explain the mystery of salvation in explicit terms to the gentile and newly initiated masses. All the while, the more ancient tradition lived on in the form of the prothesis rite, albeit now

18 This theory was also embraced by Fr. Athanasius al-Maqārī. Cf. Al-Maqārī, *Al-quddās al-ilāhī*, 1:278, 280.

19 Recent writings reflecting on the central place of Hegumen Mattā al-Miskīn in contemporary Coptic spirituality, monasticism, and theology are many. See Maged S.A. Mikhail, "Matta al-Miskīn," in *The Orthodox Christian World*, ed. Augustine Casiday (London: Routledge, 2012), 359–365; Gawdat Gabra, *The A to Z of the Coptic Church*, The A to Z Guide Series 107 (Lanham, MD: The Scarecrow Press, 2009), 177–178; Anthony O'Mahoney, "Coptic Christianity in Modern Egypt," in *The Cambridge History of Christianity*, vol. 5, *Eastern Christianity*, ed. Michael Angold (Cambridge: Cambridge University Press, 2006), 488–510, here 505–506; Samuel Rubenson, "Tradition and Renewal in Coptic Theology," in *Between Desert and City: The Coptic Orthodox Church Today*, ed. Nelly van Doorn-Harder and Kari Vogt (Eugene, OR: Wipf & Stock, 1997), 36–51.

curtailed to a merely practical preparation of the gifts.[20] A succinct summary of this theory is represented in the following passage:

> Thus, the new Christian Eucharist took on all the solemnity and glory of the ritual of "the breaking of the bread," the sacramental part of the Last Supper. And by extension, we face a duplication in the Eucharist in every motion, and every sentence, and every prayer, first in the rite of offering (*al-taqdīm*), which is called among us "the rite of the offering of the lamb" [i.e. the prothesis], and second in the rite of the new Christian Eucharist, which was called after the apostles and bishops such as the liturgy of Mark the Apostle.[21]

Later, he restates the position thus,

> In the rite of the offering (*al-taqdima*)—the presentation of the lamb [i.e. the prothesis]—the traditional pattern taken from the Lord himself was already accomplished, which is the blessing over the bread and the thanksgiving over the cup through a practical and mystical tradition without discourse for explanation or commentary. As for what the anaphora (*al-anāfūrā*) says here, it is only an indication to the institution, clarifying thereby the importance of the tradition of this pattern that was accomplished in the offering (*al-taqdīm*), and which the Church has received from the Lord himself.[22]

Inherent in Fr. Mattā's rather bold assertion are various ideas contained in the works of Hans Lietzmann and Gregory Dix, which are analyzed below.[23] Thus, Fr. Mattā is able to make a series of subsequent conclusions based on this central premise, such as identifying the prothesis rite with Lietzmann's *Herrenmahl*,[24] from which allegedly all apostolic anaphoras have descended.[25] Although the alleged Jewish antecedent of the Last Supper contained the thanksgiving over the cup at the very end, while the anaphora has it

---

[20] Fr. Mattā re-iterated this bold assertion on the origin of the prothesis rite in another shorter booklet on the subject. This booklet provides largely the same argument and sources as Fr. Mattā's work on the Eucharist, *Al-ifḫaristiyyā*. Thus, the discussion below relies on the latter work, considered Fr. Mattā's more influential and classic formulation of his theory. For the later booklet, see Mattā al-Miskīn, *Ifḫaristiyyā 'ašā' al-rabb: Quddās al-rusul al-awwal wa-huwa nawāt ǧamī' al-quddasāt* [Eucharist supper of the Lord: The first liturgy of the apostles, and it is the core of all the liturgies] (Wādī al-Naṭrūn: Dayr al-qiddīs anbā Maqār, 2000).

[21] Al-Miskīn, *Al-ifḫaristiyyā*, 603. Translations of Fr. Mattā's writings are mine.

[22] Ibid., 634.

[23] Hans Lietzmann, *Messe und Herrenmahl: Eine Studie zur Geschichte der Liturgie*, Arbeiten zur Kirchengeschichte 8 (Berlin: De Gruyter, 1955); Dix, *The Shape of the Liturgy*, 492, 495, 511.

[24] Al-Miskīn, *Al-ifḫaristiyyā*, 421.

[25] Ibid., 532.

at the beginning, he reasoned that the anaphoral thanksgiving prayer indeed comes at the end of the ancient eucharistic ritual, which in his view is the prothesis.[26] Finally, this idea of a *practical* original Eucharist lacking any explicit description of the Last Supper explains easily the absence of the words of institution from some early sources, such as Cyril of Jerusalem and the *Anaphora of Addai and Mari*.[27]

Unfortunately, this entire series of propositions stands on the outdated research of Lietzmann as well as a misreading of Dix.[28] The crux of Lietzmann's conclusions is that there were two distinguishable types of Eucharists in the Early Church, an earlier Jerusalem type and the Pauline type. While the former is closer in form to the Last Supper and is simply a breaking of bread accompanied by prayers and blessings, the latter is the more widespread and adds ideas of sacrifice and atonement to this originally pristine Jerusalem tradition. Regarding the survival of these two forms in the Christian Church, Lietzmann indicated that the Jerusalem type survived only in Egypt and can be seen in the *Anaphora of Sarapion*, while the Pauline type—witnessed first in the *Apostolic Tradition*—became the common eucharistic pattern everywhere.[29] Building on this theory, Fr. Mattā identified the Coptic prothesis rite precisely with this archaic Jerusalem type of eucharistic celebration, which he claimed the Coptic Church has preserved intact, albeit with the addition of the remainder of the liturgy to it to match developments elsewhere.

In addition, a passage in Dix's *The Shape of the Liturgy* provided additional support. The passage in question simply expresses the common knowledge that ritual motions were initially unaccompanied by prayers or chants, to which these latter elements were added later in order to impart solemnity and sometimes a theological or spiritual explanation to what is being done. The example given by Dix is the Roman offertory, and not the prothesis rite as Fr. Mattā seems to always understand the term! While the pre-Nicene Church was allegedly content with a silent offertory procession, prayers and chants were added later to explain the meaning of this movement or gesture.[30] Fr. Mattā consequently saw in the Coptic prothesis rite precisely this pre-Nicene action-without-explanation approach common at the time. He reasoned that the entire anaphora was the explicit prayer added later for explanation. It is clear that Fr. Mattā's theory of the origin of the Coptic prothesis rite subsumes in it many

26 Ibid., 572.

27 Ibid., 634.

28 Fr. Mattā acknowledges clearly that his entire work is based on the work of Lietzmann. Cf. ibid., 427n1.

29 Lietzmann, *Messe und Herrenmahl*, 260–263.

30 Dix, *The Shape of the Liturgy*, 511.

observations on early and pre-Nicene Christian worship. This ambitious view is surely founded on the consecratory character of the *Prothesis Prayer* without which Fr. Mattā would not have considered the rite a complete and sufficient eucharistic prayer. Thus, the central question becomes: Did the Coptic prothesis rite truly descend from what was originally an independent and complete eucharistic rite, which was followed immediately by the fraction and communion? In order to provide a comprehensive rebuttal of this ambitious theory, each facet of Fr. Mattā's reasoning is considered.

2.2. The Argument based on the Non-Discursiveness of the Early Eucharist

First of all, Gregory Dix was certainly correct when he referred to the offertory procession in Mopsuestia advancing "in dead silence" during the time of Theodore and Narsai, as opposed to the future covering over the action with chant,[31] or even with the offertory prayer.[32] Thus, Dix can rightfully reiterate later that the newly introduced offertory prayer "puts into words the meaning of the offertory, which the pre-Nicene Church had been content to express by the bare action."[33] The process of embellishing an originally simple liturgical action with accompanying chants and/or prayers is a common phenomenon in liturgical evolution, already observed by Anton Baumstark in his work *Vom geschichtlichen Werden der Liturgie* in 1923.[34] However, here as in most of Dix's work, the famous liturgist is speaking of the western offertory, a pre-anaphoral public procession to present the gifts and their subsequent placement on the altar by the clergy, something altogether different from the eastern prothesis rites. This point was proven definitively by Robert Taft for the Byzantine Rite and reiterated here with pertinent evidence for the Coptic prothesis.

That the prothesis—the way Fr. Mattā understood it—could have been this Ur-eucharistic celebration, performed free of accompanying chant and prayers and constituting the *entirety* of the eucharistic gathering could in no way be true for the following reasons. First, the earliest preparation of the gifts was a purely practical matter of receiving the gifts of the people and keeping them in the pastophorion until their transfer to the altar in the pre-anaphora, as was the case elsewhere in the Christian East. Even the *Prothesis Prayer* itself, the oldest ritual element of the rite, did not exist at first, and there is no

31 Ibid., 492.
32 Ibid., 495.
33 Ibid., 511.
34 Baumstark, *Vom geschichtlichen Werden der Liturgie*, 103–115; Baumstark, *On the Historical Development of the Liturgy*, 199–216.

evidence of it in the Alexandrian realm before the Ethiopic *Order of the Mystery* (ca. 5th c.). Thus, it is inconceivable that such a practical act done away from the public service would constitute the Eucharist in its fullness, and there is no evidence that this preparation was ever more than that previously. Even Dix himself noted—even lamented—the ritual solemnization of the prothesis and the transfer of gifts in the Byzantine East.[35] Second, if Fr. Mattā somehow meant a prothesis rite that was performed in the pre-anaphora similar to the western offertory, it would still be impossible to accept his assertions. As has been shown both in the Byzantine Rite and here in the Coptic tradition, the preparation of the gifts was never part of the pre-anaphora, and especially not the elements of it that he identifies as constituting a complete and "valid" eucharistic celebration. Third, it is one thing to describe certain actions as originally silent, and a whole other thing to claim that the entire eucharistic celebration was this one silent act of offering. Such an idea would go completely against all what is known of early eucharistic development, the extemporaneous prayers offered by the presider (cf. Justin's *Apology*) and the slow process of standardization of anaphoral prayers in the fourth century.[36] Indeed, the whole point of all the scholarship attempting to trace the early anaphoral prayers to Jewish ritual antecedents presupposes that the Christian Eucharist *from the very beginning* was a verbal prayer pronounced over the bread and wine![37] Finally, Fr. Mattā's theory assumes that the *Prayer of Thanksgiving* is an integral and ancient part of this supposed Jerusalem apostolic Eucharist, while in fact it has been argued already in Chapter 5 that it

35 Dix, *The Shape of the Liturgy*, 290.

36 On the evolution of standardized anaphoral texts from earlier extemporaneous prayers, see Allan Bouley, *From Freedom to Formula: The Evolution of the Eucharistic Prayer from Oral Improvisation to Written Texts*, Studies in Christian Antiquity 21 (Washington DC: Catholic University of America Press, 1981). For a recent analysis of this transition to codified texts in the Egyptian context, see Mihálykó, *The Christian Liturgical Papyri*, 227–236.

37 And, one must add, even the general idea of Jewish antecedents for the structure and/or content of Christian liturgy has been demonstrated recently to be not as straightforward as hitherto thought. According to Paul Bradshaw, modern scholarship on Jewish liturgy largely agrees that very little was standardized within Judaism by the first century, which leads scholars of early Christian worship today to expect very little by way of direct descent from Jewish to Christian prayer structures and formulas. For this and more reasons on the current state of the question, see Paul F. Bradshaw, "Jewish Influence on Early Christian Liturgy: A Reappraisal," in *Liturgies in East and West: Ecumenical Relevance of Early Liturgical Development. Acts of the International Symposium Vindobonense I, Vienna, November 17-20, 2007*, ed. Hans-Jürgen Feulner, Österreichische Studien zur Liturgiewissenschaft und Sakramententheologie 6 (Vienna: Lit Verlag, 2013), 47–59.

is an enarxis prayer, completely unrelated to the preparation of the gifts as such.

2.3. The Argument based on the Later Insertion of the Institution Narrative

Fr. Mattā al-Miskīn is also correct in observing that some earlier eucharistic witnesses lack any mention of the words of institution. This is certainly the case in the *Anaphora of Addai and Mari*,[38] and is also widely accepted as true for the liturgy described in the *Mystagogical Catecheses* attributed to Cyril of Jerusalem (4th c.),[39] and others.[40]

In fact, much has been written recently about the interpolation of the Institution Narrative into the anaphora, something that most anaphoral prayers are now believed to have initially lacked until the fourth century. Recently, the interpolation of the Institution Narrative was tied quite interestingly with the cessation of martyrdom by Maxwell Johnson.[41] In addition, Paul Bradshaw saw in the interpolation of the Institution Narrative an outcome of Christianity's shift in the fourth century to a public cult, the influx of un-instructed masses of converts, and thus the need to infuse the liturgy with a

38 The literature on the *Anaphora of Addai and Mari* is extensive, largely due to its lack of the words of institution and the ecumenical impact this has had in recent decades on the theology of eucharistic consecration in East and West. See Bryan D. Spinks, "A Tale of Two Anaphoras: Addai and Mari and Maronite Sharar," in *The Anaphoral Genesis of the Institution Narrative in Light of the Anaphora of Addai and Mari: Acts of the International Liturgy Congress, Rome 25–26 October 2011*, ed. Cesare Giraudo, OCA 295 (Rome: Pontificium Institutum Orientalium Studiorum, 2013), 259–274; Nicholas V. Russo, "The Validity of the Anaphora of *Addai and Mari*," in *Issues in Eucharistic Praying in East and West: Essays in Liturgical and Theological Analysis*, ed. Maxwell E. Johnson (Collegeville, MN: Liturgical Press, 2010), 21–62 and the literature cited there. Robert F. Taft, "Mass Without the Consecration? The Historic Agreement on the Eucharist between the Catholic Church and the Assyrian Church of the East Promulgated 26 October 2001," *Worship* 77 (2003): 482–509.

39 Emmanuel J. Cutrone, "The Liturgical Setting of the Institution Narrative in the Early Syrian Tradition," in *Time and Community: In Honor of Thomas Julian Talley*, ed. J. Neil Alexander, NPM Studies in Church Music and Liturgy (Washington DC: Pastoral Press, 1990), 105–114, and more specifically on Cyril of Jerusalem, Emmanuel J. Cutrone, "Cyril's Mystagogical Catecheses and the Evolution of the Jerusalem Anaphora," *OCP* 45 (1978): 52–64.

40 This includes *Didache 9–10, Apostolic Constitutions 7,* and the *Strasbourg Papyrus* to name a few famous documents. See Taft, "Mass Without the Consecration," 490–493.

41 Maxwell E. Johnson, "Sharing 'the Cup of Christ': The Cessation of Martyrdom and Anaphoral Development," in *Studies on the Liturgies of the Christian East: Selected Papers of the Third International Congress of the Society of Oriental Liturgy Volos, May 26–30, 2010*, ed. Steven Hawkes-Teeples, Bert Groen, and Stefanos Alexopoulos, Eastern Christian Studies 18 (Leuven: Peeters, 2013), 109–126.

catechetical element explaining the reason for the celebration and its historical roots in the Last Supper.[42]

All of this may appear to lend credence to Fr. Mattā's theory, that the ancient Jerusalem Eucharist was later embellished by the addition of explanatory prose–such as the words of institution–until finally the latter became *the* liturgy, while the simpler ancient Eucharist remained in embryonic form in the Coptic prothesis rite. However, this identification of ancient eucharistic celebration with what should properly be called the preparation and transfer of gifts–a specificity of language that was maintained so far in this work–represents the bold and unacceptable leap that is rejected here. The fact of the matter is that it is the anaphoral prayer itself that was enlarged from its simple thanksgiving over the gifts–the kind found in sources like the *Didache*, *Addai and Mari*, and other Early Church documents–to include the words of institution and even a full account of the economy of salvation. In other words, the prothesis, the preparation of the gifts and their subsequent transfer to the altar had nothing to do with this development, which, as was reiterated many times, took place at a time when the prothesis had no ritual or theological significance of the kind that would develop in subsequent centuries.

2.4. The Argument based on Lietzmann's Two Ancient Eucharistic Types

This leaves the aspect of Fr. Mattā's theory that relies upon Lietzmann's two Eucharist types, the Jerusalem and the Pauline. Already, Gregory Dix himself rejected such a sharp distinction, since to him both the non-sacramental *agape* meal and the Eucharist stem from a single Jewish source, the *chaburah* supper.[43] At any rate, today most scholars have rejected Lietzmann's theory of a sharp division between a Jewish Christian Jerusalem Eucharist and a Hellenized Christian Pauline one.[44] For the present purpose, it is sufficient once again to reiterate that neither Dix nor Lietzmann would have ever imagined this early Christian Eucharist to be the ancestor of the Coptic prothesis or any other eastern rite of preparation of the gifts. More specifically, one of Lietzmann's main characteristics of this non-sacramental Jerusalem type of meal fellowship is that it did not include

42 See for example Paul F. Bradshaw, *Eucharistic Origins*, Alcuin Club Collections 80 (Eugene, OR: Wipf & Stock, 2012), 140–141.

43 Dix, *The Shape of the Liturgy*, 95.

44 Paul. F. Bradshaw, *The Search for the Origins of Christian Worship: Sources and Methods for the Study of Early Liturgy*, 2nd ed. (Oxford: Oxford University Press, 2002), 51–53.

wine, turning Fr. Mattā's theory entirely on its head and making it inapplicable to the Eucharist in any real way.[45]

In the final analysis, Fr. Mattā al-Miskīn attempted to explain the purpose of the Coptic prothesis, which according to its new ordo is performed on the altar and essentially functions as an offering and consecration of the gifts before the anaphora. In so doing, he envisioned an ancient history of eucharistic development in which the prothesis takes center stage as the entirety of the eucharistic celebration, to be followed only by the fraction and communion. His theory, ambitious though it is, is built on a misreading of the mostly-outdated theories of earlier scholarship. Moreover, it is based on huge assumptions that ultimately fail when judged against the current knowledge of the evolution of the prothesis specifically and the Eucharist generally.

3. THE PROTHESIS PRAYER AS A MOMENT OF CONSECRATION

Hegumen Mattā al-Miskīn's fantastic attempt at explaining the *Prothesis Prayer* and rite aside, the explicit consecratory language of the prayer still poses a dilemma, at least for anyone committed to recognizing only a single moment of eucharistic consecration in the anaphoral epiclesis. Despite the long centuries of dispute between the Byzantine East and the Latin West over the issue of when the transformation of bread and wine took place, recent scholarship has come to the understanding that the change of the elements was never fixed to a single moment in the mind of early Christians. This began to change when the medieval polemics between East and West caused both sides to proclaim an official adherence to a single moment, the words of institution in the West vs. the epiclesis prayer in the East. In a recent study of the issue from the Byzantine perspective, Michael Zheltov concluded that the Byzantines–official statements notwithstanding–never really favored a single moment of consecration. Rather, multiple points in the liturgical celebration could be identified as having particular consecratory power, and these were usually associated with acts rather than words. Examples presented by Zheltov include the elevation, the commixture, and the fraction. More importantly, even the prothesis rite is included due to the consecratory character of the *Prothesis Prayer*, evident both in the Egyptian/Italo-Byzantine version found in CHR of *BAV Barberini Gr. 336* (8th c.), as well as in the Constantinopolitan version of Byzantine

[45] Lietzmann, *Messe und Herrenmahl*, 253.

BAS.[46] In order to show that such moments were indeed understood—sometimes even on a subconscious level—as somehow climactic or consecratory, Zheltov builds on the work of Taft. The latter marshalled evidence from certain Byzantine saints' *Vitae*, such as the *Life of Saint Theodore of Sykeon* (ca. 7th c.), the *Life of Saint Stephen the Sabaite* (end of 8th c.), the *Life of Saint John Chrysostom* by Symeon Metaphrastes (end of 10th c.), and the *Life of Saint Bartholomew of Simeri* (12th c.).[47] To these accounts, Zheltov added a miracle of Saint Nicholas of Myra, and the *Life of Saint Sergius of Radonezh* (15th c.).[48]

Examining Coptic sources on this matter demonstrates that the Copts too perceived various points throughout the liturgy as imbued with particular consecratory significance. The earliest reference to a consecratory moment other than the epiclesis appears in a seventh-century pastoral epistle preserved in the papyrus *P. Berlin 11346.* The epistle is written by an unidentified Egyptian bishop to his local clergy, presumably in the seventh century, according to Alberto Camplani.[49] In this letter, the anonymous bishop seems to be introducing a provision by which priests are allowed to consecrate additional *prosphorae* after the anaphora but before communion, presumably if the need arises because of the large number of communicants. In order to do so, the bishop instructs his clergy, they are to "bring the seal (ⲛ̄ϥⲛ̄ⲧⲥⲫⲣⲁⲅⲓⲥ) on the chalice of the Eucharist, that which is plunged in the holy blood of [the Lord] and he/it seals the bread saying in this way, the consecrated holy things for the saints (ⲧⲁ [...] ⲅⲓⲁⲥⲑⲉⲛⲧⲁ. ⲧⲁ ⲁⲅⲓⲁ ⲧⲟⲓⲥ ⲁⲅⲓⲟⲓⲥ)."[50] Although Camplani himself avoided entering into the complicated liturgical interpretation of this passage, it appears that the intention was for the priest to do the consignation between the consecrated chalice and the new bread oblation immediately before the *sancta sanctis*.[51] Clearly, if the consignation

46 Michael Zheltov, "The Moment of Eucharistic Consecration in Byzantine Thought," in Johnson, *Issues in Eucharistic Praying*, 263–306.

47 Taft, *The Precommunion Rites*, 211, 214, 227–228.

48 Zheltov, "The Moment of Eucharistic Consecration," 294.

49 Alberto Camplani, "A Pastoral Epistle of the Seventh Century Concerning the Eucharist (Pap. Berlin P. 11346)," in *Forschung in der Papyrussammlung. Eine Festgabe für das Neue Museum*, ed. Verena M. Lepper, Ägyptische und orientalische Papyri und Handschriften des ägyptischen Museums und Papyrussammlung Berlin 1 (Berlin: Akademie Verlag, 2012), 377–386.

50 Ibid., 379–380.

51 Such was also the interpretation in the recent Arabic edition of this epistle based on Camplani's article. Cf. Bishoy Ramzī and Christine Fawzī, "Risāla ra'awiyya 'an al-ifḫāristiyyā min al-qarn al-sābi'," [A pastoral epistle on the Eucharist from the seventh century] *Madrasat al-Iskandariyya* 18 (2015): 191–209, here 206. On the consignation of the Coptic liturgy, see Burmester, *The Egyptian Church*, 71–72.

alone sufficed to consecrate the new bread, no mention of the elevation call would have been necessary. Thus, this can be understood as witnessing clearly to the consecratory effect of the elevation in Coptic Egypt, at least in limited circumstances.[52]

Often the consecratory power of particular moments appears in the context of a eucharistic miracle in which the bread and wine are seen as a sacrificed and bleeding child on the altar at a certain moment during the liturgy, either as a form of demonstration of the real presence of Christ in the Eucharist, or as proof of the sanctity of a certain saint.[53] In a seventh-century miracle found in a saying of Abba Daniel of Scetis, a monk of simple faith, who considered the Eucharist merely symbolic of the body and blood, is shown the body of Christ as a little child already at the time of its placement on the altar, by which is presumably meant the prothesis. Later at the fraction, an angel is seen descending with a sword and pouring the child's blood into the chalice.[54] This story appears to have been quite popular in monastic circles, that it survived not only in Coptic, but in Greek[55] and

52 Another source points to a similar practice of post-anaphoral consecration, though unfortunately it is not possible to identify the exact use and liturgical context in which this took place. The papyrus *P. Oslo inv. 1665* (7th/8th c.) contains a prayer for the consecration of the chalice that mentions the presanctified body. The prayer concludes with Our Father, which makes it quite similar to the *Rite of Filling the Chalice*, usually prescribed for emergencies if the original chalice at a liturgy is spilled, or its contents found to be corrupted. On this rite, see Īrīs Ḥabīb al-Maṣrī, "The Rite of the Filling of the Chalice," *BSAC* 6 (1940): 77–90; Ramez Mikhail, "The Coptic Church and the Presanctified Liturgy: The Story of a Rejected Tradition," *Alexandria School Journal* 3 (2016): 2–30, here 16–21. For the Oslo papyrus text, with translation and commentary, see Anastasia Maravela, Ágnes Mihálykó, and Glenn Ø. Wehus, "A Coptic Liturgical Prayer for the Consecration of the Chalice," *Archiv für Papyrusforschung* 63, no. 1 (2017): 204–230. Maravela et al posit three possible uses of this prayer, thus it is arguable if this prayer is another witness to the consecratory effect of the pre-communion rites.

53 Many of the miracles included in this section are discussed in terms of their historical context and place in the dogmatic conflicts of the Chalcedonian controversy in Leslie S.B. MacCoull, "John Philoponus, *On the Pasch* (*CPG* 7267): The Egyptian Eucharist in the Sixth Century and the Armenian Connection," *Jahrbuch der Österreichischen Byzantinistik* 49 (1999): 1–12, reprinted later in MacCoull, *Documenting Christianity*, 1–12.

54 For the Coptic text of the miracle, see Marius Chaîne, *Le manuscrit de la version copte en dialecte sahidique des "Apophthegmata Patrum,"* Bibliothèque d'études coptes 6 (Cairo: Institut français d'archéologie orientale, 1960), 40–41 (Coptic), 118–119 (French). Alternatively, an English translation is found in Ward, *The Sayings of the Desert Fathers*, 53–54. For a discussion of the dogmatic as well as Ancient Egyptian themes in this story, see Jan Helderman, "Der sketische Greis, das Hostienwunder und das alte Ägypten," in *Divitiae Aegypti: Koptologische und verwandte Studien zu Ehren von Martin Krause*, ed. Căcilia Fluck et al. (Wiesbaden: Ludwig Reichert Verlag, 1995), 134–146.

55 Daniel 7 (CPG 5562). Cf. Guy, *Les Apophtegmes des Pères*, 3:40–44.

Syriac[56] as well. Other miracles seem to point to the pre-communion rites generally as times when the real presence of Christ is revealed. Examples include the Coptic Synaxarion life of John, bishop of al-Burullus, in which the bishop used to see the chalice burning with flames at the time of the consignation, when the priest is to trace the sign of the cross over the body after dipping his finger in the chalice, shortly before the fraction.[57] In another story, the fraction itself is enlisted as a climactic point in which the immolation of the child Jesus on the altar takes place. This is told in the context of a miracle that is said to have taken place in Baghdad in order to demonstrate the truth of the Christian religion to the Abbasid prince al-Hāshimī. Upon entering the church to begin one of his customary destructive raids—so the story goes—he saw the body in the form of a beautiful noble child. Later at the fraction, he saw the priest slaughter this child and pour his blood into the chalice.[58]

In other instances, the epiclesis is clearly portrayed as the moment of highest solemnity and thus conducive for a miraculous occurrence. In the biography of Pope Christodoulus (AD 1047–1077), a story is told of a certain Peter the Anchorite, who told his disciple that he has never celebrated the liturgy ever since the time when his finger became permanently dyed red with the overflowing blood from the chalice. The account as told in the *History of the Patriarchs* makes it clear that this took place when the anchorite pointed to the chalice saying "May this become the blood of Christ," in reference to the manual gesture of the priest at the epiclesis.[59] A very similar story, although featuring a different protagonist, appears in the *The Histories of the Monasteries and Churches* of Abū l-Makārim.[60] Certainly, the historical veracity of these miracles cannot be ascertained, and oftentimes the events described would have taken place much earlier than the date of the text at any rate. However, these miracles usually have as their purpose either to prove the reality of the Eucharist—sometimes explicitly against the Eucharist of an rival group—or to demonstrate the sainthood of the key figure who was

56 E.A. Wallis Budge, *The Book of Paradise Being the Histories and Sayings of the Monks and Ascetics of the Egyptian Desert by Palladius, Hieronymus and Others. The Syriac Text, According to the Recension of 'Anân-îshô' of Bêth 'Âbhê, Edited with an English Translation*, vol. 1, *English Translation*, Lady Meux Manuscript 6 (London, 1904), 819–820.

57 Basset, *Le Synaxaire arabe jacobite*, 2:488.

58 The miracle is inserted in the biography of Coptic Pope Philotheos (AD 979–1003). See *HP*, 2.2:110 (Arabic), 166 (English).

59 Atiya, *HP*, 2.3:194 (Arabic), 297 (English). The same story is repeated in the *History of the Patriarchs* by Pseudo-Yūsāb of Fuwwa: Cf. Al-Suryānī and Kāmil, *Tārīḫ al-ābā' al-baṭārika*, 116.

60 Evetts, *The Churches & Monasteries*, 304.

worthy to see such miracles. As such, it is very likely that the moment in the liturgy chosen to make this point would be one already perceived and understood by the readers as particularly special and unique. This renders these miraculous stories very insightful into how the liturgy was perceived by the Copts at various times, despite the obvious lack of historical credibility.[61]

This is not to say that official and dogmatic expressions in theological texts did not commit to a single moment, much as Zheltov observed in the Byzantine and western sources. By the fourteenth century at the latest, a single moment of eucharistic consecration is identified clearly with the descent of the Holy Spirit at the epiclesis. This is seen in the fourteenth-century anonymous *Treatise on the Eucharist*, which according to its editor Alfonso 'Abdallah as well as Georg Graf, is a Coptic treatise originating from the Monastery of Saint Antony by the Red Sea by an apparently learned anonymous monk.[62] In this treatise, which provides extensive treatment of the proper manners and customs for priests and laity during the liturgy, the author speaks more than once of the consecration of the gifts. This consecration is said to take place through, "the prayer of the priest and the descent of the Holy Spirit,"[63] "the grace [of the priesthood] and the descent of the Holy Spirit,"[64] and "through the descent of the Holy Spirit by the consecration of it [the mysteries] by the priest of God."[65] Finally, although less explicitly, a dogmatic letter on the Eucharist written by Pope Matthew IV (AD 1660–1675) and preserved in *Paris BnF Ar. 227* (AD 1671) speaks multiple times as well of the real presence of Christ after the consecration.[66] Although it is unclear what constitutes the consecration, it is clear at least that the patriarch had a particular moment in mind, after which he understood Christ to be present in the bread and wine.

Thus, while official dogmatic expressions on the one hand favored the epiclesis as the single moment of consecration, popular literature and hagiographical miracles on the other hand placed significant

61 A helpful discussion of the place of hagiography in liturgical research can be found in Taft, *Communion, Thanksgiving, and Concluding Rites*, 74–76. See also Delehaye, *Cinq leçons*; Pratsch, "Exploring the Jungle," 59–72.

62 Alfonso 'Abdallah, "Un trattato inedito sulla SS. Eucaristia (Ms. Vat. Ar. 123, 1396 A.D.) Testo originale e traduzione," *SOC. Aegyptiaca Collectanea* 12 (1967): 345–464. On this treatise, see *GCAL*, 2:453–455.

63 'Abdallah, "Un trattato inedito sulla SS. Eucaristia," 363 (Arabic), 415 (Italian).

64 Ibid., 370 (Arabic), 422 (Italian).

65 Ibid., 377 (Arabic), 431 (Italian).

66 For an Arabic text with a French translation, see Wadi Awad and Enzo Lucchesi, "Les deux lettres dogmatiques du pape copte Matthieu IV," in Youssef and Moawad, *From Old Cairo to the New World*, 185–201, here 191–192 (Arabic), 198–199 (French).

weight on many other moments in the liturgy, such as the consignation, the fraction, the elevation, and even the prothesis. Returning to the initial task, this journey through samples of Coptic and Copto-Arabic literature demonstrates the following idea clearly: The introduction of the *Prothesis Prayer* with its explicit consecratory language at such an early juncture in the liturgy is very natural in a tradition that never really committed to a single moment of consecration. After all, such well-defined dogmatic positions are a product of medieval theological thought, found explicit usually in abstract theological discourse with its requirements for specificity and exactness.

The existence of this prayer in the Coptic prothesis rite, which was certainly the case even in the privately performed old ordo, indicates clearly that the Coptic Church and its clergy perceived the very act of receiving the gifts of the people as in itself worthy of solemnization. An epicletic prayer asking Christ to shine his face upon them was thus employed for this purpose. The prothesis rite was thus certainly understood as a significant point within the overall eucharistic journey, a journey that is in fact a continuous and cohesive transformation and change from the earthly to the heavenly, which cannot be easily broken down to its constituent parts without doing violence to the overall process. This transformation requires an entire journey, from the prothesis to the precommunion rites, and even communion itself as its ultimate goal, rather than a single formula or moment.

Therefore, rather than seeking to explain the *Prothesis Prayer* either as an ancient rogue anaphoral epiclesis, or as evidence that the prothesis rite in its entirety was at some point a complete eucharistic celebration, it is more in line with the evidence and Coptic eucharistic consciousness to see in this fascinating prayer a witness to the non-spontaneous evolution of the liturgy. Quite simply, the *Prothesis Prayer* developed as an expression of the increasing solemn character of the preparation of the eucharistic gifts in Coptic piety and practice. This development is in every way consistent with the common understanding of the liturgy as a continuous and holistic journey with many notable stops along the way.

CONCLUSIONS

By its very nature, the method of structural analysis of liturgical units works by breaking down a liturgical rite under investigation into its constituent parts, and then proceeds to analyze each unit in the rite in order to understand its historical origins, and by extension its function in the overall celebration. The disadvantage—if one may call it such—of using this very useful method is that one may risk getting lost in the details, or not seeing the forest because of the trees, as it were. Now that the elements of the Coptic prothesis rite have been analyzed in as much detail as the evidence allows, one would risk leaving the job undone unless a broad birds-eye view of the evolution of the Coptic prothesis rite is provided.

The stages outlined below take into account other related structures in the Coptic liturgy such as the enarxis and the pre-anaphora, which have interacted and exerted their influence on the prothesis, and without which, the picture would be incomplete. Most of the elements in the following outline of developmental stages are arranged based on explicit evidence that was presented in the course of this study. Nonetheless, there remains some degree of uncertainty regarding certain elements, which I have taken the liberty of placing in particular stages based rather on educated conjecture. Naturally, we await the re-interpretation of existing sources by mentors and colleagues, or even the discovery of new sources. This may make it possible to adjust the following outline in its finer details, though, it is hoped, not in its broad strokes. Throughout this work, I have been speaking of three main types of the Coptic prothesis: old ordo, intermediate ordo, and new ordo, these ordos are distinguished mainly in terms of the location of the preparation of the gifts and the point at which the transfer procession took place. They can be summarized as follows:

1. Old ordo: The preparation of the gifts took place in the pastophorion, followed by a transfer procession in the pre-anaphora.
2. Intermediate ordo: The selection of the gifts took place in the pastophorion, followed immediately by a procession to the altar and the remainder of the prothesis rite.

3. New ordo: All elements of the prothesis rite take place on the altar. This includes a circular procession around the altar during the prothesis.

Since even within the so-called new ordo the rite continued to develop, culminating in the fifteenth-century reforms of Patriarch Gabriel V, I have sought below to break down this development into more than a simple tripartite outline. The historical development of the Coptic prothesis rite is presented here in the form of broad successive stages. In each stage, new elements are indicated in bold. Whenever possible, I indicate the relative date of the first appearance of an element in the sources.

1. TOWARDS A BROAD HISTORICAL VIEW

1.1. Phase 1: The Primitive Preparation of the Gifts

Based on all the evidence presented in the first two chapters, this first phase is characterized by its practical nature, which lacks most if not all signs of a fully-developed liturgical rite. One should speak more accurately of this phase as the pre-history or the kernel of what would eventually become the prothesis rite through a process of ritualization, rather than as a stage of the prothesis rite itself in the strict sense. As can be seen, the most ancient element of the rite, the *Prothesis Prayer*, had yet to be introduced. The steps below are simply the actions required to prepare the gifts in view of their future transfer in the pre-anaphora:

1. Reception of the oblations from the people and their selection
2. Mixing the chalice
3. Covering the gifts
4. Pre-anaphoral transfer procession

1.2. Phase 2: The Old Ordo (ca. 5th–8th c.)

With the introduction of the *Prothesis Prayer*, one can now speak unequivocally of a liturgical rite in the strict sense. This by necessity required the participation of a priest, although it is doubtful that at this early stage a bishop would have been involved in what was still in its essence a practical matter of preparation. In the absence of any other evidence, one must add the vesting before all these rites, which took place also in one of the pastophoria. To these would have been also added the blessing of the bread, hinted at as early as the seventh-century *Life of John of Scetis*. The fact that people brought their own offerings makes commemorations on their behalf also very logical, and indeed it is seen in the *Canons of Shenoute* among other sources. This results in the following outline:

Before the Liturgy in the pastophorion:

1. **Vesting of the clergy and assistants**
2. Reception of the oblations from the people and their selection
3. **Blessing of the bread by the celebrant (7th c.)**
4. **Commemorations (5th c.)**
5. Mixing of the chalice by the deacon
6. ***Prothesis Prayer* (ca. 5th c.)**
7. Hierarch's vesting

Enarxis Rites:

1. Psalm 116
2. *Prayer of Thanksgiving* (ca. 7th c.)
3. *Entrance Prayer* = *Absolution of the Son*

The Pre-Anaphoral Rites:

1. Hand washing
2. Prayer of the Kiss of Peace, and exchange of the kiss
3. Prayer of *accessus ad altare* (= *oratio veli*)
4. Transfer procession accompanied by processional chant(s)
5. Deposition of the gifts with altar veils on the altar
6. The anaphora and remainder of the service

1.3. Phase 3: An Old Rite in a New Place (ca. 8th–10th c.)

The third phase in this scheme corresponds to the immediate aftermath of the shift from the old ordo to the new arrangement, which over a few centuries would stabilize into the intermediate and eventually the new ordo*s*. Admittedly, there is no hard evidence in support of this phase, and it is certainly the most conjectural in this scheme. However, the highly plausible assumption underlying this phase is that such a radical shift in the rite must have taken place gradually.

First, rites traditionally associated with the pre-anaphoral *accessus ad altare* began to make their way into the prothesis rite at this time. This includes the *Prayers of Preparation,* which are identical in content to similar prayers of *accessus* elsewhere. Initially a single prayer, soon another prayer from Byzantine BAS are adopted, a familiar phenomenon of emphasis via duplication. Also, from the *accessus* rites, the hand washing is repeated, while retaining its original location in the pre-anaphora. Similarly, the exchange of blessing must have been imported from the pre-anaphora, where it is traditionally found in many liturgical traditions.

Other than the wholesale adoption of rituals from the *accessus* rites, one may notice that this scheme leaves the enarxis rites intact and distinct from the prothesis. At such an early stage, when these changes in the location of the prothesis were new, there was likely a period of time in which both major rites–prothesis and enarxis–were yet to begin mingling and their respective elements become confused. The first exception to break this rule must have been the *Prayer of Thanksgiving*, which based on the hypothesis in Chapter 5 was likely brought into the prothesis rite shortly after the shift in order to "normalize" matters, to restore it once more to a more primary position as an opening prayer, and to preface the highly solemn and consecratory *Prothesis Prayer*. Finally, the *Absolution of the Servants*, a unique prayer having no other exact parallel elsewhere in the Coptic Rite or otherwise likely developed in this formative period of the Northern Egyptian liturgy. This is especially the case given the stark confessional character of the prayer, which emphasizes the heroes of non-Chalcedonian Orthodoxy

Taken altogether, the rite likely took the following shape:

1. Vesting of presbyters and deacons
2. **Prayers of Preparation of the Altar**

In Prothesis pastophorion:

3. Selection of the oblation
4. **Hand washing**
5. Commemorations
6. Procession to the altar

Alleluia al-Qurbān + Psalm verses

At the Altar:

7. **Exchange of blessing among the clergy**
8. Blessing of the bread offering
9. Mixing of the chalice by the deacon
10. *Prothesis Prayer*
11. Covering of the oblations and exiting the sanctuary
12. ***Absolution of the Servants***

Enarxis Rites:

13. Psalm 116
14. *Thanksgiving Prayer* (brought before the *Prothesis Prayer* soon after)
15. Hierarch's vesting
16. *Entrance Prayer* = *Absolution of the Son* followed by *May you be saved*

1.4. Phase 4: Growth in a New Environment (until ca. 14th c.)

The fourth phase in this scheme combines both the intermediate ordo of Ibn Sabbāʿ and the slightly later new ordo found in Ibn Kabar and other sources of the period. Overall, this is a period of transition. While the new arrangement of celebrating the prothesis rite on the altar—at least partially in the intermediate ordo—had by then become the *de facto* order of worship, minor elements and gestures were still largely in flux, especially in terms of their relative order in the unfolding of the rite. This is an era before the ritual reforms spread through the *Ritual Order* of Gabriel V in the fifteenth century, after which a much greater uniformity can be observed in the sources. The main addition at this point would have been the practice of baptizing the oblation bread, a custom seen since Ibn Sabbāʿ in the fourteenth century but seems to have been already stable by that time.

In a broader sense, we witness here the inevitable mixing of the prothesis and enarxis rites. This is seen in the combining of *One is the Holy Father* and Psalm 116 to essentially form a single diaconal proclamation. This is also seen in the stabilization of the *Prayer of Thanksgiving* as a veritable element in the prothesis by virtue of its displacement. Finally, this is seen in the juxtaposition of the *Absolution of the Son* and the *Absolution of the Servants*, which were previously separated.

1. Vesting of presbyters and deacons 2. *Prayers of Preparation of the Altar* *In Prothesis pastophorion* (in Ibn Sabbāʿ): 3. Selection of the oblation 4. Hand washing **5. Baptism of oblation bread (14th c.)** 6. Commemorations 7. Procession to the altar (in Ibn Sabbāʿ) or around the altar	*Alleluia al-Qurbān* + Psalm verses

At the Altar:

8. Exchange of blessing among the clergy (in Ibn Kabar: Before the procession)
9. Blessing of the bread offering (later, both bread and wine).
10. Mixing the chalice by the deacon.
11. *One is the Holy Father*
12. Psalm 116
13. *Thanksgiving Prayer*
14. *Prothesis Prayer*
15. Covering the oblations and exiting the sanctuary

16. Hierarch's vesting
17. *Entrance Prayer* (= *Absolution of the Son*)
18. *Absolution of Servants*

1.5. Phase 5: The Stabilization of the Rite under Gabriel V (15th c.)

In this final phase, the rite reaches more or less its current form. Judging from the Euchologia before and after *The Ritual Order*, it is likely that this uniformity can be attributed to the liturgical activities of Patriarch Gabriel V himself. Only two elements in the following outline can be said to be rather new: 1. The repurposing of *Glory and Honor* from being part of the blessing formula over the oblations to a loud proclamation at the start of the procession, and 2. The adoption of yet another element from the anaphora, the diaconal response, "Pray for these holy honorable gifts," hitherto unattested in the prothesis.

Another noticeable tendency moving forward is the continued diminishing role of the deacon. Compared to earlier historical stages of the rite, in which deacons prepared the oblations, or at least mixed the chalice, we see the gradual assignment of these duties to the priest. By the seventeenth century at the latest, the priest had become the sole cleric responsible for mixing the chalice. As for the procession, it had become the privilege of the priest to carry the oblation bread already by the time of Gabriel V. Finally, the alleluia chant which formerly accompanied all preparatory acts until the procession has now become reduced to the interval of time between the selection of the offering and the *Glory and Honor* at the procession.

1. Vesting of presbyters and deacons
2. *Prayers of Preparation of the Altar*
3. Selection of the oblation
4. Hand washing. ⎤
5. Baptism of the oblation bread ⎬ *Alleluia al-Qurbān* + Psalm verses
6. Commemorations ⎦
7. Procession **by the priest** and deacons around the altar **with *Glory and Honor***
8. **Deacon's acclamation: "Pray for these holy honorable gifts." (post-15th c.)** accompanied with,
9. Processional Psalms
10. Exchange of blessing among the clergy
11. Blessing of the oblation bread
12. Mixing the chalice by the deacon **(by priest post-17th c.)**
13. *One is the Holy Father*

14. Psalm 116
15. *Thanksgiving Prayer*
16. *Prothesis Prayer*
17. Covering the oblations and exiting the sanctuary
18. Hierarch's vesting
19. *Entrance Prayer* (= *Absolution of the Son*)
20. *Absolution of Servants.*

2. SOME CONCLUDING THEOLOGICAL REMARKS

Liturgical rites are not mere aimless pieces of group behavior but are intelligent building blocks placed together to contribute to a larger edifice more than the sum of their parts. In this case, the edifice is the expression of faith and life of the people who developed and observed these rites precisely in order to express and reinforce certain truths about their faith concerning God, the world, and their place in it. With this in mind, it would be again insufficient to conclude this work without making some theological and pastoral observations on the rite of the prothesis, especially at this point after much of it has been elucidated through a meticulous analysis of the sources. The following remarks also stem from the author's personal experience as a practitioner and observer of the Coptic liturgical tradition, which certainly grant a unique perspective in addition to the scientific analysis of the sources adopted throughout this work.

2.1. The Demise of the Old Ordo: Consequences

It would not be difficult to evaluate the new ordo of the transfer of gifts of the Coptic liturgy in the most negative light. As I have already demonstrated, the universal witness of various liturgical traditions is unanimous that the bringing of the eucharistic gifts and their placement on the altar was originally and everywhere executed between the Liturgy of the Word and the eucharistic liturgy proper. This is the case not only in the particular regional Rites of East and West, but even in the *First Apology* of Justin Martyr from the second century.[1] Going back even further, one can find clear precedence for the familiar order of reading the Scriptures first before proceeding to bring, place, and offer the eucharistic gifts in the course of the anaphora. This is in some way what Christ himself did during his post-resurrectional encounter with the disciples in Emmaus, where he interpreted to them his own ministry from the Scriptures before he broke bread (Lk 24:27–30). This pattern continued in the life of the

[1] *1 Apol.* 65 and 67 (CPG 1073). Cf. Charles Munier, *Justin: Apologies pour les chrétiens*, SC 507 (Paris: Cerf, 2006), 302–304, and 310–311 respectively.

nascent Christian community in Jerusalem, where we find that the disciples continued in attending the temple services, followed by breaking of bread in their homes (Acts 2:46). It is scarcely a point in need of proof that the eucharistic service traditionally *started* with the reading of Scripture, to be followed by the breaking of bread, and not as is the case in the Coptic liturgy today, with the bringing of gifts followed by the Scriptures and the anaphora.

The first major consequence of the shift to the new ordo is that now, practically speaking, the offering of the gifts represented visibly in their placement on the altar is already accomplished in the very beginning of the liturgy. This can be a source of confusion, when the offering of the gifts is so far removed from the actual anaphora, itself understood as the offering of bread and wine. When the priest declares later in the anaphora of BAS, "We offer unto you these gifts from what is yours,"[2] it is difficult to see this as a moment of offering, when the gifts have been effectively offered for quite some time. On the other hand, while the gifts are referred to as oblations in the prothesis rite and are physically placed on the altar as a clear act of offering, the act is never quite identified as such or even mentioned as having taken place. Thus, in short, the new ordo creates a severing between word and act, what is done earlier without words is referenced later without an accompanying act. This, from the point of view of ritual intelligibility, is certainly problematic and cannot serve as a clear way for the ritual to show what it does, or to communicate its own meaning coherently.

This inconsistency between what is done and what the prayers communicate–or fail to communicate–strikes at the heart of the question: Can the prothesis rite in the Coptic liturgy be considered a preparatory rite, or an actual offering of the eucharistic gifts? If the answer to this question is the former, it would be perfectly understandable that the accompanying prayers, formulas, and chants do not explicitly mention the act of offering, at least not as explicitly as the anaphora itself does. This preparatory nature can be easily understood and accepted within the framework of the old ordo, where the gifts are indeed prepared and placed elsewhere and only brought to the altar at the commencement of the anaphora. However, the issue only arises within the framework of the new ordo, in which the gifts are physically placed on the altar much before the anaphora. This leaves the interpreter of the Coptic liturgy one of two hardly plausible options, either 1. The prothesis is not understood as a true offering, despite being exactly that, or 2. The Coptic liturgy has a double offering, one at the prothesis and another in the anaphora. Clearly,

2 Ṣalīb, ⲡⲓϫⲱⲙ ⲛ̀ⲧⲉ ⲡⲓⲉⲩⲭⲟⲗⲟⲅⲓⲟⲛ, 338.

the rite as it was intended to be performed provided no cause for such a dilemma.

Furthermore, such a profound shift in the order of major liturgical units could not have occurred without reverberations throughout the liturgy. While the so-called rites of *accessus ad altare* are traditionally part of the pre-anaphora, it was inevitable under the new ordo for some of these rites to be duplicated before the prothesis as well, since the celebration of the latter necessitates access to the altar. This may explain for example the recitation of the creed before the prothesis rite, in an attempt to harmonize it with the pre-anaphora, in which the creed is likewise recited. The same can certainly be said of the hand washing, which today occurs twice, before the prothesis and before the anaphora. Finally, the two prayers that accompany the preparation of the altar are nothing but prayers of *accessus ad altare*, seeking worthiness and permission for the celebrant to offer the eucharistic sacrifice despite his sinfulness and unworthiness, another traditional element of the pre-anaphora. Once more, the organic progression of the unfolding of the liturgy, building up to this point of approaching the altar, is in a way compromised when such rites associated with it are no longer unique and performed only at this juncture. In fact, to speak of an approach to the altar in the pre-anaphora may seem incomprehensible to the casual observer, or even the frequent practitioner, unless they are familiar with the pristine shape of the liturgy across multiple traditions.

Nonetheless, there remains one overlooked advantage made possible by the new ordo, and that is the public nature of the entire rite of prothesis in the Coptic liturgy. As is known, the rite of the prothesis is a second-stratum unit, which developed from an archaic simple reception of the gifts and their keeping by the deacons into the full rite it is today, with prayers, formulas, and involvement of priests. This took place in various rites in different ways, but the main result is that the basic bringing and keeping of gifts acquired rites of preparation and a certain solemnity. However, it is only in the Syrian, Coptic, and Ethiopian traditions that the gifts were no longer placed in the prothesis pastophorion after a certain point, while the Byzantine tradition retained the practice of storing the gifts elsewhere.

The result is that the rite of the prothesis that developed in the Byzantine tradition came to be a private rite, seen and participated in only by the celebrant, deacon, and assistants. In the Syrian tradition, this private nature is also maintained by the drawing of the curtain veiling the sanctuary while the priest prepares the gifts and reads the appropriate prayers. On the other hand, the Coptic tradition followed a markedly different trajectory, where the rite of the prothesis has a very public character, and where everything from the selection of the oblation to its covering on the altar following the *Prothesis Prayer* are performed publicly. Nor is the rite only observed by the people, but they also participate in it with their own responses and acclamations, which in some points even parallel those of the priest and deacon. For example, to the priest's triple blessing of the oblation after its selection, followed by the deacon's own Trinitarian acclamation "One is the Holy Father, one is the Holy Son, one is the Holy Spirit," the people in turn respond with the *doxa patri*. In my view, were the old ordo to be retained consisting in a reception and preparation of gifts in an adjacent chamber, followed by its transfer before the anaphora, it is likely that the further elaboration of the prothesis rite would have followed the private model, to be performed as a strictly clerical preparation, shielded from view and participation.

2.2. Approaching the Holy

Problems with the new ordo aside, it had become a reality for the Coptic tradition since the early middle ages, and it was inevitable, indeed necessary, that the rite adjusts accordingly. As the historical outline above has highlighted, many of the newly acquired liturgical elements are in fact rites of *accessus ad altare*, imported to this new location to adapt to the new reality of approaching the altar at this early stage. The *Prayers of Preparation of the Altar*, the hand washing, and the exchange of blessing are all manifestations of this same general adaptation.

But whether done before the anaphora immediately, or before the prothesis, the priest's ascent to the altar represents an important and crucial stage, in which he is to pause and reflect on his own sinfulness and unworthiness of this heavenly mystery, as seen first and foremost in the *Prayers of Preparation of the Altar*. As the text of these prayers communicates, this realization in turn leads him to request the grace from on high necessary for the sacrifice to be acceptable and well-pleasing on his behalf and that of others. From the very beginning of the Coptic liturgy then, the priest is reminded of some key spiritual aspects of his ministry as *leitourgos* or celebrant: 1. He is entirely unworthy and unable on his own to fulfill his ministry in a manner pleasing to God, 2. To aid him in the ministry of the altar to which he was called, God sends the grace of the Holy Spirit to cooperate with him for the well-acceptance of the offering of the church, and 3. This offering that is about to be offered for his sins and the sins of the people whom he serves is a sweet-smelling savor before God in the likeness of Christ's own sacrifice on the cross (Eph 5:2).

Thus, the priest is armed with some key theological and spiritual reflections regarding his own sinfulness, God's philanthropy in sending his Holy Spirit to his aid, and finally that the sacrifice of the Church on the altar is modeled after Christ's sacrifice. This act of eucharistic offering should transform the whole of the priest's and the Church's ministry in Christ into a continuous act of offering a sweet-smelling sacrifice on the spiritual altar of the heart.

The same is true for the hand washing. It was mentioned earlier that the hand washing is witnessed as early as the fourth century in the *Mystagogical Catecheses* commonly-attributed to Cyril of Jerusalem. This reference appears in his fifth catechetical homily, in which he writes about the deacon's offering of water to the priest, "Not at all did he give it because of bodily filth! It is not so! For we did not enter the church at first with filthy bodies, but it is a symbol that you must purify yourself from all sins and iniquities."[3] As remarked earlier, Robert Taft has argued convincingly that the washing of the hands was never a practical gesture originally, but was always meant as a spiritual act symbolizing the purity required of those that are to serve the altar.[4] As such, and as was already remarked, the washing of the hands is a veritable element of the rites of *accessus ad altare*, exactly as it functions in the pre-anaphoral rites. This is supported by the three psalm verses that accompany this ritual act (Pss 50:9–10; 25:6–7), all of which clearly link the physical act of washing to purity and repentance.

Placed within the context of other *accessus* rites in the Coptic prothesis, the hand washing then is the third step in this gradual process of the priest's ascent and entrance into the holy ministry of the altar. The first such step was the putting on of the liturgical vestments. Including a blessing received from the highest-ranking priest or bishop, vesting is an act rich in ecclesiological significance, which reminds all those about to serve of their unworthiness and their need for God's permission and grace to approach his holy altar. The second step in the *accessus* took place at the preparation of the altar. Expressed in this case in the words of the *Prayers of Preparation*, the celebrant is reminded that he stands in need of Divine grace to properly enter into the fearful ministry entrusted to him. He prays therefore for the well-acceptance of the eucharistic sacrifice, which is modeled after Christ's own sacrifice on the cross.

Finally, arriving at the threshold of the priestly actions of the prothesis rite, the priest washes his hands in an act that re-inforces what the prayers expressed earlier in words, namely, his own unfitness to approach such a sublime and fearful mystery without first cleansing

3 *Catech. Mystag* 5.2 (CPG 3686). Cf. Auguste Piédagnel, *Cyrille de Jérusalem: Catéchèses mystagogiques*, SC 126bis (Paris: Cerf, 2004), 148–149.

4 Taft and Parenti, *Il Grande Ingresso*, 320.

himself spiritually. This recalls the same idea found in the epistle to the Hebrews, "Let us draw near with a true heart in full assurance of faith, with our hearts sprinkled clean from an evil conscience and our bodies washed with pure water" (Heb 10:22). Such is the mystery of the new covenant, in which man's unworthiness and sinfulness are only one side of the Divine-human relationship, the other being God's overwhelming love for mankind that grants him the way by which he is to approach with full assurance, trusting that Christ the high priest is also Christ the spotless lamb, by whose blood, "we have confidence to enter the sanctuary" (Heb 10:19). This paradox is inherent in the rites of *accessus ad altare*, at once linking mankind's unworthiness with God's condescension in sanctifying and purifying mankind to make him fit for his service as a worshipping being in company with the saints.

Nowhere is this last element more clearly expressed than in the single non-scriptural prayer that accompanies the hand washing in some manuscripts, where the priest says, "My Lord Jesus Christ, purify our souls and our bodies and our spirits, so that we may find a share with the saints, who have pleased you since the beginning."[5] The prayer is at once a balanced reminder that our worship is both bodily and spiritual, encompassing and summing up the whole of man. One may indeed emphasize the need for spiritual cleansing as taking more precedence, but that in no way diminishes the place of the body in worship, which the prayer grants a place among the dimensions of human existence in need of purifying.

Further, the liturgy that is about to begin is not merely an earthly ritual, limited to the physical offering of bread and wine on a physical altar, for which indeed a merely physical cleansing would have been sufficient. Rather, it is in continuity with the heavenly liturgy, which the saints continuously offer before the throne of God. As such, the priest in this final act of preparation enters into the heavenly realm, not to commence or start an act of worship strictly speaking, but to partake and share in an ongoing and eternal praise of God that has indeed been active from the beginning, as the prayer declares. As the final act of *accessus ad altare*, the idea of approach will no longer be found in the subsequent elements of the rite, to be resumed once again later in the pre-anaphora.

[5] *British Library Add. 17725* (AD 1811), fol. 8r. The prayer appears also in *St. Macarius Lit. 134* (18th/19th c.) and *St. Macarius Lit. 133* (19th c.), where in the former it is attributed to Bishop Mīḫāʾīl of Samannūd. See Al-Maqārī, *Al-quddās al-ilāhī*, 1:298.

2.3. The Joyous Offering of God's People

The historical evidence of the new ordo consistently witnesses to an alleluia chant as the introductory chant of the entire liturgy, one that seems to have lasted throughout the preparatory rites and initial stages of the prothesis, particularly accompanying the selection of the offering, and presumably identified with the currently known *Alleluia al-Qurbān*. So fundamental was this alleluia to the commencement of the liturgy that the *Canons of Ps.-Athanasius* set it apart as the signal the priest must await to begin the rites.[6] One would not be exaggerating to see this chant as a call to prayer, a resounding shout not unlike the Muslim call to prayer or the blowing of a Shofar in Judaism, joyfully announcing the beginning of the feast that is the eucharistic gathering of the people of God, and its offering of its sacrifice of praise (Heb 13:15). That the chant lasted well into the rite of the prothesis is a testament to its profound influence on the overall tenor of the rite, its intended mood and character.[7]

The joyous character of the eucharistic assembly is indeed self-evident for many reasons. In the Eucharist, the Church enters into the ever-present reality of God's salvation, an act that is not merely a remembrance of the past events of his earthly life, but, "the lifting up of the Church into his parousia, the Church's participation in his heavenly glory."[8] Entering thus into this continuous festive presence of God, the Church is raised to where Christ is, sitting with him in the heavenly places (Eph 2:6).

But the Eucharist is also a sacrifice just as much as it is a heavenly celebration. As such, it would be certainly an oversight to assume a logical and self-evident link between sacrifice and joy. Indeed, in an age in which individualism is praised as a sign of a strong independent character and in which the concept of giving up anything is a sign of weakness, it is by no means immediately clear how a collective act of offering, giving, or sacrificing can be characterized as joyous or a cause for celebration. However, this is precisely the Christian message communicated so effectively from the very beginning of the liturgy. Saint Gregory of Nazianzus urged in his *Second Oration on Easter*, "Let us sacrifice ourselves to God, rather, let us sacrifice every day and in every action."[9] It is exactly this eagerness, even joy, to sacrifice and

6 Riedel and Crum, *The Canons of Athanasius of Alexandria*, 27 (Arabic), 33 (English).

7 I resume here my discussion of the topic of the introductory alleluia chant vis-à-vis the joyous character of the prothesis. See Ramez Mikhail, "Aspects of Witness in the Coptic Liturgical Tradition," *Alexandria School Journal* 1 (2014): 1–26, here 24–25.

8 Alexander Schmemann, *Introduction to Liturgical Theology*, 5th ed. (Crestwood, NY: St Vladimir's Seminary Press, 2003), 72.

9 *Or. 45*, 23 (CPG 3010) (PG 36:636). Translation mine.

offer not just bread and wine but our very selves that is the striking and paradoxical theology of sacrifice that the Church proclaims and teaches in contradistinction to the world's common understanding of sacrifice. Given the very public nature of the prothesis rite in the Coptic liturgy, this message of joyous sacrifice is highlighted as the central teachable theological truth, reinforced in every celebration of the liturgy for those participating in the rite. Whether the psalm that follows is the most clearly joyous "This is the day the Lord has made," (Ps 117:24–26) or one of the other selections emphasizing entrance (Pss 75:11; 42:4; 131:1) the Church in any case proclaims her joy at the inauguration of the day of the Lord, the icon of the unending day of the Lord's kingdom, in which humanity will be granted to enter into the sanctuary (Heb 10:19).

I say this in theory, of course, because as explained previously the current rite has relegated this solemn introductory chant to whatever interval of time remains between the prayers "Holy, Holy, Holy," Our Father, and until the priest is ready to begin the procession around the altar. In fact, in many a hasty celebration in which the celebrant rushes through the commemorations, the chant is never executed.

As the evidence has clearly demonstrated, these prayers and the chanting of *Kyrie eleison* 41 times that precedes them are elements belonging to the prayers of the hours and have nothing to do originally with the prothesis rite. Unfortunately, the chanting of *Kyrie eleison* executed during the selection of the offering is perceived today as the accepted norm, a chant that goes hand in hand with the selection of the lamb and is precisely meant to highlight the theme of the Lord's passion as the spotless lamb of Isaiah (cf. Is 53:7). Indeed, the very number 41 is meant to evoke this passion motif, which is usually interpreted as symbolic of the Lord's sufferings (39 lashes, the crown of thorns, and the piercing of his side).[10] Despite the appropriateness of this passion motif for the moment of the selection of the lamb, evidence shows that this was simply not the pristine form or original intent of the Coptic pothesis rite, a rite which has chosen rather to emphasize the joyous character of offering in crying out alleluia! For the Church's offering of herself is by necessity a deliberate identification with Christ the spotless lamb, a joyful act without which no offering can truly be called a gift.

2.4. The Commemorations: Ecclesiology in Action

Saint Paul wrote in his epistle to the Corinthians, "Because there is one bread, we who are many are one body, for we all partake of the

10 Mattā'us, *The Spirituality of the Rites of the Holy Liturgy*, 94.

one bread" (1 Cor 10:17). In fact, as I have written elsewhere, the Church's offering ultimately extends beyond those gathered on any given day to include the entire body of Christ.[11] The same ecclesiologically universal reality was noted by Alkiviadis Calivas, who wrote, "The Church as community is not limited to the faithful who constitute her membership in any given time and place. The Church catholic is present at every liturgical assembly."[12] It is precisely the Eucharist that encapsulates the entirety of the Church, or, in the words of John Zizioulas, "It is an event constitutive of the being of the Church, enabling the Church to be."[13]

This is most evident in the commemorations and precisely in the manner of their performance. Standing at the altar following the selection of the one bread of the Eucharist, the priest holds the eucharistic loaf in both hands and bows his head, silently praying for all those in particular needs, the departed, sick, travelers, or those in various difficult situations. Many priests may also remember at this time their fellow priests, family members, or the bishop that ordained them. Finally, this all-inclusive act of remembrance is brought to a conclusion by praying for the peace of the Church, the hierarchs–the Pope of Alexandria and the local bishop–and the peace of the liturgical gatherings everywhere. It is as though the one loaf, which is indeed the offering of the Church of her very self, gathers in it all the needs and hopes of the Church. Rather, it gathers in it the Church herself.

This idea was present also in such early texts as the *Didache,* where one reads, "As this piece of bread was scattered over the hills and then was brought together and made one, so let your Church be brought together from the ends of the earth into your kingdom."[14] The same understanding is communicated later in the *Anaphora of Sarapion of Thmuis,* "As this bread had been scattered on the top of the mountains and gathered together came to be one, so also gather your holy Church out of every nation and every country and every city and village and house and make one living catholic Church."[15]

At the very beginning of the prothesis rite when the liturgy publicly begins, the people of God have just arrived, both constituting the

[11] Mikhail, "Aspects of Witness," 23.

[12] Alkiviadis C. Calivas, *Essays in Theology and Liturgy,* vol 3, *Aspects of Orthodox Worship* (Brookline, MA: Holy Cross Orthodox Press, 2003), 121.

[13] John D. Zizioulas, *Being as Communion: Studies in Personhood and the Church,* Contemporary Greek Theologians 4 (Crestwood, NY: St Vladimir's Seminary Press, 1997), 21.

[14] *Didache* 9.4. (CPG 1735). Cf. Willy Rordorf and André Tuilier, *La Doctrine des douze apôtres (Didachè),* SC 248bis (Paris: Cerf, 1998), 176–177.

[15] Johnson, *The Prayers of Sarapion of Thmuis,* 48–49.

ecclesia and bringing with them all their hopes, desires, and pressing needs; in short, the human dimension of the Church meets the Divine. Before delving into any elaborate rites of complex symbolic meaning, and in full view of the assembled people, the priest reaffirms the unity of the people of God as one body in one bread, with all their needs raised as petitions to God at that very moment, because, "Nothing and no one escapes the concern of the Church at prayer because she is God's eternal witness, the sacrament of his love for everyone and everything, the sign and herald of his kingdom in the midst of the contradictions and anomalies of the fallen world."[16] This is precisely why this unity is affirmed shortly after, this time in such triumphal fashion, when the priest now elevates this one bread and proclaims it as "peace and building up of the one and only, holy, catholic, and apostolic Church of God."[17]

This ecclesiological dimension is also closely linked to the level of participation of the deaconate in the rites of the prothesis. While for most of ritual history the deacons were responsible for receiving the oblations, selecting from them what was appropriate, and in all likelihood also transferring them to the altar in the pre-anaphora, we see in the particularly Coptic evidence of later centuries a clear move towards increasing clericalization of acts and gestures. This was seen for example in the selection of the offering, which throughout all sources for the new ordo has been performed by the priest alone. Even in the fifteenth-century patriarchal liturgy, when the patriarch was in attendance but not yet vested, the oblations were brought to him outside for the selection, a sure sign of the understanding that this act should be reserved for the highest clerical rank available. Another example was the procession around the altar, which is led by the priest carrying the bread, despite earlier sources such as the *Lamp of Darkness* (14th c.) assigning this function to the deacon.

The increasing clericalization of the rite is a documented fact, and is likely the product of complex factors, not the least of which is the decline of the deaconate itself, yet it remains a movement that is not the most beneficial for communicating the ecclesiological depth of the prothesis rite, a rite that otherwise emphasizes the Church's ecclesiology quite strongly. The public nature of the prothesis contributes greatly to the involvement of the entire Church in what is ultimately its own offering. The people do not merely observe the rites performed by the priest, but they frequently respond to them with chants and hymns. Yet, diminished from this beautiful dynamic

16 Calivas, *Essays in Theology and Liturgy*, 123.

17 Ṣalīb, ⲡⲓϫⲱⲙ ⲛ̀ⲧⲉ ⲡⲓⲉⲩⲭⲟⲗⲟⲅⲓⲟⲛ, 214.

between presider and people is the ancient role of the deaconate as an integral ministry in the ecclesial community.

The importance of the deaconate in the Early Church cannot be overstated. It is clear for example in Saint Paul's greeting to the Philippians, "Paul and Timothy, servants of Christ Jesus, to all the saints in Christ Jesus who are at Philippi, with the bishops and deacons," (Phil 1:1) as well as the continuous mention of them by Saint Ignatius of Antioch, for example in his epistle *To the Trallians*, "Likewise, may everyone honor the deacons as the command of Jesus Christ and the bishop as Jesus Christ, who is the Son of the Father, and the presbyters as the assembly of God and as the band of the apostles. Without these no Church is named."[18] Commenting on the special place of honor accorded deacons in the epistles of Saint Ignatius, John Chryssavgis wrote, "Union with the ordained or ordered triadic ministry, within which the service of deacons was compared to the sacrifice of Christ, assured the very unity of the Church to Christ."[19]

Unlike such ancient notions of the importance of the deaconate, one can observe this increased prominence of the role of the presbyter/bishop as indeed a common phenomenon in later centuries. It appears for example in the Byzantine tradition in the second millennium.[20] Observed through the lens of the ancient deaconate, it is clear that the role of the deaconate today in the prothesis does not adequately reflect the importance of this rank as servants of the altar (cf. Acts 6:2).

2.5. The Prothesis Prayer: A Silent Witness to the Work of Christ

I have already seriously challenged the notion that the prothesis rite ever functioned as a self-contained eucharistic celebration. However, this idea surely owes much to the clearly epicletic character of the *Prothesis Prayer*, which is by far the most theologically profound

18 *Trall.* 3.1 (CPG 1025). Cf. Pierre Thomas Camelot, *Ignace d'Antioche, Polycarpe de Smyrne: Lettres, Martyre de Polycarpe*, SC 10bis (Paris: Cerf, 2007), 96–97. For a discussion of the deaconate as revealed in the sources of the first four centuries in particular, see John Chryssavgis, *Remembering and Reclaiming Diakonia: The Diaconate Yesterday and Today* (Brookline, MA: Holy Cross Orthodox Press, 2009), 29–65.

19 Ibid., 50.

20 Cf. Teeples, "The Prothesis of the Byzantine Divine Liturgy," 324. Teeples shows this increasing clericalization of the rite evidenced for example in the twelfth-century Latin translation of the Byzantine liturgy by Leo Tuscanus, in which the deacon asks for the priest's blessing to perform many functions previously considered his natural duty. Thomas Pott considers this move a *fait accompli* by the fourteenth century in agreement with Descoeudres. Cf. Pott, *Byzantine Liturgical Reform,* 210; Descoeudres, *Die Pastophorien im syro-byzantinischen Osten*, 113–114.

prayer of the entire rite. Especially in its Coptic modern recension, the *Prothesis Prayer* of the Egyptian tradition stands so early in the liturgical celebration as a clear testimony to the ever-present parousia of Christ throughout the eucharistic liturgy. In its central petition, the prayer asks Christ to "shine his face upon this bread and upon this cup," in what amounts to requesting his personal presence in the gifts considerably earlier than the classic epiclesis prayer of the anaphora will ask for the descent of the Holy Spirit. As such, the *Prothesis Prayer* is a strong reminder that the Coptic Church's eucharistic theology does not adhere to any single moment of consecration. A number of eucharistic miracles and other sources were advanced in support of this clear point that indeed various stages of the liturgy were understood to have significant consecratory power, even when official dogmatic expressions may make it seem otherwise. All at once, the *Prothesis Prayer*, its language, its location, all witness to Christ's consecratory work among his people, his acceptance of their offerings of their very selves, and his continuous parousia that is unbounded by time throughout the liturgical assembly.

It is unfortunate therefore that this profound expression of such central truths of the Gospel would be silenced today in actual practice, when the *Prothesis Prayer* is recited *mystically* or secretly by the celebrant. In fact, most people today are practically unaware that the so-called *presentation of the lamb* as the rite is known has any prayer of this kind. Silenced by the simultaneous chanting of the first syllable of the chant *May you be saved*, which is ultimately nothing but a ritualized *response* to the absolution to follow, the central prayer of the prothesis rite has truly become a silent witness to the Church's faith, inaccessible to all but the celebrant and that rare breed of the faithful who study the liturgy in search for meaning. It should go without saying that the ancient tradition everywhere was to recite all prayers aloud for all to hear. The common notion that certain prayers came to be read silently out of a sense of mystery and to prevent the unprepared from hearing them has been demonstrated to have no basis in historical evidence.[21] In the same vein, there is no reason to believe things were any different for the Coptic *Prothesis Prayer* in particular.

It is truly an ironic accident of liturgical development that in relation to this, the *Prayer of Thanksgiving* still retains its audible recitation, although this latter prayer is originally unrelated to the prothesis whatsoever. Although it is certainly not the goal of

[21] Robert F. Taft, "Was the Eucharistic Anaphora Recited Secretly or Aloud? The Ancient Tradition and What Became of it," in Ervine, *Worship Traditions in Armenia*, 15–57.

scholarship to meddle in the Church's organic liturgical development, nor to campaign for change, it is only hoped that the present analysis of this prayer and its history can at least restore this fundamental prayer to the consciousness of the Church and–perhaps more importantly–to liturgical catechism and instruction.

The *Prothesis Prayer*, and indeed the entire rite of the prothesis in its current public form, offers a precious snapshot of the Church's theology of offering, ecclesiology, eschatology, and the work of the Holy Trinity all at once. The need to engage more deeply with these eternal truths as they are revealed in the rite is precisely what this work has–in my view at any rate–made abundantly clear.

APPENDIX 1

THE TEXT OF THE COPTIC PROTHESIS

The following textus receptus of the Coptic prothesis rite is adapted generally from the Euchologion of Hegumen ʿAbd al-Masīḥ Ṣalīb al-Masʿūdī al-Baramūsī published in 1902,[1] and condensed for clarity. The insertion of square brackets [...] indicates that a portion of the original text has been removed to preserve the flow of the rite. The removed sections usually correspond to lengthy spiritual explanations that do not add to the reader's knowledge of the unfolding of the rite. The text has been supplemented by adding the chant *All the wise men of Israel* from the 1887 edition of the Deacon's Service Book (*kitāb ḫidmat al-šammās*) by Hegumen Philotheos Ibrahīm.[2] The text is presented here in Coptic with my own English translation in a parallel column, while the rubrics are presented only in English translation. This text is intended solely as a quick reference to the rite in its entirety for the reader's convenience. For official English translations of the Coptic liturgy, one may consult the respective Euchologion editions published by the various English-speaking Coptic Orthodox dioceses in North America, the United Kingdom, and Australia.

1. THE VESTING RITE

The priest must first examine his thoughts and condition internally and externally. Internally [...], the priest should be reconciled with the people [...]. Externally, he should be clean with respect to his body and clothing and he should wash his hands and feet. He ought to watch not to taste anything whatsoever. And the priest puts on the vestment of the priesthood, while he says the twenty-ninth psalm, "I will exalt You O Lord," and after it the ninety-second psalm, "The Lord reigns, he is clothed with majesty." Then he [the priest] greets his brothers the priests and asks them to assist him in entreating. Then he bows to the Lord before his holy sanctuary and offers an obeisance to his brothers the priests and the rest of the clergy [...].

1 Ṣalīb, ⲡⲓϫⲱⲙ ⲛ̀ⲧⲉ ⲡⲓⲉⲩⲭⲟⲗⲟⲅⲓⲟⲛ, 193–234.

2 [Ibrāhīm], *Kitāb mā yağibu ʿala l-šamāmisa*, 70.

2. THE PREPARATION OF THE ALTAR

He ascends now [to the altar] as was explained, and the eastern lamp should be lit, and likewise two candles on both sides of the altar on two candlestands. And the deacon ascends and stands opposite him. Then the priest uncovers the table from the *prospherin*, and he places the vessels before him and unties them [...]. Footnote: The custom current now is that the people first pray the prayer of the psalms of the hours, and that the preparation of the altar be done before or during this. Then he begins the *Prayer of Preparation* of the altar. He says it secretly:

ⲡ̅ⲟ̅ⲥ̅ ⲫⲏⲉⲧⲥⲱⲟⲩⲛ ⲛ̀ⲛⲓϩⲏⲧ ⲛ̀ⲧⲉ ⲟⲩⲟⲛ ⲛⲓⲃⲉⲛ ⲫⲏⲉⲑⲟⲩⲁⲃ ⲟⲩⲟϩ ⲉⲑⲙⲟⲧⲉⲛ ⲙ̀ⲙⲟϥ ϧⲉⲛ ⲛⲏⲉⲑⲟⲩⲁⲃ ⲛ̀ⲧⲁϥ. ⲫⲏⲉⲧⲟⲓ ⲛ̀ⲁⲑⲛⲟⲃⲓ ⲙ̀ⲙⲁⲩⲁⲧϥ ⲟⲩⲟϩ ⲉ̀ⲧⲉ ⲟⲩⲟⲛ ϣ̀ϫⲟⲙ ⲙ̀ⲙⲟϥ ⲉ̀ⲭⲁⲛⲟⲃⲓ ⲉ̀ⲃⲟⲗ. ⲛ̀ⲑⲟⲕ ⲫⲛⲏⲃ ⲉⲧⲥⲱⲟⲩⲛ ⲛ̀ⲧⲁⲙⲉⲧⲁⲧⲉⲙⲡϣⲁ ⲛⲉⲙ ⲧⲁⲙⲉⲧⲁⲧⲥⲟⲃϯ ⲛⲉⲙ ⲧⲁⲙⲉⲧⲁⲧϩⲓⲕⲁⲛⲟⲥ ⲉ̀ϧⲟⲩⲛ ⲉ̀ⲡⲁⲓϣⲉⲙϣⲓ ⲉⲑⲟⲩⲁⲃ ⲛ̀ⲧⲁⲕ ⲫⲁⲓ. ⲟⲩⲟϩ ⲙ̀ⲙⲟⲛ ϩⲟ ⲙ̀ⲙⲟⲓ ⲉ̀ϧⲱⲛⲧ ⲉ̀ϧⲟⲩⲛ ⲟⲩⲟϩ ⲉ̀ⲁⲟⲩⲱⲛ ⲛ̀ⲣⲱⲓ ⲙ̀ⲡⲉⲙ̀ⲑⲟ ⲙ̀ⲡⲉⲕⲱ̀ⲟⲩ ⲉ̀ⲑⲩⲟⲁⲃ. ⲁⲗⲗⲁ ⲕⲁⲧⲁ ⲡⲁ̀ϣⲁⲓ ⲛ̀ⲧⲉ ⲛⲉⲕⲙⲉⲧϣⲉⲛϩⲏⲧ ⲭⲱ ⲛⲏⲓ ⲉ̀ⲃⲟⲗ ⲁⲛⲟⲕ ϧⲁ ⲡⲓⲣⲉϥⲉⲣⲛⲟⲃⲓ. ⲟⲩⲟϩ ⲙⲏⲓⲥ ⲛⲏⲓ ⲉⲑⲣⲓϫⲓⲙⲓ ⲛ̀ⲟⲩϩⲙⲟⲧ ⲛⲉⲙ ⲟⲩⲛⲁⲓ ϧⲉⲛ ⲧⲁⲓ ⲟⲩⲛⲟⲩ ⲑⲁⲓ. ⲟⲩⲟϩ ⲟⲩⲱⲣⲡ ⲛⲏⲓ ⲉ̀ϧⲣⲏⲓ ⲛ̀ⲟⲩϫⲟⲙ ⲉ̀ⲃⲟⲗ ϧⲉⲛ ⲡϭⲓⲥⲓ

O Lord who knows the hearts of everyone [Acts 1:24; Lk 16:15], the holy one and who rests in his saints, who alone is without sin, and is able to forgive sins [Mt 9:6]. You, O Master, know my unworthiness, my unpreparedness, and my insufficiency unto this your holy service. And I do not have the face to draw near and to open my mouth before your holy glory. But according to the multitude of your compassion, forgive me the sinner [Lk 18:13]. And grant me to find grace and mercy at this hour. And send unto me power from on high,

Here the priest begins to wipe the paten and puts it in its place. Then he wipes the chalice, looks inside the throne, wipes it from the top, and places the chalice in it. Likewise, he wipes the spoon and places it on the throne south of the chalice. And he puts the veils in their places, and he is to have placed from them a veil under the paten and covered it [the paten] with another veil, and covered the chalice also with a veil. All this is while he recites the remainder of the *Prayer of Preparation* for the covering of the altar and the preparation of the vessels, saying:

ⲉⲑⲣⲓⲉⲣϩⲏⲧⲥ ⲟⲩⲟϩ ⲛ̀ⲧⲁⲥⲟⲃϯ ⲟⲩⲟϩ ⲛ̀ⲧⲁϫⲱⲕ ⲉ̀ⲃⲟⲗ ⲕⲁⲧⲁ ⲡⲉⲑⲣⲁⲛⲁⲕ ⲙ̀ⲡⲉⲕϣⲉⲙϣⲓ ⲉⲑⲟⲩⲁⲃ ⲕⲁⲧⲁ ⲡϯⲙⲁϯ ⲙ̀ⲡⲉⲕⲟⲩⲱϣ ⲉ̀ⲟⲩⲥⲑⲟⲓ ⲛ̀ⲥⲑⲟⲓⲛⲟⲩϥⲓ. ⲥⲉ ⲡⲉⲛⲛⲏⲃ ϣⲱⲡⲓ ⲛⲉⲙⲁⲛ ⲁⲣⲓϣⲫⲏⲣ ⲛ̀ⲉⲣϩⲱⲃ ⲛⲉⲙⲁⲛ ⲥⲙⲟⲩ ⲉ̀ⲣⲟⲛ. ⲛ̀ⲑⲟⲕ ⲅⲁⲣ ⲡⲉ ⲡⲭⲱ ⲉ̀ⲃⲟⲗ ⲛ̀ⲧⲉ ⲛⲉⲛⲛⲟⲃⲓ ⲫⲟⲩⲱⲓⲛⲓ ⲛ̀ⲧⲉ ⲛⲉⲛⲯⲩⲭⲏ ⲡⲉⲛⲱⲛϧ ⲛⲉⲙ ⲧⲉⲛϫⲟⲙ ⲛⲉⲙ ⲧⲉⲛⲡⲁⲣⲣⲏⲥⲓⲁ. ⲟⲩⲟϩ ⲛ̀ⲑⲟⲕ

that I may begin and prepare and fulfill your holy service as is pleasing to you, according to the pleasure of your will, unto a sweet-smelling savor [Eph 5:2]. Yes, our Master, dwell with us, cooperate with us, bless us. For you are the forgiveness of our sins, the light of our souls, our life, our strength, and our boldness. And to

ⲡⲉⲧⲉⲛⲟⲩⲱⲣⲡ ⲛⲁⲕ ⲉ̀ⲡϣⲱⲓ ⲙ̀ⲡⲓⲱⲟⲩ ⲛⲉⲙ ⲡⲓⲧⲁⲓⲟ ⲛⲉⲙ ϯⲡⲣⲟⲥⲕⲩⲛⲏⲥⲓⲥ ⲫⲓⲱⲧ ⲛⲉⲙ ⲡϣⲏⲣⲓ ⲛⲉⲙ ⲡⲓⲡⲛⲉⲩⲙⲁ ⲉⲑⲟⲩⲁⲃ. ϯⲛⲟⲩ ⲛⲉⲙ ⲛ̀ⲥⲏⲟⲩ ⲛⲓⲃⲉⲛ ⲛⲉⲙ ϣⲁ ⲉⲛⲉϩ ⲛ̀ⲧⲉ ⲛⲓⲉⲛⲉϩ ⲧⲏⲣⲟⲩ ⲁⲙⲏⲛ.	you we send up the glory, the honor, and the worship, to the Father, and the Son, and the Holy Spirit, now and at all times, and unto ages of all the ages, amen.

And when the priest has finished placing the vessels everything in its place, he says this prayer secretly after the preparation of the altar:

ⲛ̀ⲑⲟⲕ ⲡⲟ̅ⲥ̅ ⲁⲕϯ̀ⲥⲁⲃⲟⲛ ⲉ̀ⲡⲁⲓⲛⲓϣϯ ⲙ̀ⲙⲩⲥⲧⲏⲣⲓⲟⲛ ⲛ̀ⲧⲉ ⲡⲓⲟⲩϫⲁⲓ. ⲛ̀ⲑⲟⲕ ⲁⲕⲑⲁϩⲙⲉⲛ ϧⲁ ⲛⲏⲉⲧⲑⲉⲃⲓⲏⲟⲩⲧ ⲟⲩⲟϩ ⲛ̀ⲁⲧⲉⲙⲡϣⲁ ⲛ̀ⲉⲃⲓⲁⲓⲕ ⲛ̀ⲧⲁⲕ ⲉ̀ⲑⲣⲉⲛϣⲱⲡⲓ ⲛ̀ⲣⲉϥϣⲉⲙϣⲓ ⲙ̀ⲡⲉⲕⲑⲩⲥⲓⲁⲥⲧⲏⲣⲓⲟⲛ ⲉⲑⲟⲩⲁⲃ. ⲛ̀ⲑⲟⲕ ⲡⲉⲛⲛⲏⲃ ⲁ̀ⲣⲓⲧⲉⲛ ⲛ̀ϩⲓⲕⲁⲛⲟⲥ ϧⲉⲛ ϯϫⲟⲙ ⲛ̀ⲧⲉ ⲡⲉⲕⲡⲛ̅ⲁ̅ ⲉ̅ⲑ̅ⲩ̅ ⲉ̀ϫⲱⲕ ⲉ̀ⲃⲟⲗ ⲛ̀ⲧⲁⲓⲇⲓⲁⲕⲟⲛⲓⲁ ⲑⲁⲓ. ϩⲓⲛⲁ ϧⲉⲛ ⲟⲩⲙⲉⲧⲁⲧϩⲓⲧⲧⲉⲛ ⲉ̀ⲡϩⲁⲡ ⲙ̀ⲡⲉⲙⲑⲟ ⲙ̀ⲡⲉⲕⲛⲓϣϯ ⲛ̀ⲱⲟⲩ ⲛ̀ⲧⲉⲛⲓ̀ⲛⲓ ⲛⲁⲕ ⲉ̀ϧⲟⲩⲛ ⲛ̀ⲟⲩⲑⲩⲥⲓⲁ ⲛ̀ⲥⲙⲟⲩ. ⲟⲩⲱⲟⲩ ⲛⲉⲙ ⲟⲩⲛⲓϣϯ ⲙ̀ⲙⲉⲧⲥⲁⲓⲉ ϧⲉⲛ ⲡⲉⲑⲟⲩⲁⲃ ⲛ̀ⲧⲁⲕ. ⲫϯ ⲫⲏ ⲉⲧϯ ⲛ̀ⲟⲩϩⲙⲟⲧ ⲫⲏ ⲉⲑⲟⲩⲱⲣⲡ ⲛ̀ⲟⲩⲥⲱϯ ⲫⲏ ⲉⲧⲉⲣⲛ̀ⲉⲣⲅⲓⲛ ⲛ̀ϩⲱⲃ ⲛⲓⲃⲉⲛ ϧⲉⲛ ⲟⲩⲟⲛ ⲛⲓⲃⲉⲛ. ⲙⲏⲓⲥ ⲡⲟ̅ⲥ̅ ⲉⲑⲣⲉⲥϣⲱⲡⲓ ⲉⲥϣⲏⲡ ⲙ̀ⲡⲉⲕⲙⲑⲟ ⲛ̀ϫⲉ ⲧⲉⲛⲑⲩⲥⲓⲁ ⲉ̀ϩⲣⲏⲓ ⲉ̀ϫⲉⲛ ⲛⲏ ⲉ̀ⲧⲉ ⲛⲟⲩⲓ̀ ⲛ̀ⲛⲟⲃⲓ ⲛⲉⲙ ⲛⲓⲙⲉⲧⲁⲧⲉⲙⲓ ⲛ̀ⲧⲉ ⲡⲉⲕⲗⲁⲟⲥ. ⲟⲩⲟϩ ϫⲉ ⲥⲧⲟⲩⲃⲏⲟⲩⲧ ⲕⲁⲧⲁ ϯⲇⲱⲣⲉⲁ̀ ⲛ̀ⲧⲉ ⲡⲉⲕⲡⲛⲉⲩⲙⲁ ⲉⲑⲟⲩⲁⲃ ϧⲉⲛ ⲡⲓⲭⲣⲓⲥⲧⲟⲥ ⲓⲏⲥⲟⲩⲥ ⲡⲉⲛⲟ̅ⲥ̅. ⲫⲁⲓ ⲉⲧⲉ ⲉ̀ⲃⲟⲗ ϩⲓⲧⲟⲧϥ ⲉⲣⲉ ⲡⲓⲱⲟⲩ ⲛⲉⲙ ⲡⲓⲧⲁⲓⲟ ⲛⲉⲙ ⲡⲓⲁⲙⲁϩⲓ ⲛⲉⲙ ϯⲡⲣⲟⲥⲕⲩⲛⲏⲥⲓⲥ ⲉⲣⲡⲣⲉⲡⲓ ⲛⲁⲕ ⲛⲉⲙⲁϥ ⲛⲉⲙ ⲡⲓⲡⲛ̅ⲁ̅ ⲉ̅ⲑ̅ⲩ̅ ⲛ̀ⲣⲉϥⲧⲁⲛϧⲟ ⲟⲩⲟϩ ⲛ̀ⲟⲙⲟⲟⲩⲥⲓⲟⲥ ⲛⲉⲙⲁⲕ. ϯⲛⲟⲩ ⲛⲉⲙ ⲛ̀ⲥⲏⲟⲩ ⲛⲓⲃⲉⲛ ⲛⲉⲙ ϣⲁ ⲉⲛⲉϩ ⲛ̀ⲧⲉ ⲛⲓⲉⲛⲉϩ ⲧⲏⲣⲟⲩ ⲁⲙⲏⲛ.	You, O Lord, have taught us this great mystery of salvation. You called us, your lowly and unworthy servants, to become ministers of your holy altar. O our Master, make us worthy by the power of your Holy Spirit to fulfill this ministry. So that without falling into condemnation before your holy glory, we may offer unto you a sacrifice of praise [Heb 13:15], glory, and great beauty in your holy place. O God who grants grace, who sends salvation, who works everything in everyone [1 Cor 12:16]. Grant, O Lord, that our sacrifice may be acceptable before you [Phil 4:18], for my own sins and for the ignorances of your people [Heb 9:7], and that it may be pure according to the gift of your Holy Spirit [Rom 15:16], in Christ Jesus our Lord. This is he through whom the glory, the honor, the dominion, and the worship are due unto you, with him and the Holy Spirit, the giver of life, who is of one essence with you, now and at all times, and unto the ages of all ages, amen.

3. THE SELECTION OF THE OFFERING

Then the priest kisses the altar. And at the presentation of the lamb, he stands at the door of the sanctuary facing west and holding a small veil. And they present to him the lamb and the wine. He chooses the lamb, which is the bread of offering, and examines this well. [...] And he takes the lamb after inspecting it and wipes its back with a clean veil, that is, a cloth, kisses it, and places it on the right side of the altar in a silk veil. And he carefully examines the condition of the wine by smelling or allows one of those not fasting to taste it in the palm of their hand. [...] Then he gives it to the deacon, who holds it with a veil.

4. THE HAND WASHING

Then the priest washes his hands three times, while he says in the first time from Psalm 50:7:

ⲉⲕⲉ̀ⲛⲟⲩϫ ϧⲁϫⲱⲓ ⲙ̀ⲡⲉⲕϣⲉⲛϩⲓⲥⲟⲡⲟⲛ ⲉⲓⲉ̀ⲧⲟⲩⲃⲟ. ⲉⲕⲉ̀ⲣⲁϧⲧ ⲉⲛⲟⲩⲃⲁϣ ⲉϩⲟⲧⲉ ⲟⲩⲭⲓⲱⲛ.	Sprinkle upon me your hyssop, I will become pure. Wash me and I shall be whiter than snow.

And in the second time from Psalm 50:8:

ⲉⲕⲉ̀ⲑⲣⲓ ⲥⲱⲧⲉⲙ ⲉ̀ⲟⲩⲑⲉⲗⲏⲗ ⲛⲉⲙ ⲟⲩⲟⲩⲛⲟϥ ⲉⲩⲉ̀ⲑⲉⲗⲏⲗ ⲙ̀ⲙⲱⲟⲩ ⲛ̀ϫⲉ ⲛⲓⲕⲁⲥ ⲉⲧⲑⲉⲃⲓⲏⲟⲩⲧ.	You shall make me to hear joy and gladness, the humble bones shall rejoice.

And in the third time from Psalm 25:6–7:

ϯⲛⲁⲓⲁ ⲧⲟⲧ ⲉ̀ⲃⲟⲗ ϧⲉⲛ ⲡⲉⲑⲟⲩⲁⲃ. ⲟⲩⲟϩ ⲛ̀ⲧⲁⲕⲱϯ ⲉ̀ⲡⲉⲕⲙⲁⲛ̀ⲉⲣϣⲱⲟⲩϣⲓ ⲡ̅ⲟ̅ⲥ̅ ⲉ̀ⲡϫⲓⲛⲧⲁⲥⲱⲧⲉⲙ ⲉ̀ⲡϧⲣⲱⲟⲩ ⲛ̀ⲧⲉ ⲡⲉⲕⲥⲙⲟⲩ.	I will wash my hands of the holies, and I will go about your altar, O Lord, to hear the voice of your praise

And in some copies, he says in the second time from Psalm 50:9:

ⲙⲁⲧⲁⲥⲑⲟ ⲙ̀ⲡⲉⲕϩⲟ ⲥⲁⲃⲟⲗ ⲛ̀ⲛⲁⲛⲟⲃⲓ ⲟⲩⲟϩ ⲛⲁⲁⲛⲟⲙⲓⲁ ⲧⲏⲣⲟⲩ ⲉⲕⲉ̀ⲥⲟⲗϫⲟⲩ.	Turn way your face from my sins and blot out all my iniquities.

And in the third time, from Psalm 50:10:

ⲟⲩϩⲏⲧ ⲉϥⲟⲩⲁⲃ ⲉⲕⲉ̀ⲥⲟⲛⲧϥ ⲛ̀ϧⲏⲧ ⲫϯ ⲟⲩⲡⲛⲉⲩⲙⲁ ⲉϥⲥⲟⲩⲧⲱⲛ ⲁⲣⲓⲧϥ ⲙ̀ⲃⲉⲣⲓ ϧⲉⲛ ⲛⲏⲉⲧⲥⲁϧⲟⲩⲛ ⲙ̀ⲙⲟⲓ.	Create in me a pure heart, O God, and renew a right spirit in my inward parts.

5. THE BAPTISM OF THE LAMB

Then he dries his hands in a white linen clean veil only a little. And he takes the lamb on the palm of his left hand and wipes it with his right hand above and below, while saying ⲙⲏⲓⲥ ⲡ̅ⲟ̅ⲥ̅ ⲉⲑⲣⲉⲥϣⲱⲡⲓ ⲉⲥϣⲏⲡ [Grant O Lord that our sacrifice may be acceptable] in its entirety as was written above in the end of ⲛ̀ⲑⲟⲕ ⲡ̅ⲟ̅ⲥ̅ ⲁⲕ̀ⲧⲥⲁⲃⲟⲛ [You O Lord have taught us].

6. THE COMMEMORATIONS

Then he commemorates whomever he wishes, and in particular those for whom the offering has been presented, whether they be alive, departed, sick, travelling, or in adversity.
If they are alive, the priest says:

ⲁⲣⲓⲫⲙⲉⲩⲓ̀ ⲡⲟ̅ⲥ̅ ⲙ̀ⲡⲉⲕⲃⲱⲕ ⲛⲓⲙ̅ ⲁⲣⲉϩ ⲉ̀ⲣⲟϥ ϧⲉⲛ ⲟⲩⲁⲅⲅⲉⲗⲟⲥ ⲛ̀ⲧⲉ ϯϩⲓⲣⲏⲛⲏ ⲟⲩⲟϩ ⲭⲱ ⲛⲁϥ ⲛ̀ⲛⲉϥⲛⲟⲃⲓ ⲧⲏⲣⲟⲩ ⲉ̀ⲃⲟⲗ ⲟⲩⲟϩ ⲙⲁⲧⲟⲧⲕ ⲛⲉⲙⲁϥ ϧⲉⲛ ϩⲱⲃ ⲛⲓⲃⲉⲛ ⲛ̀ⲁⲅⲁⲑⲟⲛ.	Remember O Lord your servant N.N. Preserve him by the angel of peace, and forgive him all his sins, and help him in every good work.

For the departed, he says:

ⲁⲣⲓⲫⲙⲉⲩⲓ̀ ⲡⲟ̅ⲥ̅ ⲙ̀ⲡⲉⲕⲃⲱⲕ ⲛⲓⲙ̅ ⲟⲩⲟϩ ⲥⲁϩⲛⲓ ⲛⲁϥ ⲛ̀ⲟⲩⲙⲁⲛ̀ⲉⲙⲧⲟⲛ ⲛⲉⲙ ⲟⲩⲭⲃⲟⲃ ⲛⲉⲙ ⲟⲩⲁⲛⲁⲡⲁⲩⲥⲓⲥ ϧⲉⲛ ⲛⲓⲙⲁⲛ̀ϣⲱⲡⲓ ⲛ̀ⲧⲉ ⲛⲏ ⲉⲑⲟⲩⲁⲃ ⲛ̀ⲧⲁⲕ ϧⲉⲛ ⲕⲉⲛϥ ⲛ̀ⲛⲉⲛⲓⲟϯ ⲉⲑⲟⲩⲁⲃ ⲁⲃⲣⲁⲁⲙ ⲛⲉⲙ ⲓⲥⲁⲁⲕ ⲛⲉⲙ ⲓⲁⲕⲱⲃ ϧⲉⲛ ⲡⲓⲡⲁⲣⲁⲇⲓⲥⲟⲥ ⲛ̀ⲧⲉ ⲡ̀ⲟⲩⲛⲟϥ.	Remember O Lord your servant N.N. Appoint for him a place of rest, refreshment, and repose in the dwelling places of your saints, in the bosom of our holy fathers Abraham, Isaac, and Jacob, in the paradise of joy.

For the sick, he says:

ⲁⲣⲓⲫⲙⲉⲩⲓ̀ ⲡⲟ̅ⲥ̅ ⲙ̀ⲡⲉⲕⲃⲱⲕ ⲛⲓⲙ̅. ⲁⲣⲉϩ ⲉ̀ⲣⲟϥ ϧⲉⲛ ⲡⲁⲅⲅⲉⲗⲟⲥ ⲛ̀ⲧⲉ ϯϩⲏⲣⲏⲛⲏ ⲟⲩⲟϩ ⲙⲁⲧⲁⲗϭⲟϥ ⲉ̀ⲃⲟⲗ ϧⲉⲛ ⲛⲉϥϣⲱⲛⲓ ⲧⲏⲣⲟⲩ	Remember O Lord your servant N.N. Preserve him by the angel of peace and heal him of all his sicknesses.

And for the travelers by land or sea, he says what was mentioned for the sick. However, after saying ⲡⲁⲅⲅⲉⲗⲟⲥ ⲛ̀ⲧⲉ ϯϩⲏⲣⲏⲛⲏ [the angel of peace], he continues saying:

ⲟⲩⲟϩ ⲙⲁⲧⲁⲥⲑⲟϥ ⲉⲛⲏ ⲉⲧⲉ ⲛⲟⲩϥ ⲙⲁⲛ̀ϣⲱⲡⲓ ϧⲉⲛ ⲟⲩϩⲓⲣⲏⲛⲏ ⲛⲉⲙ ⲟⲩⲟⲩϫⲁⲓ	And return him to his own dwelling in peace and safety.

And for those in adversity or tribulation or prison or anything similar, he says what was mentioned previously for the sick as well. However, after saying ⲡⲁⲅⲅⲉⲗⲟⲥ ⲛ̀ⲧⲉ ϯϩⲏⲣⲏⲛⲏ [the angel of safety], he continues:

ⲟⲩⲟϩ ⲛⲁϩⲙⲉϥ ⲉ̀ⲃⲟⲗ ϧⲉⲛ ⲛⲉϥϩⲟϫϩⲉϫ ⲧⲏⲣⲟⲩ	And deliver him from all his tribulations.

And for all Christians generally, and his relatives in particular, he says:

ⲁⲣⲓⲫⲙⲉⲩⲓ̀ ⲡⲟ̅ⲥ̅ ⲛ̀ⲛⲉⲕⲉⲃⲓⲁⲓⲕ ⲛ̀ⲭⲣⲓⲥⲧⲓⲁⲛⲟⲥ ⲛ̀ⲟⲣⲑⲟⲇⲟⲝⲟⲥ ⲡⲓⲟⲩⲁⲓ ⲡⲓⲟⲩⲁⲓ ⲕⲁⲧⲁ ⲡⲉϥⲣⲁⲛ ⲛⲉⲙ ϯⲟⲩⲓ̀ ϯⲟⲩⲓ̀ ⲕⲁⲧⲁ ⲡⲉⲥⲣⲁⲛ. ⲁⲣⲓⲫⲙⲉⲩⲓ̀ ⲡⲟ̅ⲥ̅ ⲙ̀ⲡⲁⲓⲱⲧ ⲛⲉⲙ ⲧⲁⲙⲁⲩ ⲛⲉⲙ ⲛⲁⲥⲛⲏⲟⲩ ⲛⲉⲙ ⲛⲏ ⲉⲧϧⲉⲛⲧ ⲉ̀ⲣⲟⲓ ⲛ̀ⲥⲁⲣⲕⲓⲕⲟⲛ ⲛⲉⲙ ⲛⲁⲓⲟϯ	Remember O Lord your Orthodox Christian servants, each man by his name, and each woman by her name. Remember O Lord my father, my mother, my siblings, my relatives in the flesh, and my spiritual fathers.

ⲙ̀ⲡⲛⲉⲩⲙⲁⲧⲓⲕⲟⲛ ⲛⲏ ⲙⲉⲛ ⲉⲧⲟⲛϧ ⲁ̀ⲣⲉϩ ⲉ̀ⲣⲱⲟⲩ ϧⲉⲛ ⲡⲁⲅⲅⲉⲗⲟⲥ ⲛ̀ⲧⲉ ϯϩⲓⲣⲏⲛⲏ ⲛⲏ ⲇⲉ ⲉⲧⲁⲩⲉⲛⲕⲟⲧ ⲙⲁⲙ̀ⲧⲟⲛ ⲛⲱⲟⲩ.

Those who are living, protect them by the angel of peace, and those who are departed, repose them.

And for himself, he says:

ⲁⲣⲓⲫⲙⲉⲩ̀ⲓ ⲡⲟ̅ⲥ̅ ⲛ̀ⲧⲁⲙⲉⲧϫⲱⲃ ⲁ̀ⲛⲟⲕ ϧⲁ ⲡⲓϩⲏⲕⲓ ⲟⲩⲟϩ ⲭⲱ ⲛⲏⲓ ⲉ̀ⲃⲟⲗ ⲛ̀ⲛⲁⲛⲟⲃⲓ ⲉⲧⲟϣ.

Remember O Lord my weakness, I the poor, and forgive me my many sins.

7. THE PROCESSION OF THE LAMB

And when all of this has been accomplished, he wraps the lamb in a silk veil and lifts it above his head. Likewise, the serving deacon wraps the vessel of wine in a silk veil and raises it above his head behind the priest. And there is to be standing in front of each a deacon carrying a lighted candle. And they go around the altar one time, while the priest says:

ⲟⲩⲱⲟⲩ ⲛⲉⲙ ⲟⲩⲧⲁⲓⲟ ⲟⲩⲧⲁⲓⲟ ⲛⲉⲙ ⲟⲩⲱⲟⲩ ⲛ̀ϯⲡⲁⲛⲁⲅⲓⲁ ⲧⲣⲓⲁⲥ ⲫⲓⲱⲧ ⲛⲉⲙ ⲡϣⲏⲣⲓ ⲛⲉⲙ ⲡⲓⲡⲛⲉⲩⲙⲁ ⲉⲑⲟⲩⲁⲃ. ⲟⲩϩⲓⲣⲏⲛⲏ ⲛⲉⲙ ⲟⲩⲕⲱⲧ ⲉ̀ϫⲉⲛ ϯⲟⲩ̀ⲓ ⲙ̀ⲙⲁⲩⲁⲧⲥ ⲉⲑⲟⲩⲁⲃ ⲛ̀ⲕⲁⲑⲟⲗⲓⲕⲏ ⲛ̀ⲁⲡⲟⲥⲧⲟⲗⲓⲕⲏ ⲛ̀ⲉⲕⲕⲗⲏⲥⲓⲁ ⲛ̀ⲧⲉ ⲫϯ ⲁⲙⲏⲛ. ⲁⲣⲓⲫⲙⲉⲩ̀ⲓ ⲡⲟ̅ⲥ̅ ⲛ̀ⲛⲏ ⲉⲧⲁⲩ̀ⲓⲛⲓ ⲛⲁⲕ ⲉ̀ϧⲟⲩⲛ ⲛ̀ⲛⲁⲓⲇⲱⲣⲟⲛ ⲛⲉⲙ ⲛⲏ ⲉⲧⲁⲩⲉ̀ⲛⲟⲩ ⲉ̀ϫⲱⲟⲩ ⲛⲉⲙ ⲛⲏ ⲉⲧⲁⲩⲉ̀ⲛⲟⲩ ⲉ̀ⲃⲟⲗ ϩⲓⲧⲟⲧⲟⲩ ⲙⲟⲓ ⲛⲱⲟⲩ ⲧⲏⲣⲟⲩ ⲙ̀ⲡⲓⲃⲉⲭⲉ ⲡⲓⲉ̀ⲃⲟⲗ ϧⲉⲛ ⲛⲓⲫⲏⲟⲩ̀ⲓ.

Glory and honor, honor and glory [Rv 4:9] to the all-holy Trinity, the Father, the Son, and the Holy Spirit. Peace and building up [Acts 9:31] for the one and only, holy, catholic, and apostolic Church of God, amen. Remember O Lord those who have offered to you these gifts, those on whose behalf they have been offered, and those through whom they have been offered. Give them all the recompense from the heavens [Mt 5:12].

The deacon says:

ⲡⲣⲟⲥⲉⲩⲝⲁⲥⲑⲉ ⲩⲡⲉⲣ ⲧⲱⲛ ⲁⲅⲓⲱⲛ ⲧⲓⲙⲓⲱⲛ ⲇⲱⲣⲱⲛ ⲧⲟⲩⲧⲱⲛ ⲕⲉ ⲑⲩⲥⲓⲱⲛ ⲏⲙⲱⲛ ⲕⲉ ⲡⲣⲟⲥⲫⲉⲣⲟⲛⲧⲱⲛ.

Pray for these holy honorable gifts, our sacrifices, and those who offer them.

And the priest links the following with the previous saying:

ⲁⲣⲓⲫⲙⲉⲩ̀ⲓ ⲡⲟ̅ⲥ̅ ⲛ̀ⲟⲩⲟⲛ ⲛⲓⲃⲉⲛ ⲉⲧⲁⲩϩⲟⲛϩⲉⲛ ⲛⲁⲛ ⲉ̀ⲉⲣⲡⲟⲩⲙⲉⲩ̀ⲓ ϧⲉⲛ ⲛⲉⲛϯϩⲟ ⲛⲉⲙ ⲛⲉⲛⲧⲱⲃϩ ⲡⲟ̅ⲥ̅ ⲉϥⲉ̀ⲉⲣⲡⲟⲩⲙⲉⲩ̀ⲓ ϧⲉⲛ ⲧⲉϥⲙⲉⲧⲟⲩⲣⲟ ⲉⲧϧⲉⲛ ⲛⲓⲫⲏⲟⲩ̀ⲓ.

Remember O Lord everyone who has asked us to remember them in our entreaties and prayers. May the Lord remember them in his kingdom that is in the heavens.

8. PROCESSIONAL CHANTS

And during the procession of the priest with the lamb around the altar, in all Sundays—except the Sundays of the the holy forty days—and on major feasts, the fifty days, and all non-fasting days, the people say this from Psalm 117:24-26:

ⲁⲗⲗⲏⲗⲟⲩⲓⲁ ⲫⲁⲓ ⲡⲉ ⲡⲓⲉϩⲟⲟⲩ ⲉⲧⲁ ⲡ̅ⲟ̅ⲥ̅ ⲑⲁⲙⲓⲟϥ ⲙⲁⲣⲉⲛⲑⲉⲗⲏⲗ ⲛ̀ⲧⲉⲛⲟⲩⲛⲟϥ ⲙ̀ⲙⲟⲛ ⲛ̀ϧⲏⲧϥ ⲱ ⲡ̅ⲟ̅ⲥ̅ ⲉⲕⲉ̀ⲛⲁϩⲙⲉⲛ ⲱ ⲡ̅ⲟ̅ⲥ̅ ⲉⲕⲉ̀ⲥⲟⲩⲧⲉⲛ ⲛⲉⲛⲙⲱⲓⲧ. ϥ̀ⲥⲙⲁⲣⲱⲟⲩⲧ ⲛ̀ϫⲉ ⲫⲏ ⲉⲑⲛⲏⲟⲩ ϧⲉⲛ ⲫⲣⲁⲛ ⲙ̀ⲡ̅ⲟ̅ⲥ̅ ⲁⲗⲗⲏⲗⲟⲩⲓⲁ.

This is the day the Lord has made; let us rejoice and be glad in it. O Lord save us, O Lord straighten our ways. Blessed is he who comes in the name of the Lord, Alleluia.

And in all fasting days, namely, the fast of the nativity, Sundays of the holy forty days, the fast of the apostles, the fast of the Virgin, and on Wednesdays and Fridays throughout the year the people say this from Psalm 75:

ⲁⲗⲗⲏⲗⲟⲩⲓⲁ ϫⲉ ⲫⲙⲉⲩ̀ⲓ ⲛ̀ⲟⲩⲣⲱⲙⲓ ⲉϥⲉ̀ⲟⲩⲱⲛϩ ⲛⲁⲕ ⲉ̀ⲃⲟⲗ ⲡ̅ⲟ̅ⲥ̅ ⲟⲩⲟϩ ⲡⲥⲱϫⲡ ⲛ̀ⲧⲉ ⲟⲩⲙⲉⲩ̀ⲓ ⲉϥⲉⲣϣⲁⲓ ⲛⲁⲕ. ⲛⲓⲑⲩⲥⲓⲁ ⲛⲓⲡⲣⲟⲥⲫⲟⲣⲁ ϣⲟⲡⲟⲩ ⲉ̀ⲣⲟⲕ ⲁⲗⲗⲏⲗⲟⲩⲓⲁ.

The thought of man shall confess to you, O Lord, and the remainder of thought shall keep a feast to you. Accept unto you the sacrifices and the offerings, Alleluia.

And in the days of the fast of the holy forty except for its Sundays, and during the three-day fast of Nineveh, the people say this from Psalm 42:4 and from Psalm 131:1

ⲁⲗⲗⲏⲗⲟⲩⲓⲁ ⲉⲓⲉ̀ⲓ ⲉ̀ϧⲟⲩⲛ ϣⲁ ⲡⲓⲙⲁⲛ̀ⲉⲣϣⲱⲟⲩϣⲓ ⲛ̀ⲧⲉ ⲫϯ ⲛⲁϩⲣⲉⲛ ⲡ̀ϩⲟ ⲙ̀ⲫϯ ⲫⲏ ⲉⲧⲁϥϯ ⲙ̀ⲡⲟⲩⲛⲟϥ ⲛ̀ⲧⲉ ⲧⲁⲙⲉⲧⲁⲗⲟⲩ ϯⲛⲁⲟⲩⲱⲛϩ ⲛⲁⲕ ⲉ̀ⲃⲟⲗ ⲫϯ ⲡⲁⲛⲟⲩϯ ϧⲉⲛ ⲟⲩⲕⲩⲑⲁⲣⲁ ⲁⲗⲗⲏⲗⲟⲩⲓⲁ. ⲁⲣⲓⲫⲙⲉⲩ̀ⲓ ⲡ̅ⲟ̅ⲥ̅ ⲛ̀ⲇⲁⲩⲓⲇ ⲛⲉⲙ ⲧⲉϥⲙⲉⲧⲣⲉⲙⲣⲁⲩϣ ⲧⲏⲣⲥ ⲁⲗⲗⲏⲗⲟⲩⲓⲁ.

I will go in to the altar of God, before the face of God, who gave joy to my youth. I will confess you, O God my God, with a harp, alleluia. Remember O Lord David and all his meekness, Alleluia.

9. THE EXCHANGE OF BLESSING

And when the priest has completed the aforementioned circuit, he stands in his original place west of the altar and his face to the east. And he places the lamb, that is, the oblation bread, on his left hand, and bows his head to his brothers the priests, and says ⲉⲩⲗⲟⲅⲓⲧⲉ, that is, "bless [plural]," and in the singular, that is, if he who is present with him is one priest, he says ⲉⲩⲗⲟⲅⲏⲥⲟⲛ, that is, "bless [singular]." So, they also bow their heads and answer him saying, ⲛ̀ⲑⲟⲕ ⲉⲩⲗⲟⲅⲏⲥⲟⲛ, that is, you bless. And the priest turns to the oblation bread and brings the vessel of wine close to it. And the deacon holds it with his right hand with a silk cloth. And the priest signs the two together three times with the sign of the cross according to the custom.

10. THE BLESSING OF THE OBLATIONS

First, he begins saying:

ϧⲉⲛ ⲫⲣⲁⲛ ⲙ̀ⲫⲓⲱⲧ ⲛⲉⲙ ⲡϣⲏⲣⲓ ⲛⲉⲙ ⲡⲓⲡ̅ⲛ̅ⲁ̅ ⲉ̅ⲑ̅ⲩ̅ ⲟⲩⲛⲟⲩϯ ⲛ̀ⲟⲩⲱⲧ.	In the name of the Father and the Son and the Holy Spirit, one God.

Then he makes the first signing, saying:

ⲁ̀ⲥⲙⲁⲣⲱⲟⲩⲧ ⲛ̀ϫⲉ ⲫϯ ⲫⲓⲱⲧ ⲡⲓⲡⲁⲛⲧⲟⲕⲣⲁⲧⲱⲣ ⲁⲙⲏⲛ.	Blessed be God the Father the Pantocrator, amen.

And he makes the second signing, saying:

ⲁ̀ⲥⲙⲁⲣⲱⲟⲩⲧ ⲛ̀ϫⲉ ⲡⲉϥⲙⲟⲛⲟⲅⲉⲛⲏⲥ ⲛ̀ϣⲏⲣⲓ ⲓ̅ⲏ̅ⲥ̅ ⲡⲭ̅ⲥ̅ ⲡⲉⲛⲟ̅ⲥ̅ ⲁⲙⲏⲛ.	Blessed be his only-begotten Son, Jesus Christ our Lord, amen.

And in the third signing, he says:

ⲁ̀ⲥⲙⲁⲣⲱⲟⲩⲧ ⲛ̀ϫⲉ ⲡⲓⲡ̅ⲛ̅ⲁ̅ ⲉ̅ⲑ̅ⲩ̅ ⲙ̀ⲡⲁⲣⲁⲕⲗⲏⲧⲟⲛ ⲁⲙⲏⲛ.	Blessed be the Holy Spirit, the Paraclete, amen.

Then he places the oblation bread in the paten with a silk veil beneath it, saying:

ⲟⲩⲱⲟⲩ ⲛⲉⲙ ⲟⲩⲧⲁⲓⲟ ⲟⲩⲧⲁⲓⲟ ⲛⲉⲙ ⲟⲩⲱⲟⲩ ⲛ̀ϯⲡⲁⲛⲁⲅⲓⲁ ⲧⲣⲓⲁⲥ: ⲫⲓⲱⲧ ⲛⲉⲙ ⲡϣⲏⲣⲓ ⲛⲉⲙ ⲡⲓⲡ̅ⲛ̅ⲁ̅ ⲉ̅ⲑ̅ⲩ̅. ϯⲛⲟⲩ ⲛⲉⲙ ⲛ̀ⲥⲏⲟⲩ ⲛⲓⲃⲉⲛ ⲛⲉⲙ ϣⲁ ⲉⲛⲉϩ ⲛ̀ⲧⲉ ⲡⲓⲉⲛⲉϩ ⲧⲏⲣⲟⲩ ⲁⲙⲏⲛ	Glory and honor, honor and glory, to the all-holy Trinity, the Father and the Son and the Holy Spirit, now and at all times, and unto the ages of all the ages, amen.

11. THE MIXING OF THE CHALICE

Then he pours the wine in the chalice and mixes it with a small amount of water, approximately a third or a quarter or less, but no more than a third. Regarding the deacon, he says Amen after each of the three previous blessings. Afterwards, he says this at whose conclusion is Psalm 116:

ⲓⲥ ⲡⲁⲧⲏⲣ ⲁⲅⲓⲟⲥ ⲓⲥ ⲩⲓⲟⲥ ⲁⲅⲓⲟⲥ ⲉⲛ ⲡⲛⲉⲩⲙⲁ ⲁⲅⲓⲟⲛ ⲁⲙⲏⲛ. ⲉⲩⲗⲟⲅⲏⲧⲟⲥ ⲕⲩⲣⲓⲟⲥ ⲟ ⲑⲉⲟⲥ ⲓⲥ ⲧⲟⲩⲥ ⲉⲱⲛⲁⲥ ⲁⲙⲏⲛ. ⲛⲓⲉⲑⲛⲟⲥ ⲧⲏⲣⲟⲩ ⲥⲙⲟⲩ ⲡⲟ̅ⲥ̅ ⲙⲁⲣⲟⲩⲥⲙⲟⲩ ⲉ̀ⲣⲟϥ ⲛ̀ϫⲉ ⲛⲓⲗⲁⲟⲥ ⲧⲏⲣⲟⲩ ϫⲉ ⲁ ⲡⲉϥⲛⲁⲓ ⲧⲁϫⲣⲟ ⲉ̀ϩⲣⲏⲓ ⲉ̀ϫⲱⲛ ⲟⲩⲟϩ ϯⲙⲉⲑⲙⲏⲓ	One is the holy Father, one is the holy Son, one is the Holy Spirit, amen. Blessed is the Lord God, unto the ages amen. Praise the Lord, all nations. Let all the peoples praise him. For his mercy has been firmly established upon us, and the truth of

ⲛ̀ⲧⲉ ⲡ̅ⲟ̅ⲥ̅ ϣⲟⲡ ϣⲁ ⲉⲛⲉϩ ⲁⲙⲏⲛ ⲁⲗⲗⲏⲗⲟⲩⲓⲁ.	the Lord endures forever, amen alleluia.

The people say:

ⲇⲟⲝⲁ ⲡⲁⲧⲣⲓ ⲕⲉ ⲩⲓⲱ ⲕⲉ ⲁⲅⲓⲱ ⲡⲛⲉⲩⲙⲁⲧⲓ. ⲕⲉ ⲛⲩⲛ ⲕⲉ ⲁ̀ⲓ ⲕⲉ ⲓⲥ ⲧⲟⲩⲥ ⲉⲱⲛⲁⲥ ⲧⲱⲛ ⲉⲱⲛⲱⲛ ⲁⲙⲏⲛ ⲁⲗⲗⲏⲗⲟⲩⲓⲁ.	Glory to the Father and the Son and the Holy Spirit, both now and ever, and unto the ages of ages, amen alleluia.

And he [the priest] empties the vessel of wine carefully and wipes its opening with a white veil and removes it from the altar.

12. THE PRAYER OF THANKSGIVING

And after the people have said ⲇⲟⲝⲁ ⲡⲁⲧⲣⲓ [Glory to the Father] the priest says ϣⲗⲏⲗ [Pray]. And he turns to his brothers the priests then to the west and signs the people once with the sign of the cross, saying

ⲓⲣⲏⲛⲏ ⲡⲁⲥⲓ	Peace be to all.

The people say:

ⲕⲉ ⲧⲱ ⲡⲛⲉⲩⲙⲁⲧⲓ ⲥⲟⲩ	And to your spirit.

Then the priest says the *Prayer of Thanksgiving*:

ⲙⲁⲣⲉⲛϣⲉⲡϩⲙⲟⲧ ⲛ̀ⲧⲟⲧϥ ⲙ̀ⲡⲓⲣⲉϥⲉⲣⲡⲉⲑⲛⲁⲛⲉϥ ⲟⲩⲟϩ ⲛ̀ⲛⲁⲏⲧ ⲫϯ ⲫⲓⲱⲧ ⲙ̀ⲡⲉⲛⲟ̅ⲥ̅ ⲟⲩⲟϩ ⲡⲉⲛⲛⲟⲩϯ ⲟⲩⲟϩ ⲡⲉⲛⲥ̅ⲱ̅ⲣ̅ ⲓ̅ⲏ̅ⲥ̅ ⲡ̅ⲭ̅ⲥ̅. ϫⲉ ⲁϥⲉⲣⲥⲕⲉⲡⲁⲍⲓⲛ ⲉ̀ϫⲱⲛ ⲁϥⲉⲣⲃⲟⲏⲑⲓⲛ ⲉ̀ⲣⲟⲛ ⲁϥⲁⲣⲉϩ ⲉ̀ⲣⲟⲛ ⲁϥϣⲟⲡⲧⲉⲛ ⲉ̀ⲣⲟϥ ⲁϥϯⲁⲥⲟ ⲉ̀ⲣⲟⲛ ⲁϥϯⲧⲟⲧⲉⲛ ⲁϥⲉ̀ⲛⲧⲉⲛ ϣⲁ ⲉ̀ϩⲣⲏⲓ ⲉ̀ⲧⲁⲓⲟⲩⲛⲟⲩ ⲑⲁⲓ. ⲛ̀ⲑⲟϥ ⲟⲛ ⲙⲁⲣⲉⲛϯϩⲟ ⲉ̀ⲣⲟϥ ϩⲟⲡⲱⲥ ⲛ̀ⲧⲉϥⲁⲣⲉϩ ⲉ̀ⲣⲟⲛ ϧⲉⲛ ⲡⲁⲓⲉϩⲟⲟⲩ ⲉ̅ⲑ̅ⲩ̅ ⲫⲁⲓ ⲛⲉⲙ ⲛⲓⲉϩⲟⲟⲩ ⲧⲏⲣⲟⲩ ⲛ̀ⲧⲉ ⲡⲉⲛⲱⲛϧ ϧⲉⲛ ϩⲓⲣⲏⲛⲏ ⲛⲓⲃⲉⲛ ⲛ̀ϫⲉ ⲡⲓⲡⲁⲛⲧⲟⲕⲣⲁⲧⲱⲣ ⲡ̅ⲟ̅ⲥ̅ ⲡⲉⲛⲛⲟⲩϯ.	Let us give thanks to the beneficent and merciful God, the Father of our Lord, God, and Savior Jesus Christ. For he has protected us, helped us, kept us, accepted us to himself, spared us, supported us, and has brought us to this hour. Let us also ask the Pantocrator our God to keep us this holy day and all the days of our life in all peace.

The deacon says:

ⲡⲣⲟⲥⲉⲩⲝⲁⲥⲑⲉ	Pray.

The people say:

ⲕⲩⲣⲓⲉ ⲉⲗⲉⲏⲥⲟⲛ	Lord have mercy.

The priest says:

ⲫⲛⲏⲃ ⲡ̅ⲟ̅ⲥ̅ ⲫϯ ⲡⲓⲡⲁⲛⲧⲟⲕⲣⲁⲧⲱⲣ ⲫⲓⲱⲧ ⲙ̀ⲡⲉⲛⲟ̅ⲥ̅ ⲟⲩⲟϩ ⲡⲉⲛⲛⲟⲩϯ ⲟⲩⲟϩ ⲡⲉⲛⲥ̅ⲱ̅ⲣ̅ ⲓ̅ⲏ̅ⲥ̅ ⲡ̅ⲭ̅ⲥ̅. ⲧⲉⲛϣⲉⲡϩⲙⲟⲧ ⲛ̀ⲧⲟⲧⲕ ⲕⲁⲧⲁ	O Master, Lord, God the Pantocrator, the Father of our Lord, God, and Savior Jesus Christ, we

ϩⲱⲃ ⲛⲓⲃⲉⲛ ⲛⲉⲙ ⲉⲑⲃⲉ ϩⲱⲃ ⲛⲓⲃⲉⲛ ⲛⲉⲙ ϧⲉⲛ ϩⲱⲃ ⲛⲓⲃⲉⲛ. ϫⲉ ⲁⲕⲉⲣⲥⲕⲉⲡⲁⲍⲓⲛ ⲉ̀ϫⲱⲛ ⲁⲕⲉⲣⲃⲟⲏⲑⲓⲛ ⲉ̀ⲣⲟⲛ ⲁⲕⲁⲣⲉϩ ⲉ̀ⲣⲟⲛ ⲁⲕϣⲟⲡⲧⲉⲛ ⲉ̀ⲣⲟⲕ ⲁⲕϯⲁⲥⲟ ⲉ̀ⲣⲟⲛ ⲁⲕϯⲧⲟⲧⲉⲛ ⲁⲕⲉ̀ⲛⲧⲉⲛ ϣⲁ ⲉ̀ϩⲣⲏⲓ ⲉⲧⲁⲓⲟⲩⲛⲟⲩ ⲑⲁⲓ.

thank you for everything, concerning everything, and in everything, for you have covered us, helped us, kept us, accepted us to yourself, spared us, supported us, and have brought us to this hour.

The deacon says:

ⲧⲱⲃϩ ϩⲓⲛⲁ ⲛ̀ⲧⲉ ⲫϯ ⲛⲁⲓ ⲛⲁⲛ ⲛ̀ⲧⲉϥϣⲉⲛϩⲏⲧ ϧⲁⲣⲟⲛ ⲛ̀ⲧⲉϥⲥⲱⲧⲉⲙ ⲉ̀ⲣⲟⲛ ⲛ̀ⲧⲉϥⲉⲣⲃⲟⲏⲑⲓⲛ ⲉ̀ⲣⲟⲛ ⲛ̀ⲧⲉϥϭⲓ ⲛ̀ⲛⲓϯϩⲟ ⲛⲉⲙ ⲛⲓⲧⲱⲃϩ ⲛ̀ⲧⲉ ⲛⲏ ⲉ̅ⲑ̅ⲩ̅ ⲛ̀ⲧⲁϥ ⲛ̀ⲧⲟⲧⲟⲩ ⲉ̀ϩⲣⲏⲓ ⲉ̀ϫⲱⲛ ⲉ̀ⲡⲓⲁⲅⲁⲑⲟⲛ ⲛ̀ⲥⲏⲟⲩ ⲛⲓⲃⲉⲛ ⲛ̀ⲧⲉϥⲁⲓⲧⲉⲛ ⲛ̀ⲉⲙⲡϣⲁ ⲉ̀ⲑⲣⲉⲛϭⲓ ⲉ̀ⲃⲟⲗ ϧⲉⲛ ϯⲕⲟⲓⲛⲱⲛⲓⲁ ⲛ̀ⲧⲉ ⲛⲉϥⲙⲩⲥⲧⲏⲣⲓⲟⲛ ⲉⲑⲟⲩⲁⲃ ⲉⲧⲥⲙⲁⲣⲱⲟⲩⲧ ⲉ̀ⲡⲓⲭⲱ ⲉ̀ⲃⲟⲗ ⲛ̀ⲧⲉ ⲛⲉⲛⲛⲟⲃⲓ.

Pray that God may have mercy on us, have compassion on us, hear us, help us, and receive the entreaties and prayers of his saints from them on our behalf for the good at all times, and to make us worthy to receive of the communion of his holy and blessed mysteries for the forgiveness of our sins.

The people say:

ⲕⲩⲣⲓⲉ ⲉⲗⲉⲏⲥⲟⲛ

Lord have mercy.

The priest says:

ⲉⲑⲃⲉ ⲫⲁⲓ ⲧⲉⲛϯϩⲟ ⲟⲩⲟϩ ⲧⲉⲛⲧⲱⲃϩ ⲛ̀ⲧⲉⲕⲙⲉⲧⲁⲅⲁⲑⲟⲥ ⲡⲓⲙⲁⲓⲣⲱⲙⲓ ⲙⲏⲓⲥ ⲛⲁⲛ ⲉ̀ⲑⲣⲉⲛϫⲱⲕ ⲉ̀ⲃⲟⲗ ⲙ̀ⲡⲁⲓⲕⲉⲉϩⲟⲟⲩ ⲉ̅ⲑ̅ⲩ̅ ⲫⲁⲓ ⲛⲉⲙ ⲛⲓⲉϩⲟⲟⲩ ⲧⲏⲣⲟⲩ ⲛ̀ⲧⲉ ⲡⲉⲛⲱⲛϧ ϧⲉⲛ ϩⲓⲣⲏⲛⲏ ⲛⲓⲃⲉⲛ ⲛⲉⲙ ⲧⲉⲕϩⲟϯ. ⲫⲑⲟⲛⲟⲥ ⲛⲓⲃⲉⲛ ⲡⲓⲣⲁⲥⲙⲟⲥ ⲛⲓⲃⲉⲛ ⲉⲛⲉⲣⲅⲓⲁ ⲛⲓⲃⲉⲛ ⲛ̀ⲧⲉ ⲡⲥⲁⲧⲁⲛⲁⲥ ⲡⲥⲟϭⲛⲓ ⲛ̀ⲧⲉ ϩⲁⲛⲣⲱⲙⲓ ⲉⲩϩⲱⲟⲩ ⲛⲉⲙ ⲡⲧⲱⲛϥ ⲉ̀ⲡϣⲱⲓ ⲛ̀ⲧⲉ ϩⲁⲛϫⲁϫⲓ ⲛⲏ ⲉⲧϩⲏⲡ ⲛⲉⲙ ⲛⲏ ⲉⲑⲟⲩⲱⲛϩ ⲉ̀ⲃⲟⲗ ⲁⲗⲓⲧⲟⲩ ⲉ̀ⲃⲟⲗ ϩⲁⲣⲟⲛ ⲛⲉⲙ ⲉ̀ⲃⲟⲗ ϩⲁ ⲡⲉⲕⲗⲁⲟⲥ ⲧⲏⲣϥ ⲛⲉⲙ ⲉ̀ⲃⲟⲗ ϩⲁ ⲧⲁⲓⲧⲣⲁⲡⲉⲍⲁ ⲑⲁⲓ ⲛⲉⲙ ⲉ̀ⲃⲟⲗ ϩⲁ ⲡⲁⲓⲙⲁ ⲉⲑⲟⲩⲁⲃ ⲛ̀ⲧⲁⲕ ⲫⲁⲓ. ⲛⲏ ⲇⲉ ⲉⲑⲛⲁⲛⲉⲩ ⲛⲉⲙ ⲛⲏ ⲉⲧⲉⲣⲛⲟϥⲣⲓ ⲥⲁϩⲛⲓ ⲙ̀ⲙⲱⲟⲩ ⲛⲁⲛ ϫⲉ ⲛ̀ⲑⲟⲕ ⲡⲉ ⲉⲧⲁⲕϯ ⲙ̀ⲡⲓⲉⲣϣⲓϣⲓ ⲛⲁⲛ ⲉ̀ϩⲱⲙⲓ ⲉ̀ϫⲉⲛ ⲛⲓϩⲟϥ ⲛⲉⲙ ⲛⲓϭⲗⲏ ⲛⲉⲙ ⲉ̀ϫⲉⲛ ϯϫⲟⲙ ⲧⲏⲣⲥ ⲛ̀ⲧⲉ ⲡⲓϫⲁϫⲓ. ⲟⲩⲟϩ ⲙ̀ⲡⲉⲣⲉ̀ⲛⲧⲉⲛ ⲉ̀ϧⲟⲩⲛ ⲉ̀ⲡⲓⲣⲁⲥⲙⲟⲥ ⲁⲗⲗⲁ ⲛⲁϩⲙⲉⲛ ⲉ̀ⲃⲟⲗ ϩⲁ ⲡⲓⲡⲉⲧϩⲱⲟⲩ ϧⲉⲛ ⲡⲓϩⲙⲟⲧ ⲛⲉⲙ ⲛⲓⲙⲉⲧϣⲉⲛϩⲏⲧ ⲛⲉⲙ ϯⲙⲉⲧⲙⲁⲓⲣⲱⲙⲓ ⲛ̀ⲧⲉ ⲡⲉⲕⲙⲟⲛⲟⲅⲉⲛⲏⲥ ⲛ̀ϣⲏⲣⲓ ⲡⲉⲛⲟ̅ⲥ̅ ⲟⲩⲟϩ ⲡⲉⲛⲛⲟⲩϯ ⲟⲩⲟϩ ⲡⲉⲛⲥ̅ⲱ̅ⲣ̅ ⲓ̅ⲏ̅ⲥ̅ ⲡⲭ̅ⲥ̅. ⲫⲁⲓ ⲉⲧⲉ ⲉ̀ⲃⲟⲗ ϩⲓⲧⲟⲧϥ ⲉⲣⲉ ⲡⲓⲱⲟⲩ ⲛⲉⲙ ⲡⲓⲧⲁⲓⲟ ⲛⲉⲙ ⲡⲓⲁⲙⲁϩⲓ ⲛⲉⲙ

Therefore, we ask and entreat your goodness, O lover of mankind, grant us also to complete this holy day and all the days of our life in all peace and your fear. All envy, all temptation, all the work of Satan, the counsel of wicked men and the rising up of enemies, hidden and manifest, take them away from us, and from all your people, and from this table, and from this, your holy place. But those things which are good and profitable do provide for us, for it is you who have given us the authority to tread on serpents and scorpions, and upon all the power of the enemy [Lk 10:19] And lead us not into temptation, but deliver us from the evil one [Mt 6:13], through the grace, compassion and love of mankind, of your only-begotten Son, our Lord, God, and Savior, Jesus Christ. Through whom the glory, the honor, the dominion, and the worship are due unto you, with him and the Holy Spirit, the

ϯⲡⲣⲟⲥⲕⲩⲛⲏⲥⲓⲥ ⲉⲣⲡⲣⲉⲡⲓ ⲛⲁⲕ ⲛⲉⲙⲁϥ ⲛⲉⲙ ⲡⲓⲡ̅ⲛ̅ⲁ̅ ⲉ̅ⲑ̅ⲩ̅ ⲛ̀ⲣⲉϥⲧⲁⲛϧⲟ ⲟⲩⲟϩ ⲛ̀ⲟⲙⲟⲟⲩⲥⲓⲟⲥ ⲛⲉⲙⲁⲕ. ϯⲛⲟⲩ ⲛⲉⲙ ⲛ̀ⲥⲏⲟⲩ ⲛⲓⲃⲉⲛ ⲛⲉⲙ ϣⲁ ⲉⲛⲉϩ ⲛ̀ⲧⲉ ⲛⲓⲉⲛⲉϩ ⲧⲏⲣⲟⲩ ⲁⲙⲏⲛ.

giver of life, who is of one essence with you, now and at all times, and unto the age of all ages, amen.

13. THE PROTHESIS PRAYER

And after this, the people say the following with its known melody:

ⲥⲱⲑⲏⲥ ⲁⲙⲏⲛ ⲕⲉ ⲧⲱ ⲡⲛⲉⲩⲙⲁⲧⲓ ⲥⲟⲩ

May you be saved, amen, and with your spirit.

And in the presence of the bishop or another hierarch, the people chant:

ⲛⲓⲥⲁⲃⲉⲩ ⲧⲏⲣⲟⲩ ⲛ̀ⲧⲉ ⲡⲓⲥⲣⲁⲏⲗ ⲛⲏ ⲉⲧⲉⲣϩⲱⲃ ⲉ̀ⲛⲓⲕⲁⲡ ⲛ̀ⲛⲟⲩⲃ ⲙⲁⲑⲁⲙⲓⲟ ⲛ̀ⲟⲩϣⲑⲏⲛ ⲛ̀ⲁⲁⲣⲱⲛ ⲕⲁⲧⲁ ⲡⲧⲁⲓⲟ ⲛ̀ϯⲙⲉⲧⲟⲩⲏⲃ ⲙ̀ⲡⲉⲛⲓⲱⲧ ⲉⲧⲧⲁⲓⲏⲟⲩⲧ ⲛ̀ⲁⲣⲭⲏⲉⲣⲉⲩⲥ ⲡⲁⲡⲁ ⲁⲃⲃⲁ [...] ⲛⲉⲙ ⲡⲉⲛⲓⲱⲧ ⲛ̀ⲉⲡⲓⲥⲕⲟⲡⲟⲥ ⲁⲃⲃⲁ [...] ⲛⲓⲙⲉⲛⲣⲁϯ ⲛ̀ⲧⲉ ⲡⲓⲭⲣⲓⲥⲧⲟⲥ.

All the wise men of Israel, who weave golden threads, make an Aaronic garment [Ex 28:1–5] according to the honor of the priesthood of our honorable father, the high priest, Pope Abba N.N. and our father the bishop Abba N.N. the beloved of Christ.

Meanwhile, the priest says the prayer of the offering of the bread and the chalice to the Son inaudibly:

ⲫⲏⲏⲃ ⲡ̅ⲟ̅ⲥ̅ ⲓ̅ⲏ̅ⲥ̅ ⲡ̅ⲭ̅ⲥ̅ ⲡⲓϣⲫⲏⲣ ⲛ̀ⲁⲓⲇⲓⲟⲥ ⲟⲩⲟϩ ⲡⲗⲟⲅⲟⲥ ⲛ̀ⲧⲉ ⲡⲓⲁⲧⲑⲱⲗⲉⲃ ⲫⲓⲱⲧ ⲛ̀ⲟⲙⲟⲟⲩⲥⲓⲟⲥ ⲛⲉⲙⲁϥ ⲛⲉⲙ ⲡⲓⲡⲛⲉⲩⲙⲁ ⲉⲑⲟⲩⲁⲃ. ⲛ̀ⲑⲟⲕ ⲅⲁⲣ ⲡⲉ ⲡⲓⲱⲓⲕ ⲉⲧⲟⲛϧ ⲉⲧⲁϥⲓ̀ ⲉ̀ⲡⲉⲥⲏⲧ ⲉ̀ⲃⲟⲗ ϧⲉⲛ ⲧⲫⲉ ⲟⲩⲟϩ ⲁⲕⲉⲣϣⲟⲣⲡ ⲛ̀ⲭⲁⲕ ⲛ̀ⲟⲩϩⲓⲏⲃ ⲛ̀ⲁⲧⲁϭⲛⲓ ⲉ̀ϩⲣⲏⲓ ⲉ̀ϫⲉⲛ ⲡⲱⲛϧ ⲙ̀ⲡⲓⲕⲟⲥⲙⲟⲥ. ⲧⲉⲛϯϩⲟ ⲟⲩⲟϩ ⲧⲉⲛⲧⲱⲃϩ ⲛ̀ⲧⲉⲕⲙⲉⲧⲁⲅⲁⲑⲟⲥ ⲡⲓⲙⲁⲓⲣⲱⲙⲓ

O Master Lord Jesus Christ, the co-eternal Logos of the immaculate Father, who is co-essential with him and the Holy Spirit, for you are the living bread, which came down from heaven [Jn 6:51], and has made yourself a spotless lamb for the life of the world [Jn 1:29]. We ask and entreat your goodness, O lover of mankind,

Here, the priest points to the bread placed before him in the paten saying:

ⲟⲩⲱⲛϩ ⲙ̀ⲡⲉⲕϩⲟ ⲉ̀ϩⲣⲏⲓ ⲉ̀ϫⲉⲛ ⲡⲁⲓⲱⲓⲕ ⲫⲁⲓ

Shine your face upon this bread

And he points to the chalice filled with wine, saying:

ⲛⲉⲙ ⲉ̀ϫⲉⲛ ⲡⲁⲓⲁⲫⲟⲧ ⲫⲁⲓ ⲛⲁⲓ ⲉⲧⲁⲛⲭⲁⲩ

And upon this cup, these which have been placed

Then he points to the altar saying:

ⲉ̀ϧⲣⲏⲓ ⲉ̀ϫⲉⲛ ⲧⲁⲓⲧⲣⲁⲡⲉⲍⲁ ⲛ̀ⲓⲉⲣⲁⲧⲓⲕⲏ ⲛ̀ⲧⲁⲕ ⲑⲁⲓ.

upon this your priestly table:

Here, he signs the bread and the chalice together three crosses. In the first, he says:

ⲥⲙⲟⲩ ⲉ̀ⲣⲱⲟⲩ

Bless them,

In the second, he says:

ⲁⲣⲓⲁⲅⲓⲁⲍⲓⲛ ⲙ̀ⲙⲱⲟⲩ

Sanctify them,

In the third he says:

ⲙⲁⲧⲟⲩⲃⲱⲟⲩ ⲟⲩⲟϩ ⲟⲩⲟⲑⲃⲟⲩ.

Purify and change them.

Then he points to the bread, saying:

ϩⲓⲛⲁ ⲡⲁⲓⲱⲓⲕ ⲙⲉⲛ ⲛ̀ⲧⲉϥϣⲱⲡⲓ ⲛ̀ⲑⲟϥ ⲡⲉ ⲡⲉⲕⲥⲱⲙⲁ ⲉⲑⲟⲩⲁⲃ,

So that this bread may become your holy body,

Then he points to the chalice, saying:

ⲡⲓⲑⲱⲧ ⲇⲉ ⲉⲧϧⲉⲛ ⲡⲁⲓⲁⲫⲟⲧ ⲛ̀ⲑⲟϥ ⲡⲉ ⲡⲉⲕⲥⲛⲟϥ ⲉⲧⲧⲁⲓⲏⲟⲩⲧ.

and the mixture in this cup your honored blood.

Then he continues the *Prothesis Prayer* saying:

ⲟⲩⲟϩ ⲙⲁⲣⲟⲩϣⲱⲡⲓ ⲛⲁⲛ ⲧⲏⲣⲟⲩ ⲉⲩⲙⲉⲧⲁⲗⲩⲙⲯⲓⲥ ⲛⲉⲙ ⲟⲩⲧⲁⲗϭⲟ ⲛⲉⲙ ⲟⲩⲥⲱⲧⲏⲣⲓⲁ ⲛ̀ⲧⲉ ⲛⲉⲛⲯⲩⲭⲏ ⲛⲉⲙ ⲛⲉⲛⲥⲱⲙⲁ ⲛⲉⲙ ⲛⲉⲛⲡⲛⲉⲩⲙⲁ. ϫⲉ ⲛ̀ⲑⲟⲕ ⲅⲁⲣ ⲡⲉ ⲡⲉⲛⲛⲟⲩϯ ⲉⲣⲉ ⲡⲓⲱⲟⲩ ⲉⲣⲡⲣⲉⲡⲓ ⲛⲁⲕ ⲛⲉⲙ ⲡⲉⲕⲓⲱⲧ ⲛ̀ⲁⲅⲁⲑⲟⲥ ⲛⲉⲙ ⲡⲓⲡⲛⲉⲩⲙⲁ ⲉⲑⲟⲩⲁⲃ ⲛ̀ⲣⲉϥⲧⲁⲛϧⲟ ⲟⲩⲟϩ ⲛ̀ⲟⲙⲟⲟⲩⲥⲓⲟⲥ ⲛⲉⲙⲁⲕ ϯⲛⲟⲩ ⲛⲉⲙ ⲛ̀ⲥⲏⲟⲩ ⲛⲓⲃⲉⲛ ⲛⲉⲙ ϣⲁ ⲉⲛⲉϩ ⲛ̀ⲧⲉ ⲛⲓⲉⲛⲉϩ ⲧⲏⲣⲟⲩ ⲁⲙⲏⲛ.

And may they become unto all of us communion, healing, and salvation of our souls, our bodies, and our spirits. For you are our God, and to you belongs glory with your good Father and the Holy Spirit the life-giver and co-essential with you. Now and at all times and unto ages of all ages, amen.

14. THE COVERING OF THE GIFTS

After this, the priest covers the bread in the paten with a clean veil and likewise the chalice. Then he and the deacon opposite him cover everything with the *prospherin*, and he places a veil over the *prospherin*.

And if he has covered everything carefully and with the utmost caution with the *prospherin* as explained, he kisses the altar and moves to its southern side. He bows to the east, thankging God who has made him worthy of this pure service. Then he rises, kisses the altar, and goes to the northern side. There, the serving deacon makes a prostration to him and raises his head. The priest then extends his hand and blesses him. Both of them kiss the altar and descend, together with the rest of the servants, while each of them facing east and their backs to the west. Their descent must always be with their left foot first and their ascent with the right.

15. THE ABSOLUTIONS

Then they sit before the door of the sanctuary bowing their heads. One of the priests that are present comes and reads the absolution over them. If the father the patriarch or metropolitan or bishop is present, he reads it. However, if it did not occur that another priest or a hierarch is present, then the celebrant priest stands behind the servants and reads the absolution. If it was the Liturgy of Saints Basil or Cyril, the priest says the *Absolution of the Son* inaudibly:

ⲫⲛⲏⲃ ⲡⲟ̅ⲥ̅ ⲓⲏⲥⲟⲩⲥ ⲡⲭ̅ⲥ̅ ⲡⲓⲙⲟⲛⲟⲅⲉⲛⲏⲥ ⲛ̀ϣⲏⲣⲓ ⲟⲩⲟϩ ⲡⲗⲟⲅⲟⲥ ⲛ̀ⲧⲉ ⲫ̅ϯ̅ ⲫⲓⲱⲧ ⲫⲏ ⲉⲧⲁϥⲥⲱⲗⲡ ⲛ̀ⲥⲛⲁⲩϩ ⲛⲓⲃⲉⲛ ⲛ̀ⲧⲉ ⲛⲉⲛⲛⲟⲃⲓ ϩⲓⲧⲉⲛ ⲛⲉϥⲙⲕⲁⲩϩ ⲛ̀ⲟⲩϫⲁⲓ ⲛ̀ⲣⲉϥⲧⲁⲛϧⲟ. ⲫⲏ ⲉⲧⲁϥⲛⲓϥⲓ ⲉ̀ϧⲟⲩⲛ ϧⲉⲛ ⲡϩⲟ ⲛ̀ⲛⲉϥⲁⲅⲓⲟⲥ ⲙ̀ⲙⲁⲑⲏⲧⲏⲥ ⲟⲩⲟϩ ⲛ̀ⲁⲡⲟⲥⲧⲟⲗⲟⲥ ⲉⲑⲟⲩⲁⲃ ⲉ̀ⲁϥϫⲟⲥ ⲛⲱⲟⲩ. ϫⲉ ϭⲓ ⲛⲱⲧⲉⲛ ⲛ̀ⲟⲩⲡ̅ⲛ̅ⲁ̅ ⲉϥⲟⲩⲁⲃ ⲛⲏ ⲉⲧⲉⲧⲉⲛⲛⲁⲭⲁ ⲛⲟⲩⲛⲟⲃⲓ ⲛⲱⲟⲩ ⲉ̀ⲃⲟⲗ ⲥⲉⲭⲏ ⲛⲱⲟⲩ ⲉ̀ⲃⲟⲗ ⲟⲩⲟϩ ⲛⲏ ⲉⲧⲉⲧⲉⲛⲛⲁⲁⲙⲟⲛⲓ ⲙ̀ⲙⲱⲟⲩ ⲥⲉⲛⲁⲁⲙⲟⲛⲓ ⲙ̀ⲙⲱⲟⲩ. ⲛ̀ⲑⲟⲕ ⲟⲛ ϯⲛⲟⲩ ⲡⲉⲛⲛⲏⲃ ϩⲓⲧⲉⲛ ⲛⲉⲕⲁⲡⲟⲥⲧⲟⲗⲟⲥ ⲉ̅ⲑ̅ⲩ̅ ⲁⲕⲉⲣϩⲙⲟⲧ ⲛ̀ⲛⲏ ⲉⲧⲉⲣϩⲱⲃ ϧⲉⲛ ⲟⲩⲙⲉⲧⲟⲩⲏⲃ ⲕⲁⲧⲁ ⲥⲏⲟⲩ ϧⲉⲛ ⲧⲉⲕⲉⲕⲕⲗⲏⲥⲓⲁ ⲉ̅ⲑ̅ⲩ̅ ⲉ̀ⲭⲁ ⲛⲟⲃⲓ ⲉ̀ⲃⲟⲗ ϩⲓϫⲉⲛ ⲡⲓⲕⲁϩⲓ ⲟⲩⲟϩ ⲉ̀ⲥⲱⲛϩ ⲟⲩⲟϩ ⲉ̀ⲃⲱⲗ ⲉ̀ⲃⲟⲗ ⲛ̀ⲥⲛⲁⲩϩ ⲛⲓⲃⲉⲛ ⲛ̀ⲧⲉ ϯⲁⲇⲓⲕⲓⲁ. ϯⲛⲟⲩ ⲟⲛ ⲧⲉⲛϯϩⲟ ⲟⲩⲟϩ ⲧⲉⲛⲧⲱⲃϩ ⲛ̀ⲧⲉⲕⲙⲉⲧⲁⲅⲁⲑⲟⲥ ⲡⲓⲙⲁⲓⲣⲱⲙⲓ ⲉ̀ϩⲣⲏⲓ ⲉ̀ϫⲉⲛ ⲛⲉⲕⲉⲃⲓⲁⲓⲕ ⲛⲁⲓⲟϯ ⲛⲉⲙ ⲛⲁⲥⲛⲏⲟⲩ ⲛⲉⲙ ⲧⲁⲙⲉⲧϫⲱⲃ ⲛⲁⲓ ⲉⲧⲕⲱⲗϫ ⲛ̀ⲛⲟⲩⲁⲫⲏⲟⲩ̀ⲓ ⲙ̀ⲡⲉⲙⲑⲟ ⲙ̀ⲡⲉⲕⲱⲟⲩ ⲉ̅ⲑ̅ⲩ̅. ⲥⲁϩⲛⲓ ⲛⲁⲛ ⲙ̀ⲡⲉⲕⲛⲁⲓ ⲟⲩⲟϩ ⲥⲱⲗⲡ ⲛ̀ⲥⲛⲁⲩϩ ⲛⲓⲃⲉⲛ ⲛ̀ⲧⲉ ⲛⲉⲛⲛⲟⲃⲓ. ⲓⲥϫⲉ ⲇⲉ ⲁⲛⲉⲣ ϩ̀ⲗⲓ ⲛ̀ⲛⲟⲃⲓ ⲉ̀ⲣⲟⲕ ϧⲉⲛ ⲟⲩⲉⲙⲓ ⲓⲉ ϧⲉⲛ ⲟⲩⲙⲉⲧⲁⲧⲉⲙⲓ ⲓⲉ ϧⲉⲛ ⲟⲩⲙⲉⲧϣⲗⲁϩ ⲛ̀ϩⲏⲧ ⲓⲧⲉ ϧⲉⲛ ⲡϩⲱⲃ ⲓⲧⲉ ϧⲉⲛ ⲡⲥⲁϫⲓ ⲓⲧⲉ ⲉ̀ⲃⲟⲗ ϧⲉⲛ ⲟⲩⲙⲉⲧⲕⲟⲩϫⲓ ⲛ̀ϩⲏⲧ. ⲛ̀ⲑⲟⲕ ⲫⲛⲏⲃ ⲫⲏ ⲉⲧⲥⲱⲟⲩⲛ ⲛ̀ⲑⲙⲉⲧⲁⲥⲑⲉⲛⲏⲥ ⲛ̀ⲧⲉ ⲛⲓⲣⲱⲙⲓ ϩⲱⲥ ⲁⲅⲁⲑⲟⲥ ⲟⲩⲟϩ ⲙ̀ⲙⲁⲓⲣⲱⲙⲓ

O Master, Lord Jesus Christ, the only-begotten Son and Logos of God the Father, who has broken every bond of our sins through his saving, life-giving sufferings. Who breathed into the face of his saints the disciples and holy apostles, saying to them, "Receive unto you the Holy Spirit. If you forgive the sins of any, they are forgiven. If you bind the sins of any, they are bound." [Jn 20:22–23] You also now, O our Master, have given grace through your holy apostles to those who for a time work in the priesthood in your holy Church to forgive sin upon the earth and to bind and to loosen every bond of iniquity. Now also we ask and entreat your goodness, O lover of mankind, for your servants, my fathers, my brothers, and my weakness, those who are bowing their heads before your holy glory. Dispense to us your mercy and break every bond of our sins, and if we have committed any sin against you knowingly or unknowingly, or through cowardice, or in deed or word, or from pusillanimity, O Master who knows the weakness of men, as a good one

ⲫϯ ⲁⲣⲓⲭⲁⲣⲓⲍⲉⲥⲑⲉ ⲛⲁⲛ ⲙ̀ⲡⲭⲱ ⲉ̀ⲃⲟⲗ ⲛ̀ⲧⲉ ⲛⲉⲛⲛⲟⲃⲓ. ⲥⲙⲟⲩ ⲉ̀ⲣⲟⲛ ⲙⲁⲧⲟⲩⲃⲟⲛ ⲁⲣⲓⲧⲉⲛ ⲛ̀ⲣⲉⲙϩⲉ ⲙⲁϩⲧⲉⲛ ⲉ̀ⲃⲟⲗ ϧⲉⲛ ⲧⲉⲕϩⲟϯ ⲟⲩⲟϩ ⲥⲟⲩⲧⲱⲛ ⲉ̀ϧⲟⲩⲛ ⲉ̀ⲡⲉⲕⲟⲩⲱϣ ⲉ̅ⲑ̅ⲩ̅ ⲛ̀ⲁⲅⲁⲑⲟⲛ. ϫⲉ ⲛ̀ⲑⲟⲕ ⲅⲁⲣ ⲡⲉ ⲡⲉⲛⲛⲟⲩϯ ⲉ̀ⲣⲉ ⲡⲓⲱⲟⲩ ⲛⲉⲙ ⲡⲓⲧⲁⲓⲟ ⲛⲉⲙ ⲡⲓⲁⲙⲁϩⲓ ⲛⲉⲙ ϯⲡⲣⲟⲥⲕⲩⲛⲏⲥⲓⲥ ⲉⲣⲡⲣⲉⲡⲓ ⲛⲁⲕ ⲛⲉⲙ ⲡⲉⲕⲓⲱⲧ ⲛ̀ⲁⲅⲁⲑⲟⲥ ⲛⲉⲙ ⲡⲓⲡ̅ⲛ̅ⲁ̅ ⲉ̅ⲑ̅ⲩ̅ ⲛ̀ⲣⲉϥⲧⲁⲛϧⲟ ⲟⲩⲟϩ ⲛ̀ⲟⲙⲟⲟⲩⲥⲓⲟⲥ ⲛⲉⲙⲁⲕ. ϯⲛⲟⲩ ⲛⲉⲙ ⲛ̀ⲥⲏⲟⲩ ⲛⲓⲃⲉⲛ ⲛⲉⲙ ϣⲁ ⲉⲛⲉϩ ⲛ̀ⲧⲉ ⲛⲓⲉⲛⲉϩ ⲧⲏⲣⲟⲩ ⲁⲙⲏⲛ.

and lover of man, O God, grant us the forgiveness of our sins. Bless us, purify us, absolve us, and all your people. Fill us with your fear and direct us towards your holy good will, for you are our God, and the glory, the honor, the dominion, and the worship are due unto you, with your good Father and the Holy Spirit, the giver of life, who is of one essence with you, now and at all times and unto the age of all ages, amen.

But if it were the Liturgy of Saint Gregory, he reads the *Absolution of the Father* secretly instead of the previous absolution:

ⲫⲏⲏⲃ ⲡ̅ⲟ̅ⲥ̅ ⲫϯ ⲡⲓⲡⲁⲛⲧⲟⲕⲣⲁⲧⲱⲣ ⲡⲓⲣⲉϥⲧⲁⲗϭⲟ ⲛ̀ⲧⲉ ⲛⲉⲛⲯⲩⲭⲏ ⲛⲉⲙ ⲛⲉⲛⲥⲱⲙⲁ ⲛⲉⲙ ⲛⲉⲛⲡⲛⲉⲩⲙⲁ. ⲛ̀ⲑⲟⲕ ⲡⲉ ⲉⲧⲁⲕϫⲟⲥ ⲙ̀ⲡⲉⲛⲓⲱⲧ ⲡⲉⲧⲣⲟⲥ ⲉ̀ⲃⲟⲗ ϧⲉⲛ ⲣⲱϥ ⲙ̀ⲡⲉⲕⲙⲟⲛⲟⲅⲉⲛⲏⲥ ⲛ̀ϣⲏⲣⲓ ⲡⲉⲛ̅ⲟ̅ⲥ̅ ⲟⲩⲟϩ ⲡⲉⲛⲛⲟⲩϯ ⲟⲩⲟϩ ⲡⲉⲛⲥⲱⲧⲏⲣ ⲓⲏⲥⲟⲩⲥ ⲡⲓⲭⲣⲓⲥⲧⲟⲥ. ϫⲉ ⲛ̀ⲑⲟⲕ ⲡⲉ ⲡⲉⲧⲣⲟⲥ ⲉⲓⲉ̀ⲕⲱⲧ ⲛ̀ⲧⲁⲉⲕⲕⲗⲏⲥⲓⲁ ⲉ̀ϩⲣⲏⲓ ⲉ̀ϫⲉⲛ ⲧⲁⲓⲡⲉⲧⲣⲁ ⲟⲩⲟϩ ⲛⲓⲡⲩⲗⲏ ⲛ̀ⲧⲉ ⲁⲙⲉⲛϯ ⲛ̀ⲛⲟⲩϣ̀ϫⲉⲙϫⲟⲙ ⲉ̀ⲣⲟⲥ. ⲉⲓⲉ̀ϯ ϫⲉ ⲛⲁⲕ ⲛ̀ⲛⲓϣⲟϣⲧ ⲛ̀ⲧⲉ ⲑⲙⲉⲧⲟⲩⲣⲟ ⲛ̀ⲧⲉ ⲛⲓⲫⲏⲟⲩ̀ⲓ. ⲛⲏ ⲉⲧⲉⲕⲛⲁⲥⲟⲛϩⲟⲩ ϩⲓϫⲉⲛ ⲡⲓⲕⲁϩⲓ ⲉⲩⲉ̀ϣⲱⲡⲓ ⲉⲩⲥⲱⲛϩ ϧⲉⲛ ⲛⲓⲫⲏⲟⲩ̀ⲓ ⲟⲩⲟϩ ⲛⲏ ⲉⲧⲉⲕⲛⲁⲃⲟⲗⲟⲩ ⲉ̀ⲃⲟⲗ ϩⲓϫⲉⲛ ⲡⲓⲕⲁϩⲓ ⲉⲩⲉ̀ϣⲱⲡⲓ ⲉⲩⲃⲏⲗ ϧⲉⲛ ⲛⲓⲫⲏⲟⲩ̀ⲓ. ⲙⲁⲣⲟⲩϣⲱⲡⲓ ⲟⲩⲛ ⲫⲏⲏⲃ ⲛ̀ϫⲉ ⲛⲉⲕⲉⲃⲓⲁⲓⲕ ⲛⲁⲓⲟϯ ⲛⲉⲙ ⲛⲁⲥⲛⲏⲟⲩ ⲛⲉⲙ ⲧⲁⲙⲉⲧϫⲱⲃ ⲉⲩⲃⲏⲗ ⲉ̀ⲃⲟⲗ ϧⲉⲛ ⲣⲱⲓ ϩⲓⲧⲉⲛ ⲡⲉⲕⲡⲛⲉⲩⲙⲁ ⲉⲑⲟⲩⲁⲃ ⲡⲓⲁⲅⲁⲑⲟⲥ ⲟⲩⲟϩ ⲙ̀ⲙⲁⲓⲣⲱⲙⲓ. ⲫϯ ⲫⲏ ⲉⲧⲱⲗⲓ ⲙ̀ⲫⲛⲟⲃⲓ ⲛ̀ⲧⲉ ⲡⲓⲕⲟⲥⲙⲟⲥ ⲁⲣⲓϣⲟⲣⲡ ⲛ̀ϭⲓ ⲛ̀ⲑⲙⲉⲧⲁⲛⲟⲓⲁ ⲛ̀ⲧⲉ ⲛⲉⲕⲉⲃⲓⲁⲓⲕ ⲛ̀ⲧⲟⲧⲟⲩ ⲉ̀ⲟⲩⲟⲩⲱⲓⲛⲓ ⲛ̀ⲧⲉ ⲡⲉⲙⲓ ⲛⲉⲙ ⲟⲩⲭⲱ ⲉ̀ⲃⲟⲗ ⲛ̀ⲧⲉ ⲛⲓⲛⲟⲃⲓ. ϫⲉ ⲛ̀ⲑⲟⲕ ⲟⲩⲛⲟⲩϯ ⲛ̀ⲣⲉϥϣⲉⲛϩⲏⲧ ⲟⲩⲟϩ ⲛ̀ⲛⲁⲏⲧ ⲛ̀ⲑⲟⲕ ⲟⲩⲣⲉϥⲱⲟⲩⲛϩⲏⲧ ⲛⲁϣⲉ ⲡⲉⲕⲛⲁⲓ ⲟⲩⲟϩ ⲛ̀ⲑⲙⲏⲓ. ⲓⲥϫⲉ ⲇⲉ ⲁⲛⲉⲣⲛⲟⲃⲓ ⲉ̀ⲣⲟⲕ ⲓⲧⲉ ϧⲉⲛ ⲡⲥⲁϫⲓ ⲓⲧⲉ ϧⲉⲛ ⲛⲓϩⲃⲏⲟⲩⲓ ⲁⲣⲓⲥⲩⲛⲭⲱⲣⲓⲛ ⲭⲱ ⲛⲁⲛ ⲉ̀ⲃⲟⲗ ϩⲱⲥ ⲁⲅⲁⲑⲟⲥ ⲟⲩⲟϩ ⲙ̀ⲙⲁⲓⲣⲱⲙⲓ. ⲫϯ ⲁⲣⲓⲧⲉⲛ ⲛ̀ⲣⲉⲙϩⲉ ⲛⲉⲙ ⲡⲉⲕⲗⲁⲟⲥ ⲧⲏⲣϥ ⲛ̀ⲣⲉⲙϩⲉ ⲉ̀ⲃⲟⲗ ϩⲁ ⲛⲟⲃⲓ ⲛⲓⲃⲉⲛ ⲛⲉⲙ ⲉ̀ⲃⲟⲗ ϩⲁ

O Master, Lord God the Pantocrator, healer of our souls, our bodies, and our spirits. You are he who said to our father Peter, from the mouth of your only-begotten Son, our Lord, God, and Savior Jesus Christ, "You are Peter, and on this rock, I will build my Church, and the gates of hades shall not prevail against it. I will give you the keys of the kingdom of the heavens. That which you bind on earth shall be bound in the heavens, and that which you loose on earth shall be loosed in the heavens." [Mt 16:18–19] Therefore, Master, let your servants, my fathers, my brothers, and my weakness, be absolved by my mouth, through your Holy Spirit, O good one and lover of man. O God, who takes away the sin of the world [Jn 1:29], hasten to accept the repentance of your servants, unto a light of understanding and forgiveness of sins. For you are a compassionate and merciful God. You are longsuffering. Your mercy is great and true [Ps 85:15]. If we have sinned against you, either by word or by deed, pardon and forgive us, as a good one and lover of mankind. O God, absolve us, and absolve all your

ⲥⲁϩⲟⲩⲓ ⲛⲓⲃⲉⲛ ⲛⲉⲙ ⲉ̀ⲃⲟⲗ ϩⲁ ϫⲱⲗ ⲉ̀ⲃⲟⲗ ⲛⲓⲃⲉⲛ ⲛⲉⲙ ⲉ̀ⲃⲟⲗ ϩⲁ ⲱⲣⲕ ⲛ̀ⲛⲟⲩϫ ⲛⲓⲃⲉⲛ ⲛⲉⲙ ⲉ̀ⲃⲟⲗ ϩⲁ ϫⲓⲛⲉⲣⲁⲡⲁⲛⲧⲁⲛ ⲛⲓⲃⲉⲛ ⲛ̀ⲧⲉ ⲛⲓϩⲉⲣⲉⲧⲓⲕⲟⲥ ⲛⲉⲙ ⲛⲓⲉⲑⲛⲓⲕⲟⲥ. ⲁⲣⲓⲭⲁⲣⲓⲍⲉⲥⲑⲉ ⲛⲁⲛ ⲡⲉⲛⲛⲏⲃ ⲛ̀ⲟⲩⲛⲟⲩⲥ ⲛⲉⲙ ⲟⲩϫⲟⲙ ⲛⲉⲙ ⲟⲩⲕⲁϯ ⲉⲑⲣⲉⲛⲫⲱⲧ ϣⲁ ⲉ̀ⲃⲟⲗ ⲉ̀ⲃⲟⲗ ϩⲁ ϩⲱⲃ ⲛⲓⲃⲉⲛ ⲉ̀ⲧϩⲱⲟⲩ ⲛ̀ⲧⲉ ⲡⲓⲁⲛⲧⲓⲕⲓⲙⲉⲛⲟⲥ ⲟⲩⲟϩ ⲙⲏⲓⲥ ⲛⲁⲛ ⲉⲑⲣⲉⲛⲓ̀ⲣⲓ ⲙ̀ⲡⲉⲑⲣⲁⲛⲁⲕ ⲛ̀ⲥⲏⲟⲩ ⲛⲓⲃⲉⲛ. ⲥ̀ϧⲉ ⲡⲉⲛⲣⲁⲛ ⲛⲉⲙ ⲡⲭⲟⲣⲟⲥ ⲧⲏⲣϥ ⲛ̀ⲧⲉ ⲛⲏ ⲉⲑⲟⲩⲁⲃ ⲛ̀ⲧⲁⲕ ⲛ̀ϩⲣⲏⲓ ϧⲉⲛ ⲑⲙⲉⲧⲟⲩⲣⲟ ⲛ̀ⲧⲉ ⲛⲓⲫⲏⲟⲩⲓ̀ ϧⲉⲛ ⲡⲓⲭⲣⲓⲥⲧⲟⲥ ⲓⲏⲥⲟⲩⲥ ⲡⲉⲛⲟ̅ⲥ̅ ⲫⲁⲓ ⲉ̀ⲧⲉ ⲉ̀ⲃⲟⲗ ϩⲓⲧⲟⲧϥ ⲉⲣⲉ ⲡⲓⲱⲟⲩ ⲛⲉⲙ ⲡⲓⲧⲁⲓⲟ ⲛⲉⲙ ⲡⲓⲁⲙⲁϩⲓ ⲛⲉⲙ ϯⲡⲣⲟⲥⲕⲩⲛⲏⲥⲓⲥ ⲉⲣⲡⲣⲉⲡⲓ ⲛⲁⲕ ⲛⲉⲙⲁϥ ⲛⲉⲙ ⲡⲓⲡ̅ⲛ̅ⲁ̅ ⲉ̅ⲑ̅ⲩ̅ ⲛ̀ⲣⲉϥⲧⲁⲛϧⲟ ⲟⲩⲟϩ ⲛ̀ⲟⲙⲟⲟⲩⲥⲓⲟⲥ ⲛⲉⲙⲁⲕ. ϯⲛⲟⲩ ⲛⲉⲙ ⲛ̀ⲥⲏⲟⲩ ⲛⲓⲃⲉⲛ ⲛⲉⲙ ϣⲁ ⲉⲛⲉϩ ⲛ̀ⲧⲉ ⲛⲓⲉⲛⲉϩ ⲧⲏⲣⲟⲩ ⲁⲙⲏⲛ.

people from every sin, and from every curse, and from every denial, and from every false oath, and from every encounter with the heretics and the heathen. O our Master, grant us a reason and strength and understanding to flee from every evil deed of the adversary, and grant us to do what is pleasing to you at all times. Inscribe our names with all the choir of your saints in the kingdom of the heavens [Lk 10:20] in Christ Jesus our Lord. Through whom the glory, the honor, the dominion, and the worship are due unto you, with him and the Holy Spirit, the giver of life, who is of one essence with you, now and at all times, and unto the age of all ages, amen.

And after either absolution, he says the *Absolution of the Servants* inaudibly:

ⲛⲉⲕⲉⲃⲓⲁⲓⲕ ⲛ̀ⲣⲉϥϣⲉⲙϣⲓ ⲛ̀ⲧⲉ ⲡⲁⲓⲉϩⲟⲟⲩ ⲫⲁⲓ ⲡⲓϩⲓⲅⲟⲩⲙⲉⲛⲟⲥ ⲡⲓⲡⲣⲉⲥⲃⲩⲧⲉⲣⲟⲥ ⲛⲉⲙ ⲡⲓⲇⲓⲁⲕⲱⲛ ⲛⲉⲙ ⲡⲓⲕⲗⲏⲣⲟⲥ ⲛⲉⲙ ⲡⲓⲗⲁⲟⲥ ⲧⲏⲣϥ ⲛⲉⲙ ⲧⲁⲙⲉⲧϫⲱⲃ. ⲉⲩⲉ̀ϣⲱⲡⲓ ⲉⲩⲟⲓ ⲛ̀ⲉⲣⲙⲏϩⲉ ⲉ̀ⲃⲟⲗ ϧⲉⲛ ⲣⲱⲥ ⲛ̀ϯⲡⲁⲛⲁⲅⲓⲁ ⲧⲣⲓⲁⲥ ⲫⲓⲱⲧ ⲛⲉⲙ ⲡϣⲏⲣⲓ ⲛⲉⲙ ⲡⲓⲡⲛⲉⲩⲙⲁ ⲉⲑⲟⲩⲁⲃ. ⲛⲉⲙ ⲉ̀ⲃⲟⲗ ϧⲉⲛ ⲣⲱⲥ ⲛ̀ϯⲟⲩⲓ̀ ⲙ̀ⲙⲁⲩⲁⲧⲥ ⲉⲑⲟⲩⲁⲃ ⲛ̀ⲕⲁⲑⲟⲗⲓⲕⲏ ⲛ̀ⲁⲡⲟⲥⲧⲟⲗⲓⲕⲏ ⲛ̀ⲉⲕⲕⲗⲏⲥⲓⲁ. ⲛⲉⲙ ⲉ̀ⲃⲟⲗ ϧⲉⲛ ⲣⲱⲟⲩ ⲙ̀ⲡⲓⲓ̅ⲃ̅ ⲛ̀ⲁⲡⲟⲥⲧⲟⲗⲟⲥ. ⲛⲉⲙ ⲉ̀ⲃⲟⲗ ϧⲉⲛ ⲣⲱϥ ⲙ̀ⲡⲓⲑⲉⲱⲣⲓⲙⲟⲥ ⲛ̀ⲉⲩⲁⲅⲅⲉⲗⲓⲥⲧⲏⲥ ⲙⲁⲣⲕⲟⲥ ⲡⲓⲁⲡⲟⲥⲧⲟⲗⲟⲥ ⲉⲑⲟⲩⲁⲃ ⲟⲩⲟϩ ⲙ̀ⲙⲁⲣⲧⲩⲣⲟⲥ. ⲛⲉⲙ ⲡⲓⲡⲁⲧⲣⲓⲁⲣⲭⲏⲥ ⲉⲑⲟⲩⲁⲃ ⲥⲉⲩⲏⲣⲟⲥ ⲛⲉⲙ ⲡⲉⲛⲥⲁϧ ⲇⲓⲟⲥⲕⲟⲣⲟⲥ ⲛⲉⲙ ⲡⲓⲁⲅⲓⲟⲥ ⲁⲑⲁⲛⲁⲥⲓⲟⲥ ⲡⲓⲁⲡⲟⲥⲧⲟⲗⲓⲕⲟⲥ ⲛⲉⲙ ⲡⲓⲁⲅⲓⲟⲥ ⲡⲉⲧⲣⲟⲥ ⲓⲉⲣⲟⲙⲁⲣⲧⲩⲣⲟⲥ ⲡⲓⲁⲣⲭⲏⲉ̀ⲣⲉⲩⲥ ⲛⲉⲙ ⲡⲓⲁⲅⲓⲟⲥ ⲓⲱⲁⲛⲛⲏⲥ ⲡⲓⲭⲣⲩⲥⲟⲥⲧⲟⲙⲟⲥ ⲛⲉⲙ ⲡⲓⲁⲅⲓⲟⲥ ⲕⲩⲣⲓⲗⲗⲟⲥ ⲛⲉⲙ ⲡⲓⲁⲅⲓⲟⲥ ⲃⲁⲥⲓⲗⲓⲟⲥ ⲛⲉⲙ ⲡⲓⲁⲅⲓⲟⲥ ⲅⲣⲏⲅⲟⲣⲓⲟⲥ. ⲛⲉⲙ ⲉ̀ⲃⲟⲗ ϧⲉⲛ ⲣⲱⲟⲩ ⲙ̀ⲡⲓⲧ̅ⲓ̅ⲏ̅ ⲉⲧⲁⲩⲑⲱⲟⲩϯ ϧⲉⲛ ⲛⲓⲕⲉⲁ ⲛⲉⲙ ⲡⲓⲣ̅ⲛ̅ ⲛ̀ⲧⲉ ⲕⲱⲥⲧⲁⲛⲧⲓⲛⲟⲩⲡⲟⲗⲓⲥ ⲛⲉⲙ ⲡⲓⲥ̅ ⲛ̀ⲧⲉ

May your servants, the ministers of this day, the hegumen, the priest, the deacon, the clergy, all the people, and my weakness, be absolved from the mouth of the all-holy Trinity, the Father and the Son and the Holy Spirit; and from the mouth of the one and only, Holy, catholic and apostolic Church. And from the mouths of the twelve apostles; and from the mouth of the beholder of God the Evangelist Mark, the holy apostle and martyr; the patriarch Saint Severus, our teacher Dioscorus, Saint Athanasius the apostolic, Saint Peter the hieromartyr the high priest, Saint John Chrysostom, Saint Cyril, Saint Basil, and Saint Gregory. And from the mouths of the three hundred and eighteen assembled at Nicea, the one hundred and fifty at Constantinople, and the two hundred at Ephesus. And from the mouth of our honorable father the

ⲉⲫⲉⲥⲟⲥ. ⲛⲉⲙ ⲉ̀ⲃⲟⲗ ϧⲉⲛ ⲣⲱϥ ⲙ̀ⲡⲉⲛⲓⲱⲧ ⲉⲧⲧⲁⲛⲟⲩⲧ ⲛ̀ⲁⲣⲭⲏⲉ̀ⲣⲉⲩⲥ ⲁⲃⲃⲁ ⲛ̅ⲓ̅ⲙ̅. ⲛⲉⲙ ⲉ̀ⲃⲟⲗ ϧⲉⲛ ⲣⲱⲥ ⲛ̀ⲧⲁⲙⲉⲧⲉⲗⲁⲭⲓⲥⲧⲟⲥ. ϫⲉ ϥ̀ⲥⲙⲁⲣⲱⲟⲩⲧ ⲟⲩⲟϩ ϥ̀ⲙⲉϩ ⲛ̀ⲱⲟⲩ ⲛ̀ϫⲉ ⲡⲉⲕⲣⲁⲛ ⲉⲑⲟⲩⲁⲃ ⲫⲓⲱⲧ ⲛⲉⲙ ⲡϣⲏⲣⲓ ⲛⲉⲙ ⲡⲓⲡⲛⲉⲩⲙⲁ ⲉⲑⲟⲩⲁⲃ ϯⲛⲟⲩ ⲛⲉⲙ ⲛ̀ⲥⲏⲟⲩ ⲛⲓⲃⲉⲛ ⲛⲉⲙ ϣⲁ ⲉⲛⲉϩ ⲛ̀ⲧⲉ ⲛⲓⲉⲛⲉϩ ⲧⲏⲣⲟⲩ ⲁⲙⲏⲛ.

high priest Abba N.N. and from the mouth of my lowliness. For blessed and full of glory is your holy Name, O Father and Son and Holy Spirit, now and at all times and unto the age of all ages, amen.

APPENDIX 2

CHRONOLOGICAL LIST OF LITURGICAL MANUSCRIPTS

The following list contains references to all the liturgical manuscripts used in the preparation of this work arranged chronologically. In the course of preparing this list, a few decisions were made. First, only liturgical manuscripts are included in this list, that is, manuscripts that can be and/or were used in the performance of a liturgical rite. This means that any references to non-liturgical manuscripts (e.g. manuscripts of the literary, canonical, and hagiographical genres) are not included. Sometimes this has made it necessary to make some difficult decisions when a manuscript's genre was not quite straightforward. For example, none of the manuscripts of liturgical commentaries or descriptions of service, such as Ibn Kabar, Ibn Sabbāʿ, or Gabriel V are included below. Similarly, the codex *Paris BnF Ar. 100* (14th c.), which contains accounts of the consecration of the chrism by various patriarchs was excluded, since the manuscript itself should be more accurately considered of an epistolary kind, rather than a liturgical manuscript strictly speaking. For a comprehensive list of all manuscripts referenced in this work, including non-liturgical ones, the reader is referred to the manuscripts index.

Throughout the course of this work, manuscripts of various languages were referenced (e.g. Coptic, Arabic, Greek, Syriac, and Ethiopic). Rather than group the manuscripts by language, it was decided to group them by liturgical tradition for clarity. As has been explained in the introduction, the Coptic liturgical tradition is known to us through manuscripts in three languages: Coptic, Greek, and Arabic. At the same time, this research has found ample comparative material in the Byzantine liturgical tradition, itself in large part preserved in Greek manuscripts. Thus, it would not be practical to group all Greek manuscripts together, some of which belong to the Coptic tradition and others to the Byzantine.

Besides the numerous manuscript catalogues that were consulted in compiling this list, the dating of manuscripts belonging to the

Coptic Rite is mostly based on Budde's study,[1] with a few dates supplied by Fr. Wadīʿ al-Fransiskānī's article on the Arabic translations of the Coptic liturgy.[2] In a few cases, the catalogues did not provide even an approximate date. In such cases, the date was estimated based on script, internal liturgical evidence, and/or acquisition history. I am thankful for Mr. Hany N. Takla for lending his expert opinion in this regard.

For Byzantine mansucripts, the dates as well as the bibliography are based on the list in *Il Grande Ingresso* by Robert F. Taft and Stefano Parenti,[3] and/or Jacob's "Histoire du formulaire."[4] Whenever possible, the footnotes refer the reader to the description of the manuscript in scholarly literature.

The contents or type of each manuscript (e.g. Diaconicon, horologion, pontifical, etc.) are indicated in square brackets. When no such indication is given, the reader may assume the manuscript is an Euchologion (i.e. A book providing at least the prayers for the priest for the eucharistic liturgy). When applicable, the catalogue number of a manuscript is indicated after its more common shelf number. Unless explicitly stated, Coptic manuscripts are of the Coptic recension of BAS and Byzantine manuscripts are that of CHR. An asterisk (*) marks that a manuscript was examined directly or in a digital reproduction, rather than in an edition or based on a description found in scholarly literature.

1. COPTIC MANUSCRIPTS

6th Century

P. ÖNB K. 4854 [Sahidic fragment][5]

7th–8th Century

P. Berlin 709 and *9444+4790* [Sahidic fragment][6]
P. Oslo inv. 1665 [Sahidic fragment][7]

1 Budde, *Die ägyptische Basilios-Anaphora*, 140.
2 Al-Fransiskānī, "Aqdam al-tarǧamāt al-ʿarabiyya," 227–233.
3 Taft and Parenti, *Il Grande Ingresso*, 700–730.
4 Jacob, "Histoire du formulaire," 507–588.
5 Henner, *Fragmenta Liturgica Coptica*, 40.
6 Mihálykó, "Two Coptic Prayers on Ostracon," 145–155.
7 Maravela, Mihálykó, and Wehus, "A Coptic Liturgical Prayer," 204–230.

9th Century

**MLM M574* (AD 897–898) (= Depuydt 59) [*hermeniae* and Horologion][8]

9th–11th Century

P. Naqlun II 20 [Diaconicon][9]

10th Century

British Library Or. 4718(1) (= Crum 511) [Sahidic fragment][10]

10th–11th Century

**British Library Or. 3580A (11)* (= Crum 154) [Sahidic Diaconicon fragment][11]
**Paris BnF Copt. 129(20)*, fol. 156–157 [Sahidic fragment][12]

11th Century

**British Library Or. 3580A (7)* (= Crum 150) [Sahidic fragment][13]

11th–12th Century

Prague Or. Inst. MS I p. 1–3 [Sahidic fragment][14]

12th–13th Centuries

**RMO Copt. 85* (= Insinger 40) [Sahidic typikon][15]

8 Depuydt, *Catalogue of Coptic Manuscripts*, 113–121; Quecke, *Untersuchungen*, 91–104.

9 Derda, *Deir el-Naqlun*, 2:70–71.

10 Crum, *Catalogue of the Coptic Manuscripts*, 245–246; Quecke, "Zum 'Gebet der Lossprechung des Vaters'," 70–71. The dating of this fragment to the tenth century is based on the judgement of Quecke in the article cited.

11 Crum, *Catalogue of the Coptic Manuscripts*, 39–41; Henner, *Fragmenta Liturgica Coptica*, 142–143. The dating of this fragment is estimated here based on paleographical comparison to other Sahidic parchment fragments, namely, *ÖNB K. 9390* and *ÖNB K. 9761*, dated to the tenth and eleventh century respectively by Rodolphe Kasser. See Rodolphe Kasser, "Paleography," *CE*, 8:A175b–A184a, fig. 5a, 5b. I wish to thank Hany N. Takla for this reference.

12 Mihálykó, "Witnesses of A 'Prayer of Offering'," 129–131.

13 Crum, *Catalogue of the Coptic Manuscripts*, 35; Henner, *Fragmenta Liturgica Coptica*, 8.

14 Hažmuková, "Miscellaneous Coptic Prayers," 325–327.

15 Pleyte and Boeser, *Manuscrits coptes*, 217–228.

13th Century

Coptic Museum Lit. 361 (AD 1234) (= Simaika 141) [Horologion][16]
**BAV Vatican Copt. 17* (AD 1288)[17]
**British Library Or. 1239* (= Crum 788)[18]
**Bodleian Hunt. 360* (= Uri 34)[19]
**Coptic Museum Lit. 463* (= New 340)[20]
Rylands Copt. 426 (= Crum 59)[21]
**Sinai Ar. 184* [Horologion][22]
**Sinai Ar. 389* [Horologion][23]

13th–14th Century

**Hamburg Bishoy Euchol. 7*[24]

16 Marcus Simaika and Yassa ʿabd al-Masiḥ, *Catalogue of the Coptic and Arabic Manuscripts in the Coptic Museum, the Patriarchate, the Principal Churches of Cairo and Alexandria and the Monasteries of Egypt*, vol. 1 (Cairo: Government Press, 1939), 71; Burmester, *The Horologion of the Egyptian Church*, xxxv; Hanna, "Το Ωρολόγιον της Κοπτικής Ορθόδοξης Εκκλησίας," 20.

17 Adolph Hebbelynck and Arnold van Lantschoot, *Codices Coptici Vaticani Barberiniani Borgiani* Rossiani, vol. 1, *Codices Coptici Vaticani* (Vatican City: Biblioteca Vaticana, 1937), 58–63; Budde, *Die ägyptische Basilios-Anaphora*, 111; Wadi, "Testo della Traduzione Araba," 131.

18 Crum, *Catalogue of the Coptic Manuscripts*, 340; Budde, *Die ägyptische Basilios-Anaphora*, 108–109.

19 Joanne Uri, *Bibliothecae Bodleianae codicum manuscriptorum orientalium, videlicet Hebraicorum, Chaldaicorum, Syriacorum, Aethiopicorum, Arabicorum, Persicorum, Turcicorum, Copticorumque Catalogus*, vol. 1 (Oxford, 1787), 324; *LEW*, 112; Budde, *Die ägyptische Basilios-Anaphora*, 112.

20 Samiha abd el-Shaheed abd el-Nour, "Supplement to the Catalogue of the Manuscripts in the Coptic Museum: Section IV–Liturgica (Part 1)," *BSAC* 39 (2000): 181–200, here 189; William F. Macomber, *Final Inventory of the Microfilmed Manuscripts of the Coptic Museum Old Cairo, Egypt: Rolls B12–17 Manuscripts in Arabic, Coptic (Bohairic, Oxyrhynchite [1], Sahidic) Greek* (Provo, UT: Harold B. Lee Library Brigham Young University, 1995), 82–83.

21 W.E. Crum, *Catalogue of the Coptic Manuscripts in the Collection of the John Rylands Library Manchester* (Manchester: University Press, 1909), 200; Rodwell, *The Liturgies of S. Basil, S. Gregory, and S. Cyril*, iii–iv; Budde, *Die ägyptische Basilios-Anaphora*, 109–111.

22 Aziz S. Atiya, *Al-fahāris al-taḥlīliyya li-maḥṭūṭāt ṭūr sīnā al-ʿarabīyya* [The analytical indices of the Arabic manuscripts of Mount Sinai] (Alexandria, 1970), 368; Quecke, "Ein koptisch-arabisches Horologion," 112n50.

23 Quecke, "Ein koptisch-arabisches Horologion," 112n50.

24 O.H.E. Burmester, *Koptische Handschriften 1: Die Handschriftenfragmente der Staats- und Universitätsbibliothek Hamburg*, vol. 1, Verzeichnis der orientalischen Handschriften in Deutschland 21.1 (Wiesbaden: Franz Steiner Verlag, 1975), 104–106.

**Hamburg Macarius Euchol. 46* (= Störk 109) [Diaconicon][25]
**Bodleian Hunt. 572* (= Uri 35)[26]
**Bodleian Ind. Inst. Copt. 4*[27]
**Paris BnF Copt. 28* (= Delaporte 63)[28]

14th Century

**BAV Vatican Copt. 28* (AD 1306) [Diaconicon][29]
**Paris BnF Copt. 82* (AD 1307) (= Delaporte 67)[30]
BAV Vatican Copt. 40 (AD 1334) [Horologion][31]
**Coptic Museum Lit. 253* (AD 1364) (= Simaika 142) [pontifical][32]
**BAV Borgia Copt. 7* (AD 1379)[33]
BAV Barberini Or. 17 (AD 1396) [Horologion][34]
**BAV Vatican Copt. 24*[35]
**BAV Vatican Copt. 25*, fol. 8r–11v[36]
**BAV Vatican Copt. 38* [Diaconicon][37]

[25] Lothar Störk, *Koptische Handschriften 2: Die Handschriften der Staats- und Universitätsbibliothek Hamburg*, vol. 2, *Die Handschriften aus Dair Anbā Maqār*, Verzeichnis der orientalischen Handschriften in Deutschland 21.2 (Stuttgart: Franz Steiner Verlag, 1995), 255–256.

[26] Uri, *Bibliothecae Bodleianae*, 324; *LEW*, lxx; Budde, *Die ägyptische Basilios-Anaphora*, 114–115.

[27] Malan, *The Divine ΕΥΧΟΛΟΓΙΟΝ*, iv–vii; Budde, *Die ägyptische Basilios-Anaphora*, 113.

[28] Louis Delaporte, "Catalogue sommaire des manuscrits coptes de la Bibliothèque Nationale," *Revue de l'Orient Chrétien* 16 (1911): 85–99, 155–160, 239–248, 368–395, here 85–86; Al-Fransiskānī, "Aqdam al-tarǧamāt al-ʿarabiyya," 228. The dating of this manuscript was identified based on the expert opinion of Mr. Hany N. Takla.

[29] Hebbelynck and Van Lantschoot, *Codices Coptici Vaticani*, 98–105; Budde, *Die ägyptische Basilios-Anaphora*, 114–115, 116–117.

[30] Delaporte, "Catalogue sommaire des manuscrits coptes," 92; Budde, *Die ägyptische Basilios-Anaphora*, 115–116.

[31] Hebbelynck and Van Lantschoot, *Codices Coptici Vaticani*, 211–214; Ṭūḫī, ⲟⲩϫⲱⲙ ⲛ̀ⲧⲉ ⲛⲓⲉⲩⲭⲏ ⲙ̀ⲡⲓⲉ̀ϩⲟⲟⲩ ⲛⲉⲙ ⲡⲓⲉ̀ϫⲱⲣϩ ⲛ̀ⲍ̅.

[32] Simaika and ʿAbd al-Masiḥ, *Catalogue of the Coptic and Arabic Manuscripts*, 1:72; Burmester, *The Rite of Consecration of the Patriarch of Alexandria*, 1–8; Burmester, *Ordination Rites of the Coptic Church: Text According to MS. 253 Lit., Coptic Museum* (Cairo: [Société d'archéologie copte], 1985).

[33] Arnold van Lantschoot, *Codices Coptici Vaticani Barberiniani Borgiani Rossiani*, vol. 2, *Codices Barberiniani orientales 2 et 17 Borgiani Coptici 1–108* (Vatican City: Biblioteca Vaticana, 1947), 36–45; Budde, *Die ägyptische Basilios-Anaphora*, 116.

[34] Van Lantschoot, *Codices Coptici Vaticani*, 4–10; Quecke, "Ein koptisch-arabisches Horologion," 112n50.

[35] Hebbelynck and Van Lantschoot, *Codices Coptici Vaticani*, 82–85; Budde, *Die ägyptische Basilios-Anaphora*, 113–114.

[36] Hebbelynck and Van Lantschoot, *Codices Coptici Vaticani*, 85–90; Budde, *Die ägyptische Basilios-Anaphora*, 114.

[37] Hebbelynck and Van Lantschoot, *Codices Coptici Vaticani*, 180–190; Budde, *Die ägyptische Basilios-Anaphora*, 117.

**Bodleian Marsh 5* (= Uri 41)[38]
Coptic Museum Inv. 20 [Greek BAS][39]
**Kacmarcik Codex* [Greek BAS][40]
**Paris BnF Gr. 325* [Greek BAS][41]
St. Macarius Lit. 438 (= Zanetti 221) [Horologion][42]

14th–15th Century

**Hamburg Macarius Hymns 30* (= Störk 193) [Psalmodia/Diaconicon][43]

15th Century

**Coptic Patriarchate Lit. 73* (AD 1444) (= Simaika 742) [hymnal][44]
**Coptic Patriarchate Lit. 74* (AD 1444) (= Simaika 743) [hymnal][45]
**BAV Vatican Copt. 27* [Diaconicon][46]
**Paris BnF Copt. 24* (= Delaporte 64)[47]
**Paris BnF Copt. 31* (= Delaporte 66)[48]
**Paris BnF Copt. 39* (= Delaporte 73)[49]

15th–16th Century

**Bodleian Copt. f. 3*[50]

38 Uri, *Bibliothecae Bodleianae,* 325; *LEW,* lxx; Budde, *Die ägyptische Basilios-Anaphora,* 115.
39 Evelyn-White, *The Monasteries of the Wadi 'N Natrun,* 1:200–206; Brakmann, "Zu den Fragmenten," 118–143; Budde, *Die ägyptische Basilios-Anaphora,* 76–77.
40 Macomber, "The Kacmarcik Codex," 391–395; Macomber, "The Greek Text," 308–314; Macomber, "The Anaphora of Saint Mark," 75–76; Budde, *Die ägyptische Basilios-Anaphora,* 77–82.
41 Renaudot, *Liturgiarum Orientalium Collectio,* 1:1–25; Brakmann, "Zur Stellung des Parisinus graecus 325," 97–110; Budde, *Die ägyptische Basilios-Anaphora,* 72–76.
42 Zanetti, "Horologion copte et vêpres byzantines," 237–240.
43 Störk, *Koptische Handschriften,* 2:399–402
44 Simaika and 'Abd al-Masiḥ, *Catalogue of the Coptic and Arabic Manuscripts,* 2:339; Samuel, *Tartīb al- bī'a,* 1:[i–ii].
45 Simaika and 'Abd al-Masiḥ, *Catalogue of the Coptic and Arabic Manuscripts,* 2:339; Samuel, *Tartīb al- bī'a,* 1:[i–ii].
46 Hebbelynck and Van Lantschoot, *Codices Coptici Vaticani,* 93–98; Budde, *Die ägyptische Basilios-Anaphora,* 119.
47 Delaporte, "Catalogue sommaire des manuscrits coptes," 86–88; Al-Fransiskānī, "Aqdam al-tarǧamāt al-'arabiyya," 228.
48 Delaporte, "Catalogue sommaire des manuscrits coptes," 89–91; Budde, *Die ägyptische Basilios-Anaphora,* 120.
49 Delaporte, "Catalogue sommaire des manuscrits coptes," 98–99; Al-Fransiskānī, "Aqdam al-tarǧamāt al-'arabiyya," 232. The dating of this manuscript was identified based on the expert opinion of Mr. Hany N. Takla.
50 The dating of this manuscript was identified based on the expert opinion of Mr. Hany N. Takla.

**Paris BnF Copt. 25* (= Delaporte 75)[51]

16th Century

Baramūs 6/278 (AD 1514) [hymnal][52]
**Paris BnF Copt. 26* (before AD 1523) (= Delaporte 65)[53]
**Paris BnF Copt. 73* (AD 1528) (= Delaporte 74)[54]
**BAV Vatican Copt. 18* (AD 1531)[55]
**Suryān Lit. 466* (AD 1573)
Coptic Patriarchate Lit. 172 (AD 1599) (= Simaika 762) [Greek BAS][56]

17th Century

**Suryān Lit. 468* (AD 1601)
**BAV Vatican Copt. 26* (AD 1616)[57]
**Suryān Lit. 469* (before AD 1623)
**Paris BnF Copt. 29* (AD 1639) (= Delaporte 72)[58]
**Paris BnF Copt. 30* (AD 1642) (= Delaporte 76)[59]
**Suryān Lit. 465* (AD 1645)
**Suryān Lit. 472* (AD 1659)
**Suryān Lit. 473* (AD 1659)
St. Antony Codex (AD 1661) [hymnal][60]
**Suryān Lit. 474* (AD 1666)
**Coptic Patriarchate Lit. 331* (AD 1678) (= Simaika 790)[61]

51 Delaporte, "Catalogue sommaire des manuscrits coptes," 156–158; Al-Fransiskānī, "Aqdam al-tarǧamāt al-ʿarabiyya," 232. The dating of this manuscript was identified based on the expert opinion of Mr. Hany N. Takla.
52 Samuel, *Tartīb al- bīʿa*, 1:[i–ii].
53 Delaporte, "Catalogue sommaire des manuscrits coptes," 88–89; Al-Fransiskānī, "Aqdam al-tarǧamāt al-ʿarabiyya," 232. The dating of this manuscript was identified based on the expert opinion of Mr. Hany N. Takla.
54 Delaporte, "Catalogue sommaire des manuscrits coptes," 155–156; Al-Fransiskānī, "Aqdam al-tarǧamāt al-ʿarabiyya," 228.
55 Hebbelynck and Van Lantschoot, *Codices Coptici Vaticani*, 63–68; Budde, *Die ägyptische Basilios-Anaphora*, 120–121.
56 Simaika and ʿAbd al-Masiḥ, *Catalogue of the Coptic and Arabic Manuscripts*, 2:346; Dous, "Η Αλεξανδρινή Θεία Λειτουργία," 58–59; Budde, *Die ägyptische Basilios-Anaphora*, 82–84.
57 Hebbelynck and Van Lantschoot, *Codices Coptici Vaticani*, 90–93; Budde, *Die ägyptische Basilios-Anaphora*, 121–122.
58 Delaporte, "Catalogue sommaire des manuscrits coptes," 96–97; Al-Fransiskānī, "Aqdam al-tarǧamāt al-ʿarabiyya," 228.
59 Delaporte, "Catalogue sommaire des manuscrits coptes," 158; Al-Fransiskānī, "Aqdam al-tarǧamāt al-ʿarabiyya," 228.
60 Samuel, *Tartīb al- bīʿa*, 1:[i–ii].
61 Simaika and ʿAbd al-Masiḥ, *Catalogue of the Coptic and Arabic Manuscripts*, 2:357–358.

Suryān Monastery Codex (AD 1698) [hymnal][62]
**BAV Vatican Copt. 25*, fol. 1r–7v, 12r–18r[63]
St. Macarius Lit. 440 (= Zanetti 223) [Horologion][64]

17th–18th Century

**British Library Or. 429* (= Crum 789)[65]
**Hamburg Macarius Euchol. 30* (= Störk 93)[66]

18th Century

**BAV Vatican Copt. 19* (AD 1715)[67]
Alexandria Coptic Patriarchate Codex (AD 1716) [hymnal][68]
**British Library Or. 431* (AD 1718) (= Crum 793)[69]
**BAV Vatican Copt. 99* (AD 1718–1726)[70]
**BAV Vatican Copt. 78* (AD 1722)[71]
**BAV Vatican Copt. 81* (AD 1722)[72]
**British Library Or. 8778* (AD 1726) (= Layton 228)[73]
**Rylands Copt. 427* (AD 1749) (= Crum 19)[74]
**Coptic Museum Lit. 344* (AD 1752) (= Simaika 227)[75]
**Suryān Lit. 481* (AD 1752)
**Suryān Lit. 457* (AD 1758)
**Suryān Lit. 485* (AD 1784)
**Suryān Lit. 482* (AD 1787)

62 Samuel, *Tartīb al- bīʿa*, 1:[i–ii].
63 Hebbelynck and Van Lantschoot, *Codices Coptici Vaticani*, 85–90; Budde, *Die ägyptische Basilios-Anaphora*, 114.
64 Zanetti, "Horologion copte et vêpres byzantines," 240–241.
65 Crum, *Catalogue of the Coptic Manuscripts*, 340–341; Al-Fransiskānī, "Aqdam al-tarǧamāt al-ʿarabiyya," 233. The dating of this manuscript was identified based on the expert opinion of Mr. Hany N. Takla.
66 Störk, *Koptische Handschriften*, 2:237.
67 Hebbelynck and Van Lantschoot, *Codices Coptici Vaticani*, 68–71; Budde, *Die ägyptische Basilios-Anaphora*, 123–124.
68 Samuel, *Tartīb al- bīʿa*, 1:[i–ii].
69 Crum, *Catalogue of the Coptic Manuscripts*, 342; Al-Fransiskānī, "Aqdam al-tarǧamāt al-ʿarabiyya," 229.
70 Hebbelynck and Van Lantschoot, *Codices Coptici Vaticani*, 668–672; Budde, *Die ägyptische Basilios-Anaphora*, 124.
71 Hebbelynck and Van Lantschoot, *Codices Coptici Vaticani*, 556–568; Al-Fransiskānī, "Aqdam al-tarǧamāt al-ʿarabiyya," 229.
72 Hebbelynck and Van Lantschoot, *Codices Coptici Vaticani*, 569–571; Al-Fransiskānī, "Aqdam al-tarǧamāt al-ʿarabiyya," 229.
73 Bentley Layton, *Catalogue of Coptic Literary Manuscripts in the British Library Acquired Since the Year 1906* (London: British Library, 1987), 354–356.
74 W.E. Crum, *Catalogue of the Coptic Manuscripts–John Rylands Library*, 201; Al-Fransiskānī, "Aqdam al-tarǧamāt al-ʿarabiyya," 229.
75 Simaika and ʿAbd al-Masiḥ, *Catalogue of the Coptic and Arabic Manuscripts*, 1:106.

Suryān Lit. 459 (AD 1788)
**Suryān Lit. 477* (AD 1792)
**Suryān Lit. 461* (AD 1795)
**Coptic Museum Lit. 80* (AD 1796) (= Simaika 244)[76]
Abnūb St. Mīnā Lit. 1 [Greek BAS][77]
**Coptic Museum Lit. 265* (= Simaika 263)[78]
**Coptic Museum Lit. 338* (= Simaika 266)[79]
Coptic Patriarchate Lit. 175 (= Simaika 767) [Greek BAS][80]
Coptic Patriarchate Lit. 184 (= Simaika 771) [Greek BAS][81]
**St. Macarius Lit. 147* (= Zanetti 191)[82]

18th–19th Century

**Coptic Museum Supp. Lit. 432*[83]
**Hamburg Bishoy Euchol. 6*[84]
**St. Macarius Lit. 134* (= Zanetti 178)[85]

19th Century

**British Library Add. 17725* (AD 1811) (= Crum 791)[86]

76 Simaika and ʿAbd al-Masiḥ, *Catalogue of the Coptic and Arabic Manuscripts*, 1:113; Al-Fransiskānī, "Aqdam al-tarǧamāt al-ʿarabiyya," 229.

77 Dous, "Η Αλεξανδρινή Θεία Λειτουργία," 61–62; Budde, *Die ägyptische Basilios-Anaphora*, 86.

78 Simaika and ʿAbd al-Masiḥ, *Catalogue of the Coptic and Arabic Manuscripts*, 1:119; Al-Fransiskānī, "Aqdam al-tarǧamāt al-ʿarabiyya," 229.

79 Simaika and ʿabd al-Masiḥ, *Catalogue of the Coptic and Arabic Manuscripts*, 1:121.

80 Simaika and ʿAbd al-Masiḥ, *Catalogue of the Coptic and Arabic Manuscripts*, 2:347–348; Dous, "Η Αλεξανδρινή Θεία Λειτουργία," 60–61; Budde, *Die ägyptische Basilios-Anaphora*, 85–86.

81 Simaika and ʿAbd al-Masiḥ, *Catalogue of the Coptic and Arabic Manuscripts*, 2:349; Dous, "Η Αλεξανδρινή Θεία Λειτουργία," 59–60; Budde, *Die ägyptische Basilios-Anaphora*, 84–85.

82 Ugo Zanetti, *Les Manuscrits de Dair Abū Maqār: Inventaire*, Cahiers d'orientalisme 11 (Geneva: Patrick Cramer, 1986), 31; Al-Maqārī, *Al-quddās al-ilāhī*, 1:103.

83 Samiha abd el-Shaheed abd el-Nour, "Supplement to the Catalogue of the Manuscripts in the Coptic Museum: Section 4—Liturgical (Part 4)," *BSAC* 44 (2005): 69–80, here 75; William F. Macomber, *Final Inventory of the Microfilmed Manuscripts of the Coptic Museum Old Cairo, Egypt: Rolls 7–11 Manuscripts in Arabic, Coptic (Bohairic, Oxyrhynchite [1], Sahidic) Greek* (Provo, UT: Harold B. Lee Library Brigham Young University, 1995), 4–5. This manuscript was not cataloged by Marcus Simaika and is listed here using its new catalogue number.

84 Burmester, *Koptische Handschriften*, 1:103.

85 Zanetti, *Les Manuscrits de Dair Abū Maqār*, 30; Al-Maqārī, *Al-quddās al-ilāhī*, 1:102.

86 Crum, *Catalogue of the Coptic Manuscripts*, 341; Al-Fransiskānī, "Aqdam al-tarǧamāt al-ʿarabiyya," 230.

St. Paul Lit. 201 (AD 1818) [Greek BAS][87]
St. Antony Lit. 55 (AD 1824) [Greek BAS][88]
**British Library Or. 430* (AD 1832) (= Crum 790)[89]
**Suryān Lit. 484* (AD 1841)
**St. Macarius Lit. 156* (AD 1852) (= Zanetti 200) [Greek BAS][90]
**Coptic Museum Lit. 412* (AD 1867) (= New 356)[91]
**British Library Or. 5282* (AD 1872) (= Crum 817)[92]
**Beinecke Copt. 21* (AD 1877)
**Cairo Franciscan Center 248* (AD 1878)[93]
**St. Macarius Lit. 155* (AD 1894) (= Zanetti 199) [Greek BAS][94]
**Beinecke Copt. 20*
**Coptic Museum Lit. 462* (= New 345)[95]
Coptic Patriarchate Lit. 90 (= Simaika 977) [pontifical][96]
**St. Macarius Lit. 133* (= Zanetti 177)[97]
**St. Macarius Lit. 136* (= Zanetti 180)[98]
Virgin Mary Monastery al-Muḥarraq Lit. 13 [Greek BAS][99]

87 Dous, "Η Αλεξανδρινή Θεία Λειτουργία," 63–64; Budde, *Die ägyptische Basilios-Anaphora*, 87.

88 Dous, "Η Αλεξανδρινή Θεία Λειτουργία," 65–66; Budde, *Die ägyptische Basilios-Anaphora*, 87.

89 Crum, *Catalogue of the Coptic Manuscripts*, 341; Al-Fransiskānī, "Aqdam al-tarǧamāt al-ʿarabiyya," 230.

90 Zanetti, *Les Manuscrits de Dair Abū Maqār*, 31; Dous, "Η Αλεξανδρινή Θεία Λειτουργία," 68. Budde, *Die ägyptische Basilios-Anaphora*, 88.

91 William F. Macomber, *Final Inventory of the Microfilmed Manuscripts of the Coptic Museum Old Cairo, Egypt: Rolls B1–6 Manuscripts in Arabic, Coptic (Bohairic, Oxyrhynchite [1], Sahidic) Greek* (Provo, UT: Harold B. Lee Library Brigham Young University, 1995), 137–138.

92 Crum, *Catalogue of the Coptic Manuscripts*, 345–346; Al-Fransiskānī, "Aqdam al-tarǧamāt al-ʿarabiyya," 230.

93 William F. Macomber, *Catalogue of the Christian Arabic Manuscripts of the Franciscan Center of Christian Oriental Studies, Muski, Cairo*, Studia Orientalia Christiana (Cairo: Centre franciscain d'études orientales chrétiennes, 1984), 52.

94 Dous, "Η Αλεξανδρινή Θεία Λειτουργία," 66–67; Budde, *Die ägyptische Basilios-Anaphora*, 87–88.

95 ʿAbd el-Nour, "Supplement to the Catalogue: Section IV–Liturgica (Part 1)," 191; Macomber, *Final Inventory, Rolls B1–6, 128*–129.

96 Simaika and ʿAbd al-Masiḥ, *Catalogue of the Coptic and Arabic Manuscripts*, 2:437; Burmester, *The Rite of Consecration of the Patriarch of Alexandria*, 49–50, 85–88.

97 Zanetti, *Les Manuscrits de Dair Abū Maqār*, 30; Al-Maqārī, *Al-quddās al-ilāhī*, 1:101–102.

98 Zanetti, *Les Manuscrits de Dair Abū Maqār*, 30; Al-Maqārī, *Al-quddās al-ilāhī*, 1:102–103.

99 Dous, "Η Αλεξανδρινή Θεία Λειτουργία," 62–63; Budde, *Die ägyptische Basilios-Anaphora*, 86.

20th Century

Coptic Patriarchate Lit. 117 (AD 1910) (= Simaika 1035) [hymnal][100]
**Coptic Museum Lit. 16* (AD 1928–1942) (= Simaika 250)[101]

2. BYZANTINE MANUSCRIPTS

8th Century

**BAV Barberini Gr. 336*[102]

8th–9th Century

Sinai Gr. NE/ΜΓ 118 [JAS][103]

9th Century

**BAV Vatican Gr. 2282* [JAS][104]

9th–10th Century

Sinai Geo. O. 53 [JAS][105]

10th Century

Sinai Geo. N. 26 (AD 965–973) [JAS][106]
Graz Universitätsbibliothek 2058/4 (AD 985) [JAS][107]
Grottaferrata Γβ IV[108]
Grottaferrata Γβ VII[109]
The Latin translation of Byzantine BAS of Johannisberg[110]
Pyromalus Codex [Byzantine BAS][111]

100 Simaika and ʿAbd al-Masiḥ, *Catalogue of the Coptic and Arabic Manuscripts*, 2:460; Samuel, *Tartīb al- bīʿa*, 1:[i–ii].

101 Simaika and ʿAbd al-Masiḥ, *Catalogue of the Coptic and Arabic Manuscripts*, 1:115.

102 Parenti and Velkovska, *L'Eucologio Barberini gr. 336.* 19–34; Jacob, "Histoire du formulaire," 63–119.

103 Kazamias, *Η Θεία Λειτουργία του Αγίου Ιακώβου*, 58–59.

104 Mercier, *La Liturgie de Saint Jacques*, 20.

105 Khevsuriani et al., *Liturgia Ibero-Graeca Sancti Iacobi*, 20–21.

106 Ibid, 19; Taft and Parenti, *Il Grande Ingresso*, 729n381.

107 Khevsuriani et al., *Liturgia Ibero-Graeca Sancti Iacobi*, 22–23.

108 Jacob, "Histoire du formulaire," 170–183; Taft and Parenti, *Il Grande Ingresso*, 704n20.

109 Jacob, "Histoire du formulaire," 120–136; Passarelli, *L'Eucologio Cryptense Γ.β. VII*, 21–34; Taft and Parenti, *Il Grande Ingresso*, 704n22.

110 Taft and Parenti, *Il Grande Ingresso*, 63–64.

111 Goar, *ΕΥΧΟΛΟΓΙΟΝ*, 153-156; Taft and Parenti, *Il Grande Ingresso*, 703.

Sinai Geo. N. 63 [JAS][112]
St. Petersburg NLR 226[113]

11th Century

Messina Gr. 160[114]
Messina Gr. 177 [JAS, Melkite MARK][115]
Sinai Glagol. 37[116]
Sinai Gr. NE/E 24 [JAS][117]

11th–12th Century

Sinai Gr. NE/E 80 [JAS][118]

12th Century

Sinai Gr. 1040 (AD 1156–1169) [Diaconicon][119]
The Latin version of Leo Tuscanus (AD 1173–1174)[120]
**BAV Vatican Gr. 2005* (AD 1194–1195)[121]
**BAV Vatican Gr. 1970* [Melkite MARK][122]
Grottaferrata Γβ VIII[123]

13th Century

**BAV Vatican Gr. 2281* (AD 1207) [Melkite MARK][124]
Ambrosiana Gr. 276 [PRES][125]

112 Khevsuriani et al., *Liturgia Ibero-Graeca Sancti Iacobi*, 22.
113 Jacob, "Histoire du formulaire," 137–169; Jacob, "L'euchologe de Porphyre Uspenski," 174–176; Taft and Parenti, *Il Grande Ingresso*, 704n19.
114 Jacob, "Histoire du formulaire," 184–191; Taft and Parenti, *Il Grande Ingresso*, 705n42.
115 Cuming, *The Liturgy of St Mark*, xxix–xxx; Taft and Parenti, *Il Grande Ingresso*, 704n29.
116 Frček, *Euchologium Sinaiticum*; Parenti, "Influssi italo-greci," 150–152; Taft and Parenti, *Il Grande Ingresso*, 724n315.
117 Kazamias, *Η Θεία Λειτουργία του Αγίου Ιακώβου*, 47–50.
118 Ibid., 60.
119 Ibid., 54–56; Taft and Parenti, *Il Grande Ingresso*, 708n73.
120 Taft and Parenti, *Il Grande Ingresso*, 724.
121 Ibid., 709n89.
122 Cuming, *The Liturgy of St Mark*, xxx; Taft and Parenti, *Il Grande Ingresso*, 707, 60.
123 Jacob, "Histoire du formulaire," 524–525; Taft and Parenti, *Il Grande Ingresso*, 707, 69.
124 Cuming, *The Liturgy of St Mark*, xxx.
125 Alexopoulos, *The Presanctified Liturgy*, 337; Taft and Parenti, *Il Grande Ingresso*, 711n130, identified as *Ambrosiana E 20 sup.*

Arabic CHR manuscript edited by Bacha (AD 1260)[126]
Grottaferrata Γβ XIII[127]
**Sinai Ar. 237* [MARK and MARK PRES][128]

15th Century

Munich Bayerische Staatsbibliothek Gr. 540 (AD 1416) [PRES][129]

16th Century

Strasbourg Gr. 1899 (AD 1523)[130]
**BAV Ottoboni Gr. 384* (AD 1581) [PETER][131]
BAV Vatican Borghes. Ser. I 506 (AD 1581) [PETER][132]
Greek Orthodox Patriarchate of Alexandria 173/36, Pegas Manuscript (AD 1586) [Melkite MARK][133]
**BAV Ottoboni Gr. 189* [PETER][134]
BAV Vatican Gr. 2012[135]
Modena Gr. 16[136]
Paris BnF Gr. 322 [PETER][137]

19th Century

BAV Borgia Gr. 24 (AD 1880) [JAS][138]

126 Bacha, "Notions génerales sur les versions arabes"; Jacob, "Histoire du formulaire," 297–301.
127 Jacob, "Histoire du formulaire," 535–536; Taft and Parenti, *Il Grande Ingresso*, 711n125.
128 Atiya, *Al-fahāris al-taḥlīliyya*, 446–451.
129 Parenti, ""Influssi italo-greci," 165; Taft and Parenti, *Il Grande Ingresso*, 716n188.
130 Parenti, ""Influssi italo-greci," 164.
131 Codrington, *The Liturgy of Saint Peter*, 163–164.
132 Ibid., 137.
133 Cuming, *The Liturgy of St Mark*, xxxi.
134 Codrington, *The Liturgy of Saint Peter*, 13.
135 Jacob, "Histoire du formulaire," 576; Taft and Parenti, *Il Grande Ingresso*, 718n222.
136 Parenti, ""Influssi italo-greci," 163.
137 Ibid., 12–13.
138 Mercier, *La Liturgie de Saint Jacques*, 21–22. This manuscript is a copy of the earlier *Messina Gr. 177* (11th c.). See Taft and Parenti, *Il Grande Ingresso*, 704n29.

3. ETHIOPIAN MANUSCRIPTS

17th Century

British Library Or. 545 (AD 1670–1675)[139]
Uppsala Or. Ethiop. 20–23[140]

18th Century

British Library Or. 546 (AD 1730–1737)[141]
British Library Or. 547 (AD 1784–1800)[142]

19th Century

British Library Or. 548 (AD 1855–1868)[143]

4. SYRIAC MANUSCRIPTS

8th–9th Century

Codex Syr. 303 of Bibliotheca Rahmani[144]

139 William Wright, *Catalogue of the Ethiopic Manuscripts in the British Museum Acquired Since the Year 1847* (London, 1877), 88
140 Fritsch, "The Preparation of the Gifts," 123n51.
141 Ibid., 90
142 Ibid., 90–91
143 Ibid., 91
144 Taft and Parenti, *Il Grande Ingresso*, 138–140.

APPENDIX 3

PLANS AND FIGURES

The church plans provided here are a few examples of the architectural feature of pastophoria, which was otherwise ubiquitous in the architectural landscape of Egyptian churches in the early medieval period. This architectural feature, discussed at length in Chapter 1, represented a major aspect in analyzing the preparation and transfer of the eucharistic gifts in the Coptic tradition. Notable in all the following plans is the existence of such lateral apsidal rooms called pastophoria and their respective entryways to the nave, the apse, or both, in each example.

1. Church of the Virgin in the Baramūs Monastery

The plan of the church is based on Grossmann, *Christliche Architektur in Ägypten*, fig. 118. The original church, notably without internal passageways between pastophoria and apse, was built in the early years of the seventh century. A detailed description of the church can be found in ibid., 499–501. For a plan of the original church, see Peter Grossmann, "Dayr al-Baramūs, Architecture," *CE*, 3:791b–793a; Peter Grossmann, "On the Architecture at Wādī al-Naṭrūn," in *Christianity and Monasticism in Wadi al-Natrun: Essays from the 2002 International Symposium of the Saint Mark Foundation and the Saint Shenouda the Archimandrite Coptic Society*, ed. Maged S.A. Mikhail and Mark Moussa (Cairo: The American University in Cairo Press, 2009), 159–184, here 170, 182. A brief history and plans of the monastery and the church can also be found in Gawdat Gabra, *Coptic Monasteries: Egypt's Monastic Art and Architecture* (Cairo: The American University in Cairo Press, 2002), 23–28.

The plan given here corresponds to the original church before the addition of a choir screen and the opening of passageways between the pastophoria and the apse.

2. The Single-Aisle Church in the Temple in Taposiris Magna

This small late fourth/early-fifth century church was built on the grounds of a Roman military camp in the city of Taposiris Magna on Lake Maryūṭ near Alexandria. The plan is based on Grossmann, *Christliche Architektur in Ägypten,* fig. 3 and the description on pages 381–383. Further information on the city and the excavations at Taposiris Magna can be consulted in Peter Grossmann, "Abuṣir," *CE,* 1:34b–36b and in Grossmann, "Abusir," in *The Eerdmans Encyclopedia of Early Christian Art and Archaeology,* 1:7. A more detailed discussion of the site, its history, and excavation, is available in Győző Vörös, *Taposiris Magna: Port of Isis, Hungarian Excavations at Alexandria (1998–2001)* (Budapest: Egypt Excavation Society of Hungary, 2001), 30–83, with numerous plans throughout distinguishing two relative phases of construction. See also Győző Vörös, *Taposiris Magna: 1998–2004* (Budapest, Egypt Excavation Society of Hungary, 2004), 142–145.

It is important to note with regards to this church that the exact place of the altar remains unknown. The northeastern pastophorion housed a water basin, which may have been used for the ritual hand washing. As the plan shows, pastophoria are accessible through narrow passageways directly from the nave. No route seems have led directly into the apse.

3. Pastophoria Entryways in Ethiopia

Ethiopian churches provide a more complete record of the evolution of pastophoria entryways over time. All four plans in this figure are based on Fritsch, "The Preparation of the Gifts," 115. See also the discussion and plans in Fritsch and Gervers, "Pastophoria and Altars," 12–14. For a more detailed plan of the ancient church in Adulis, the main port of Aksum, see Marilyn E. Heldman, "Church Buildings," *EAE,* 1:737. This ancient church featured lateral pastophoria on each side of the apse opening only towards the nave. A medieval church in Gāzēn (East Təgray) named after John the Baptist (Yoḥannes Maṭmeq) begins to depart from this ancient design with additional narrow passageways between pastophoria and apse. See Wolbert Smidt, "Təgray," *EAE,* 4:888–895, here 892. On the other hand, the northern church in Dəgum on the plain of Ḥawzen reverses this disposition with wide passageways between pastophoria and apse, while the former are entirely closed off to the nave. For this, see Ewa Balicka Witakowska, "Dəgum," *EAE,* 2:126–127. Finally, the church of Giyorgis Zāramā, located in the mountain fortress of Ǝmäkina in Lasta represents the final stage of this development, with pastophoria opening to both apse and nave. For the latter, see Ewa Balicka-Witakowska, "Ǝmäkina Churches," *EAE*, 2:269–270.

4. Church number D (CHD87) in Narmuthis (Madīnat Māḍī)

This church is among a number of excavated remains in the ancient site of Narmuthis on the southwest edge of the Fayyūm. It is characteristic for its five-aisle nave and for its unevenly sized pastophoria flanking the apse. As the plan shows, these pastophoria were only accessible from the nave. The plan is based on Grossmann, *Christliche Architektur in Ägypten*, fig. 42 and the description on pages 421–422. More information on the abandoned site of Narmuthis, known in Arabic as Madīnat Māḍī can be found in Edda Bresciani and Peter Grossmann, "Madīnat Māḍī," *CE*, 5:1497b–1499a.

5. The Underground Church in the Monastery of Abū Fānā

The ruins of the Monastery of Abū Fānā are located in Southern Egypt, northwest of Ašmūnayn in modern-day Al-Minyā, where presumably a saint by the name of Abba Bane in the fourth century and mentioned in the *Apophthegmata Patrum*. Among the churches in this monastery is small underground chapel with a single aisle, going back to the late fourth century and thus considered one of the oldest monastic churches in Egypt. The plan given here is based on the first phase of the building as given in Grossmann, *Christliche Architektur in Ägypten*, fig. 134 and the description on page 516. Based on this reconstruction, the sanctuary area consisted of a central apse surrounded by sharply divided pastophoria to the north and south. For more information on the monastery, see Peter Grossmann, "Dayr Abū Fānah, Architecture," *CE* 3:699a–700b.

6. The Prepared Coptic Altar

The image of the altar shows a closeup of the Coptic altar after its preparation for the prothesis rite and the eucharistic liturgy. From east to west, one can see the prominent wooden chalice throne with icons of Christ and the saints around its perimeter. The chalice throne houses the chalice, which is not visible in the photograph. As explained in Chapter 3, the chalice is covered with two eucharistic cloths, one with a circular opening the equal to the diameter of the chalice and an additional one on top entirely covering the chalice. To the west of that and directly in front of the priest lies the paten. In the photograph, it is also covered with two cloths, each folded into triangles. The paten rests on top of a red cloth. In addition, five other cloths can be seen in the image, two white ones on either side of the red cloth and three more placed at right angles at the edge of the altar and pointing downwards.

The photograph was taken on 16 January 2016 at Holy Virgin Mary and Saint Pishoy Coptic Orthodox Church in Los Angeles, California through the kind permission of Fr. James Efrayem Soliman.

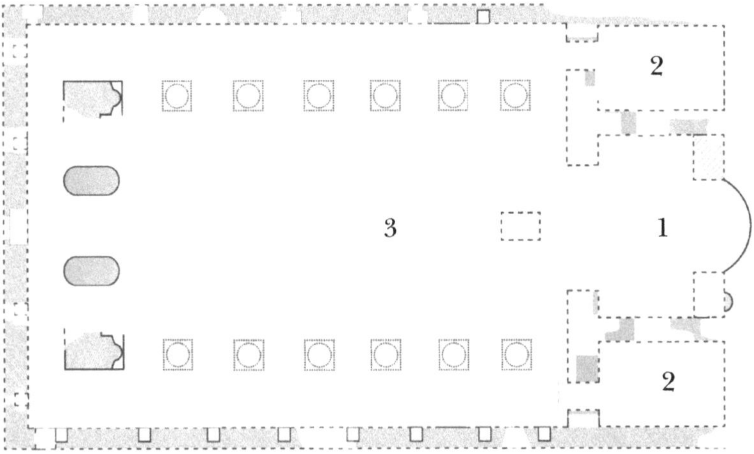

Church of the Virgin in the Baramūs Monastery

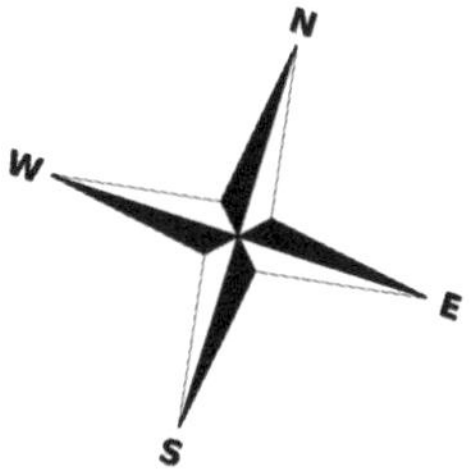

1. Apse
2. Pastophoria
3. Nave

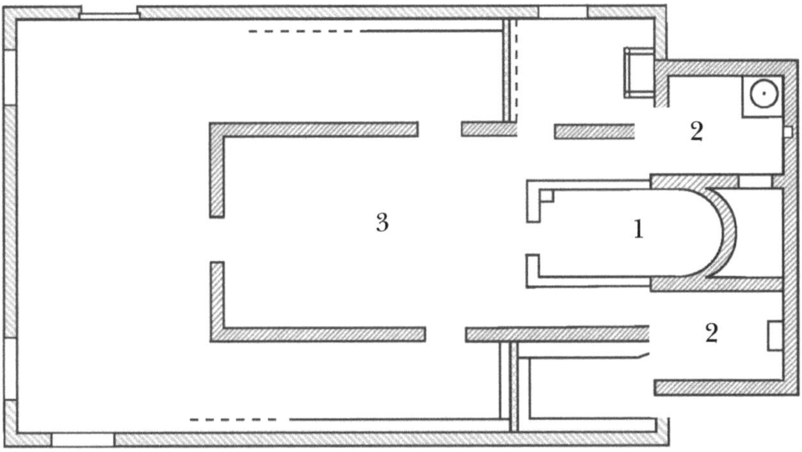

The Single-Aisle Church in the Temple
in Taposiris Magna

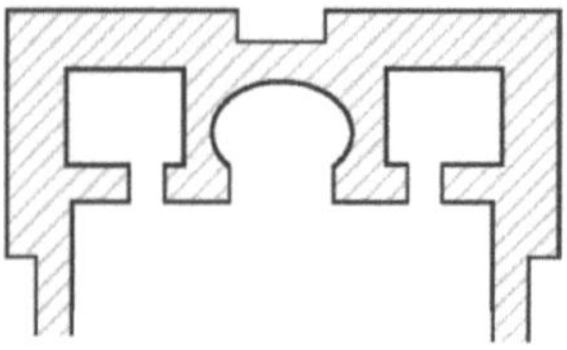

Adulis,
Aksum

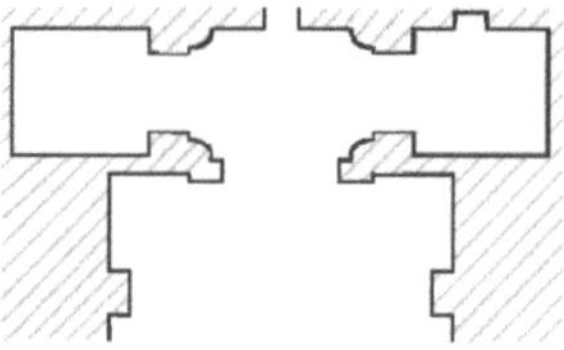

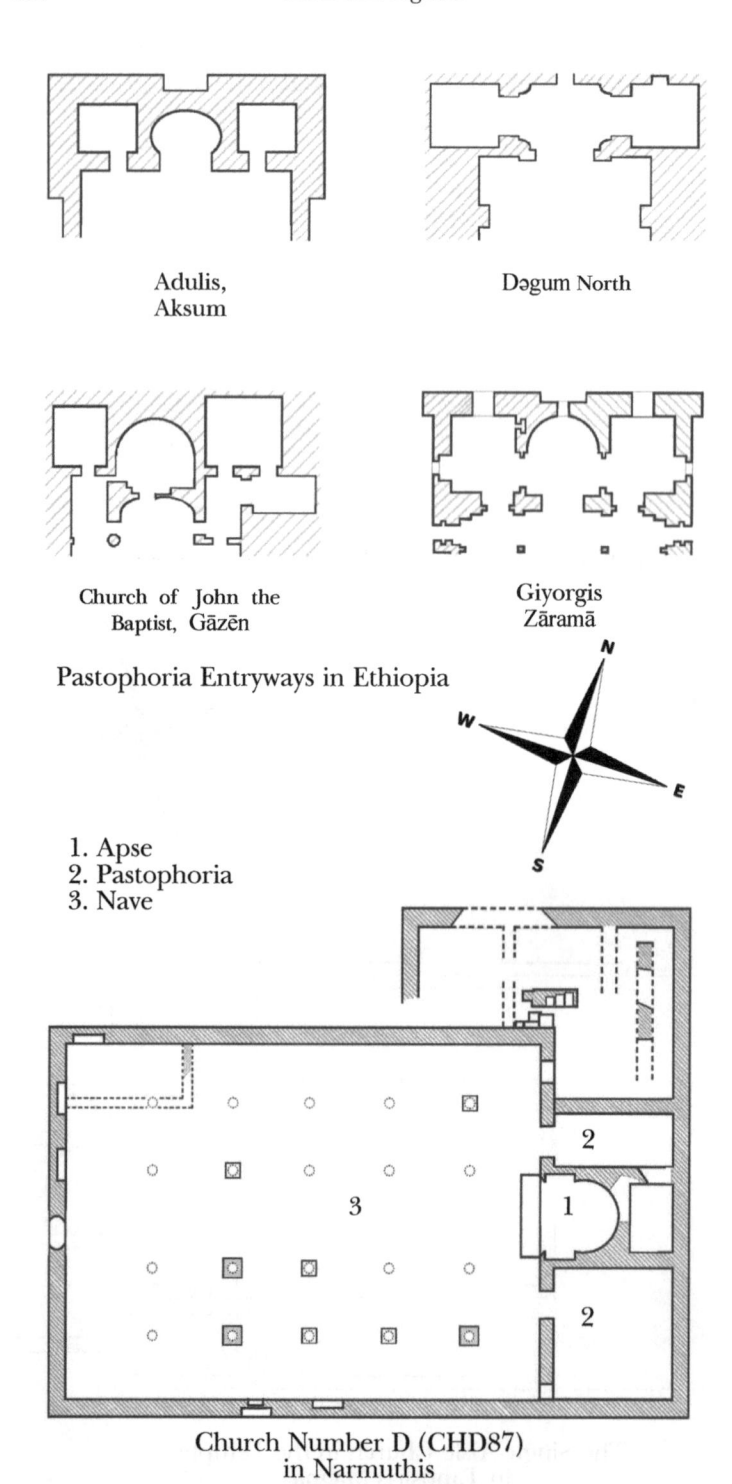

Dəgum North

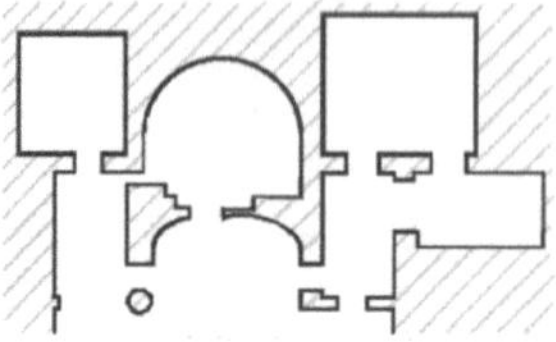

Church of John the
Baptist, Gāzēn

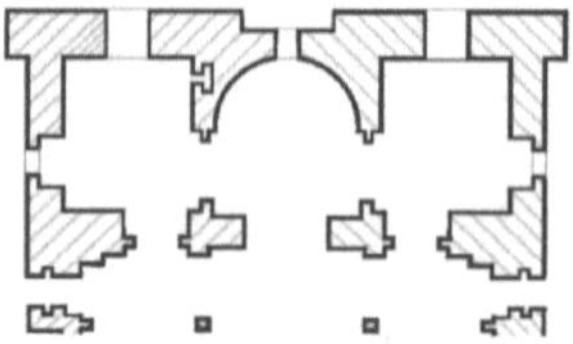

Giyorgis
Zāramā

Pastophoria Entryways in Ethiopia

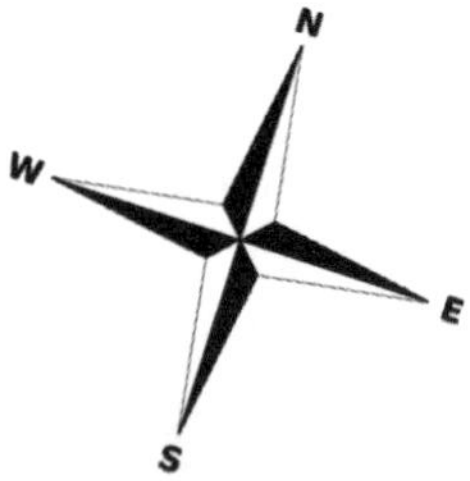

1. Apse
2. Pastophoria
3. Nave

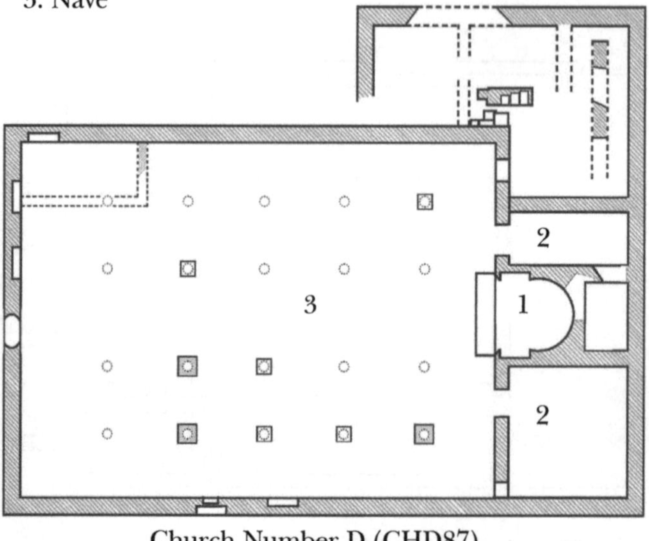

Church Number D (CHD87)
in Narmuthis

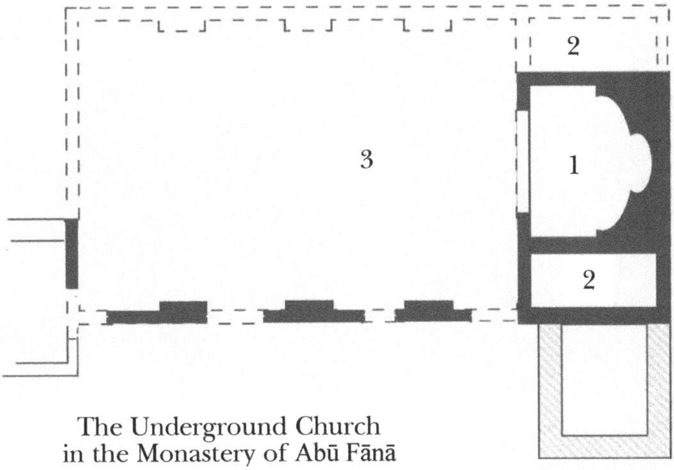

The Underground Church
in the Monastery of Abū Fānā

1. Apse
2. Pastophoria
3. Nave

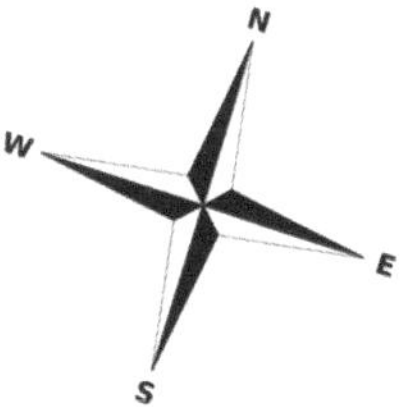

The Prepared Coptic Altar

BIBLIOGRAPHY

'Abdallah, Alfonso. *L'ordinamento liturgico di Gabriele V, 88° Patriarca Copto (1409-1427).* SOC, Aegyptiaca. Cairo: Edizioni del Centro Francescano di Studi Orientali Cristiani, 1962.

'Abdallah, Alfonso. "Un trattato inedito sulla SS. Eucaristia (Ms. Vat. Ar. 123, 1396 A.D.) Testo originale e traduzione." *SOC. Aegyptiaca Collectanea* 12 (1967): 345-464.

'Abd el-Nour, Samiha abd el-Shaheed. "Supplement to the Catalogue of the Manuscripts in the Coptic Museum: Section IV—Liturgica (Part 1)." *BSAC* 39 (2000): 181-200.

'Abd el-Nour, Samiha abd el-Shaheed. "Supplement to the Catalogue of the Manuscripts in the Coptic Museum: Section 4—Liturgical (Part 4)." *BSAC* 44 (2005): 69-80.

Adams, William Y. *Nubia: Corridor to Africa.* Princeton, NJ: Princeton University Press, 1977.

Adams, William Y. "Nubian Church Organization." *CE,* 6:1813a-1814a.

'Ādil, Rafīq. "Al-iṭār al-'ām li-šakl wa-tartīb ṭaqs al-baṣḫa al-muqaddassa fī l-qarn al-rābi' 'ašar [The general framework for the structure and order of the rite of the Holy Pascha in the 14th century]." *Madrasat al-iskandariyya* 13 (2013): 179-207.

'Ādil, Rafīq. "Al-kutub al-lītūrǧiyya bayn al-maḫṭūṭ wa-l-maṭbū'. Taṭawurihā wa-marāḥil taqnīnuhā [Liturgical books between the manuscript and the printed, their evolution and stages of standardization]." *Madrasat al-iskandariyya* 16 (2014): 191-224.

'Ādil, Rafīq. "Ṭaqs al-baṣḫa al-muqaddassa fī l-kanīsa al-qibṭiyya: Simātuhu al-aṣliyya wa-taṭawuruhu 'abr al-'uṣūr [The rite of Holy Pascha in the Coptic Church: Its original characteristics and its evolution throughout the ages]." *Madrasat al-iskandariyya* 6 (2010): 189-215.

'Ādil, Rafīq. "Tartīb wa-šarḥ al-quddās al-ilāhī 'ind al-ābā' al-aqbāṭ [The order and explanation of the divine liturgy among the Coptic fathers]." *Madrasat al-iskandariyya* 18 (2015): 219-241.

Alexopoulos, Stefanos. "The Influence of Iconoclasm on Liturgy: A Case Study." In *Worship Traditions in Armenia and the Neighboring Christian East: An International Symposium in Honor of the 40th Anniversary of St Nerses Armenian Seminary,* edited by Roberta R. Ervine, 127–137. AVANT Series 3. Crestwood, NY: St Vladimir's Seminary Press, 2006.

Alexopoulos, Stefanos. "Modern Greek Liturgical Scholarship: A Selective Bibliography (2000–2009)." In *ΤΟΞΟΤΗΣ: Studies for Stefano Parenti*, edited by Daniel Galadza, Nina Glibetic, and Gabriel Radle, 19–47. Ἀνάλεκτα Κρυπτοφέῤῥης 9. Grottaferrata: Monastero Esarchico, 2010.

Alexopoulos, Stefanos. *The Presanctified Liturgy in the Byzantine Rite: A Comparative Analysis of its Origins, Evolution, and Structural Components.* Liturgia Condenda 21. Leuven: Peeters, 2009.

Alikin, Valeriy A. *The Earliest History of the Christian Gathering: Origin, Development and Content of the Christian Gathering in the First to Third Centuries.* Supplements to Vigiliae Christianae 102. Leiden: Brill, 2010.

Amélineau, Émile, ed. *Oeuvres de Schenoudi: Texte copte et traduction française.* 2 volumes. Paris: Ernest Leroux, 1907–1914.

Arras, Victor, ed. *Quadraginta historiae monachorum.* CSCO 505, Scriptores Aethiopici 85. Leuven: Peeters, 1988.

Assfalg, Julius. *Die Ordnung des Priestertums: Ein altes liturgisches Handbuch der koptischen Kirche.* Publications du Centre d'etudes orientales de la Custodie Franciscaine de Terre-Sainte, Coptica 1. Cairo: [Centre d'etudes orientales de la Custodie Franciscaine de Terre-Sainte], 1955.

Atanassova, Diliana. "The Primary Sources of Southern Egyptian Liturgy: Retrospect and Prospect." In *Rites and Rituals of the Christian East: Proceedings of the Fourth International Congress of the Society of Oriental Liturgy, Lebanon, 10–15 July 2012,* edited by Bert Groen et al, 47–96. Eastern Christian Studies 22. Leuven: Peeters, 2014.

Atiya, Aziz S. "Alexandria, Historic Churches in." *CE,* 1:92b–95b.

Atiya, Aziz S. *Al-fahāris al-taḥlīliyya li-maḫṭūṭāt ṭūr sīnā al-'arabīyya* [The analytical indices of the Arabic manuscripts of Mount Sinai]. Alexandria, 1970.

'Awaḍ, Ǧirǧis Fīlūṯā'us. *Kitāb sirr al-ṯālūṯ fī ḫidmat al-kahanūt: Ta'līf aḥad 'ulamā' al-kanīsa al-qibṭiyya fī l-qurūn al-wūsṭā* [The book of the mystery of the Trinity in the service of the priesthood, composed by one of the scholars of the Coptic Church in the middle ages]. Cairo: Al-maṭba'a al-miṣriyya al-ahliyya al-ḥadīṯa, 1942.

Awaḍ, Wadī'. "Al-Shams ibn Kabar." *CMR,* 4:762–766.

Awad, Wadi. "Testo della Traduzione Araba della Messa Copta di San Basilio Secondo un Manoscritto del 1288." *SOC Collectanea* 41 (2008): 129–149.

Awad, Wadi and Enzo Lucchesi. "Les deux lettres dogmatiques du pape copte Matthieu IV." In *From Old Cairo to the New World: Coptic Studies Presented to Gawdat Gabra on the Occasion of his Sixty-Fifth Birthday*, edited by Youhanna Nessim Youssef and Samuel Moawad, 185–201. Colloquia Antiqua 9. Leuven: Peeters, 2013.

Bacha, Constantin. "*Notions générales sur les versions arabes de la liturgie de S. Jean Chrysostome suivies d'une ancienne version inédite.*" In *ΧΡΥΣΟΣΤΟΜΙΚΑ*: *Studi e ricerche intorno a S. Giovanni Crisostomo a cura del comitato per il XV° centenario della sua morte*, 405–471. Rome: Libreria Pustet, 1908.

Bagnall, Roger S. *Egypt in Late Antiquity.* Princeton, NJ: Princeton University Press, 1993.

Balicka-Witakowska, Ewa. "Dəgum." *EAE*, 2:126–127.

Balicka-Witakowska, Ewa. "Ǝmäkina Churches." *EAE*, 2:269–270.

Balicka-Witakowska, Ewa. "Mika'el 'Amba." *EAE*, 3:959–961.

al-Baramūsī, Mīṣā'īl. "Ḫūlāǧī al-qummuṣ 'Abd al-Masīḥ Ṣālīb al-Baramūsī al-Mas'ūdī al-maṭbū' sanat 1902 [The Euchologion of Hegumen 'Abd al-Masīḥ Ṣālīb al-Baramūsī al-Mas'ūdī printed in 1902]." *Madrasat al-iskandariyya* 22 (2017): 165–196.

Barnāmaǧ ḥaflat risāmat ġibṭat al-ḥabr al-ǧalīl al-anbā Kīrillus al-sādis bābā al-iskandariyya wa-baṭrīyark al-kirāza al-marqusiyya [The program of the ordination ceremony of His Beatitude the honored prelate Anba Kīrillus VI, Pope of Alexandria and Patriarch of the see of Mark]. Al-Faǧǧāla: Maṭba'at Samīr, 1959.

Basset, René. *Le Synaxaire arabe jacobite (I. Mois de Tout et de Babeh).* PO 1.3 (3). Turnhout: Brepols, 1980.

Basset, René. *Le Synaxaire arabe jacobite (II. Mois de Hatour et de Kihak).* PO 3.3 (13). Turnhout: Brepols, 1982.

Basset, René. *Le Synaxaire arabe jacobite (rédaction copte) (IV. Les mois de Barmahat, Barmoudah et Bachons).* PO 16.2 (78). Turnhout: Brepols, 1976.

Baumeister, Theofried. "Martyrology." *CE*, 5:1549b–1550b.

Baumstark, Anton. *Comparative Liturgy.* Translated by F. L. Cross. Westminster, MD: A.R. Mowbray, 1958.

Baumstark, Anton. *On the Historical Development of the Liturgy.* Translated by Fritz West. Collegeville, MN: Liturgical Press, 2011.

Baumstark, Anton. *Vom geschichtlichen Werden der Liturgie.* Ecclesia Orans 10. Freiburg im Breisgau: Herder, 1923.

Bausi, Alessandro. "Monastic Literature." *EAE*, 3:993–999.

Bausi, Alessandro, et al., eds. *Comparative Oriental Manuscript Studies: An Introduction.* Hamburg: COMSt, 2015.

Bausi, Alessandro and Gianfranco Fiaccadori. "Täsfa Ṣəyon." *EAE*, 5:525–528.

Bénazeth, Dominique. "De l'autel au musée. Quelques objets liturgiques conserves au Musée Copte du Caire." In *Egypt 1350 BC–AD 1800: Art Historical and Archeological Studies for Gawdat Gabra*, edited by Marianne Eaton-Krauss, Cäcilia Fluck, and Gertrud J.M. van Loon, 35–52. Sprachen und Kulturen des Christlichen Orients 20. Wiesbaden: Ludwig Reichert Verlag, 2011.

Beylot, Robert. "Sermon éthiopien anonyme sur l'eucharistie." *Abbay* 12 (1983): 79–116.

Blass, F. and A. Debrunner. *A Greek Grammar of the New Testament and Other Early Christian Literature*. Translated by Robert W. Funk. Cambridge: Cambridge University Press, 1961.

Boderie, Guy Lefèvre de la. *D. Severi Alexandrini quondam patriarchae de ritibus baptismi, et sacrae synaxis apud Syros christianos receptis*. Antwerp, 1572.

Bolman, Elizabeth S. "The Iconography of the Eucharist? Early Byzantine Painting, the *Prothesis*, and the Red Monastery." In *ΑΝΑΘΗΜΑΤΑ ΕΟΡΤΙΚΑ: Studies in Honor of Thomas F. Mathews*, edited by Joseph D. Alchermes, Helen C. Evans, and Thelma K. Thomas, 57–66. Mainz: Philipp von Zabern, 2009.

Bolman, Elizabeth S. "Preparation of the Eucharist: Paintings in the Side Chambers." In *The Red Monastery Church: Beauty and Asceticism in Upper Egypt*, edited by Elizabeth S. Bolman, 183–189. New Haven, CT: Yale University Press, 2016.

Bolman, Elizabeth S. "The Red Monastery Conservation Project, 2006 and 2007 Campaigns: Contributing to the Corpus of Late Antique Art." In *Christianity and Monasticism in Upper Egypt*, edited by Gawdat Gabra and Hany N. Takla, 305–318. Volume 1, *Akhmim and Sohag*. Cairo: The American University in Cairo Press, 2008.

Bornert, René. *Les commentaires byzantins de la Divine Liturgie du VIIe au XVe siècle*. Archives de l'Orient Chrétien 9. Paris: Institut français d'études byzantines, 1966.

Bouley, Allan. *From Freedom to Formula: The Evolution of the Eucharistic Prayer from Oral Improvisation to Written Texts*. Studies in Christian Antiquity 21. Washington DC: Catholic University of America Press, 1981.

Boulluec, Alain le. *Clément d'Alexandrie: Les Stromates VII*. SC 428. Paris: Cerf, 1997.

Bradshaw, Paul F. "Cathedral and Monastic: What's in a Name?" *Worship* 77 (2003): 341–353.

Bradshaw, Paul F. *Daily Prayer in the Early Church: A Study of the Origin and Early Development of the Divine Office*. Eugene, OR: Wipf & Stock, 1981.

Bradshaw, Paul F. *Eucharistic Origins.* Alcuin Club Collections 80. Eugene, OR: Wipf & Stock, 2012.
Bradshaw, Paul F. "Jewish Influence on Early Christian Liturgy: A Reappraisal." In *Liturgies in East and West: Ecumenical Relevance of Early Liturgical Development. Acts of the International Symposium Vindobonense I, Vienna, November 17–20, 2007,* edited by Hans-Jürgen Feulner, 47–59. Österreichische Studien zur Liturgiewissenschaft und Sakramententheologie 6. Vienna: Lit Verlag, 2013.
Bradshaw, Paul. F. *The Search for the Origins of Christian Worship: Sources and Methods for the Study of Early Liturgy.* 2nd edition. Oxford: Oxford University Press, 2002.
Bradshaw, Paul F., Maxwell E. Johnson, and L. Edward Phillips. *The Apostolic Tradition: A Commentary.* Edited by Harold W. Attridge. Hermeneia–A Critical and Historical Commentary on the Bible. Minneapolis, MN: Fortress Press, 2002.
Brakke, David and Andrew Crislip. *Selected Discourses of Shenoute the Great: Community, Theology, and Social Conflict in Late Antique Egypt.* Cambridge: Cambridge University Press, 2015.
Brakmann, Heinzgerd. "Das alexandrinische Eucharistiegebet auf Wiener Papyrusfragmenten." *Jahrbuch für Antike und Christentum* 39 (1996): 149–164.
Brakmann, Heinzgerd. "Defunctus adhuc loquitur: Gottesdienst und Gebetsliteratur der untergegangenen Kirche in Nubien." *Archiv für Liturgiewissenschaft* 48 (2006): 283–333.
Brakmann, Heinzgerd. "Le déroulement de la Messe copte: Structure et histoire." In *L'Eucharistie: Célébrations, rites, piétés: Conférences Saint-Serge, XLIe semaine d'études liturgiques, Paris, 28 Juin–1 Juillet 1994,* edited by Achille M. Triacca and Alessandro Pistoia, 107–132. BEL.S 79. Rome: Edizioni Liturgiche, 1995.
Brakmann, Heinzgerd. "Le forme cultuali dell'antica Chiesa di Alessandria e la successive tradizione rituale della Chiesa copta." In *Popoli, Religioni e Chiese lungo il corso del Nilo: Dal Faraone Cristiano al Leone di Giuda,* edited by Cesare Alzati and Luciano Vaccaro, 247–264. Storia Religiosa Euro-Mediterranea 4. Vatican City: Liberia Editrice Vaticana, 2015.
Brakmann, Heinzgerd. "Hagiographie im Dienst hierarchischer Ambitionen. Eine ägyptische Wundererzählung im Umfeld der Vita *BHO* 1062 des Severos von Antiochien." In *Ægyptus Christiana: Mélanges d'hagiographie égyptienne et orientale dédiés à la mémoire du P. Paul Devos, Bollandiste,* edited by Ugo Zanetti and Enzo Lucchesi, 279–286. Cahiers d'orientalisme 25. Geneva: Patrick Cramer, 2004.

Brakmann, Heinzgerd. "La 'Mystagogie' de la liturgie alexandrine et copte." In *Mystagogie: pensée liturgique d'aujourd'hui et liturgie ancienne, Conférences Saint-Serge, 39e semaine d'Études liturgiques, Paris, 30 juin–3 juillet 1992*, edited by Achille M. Triacca and Alessandro Pistoia, 55–65. BEL.S 70. Rome: Edizioni Liturgiche, 1992.

Brakmann, Heinzgerd. "Neue Funde und Forschungen zur Liturgie der Kopten (1988–1992)." In *Acts of the Fifth International Congress of Coptic Studies, Washington, 12–15 August 1992*, edited by Tito Orlandi, 9–32. Volume 1, *Reports on Recent Research.* Rome: CIM, 1993.

Brakmann, Heinzgerd. "Neue Funde und Forschungen zur Liturgie der Kopten (1992–1996)." In *Ägypten und Nubien in spätantiker und christlicher Zeit: Akten des 6. Internationalen Koptologenkongresses Münster, 20.–26. Juli 1996*, edited by Stephen Emmel, et al, 451–464. Volume 1, *Materielle Kultur, Kunst und religiöses Leben.* Sprachen und Kulturen des Christlichen Orients 6.1. Wiesbaden: Ludwig Reichert Verlag, 1999.

Brakmann, Heinzgerd. "Neue Funde und Forschungen zur Liturgie der Kopten, (1996–2000)." In *Coptic Studies on the Threshold of a New Millennium II: Proceedings of the Seventh International Congress of Coptic Studies, Leiden, 27 August–2 September 2000*, edited by Mat Immerzeel and Jacques van der Vliet, 575–606. Orientalia Lovaniensia Analecta 133. Leuven: Peeters, 2004.

Brakmann, Heinzgerd. "Neue Funde und Forschungen zur Liturgie der Kopten (2000–2004)." In *Huitième congrès international d'études coptes (Paris 2004) I. Bilans et perspectives 2000–2004*, edited by Anne Boud'hors and Denyse Vaillancourt, 127–149. Cahiers de la Bibliothèque copte 15. Paris: De Boccard, 2006.

Brakmann, Heinzgerd. "New Discoveries and Studies in the Liturgy of the Copts (2004–2012)." In *Coptic Society, Literature and Religion from Late Antiquity to Modern Times: Proceedings of the Tenth International Congress of Coptic Studies, Rome, September 17th–22nd, 2012 and Plenary Reports of the Ninth International Congress of Coptic Studies, Cairo, September 15th–19th, 2008*, edited by Paola Buzi, Alberto Camplani and Federico Contardi, 457–481. Volume 1. Orientalia Lovaniensia Analecta 247. Leuven: Peeters, 2016.

Brakmann, Heinzgerd. "Zu den Fragmenten einer griechischen Basileios-Liturgie aus dem koptischen Makarios-Kloster." *OC* 66 (1982): 118–143.

Brakmann, Heinzgerd. "Zur Stellung des Parisinus graecus 325 in der Geschichte der alexandrinisch-ägyptischen Liturgie." *Studi sull'Oriente Cristiano* 3 (1999): 97–110.

Brakmann, Heinzgerd. "Zwischen Pharos und Wüste: Die Erforschung alexandrinisch-ägyptischer Liturgie durch und nach Anton Baumstark (1872–1948)." In *Acts of the International Congress: Comparative Liturgy Fifty Years after Anton Baumstark (1872–1948), Rome, 25–29 September 1998*, edited by Robert F. Taft and Gabriele Winkler, 323–376. OCA 265. Rome: Pontificio Istituto Orientale, 2001.

Braun, Joseph. *Das christliche Altargerät in seinem Sein und in seiner Entwicklung*. Munich: M. Hueber, 1932.

Bresciani, Edda and Peter Grossmann. "Madīnat Māḍī." *CE*, 5:1497b–1499a.

Brooks, Ernest Walter, ed. *A Collection of Letters of Severus of Antioch from Numerous Syriac Manuscripts*. Volume 2. PO 14 (67). Turnhout: Brepols, 2003.

Brooks, Ernest Walter, ed. *The Sixth Book of the Select Letters of Severus Patriarch of Antioch in the Syriac Version of Athanasius of Nisibis*. 2 volumes. Oxford: Williams & Norgate, 1902–1903.

Budde, Achim. *Die ägyptische Basilios-Anaphora: Text, Kommentar, Geschichte*. JThF 7. Münster: Aschendorff, 2004.

Budde, Achim. "The Kacmarcik Codex as a Document of a Reformed Orthography in Greek Texts of the Coptic Church." *Journal of Coptic Studies* 7 (2005): 125–130.

Budde, Achim. "P. Naqlun 10/95 und seine Bedeutung für die Pflege des Griechischen in der Liturgie der koptischen Kirche." *OC* 86 (2002): 69–72.

Budge, E.A. Wallis. *The Book of Paradise Being the Histories and Sayings of the Monks and Ascetics of the Egyptian Desert by Palladius, Hieronymus and Others. The Syriac Text, According to the Recension of 'Anân-îshô' of Bêth 'Âbhê, Edited with an English Translation*. Volume 1, *English Translation*. Lady Meux Manuscript 6. London, 1904.

Budge, E.A. Wallis, ed. *Coptic Martyrdoms etc. in the Dialect of Upper Egypt*. Volume 1. Oxford, 1914.

Budge, E. A. Wallis, ed. *Miscellaneous Coptic Texts in the Dialect of Upper Egypt*. London: British Museum, 1915.

Burmester, O.H.E. "The Baptismal Rite of the Coptic Church (A Critical Study)." *BSAC* 11 (1945): 27–86.

Burmester, O.H.E. "The Canonical Hours of the Coptic Church." *OCP* 2, no. 1/2 (1936): 78–100.

Burmester, O.H.E. "The Canons of Christodulos, Patriarch of Alexandria (1047–1077)." *Le Muséon* 45 (1932): 71–84.

Burmester, O.H.E. "The Canons of Cyril II, LXVII Patriarch of Alexandria." *Le Muséon* 49 (1936): 245–288.

Burmester, O.H.E. "The Canons of Cyril III Ibn Laklak, 75th Patriarch of Alexandria." *BSAC* 14 (1950): 113–150.

Burmester, O.H.E. "The Canons of Cyril III Ibn Laqlaq, 75th Patriarch of Alexandria." *BSAC* 12 (1946–1947): 81–136.

Burmester, O.H.E. "The Canons of Gabriel Ibn Turaik LXX Patriarch of Alexandria." *Le Muséon* 36 (1933): 43–54.

Burmester, O.H.E. "The Canons of Gabriel Ibn Turaik, LXX Patriarch of Alexandria." *OCP* 1 (1935): 5–45.

Burmester, O.H.E. "The Coptic and Arabic Versions of the Mystagogia." *Le Muséon* 46 (1933): 203–235.

Burmester, O.H.E. "A Coptic Lectionary Poem (from MS. 408, Coptic Museum, Cairo)." *Le Muséon* 45 (1932): 21–70.

Burmester, O.H.E. "The Copts in Cyprus." *BSAC* 7 (1942): 9–13.

Burmester, O.H.E. *The Egyptian or Coptic Church: A Detailed Description of Her Liturgical Services and the Rites and Ceremonies Observed in the Administration of Her Sacraments.* Publications de la Société d'archéologie copte: Textes et documents. Cairo: [La Société d'archéologie copte], 1967.

Burmester, O.H.E. "Fragments of a Late 12th to Early 13th Century Bohairic Euchologion from the Monastery of St. Macarius in Scetis." *BSAC* 19 (1967–1968): 17–47.

Burmester, O.H.E. "The Greek Kīrugmata Versicles & Responses and Hymns in the Coptic Liturgy." *OCP* 2, no. 3/4 (1936): 363–394.

Burmester, O.H.E. *The Horologion of the Egyptian Church: Coptic and Arabic Text from a Mediaeval Manuscript.* SOC Aegyptiaca. Cairo: Edizioni del Centro Francescano di Studi Orientali Cristiani, 1973.

Burmester, O.H.E. *Koptische Handschriften 1: Die Handschriftenfragmente der Staats- und Universitätsbibliothek Hamburg.* Volume 1. Verzeichnis der orientalischen Handschriften in Deutschland 21.1. Wiesbaden: Franz Steiner Verlag, 1975.

Burmester, O.H.E. "The Liturgy *Coram Patriarcha aut Episcopo* in the Coptic Church." *Le Muséon* 49 (1936): 79–84.

Burmester, O.H.E. "An Offertory-Consecratory Prayer in the Greek and Coptic Liturgy of Saint Mark." *BSAC* 17 (1963–1964): 23–33.

Burmester, O.H.E. "The Office of Genuflection on Whitsunday." *Le Muséon* 47 (1934): 205–257.

Burmester, O.H.E. *Ordination Rites of the Coptic Church: Text According to MS. 253 Lit., Coptic Museum.* Cairo: [Société d'archéologie copte], 1985.

Burmester, O.H.E. *The Rite of Consecration of the Patriarch of Alexandria: Text According to MS. 253 Lit., Coptic Museum.* Cairo: Société d'archéologie copte, 1960.

Burmester, O.H.E. "Two Services of the Coptic Church Attributed to Peter, Bishop of Behnesā." *Le Muséon* 45 (1932): 235–254.

Burmester, O.H.E. "Vesting Prayers and Ceremonies of the Coptic Church." *OCP* 1 (1935): 305–314.

Bute, John Marquess of. *The Coptic Morning Service for the Lord's Day.* London, 1882.

Butler, Alfred J. *The Ancient Coptic Churches of Egypt.* 2 volumes. Oxford, 1884.

Butler, Cuthbert. *The Lausiac History of Palladius II: The Greek Text Edited with Introduction and Notes.* Texts and Studies Contributions to Biblical and Patristic Literature 6. Cambridge: Cambridge University Press, 1904.

Calivas, Alkiviadis C. *Essays in Theology and Liturgy.* Volume 3, *Aspects of Orthodox Worship.* Brookline, MA: Holy Cross Orthodox Press, 2003.

Camelot, Pierre Thomas. *Ignace d'Antioche, Polycarpe de Smyrne: Lettres, Martyre de Polycarpe.* SC 10bis. Paris: Cerf, 2007.

Camplani, Alberto. "A Pastoral Epistle of the Seventh Century Concerning the Eucharist (Pap. Berlin P. 11346)." In *Forschung in der Papyrussammlung. Eine Festgabe für das Neue Museum,* edited by Verena M. Lepper, 377–386. Ägyptische und orientalische Papyri und Handschriften des ägyptischen Museums und Papyrussammlung Berlin 1. Berlin: Akademie Verlag, 2012.

Camplani, Alberto and Federico Contardi. "The Canons Attributed to Basil of Caesarea: A New Coptic Codex." In *Coptic Society, Literature and Religion from Late Antiquity to Modern Times: Proceedings of the Tenth International Congress of Coptic Studies, Rome, September 17th–22nd, 2012 and Plenary Reports of the Ninth International Congress of Coptic Studies, Cairo, September 15th–19th, 2008,* edited by Paola Buzi, Alberto Camplani and Federico Contardi, 979–992. Volume 2. Orientalia Lovaniensia Analecta 247. Leuven: Peeters, 2016.

Chaîne, Marius. *Le manuscrit de la version copte en dialecte sahidique des "Apophthegmata Patrum".* Bibliothèque d'études coptes 6. Cairo: Institut français d'archéologie orientale, 1960.

Chéhab, Mamdouh. "Traduction de la version arabe de la messe copte de s. Basile. Vatican copte 17 (1288 AD)." *SOC Collectanea* 44 (2011): 49–68.

Chryssavgis, John. *Remembering and Reclaiming Diakonia: The Diaconate Yesterday and Today.* Brookline, MA: Holy Cross Orthodox Press, 2009.

Clédat, Jean. *Le monastère et la nécropole de Baouit.* Volume 2. Mémoires publiés par les members de l'Institut français d'archéologie orientale du Caire 39. Cairo: l'Institut français d'archéologie orientale, 1916.

Codrington, H.W. *The Liturgy of Saint Peter.* Liturgiegeschichtliche Quellen und Forschungen 30. Münster: Aschendorff, 1936.

Cody, Aelred. "L'eucharistie et les heures canoniales ches les Syriens jacobites. Une description des cérémonies." *L'Orient Syrien* 12 (1967): 55–81.

Colin, Gérard. *Le Synaxaire éthiopien: Mois de Ṭerr.* PO 45.1. Turnhout: Brepols, 1990.

Connolly, R. H. *Didascalia Apostolorum: The Syriac Version Translated and Accompanied by the Verona Latin Fragments.* Oxford: The Clarendon Press, 1929.

Connolly, R. H. *The Liturgical Homilies of Narsai: Translated into English with an Introduction.* Texts and Studies Contributions to Biblical and Patristic Literature 8.1. Cambridge: Cambridge University Press, 1909.

Connolly, R. H. and H. W. Codrington. *Two Commentaries on the Jacobite Liturgy by George Bishop of the Arab Tribes and Moses Bār Kēpha: Together with the Syriac Anaphora of St. James and a Document Entitled the Book of Life.* Oxford: Williams & Norgate, 1913.

Coquin, René-Georges. *Les canons d'Hippolyte: Édition critique de la version arabe, introduction et traduction française.* PO 31.2. Paris: Firmin-Didot, 1966.

Coquin, René-Georges. "Canons of Pseudo-Athanasius." *CE,* 2:458b–459a.

Coquin, René-Georges. "Les formes de participation du peuple dans le rit copte." *Proche Orient chrétien* 18 (1968): 122–139.

Coquin, René-Georges. "Vestiges de concélébration ches les Melkites, les Coptes et les Éthiopiens." *Le Muséon* 80 (1967): 37–46.

Coquin, René-Georges and Maurice Martin, "Dayr Nahya." *CE,* 2:843b–844a.

Cramer, Maria. "Studien zu koptischen Pascha-Büchern: Der Ritus der Karwoche in der koptischen Kirche." *OC* 47 (1963): 118–130.

Crum, W.E. *Catalogue of the Coptic Manuscripts in the British Museum.* London: British Museum, 1906.

Crum, W. E. *Catalogue of the Coptic Manuscripts in the Collection of the John Rylands Library Manchester.* Manchester: University Press, 1909.

Crum, W. E. *Coptic Ostraca from the Collections of the Egypt Exploration Fund, the Cairo Museum and Others.* London, 1902.

Cuming, Geoffrey J. *The Liturgy of St Mark: Edited from the Manuscripts with a Commentary.* OCA 234. Rome: Pontificium Institutum Studiorum Orientalium, 1990.

Cutrone, Emmanuel J. "Cyril's Mystagogical Catecheses and the Evolution of the Jerusalem Anaphora" *OCP* 45 (1978): 52–64.

Cutrone, Emmanuel J. "The Liturgical Setting of the Institution Narrative in the Early Syrian Tradition." In *Time and Community: In Honor of Thomas Julian Talley,* edited by J. Neil Alexander, 105–114. NPM Studies in Church Music and Liturgy. Washington DC: Pastoral Press, 1990.

Dā'ūd, Marqus. *Al-disqūliyya aw ta'ālīm al-rusul.* 5th edition. Cairo: Maktabat al-maḥabba, 1979.

Dā'ūd, Marqus. *The Liturgy of the Ethiopian Church.* Cairo: The Egyptian Book Press, 1959.

Davis, Stephen J. *Coptic Christology in Practice: Incarnation and Divine Participation in Late Antique and Medieval Egypt.* Oxford Early Christian Studies. Oxford: Oxford University Press, 2008.

Delaporte, Louis. "Catalogue sommaire des manuscrits coptes de la Bibliothèque Nationale." *Revue de l'Orient Chrétien* 16 (1911): 85–99, 155–160, 239–248, 368–395.

Delehaye, Hippolyte. *Cinq leçons sur la méthode hagiographique.* Subsidia Hagiographica 21. Brussels: Société des Bollandistes, 1934.

den Heijer, Johannes. *Mawhub ibn Mansur ibn Mufarrig et l'historiographie copto-arabe: Études sur la composition de l'Histoire des Patriarches d'Alexandrie.* CSCO 513, Subsidia 83. Louvain: Peeters, 1989.

Depuydt, Leo. *Catalogue of Coptic Manuscripts in the Pierpont Morgan Library.* 2 volumes. Oriental Series 1–2, Corpus of Illuminated Manuscripts 4–5. Leuven: Peeters, 1993.

Derda, Tomasz, ed. *Deir el-Naqlun: The Greek Papyri.* Volume 2 (P. Naqlun II). With contributions by Jakub Urbanik and Jaques van der Vliet. Supplements to the Journal of Juristic Papyrology 9. Warsaw: Warsaw University, Faculty of Law and Administration, Institute of Archaeology, Department of Papyrology, 2008.

Descoeudres, Georges. *Die Pastophorien im syro-byzantinischen Osten: Eine Untersuchung zu architektur- und liturgiegeschichtlichen Problemen.* Schriften zur Geistesgeschichte des östlichen Europa 16. Wiesbaden: Otto Harrassowitz, 1983.

Descourtieux, Patrick. *Clément d'Alexandrie: Les Stromates VI.* SC 446. Paris: Cerf, 1999.

Dix, Gregory. *The Shape of the Liturgy.* London: Bloomsbury, 2005.

Dorry, Mennat Allah el-. "Wine Production in Medieval Egypt: The Case of the Coptic Church." In *Studies in Coptic Culture: Transmission and Interaction*, edited by Mariam Ayad, 55–63. Cairo: The American University in Cairo Press, 2016.

Dous, Roshdi Wassef Behman. "Ο Αγιασμός των υδάτων του Νείλου Ποταμού στην Αλεξανδρινή Λειτουργική Παράδοση." Doctoral dissertation, Aristotle University of Thessaloniki, 2011.

Dous, Roshdi Wassef Behman. "Η Αλεξανδρινή Θεία Λειτουργία του Αγίου Βασιλείου κατά την Κοπτική Παράδοση: Κριτική Έκδοση." Doctoral dissertation, Aristotle University of Thessaloniki, 1997.

Dous, Roshdi Wassef Behman. "History of Making the Holy Chrism in the Coptic Orthodox Church since Pope Athanasius (326–378) until Pope Shenouda the 3rd (1971–)." *Hallesche Beiträge zur Orientwissenschaft* 44 (2007): 27–63.

Drescher, James. "Graeco-Coptica." *Le Muséon* 82 (1969): 85–100.

Dugmore, C. W. *The Influence of the Synagogue upon the Divine Office*. Alcuin Club Collections 5. [London]: The Faith Press, 1964.

Engberding, Hieronymus. "Neues Licht über die Geschichte des Textes der ägyptischen Markusliturgie." *OC* 40 (1956): 51–68.

Engberding, Hieronymus. "Der Nil in der liturgischen Frömmigkeit des christlichen Ostens." *OC* 37 (1953): 56–88.

Engberding, Hieronymus. "Ein Problem in der Homologia vor der hl. Kommunion in der ägyptischen Liturgie." *OCP* 2 (1936): 145–154.

Engberding, Hieronymus. "Untersuchungen zu den jüngst veröffentlichten Bruchstücken ṣa'idischer Liturgie." *OC* 43 (1959): 59–102.

Evelyn-White, Hugh G. *The Monasteries of the Wadi 'N Natrūn Part I: New Coptic Texts from the Monastery of Saint Macarius*. Publications of the Metropolitan Museum of Art Egyptian Expedition 2. New York: Metropolitan Museum of Art, 1926.

Evelyn-White, Hugh G. *The Monasteries of the Wādi 'N Natrūn Part II: The History of the Monasteries of Nitria and of Scetis*. Publications of the Metropolitan Museum of Art Egyptian Expedition 4. New York: Metropolitan Museum of Art, 1932.

Evetts, B.T.A. *The Churches & Monasteries of Egypt and Some Neighbouring Countries Attributed to Abū Ṣāliḥ the Armenian*. Oxford, 1895.

Fanous, Daniel. *A Silent Patriarch: Kyrillos VI (1902–1971) Life and Legacy*. Yonkers, NY: St. Vladimir's Seminary Press, 2019.

Feulner, Hans-Jürgen. "The Anglican Use within the Western Liturgical Tradition: Importance and Ecumenical Relevance from the Perspective of Comparative Liturgy." In *Anglicans and the Roman Catholic Church: Reflections on Recent Developments,* edited by Stephen E. Cavanaugh, 184–224. San Francisco, CA: Ignatius Press, 2011.

Fiey, Jean Maurice. "Coptes et syriaques: contacts et échanges." *SOC Collectanea* 15 (1972–1973): 295-365.

Förster, Hans. *Wörterbuch der griechischen Wörter in den koptischen dokumentarischen Texten.* Texte und Untersuchungen zur Geschichte der altchristlichen Literatur 148. Berlin: Walter de Gruyter, 2002.

al-Fransiskānī, Wadi'. "Aqdam al-tarğamāt al-'arabiyya (Qurūn 12–14) li-quddāsāt al-kanīsa al-qibṭiyya [The oldest Arabic translations (12th–14th centuries) of the liturgies of the Coptic Church]." *Madrasat al-iskandariyya* 7 (2011): 217–235.

Frček, Jean. *Euchologium Sinaiticum: Texte Slave avec sources grecques et traduction française.* PO 25.3 (123). Turnhout: Brepols, 1989.

Frend, W. H. C. and I.A. Muirhead. "The Greek Manuscripts from the Cathedral of Q'asr Ibrim." *Le Muséon* 89 (1976): 43–49.

Fritsch, Emmanuel. "The Altar in the Ethiopian Church: History, Forms and Meanings." In *Inquiries into Eastern Christian Worship: Selected Papers of the Second International Congress of the Society of Oriental Liturgy, Rome, 17–21 September 2008*, edited by Bert Groen, Steven Hawkes-Teeples, and Stefanos Alexopoulos, 443–510. Eastern Christian Studies 12. Leuven: Peeters, 2012.

Fritsch, Emmanuel. "The Churches of Lalibäla (Ethiopia) Witnesses of Liturgical Changes." *BBGG III* 5 (2008): 69–112.

Fritsch, Emmanuel. "Concelebration of the Eucharistic Liturgy in the Ethiopian Tradition." In *Studies on the Liturgies of the Christian East: Selected Papers of the Third International Congress of the Society of Oriental Liturgy Volos, May 26–30, 2010*, edited by Steven Hawkes-Teeples, Bert Groen, and Stefanos Alexopoulos, 11–29. Eastern Christian Studies 18. Leuven: Peeters, 2013.

Fritsch, Emmanuel. "The Order of the Mystery: An Ancient Catechesis Preserved in BnF Ethiopic Ms d'Abbadie 66–66bis (Fifteenth Century) with a Liturgical Commentary." In *Studies in Oriental Liturgy: Proceedings of the Fifth International Congress of the Society of Oriental Liturgy, New York, 10–15 June 2014*, edited by Bert Groen, et al, 195–263. Eastern Christian Studies 28. Leuven: Peeters, 2019.

Fritsch, Emmanuel. "The Preparation of the Gifts and the Pre-Anaphora in the Ethiopian Eucharistic Liturgy in Around A.D. 1100." In *Rites and Rituals of the Christian East: Proceedings of the Fourth International Congress of the Society of Oriental*

Liturgy, Lebanon, 10–15 July 2012, edited by Bert Groen et al, 97–152. Eastern Christian Studies 22. Leuven: Peeters, 2014.

Fritsch, Emmanuel and Michael Gervers. "*Pastophoria* and Altars: Interaction in Ethiopian Liturgy and Church Architecture." *Aethiopica* 10 (2007): 7–51.

Frøyshov, Stig Simeon. "The Cathedral-Monastic Distinction Revisited. Part I: Was Egyptian Desert Liturgy a Pure Monastic Office?" *Studia Liturgica* 37 (2007): 198–216.

Funk, Franciscus Xaverius, ed. *Didascalia et Constitutiones Apostolorum*. 2 volumes. Paderborn: In libraria Ferdinandi Schoeningh, 1906.

Gabra, Gawdat. *The A to Z of the Coptic Church*. The A to Z Guide Series 107. Lanham, MD: The Scarecrow Press, 2009.

Gabra, Gawdat. *Coptic Monasteries: Egypt's Monastic Art and Architecture*. Cairo: The American University in Cairo Press, 2002.

Galadza, Daniel. *Liturgy and Byzantinization in Jerusalem*. Oxford Early Christian Studies. Oxford: Oxford University Press, 2018.

Gémayel, Pierre-Edmond. *Avant-Messe maronite. Histoire et structure*. OCA 174. Rome: Pontificium Institutum Orientalium Studiorum, 1965.

Getcha, Job. *The Typikon Decoded: An Explanation of Byzantine Liturgical Practice*. Orthodox Liturgy Series 3. Yonkers, NY: St Vladimir's Seminary Press, 2012.

Gibson, Margaret Dunlop. *The Didascalia Apostolorum in English*. Horae Semiticae 2. London: Cambridge University Press, 1903.

Ǧirǧis, Marqus. *Al-durr al-ṯamīn fī iḍāḥ al-dīn* [The precious pearl in elucidating the faith]. 2nd edition. Cairo, [1992].

Goar, Jacques. *ΕΥΧΟΛΟΓΙΟΝ sive Rituale Graecorum complectens ritus et ordines Divinae Liturgiae, officiorum, sacramentorum, consecrationum, benedictionum, funerum, orationum, &c. cuilibet personae, statui vel tempori congruos, juxta usum Orientalis Ecclesiae*. 2nd edition. Graz: Akademische Druck- und Verlagsanstalt, 1960.

Goodspeed, Edgar J. *The Conflict of Severus Patriarch of Antioch by Athanasius: Ethiopic Text Edited and Translated*. PO 4.6 (20). Turnhout: Brepols, 2003.

Graf, Georg. "Ein alter Kelchthron in der Kirche Abū Sēfēn (mit einer Tafel)." *BSAC* 4 (1938): 29–36.

Graf, Georg. "Liturgische Anweisungen des koptischen Patriarchen Kyrillos ibn Laklak." *Jahrbuch für Liturgiewissenschaft* 4 (1924): 119–134.

Graf, Georg. *Verzeichnis arabischer kirchlicher Termini*. 2nd edition. CSCO 147, Subsidia 8. Louvain: Secrétariat du Corpus, 1954.

Grand'Henry, Jacques. "Christian Middle Arabic." In *Encyclopedia of Arabic Language and Linguistics*. Volume 1, A–Ed, edited by Kees Versteegh, et al, 383–387. Leiden: Brill, 2006.

Grossmann, Peter. "Abusir." In *The Eerdmans Encyclopedia of Early Christian Art and Archaeology*. Volume 1, A–J, edited by Paul Corby Finney, 7. Grand Rapids, MI: William B. Eerdmans Publishing Company, 2017.

Grossmann, Peter. "Architecture: Egypt (3rd–7th c. A.D.)." In *The Eerdmans Encyclopedia of Early Christian Art and Archaeology*. Volume 1, A–J, edited by Paul Corby Finney, 108–110. Grand Rapids, MI: William B. Eerdmans Publishing Company, 2017.

Grossmann, Peter. "Babylon." *CE*, 2:317a–323b.

Grossmann, Peter. *Christliche Architektur in Ägypten*. Handbuch der Orientalistik, Section 1: The Near and Middle East 62. Leiden: Brill, 2002.

Grossmann, Peter. "Dayr Abū Fānah, Architecture." *CE* 3:699a–700b.

Grossmann, Peter. "Dayr al-Baramūs, Architecture." *CE*, 3:791b–793a.

Grossmann, Peter. "Dayr al-Quṣayr." *CE*, 3:853a–855b.

Grossmann, Peter. "On the Architecture at Wādī al-Naṭrūn." In *Christianity and Monasticism in Wadi al-Natrun: Essays from the 2002 International Symposium of the Saint Mark Foundation and the Saint Shenouda the Archimandrite Coptic Society*, edited by Maged S.A. Mikhail and Mark Moussa, 159–184. Cairo: The American University in Cairo Press, 2009.

Grossmann, Peter. "Pastophorium." *CE*, 1:216a–217a.

Grumel, Venance. "Les Réponses canoniques à Marc d'Alexandrie, leur caractère officiel, leur double redaction." *Échos d'Orient* 38 (1939): 321–333.

Guy, Jean-Claude. *Les Apophtegmes des Pères. Collection systématique, chapitres X–XVI*. Volume 2. SC 474. Paris: Cerf, 2003.

Guy, Jean-Claude. *Les Apophtegmes des Pères. Collection systématique, chapitres XVII–XXI*. Volume 3. SC 498. Paris: Cerf, 2005.

Guy, Jean-Claude. *Jean Cassien, Institutions cénobitiques: Texte latin revu, introduction, traduction et notes*. SC 109. Paris: Cerf, 1965.

Haas, Christopher. *Alexandria in Late Antiquity: Topography and Social Conflict*. Ancient Society and History. Baltimore, MD: Johns Hopkins University Press, 1997.

Hammerschmidt, Ernst. *Die koptische Gregoriosanaphora: Syrische und griechische Einflüsse auf eine ägyptische Liturgie*. Berliner byzantinistische Arbeiten 8. Berlin: Akademie Verlag, 1957.

Hammerschmidt, Ernst. *Studies in the Ethiopic Anaphoras.* 2nd revised edition. Berliner Byzantinische Arbeiten 25. Berlin: Akademie Verlag, 1988.

Hammerstaedt, Jürgen. *Griechische Anaphorenfragmente aus Ägypten und Nubien.* Papyrologica Coloniensa 28. Opladen: Westdeutscher Verlag, 1999.

Hanna, Maged Soubhy Rezk. "Το Ωρολόγιον της Κοπτικής Ορθόδοξης Εκκλησίας κατά τον Codex Parisinus 107 Arabe." Doctoral dissertation, National and Kapodistrian University of Athens, 2005.

Hawkes-Teeples, Steven. "The Prothesis of the Byzantine Divine Liturgy: What Has Been Done and What Remains." In *Rites and Rituals of the Christian East: Proceedings of the Fourth International Congress of the Society of Oriental Liturgy, Lebanon, 10–15 July 2012,* edited by Bert Groen, Daniel Galadza, Nina Glibetic, and Gabriel Radle, 317–327. Eastern Christian Studies 22. Leuven: Peeters, 2014.

Hažmuková, Valerie. "Miscellaneous Coptic Prayers." *Archiv Orientální* 8 (1936): 318–333.

Hebbelynck, Adolph and Arnold van Lantschoot. *Codices Coptici Vaticani Barberiniani Borgiani* Rossiani. Volume 1, *Codices Coptici Vaticani.* Vatican City: Biblioteca Vaticana, 1937.

Helderman, Jan. "Der sketische Greis, das Hostienwunder und das alte Ägypten." In *Divitiae Aegypti: Koptologische und verwandte Studien zu Ehren von Martin Krause,* edited by Cäcilia Fluck, et al, 134–146. Wiesbaden: Ludwig Reichert Verlag, 1995.

Heldman, Marilyn E. "Church Buildings." *EAE,* 1:737–740.

Henner, Jutta. *Fragmenta Liturgica Coptica: Editionen und Kommentar liturgischer Texte der koptischen Kirche des ersten Jahrtausends.* Studien und Texte zu Antike und Christentum 5. Tübingen: Mohr Siebeck, 2000.

Hill, Robert C. *St. Cyril of Alexandria: Commentary on the Twelve Prophets.* Volume 3. The Fathers of the Church 124. Washington, DC: Catholic University of America Press, 2007.

Horner, George William. *The Statutes of the Apostles or Canones Ecclesiastici: Edited with Translation and Collation from Ethiopic and Arabic MSS.; also a Translation of the Saidic and Collation of the Bohairic Versions; and Saidic Fragments.* London: Williams & Norgate, 1904.

Hyvernat, Henri. *Bybliothecae Pierpont Morgan Codices Coptici photographice expressi.* Volume 13. Rome, 1922.

[Ibrāhīm, Philotheos]. *Ḫulāǧī al-qiddīs Basīliyūs* [The Euchologion of Saint Basil]. Cairo, 1887.

[Ibrāhīm, Philotheos]. *Kitāb mā yağibu 'ala l-šamāmisa min al-qirā'a fī l-ḫidma wa-l-tarātīl* [The book of what the deacons ought to read in the service and the chants]. Cairo, 1887.

Innemée, Karel C. *Ecclesiastical Dress in the Medieval Near East.* Studies in Textile and Costume History 1. Leiden: Brill, 1992.

Innemée, Karel C. "A Newly Discovered Mural Painting in Deir al-Surian" *Eastern Chrisitan Art* 1 (2004): 61–66.

Jacob, André. "L'euchologe de Porphyre Uspenski Cod. Leningr. Gr. 226 (Xe siècle)." *Le Muséon* 68 (1965): 173–214.

Jacob, André. "L'evoluzione dei libri liturgici bizantini in Calabria e in Sicilia dall'VIII al XVI secolo, con particolare riguardo ai riti eucaristici." In *Calabria bizantina. Vita religiosa e strutture amministrative, Atti del primo e secondo Incontro di studi bizantini,* 47–69. Reggio Calabria: Edizioni Parallelo, 1974.

Jacob, André. "Histoire du formulaire grec de la liturgie de saint Jean Chrysostome." Doctoral dissertation, Université de Louvain, 1968.

Jacob, André. "La tradition manuscrite de la liturgie de Saint Jean Chrysostome (VIIIe–XIIe siècles)." In *Eucharisties d'Orient et d'Occident. Semaine liturgique de l'Institut Saint-Serge 2,* edited by Bernard Botte, et al, 109–138. Lex Orandi 47. Paris: Cerf, 1970.

Johnson, Maxwell E. *The Prayers of Sarapion of Thmuis: A Literary, Liturgical, and Theological Analysis.* OCA 249. Rome: Pontificio Istituto Orientale, 1995.

Johnson, Maxwell E. *The Rites of Christian Initiation: Their Evolution and Interpretation.* Rev. ed. Collegeville, MN: Liturgical Press, 2007.

Johnson, Maxwell E. "Sharing 'the Cup of Christ': The Cessation of Martyrdom and Anaphoral Development." In *Studies on the Liturgies of the Christian East: Selected Papers of the Third International Congress of the Society of Oriental Liturgy Volos, May 26–30, 2010,* edited by Steven Hawkes-Teeples, Bert Groen, and Stefanos Alexopoulos, 109–126. Eastern Christian Studies 18. Leuven: Peeters, 2013.

Jungmann, Josef A. *The Early Liturgy to the Time of Gregory the Great.* Notre Dame, IN: University of Notre Dame Press, 1959.

Kasser, Rudolphe. "Paleography." *CE,* 8:A175b–A184a.

Kaufhold, Hubert. "Sources of Canon Law in the Eastern Churches." In *The History of Byzantine and Eastern Canon Law to 1500,* edited by Wilfried Hartmann and Kenneth Pennington, 215–342. History of Medieval Canon Law. Washington DC: Catholic University of America Press, 2012.

Kazamias, Alkiviades. *Η Θεία Λειτουργία του Αγίου Ιακώβου του Αδελφοθέου και τα Νέα Σιναϊτικά Χειρόγραφα.* Thessaloniki: Ἵδρυμα Ὄρους Σινᾶ, 2006.

Khevsuriani, Lili, et al. *Liturgia Ibero-Graeca Sancti Iacobi: Editio, translatio, retroversio, commentarii.* JThF 17. Münster: Aschendorff, 2011.

Khouri-Sarkis, Gabriel. "L'anaphore syriaque de s. Jacques. Notes." *L'Orient Syrien* 7 (1962): 287–296.

Khouri-Sarkis, Gabriel. *La Liturgie syrienne. Anaphore des douze apôtres.* Paris: Mission Syrienne, 1950.

Klinghardt, Matthias. *Gemeinschaftsmahl und Mahlgemeinschaft: Soziologie und Liturgie frühchristlicher Mahlfeiern.* Texte und Arbeiten zum neutestamentlichen Zeitalter 13. Tübingen: Francke Verlag, 1996.

Knowles, Peter. "A Renaissance in the Study of Byzantine Liturgy?" *Worship* 68 (1994): 232–41.

Koetschau, Paul. *Origenes Werke.* Volume 2, *Buch V–VII gegen Celsus, die Schrift vom Gebet.* GCS 3. Leipzig, 1899.

Kubińska, Jadwiga. "Prothesis de la cathédrale de Faras. Documents et recherches." *Revue des Archéologues et Historiens d'Art de Louvain* 9 (1976): 7–37.

Lagarde, Paul de. *Aegyptiaca.* Göttingen, 1883.

Łajtar, Adam. "Varia Nubica III: Ein liturgisches Gebet aus Qasr Ibrim." *Zeitschrift für Papyrologie und Epigraphik* 112 (1996): 140–142.

Łajtar, Adam and Dobrochna Zielińska. "The Northern Pastophorium of Nubian Churches: Ideology and Function (On the Basis of Inscriptions and Paintings)." In *Aegyptus et Nubia Christiana: The Włodzimierz Godlewski Jubilee Volume on the Occasion of his 70th Birthday,* edited by Adam Łajtar, Artur Obluski, and Iwona Zych, 435–457. Warsaw: Polish Centre of Mediterranean Archaeology, 2016.

Łajtar, Adam and Grzegorz Ochała. "Two Wall Inscriptions from the Faras Cathedral with Lists of People and Goods." In *Nubian Voices II: New Texts and Studies of Christian Nubian Culture,* edited by Adam Łajtar, Grzegorz Ochała, and Jacques van der Vliet, 73–102. Supplements to the Journal of Juristic Papyrology 27. Warsaw: Faculty of Law and Administration University of Warsaw / Institute of Archaeology / The Raphael Taubenschlag Foundation, 2015.

Łajtar, Adam and Jacques van der Vliet. *Empowering the Dead in Christian Nubia: The Texts from a Medieval Funerary Complex in Dongola.* Supplements to the Journal of Juristic Papyrology 32. Warsaw: Faculty of Law and Administration University of Warsaw / Institute of Archaeology / The Raphael Taubenschlag Foundation, 2017.

Lampe, G.W.H. *A Patristic Greek Lexicon*. Oxford: The Clarendon Press, 1961.

Langen, Linda. "A Mysterious Altar-Casket in Abu Sefein Church in Old-Cairo." *BSAC* 28 (1986–1989): 75–79.

Lanne, Emmanuel. *Le grand euchologe du Monastère Blanc: Texte copte édité avec traduction française*. PO 28.2 (135). Turnhout: Brepols, 2003.

Lanne, Lanne. "Textes et rites de la liturgie pascale dans l'ancienne église copte." *L'Orient Syrien* 6 (1961): 279–300.

Larin, Vassa. "The Bishop as Minister of the Prothesis? Reconsidering the Evidence in Byzantine and Muscovite Sources." In *Inquiries into Eastern Christian Worship: Selected Papers of the Second International Congress of the Society of Oriental Liturgy, Rome, 17–21 September 2008*, edited by Bert Groen, Steven Hawkes-Teeples, and Stefanos Alexopoulos, 319–330. Eastern Christian Studies 12. Leuven: Peeters, 2012.

Larin, Vassa. *The Byzantine Hierarchical Divine Liturgy in Arsenij Suxanov's Proskinitarij: Text, Translation, and Analysis of the Entrance Rites*. OCA 286. Rome: Pontificio Istituto Orientale, 2010.

Layton, Bentley. *The Canons of our Fathers: Monastic Rules of Shenoute*. Oxford Early Christian Studies. Oxford: Oxford University Press, 2014.

Layton, Bentley. *Catalogue of Coptic Literary Manuscripts in the British Library Acquired Since the Year 1906*. London: British Library, 1987.

Leipoldt, Iohannes, ed. *Sinuthii archimandritae vita et opera omnia*. CSCO 42, Scriptores Coptici, Ser. 2, volume 4. Paris: [E Typographeo reipublica], 1908.

Lewicka, Paulina B. "Alcohol and its Consumption in Medieval Cairo. The Story of a Habit." *Studia Arabistyczne i Islamistyczne* 12 (2004): 55–98.

Liddell, Henry George, and Robert Scott. *A Greek-English Lexicon*. Revised and augmented thoroughly by Sir Henry Stuart Jones with a revised supplement. Oxford: Clarendon Press, 1996.

Lietzmann, Hans. *Messe und Herrenmahl: Eine Studie zur Geschichte der Liturgie*. Arbeiten zur Kirchengeschichte 8. Berlin: De Gruyter, 1955.

Lucchesi, Enzo. "Trois nouveaux fragments coptes de la vie de Paul de Tamma par Ezéchiel." In *Ægyptus Christiana: Mélanges d'hagiographie égyptienne et orientale dédiés à la mémoire du P. Paul Devos, Bollandiste*, edited by Ugo Zanetti and Enzo Lucchesi, 211–224. Cahiers d'orientalisme 25. Geneva: Patrick Cramer, 2004.

MacCoull, Leslie S.B. "1. *Apa Abraham*: *Testament* of Apa Abraham, Bishop of Hermonthis, for the Monastery of St. Phoibammon near Thebes, Egypt." In *Byzantine Monastic Foundation Documents: A Complete Translation of the Surviving Founders' Typika and Testaments*, edited by John Thomas and Angela Constantinides Hero, 51–58. Volume 1. Dumbarton Oaks Studies 35. Washington DC: Dumbarton Oaks Research Library and Collection, 2000.

MacCoull, Leslie S.B. *Documenting Christianity in Egypt, Sixth to Fourteenth Centuries*. Variorum Collected Studies Series CS 981. Burlington, VT: Ashgate Variorum, 2011.

MacCoull, Leslie S.B. "'A Dwelling Place of Christ, a Healing Place of Knowledge': The Non-Chalcedonian Eucharist in Late Antique Egypt and its Setting." In *Varieties of Devotion in the Middle Ages and Renaissance*, edited by Susan C. Karant-Nunn, 1–16. Arizona Studies in the Middle Ages and the Renaissance 7. Turnhout: Brepols, 2003.

MacCoull, Leslie S.B. "John Philoponus, *On the Pasch* (*CPG* 7267): The Egyptian Eucharist in the Sixth Century and the Armenian Connection." *Jahrbuch der Österreichischen Byzantinistik* 49 (1999): 1–12.

Macomber, William F. "The Anaphora of Saint Mark according to the Kacmarcik Codex." *OCP* 45 (1979): 75–98.

Macomber, William F. *Catalogue of the Christian Arabic Manuscripts of the Franciscan Center of Christian Oriental Studies, Muski, Cairo*. Studia Orientalia Christiana. Cairo: Centre franciscain d'études orientales chrétiennes, 1984.

Macomber, William F. *Final Inventory of the Microfilmed Manuscripts of the Coptic Museum Old Cairo, Egypt: Rolls B1–6 Manuscripts in Arabic, Coptic (Bohairic, Oxyrhynchite [1], Sahidic) Greek*. Provo, UT: Harold B. Lee Library Brigham Young University, 1995.

Macomber, William F. *Final Inventory of the Microfilmed Manuscripts of the Coptic Museum Old Cairo, Egypt: Rolls B7–11 Manuscripts in Arabic, Coptic (Bohairic, Oxyrhynchite [1], Sahidic) Greek*. Provo, UT: Harold B. Lee Library Brigham Young University, 1995.

Macomber, William F. *Final Inventory of the Microfilmed Manuscripts of the Coptic Museum Old Cairo, Egypt: Rolls B12–17 Manuscripts in Arabic, Coptic (Bohairic, Oxyrhynchite [1], Sahidic) Greek*. Provo, UT: Harold B. Lee Library Brigham Young University, 1995.

Macomber, William F. "The Greek Text of the Coptic Mass and of the Anaphoras of Basil and Gregory according to the Kacmarcik Codex." *OCP* 43 (1977): 308–334.

Macomber, William F. "The Kacmarcik Codex. A 14th Century Greek-Arabic Manuscript of the Coptic Mass." *Le Muséon* 88 (1975): 391–395.

Malan, Solomon Caesar. *The Divine ΕΥΧΟΛΟΓΙΟΝ, and the Divine Liturgy of S. Gregory the Theologian; Translated from an Old Coptic Manuscript.* Original Documents of the Coptic Church 6. London, 1875.

Mandalà, Marco. *La protesi della liturgia nel rito bizantino-greco.* Grottaferrata: Scuola Tipografica Italo-Orientale S. Nilo, 1935.

al-Maqārī, Athanasius. *Qawānīn al-bābā aṯanāsiyūs baṭriyark al-iskandariyya* [The canons of Pope Athanasius the patriarch of Alexandria]. Maṣādir ṭuqūs al-kanīsa 1.10. Cairo: Dār nūbār, 2006.

al-Maqārī, Athanasius. *Al-quddās al-ilāhī: Sirr malakūt allāh* [The Divine Liturgy: The mystery of the kingdom of God]. 2nd edition. 2 volumes. Ṭuqūs asrār wa-ṣalawāt al-kanīsa 3.5–6. Cairo: Dār nūbār, 2011.

al-Maqārī, Athanasius. *Sabt al-faraḥ wa-l-nūr: Al-tārīḫ al-ṭaqsī/ ṭuqūs al-ṣalawāt* [The Saturday of joy and light: The ritual history/the rites of the prayers]. Ṭuqūs aṣwām wa-a'yād al-kanīsa 4.7. Cairo: maṭābi' al-nūbār, 2012.

al-Maqārī, Athanasius. *Sirr al-rūḥ al-qudus wa-l-mayrūn al-muqaddas* [The mystery of the Holy Spirit and the holy chrism]. Ṭuqūs asrār wa-ṣalawāt al-kanīsa 3.2. Cairo: Dār nūbār, 2007.

al-Maqārī, Athanasius. *Ṣawm nīnawa wa-l-ṣawm al-kabīr* [The fast of Nineveh and the great fast]. Ṭuqūs aṣwām wa-a'yād al-kanīsa 4.4. Cairo: Šarikat al-ṭibā'a al-miṣriyya, 2009.

Maraval, Pierre. *Égérie, Journal de voyage (Itinéraire): Introduction, texte critique, traduction, notes et cartes.* SC 296. Paris: Cerf, 2017.

Maravela, Anastasia, Ágnes Mihálykó, and Glenn Ø. Wehus. "A Coptic Liturgical Prayer for the Consecration of the Chalice." *Archiv für Papyrusforschung* 63, no. 1 (2017): 204–230.

Martin, Annick and Pierre Canivet. *Théodoret de Cyr: Histoire ecclésiastique I (Livres I–II).* SC 501. Paris: Cerf, 2006.

al-Maṣrī, Īrīs Ḥabīb. "The Rite of the Filling of the Chalice." *BSAC* 6 (1940): 77–90.

Mathews, Thomas F. *The Early Churches of Constantinople: Architecture and Liturgy.* University Park, PA: Pennsylvania State University Press, 1971.

Mattā'us. *Al-qarārāt al-maǧma'iyya al-ḫāṣṣa bi-l-ṭuqūs al-kanasiyya* [The synodical decisions concerned with ecclesiastical rites]. Dayr Al-Suryān, 2001.

Mattā'us. *The Spirituality of the Rites of the Holy Liturgy in the Coptic Orthodox Church.* Alexandria, n.d.

McKenna, John H. *The Eucharistic Epiclesis: A Detailed History from the Patristic to the Modern Era.* 2nd edition. Chicago, IL: Hillenbrand Books, 2009.

Meinardus, Otto F.A. *Two Thousand Years of Coptic Christianity.* Cairo: American University in Cairo Press, 1999.

Mercer, Samuel A.B. *The Ethiopic Liturgy: Its Sources, Development, and Present Form.* The Hale Lectures 1914–5. London: A. R. Mowbray, 1915.

Mercier, B. Charles. *La Liturgie de Saint Jacques: Édition critique du texte grec avec traduction latine.* PO 26.2 (126). Turnhout: Brepols, 1997.

Metzger, Marcel. *Les constitutions apostoliques.* volume 3, *Livres 7-8: Introduction, texte critique, traduction et notes.* SC 336. Paris: Cerf, 2008.

Meyendorff, Paul. *St Germanus of Constantinople on the Divine Liturgy: The Greek Text with Translation, Introduction, and Commentary.* Popular Patristics Series 8. Crestwood, NY: St. Vladimir's Seminary Press, 1984.

Mihálykó, Ágnes T. *The Christian Liturgical Papyri: An Introduction.* Studien und Texte zu Antike und Christentum 114. Tübingen: Mohr Siebeck, 2019.

Mihálykó, Ágnes T. "Two Coptic Prayers on Ostracon (P. Berol. 709 and 9444+4790)." *Archiv für Papyrusforschung* 65, no. 1 (2019): 133–155.

Mihálykó, Ágnes T. "Witnesses of A 'Prayer of Offering' in Sahidic from the White Monastery and the Thebaid." *Journal of Coptic Studies* 17 (2015): 127–139.

Mikhail, Maged S.A. *From Byzantine to Islamic Egypt: Religion, Identity and Politics after the Arab Conquest.* Library of Middle East History 45. London: I.B. Tauris, 2014.

Mikhail, Maged S.A. "Matta al-Miskīn." In *The Orthodox Christian World,* edited by Augustine Casiday, 359–365. London: Routledge, 2012.

Mikhail, Ramez. "'And they Shall Stand Bareheaded': On the Historical Development of Liturgical Head-Covering in the Coptic Rite." Forthcoming in Proceedings of the Eleventh International Congress of Coptic Studies, Claremont, California, July 25th–30th, 2016.

Mikhail, Ramez. "Aspects of Witness in the Coptic Liturgical Tradition." *Alexandria School Journal* 1 (2014): 1–26.

Mikhail, Ramez. "The Coptic Church and the Presanctified Liturgy: The Story of a Rejected Tradition." *Alexandria School Journal* 3 (2016): 2–30.

Mikhail, Ramez. "The Liturgy *Coram Patriarcha* Revisited: The Prothesis of the Coptic Patriarchal Liturgy in Sources of the 15th–16th Centuries." *Le Muséon* 131, no. 3-4 (2018): 279–312.

Mikhail, Ramez. "On Evening Worship in Egypt: A Theological Evaluation of Contemporary Practice in Light of Patristic and Medieval Sources." *Coptica* 12 (2013): 77–94.

Mikhail, Ramez. "The Presanctified Liturgy of the Apostle Mark in *Sinai Arabic 237:* Text and Commentary." *BBGG III* 12 (2015): 163–214.

Mikhail, Ramez. "Towards a History of Liturgical Vestments in the Coptic Rite: I-Minor Orders, Deacons, and Presbyters." *Coptica* 15 (2016): 55–70.

Mikhail, Ramez. "Towards a History of Liturgical Vestments in the Coptic Rite: II-Bishops and Patriarchs." *Coptica* 16 (2017): 55–66.

al-Miskīn, Mattā. *Ifḫaristiyyā 'ašā' al-rabb: Quddās al-rusul al-awwal wa-huwa nawāt ǧamī' al-quddasāt* [Eucharist supper of the Lord: The first liturgy of the apostles, and it is the core of all the liturgies]. Wādī al-Naṭrūn: Dayr al-qiddīs anbā Maqār, 2000.

al-Miskīn, Mattā. *Al-ifḫāristiyyā 'ašā' al-rabb* [The Eucharist the supper of the Lord]. 3rd edition. Wādī al-Naṭrūn: Dayr al-qiddīs anbā Maqār, 2007.

Mistrīḥ, Vincentio. *Yūḥannā ibn Abī Zakarīā ibn Sibā', Pretiosa margarita de scientiis ecclesiasticis.* SOC, Aegyptiaca. Cairo: Centrum Franciscanum Studiorum Orientalium Christianorum, 1966.

Moawad, Samuel. "Liturgische Hinweise in koptischen literarischen Werken." In *From Old Cairo to the New World: Coptic Studies Presented to Gawdat Gabra on the Occasion of his Sixty-Fifth Birthday,* edited by Youhanna Nessim Youssef and Samuel Moawad, 125–145. Colloquia Antiqua 9. Leuven: Peeters, 2013.

Monastery of the Virgin Mary al-Muḥarraq. *Kitāb al-ḫūlāǧī al-muqaddas: Al-ṯalāṯat al-quddāsāt lil-qiddīsīn bāsīlyūs wa-iġrīġūryūs wa-kīrillus wa-yalīhum tartīb ta'mīr al-ka's wa-ṣalawāt uḫra mutanawi'a* [The book of the Holy Euchologion: The three liturgies of Saints Basil, Gregory, and Cyril, followed by the rite of the filling of the chalice, and miscellaneous other prayers]. 5th edition. [Asyūṭ]: The Monastery of the Virgin Mary al-Muḥarraq, 2014.

Muksuris, Stelyios S. *Economia & Eschatology: Liturgical Mystagogy in the Byzantine Prothesis Rite.* Brookline, MA: Holy Cross Orthodox Press, 2013.

Munier, Charles. *Justin: Apologies pour les chrétiens.* SC 507. Paris: Cerf, 2006.

Nasrallah, Joseph. "La liturgie des Patriarcats melchites de 969 à 1300." *OC* 71 (1987): 156–181.

Nicolotti, Andrea. "Forme di partecipazione alla liturgia eucaristica nel rito copto." In *Liturgia e partecipazione: Forme del coinvolgimento rituale*, edited by Luigi Girardi, 223–267. Caro salutis cardo. Contributi 27. Padua: Messaggero, 2013.

Nosnitsin, Denis. "Mika'el I." *EAE*, 3:953.

O'Leary, De Lacy Evans. *The Daily Office and Theotokia of the Coptic Church*. London: Simpkin, Marshall, Hamilton, Kent, 1911.

O'Mahoney, Anthony. "Coptic Christianity in Modern Egypt." In *The Cambridge History of Christianity*, edited by Michael Angold, 488–510. Volume 5, *Eastern Christianity*. Cambridge: Cambridge University Press, 2006.

Orlandi, Tito. "Hagiography, Coptic." *CE*, 4:1191a–1197b.

Papaconstantinou, Arietta. "Hagiography in Coptic." In *The Ashgate Research Companion to Byzantine Hagiography*, edited by Stephanos Efthymiadis, 323–343. Volume 1, *Periods and Places*. Farnham, Surrey, England: Ashgate, 2011.

Parenti, Stefano. "Influssi italo-greci nei testi eucaristici bizantini dei 'Fogli Slavi' del Sinai (XI sec.)." *OCP* 57 (1991): 145–177.

Parenti, Stefano. "Vino e olio nelle liturgie bizantine." In *Olio e vino nell'alto Medioevo. Spoleto, 20–26 aprile 2006*, 1251–1289. Settimane di studio della Fondazione Centro italiano di studi sull'alto Medioevo 54. Spoleto: Fondazione Centro italiano di studi sull'alto Medioevo, 2007.

Parenti, Stefano. "La 'vittoria' nella chiesa di Constantinopoli della Liturgia di Crisostomo sulla Liturgia di Basilio." In *A Oriente e Occidente di Constantinopoli. Temi e problemi liturgici di ieri e di oggi*, edited by Stefano Parenti, 27–73. Monumenta, Studia, Instrumenta Liturgica 54. Vatican City: Libreria editrice vaticana, 2010.

Parenti, Stefano and Elena Velkovska, eds. *L'Eucologio Barberini gr. 336*. 2nd rev. ed. BEL.S 80. Rome: Edizioni Liturgiche, 2000.

Passarelli, Gaetano. *L'Eucologio Cryptense Γ.β. VII (sec. X)*. Ἀνάλεκτα Βλατάδων 36. Thessaloniki: Πατριαρχηκόν Ἵδρυμα Πατερικῶν Μελετῶν, 1982.

Patrich, Joseph. "The Transfer of Gifts in the Early Christian Churches of Palestine: Archaeological and Literary Evidence for the Evolution of the "Great Entrance"." In *Pèlerinages et lieux saints dans l'Antiquité et le Moyen-Âge: Mélanges offerts à Pierre Maraval*, edited by Béatrice Caseau, Jean-Claude Cheynet, and Vincent Déroche, 341–393. Monographies 3. Paris: Association des amis du Centre d'histoire et civilisation de Byzance, 2006.

Phountoules, Ioannes. *Απαντήσεις εις Λειτουργικάς Απορίας* [Answers to liturgical questions]. 6th edition. Volume 1 (1–150). Athens: Ἀποστολική Διακονία τής Ἐκκλησίας τής Ἑλλάδος, 2006.

Phountoules, Ioannes. *Απαντήσεις εις Λειτουργικάς Απορίας* [Answers to liturgical questions]. 4th edition. Volume 3 (301–400). Athens: Ἀποστολική Διακονία τῆς Ἐκκλησίας τῆς Ἑλλάδος, 2006.

Phountoules, Ioannes. *Τελετουργικά Θέματα* [Teleturgic topics]. 2nd edition. Volume 1. Λογική Λατρεία 12. Athens: Ἀποστολική Διακονία τῆς Ἐκκλησίας τῆς Ἑλλάδος, 2009.

Piédagnel, Auguste. *Cyrille de Jérusalem: Catéchèses mystagogiques.* SC 126bis. Paris: Cerf, 2004.

Pleyte, W. and P.A.A. Boeser. *Manuscrits coptes du Musée d'Antiquités des Pays-Bas à Leide.* Leiden: E.J. Brill, 1897.

Porcher, Ernest, ed. *Vie d'Isaac, Patriarche d'Alexandrie de 686 a 689.* PO 11.3 (54). Turnhout: Brepols, 2003.

Pott, Thomas. *Byzantine Liturgical Reform: A Study of Liturgical Change in the Byzantine Tradition.* Orthodox Liturgy Series 2. Crestwood, NY: St Vladimir's Seminary Press, 2010.

Pratsch, Thomas. "Exploring the Jungle: Hagiographical Literature between Fact and Fiction." In *Fifty Years of Prosopography: The Later Roman Empire, Byzantium and Beyond,* edited by Averil Cameron, 59–72. Proceedings of the British Academy 118. Oxford: Oxford University Press, 2003.

Qilāda, William Sulaymān. *Ta'ālīm al-rusul al-disqūliyya.* 2nd edition. Cairo: Dār al-ṯaqāfa, 1989.

Quecke, Hans. "Ein koptisch-arabisches Horologion in der Bibliothek des Katharinenklosters auf dem Sinai (Cod. Sin. ar. 389)." *Le Muséon* 78 (1965): 99–117.

Quecke, Hans. "Psalmverse als »Hymnen« in der koptischen Liturgie?" In *Christianisme d'Egypte: Hommages à René-Georges Coquin,* edited by [Jean-Marc Rosenstiehl], 101–114. Cahiers de la Bibliothèque copte 9. Paris: Éditions Peeters, 1995.

Quecke, Hans. "Ein saidischer Zeuge der Markusliturgie (Brit. Mus. Nr. 54 036)." *OCP* 37 (1971): 40–57.

Quecke, Hans. *Untersuchungen zum koptischen Stundengebet.* Publications de l'Institut orientaliste de Louvain 3. Louvain: Université catholique de Louvain, Institut orientaliste, 1970.

Quecke, Hans. "Zum 'Gebet der Lossprechung des Vaters' in der ägyptischen Basilius-Liturgie. Ein bisher unbeachteter Textzeuge: Brit. Libr., Ms. Or. 4718(1) 3." *Orientalia* 48 (1979): 68–81.

Rackham, Harris. *Pliny Natural History: With an English Translation in Ten Volumes.* Volume 4, *Books 12–16.* The Loeb Classical Library 370. Cambridge, MA: Harvard University Press, 1986.

Radle, Gabriel. "The Byzantine Marriage Tradition in Calabria: *Vatican Reginensis Gr. 75* (a. 982/3)." *BBGG III* 9 (2012): 221–245.

Radle, Gabriel. "The History of Nuptial Rites in the Byzantine Periphery." Doctoral dissertation Pontificio Istituto Orientale, 2012.

Radle, Gabriel. "The Liturgical Ties between Egypt and Southern Italy: A Preliminary Investigation." In *Ⲥⲩⲛⲁⲝⲓⲥ ⲕⲁⲑⲟⲗⲓⲕⲏ: Beiträge zu Gottesdienst und Geschichte der fünf altkirchlichen Patriarchate für Heinzgerd Brakmann zum 70. Geburtstag*, edited by Diliana Atanassova and Tinatin Chronz, 618–631. Orientalia-Patristica-Oecumenica 6.2. Vienna: Lit Verlag, 2014.

Radle, Gabriel. "Uncovering the Alexandrian Greek Rite of Marriage: The Liturgical Evidence of *Sinai NF/MG 67* (9th/10th c.)." *Ecclesia Orans* 28 (2011): 49–73.

Rahmani, Ignatius Ephraem. *Les liturgies orientales et occidentales, étudiées séparément et comparées entre elles.* Beirut: Patriarcale Syrienne, 1929.

Ramzī, Bishoy, and Christine Fawzī. "Risāla ra'awiyya 'an al-ifḫāristiyyā min al-qarn al-sābi' [A pastoral epistle on the Eucharist from the seventh century]." *Madrasat al-iskandariyya* 18 (2015): 191–209.

Ramzī, Fādī Ra'fat. "Tartīb al-quddās wa-l-qurbān (1): Naṣṣ al-bāb al-sābi' 'ašar min miṣbāḥ al-ẓulma fī īḍāḥ al-ḫidma ḥasab maḫṭūṭ bārīs [The order of the liturgy and the oblation (1): The text of the seventeenth chapter of the lamp of darkness in the elucidation of the service according to the Paris manuscript]." *Madrasat al-iskandariyya* 17 (2014): 193–214.

Renaudot, Eusèbe. *Liturgiarum Orientalium Collectio.* 2nd edition. 2 volumes. Frankfurt, 1847.

Renoux, Charles. "L'hymne des saints dons dans l'Octoéchos géorgien ancient." In *Θυσία αἰνέσεως. Mélanges liturgiques offerts à la mémoire de l'Archevêque Georges Wagner (1930–1993)*, edited by Job Getcha and André Lossky, 293–314. Analecta Sergiana 2. Paris: Institut de théologie orthodoxe, 2005.

Rentel, Alexander. "The 14th Century Patriarchal Liturgical Diataxis of Dimitrios Gemistos: Edition and Commentary." Doctoral dissertation, Pontifical Oriental Institute, 2003.

Riedel, Wilhelm. *Die Kirchenrechtsquellen des Patriarchats Alexandrien.* Leipzig: A. Deichert'sche Verlagsbuchhandlung Nachf. 1900.

Riedel, Wilhelm, and W.E Crum. *The Canons of Athanasius of Alexandria: The Arabic and Coptic Versions.* Oxford: Williams & Norgate, 1904.

Roca-Puig, Ramón. *Anàfora de Barcelona i altres pregàries: Missa del segle IV.* 3rd edition. Barcelona, 1999.

Rodwell, John M. *The Liturgies of S. Basil, S. Gregory, and S. Cyril, Translated from a Coptic Manuscript of the Thirteenth Century.*

Occasional Paper of the Eastern Church Association 12. London, 1870.

Rordorf, Willy and André Tuilier. *La Doctrine des douze apôtres (Didachè).* SC 248bis. Paris: Cerf, 1998.

Rubenson, Samuel. "Tradition and Renewal in Coptic Theology." In *Between Desert and City: The Coptic Orthodox Church Today*, edited by Nelly van Doorn-Harder and Kari Vogt, 36–51. Eugene, OR: Wipf & Stock, 1997.

Rubenson, Samuel. "Translating the Tradition: Some Remarks on the Arabization of the Patristic Heritage in Egypt." *Medieval Encounters* 2, no. 1 (1996): 4–14.

Russo, Nicholas V. "The Validity of the Anaphora of *Addai and Mari.*" In *Issues in Eucharistic Praying in East and West: Essays in Liturgical and Theological Analysis*, edited by Maxwell E. Johnson, 21–61. Collegeville, MN: Liturgical Press, 2010.

Sākā, Isḥaq. *Tafsīr ṭaqs al-kanīsa al-siryāniyya al-urṯuḏuksiyya al-anṭakiyya* [Explanation of the rite of the Syrian Antiochian Orthodox Church]. 3rd rev. ed. Lebanon: Manšūrāt Dayr Mār Ya'qūb al-Barād'ī lil-Rāhibāt al-Suryānīyāt al-Urṯuḏuksiyāt, 2003.

Salāma, Yūḥannā. *Al-la'āli' al-nafīsa fī šarḥ ṭuqūs wa-mu'taqadāt al-kanīsa* [The precious pearls in the explanation of the rites and beliefs of the Church]. 3rd edition. Volume 1. Cairo: Maktabat Mār Ǧirǧis bi-šīkūlānī, 1965.

Ṣalīb, 'Abd al-Masīḥ. ⲡⲓϫⲱⲙ ⲛ̀ⲧⲉ ⲡⲓⲉⲩⲭⲟⲗⲟⲅⲓⲟⲛ ⲉⲑⲟⲩⲁⲃ ⲉ̀ⲧⲉ ⲫⲁⲓ ⲡⲉ ⲡⲓϫⲱⲙ ⲛ̀ⲧⲉ ϯϣⲟⲙϯ ⲛ̀ⲁⲛⲁⲫⲟⲣⲁ ⲛ̀ⲧⲉ ⲡⲓⲁⲅⲓⲟⲥ ⲃⲁⲥⲓⲗⲓⲟⲥ ⲛⲉⲙ ⲡⲓⲁⲅⲓⲟⲥ ⲅⲣⲏⲅⲟⲣⲓⲟⲥ ⲛⲉⲙ ⲡⲓⲁⲅⲓⲟⲥ ⲕⲩⲣⲓⲗⲗⲟⲥ ⲛⲉⲙ ϩⲁⲛⲕⲉⲉⲩⲭⲏ ⲉⲩⲟⲩⲁⲃ [The book of the Holy Euchologion, which is the book of the three Anaphoras of Saint Basil and Saint Gregory and Saint Cyril, and other holy prayers]. Cairo: 'Ayn šams, 1902.

Samir, Kussaim. "Contribution à l'étude du Moyen Arabe des Coptes." *Le Muséon* 80 (1967): 153–209.

Samir, Samir Khalil. "L'Encyclopédie liturgique d'Ibn Kabar († 1324) et son apologie d'usages coptes." In *Crossroad of Cultures: Studies in Liturgy and Patristics in Honor of Gabriele Winkler*, edited by Hans-Jürgen Feulner, Elena Velkovska, and Robert F. Taft, 619–655. OCA 260. Rome: Pontificio Istituto Orientale, 2000.

Samir, Samir Khalil, "Gabriel V." *CE*, 4:1130a–1133a.

Samuel, ed. *Tartīb al-bī'a: 'an maḫṭūṭāt al-baṭriyarkiyya bi-miṣr wa-l-iskandariyya wa-maḫṭūṭāt al-adyira wa-l-kanā'is* [The church order: From the manuscripts of the Patriarchate in Cairo and Alexandria, and the manuscripts of the monasteries and churches]. 3 volumes. [Cairo], 2000.

Schmelz, Georg. *Kirchliche Amtsträger im spätantiken Ägypten nach den Aussagen der griechischen und koptischen Papyri und*

Ostraka. Archiv für Papyrusforschung und verwandte Gebiete 13. Munich: K. G. Saur, 2002.

Schmemann, Alexander. *Introduction to Liturgical Theology*. 5th edition. Crestwood, NY: St Vladimir's Seminary Press, 2003.

Schulz, Hans-Joachim. *The Byzantine Liturgy: Symbolic Structure and Faith Expression*. Translated by Matthew J. O'Connell. New York: Pueblo Publishing, 1986.

Schulz, Hans-Joachim. *Die byzantinische Liturgie: Glaubenszeugnis und Symbolgestalt*. 3rd revised edition. Sophia: Quellen östlicher Theologie 5. Trier: Paulinus, 2000.

Seybold, Christian Friedrich. *Severus ibn al Muqaffa' alexandrinische Patriarchengeschichte von S. Marcus bis Michael I, 61–767 nach der ältesten 1266 geschriebenen Hamburger Handschrift*. Veröffentlichungen aus der Hamburger Stadtbibliothek 3. Hamburg: Lucas Gräfe, 1912.

Simaika, Marcus and Yassa 'abd al-Masiḥ. *Catalogue of the Coptic and Arabic Manuscripts in the Coptic Museum, the Patriarchate, the Principal Churches of Cairo and Alexandria and the Monasteries of Egypt*. 3 volumes. Cairo: Government Press, 1939.

Smidt, Wolbert. "Təgray." *EAE*, 4:888–895.

Smith, Dennis E. *From Symposium to Eucharist: The Banquet in the Early Christian World*. Minneapolis, MN: Fortress Press, 2003.

Stegmüller, Otto. "Christliche Texte aus der Berliner Papyrussammlung." *Aegyptus* 17 (1937): 452–462.

Störk, Lothar. *Koptische Handschriften 2: Die Handschriften der Staats- und Universitätsbibliothek Hamburg*. Volume 2, *Die Handschriften aus Dair Anbā Maqār*. Verzeichnis der orientalischen Handschriften in Deutschland 21.2. Stuttgart: Franz Steiner Verlag, 1995.

Suciu, Alin. "À propos de la datation du manuscrit contenant le grand euchologe du Monastère Blanc." *Vigiliae Christianae* 65 (2011): 189–198.

al-Suryānī, Samuel and Nabīh Kāmil. *Tārīḫ al-ābā' al-baṭārika li-l-anbā Yūsāb usquf Fuwwa* [The history of the fathers the patriarchs of Anba Yūsāb bishop of Fuwwa]. Cairo, 1987.

Swainson, Charles Anthony. *The Greek Liturgies Chiefly from Original Authorities*. Cambridge, 1884.

Swanson, Mark N. *The Coptic Papacy in Islamic Egypt (641–1517)*. The Popes of Egypt 2. Cairo: The American University in Cairo Press, 2010.

Swanson, Mark N. "Ibn Sabbā'." *CMR*, 4:918–923.

Swanson, Mark N. "*Kitāb al-īḍāḥ*." *CMR*, 3:265–269.

Swanson, Mark N. "Sāwīrus ibn al-Muqaffa'." *CMR*, 2:491–509.

Taft, Robert F. "Anton Baumstark's Comparative Liturgy Revisited." In *Acts of the International Congress: Comparative Liturgy Fifty Years after Anton Baumstark (1872–1948), Rome, 25–29 September 1998.* edited by Robert F. Taft and Gabriele Winkler, 191–232. OCA 265. Rome: Pontificio Istituto Orientale, 2001.

Taft, Robert F. "Byzantine Communion Spoons: A Review of the Evidence." *Dumbarton Oaks Papers* 50 (1996): 209–238.

Taft, Robert F. *The Byzantine Rite: A Short History.* American Essays in Liturgy. Collegeville, MN: Liturgical Press, 1992.

Taft, Robert F. "Cathedral vs. Monastic Liturgy in the Christian East: Vindicating a Distinction." *BBGG III* 2 (2005): 173–219.

Taft, Robert F. "The Dialogue before the Anaphora in the Byzantine Eucharistic Liturgy III: 'Let us Give Thanks to the Lord–It is Fitting and Right'." *OCP* 55 (1989): 63–74.

Taft, Robert F. "Eucharistic Concelebration in Greek Orthodoxy Yesterday and Today." In *Studies on the Liturgies of the Christian East: Selected Papers of the Third International Congress of the Society of Oriental Liturgy Volos, May 26–30, 2010*, edited by Steven Hawkes-Teeples, Bert Groen, and Stefanos Alexopoulos, 259–277. Eastern Christian Studies 18. Leuven: Peeters, 2013.

Taft, Robert F. "From Logos to Spirit: On the Early History of the Epiclesis." In *Gratias Agamus: Studien zum eucharistischen Hochgebet: Für Balthasar Fischer*, edited by Andreas Heinz and Heinrich Rennings, 489–502. Freiburg: Herder, 1992.

Taft, Robert F. *A History of the Liturgy of St. John Chrysostom.* Volume 2, *The Great Entrance: A History of the Transfer of Gifts and other Pre-anaphral [sic.] Rites.* 4th edition. OCA 200. Rome: Pontificio Istituto Orientale, 2004.

Taft, Robert F. *A History of the Liturgy of St. John Chrysostom.* Volume 4, *The Diptychs.* OCA 238. Rome: Pontificium Institutum Studiorum Orientalium, 1991.

Taft, Robert F. *A History of the Liturgy of St. John Chrysostom.* Volume 5, *The Precommunion Rites.* OCA 261. Rome: Pontificio Istituto Orientale, 2000.

Taft, Robert F. *A History of the Liturgy of St. John Chrysostom.* Volume 6, *The Communion, Thanksgiving, and Concluding Rites.* OCA 281. Rome: Pontificio Istituto Orientale, 2008.

Taft, Robert F. "How Liturgies Grow: The Evolution of the Byzantine Divine Liturgy." In *Beyond East and West: Problems in Liturgical Understanding.* 2nd edition, edited by Robert F. Taft, 203–232. Rome: Edizioni Orientalia Christiana, 2001.

Taft, Robert F. "Is the Liturgy Described in the Mystagogia of Maximus Confessor Byzantine, Palestinian or Neither?" *BBGG III* 8 (2011): 223–270.

Taft, Robert F. *Liturgy in Byzantium and Beyond.* Hampshire, UK: Variorum, 1995.

Taft, Robert F. "The Liturgy of the Great Church: An Initial Synthesis of Structure and Interpretation on the Eve of Iconoclasm." *Dumbarton Oaks Papers* 34–35 (1980–1981): 45–75.

Taft, Robert F. *The Liturgy of the Hours in East and West: The Origins of the Divine Office and its Meaning for Today.* 2nd revised edition. Collegeville, MN: Liturgical Press, 1993.

Taft, Robert F. "Mass Without the Consecration? The Historic Agreement on the Eucharist between the Catholic Church and the Assyrian Church of the East Promulgated 26 October 2001." *Worship* 77 (2003): 482–509.

Taft, Robert F. "Praise in the Desert: The Coptic Monastic Office Yesterday and Today." *Worship* 56 (1982): 513–536.

Taft, Robert F. "*Quaestiones disputatae:* The Skeuophylakion of Hagia Sophia and the Entrances of the Liturgy Revisited." *OC* 81 (1997): 1–35.

Taft, Robert F. "The Structural Analysis of Liturgical Units: An Essay in Methodology." In *Beyond East and West: Problems in Liturgical Understanding.* 2nd edition, edited by Robert F. Taft, 187–202. Rome: Edizioni Orientalia Christiana, 2001.

Taft, Robert F. "Textual Problems in the Diaconal Admonition before the Anaphora in the Byzantine Tradition." *OCP* 49 (1983): 340–365.

Taft, Robert F. "Was the Eucharistic Anaphora Recited Secretly or Aloud? The Ancient Tradition and What Became of it." In *Worship Traditions in Armenia and the Neighboring Christian East: An International Symposium in Honor of the 40th Anniversary of St Nerses Armenian Seminary,* edited by Roberta R. Ervine, 15–57. AVANT Series 3. Crestwood, NY: St Vladimir's Seminary Press, 2006.

Taft, Robert F., and Stefano Parenti. *Il Grande Ingresso: Edizione italiana rivista, ampliata e aggiornata.* Ἀνάλεκτα Κρυπτοφέρρης 10. Grottaferrata: Monastero Esarchico, 2014.

Tarnanidis, Ioannis C. *The Slavonic Manuscripts Discovered in 1975 at St Catherine's Monastery on Mount Sinai.* Thessaloniki: Saint Catherine's Monastery, 1988.

Tattam, Henry. *The Apostolical Constitutions or Canons of the Apostles in Coptic with an English Translation.* London, 1848.

Till, Walter and Johannes Leipoldt. *Der koptische Text der Kirchenordnung Hippolyts.* Texte und Untersuchungen zur Geschichte der altchristlichen Literatur 58. Berlin: Akademie Verlag, 1954.

Timm, Stefan. *Das christlich-koptische Ägypten in arabischer Zeit: Eine Sammlung christlicher Stätten in Ägypten in arabischer Zeit, unter Ausschluß von Alexandria, Kairo, des Apa-Mena-Klosters (Dēr Abū Mina), der Skētis (Wādi n-Naṭrūn) und der Sinai-Region.* 6 volumes. Beihefte zum Tübinger Atlas des Vorderen Orients, Reihe B, (Geisteswissenschaften) 41.1–6. Wiesbaden: Ludwig Reichert Verlag, 1984–1991.

Tisserant, Eugène, Louis Villecourt, and Gaston Wiet. “Recherches sur la personnalité et la vie d’Abul Barakat Ibn Kubr.” *Revue de l’Orient chrétien* 22 (1921–22): 373–394.

Tornberg, Carl Johan. *Codices Arabici, Persici et Turcici Bibliothecae Regiae Universitatis Upsaliensis.* Uppsala, 1849.

al-Ṭūḫī, Raphael. ⲡⲓϫⲱⲙ ⲛ̀ⲧⲉ ⲡⲓϣⲟⲙⲧ ⲛ̀ⲁⲛⲁⲫⲟⲣⲁ ⲉ̀ⲧⲉ ⲛⲁⲓ ⲛⲉ ⲙ̀ⲡⲓⲁⲅⲓⲟⲥ ⲃⲁⲥⲓⲗⲓⲟⲥ ⲛⲉⲙ ⲡⲓⲁⲅⲓⲟⲥ ⲅⲣⲏⲅⲟⲣⲓⲟⲥ ⲡⲓⲑⲉⲟⲗⲟⲅⲟⲥ ⲛⲉⲙ ⲡⲓⲁⲅⲓⲟⲥ ⲕⲩⲣⲓⲗⲗⲟⲥ ⲛⲉⲙ ⲛⲓⲕⲉ ⲉⲩⲭⲏ ⲉⲑⲟⲩⲁⲃ [The book of the three anaphoras, which are of Saint Basil and Saint Gregory the Theologian and Saint Cyril, and other holy prayers]. Rome, 1736.

al-Ṭūḫī, Raphael. ⲟⲩϫⲱⲙ ⲛ̀ⲧⲉ ⲛⲓⲉⲩⲭⲏ ⲙ̀ⲡⲓⲉϩⲟⲟⲩ ⲛⲉⲙ ⲡⲓⲉϫⲱⲣϩ ⲛ̀ⲍ̅ [The book of the seven prayers of the day and night]. Rome, 1750.

Uri, Joanne. *Bibliothecae Bodleianae codicum manuscriptorum orientalium, videlicet Hebraicorum, Chaldaicorum, Syriacorum, Aethiopicorum, Arabicorum, Persicorum, Turcicorum, Copticorumque Catalogus.* Volume 1. Oxford, 1787.

Van Esbroeck, Michel. “Victor Stratelates, Saint—Coptic Tradition.” *CE* 7:2303a–2305a.

Van Lantschoot, Arnold. *Codices Coptici Vaticani Barberiniani Borgiani Rossiani.* Volume 2, *Codices Barberiniani orientales 2 et 17 Borgiani Coptici 1–108.* Vatican City: Biblioteca Vatican, 1947.

Van Lantschoot, Arnold. “Le ms. Vatican copte 44 et le livre du Chrême (ms. Paris arabe 100).” *Le Muséon* 45 (1932): 181–234.

Van Loon, Gertrud J. M. “The Meeting of Abraham and Melchizedek and the Communion of the Apostles.” In *Coptic Studies on the Threshold of a New Millennium II: Proceedings of the Seventh International Congress of Coptic Studies, Leiden, 27 August–2 September 2000,* edited by Mat Immerzeel and Jacques van der Vliet, 1373–1392. Orientalia Lovaniensia Analecta 133. Leuven: Peeters, 2004.

Varghese, Baby. “Early History of the Preparation Rites in the Syrian Orthodox Anaphora.” In *Symposium Syriacum VII: Uppsala University, Department of Asian and African Languages, 11–14 August 1996,* edited by René Lavenant, 127–138. OCA 256. Rome: Pontificio Istituto Orientale, 1998.

Veilleux, Armand. *La liturgie dans le cénobitisme pachômien au quatrième siècle.* Studia Anselmiana 57. Rome: I.B.C. Liberia Herder, 1968.

Veilleux, Armand. *Pachomian Koinonia.* 3 volumes. Cistercian Studies 45–47. Kalamazoo, MI: Cistercian Publications, 1980–1982.

Verhelst, Stéphane. "La déposition des oblats sur l'autel en Syrie-Palestine. Contribution à l'histoire de la prothesis." *OC* 82 (1998): 184–203.

Verrone, Kerry E. *Mighty Deeds and Miracles by Saint Apa Phoebammon: Edition and Translation of Coptic Manuscript M582 ff. 21r–30r in the Pierpont Morgan Library.* Providence, RI: Brown University, 2002.

Viaud, Gérard. "La procession des deux fêtes de la Croix et du Dimanche des Rameaux dans l'Église copte d'après un manuscrit du monastère Al-Baramûs et du monastère Al-Muḥarraq." *BSAC* 19 (1970): 211–226.

Villecourt, Louis. "La lettre de Macaire, évêque de Memphis, sur la liturgie antique du chrême et du baptême à Alexandrie." *Le Muséon* 36 (1923): 33–46.

Villecourt, Louis. "Les observances liturgiques et la discipline du jeûne dans l'Eglise copte (Ch. XVI–XIX de la Lampe des ténèbres)." *Le Muséon* 36 (1923): 249–292.

Villecourt, Louis. "Les observances liturgiques et la discipline du jeûne dans l'Eglise copte." *Le Muséon* 37 (1924): 201–280.

Viscuso, Patrick Demetrios. *A Guide for a Church under Islam: The Sixty-Six Canonical Questions Attributed to Theodōros Balsamōn.* Brookline, MA: Holy Cross Orthodox Press, 2014.

Vööbus, Arthur. *The Synodicon in the West Syrian Tradition I.* CSCO 367–368, Scriptores Syri 161–162. Louvain: Secrétariat du Corpus SCO, 1975.

Vörös, Győző. *Taposiris Magna: 1998–2004.* Budapest, Egypt Excavation Society of Hungary, 2004.

Vörös, Győző. *Taposiris Magna: Port of Isis, Hungarian Excavations at Alexandria (1998–2001).* Budapest: Egypt Excavation Society of Hungary, 2001.

Ward Benedicta, tra. *The Sayings of the Desert Fathers: The Alphabetical Listing.* Revised edition. Cistercian Studies 59. Kalamazoo, MI: Cistercian Publications, 1984.

Wehr, Hans. *A Dictionary of Modern Written Arabic (Arabic-English).* Edited by J. Milton Cowan. 4th Edition. Wiesbaden, Otto Harrassowitz, 1979.

West, Fritz. *The Comparative Liturgy of Anton Baumstark.* Alcuin/GROW Liturgical Study 31. Nottingham, England: Grove Books, 1995.

Wright, William. *Catalogue of the Ethiopic Manuscripts in the British Museum Acquired Since the Year 1847.* London, 1877.

Youssef, Youhanna Nessim. "The Ark/Tabernacle/Throne/Chalice-Stand in the Coptic Church (Revisited)." *Ancient Near Eastern Studies* 48 (2011): 251–259.

Youssef, Youhanna Nessim and Ugo Zanetti. *La consécration du Myron par Gabriel IV 86e Patriarche d'Alexandrie en 1374 A.D.* JThF 20. Münster: Aschendorff, 2014.

Zanetti, Ugo. "Deux prières de la fraction de la liturgie Grégoire, en grec et en copte." *OCP* 78 (2012): 291–333.

Zanetti, Ugo. "Esquisse d'une typologie des euchologes coptes bohaïriques." *Le Muséon* 100 (1987): 407–418.

Zanetti, Ugo. "Horologion copte et vêpres byzantines." *Le Muséon* 102 (1989): 237–254.

Zanetti, Ugo. "Is the Ethiopian Holy Week Service Translated from Sahidic? Towards a Study of the *Gebra Ḥemāmāt.*" In *Proceedings of the Eleventh International Conference of Ethiopian Studies, Addis Ababa, April 1–6 1991,* edited by Bahru Zewde, Richard Pankhurst, and Taddese Beyene, 765–783. Volume 1. Adis Ababa: Institute of Ethiopian Studies, 1994.

Zanetti, Ugo. "La liturgie dans les monastères de Shenoute." *BSAC* 53 (2014): 167–224.

Zanetti, Ugo. "Liturgy in the White Monastery." In *Christianity and Monasticism in Upper Egypt,* edited by Gawdat Gabra and Hany N. Takla, 201–210. Volume 1, *Akhmim and Sohag.* Cairo: The American University in Cairo Press, 2008.

Zanetti, Ugo. *Les Manuscrits de Dair Abū Maqār: Inventaire.* Cahiers d'orientalisme 11. Geneva: Patrick Cramer, 1986.

Zanetti, Ugo. "Questions liturgiques dans les 'Canons de Shenoute'." *OCP* 82 (2016): 67–99.

Zanetti, Ugo. *Saint Jean, higoumène de Scété (VIIe siècle) Vie arabe et épitomé éthiopien.* Subsidia Hagiographica 94. Brussels: Société des Bollandistes, 2015.

Zanetti, Ugo. "La Vie de Saint Jean, higoumène de Scété au VIIe siècle" *Analecta Bollandiana* 114 (1996): 273–405.

Zheltov, Michael. "The Anaphora and the Thanksgiving Prayer from the Barcelona Papyrus: An Underestimated Testimony to the Anaphoral History in the Fourth Century." *Vigiliae Christianae* 62 (2008): 467–504.

Zheltov, Michael. "The Byzantine Manuscripts of the Liturgy of Mark in the Sinai New Finds." In ⲤⲨⲚⲀⲜⲒⲤ ⲔⲀⲐⲞⲖⲒⲔⲎ: *Beiträge zu Gottesdienst und Geschichte der fünf altkirchlichen Patriarchate für Heinzgerd Brakmann zum 70. Geburtstag,* edited by Diliana

Atanassova and Tinatin Chronz, 801–808. Orientalia-Patristica-Oecumenica 6.2. Vienna: Lit Verlag, 2014.

Zheltov, Michael. "The Moment of Eucharistic Consecration in Byzantine Thought." In *Issues in Eucharistic Praying in East and West: Essays in Liturgical and Theological Analysis*, edited by Maxwell E. Johnson, 263–306. Collegeville, MN: Liturgical Press, 2010.

Zizioulas, John D. *Being as Communion: Studies in Personhood and the Church.* Contemporary Greek Theologians 4. Crestwood, NY: St Vladimir's Seminary Press, 1997.

BIBLICAL INDEX

Exodus
12:5, 118
15:1–21, 184
16:33, 127
27:20–21, 142
28:1–5, 339, 340, 407
Psalms
5:8, 112
18:12–13, 226
18:14, 103
23:7–10, 114
25:6–7, 210, 224, 225, 387, 400
29, 134, 136, 137, 397
42:4, 25, 111–113, 211, 252, 390, 403
50, 200, 226
50:7, 225, 400
50:8, 225, 400
50:9, 226, 400
50:9–10, 210, 224, 387
50:10, 226, 400
50:11–12, 210, 224,
75:10, 25
75:11, 111, 195, 211, 252, 390
85:15, 348, 410
87:1–3, 5 334
92, 134, 397
103, 187, 189
116, 25, 187, 257, 282, 287–9, 308, 333, 379, 380, 381, 383, 404
117:15, 103
117:24–26, 25, 113, 195, 211, 252, 390, 403
117:26, 114
129, 187, 189
131:1, 25, 111, 211, 252, 390, 403
131:1–3, 7 112
135, 184
140, 187, 189
141, 187, 189
148–150, 184
Isaiah
6:3, 115
53:7, 390
Daniel
3:52–90, 184
Matthew
4:23, 351
5:12, 248, 402
5:23–24, 117
6:13, 293, 305, 406
9:6, 154, 155, 398
16:18–19, 348, 410,
Luke
10:19, 293, 297, 305, 406
10:20, 348, 411
16:15, 154, 155, 398
18:13, 154, 155, 398
24:27–30, 383
John
1:15–17, 229
1:29, 229
6:51, 315, 407
20:22–23, 346, 351, 409
Acts
1:24, 154, 155, 398
2:46, 384
3:1, 176
6:2, 393
9:31, 248, 402

10:9, 176, 177
Romans
12:15, 66
15:16, 156, 157, 399
1 Corinthians
10:17, 391
12:16, 156, 157, 399
Ephesians
2:6, 389
5:2, 154, 155, 386, 398
Philippians
1:1, 393
3:16, 66
4:18, 156, 157
1 Thessalonians
5:17, 176, 177, 191
Hebrews
9:7, 156, 157, 399
10:19, 388, 390
10:22, 388
13:15, 156, 389, 399
Revelation
4:9, 248, 402

MANUSCRIPTS INDEX

Abnūb
St. Mina Lit. 1 (18th c.), 38, 299, 421
Alexandria
Alexandria Coptic Patriarchate Codex (1716), 112, 420
Coptic Ms. 1, 182
Greek Orthodox Patriarchate 173/36 (1586), 34, 292, 294, 425
Asyūṭ
Virgin Mary Monastery al-Muḥarraq Lit. 13 (19th c.), 38, 422
Berlin
P. Berlin 709 and *9444+4790* (7th/8th c.), 300, 414
P. Berlin 11346 (7th c.), 372
P. Berlin 12683 (597–626), 334
Cairo
Coptic Museum Inv. 20 (14th c.), 37, 322, 360, 418
Coptic Museum Lit. 16 (1928–42), 214, 222, 226, 228, 236, 246, 261, 270, 283, 291, 314, 423
Coptic Museum Lit. 80 (1796), 214, 221, 226, 228, 236, 246, 265, 270, 283, 291, 313, 421
Coptic Museum Lit. 253 (1364), 128, 136, 417
Coptic Museum Lit. 265 (18th c.), 215, 222, 228, 235, 245, 250, 265, 270, 284, 288, 292, 315, 338, 345, 421
Coptic Museum Lit. 338 (18th c.), 159, 421
Coptic Museum Lit. 344 (1752), 216, 221, 228, 231, 235, 246, 249, 284, 292, 314, 420
Coptic Museum Lit. 361 (1234), 202, 416
Coptic Museum Lit. 412 (1867), 214, 222, 228, 236, 245, 250, 261, 265, 270, 284, 292, 315, 422
Coptic Museum Lit. 462 (19th c.), 213, 288, 291, 314, 315, 338, 422
Coptic Museum Lit. 463 (13th c.), 64, 352, 416
Coptic Museum Supp. Lit. 432 (18th/19th c.), 360, 421
Coptic Patriarchate Lit. 73 (1444), 43, 112, 418
Coptic Patriarchate Lit. 74 (1444), 43, 44, 195, 217, 223, 239, 241, 270, 271, 292, 306, 307, 308, 309, 313, 338, 341, 418
Coptic Patriarchate Lit. 90 (19th c.), 136, 422
Coptic Patriarchate Lit. 117 (1910), 112, 423
Coptic Patriarchate Lit. 160 (1851), 167
Coptic Patriarchate Lit. 172 (1599), 299, 419
Coptic Patriarchate Lit. 175 (18th c.), 38, 421
Coptic Patriarchate Lit. 184 (18th c.) 38, 299, 421
Coptic Patriarchate Lit. 331 (1678), 157, 158, 214, 215, 219, 292, 313, 419

Coptic Patriarchate Lit. 367 (1493), 283
Coptic Patriarchate Theo. 110 (1562), 283
Egypt National Library Theology 221 (1750), 42
Franciscan Center 248 (1878), 283, 422
P. Naqlun II 20 (9th/11th c.), 39, 67, 304, 415
Collegeville
EMML 746 (20th c.), 95
Kacmarcik Codex (14th c.), 38, 154, 157, 212, 297, 299, 313, 322, 335, 351, 418
Graz
Universitätsbibliothek 2058/4 (985), 164, 423
Grottaferrata
Grottaferrata Γβ IV (10th c.), 163, 316, 423
Grottaferrata Γβ VII (10th c.), 317, 423
Grottaferrata Γβ VIII (12th c.), 317, 424
Grottaferrata Γβ XIII (13th c.), 317, 425
Hamburg
Hamburg 304 (Or. 26) (1266), 300
Hamburg Bishoy Euchol. 6 (18th/19th c.), 313, 421
Hamburg Bishoy Euchol. 7 (13th/14th c.), 330, 416
Hamburg Macarius Euchol. 30 (17th/18th c.), 314, 420
Hamburg Macarius Euchol. 46 (13th/14th c.), 338, 417
Hamburg Macarius Hymns 30 (14th/15th c.), 338, 418
Leiden
P. Leiden Inst. 13 (7th/8th c.), 129
RMO Copt. 85 (12th/13th c.), 102, 110, 114, 415
London
British Library Add. 17725 (1811), 216, 222, 226, 228, 231, 245, 248, 249, 251, 261, 265, 270, 288, 289, 291, 314, 345, 388, 421
British Library Or. 429 (17th/18th c.), 221, 235, 245, 265, 270, 283, 291, 313, 338, 345, 420
British Library Or. 430 (1832), 214, 222, 228, 235, 245, 250, 261, 265, 270, 284, 292, 314, 338, 345, 422
British Library Or. 431 (1718), 270, 283, 288, 289, 313, 338, 353, 420
British Library Or. 545 (1670–5), 153, 263, 273, 285, 426
British Library Or. 546 (1730–7), 153, 273, 426
British Library Or. 547 (1784–1800), 153, 426
British Library Or. 548 (1855–68), 153, 426
British Library Or. 768 (18th c.), 95
British Library Or. 1239 (13th c.), 40, 147, 158, 159, 212, 330, 332, 352, 416
British Library Or. 1320 (1006), 92, 177
British Library Or. 3580A (7) (11th c.), 328, 360, 361, 415
British Library Or. 3580A (11) (10th/11th c.), 65, 415
British Library Or. 4718(1) (10th c.), 350, 415
British Library Or. 5282 (1872), 270, 313, 422
British Library Or. 7022 (951), 142
British Library Or. 7029 (992), 63

British Library Or. 7597 (10th c.), 64
British Library Or. 8778 (1726), 291, 305, 314, 420
Manchester
Rylands Copt. 426 (13th c.), 45, 212, 287, 288, 291, 330, 352, 416
Rylands Copt. 427 (1749), 214, 221, 226, 228, 236, 245, 265, 270, 283, 291, 314, 345, 420
Messina
Messina Gr. 160 (11th c.), 316, 424
Messina Gr. 177 (11th c.), 34, 292, 294, 424, 425
Milan
Ambrosiana Gr. 276 (13th c.), 317, 424
Modena
Modena Gr. 16 (16th c.), 317, 425
Munich
Bayerische Staatsbibliothek Gr. 540 (1416), 317, 425
New Haven
Beinecke Copt. 20 (19th c.), 314, 422
Beinecke Copt. 21 (1877), 158, 291, 314, 422
New York
MLM M574 (897-898), 183-5, 415
MLM M582 (822-914), 56
Oslo
P. Oslo inv. 1665 (7th/8th c.), 373, 414
Oxford
Bodleian Copt. f. 3 (15th/16th c.), 338, 418
Bodleian Hunt. 360 (13th c.), 46, 56, 65, 147, 158, 159, 212, 250, 292, 303, 304, 305, 313, 326, 330, 352, 416
Bodleian Hunt. 572 (13th/14th c.), 157, 212, 267, 291, 304, 330, 353, 417
Bodleian Ind. Inst. Copt. 4 (13th/14th c.), 45, 157, 212, 291, 304, 330, 417
Bodleian Marsh 5 (14th c.), 46, 158, 212, 292, 353, 418
Bodleian Syr. E5, 152
Paris
BnF Ar. 98 (17th c.), 42, 43, 111, 121, 122, 130, 137, 138, 139, 141, 148, 194, 214, 221, 227, 230, 234, 239, 244, 248, 250, 260, 264, 269, 270, 279, 282, 287, 314, 335, 345, 346
BnF Ar. 100 (14th c.), 24, 96-9, 188, 189, 413
BnF Ar. 170 (13th c.), 130
BnF Ar. 203 (1363-69), 41, 44, 121, 130, 137, 140, 144, 186, 187, 188, 213, 222, 243, 248, 260, 264, 267, 269, 279, 281, 282, 287, 314, 334, 335, 338, 345
BnF Ar. 207 (14th c.), 24, 42, 113, 118, 130, 137, 139, 140, 147, 190-2, 220, 229, 238, 253, 260, 264, 278, 281, 287, 306, 331, 336, 340, 341, 344, 345, 359
BnF Ar. 227 (1671), 375
BnF Ar. 251 (1353), 58, 65, 181, 182, 183, 279
BnF Ar. 301 (15th c.), 301
BnF Ar. 302 (15th c.), 301
BnF Ar. 6147 (17th c.), 282
BnF Copt. 24 (15th c.), 157, 212, 291, 360, 418
BnF Copt. 25 (15th/16th c.), 291, 314, 329, 353, 419
BnF Copt. 26 (b. 1523), 45, 291, 313, 315, 360, 419
BnF Copt. 28 (13th/14th c.), 291, 314, 330, 417

BnF Copt. 29 (1639), 158, 160, 291, 303, 313, 338, 353, 419
BnF Copt. 30 (1642), 158, 159, 215, 221, 228, 236, 245, 261, 265, 270, 292, 303, 313, 338, 419
BnF Copt. 31 (15th c.), 212, 291, 314, 418
BnF Copt. 39 (15th c.), 292, 304, 314, 360, 418
BnF Copt. 73 (1528), 157, 291, 313, 360, 419
BnF Copt. 82 (1307), 157, 212, 292, 304, 313, 352, 417
BnF Copt. 129(20) (10th/11th c.), 328, 415
BnF Copt. 130(3), 55
BnF Eth. d'Abbadie 66–66bis (15th c.), 94
BnF Gr. 322 (16th c.), 317, 425
BnF Gr. 325 (14th c.), 37, 162, 165, 166, 335, 418
Prague
P. Prag II 178 (5th/6th c.), 130
Prague Or. Inst. MS I p. 1–3 (11th/12th c.), 300, 415
Red Sea
St. Antony Codex (1661), 112, 419
St. Antony Lit. 55 (1824), 38, 422
St. Paul Lit. 201 (1818), 38, 422
Scetis
Baramūs 6/278 (1514), 44, 112, 195, 218, 223, 271, 282, 307, 308, 313, 341, 419
St. Macarius Hagiography 35 (1549), 72
St. Macarius Lit. 133 (19th c.), 222, 226, 228, 231, 246, 388, 422
St. Macarius Lit. 134 (18th/19th c.), 222, 226, 228, 231, 245, 388, 421
St. Macarius Lit. 136 (19th c.), 222, 226, 228, 246, 422
St. Macarius Lit. 147 (18th c.), 222, 228, 245, 421
St. Macarius Lit. 155 (1894), 38, 213, 299, 422
St. Macarius Lit. 156 (1852), 38, 422
St. Macarius Lit. 438 (14th c.), 187, 418
St. Macarius Lit. 440 (17th c.), 187, 420
Suryān Lit. 457 (1758), 157, 313, 420
Suryān Lit. 459 (1788), 314, 421
Suryān Lit. 461 (1795), 158, 421
Suryān Lit. 465 (1645), 158, 314, 419
Suryān Lit. 466 (1573), 157, 313, 419
Suryān Lit. 468 (1601), 157, 313, 419
Suryān Lit. 469 (b. 1623), 157, 291, 313, 419
Suryān Lit. 472 (1659), 157, 313, 419
Suryān Lit. 473 (1659), 157, 313, 419
Suryān Lit. 474 (1666), 157, 313, 419
Suryān Lit. 477 (1792), 158, 314, 421
Suryān Lit. 481 (1752), 157, 313, 420
Suryān Lit. 482 (1787), 157, 313, 420
Suryān Lit. 484 (1841), 157, 313, 422
Suryān Lit. 485 (1784), 283, 315, 420
Suryān Monastery Codex (1698), 112, 420
Sinai
Sinai Ar. 184 (13th c.), 202, 416
Sinai Ar. 237 (13th c.), 34, 294–5, 321, 425

Sinai Ar. 389 (13th c.), 202–3, 416
Sinai Geo. N. 26 (965–73), 164, 423
Sinai Geo. N. 63 (10th c.), 164, 424
Sinai Geo. O. 53 (9th/10th c.), 164, 423
Sinai Glagol. 37 (11th c.), 316, 329, 361, 424
Sinai Gr. 1040 (1156–69), 164, 424
Sinai Gr. NE/E 24 (11th c.), 164, 424
Sinai Gr. NE/E 80 (11th/12th c.), 163, 424
Sinai Gr. NE/MΓ 118 (8th/9th c.), 163, 423

St. Petersburg
NLR 226 (10th c.), 316, 424

Strasbourg
Strasbourg Gr. 1899 (1523), 317, 425

Sweden
Uppsala O. Vet. 12 (1546), 41, 44, 121, 187, 218, 226, 244, 269–71, 282, 306, 307, 308, 342, 355
Uppsala Or. Ethiop 20–23 (17th c.), 285, 426

Turin
Codex XIII, 182

Vatican City
BAV Barberini Gr. 336 (8th c.), 25, 106, 107, 161, 162, 167, 316, 317, 318, 325, 326, 327, 330, 371, 423
BAV Barberini Or. 17 (1396), 203, 417
BAV Borgia Ar. 22 (1295), 57
BAV Borgia Copt. 7 (1379), 157, 212, 292, 304, 305, 313, 352, 360, 417
BAV Borgia Gr. 24 (1880), 165, 425
BAV Ottoboni Gr. 189 (16th c.), 317, 425
BAV Ottoboni Gr. 384 (1581), 317, 425
BAV Vatican Ar. 117 (1323), 40, 131, 143, 259, 314, 326
BAV Vatican Borghes. Ser. I 506 (1581), 317, 425
BAV Vatican Copt. 17 (1288), 46, 64, 147, 149, 157, 159, 195, 212, 291, 304, 313, 326, 330, 352, 416
BAV Vatican Copt. 18 (1531), 158, 214, 221, 227, 228, 236, 245, 250, 265, 270, 283, 284, 288, 291, 292, 313, 338, 345, 419
BAV Vatican Copt. 19 (1715), 305, 314, 323, 420
BAV Vatican Copt. 24 (14th c.), 212, 292, 352, 417
BAV Vatican Copt. 25 (14th c.), 158, 160, 212, 246, 265, 268, 269, 270, 274, 291, 305, 306, 313, 417, 420
BAV Vatican Copt. 26 (1616), 157, 313, 419
BAV Vatican Copt. 27 (15th c.), 116, 250, 287, 335, 338, 344, 418
BAV Vatican Copt. 28 (1306), 116, 250, 287, 289, 304, 336, 338, 344, 417
BAV Vatican Copt. 38 (14th c.), 283, 288, 335, 338, 344, 417
BAV Vatican Copt. 40 (1334), 203, 417
BAV Vatican Copt. 62 (9th–10th c.), 74
BAV Vatican Copt. 78 (1722), 291, 305, 314, 420
BAV Vatican Copt. 81 (1722), 305, 314, 420
BAV Vatican Copt. 99 (1718–26), 214, 221, 226, 228, 236, 245, 265, 270, 283, 291, 420

BAV Vatican Gr. 1970 (12th c.), 34, 165, 292, 294, 295, 297, 299, 317, 320, 326, 330, 331, 424
BAV Vatican Gr. 2005 (1194–5), 317, 424
BAV Vatican Gr. 2012 (16th c.), 317, 425
BAV Vatican Gr. 2281 (1207), 25, 34, 65, 165, 292, 294, 295, 296, 297, 309, 319, 326, 330, 424
BAV Vatican Gr. 2282 (9th c.), 164, 423

Vienna
P. ÖNB K. 4854 (6th c.), 66, 414
P. ÖNB K. 9390 (10th c.), 415
P. ÖNB K. 9761 (11th c.), 415

GENERAL INDEX

‘Abd al-Masīḥ Ṣalīb, Euchologion of (*editio typica*), 13, 36, 46, 48, 65, 116, 134, 135, 140–2, 144, 145, 148, 149, 154, 157, 166–7, 175, 196, 204, 209, 210, 211, 226, 230, 231, 235, 240, 246,248, 249, 250, 252, 257, 258, 262, 269, 279, 287, 293, 313, 315, 339, 346, 397
ablutions. *See under* washing, ritual
Abraham ibn Zur‘a, Pope, 33, 85, 87
Abraham of Hermonthis, Bishop, 232–3, 278–9
Absolution(s)
function of, 354–6; of the Father, 25–6, 311, 335, 345–6, 347–8, 350–4, 410–1; of the servants, 25–6, 346, 349–50, 352–7, 380, 381, 411–2; of the Son, 25–6, 311, 345–7, 349, 351–6, 379, 380, 381, 382, 383, 409–10; origin in prothesis, 350–4
accessus ad altare, prayers of
in *Addai and Mari*, 164; in Byzantine liturgies, 161–3; in Roman Mass, 161; in West-Syrian liturgies, 164
accessus ad altare, rites of
duplication in Coptic new ordo, 171, 220, 224, 263, 379
Addai and Mari, anaphora of, 164, 366, 369, 370
‘Ādil, Rafīq, 36, 43, 193
Adulis (Ethiopia), 79
Ağbiyya, 53, 184, 187, 188, 203. *See also* Horologion
Aksum, 79, 108, 428
Aksumite Collection, 56, 300, 301
Alexandria, liturgy in, 31–2, 33–4, 35, 99, 101, 110, 301
Alexopoulos, Stefanos, 81, 199, 324
Alleluia al-Qurbān (chant), 113–4, 117, 148, 237, 240, 241, 242, 251, 253, 380, 381, 382, 389
All the wise men of Israel, 25, 311, 312, 339–42, 407
altar preparation (prayers)
comparison between Coptic and Greek Egyptian BAS, 159–60; origins, 167–72; title in manuscripts, 157–9
altar, preparation of the
from the comparative method, 150–4; in ‘Abd al-Masīḥ’s Euchologion, 141–5; in Byzantine Rite, 151; in current usage, 145–6; in Ethiopian Rite, 152–3; in Gabriel V, 147–8; in Ibn Sabbā‘, 147; in Roman Rite, 151; in Syro-Antiochene Rite, 151–2; vis-à-vis preparation of the gifts, 153
Angelion (church), 99, 100, 101
Annunciation, Feast of the, 192, 193
Apologia contra Arianos, 70–1
Apollo (Bawīṭ), Monastery of, 85, 129

Apophthegmata Patrum, 336–7, 373
Apostolic Constitutions, 66, 69–70, 77, 89, 92, 104, 151, 223–4, 280, 369
Apostolic Tradition, 92–3, 104, 177–8, 280, 366
Arab conquest, 101, 276
Arabization, 37, 39
Armenian Rite, 54, 101, 102, 115–6, 161, 272
aspasmos chants, 103, 116
Atanassova, Diliana, 32, 102, 103
Athanasius of Alexandria, 14, 58, 63, 70, 71, 349, 352, 353, 354, 411
Athanasius II, Pope, 58
Ayyubids, 86–7

baptism of the lamb, 227–32, 254, 381, 382, 400
al-Baramūs, Monastery of
Church of the Virgin, 73, 74, 85, 427
Basil the Great, Liturgy of
Byzantine BAS, 162, 163, 165, 166, 167, 168, 171, 172, 173, 259, 260, 324, 325, 329, 343, 379, 423; Coptic BAS, 64, 71, 116, 361
basin, water (church), 137, 138
Baumstark, Anton, 49, 62, 114, 179, 367; *Angleichung*, 203, 250; laws of (general), 49, 113; emphasis by duplication, 171, 172, 173, 379; enrichment then retrograde simplification, 354, 357; retention of ancient practices, 113, 193, 200, 344
blessing, exchange of
in East and West, 262–3; in hagiography, 263; in medieval sources, 263–5; significance of, 265–6
Bolman, Elizabeth, 84, 128
Book of the Chrism, The, 96
Bornert, René, 131
Bradshaw, Paul F., 93, 176, 177, 178, 179, 368, 369, 370
Brakmann, Heinzgerd, 10, 27, 29, 30, 31, 33–4, 35, 37–8, 40, 45–6, 80–1, 93–4, 95, 110, 149, 242, 260, 272, 301, 324, 327, 360
Brightman, F.E., 27, 46, 63, 152, 153, 263, 267, 285, 323
Budde, Achim, 37–8, 40, 66, 67, 267, 283, 414
Budge, E.A. Wallis, 63, 64, 142, 374
Burmester, O.H.E., 26, 44, 45, 125, 126, 127, 129, 130, 139, 144, 158, 189, 192, 193, 195, 200, 201, 202, 209, 210, 211, 249, 287, 302, 303, 304, 306, 312, 336, 344, 360, 361, 372
Bute, John Marquess of, 45, 240
Butler, Alfred J., 59, 125, 126, 127, 128, 129, 132
Byzantinization, 37, 178, 259, 260, 326

Cairo, 27, 32, 35, 42, 85, 128, 214, 215, 256, 261, 276, 277, 283, 333
Calivas, Alkiviadis, 391, 392
canons, medieval, 47. See also under respective titles.
Canons of Hippolytus, 93
Canons of the Apostles, 92, 223
catechumens, 69, 70, 71, 94, 97, 98, 99, 100, 101, 106, 110, 258
Chalcedon, conflict after, 32, 57, 101, 353, 373
chalice, eucharistic (general), 127
chalice, mixing of, 26, 233, 258, 272, 273, 275–90, 302, 308, 333, 378, 379, 380, 381, 382,

404–5; deacon's response during, 286–90; in East and West, 284–6; in Euchologia, 283–4; in medieval guides, 281–3; response as duplication from pre-communion, 288–90
cherubic hymn (Cherubicon), 111, 114, 161, 165
Christodoulus, Pope, 14, 32, 47, 58–60, 85, 89, 374
churches (building)
ancient Ethiopian, 73–4, 79–80, 86, 107–8; in Nubia, 81–2; in Old Cairo, 85–6; monastic Coptic, 73–4, 85, 89; with three altars, 85–9
Chrysostom, liturgy of Saint John (CHR), 19, 66, 161, 162, 163, 259, 316, 317, 324, 325, 326, 329, 330, 331, 356, 371, 414, 425
Clement of Alexandria, 176–7, 299
clericalization, increased in prothesis, 219, 271, 280, 282, 283, 286, 350, 392–3
cloths, altar, 130–2, 144–6, 150–1, 253
codicology, 99
Cody, Aelred, 198
commemorations, in Byzantine liturgy, 236; in Ethiopian liturgy, 236–7; in Gabriel V, 233–5; in Ibn Kabar, 233; in the West, 236
concelebration, 217–8
consecration, in theological texts, 375–6; in pre-communion, 372–4; patriarchal, 136; verbs of, 317, 319, 323
Constantinople, liturgy of, 78, 106, 131, 162, 163, 171, 198, 324, 325, 327, 345
Coptic Liturgy, Arabic translation of. *See under* Arabic language; Greek recension of, 37–8, 154, 213; Bohairic recension of, 38–9; patriarchal, 43–5, 195, 217–9, 223, 270–2, 282, 306–7, 308, 341–2, 344, 354, 392
Coquin, René-Georges, 58, 93, 218, 259, 335, 336
Cosmas III, Pope, 97, 100
Cramer, Maria, 193
crosses, performed by priest during liturgy, 267
Cuming, Geoffrey J., 34, 56, 167, 294, 324, 328, 330, 331, 360–1
Cyprus, Coptic community in, 37, 158, 212
Cyril, Liturgy of. *See under* Mark, liturgy of
Cyril II, Pope, 47, 60
Cyril III ibn Laqlaq, Pope, 40, 47, 314
Cyril of Alexandria, 62–3, 164, 353–4
Cyril of Jerusalem, 366, 369, 387

daily office. *See also* liturgy of the hours; cathedral and monastic, 179, 183, 187, 189, 197–8, 200
Dā'ūd, Marqus, 57, 247
Davis, Stephen J., 11, 131, 278
deacon, as minister of the chalice. *See* chalice, minister of; position across from celebrant, 258–61
De lingua, 55, 232
Demetrius Gemistos, 343
Descoeudres, Georges, 23, 78, 88, 236, 253, 280, 284, 285, 326, 327, 363, 393
diaconicon (book), 46, 116, 414, 415, 417, 418, 424
diaconicon (room), 70, 76

Didascalia Apostolorum, 27, 68–9, 89, 280
Didascalia Arabica, 57, 69, 76
Dix, Gregory, 27, 62, 365–8, 370
el-Dorry, Mennat Allah, 277
Dous, Roshdi W.B., 29–30, 34, 38, 71, 100, 122, 154, 167, 299
Drescher, James, 126

ecclesiology, 23, 387, 390–3
Egeria, diary of, 178
Eis pater. See under chalice, deacon's response during mixing of
enarxis, 26, 35, 258, 288, 289, 290, 291, 295, 301, 303, 308, 309, 312, 313, 314, 330, 331, 333, 342, 344, 350, 355, 357, 369, 377, 379, 380, 381
Engberding, Hieronymus, 34, 37, 324, 328, 330, 352, 353, 356, 360, 361
epiclesis prayer, 81, 218, 312, 319, 324, 327–30, 331, 356, 359, 360–2, 364, 371, 372, 374, 375, 376, 394
eucharistic gifts, covering of, 334, 344–5, 380, 408–9; deposition (placement) of, 23–4, 29, 54, 55, 64, 78, 79, 80, 82, 91, 104–9, 111, 122, 123, 165, 171, 173, 207, 208, 236, 247, 272–3, 302, 362, 367, 373, 379, 383–4; transfer of the. *See under* transfer
eucharistic gifts, blessing of, 211, 266–75, 332, 404; in current practice, 208, 211, 404; in East and West, 272–3; in Ibn Kabar, 267–8; in John of Scetis, 72–3, 266; in patriarchal liturgy, 270–2; origins of, 274–5; significance of, 271–2; trinitarian, 268–70
eucharistic gifts, preparation of by the people, 55–62; in Isaac of Alexandria, 74–6; in John of Scetis, 72–4
eucharistic gifts, selection of, 115, 121–2, 141, 148, 207, 212–20, 222–5, 253–5, 258, 264, 265–6, 271, 333, 377, 380, 381, 382, 385–6, 392, 399–400; additional acts and prayers at, 219–20; chant during, 111, 117, 175, 204, 237–42, 389–90; in current practice, 209–10; in Euchologia manuscripts, 212; in Gabriel V, 214–5; in Ibn Kabar, 213–4; in patriarchal liturgy, 217–19
eucharistic gifts, transfer of, 54, 55, 78, 91–109, 117–123, 151, 242, 258, 266; chant at the, 109–117; in Ancient Church Orders, 92–93; in Byzantium, 106–7. *See also* Great Entrance; in Ethiopia, 107–9; in Gabriel V, 121–2; in Ibn Kabar, 120–1; in Ibn Sabbā‘, 117–9; in Jacob of Wasīm, 95; in Justin, 91–2; in Rome, 109; in Southern Egypt, 102–3; in Syria-Antioch, 104–6; in *The Letter of Macarius*, 95–101; in *The Order of the Mystery*, 93–5
Euchologium Sinaiticum, 316, 329, 331, 361–2, 424
Eutychus, Patriarch of Constantinople, 107, 284, 285, 325, 326–7

Faras Cathedral, 60, 81, 82, 318
Fatimids, 85, 87
Feulner, Hans-Jürgen, 10, 50
al-Fransīskānī, Wadī‘ (‘Awaḍ), 39–40, 46, 414

Fritsch, Emmanuel, 73, 79–80, 85, 86, 87, 94, 107–8, 110, 115, 119, 152, 155, 222, 237, 247, 261, 273, 285
Frøyshov, Stig Simeon, 179

Gabriel II ibn Turaik, Pope, 32, 47, 143, 193
Gabriel IV, Pope, 215, 283
Gabriel V, Pope, 13, 42, 122, 123, 141, 378. See also *The Ritual Order*
Galadza, Daniel, 10, 178, 260
Gémayel, Pierre-Edmond, 104–5
Germanus, Patriarch of Constantinople, 131, 284, 343
Glory and honor, 24, 135, 139, 210, 216, 242–3, 246, 248–51, 252–3, 264, 267–70, 273, 274–5, 382, 402, 404
Graf, Georg, 19, 40, 53, 57, 68–9, 128–9, 375
Great Entrance (Byzantine), 28, 62, 69, 102, 106–7, 114, 151, 163, 224, 284, 325, 327, 330; as burial procession, 104; in Syro-Palestinian churches, 77–8, 151
Great Euchologion of the White Monastery, 32, 102
Gregory the Theologian, Liturgy of (GREG), 19, 25, 32, 37, 38, 45, 64, 162, 165, 166, 168, 169, 170, 171, 172, 346, 350, 361, 410
Grossmann, Peter, 48, 68, 73, 75, 82–6, 88, 427, 428, 429
Guide to the Beginners, The, 40, 143, 259, 260, 261, 267, 268, 313–4, 326

Hagia Sophia, 78, 106–7
hagiography, 36, 47–8, 68, 126, 263, 373–5
Ḫā'īl III, Pope, 119–20
Al-Ḥākim, Caliph, 86, 276
hand washing, 141, 161, 203, 207, 213–4, 215, 216, 220–32, 240, 247, 253, 254–5, 333, 379, 380, 381–2, 385, 386, 387, 388, 400; duplicated from pre-anaphora, 223–4; in Euchologia manuscripts, 221–2; in Gabriel V, 221; in Ibn Sabbā', 220; place in the unfolding of the prothesis, 222–5; psalms and prayers during, 225–7
Hanna, Maged (Basilios), 202, 299
Hawkes-Teeples, Steven, 23, 229, 236
hermenia (chant), 183, 415
Hermopolis Magna, church of, 83
Historia ecclesiastica (Theodoret), 70–1, 89, 98
Historia monachorum, 63, 280
Histories of the Monasteries and Churches, The, 85, 259, 374
History of the Patriarchs, 20, 59–60, 74, 75, 120, 276, 300–1, 374
Holy Week, 189, 192, 193, 195, 200
Horologion. 53, 140, 144, 146, 175, 179, 181, 183, 184, 185, 188, 189, 193, 197, 200, 201, 202, 204, 209, 241–2, 302, 415, 416, 417, 418, 420. See also *Aǧbiyya*
Hosts of Angels, The (chant), 94, 110, 114–5, 116–7, 327
hours, little (third, sixth, and ninth), 175–204; in Byzantine liturgy, 198–9; in Coptic practice, 200–4; in Gabriel V, 194–5; in Ibn Sabbā', 190–4; in Pachomian monasteries, 180–1; in Ps.-Basil, 181–3; in Roman Mass, 199; in Scetis,

178–80; in Shenoute, 180–1; in the Early Church, 176–8; in the Fayyūm, 183–5 ; in Ibn Kabar, 186–90; in West-Syrian liturgy, 197–8; issues in Coptic practice, 201–4

Ibn Kabar, Abū l-Barakāt. See under *Lamp of Darkness, The*
Ibn Sabbā', Yūḥannā (ibn Abī Zakariyyā). See under *Precious Jewel, The*
Ibrahīm, Philotheos, 46, 397
incense, blessing of, 134–5, 139, 269; *Evening Raising of* (vespers), 134, 137, 139, 186, 189–90, 194, 195, 274, 289, 302, 307; *Morning Raising of* (matins), 24, 137, 139, 144, 146, 173, 175, 186, 187–8, 189–90, 194, 195, 274, 300, 302
Innemée, Karel C., 87, 133, 136
Institution Narrative, 218, 369–70
intermediate ordo, 117–9, 120, 191, 225, 238, 239, 241, 242, 266, 308, 331, 333, 377, 381

Jacob, André, 316, 324, 329, 356, 361–2, 414
Jacob of Wasīm, 29, 95, 143
James, liturgy of (JAS), 20, 66, 88, 163–4, 165, 166, 259, 260, 262, 326, 423, 424, 425
Jerusalem (hagiopolite), liturgy of, 66, 101, 163, 178; transfer chants, 110, 115
John Cassian, 179–80
John III, Pope, 72, 300
John of Bostra, 164, 167
John of Dara, 105
John of Scetis, 72–4, 89, 266, 271, 274, 378
John of Tella, 104, 105, 285
John Scholasticus, 77, 151
Johnson, Maxwell E., 36, 101, 328, 369
Jungmann, Josef A., 21, 27–8, 62, 109, 236, 273, 286, 362
Justin Martyr, 91–2, 104, 108, 278, 286, 368, 383

Kaufhold, Hubert, 47, 57, 58, 69, 92
Khouri-Sarkis, Gabriel, 104
kiss of peace (pax), 64, 67, 91–2, 102, 103, 116, 117, 161, 164, 262, 379
Kitāb al-īḍāḥ (*The Book of Elucidation*), 130–1, 278
Kīrillus VI, Pope, 136

Łajtar, Adam, 60, 81, 319
lamb. *See under* offering
lamp, eastern, 142–3, 148, 149, 398
Lamp of Darkness, The (*miṣbāḥ al-ẓulma*), 40–2, 44, 120–1, 128, 130, 140, 147, 186–90, 213–4, 222–3, 227, 233, 242–4, 248, 251, 260, 264, 266, 267–8, 269, 271, 274, 279, 281–2, 287, 306, 308, 314, 334–5, 338, 344, 381, 392
lamp-lighting, psalms (Byzantine), 187
language, Arabic, 14, 30–1, 39–40, 159, 293; Coptic, 30; Greek, 14, 29, 30–1, 37–8, 65–7, 80, 304, 336–8
Larin, Vassa, 136
Lausiac History, 179–80
Lent, 97, 111–3, 188, 197–8, 199, 200, 202, 211, 239, 252, 334
Lewicka, Paulina, 276–7
Lietzmann, Hans, 365–6, 370–1
life of Christ, symbolized in prothesis, 130–2, 227–8, 229–

30, 232, 244, 253–4, 278, 280, 286, 344–5, 390
Life of Isaac of Alexandria, 74–6, 89, 100, 130
litanies. *See under* prayer
liturgy
commentaries on, 84, 105, 131–2, 151, 229–30, 247, 253–4, 267–8, 284, 290–1, 343; Northern Egyptian, 32–3, 35, 54, 103, 133, 150, 208, 212, 338, 339, 354, 380; of the hours, 53, 175–6, 175–204, 289. *See also* Horologion and *Aǧbiyya*; of the word, 45, 54, 132, 140, 162, 165, 207, 217, 242, 271, 311, 312, 333, 335, 336, 339, 351, 352, 355, 357, 383; study of, 27, 48–50

Macarius, Monastery of Saint, 21, 33, 99, 176, 189, 193, 201,
Macarius of Manūf al-ʿuliyā, 29, 30, 96–101, 103, 108, 109, 117, 119, 120, 121, 123, 188, 242
Malan, Solomon Caesar, 45, 291, 417
Mamluks, 41, 82, 86, 87
Mandalà, Marco, 362–3
al-Maqārī, Fr. Athanasius, 30, 58, 67, 96, 98, 101, 112, 119, 122, 196, 222, 223, 228–30, 267, 291, 338, 364
Mark, liturgy of
Coptic MARK/CYRIL, 19, 30, 32, 45, 55, 64, 164, 167, 267, 346, 356, 359, 360–1
Melkite MARK, 21, 25, 34, 56, 65, 164, 165, 231, 259–60, 261, 290, 292, 294–9, 301, 303, 309, 312, 318–21, 324, 326, 330–1, 350–3, 354, 424, 425
Presanctified liturgy of, 21, 34, 294–5, 425
Mark, cathedral of St. (Alexandria), 75, 300
Mathews, Thomas F., 78
matins. *See incense, raising of*
Mattā al-Miskīn, Hegumen, 291, 299, 359, 360, 363, 364–71
Mattāʾus, Bishop, 229–30, 254, 291, 390
Maximus the Confessor. *See under* Mystagogia (Maximus)
May you be saved, 334–9; function in Coptic liturgy, 336–9; in monastic literature, 336–7
Melkite Liturgy, 34. *See also* Melkite MARK
Meyendorff, Paul, 131, 284
Michael, Archangel, 63, 84
Michael, Monastery of the Archangel (al-Ḥāmūlī), 102, 183
Mihálykó, Ágnes T., 102, 300, 329, 334, 368, 373, 414, 415
Mikhail, Maged S.A., 31, 235, 364
Mikhail, Ramez, 34, 43, 133, 187, 195, 217, 218, 223, 270, 271, 282, 289, 295, 307, 341, 342, 373, 389, 391
Mīḫāʾīl of Samannūd, 215–7, 226, 231, 249, 300, 388
miracles, eucharistic, 72, 271–2, 372–5, 394
Moses bar Kepha, 105, 108, 151, 247, 267
Muksuris, Stelyios, 363
myron (chrism), 96–100, 126, 128, 188–9, 215, 335–6
Mystagogia (Maximus), 77–8, 106, 131, 132, 151, 326, 327
Mystagogy (chrism), 96
Mystery of the Trinity, The, 282, 283, 308

Nasrallah, Joseph, 260

neo-alexandrinische Liturgie. See Northern Egyptian Liturgy
new ordo, 54, 75, 77, 78, 79, 80, 89, 91, 100, 101, 104, 105, 107, 108, 111, 113, 115, 116, 119–23, 133, 171, 172, 207–8, 211, 219, 220, 223, 225, 237, 240, 242, 243, 247, 253, 255, 258, 263, 266, 289, 291, 312, 331, 333, 344, 350, 355–6, 357, 371, 378–9, 379, 381, 383–6, 389, 392
Nicholas of Andida, 131, 284
nomocanons, 57, 183
Nubia, Christianity in, 80; Liturgy of, 35, 60, 70, 80–2, 89, 129, 318–9; Presanctified liturgy in, 81–2, 319

oblations. *See under* eucharistic gifts
offering. *See under* eucharistic gifts
old ordo, 54, 68, 77, 78, 80, 89, 91, 96, 98, 100, 101, 104, 105, 107, 111, 113, 115, 116, 117, 119, 120, 123, 133, 153, 207–8, 211, 216, 220, 223, 225, 237, 242, 247, 252, 254, 258, 263, 266, 289, 291, 308, 309, 331, 333, 343, 355, 376, 377, 378, 379, 383–6
oratio veli. See prayer of the veil
Order of the Mystery, 93–5, 110, 114, 115, 116, 301, 327, 329, 368
Order of the Priesthood (*Tartīb al-kahanūt*), 13, 43, 61, 76–7, 89, 126, 127, 128, 130, 131, 137, 139, 260, 274
Origen of Alexandria, 176–7

Parenti, Stefano, 28, 316–7, 324, 329, 414
pastophorion (pl. pastophoria), 70, 150, 153, 427, 428, 429; in Syro-Byzantine churches, 70, 77–9, 105, 107; in Egypt, 26, 49, 73–4, 75–6, 77, 82–9, 91–2, 101, 111, 114, 117, 119, 207, 211, 225, 239, 242, 264, 266, 281, 308, 331–2, 333, 355, 357, 367, 377–8, 379, 380, 381, 385; in Ethiopia, 79–80, 107–9, 216, 247; in Nubia, 80–2, 318; in Red Monastery. *See under* Red Monastery; in Scetis, 85, 87, 89; in Southern Egypt, 83, 85, 89; in urban churches, 82, 85; in White Monastery. *See under* White Monastery; origin in Egypt, 83. *See also* churches (building)
paten, 25, 26, 81, 104, 118, 119, 126, 127, 130, 145, 146, 148, 149, 152, 153, 211, 229, 243, 247, 248, 251, 253, 254, 257, 258, 270, 274, 275, 282, 311, 341, 342, 343, 344, 398, 404, 407, 408
Patrich, Joseph, 70, 77, 78, 151
Peter, the Byzantine Liturgy of (PETER), 21, 163, 317, 318, 425
Peter of Bahnasā, Bishop, 193
Peter V, Pope, 96, 189
Phoebammon, Miracles of Apa, 56, 88, 142–3
Phountoules, Ioannes, 162, 198–9, 363
Pott, Thomas, 11, 23, 253, 284, 393
prayer, *of faithful* (Byzantine), 161, 162, 163, 165, 167, 168, 172, 173; of incense, 81, 300, 339, 351; of oblations, 29, 55, 194; of thanksgiving. *See under* Thanksgiving, prayer of;

of the kiss, 116, 379; of the veil (*oratio veli*), 73, 158, 159, 162, 164, 165, 166, 167, 168, 169–70, 172, 379; proskomide (Byzantine), 107, 162, 163, 165, 166; three (peace, hierarchs, assemblies), 210, 231–2, 352
pre-anaphoral, rites, 45, 50, 75, 77, 98, 105, 117, 161–2, 171–2, 173, 203, 207, 220, 223, 224, 225, 237, 263, 273, 352, 363, 368, 377, 379, 385, 387, 388, 392; transfer of gifts, 28–30, 63, 64, 66, 82, 88, 91–2, 93, 94, 95, 99, 102, 103, 108, 151, 280, 367. *See also* old ordo
Precious Jewel, The (*al-ǧawhara al-nafīsa*), 13, 24, 29–30, 41–2, 108, 113, 118–20, 130, 138, 139, 140, 147, 149, 190–4, 207, 220, 225, 227, 229, 232, 233, 238–9, 241, 242, 252, 253, 255, 260, 264, 266, 267, 274, 278, 279, 281–2, 287, 306, 308, 309, 331, 336, 339, 340, 344, 345, 359, 381
Presanctified Gifts, Liturgy of, 21, 34, 81, 82, 295, 317, 318, 319, 373, 424, 425
procession, offertory (pre-anaphora), 28, 30, 55, 62–8, 82, 88, 109, 273, 366, 367
procession of the lamb (the gifts), 26, 29, 210, 240, 241, 242–7, 248, 251, 254, 271, 308, 332, 402; in Ethiopian liturgy, 247; in Euchologia manuscripts, 245–6; in Gabriel V, 244–5; in Ibn Kabar, 242–4; response at the, 249
proskomide, 30. *See also* prayer, *proskomide*
prospherin veil, 25, 130, 132, 142, 144, 146, 148, 149, 159, 311, 341, 344, 345, 359, 398, 408
Prothesis Prayer, 25, 26, 45, 46, 53, 81, 88, 94, 159, 208, 211, 255, 280, 289, 290, 302, 309, 311–33, 356–7, 378, 379, 380, 381, 383, 393–54, 407–8; ancient recension of, 316–7; as a moment of consecration, 371–6; as an epiclesis prayer, 360–2; chants accompanying the, 333–44; intermediate recension of, 318–21; introduction in Constantinople, 324–7; location in Melkite MARK, 330–1; modern recension of, 322–3; moved in new ordo, 331–3; origin of, 323–30; place in the liturgy, 330–3; text of, 315, 407–8; title of, 313–5
prothesis rite, as a complete ancient anaphora, 362–71; as a joyous offering, 389–90; as a preparatory rite, 255, 343, 360, 384. *See also* rites, preparatory; as a public ceremony, 23, 255, 385–6, 389, 392; Byzantine rite of, 23, 28, 131, 253, 272, 280, 284–5, 362–3
psalmody, biblical, 114, 180
Psalms, processional, 111–5, 251–3, 382
Ps.-Athanasius, canons of, 58, 232, 237–8, 389
Ps.-Basil, canons of, 65, 181–3, 279, 280
Ps.-Dionysius the Areopagite, 132, 224
Ps.-Narsai, 104, 285, 289, 367
Ps.-Sāwīrus of al-Ašmunayn, 13, 43, 130, 260, 278

Quecke, Hans, 103, 180, 183, 184, 185, 350, 361, 415, 416, 417,
qurbān. *See under* eucharistic gifts

Radle, Gabriel, 25, 34, 325, 326
Rahmani, Ignatius Ephraem, 104, 285, 426
Red Monastery, 83–4, 128, 129
Renaudot, Eusèbe, 37, 45, 162, 164, 165–6, 335, 418
Riedel, Wilhelm, 58, 279
rites, preparatory, 24, 53–4, 133–173, 201, 203, 207, 223, 224, 225, 229, 232, 233, 254, 255, 332, 343, 382, 384
Ritual Order, the (*al-tartīb al-ṭaqsī*), 13, 30, 32, 42–3, 111, 121–3, 130, 138, 139, 140–1, 147–8, 149, 194–6, 213, 214–5, 218, 221, 222, 225, 226, 227, 228, 230, 239, 244–5, 248, 250, 252, 255, 260, 264, 269, 270, 274, 279, 282, 287, 314, 335, 344, 345, 346, 354, 381, 382
Roman Rite, 109, 113, 114, 143, 151, 153, 161, 199, 262–3, 273, 285–6, 362–3, 366

Samir, Samir Khalil, 40, 42, 122
sancta sanctis, 289–90, 308, 372
Sarapion of Thmuis, prayers of, 36, 292, 303, 328, 354, 366, 391
Scetis. *See* Wādī al-Naṭrūn
Schmelz, Georg, 126, 127, 129, 130, 143
Schulz, Hans-Joachim, 363
Severus of Antioch, 33, 46, 63–4, 105–6, 151, 158, 271–2, 353–4
Shenoute of Atripe, 55, 180–1, 232; canons of, 56, 88, 181, 232, 379
Sinai New Finds, 21, 34, 163, 164, 292, 329
skeuophylakion, 78, 79, 106, 107
sōthēs amēn. See under *May you be saved*
Southern Egypt, Liturgy of, 32–3, 102–3, 179, 180–1, 183–5, 328–9, 334–5
Southern Italy, Liturgy of, 25, 34, 163, 312, 316–7, 325
spoon, communion, 125, 128–30, 145, 148, 149, 152, 153, 273, 398
star (*asteriskos*), 126–7, 146, 152
Statutes of the Apostles, Ethiopic, 56, 92
Suciu, Alin, 32, 103
Swanson, Mark N., 41, 43, 59, 60, 87, 120, 131, 276
Symeon of Thessaloniki, 131, 198, 284
Synaxarion, (Copto-)Arabic, 263, 271, 374, 120
Synodicon, West-Syrian, 267, 268
Syriac, liturgical influence, 33, 86, 89, 153, 273; Liturgy. *See under* West-Syrian Rite; monks in Scetis, 87–8, 89
Syro-Byzantine, 69, 77–9, 88, 89, 93, 312
Syrians, Monastery of the (al-Suryān), 9, 11, 22, 87, 88,

Taft, Robert F., 28, 47, 48–50, 53–4, 62, 63, 67, 69, 78, 82, 88, 106, 107, 114, 129, 132, 151, 162, 163, 171, 177, 178, 179, 181, 198, 201, 222, 224, 278, 324, 325, 327, 367, 369, 372, 387, 414
Taposiris Magna (Abūṣīr), church of, 75, 84, 89, 428

Tartīb al-bī'a, 43, 44, 112, 195, 217, 218, 223, 271, 282, 307, 341, 342, 418, 419, 420, 423
Täsfa Ṣəyon, 216–7
Tertullian, 177
Testamentum Domini, 57, 77, 93, 96, 104, 151, 232
Thanksgiving, Prayer of, 25, 26, 45, 208, 212, 235, 255, 258, 275, 290–307, 336, 339, 341, 342, 342, 355, 356, 357, 368, 394; concluding doxology of, 305–7; deacon's responses during, 303–5; in Alexandrian Melkite liturgy, 290, 294–9, 303; origins, 299–302; place in the unfolding of the liturgy, 302–3, 308–9, 330, 331–2, 379, 380, 381; text in Euchologion, 292–4, 405–7; title, 291–2
Theodore Balsamon, 259–60
Theodore of Mopsuestia, 104, 224, 289, 367
theotokia (chant), 186, 187, 192
throne, chalice (altar), 125, 127–8, 129, 145, 146, 148, 149, 257, 275, 311, 342, 398
triple-altar churches, 87, 89, 79, 100, 101
Trisagion, 115, 116, 184, 201, 202, 203
al-Ṭūḫī, Raphael, 45, 46, 140, 141, 149, 157, 167, 195, 203, 223, 239, 240, 246, 338, 344, 417
typika (White Monastery), 102, 185

Varghese, Baby, 106, 285
Veilleux, Armand, 180
veils, altar. *See under* cloths, altar
Verhelst, Stéphane, 104, 105, 106
vessels, eucharistic, 105, 106, 118, 119, 123, 125–30, 141, 142, 144, 145, 147, 148, 149, 150, 151–3, 154, 159, 160, 172–3, 260, 398–9
vesting, generally, 24, 25, 26, 53, 106, 113, 134–41, 151, 207, 269, 274, 333, 378, 379, 380, 381, 382, 387, 397; of bishops, 136, 140, 218, 223, 311, 339–44, 379, 380, 382, 383; time of, 140–1
vestments, liturgical, 99, 106, 133, 134–41, 143, 191, 257, 269, 339–44, 387, 397
Vliet, Jacques van der, 39, 67, 318–9

Wādī al-Naṭrūn (Scetis), 9, 27, 32, 33, 35, 39, 72–4, 85, 87, 89, 95, 100, 108, 144, 158, 176, 179, 193, 201, 212, 268, 274, 299, 332, 338
washing, ritual (upon entering church), 137, 138, 222
West-Syrian Rite, 23, 57, 78, 104, 105, 106, 108, 136, 143, 153, 164, 197, 247, 262, 272, 273, 285, 288, 326
White Monastery, 32, 102, 103, 110, 114, 115, 180, 328, 329; pastophoria in church of, 83, 85, 89
wine, mixing with water, 278–86 prohibition of, 275–7

Youssef, Youhanna N., 125, 128, 337

Zakhary, Milad, 41–2
Zanetti, Ugo, 10, 40, 72–3, 103, 181, 183, 187, 232, 337
Zheltov, Michael, 34, 36, 292, 371–2, 375
Zizioulas, John, 391